MORTGAGE
AND LOAN
PAYMENT
GUIDE

MORTGAGE AND LOAN PAYMENT GUIDE

MICHAEL E. DUGAN

Gramercy Books
New York • Avenel

Published by Gramercy Books,
distributed by Outlet Book Company, Inc.
a Random House Company,
40 Engelhard Avenue
Avenel, New Jersey 07001

Random House
New York • Toronto • London • Sydney • Auckland

Printed and bound in the United States

Library of Congress Cataloging-in-Publication Data
Dugan, Michael E.
Mortgage and loan payment guide / by Michael E. Dugan.
p.   cm.
ISBN 0-517-10029-0
1. Interest—Tables. I. Title.
HG1632.D84   1993
332.8'2—dc20   93-24874
CIP
8 7 6 5 4 3 2 1

Introduction

The society in which we live makes great use of borrowed money. Most people, at one time or another, borrow a significant amount of money to buy a home or a car. This pocket-size reference book will provide valuable assistance to anyone who borrows money. Neither a mathematical background nor any expertise is required. The easy-to-read tables are designed to be used without formulas.

The introduction to each of the two sections—the monthly payment tables and the annual amortization tables—provides simple instructions for its use and includes a helpful example. Read the example and then follow the instructions to solve the problem. Then use the same method to answer your specific questions.

Please note that when borrowing or investing money, different methods of rounding off numbers will cause variances of a few cents.

MICHAEL E. DUGAN

Monthly Payment Tables

The tables in this section are designed to help you determine the feasibility of making a considered loan. The tables are based on the assumption of a normal mortgage at a specified interest rate for a specific period of time. The assumption is also made that the payments will remain constant for the entire period of the mortgage and that payments will begin one month after the mortgage is finalized. The example that follows will help you understand how to use the tables.

Mrs. Jones wishes to purchase a house for $120,000. She has money to pay $20,000 down, as well as all the additional fees. The bank has agreed to loan her $100,000 at 10.5% interest with monthly payments for 25 years. What would Mrs. Jones have to pay each month to repay the $100,000 loan with interest?

Mrs. Jones must turn to the payment tables marked 10.5%. She must then find the column marked 25 years and follow it down the page until she reaches the row that aligns with $100,000. On the 10.5% page, $100,000 and 25 years meet at $944.18. The monthly payment for principal and interest would be $944.18.

3.00%　　　MONTHLY PAYMENTS

AMOUNT	1 YEAR	2 YEARS	3 YEARS	4 YEARS	5 YEARS	6 YEARS	7 YEARS
100	8.47	4.30	2.91	2.21	1.80	1.52	1.32
200	16.94	8.60	5.82	4.43	3.59	3.04	2.64
500	42.35	21.49	14.54	11.07	8.98	7.60	6.61
1000	84.69	42.98	29.08	22.13	17.97	15.19	13.21
2000	169.39	85.96	58.16	44.27	35.94	30.39	26.43
3000	254.08	128.94	87.24	66.40	53.91	45.58	39.64
4000	338.77	171.92	116.32	88.54	71.87	60.77	52.85
5000	423.47	214.91	145.41	110.67	89.84	75.97	66.07
6000	508.16	257.89	174.49	132.81	107.81	91.16	79.28
7000	592.86	300.87	203.57	154.94	125.78	106.36	92.49
8000	677.55	343.85	232.65	177.07	143.75	121.55	105.71
9000	762.24	386.83	261.73	199.21	161.72	136.74	118.92
10000	846.94	429.81	290.81	221.34	179.69	151.94	132.13
11000	931.63	472.79	319.89	243.48	197.66	167.13	145.35
12000	1016.32	515.77	348.97	265.61	215.62	182.32	158.56
13000	1101.02	558.76	378.06	287.75	233.59	197.52	171.77
14000	1185.71	601.74	407.14	309.88	251.56	212.71	184.99
15000	1270.41	644.72	436.22	332.01	269.53	227.91	198.20
20000	1693.87	859.62	581.62	442.69	359.37	303.87	264.27
25000	2117.34	1074.53	727.03	553.36	449.22	379.84	330.33
30000	2540.81	1289.44	872.44	664.03	539.06	455.81	396.40
35000	2964.28	1504.34	1017.84	774.70	628.90	531.78	462.47
40000	3387.75	1719.25	1163.25	885.37	718.75	607.75	528.53
45000	3811.22	1934.15	1308.65	996.04	808.59	683.72	594.60
50000	4234.68	2149.06	1454.06	1106.72	898.43	759.68	660.67
55000	4658.15	2363.97	1599.47	1217.39	988.28	835.65	726.73
56000	4742.85	2406.95	1628.55	1239.52	1006.25	850.85	739.94
57000	4827.54	2449.93	1657.63	1261.66	1024.22	866.04	753.16
58000	4912.23	2492.91	1686.71	1283.79	1042.18	881.23	766.37
59000	4996.93	2535.89	1715.79	1305.93	1060.15	896.43	779.58
60000	5081.62	2578.87	1744.87	1328.06	1078.12	911.62	792.80
61000	5166.32	2621.85	1773.95	1350.19	1096.09	926.81	806.01
62000	5251.01	2664.84	1803.03	1372.33	1114.06	942.01	819.22
63000	5335.70	2707.82	1832.12	1394.46	1132.03	957.20	832.44
64000	5420.40	2750.80	1861.20	1416.60	1150.00	972.40	845.65
65000	5505.09	2793.78	1890.28	1438.73	1167.96	987.59	858.86
70000	5928.56	3008.68	2035.68	1549.40	1257.81	1063.56	924.93
75000	6352.03	3223.59	2181.09	1660.07	1347.65	1139.53	991.00
80000	6775.50	3438.50	2326.50	1770.75	1437.50	1215.49	1057.06
85000	7198.96	3653.40	2471.90	1881.42	1527.34	1291.46	1123.13
90000	7622.43	3868.31	2617.31	1992.09	1617.18	1367.43	1189.20
95000	8045.90	4083.22	2762.71	2102.76	1707.03	1443.40	1255.26
100000	8469.37	4298.12	2908.12	2213.43	1796.87	1519.37	1321.33
105000	8892.84	4513.03	3053.53	2324.10	1886.71	1595.34	1387.40
110000	9316.31	4727.93	3198.93	2434.78	1976.56	1671.30	1453.46
120000	10163.24	5157.75	3489.75	2656.12	2156.24	1823.24	1585.60
130000	11010.18	5587.56	3780.56	2877.46	2335.93	1975.18	1717.73
140000	11857.12	6017.37	4071.37	3098.81	2515.62	2127.11	1849.86
150000	12704.05	6447.18	4362.18	3320.15	2695.30	2279.05	1982.00
160000	13550.99	6876.99	4652.99	3541.49	2874.99	2430.99	2114.13
175000	14821.40	7521.71	5089.21	3873.51	3144.52	2658.89	2312.33
200000	16938.74	8596.24	5816.24	4426.87	3593.74	3038.74	2642.66
250000	21173.42	10745.30	7270.30	5533.58	4492.17	3798.42	3303.33
500000	42346.85	21490.61	14540.60	11067.16	8984.35	7596.84	6606.65
1000000	84693.70	42981.21	29081.21	22134.33	17968.69	15193.68	13213.30

MONTHLY PAYMENTS   3.00%

AMOUNT	8 YEARS	9 YEARS	10 YEARS	11 YEARS	12 YEARS	13 YEARS	14 YEARS
100	1.17	1.06	0.97	0.89	0.83	0.77	0.73
200	2.35	2.12	1.93	1.78	1.66	1.55	1.46
500	5.86	5.29	4.83	4.45	4.14	3.87	3.65
1000	11.73	10.58	9.66	8.90	8.28	7.75	7.30
2000	23.46	21.15	19.31	17.81	16.56	15.50	14.59
3000	35.19	31.73	28.97	26.71	24.83	23.25	21.89
4000	46.92	42.31	38.62	35.62	33.11	31.00	29.19
5000	58.65	52.88	48.28	44.52	41.39	38.75	36.48
6000	70.38	63.46	57.94	53.42	49.67	46.50	43.78
7000	82.11	74.04	67.59	62.33	57.95	54.24	51.08
8000	93.84	84.62	77.25	71.23	66.22	61.99	58.38
9000	105.57	95.19	86.90	80.13	74.50	69.74	65.67
10000	117.30	105.77	96.56	89.04	82.78	77.49	72.97
11000	129.03	116.35	106.22	97.94	91.06	85.24	80.27
12000	140.75	126.92	115.87	106.85	99.33	92.99	87.56
13000	152.48	137.50	125.53	115.75	107.61	100.74	94.86
14000	164.21	148.08	135.19	124.65	115.89	108.49	102.16
15000	175.94	158.65	144.84	133.56	124.17	116.24	109.45
20000	234.59	211.54	193.12	178.08	165.56	154.98	145.94
25000	293.24	264.42	241.40	222.59	206.95	193.73	182.42
30000	351.89	317.31	289.68	267.11	248.34	232.48	218.91
35000	410.54	370.19	337.96	311.63	289.73	271.22	255.39
40000	469.18	423.08	386.24	356.15	331.11	309.97	291.88
45000	527.83	475.96	434.52	400.67	372.50	348.71	328.36
50000	586.48	528.85	482.80	445.19	413.89	387.46	364.85
55000	645.13	581.73	531.08	489.71	455.28	426.21	401.33
56000	656.86	592.31	540.74	498.61	463.56	433.96	408.63
57000	668.59	602.89	550.40	507.51	471.84	441.70	415.93
58000	680.32	613.46	560.05	516.42	480.12	449.45	423.22
59000	692.04	624.04	569.71	525.32	488.39	457.20	430.52
60000	703.77	634.62	579.36	534.23	496.67	464.95	437.82
61000	715.50	645.19	589.02	543.13	504.95	472.70	445.11
62000	727.23	655.77	598.68	552.03	513.23	480.45	452.41
63000	738.96	666.35	608.33	560.94	521.51	488.20	459.71
64000	750.69	676.92	617.99	569.84	529.78	495.95	467.01
65000	762.42	687.50	627.64	578.74	538.06	503.70	474.30
70000	821.07	740.39	675.93	623.26	579.45	542.44	510.79
75000	879.72	793.27	724.21	667.78	620.84	581.19	547.27
80000	938.37	846.16	772.49	712.30	662.23	619.94	583.76
85000	997.01	899.04	820.77	756.82	703.62	658.68	620.24
90000	1055.66	951.92	869.05	801.34	745.01	697.43	656.73
95000	1114.31	1004.81	917.33	845.86	786.40	736.17	693.21
100000	1172.96	1057.69	965.61	890.38	827.79	774.92	729.70
105000	1231.61	1110.58	1013.89	934.90	869.18	813.67	766.18
110000	1290.25	1163.46	1062.17	979.41	910.57	852.41	802.66
120000	1407.55	1269.23	1158.73	1068.45	993.34	929.91	875.63
130000	1524.84	1375.00	1255.29	1157.49	1076.12	1007.40	948.60
140000	1642.14	1480.77	1351.85	1246.53	1158.90	1084.89	1021.57
150000	1759.44	1586.54	1448.41	1335.56	1241.68	1162.38	1094.54
160000	1876.73	1692.31	1544.97	1424.60	1324.46	1239.87	1167.51
175000	2052.68	1850.96	1689.81	1558.16	1448.63	1356.11	1276.97
200000	2345.91	2115.39	1931.21	1780.75	1655.57	1549.84	1459.39
250000	2932.39	2644.24	2414.02	2225.94	2069.47	1937.30	1824.24
500000	5864.79	5288.47	4828.04	4451.88	4138.93	3874.61	3648.48
1000000	11729.57	10576.94	9656.07	8903.76	8277.87	7749.21	7296.95

3.00% MONTHLY PAYMENTS

AMOUNT	15 YEARS	16 YEARS	17 YEARS	18 YEARS	19 YEARS	20 YEARS	21 YEARS
100	0.69	0.66	0.63	0.60	0.58	0.55	0.54
200	1.38	1.31	1.25	1.20	1.15	1.11	1.07
500	3.45	3.28	3.13	3.00	2.88	2.77	2.68
1000	6.91	6.56	6.26	6.00	5.76	5.55	5.35
2000	13.81	13.13	12.53	11.99	11.52	11.09	10.71
3000	20.72	19.69	18.79	17.99	17.28	16.64	16.06
4000	27.62	26.26	25.05	23.99	23.04	22.18	21.41
5000	34.53	32.82	31.32	29.99	28.80	27.73	26.77
6000	41.43	39.39	37.58	35.98	34.56	33.28	32.12
7000	48.34	45.95	43.85	41.98	40.32	38.82	37.47
8000	55.25	52.51	50.11	47.98	46.08	44.37	42.83
9000	62.15	59.08	56.37	53.98	51.83	49.91	48.18
10000	69.06	65.64	62.64	59.97	57.59	55.46	53.53
11000	75.96	72.21	68.90	65.97	63.35	61.01	58.89
12000	82.87	78.77	75.16	71.97	69.11	66.55	64.24
13000	89.78	85.34	81.43	77.96	74.87	72.10	69.59
14000	96.68	91.90	87.69	83.96	80.63	77.64	74.95
15000	103.59	98.47	93.96	89.96	86.39	83.19	80.30
20000	138.12	131.29	125.27	119.94	115.19	110.92	107.07
25000	172.65	164.11	156.59	149.93	143.99	138.65	133.84
30000	207.17	196.93	187.91	179.92	172.78	166.38	160.60
35000	241.70	229.75	219.23	209.90	201.58	194.11	187.37
40000	276.23	262.57	250.55	239.89	230.38	221.84	214.14
45000	310.76	295.40	281.87	269.88	259.17	249.57	240.90
50000	345.29	328.22	313.19	299.86	287.97	277.30	267.67
55000	379.82	361.04	344.51	329.85	316.77	305.03	294.44
56000	386.73	367.60	350.77	335.85	322.53	310.57	299.79
57000	393.63	374.17	357.03	341.84	328.29	316.12	305.15
58000	400.54	380.73	363.30	347.84	334.05	321.67	310.50
59000	407.44	387.30	369.56	353.84	339.81	327.21	315.85
60000	414.35	393.86	375.82	359.83	345.56	332.76	321.21
61000	421.25	400.42	382.09	365.83	351.32	338.30	326.56
62000	428.16	406.99	388.35	371.83	357.08	343.85	331.91
63000	435.07	413.55	394.62	377.83	362.84	349.40	337.27
64000	441.97	420.12	400.88	383.82	368.60	354.94	342.62
65000	448.88	426.68	407.14	389.82	374.36	360.49	347.97
70000	483.41	459.50	438.46	419.81	403.16	388.22	374.74
75000	517.94	492.33	469.78	449.79	431.96	415.95	401.51
80000	552.47	525.15	501.10	479.78	460.75	443.68	428.28
85000	586.99	557.97	532.42	509.76	489.55	471.41	455.04
90000	621.52	590.79	563.74	539.75	518.35	499.14	481.81
95000	656.05	623.61	595.06	569.74	547.14	526.87	508.58
100000	690.58	656.43	626.37	599.72	575.94	554.60	535.34
105000	725.11	689.26	657.69	629.71	604.74	582.33	562.11
110000	759.64	722.08	689.01	659.70	633.54	610.06	588.88
120000	828.70	787.72	751.65	719.67	691.13	665.52	642.41
130000	897.76	853.36	814.29	779.64	748.72	720.98	695.95
140000	966.81	919.01	876.92	839.61	806.32	776.44	749.48
150000	1035.87	984.65	939.56	899.58	863.91	831.90	803.02
160000	1104.93	1050.29	1002.20	959.56	921.51	887.36	856.55
175000	1208.52	1148.76	1096.16	1049.52	1007.90	970.55	936.85
200000	1381.16	1312.87	1252.75	1199.45	1151.88	1109.20	1070.69
250000	1726.45	1641.08	1565.94	1499.31	1439.85	1386.49	1338.36
500000	3452.91	3282.17	3131.87	2998.62	2879.71	2772.99	2676.72
1000000	6905.82	6564.34	6263.75	5997.23	5759.41	5545.98	5353.44

MONTHLY PAYMENTS 3.00%

AMOUNT	22 YEARS	23 YEARS	24 YEARS	25 YEARS	30 YEARS	35 YEARS	40 YEARS
100	0.52	0.50	0.49	0.47	0.42	0.38	0.36
200	1.04	1.00	0.98	0.95	0.84	0.77	0.72
500	2.59	2.51	2.44	2.37	2.11	1.92	1.79
1000	5.18	5.02	4.88	4.74	4.22	3.85	3.58
2000	10.36	10.04	9.75	9.48	8.43	7.70	7.16
3000	15.54	15.06	14.63	14.23	12.65	11.55	10.74
4000	20.72	20.08	19.50	18.97	16.86	15.39	14.32
5000	25.89	25.10	24.38	23.71	21.08	19.24	17.90
6000	31.07	30.12	29.25	28.45	25.30	23.09	21.48
7000	36.25	35.14	34.13	33.19	29.51	26.94	25.06
8000	41.43	40.16	39.00	37.94	33.73	30.79	28.64
9000	46.61	45.18	43.88	42.68	37.94	34.64	32.22
10000	51.79	50.20	48.75	47.42	42.16	38.49	35.80
11000	56.97	55.22	53.63	52.16	46.38	42.33	39.38
12000	62.15	60.24	58.50	56.91	50.59	46.18	42.96
13000	67.33	65.26	63.38	61.65	54.81	50.03	46.54
14000	72.51	70.28	68.25	66.39	59.02	53.88	50.12
15000	77.68	75.30	73.13	71.13	63.24	57.73	53.70
20000	103.58	100.40	97.50	94.84	84.32	76.97	71.60
25000	129.47	125.50	121.88	118.55	105.40	96.21	89.50
30000	155.37	150.60	146.25	142.26	126.48	115.46	107.40
35000	181.26	175.71	170.63	165.97	147.56	134.70	125.29
40000	207.16	200.81	195.00	189.68	168.64	153.94	143.19
45000	233.05	225.91	219.38	213.40	189.72	173.18	161.09
50000	258.95	251.01	243.75	237.11	210.80	192.43	178.99
55000	284.84	276.11	268.13	260.82	231.88	211.67	196.89
56000	290.02	281.13	273.01	265.56	236.10	215.52	200.47
57000	295.20	286.15	277.88	270.30	240.31	219.36	204.05
58000	300.38	291.17	282.76	275.04	244.53	223.21	207.63
59000	305.56	296.19	287.63	279.78	248.75	227.06	211.21
60000	310.74	301.21	292.51	284.53	252.96	230.91	214.79
61000	315.92	306.23	297.38	289.27	257.18	234.76	218.37
62000	321.10	311.25	302.26	294.01	261.39	238.61	221.95
63000	326.27	316.27	307.13	298.75	265.61	242.46	225.53
64000	331.45	321.29	312.01	303.50	269.83	246.30	229.11
65000	336.63	326.31	316.88	308.24	274.04	250.15	232.69
70000	362.53	351.41	341.26	331.95	295.12	269.40	250.59
75000	388.42	376.51	365.63	355.66	316.20	288.64	268.49
80000	414.32	401.61	390.01	379.37	337.28	307.88	286.39
85000	440.21	426.71	414.38	403.08	358.36	327.12	304.29
90000	466.11	451.81	438.76	426.79	379.44	346.37	322.19
95000	492.00	476.92	463.13	450.50	400.52	365.61	340.09
100000	517.90	502.02	487.51	474.21	421.60	384.85	357.98
105000	543.79	527.12	511.89	497.92	442.68	404.09	375.88
110000	569.69	552.22	536.26	521.63	463.76	423.34	393.78
120000	621.47	602.42	585.01	569.05	505.92	461.82	429.58
130000	673.26	652.62	633.76	616.47	548.09	500.31	465.38
140000	725.05	702.82	682.51	663.90	590.25	538.79	501.18
150000	776.84	753.02	731.26	711.32	632.41	577.28	536.98
160000	828.63	803.23	780.02	758.74	674.57	615.76	572.78
175000	906.32	878.53	853.14	829.87	737.81	673.49	626.47
200000	1035.79	1004.03	975.02	948.42	843.21	769.70	715.97
250000	1294.74	1255.04	1218.77	1185.53	1054.01	962.13	894.96
500000	2589.48	2510.08	2437.55	2371.06	2108.02	1924.25	1789.92
1000000	5178.96	5020.16	4875.10	4742.11	4216.04	3848.50	3579.84

3.50% MONTHLY PAYMENTS

AMOUNT	1 YEAR	2 YEARS	3 YEARS	4 YEARS	5 YEARS	6 YEARS	7 YEARS
100	8.49	4.32	2.93	2.24	1.82	1.54	1.34
200	16.98	8.64	5.86	4.47	3.64	3.08	2.69
500	42.46	21.60	14.65	11.18	9.10	7.71	6.72
1000	84.92	43.20	29.30	22.36	18.19	15.42	13.44
2000	169.84	86.41	58.60	44.71	36.38	30.84	26.88
3000	254.76	129.61	87.91	67.07	54.58	46.26	40.32
4000	339.69	172.81	117.21	89.42	72.77	61.67	53.76
5000	424.61	216.01	146.51	111.78	90.96	77.09	67.20
6000	509.53	259.22	175.81	134.14	109.15	92.51	80.64
7000	594.45	302.42	205.11	156.49	127.34	107.93	94.08
8000	679.37	345.62	234.42	178.85	145.53	123.35	107.52
9000	764.29	388.82	263.72	201.20	163.73	138.77	120.96
10000	849.22	432.03	293.02	223.56	181.92	154.18	134.40
11000	934.14	475.23	322.32	245.92	200.11	169.60	147.84
12000	1019.06	518.43	351.62	268.27	218.30	185.02	161.28
13000	1103.98	561.64	380.93	290.63	236.49	200.44	174.72
14000	1188.90	604.84	410.23	312.98	254.68	215.86	188.16
15000	1273.82	648.04	439.53	335.34	272.88	231.28	201.60
20000	1698.43	864.05	586.04	447.12	363.83	308.37	268.80
25000	2123.04	1080.07	732.55	558.90	454.79	385.46	336.00
30000	2547.65	1296.08	879.06	670.68	545.75	462.55	403.20
35000	2972.26	1512.10	1025.57	782.46	636.71	539.64	470.39
40000	3396.87	1728.11	1172.08	894.24	727.67	616.74	537.59
45000	3821.47	1944.12	1318.59	1006.02	818.63	693.83	604.79
50000	4246.08	2160.14	1465.10	1117.80	909.59	770.92	671.99
55000	4670.69	2376.15	1611.61	1229.58	1000.55	848.01	739.19
56000	4755.61	2419.35	1640.92	1251.94	1018.74	863.43	752.63
57000	4840.53	2462.56	1670.22	1274.29	1036.93	878.85	766.07
58000	4925.45	2505.76	1699.52	1296.65	1055.12	894.27	779.51
59000	5010.38	2548.96	1728.82	1319.00	1073.31	909.69	792.95
60000	5095.30	2592.16	1758.12	1341.36	1091.50	925.10	806.39
61000	5180.22	2635.37	1787.43	1363.72	1109.70	940.52	819.83
62000	5265.14	2678.57	1816.73	1386.07	1127.89	955.94	833.27
63000	5350.06	2721.77	1846.03	1408.43	1146.08	971.36	846.71
64000	5434.98	2764.97	1875.33	1430.78	1164.27	986.78	860.15
65000	5519.91	2808.18	1904.64	1453.14	1182.46	1002.20	873.59
70000	5944.51	3024.19	2051.15	1564.92	1273.42	1079.29	940.79
75000	6369.12	3240.20	2197.66	1676.70	1364.38	1156.38	1007.99
80000	6793.73	3456.22	2344.17	1788.48	1455.34	1233.47	1075.19
85000	7218.34	3672.23	2490.68	1900.26	1546.30	1310.56	1142.39
90000	7642.95	3888.24	2637.19	2012.04	1637.26	1387.66	1209.59
95000	8067.55	4104.26	2783.70	2123.82	1728.22	1464.75	1276.79
100000	8492.16	4320.27	2930.21	2235.60	1819.17	1541.84	1343.99
105000	8916.77	4536.29	3076.72	2347.38	1910.13	1618.93	1411.18
110000	9341.38	4752.30	3223.23	2459.16	2001.09	1696.02	1478.38
120000	10190.60	5184.33	3516.25	2682.72	2183.01	1850.21	1612.78
130000	11039.81	5616.35	3809.27	2906.28	2364.93	2004.39	1747.18
140000	11889.03	6048.38	4102.29	3129.84	2546.84	2158.58	1881.58
150000	12738.24	6480.41	4395.31	3353.40	2728.76	2312.76	2015.98
160000	13587.46	6912.44	4688.33	3576.96	2910.68	2466.94	2150.38
175000	14861.29	7560.48	5127.86	3912.30	3183.56	2698.22	2351.97
200000	16984.33	8640.54	5860.42	4471.20	3638.35	3083.68	2687.97
250000	21230.41	10800.68	7325.52	5589.00	4547.94	3854.60	3359.96
500000	42460.81	21601.36	14651.04	11178.00	9095.87	7709.20	6719.93
1000000	84921.63	43202.72	29302.08	22356.00	18191.74	15418.40	13439.85

MONTHLY PAYMENTS   3.50%

AMOUNT	8 YEARS	9 YEARS	10 YEARS	11 YEARS	12 YEARS	13 YEARS	14 YEARS
100	1.20	1.08	0.99	0.91	0.85	0.80	0.75
200	2.39	2.16	1.98	1.83	1.70	1.60	1.51
500	5.98	5.40	4.94	4.57	4.26	3.99	3.77
1000	11.96	10.81	9.89	9.14	8.51	7.99	7.54
2000	23.92	21.61	19.78	18.28	17.03	15.98	15.08
3000	35.87	32.42	29.67	27.42	25.54	23.96	22.61
4000	47.83	43.23	39.55	36.55	34.06	31.95	30.15
5000	59.79	54.04	49.44	45.69	42.57	39.94	37.69
6000	71.75	64.84	59.33	54.83	51.09	47.93	45.23
7000	83.71	75.65	69.22	63.97	59.60	55.92	52.76
8000	95.66	86.46	79.11	73.11	68.12	63.90	60.30
9000	107.62	97.27	89.00	82.25	76.63	71.89	67.84
10000	119.58	108.07	98.89	91.38	85.15	79.88	75.38
11000	131.54	118.88	108.77	100.52	93.66	87.87	82.92
12000	143.50	129.69	118.66	109.66	102.17	95.86	90.45
13000	155.45	140.50	128.55	118.80	110.69	103.84	97.99
14000	167.41	151.30	138.44	127.94	119.20	111.83	105.53
15000	179.37	162.11	148.33	137.08	127.72	119.82	113.07
20000	239.16	216.15	197.77	182.77	170.29	159.76	150.76
25000	298.95	270.19	247.21	228.46	212.86	199.70	188.45
30000	358.74	324.22	296.66	274.15	255.44	239.64	226.14
35000	418.53	378.26	346.10	319.84	298.01	279.58	263.82
40000	478.32	432.30	395.54	365.53	340.58	319.52	301.51
45000	538.11	486.33	444.99	411.23	383.15	359.46	339.20
50000	597.90	540.37	494.43	456.92	425.73	399.40	376.89
55000	657.69	594.41	543.87	502.61	468.30	439.34	414.58
56000	669.65	605.22	553.76	511.75	476.81	447.33	422.12
57000	681.61	616.02	563.65	520.89	485.33	455.32	429.66
58000	693.57	626.83	573.54	530.02	493.84	463.30	437.19
59000	705.53	637.64	583.43	539.16	502.36	471.29	444.73
60000	717.48	648.44	593.32	548.30	510.87	479.28	452.27
61000	729.44	659.25	603.20	557.44	519.39	487.27	459.81
62000	741.40	670.06	613.09	566.58	527.90	495.26	467.35
63000	753.36	680.87	622.98	575.72	536.42	503.24	474.88
64000	765.32	691.67	632.87	584.85	544.93	511.23	482.42
65000	777.27	702.48	642.76	593.99	553.44	519.22	489.96
70000	837.06	756.52	692.20	639.68	596.02	559.16	527.65
75000	896.85	810.56	741.64	685.38	638.59	599.10	565.34
80000	956.64	864.59	791.09	731.07	681.16	639.04	603.03
85000	1016.43	918.63	840.53	776.76	723.74	678.98	640.72
90000	1076.22	972.67	889.97	822.45	766.31	718.92	678.41
95000	1136.01	1026.70	939.42	868.14	808.88	758.86	716.10
100000	1195.81	1080.74	988.86	913.83	851.45	798.80	753.78
105000	1255.60	1134.78	1038.30	959.53	894.03	838.74	791.47
110000	1315.39	1188.82	1087.74	1005.22	936.60	878.68	829.16
120000	1434.97	1296.89	1186.63	1096.60	1021.74	958.56	904.54
130000	1554.55	1404.96	1285.52	1187.98	1106.89	1038.44	979.92
140000	1674.13	1513.04	1384.40	1279.37	1192.04	1118.32	1055.30
150000	1793.71	1621.11	1463.29	1370.75	1277.18	1198.20	1130.68
160000	1913.29	1729.19	1582.17	1462.14	1362.33	1278.08	1206.05
175000	2092.66	1891.30	1730.50	1599.21	1490.04	1397.90	1319.12
200000	2391.61	2161.48	1977.72	1827.67	1702.91	1597.60	1507.57
250000	2989.51	2701.85	2472.15	2284.59	2128.63	1997.00	1884.46
500000	5979.03	5403.71	4944.29	4569.17	4257.27	3993.99	3768.92
1000000	11958.05	10807.41	9888.59	9138.34	8514.54	7987.98	7537.84

3.50%　　　　MONTHLY PAYMENTS

AMOUNT	15 YEARS	16 YEARS	17 YEARS	18 YEARS	19 YEARS	20 YEARS	21 YEARS
100	0.71	0.68	0.65	0.62	0.60	0.58	0.56
200	1.43	1.36	1.30	1.25	1.20	1.16	1.12
500	3.57	3.40	3.26	3.12	3.01	2.90	2.80
1000	7.15	6.81	6.51	6.25	6.01	5.80	5.61
2000	14.30	13.62	13.02	12.49	12.02	11.60	11.22
3000	21.45	20.43	19.53	18.74	18.03	17.40	16.83
4000	28.60	27.24	26.04	24.99	24.04	23.20	22.44
5000	35.74	34.05	32.56	31.23	30.05	29.00	28.05
6000	42.89	40.86	39.07	37.48	36.07	34.80	33.66
7000	50.04	47.67	45.58	43.73	42.08	40.60	39.26
8000	57.19	54.48	52.09	49.97	48.09	46.40	44.87
9000	64.34	61.29	58.60	56.22	54.10	52.20	50.48
10000	71.49	68.09	65.11	62.47	60.11	58.00	56.09
11000	78.64	74.90	71.62	68.71	66.12	63.80	61.70
12000	85.79	81.71	78.13	74.96	72.13	69.60	67.31
13000	92.93	88.52	84.64	81.21	78.14	75.39	72.92
14000	100.08	95.33	91.15	87.45	84.15	81.19	78.53
15000	107.23	102.14	97.67	93.70	90.16	86.99	84.14
20000	142.98	136.19	130.22	124.93	120.22	115.99	112.18
25000	178.72	170.24	162.78	156.17	150.27	144.99	140.23
30000	214.46	204.28	195.33	187.40	180.33	173.99	168.28
35000	250.21	238.33	227.89	218.63	210.38	202.99	196.32
40000	285.95	272.38	260.44	249.86	240.44	231.98	224.37
45000	321.70	306.43	293.00	281.10	270.49	260.98	252.41
50000	357.44	340.47	325.55	312.33	300.55	289.98	280.46
55000	393.19	374.52	358.11	343.56	330.60	318.98	308.50
56000	400.33	381.33	364.62	349.81	336.61	324.78	314.11
57000	407.48	388.14	371.13	356.06	342.62	330.58	319.72
58000	414.63	394.95	377.64	362.30	348.63	336.38	325.33
59000	421.78	401.76	384.15	368.55	354.64	342.18	330.94
60000	428.93	408.57	390.66	374.80	360.65	347.98	336.55
61000	436.08	415.38	397.17	381.04	366.67	353.78	342.16
62000	443.23	422.19	403.68	387.29	372.68	359.58	347.77
63000	450.38	429.00	410.19	393.54	378.69	365.37	353.38
64000	457.52	435.81	416.70	399.78	384.70	371.17	358.99
65000	464.67	442.62	423.22	406.03	390.71	376.97	364.60
70000	500.42	476.66	455.77	437.26	420.76	405.97	392.64
75000	536.16	510.71	488.33	468.50	450.82	434.97	420.69
80000	571.91	544.76	520.88	499.73	480.87	463.97	448.73
85000	607.65	578.80	553.44	530.96	510.93	492.97	476.78
90000	643.39	612.85	585.99	562.20	540.98	521.96	504.83
95000	679.14	646.90	618.55	593.43	571.04	550.96	532.87
100000	714.88	680.95	651.10	624.66	601.09	579.96	560.92
105000	750.63	714.99	683.66	655.89	631.15	608.96	588.96
110000	786.37	749.04	716.21	687.13	661.20	637.96	617.01
120000	857.86	817.14	781.32	749.59	721.31	695.95	673.10
130000	929.35	885.23	846.43	812.06	781.42	753.95	729.19
140000	1000.84	953.33	911.54	874.53	841.53	811.94	785.28
150000	1072.32	1021.42	976.65	936.99	901.64	869.94	841.38
160000	1143.81	1089.51	1041.76	999.46	961.75	927.94	897.47
175000	1251.04	1191.66	1139.43	1093.16	1051.91	1014.93	981.61
200000	1429.77	1361.89	1302.20	1249.32	1202.18	1159.92	1121.84
250000	1787.21	1702.37	1627.75	1561.65	1502.73	1449.90	1402.29
500000	3574.41	3404.73	3255.50	3123.31	3005.46	2899.80	2804.59
1000000	7148.83	6809.47	6511.00	6246.61	6010.91	5799.60	5609.18

MONTHLY PAYMENTS 3.50%

AMOUNT	22 YEARS	23 YEARS	24 YEARS	25 YEARS	30 YEARS	35 YEARS	40 YEARS
100	0.54	0.53	0.51	0.50	0.45	0.41	0.39
200	1.09	1.06	1.03	1.00	0.90	0.83	0.77
500	2.72	2.64	2.57	2.50	2.25	2.07	1.94
1000	5.44	5.28	5.14	5.01	4.49	4.13	3.87
2000	10.87	10.56	10.27	10.01	8.98	8.27	7.75
3000	16.31	15.84	15.41	15.02	13.47	12.40	11.62
4000	21.75	21.12	20.55	20.02	17.96	16.53	15.50
5000	27.18	26.40	25.69	25.03	22.45	20.66	19.37
6000	32.62	31.68	30.82	30.04	26.94	24.80	23.24
7000	38.06	36.96	35.96	35.04	31.43	28.93	27.12
8000	43.49	42.24	41.10	40.05	35.92	33.06	30.99
9000	48.93	47.52	46.23	45.06	40.41	37.20	34.87
10000	54.37	52.80	51.37	50.06	44.90	41.33	38.74
11000	59.80	58.08	56.51	55.07	49.39	45.46	42.61
12000	65.24	63.36	61.65	60.07	53.89	49.59	46.49
13000	70.68	68.64	66.78	65.08	58.38	53.73	50.36
14000	76.12	73.92	71.92	70.09	62.87	57.86	54.23
15000	81.55	79.20	77.06	75.09	67.36	61.99	58.11
20000	108.74	105.60	102.74	100.12	89.81	82.66	77.48
25000	135.92	132.00	128.43	125.16	112.26	103.32	96.85
30000	163.10	158.40	154.11	150.19	134.71	123.99	116.22
35000	190.29	184.80	179.80	175.22	157.17	144.65	135.59
40000	217.47	211.20	205.49	200.25	179.62	165.32	154.96
45000	244.66	237.60	231.17	225.28	202.07	185.98	174.33
50000	271.84	264.01	256.86	250.31	224.52	206.65	193.70
55000	299.02	290.41	282.54	275.34	246.97	227.31	213.07
56000	304.46	295.69	287.68	280.35	251.47	231.44	216.94
57000	309.90	300.97	292.82	285.36	255.96	235.58	220.81
58000	315.33	306.25	297.95	290.36	260.45	239.71	224.69
59000	320.77	311.53	303.09	295.37	264.94	243.84	228.56
60000	326.21	316.81	308.23	300.37	269.43	247.97	232.43
61000	331.64	322.09	313.37	305.38	273.92	252.11	236.31
62000	337.08	327.37	318.50	310.39	278.41	256.24	240.18
63000	342.52	332.65	323.64	315.39	282.90	260.37	244.06
64000	347.96	337.93	328.78	320.40	287.39	264.51	247.93
65000	353.39	343.21	333.91	325.41	291.88	268.64	251.80
70000	380.58	369.61	359.60	350.44	314.33	289.30	271.17
75000	407.76	396.01	385.29	375.47	336.78	309.97	290.54
80000	434.94	422.41	410.97	400.50	359.24	330.63	309.91
85000	462.13	448.81	436.66	425.53	381.69	351.30	329.28
90000	489.31	475.21	462.34	450.56	404.14	371.96	348.65
95000	516.50	501.61	488.03	475.59	426.59	392.63	368.02
100000	543.68	528.01	513.71	500.62	449.04	413.29	387.39
105000	570.86	554.41	539.40	525.65	471.50	433.96	406.76
110000	598.05	580.81	565.08	550.69	493.95	454.62	426.13
120000	652.42	633.61	616.46	600.75	538.85	495.95	464.87
130000	706.78	686.41	667.83	650.81	583.76	537.28	503.61
140000	761.15	739.21	719.20	700.87	628.66	578.61	542.35
150000	815.52	792.02	770.57	750.94	673.57	619.94	581.09
160000	869.89	844.82	821.94	801.00	718.47	661.27	619.83
175000	951.45	924.02	899.00	876.09	785.83	723.26	677.93
200000	1087.36	1056.02	1027.43	1001.25	898.09	826.58	774.78
250000	1359.20	1320.03	1284.28	1251.56	1122.61	1033.23	968.48
500000	2718.40	2640.05	2568.57	2503.12	2245.22	2066.45	1936.95
1000000	5436.80	5280.11	5137.14	5006.24	4490.45	4132.91	3873.91

4.00% MONTHLY PAYMENTS

AMOUNT	1 YEAR	2 YEARS	3 YEARS	4 YEARS	5 YEARS	6 YEARS	7 YEARS
100	8.51	4.34	2.95	2.26	1.84	1.56	1.37
200	17.03	8.68	5.90	4.52	3.68	3.13	2.73
500	42.57	21.71	14.76	11.29	9.21	7.82	6.83
1000	85.15	43.42	29.52	22.58	18.42	15.65	13.67
2000	170.30	86.85	59.05	45.16	36.83	31.29	27.34
3000	255.45	130.27	88.57	67.74	55.25	46.94	41.01
4000	340.60	173.70	118.10	90.32	73.67	62.58	54.68
5000	425.75	217.12	147.62	112.90	92.08	78.23	68.34
6000	510.90	260.55	177.14	135.47	110.50	93.87	82.01
7000	596.05	303.97	206.67	158.05	128.92	109.52	95.68
8000	681.20	347.40	236.19	180.63	147.33	125.16	109.35
9000	766.35	390.82	265.72	203.21	165.75	140.81	123.02
10000	851.50	434.25	295.24	225.79	184.17	156.45	136.69
11000	936.65	477.67	324.76	248.37	202.58	172.10	150.36
12000	1021.80	521.10	354.29	270.95	221.00	187.74	164.03
13000	1106.95	564.52	383.81	293.53	239.41	203.39	177.69
14000	1192.10	607.95	413.34	316.11	257.83	219.03	191.36
15000	1277.25	651.37	442.86	338.69	276.25	234.68	205.03
20000	1703.00	868.50	590.48	451.58	368.33	312.90	273.38
25000	2128.75	1085.62	738.10	564.48	460.41	391.13	341.72
30000	2554.50	1302.75	885.72	677.37	552.50	469.36	410.06
35000	2980.25	1519.87	1033.34	790.27	644.58	547.58	478.41
40000	3406.00	1737.00	1180.96	903.16	736.66	625.81	546.75
45000	3831.75	1954.12	1328.58	1016.06	828.74	704.03	615.10
50000	4257.50	2171.25	1476.20	1128.95	920.83	782.26	683.44
55000	4683.24	2388.37	1623.82	1241.85	1012.91	860.49	751.78
56000	4768.39	2431.80	1653.34	1264.43	1031.33	876.13	765.45
57000	4853.54	2475.22	1682.87	1287.01	1049.74	891.78	779.12
58000	4938.69	2518.65	1712.39	1309.59	1068.16	907.42	792.79
59000	5023.84	2562.07	1741.92	1332.16	1086.57	923.07	806.46
60000	5108.99	2605.50	1771.44	1354.74	1104.99	938.71	820.13
61000	5194.14	2648.92	1800.96	1377.32	1123.41	954.36	833.80
62000	5279.29	2692.35	1830.49	1399.90	1141.82	970.00	847.47
63000	5364.44	2735.77	1860.01	1422.48	1160.24	985.65	861.13
64000	5449.59	2779.20	1889.54	1445.06	1178.66	1001.29	874.80
65000	5534.74	2822.62	1919.06	1467.64	1197.07	1016.94	888.47
70000	5960.49	3039.74	2066.68	1580.53	1289.16	1095.16	956.82
75000	6386.24	3256.87	2214.30	1693.43	1381.24	1173.39	1025.16
80000	6811.99	3473.99	2361.92	1806.32	1473.32	1251.61	1093.50
85000	7237.74	3691.12	2509.54	1919.22	1565.40	1329.84	1161.85
90000	7663.49	3908.24	2657.16	2032.11	1657.49	1408.07	1230.19
95000	8089.24	4125.37	2804.78	2145.01	1749.57	1486.29	1298.54
100000	8514.99	4342.49	2952.40	2257.91	1841.65	1564.52	1366.88
105000	8940.74	4559.62	3100.02	2370.80	1933.73	1642.74	1435.22
110000	9366.49	4776.74	3247.64	2483.70	2025.82	1720.97	1503.57
120000	10217.99	5210.99	3542.88	2709.49	2209.98	1877.42	1640.26
130000	11069.49	5645.24	3838.12	2935.28	2394.15	2033.87	1776.94
140000	11920.99	6079.49	4133.36	3161.07	2578.31	2190.33	1913.63
150000	12772.49	6513.74	4428.60	3386.86	2762.48	2346.78	2050.32
160000	13623.98	6947.99	4723.84	3612.65	2946.64	2503.23	2187.01
175000	14901.23	7599.36	5166.70	3951.33	3222.89	2737.91	2392.04
200000	17029.98	8684.98	5904.80	4515.81	3683.30	3129.04	2733.76
250000	21287.48	10856.23	7381.00	5644.76	4604.13	3911.30	3417.20
500000	42574.95	21712.46	14761.99	11289.53	9208.26	7822.59	6834.40
1000000	85149.90	43424.92	29523.99	22579.05	18416.52	15645.18	13668.81

MONTHLY PAYMENTS   4.00%

AMOUNT	8 YEARS	9 YEARS	10 YEARS	11 YEARS	12 YEARS	13 YEARS	14 YEARS
100	1.22	1.10	1.01	0.94	0.88	0.82	0.78
200	2.44	2.21	2.02	1.88	1.75	1.65	1.56
500	6.09	5.52	5.06	4.69	4.38	4.12	3.89
1000	12.19	11.04	10.12	9.38	8.76	8.23	7.78
2000	24.38	22.08	20.25	18.75	17.51	16.46	15.57
3000	36.57	33.12	30.37	28.13	26.27	24.69	23.35
4000	48.76	44.16	40.50	37.51	35.02	32.92	31.13
5000	60.95	55.20	50.62	46.88	43.78	41.16	38.92
6000	73.14	66.25	60.75	56.26	52.53	49.39	46.70
7000	85.32	77.29	70.87	65.64	61.29	57.62	54.48
8000	97.51	88.33	81.00	75.01	70.04	65.85	62.27
9000	109.70	99.37	91.12	84.39	78.80	74.08	70.05
10000	121.89	110.41	101.25	93.77	87.55	82.31	77.83
11000	134.08	121.45	111.37	103.14	96.31	90.54	85.62
12000	146.27	132.49	121.49	112.52	105.06	98.77	93.40
13000	158.46	143.53	131.62	121.90	113.82	107.01	101.18
14000	170.65	154.57	141.74	131.27	122.57	115.24	108.97
15000	182.84	165.61	151.87	140.65	131.33	123.47	116.75
20000	243.79	220.82	202.49	187.53	175.11	164.62	155.67
25000	304.73	276.02	253.11	234.42	218.88	205.78	194.59
30000	365.68	331.23	303.74	281.30	262.66	246.93	233.50
35000	426.62	386.43	354.36	328.18	306.43	288.09	272.42
40000	487.57	441.64	404.98	375.07	350.21	329.25	311.34
45000	548.52	496.84	455.60	421.95	393.99	370.40	350.26
50000	609.46	552.05	506.23	468.83	437.76	411.56	389.17
55000	670.41	607.25	556.85	515.72	481.54	452.71	428.09
56000	682.60	618.29	566.97	525.09	490.30	460.95	435.87
57000	694.79	629.34	577.10	534.47	499.05	469.18	443.66
58000	706.98	640.38	587.22	543.85	507.81	477.41	451.44
59000	719.17	651.42	597.35	553.22	516.56	485.64	459.22
60000	731.36	662.46	607.47	562.60	525.32	493.87	467.01
61000	743.55	673.50	617.60	571.98	534.07	502.10	474.79
62000	755.74	684.54	627.72	581.35	542.83	510.33	482.57
63000	767.92	695.58	637.84	590.73	551.58	518.56	490.36
64000	780.11	706.62	647.97	600.11	560.34	526.79	498.14
65000	792.30	717.66	658.09	609.48	569.09	535.03	505.92
70000	853.25	772.87	708.72	656.37	612.87	576.18	544.84
75000	914.20	828.07	759.34	703.25	656.65	617.34	583.76
80000	975.14	883.28	809.96	750.13	700.42	658.49	622.68
85000	1036.09	938.48	860.58	797.02	744.20	699.65	661.59
90000	1097.03	993.69	911.21	843.90	787.98	740.80	700.51
95000	1157.98	1048.89	961.83	890.78	831.75	781.96	739.43
100000	1218.93	1104.10	1012.45	937.67	875.53	823.12	778.35
105000	1279.87	1159.30	1063.07	984.55	919.30	864.27	817.26
110000	1340.82	1214.51	1113.70	1031.43	963.08	905.43	856.18
120000	1462.71	1324.92	1214.94	1125.20	1050.63	987.74	934.01
130000	1584.61	1435.33	1316.19	1218.97	1138.19	1070.05	1011.85
140000	1706.50	1545.74	1417.43	1312.73	1225.74	1152.36	1089.68
150000	1828.39	1656.15	1518.68	1406.50	1313.29	1234.67	1167.52
160000	1950.28	1766.56	1619.92	1500.27	1400.85	1316.99	1245.35
175000	2133.12	1932.17	1771.79	1640.92	1532.17	1440.45	1362.10
200000	2437.86	2208.19	2024.90	1875.33	1751.06	1646.23	1556.69
250000	3047.32	2760.24	2531.13	2344.17	2188.82	2057.79	1945.86
500000	6094.64	5520.48	5062.26	4688.34	4377.64	4115.58	3891.73
1000000	12189.28	11040.97	10124.51	9376.67	8755.28	8231.16	7783.46

4.00%　　　MONTHLY PAYMENTS

AMOUNT	15 YEAR	16 YEARS	17 YEARS	18 YEARS	19 YEARS	20 YEARS	21 YEARS
100	0.74	0.71	0.68	0.65	0.63	0.61	0.59
200	1.48	1.41	1.35	1.30	1.25	1.21	1.17
500	3.70	3.53	3.38	3.25	3.13	3.03	2.94
1000	7.40	7.06	6.76	6.50	6.27	6.06	5.87
2000	14.79	14.12	13.53	13.00	12.54	12.12	11.74
3000	22.19	21.18	20.29	19.51	18.81	18.18	17.62
4000	29.59	28.24	27.06	26.01	25.07	24.24	23.49
5000	36.98	35.30	33.82	32.51	31.34	30.30	29.36
6000	44.38	42.36	40.58	39.01	37.61	36.36	35.23
7000	51.78	49.42	47.35	45.51	43.88	42.42	41.10
8000	59.18	56.48	54.11	52.02	50.15	48.48	46.97
9000	66.57	63.54	60.88	58.52	56.42	54.54	52.85
10000	73.97	70.60	67.64	65.02	62.69	60.60	58.72
11000	81.37	77.66	74.40	71.52	68.96	66.66	64.59
12000	88.76	84.72	81.17	78.02	75.22	72.72	70.46
13000	96.16	91.78	87.93	84.53	81.49	78.78	76.33
14000	103.56	98.84	94.70	91.03	87.76	84.84	82.21
15000	110.95	105.90	101.46	97.53	94.03	90.90	88.08
20000	147.94	141.20	135.28	130.04	125.37	121.20	117.44
25000	184.92	176.50	169.10	162.55	156.72	151.50	146.79
30000	221.91	211.80	202.92	195.06	188.06	181.79	176.15
35000	258.89	247.10	236.74	227.57	219.40	212.09	205.51
40000	295.88	282.40	270.56	260.08	250.75	242.39	234.87
45000	332.86	317.70	304.38	292.59	282.09	272.69	264.23
50000	369.84	353.00	338.20	325.10	313.44	302.99	293.59
55000	406.83	388.30	372.02	357.61	344.78	333.29	322.95
56000	414.23	395.36	378.78	364.11	351.05	339.35	328.82
57000	421.62	402.42	385.54	370.61	357.32	345.41	334.69
58000	429.02	409.48	392.31	377.11	363.58	351.47	340.56
59000	436.42	416.54	399.07	383.62	369.85	357.53	346.44
60000	443.81	423.60	405.84	390.12	376.12	363.59	352.31
61000	451.21	430.66	412.60	396.62	382.39	369.65	358.18
62000	458.61	437.72	419.36	403.12	388.66	375.71	364.05
63000	466.00	444.78	426.13	409.62	394.93	381.77	369.92
64000	473.40	451.84	432.89	416.13	401.20	387.83	375.79
65000	480.80	458.90	439.66	422.63	407.47	393.89	381.67
70000	517.78	494.20	473.48	455.14	438.81	424.19	411.03
75000	554.77	529.50	507.30	487.65	470.15	454.49	440.38
80000	591.75	564.80	541.11	520.16	501.50	484.78	469.74
85000	628.73	600.10	574.93	552.67	532.84	515.08	499.10
90000	665.72	635.40	608.75	585.18	564.18	545.38	528.46
95000	702.70	670.70	642.57	617.69	595.53	575.68	557.82
100000	739.69	706.00	676.39	650.20	626.87	605.98	587.18
105000	776.67	741.30	710.21	682.71	658.21	636.28	616.54
110000	813.66	776.60	744.03	715.22	689.56	666.58	645.90
120000	887.63	847.20	811.67	780.24	752.24	727.18	704.61
130000	961.59	917.80	879.31	845.26	814.93	787.77	763.33
140000	1035.56	988.39	946.95	910.28	877.62	848.37	822.05
150000	1109.53	1058.99	1014.59	975.30	940.31	908.97	880.77
160000	1183.50	1129.59	1082.23	1040.32	1002.99	969.57	939.49
175000	1294.45	1235.49	1183.69	1137.85	1097.02	1060.47	1027.56
200000	1479.38	1411.99	1352.79	1300.40	1253.74	1211.96	1174.36
250000	1849.22	1764.99	1690.98	1625.49	1567.18	1514.95	1467.95
500000	3698.44	3529.98	3381.97	3250.99	3134.35	3029.90	2935.90
1000000	7396.88	7059.96	6763.93	6501.98	6268.70	6059.80	5871.79

MONTHLY PAYMENTS 4.00%

AMOUNT	22 YEARS	23 YEARS	24 YEARS	25 YEARS	30 YEARS	35 YEARS	40 YEARS
100	0.57	0.55	0.54	0.53	0.48	0.44	0.42
200	1.14	1.11	1.08	1.06	0.95	0.89	0.84
500	2.85	2.77	2.70	2.64	2.39	2.21	2.09
1000	5.70	5.55	5.41	5.28	4.77	4.43	4.18
2000	11.40	11.10	10.81	10.56	9.55	8.86	8.36
3000	17.11	16.64	16.22	15.84	14.32	13.28	12.54
4000	22.81	22.19	21.63	21.11	19.10	17.71	16.72
5000	28.51	27.74	27.03	26.39	23.87	22.14	20.90
6000	34.21	33.29	32.44	31.67	28.64	26.57	25.08
7000	39.91	38.83	37.85	36.95	33.42	30.99	29.26
8000	45.61	44.38	43.26	42.23	38.19	35.42	33.44
9000	51.32	49.93	48.66	47.51	42.97	39.85	37.61
10000	57.02	55.48	54.07	52.78	47.74	44.28	41.79
11000	62.72	61.02	59.48	58.06	52.52	48.71	45.97
12000	68.42	66.57	64.88	63.34	57.29	53.13	50.15
13000	74.12	72.12	70.29	68.62	62.06	57.56	54.33
14000	79.83	77.67	75.70	73.90	66.84	61.99	58.51
15000	85.53	83.21	81.10	79.18	71.61	66.42	62.69
20000	114.04	110.95	108.14	105.57	95.48	88.55	83.59
25000	142.55	138.69	135.17	131.96	119.35	110.69	104.48
30000	171.05	166.43	162.21	158.35	143.22	132.83	125.38
35000	199.56	194.16	189.24	184.74	167.10	154.97	146.28
40000	228.07	221.90	216.28	211.13	190.97	177.11	167.18
45000	256.58	249.64	243.31	237.53	214.84	199.25	188.07
50000	285.09	277.38	270.35	263.92	238.71	221.39	208.97
55000	313.60	305.11	297.38	290.31	262.58	243.53	229.87
56000	319.30	310.66	302.79	295.59	267.35	247.95	234.05
57000	325.00	316.21	308.19	300.87	272.13	252.38	238.22
58000	330.71	321.76	313.60	306.15	276.90	256.81	242.40
59000	336.41	327.30	319.01	311.42	281.68	261.24	246.58
60000	342.11	332.85	324.41	316.70	286.45	265.66	250.76
61000	347.81	338.40	329.82	321.98	291.22	270.09	254.94
62000	353.51	343.95	335.23	327.26	296.00	274.52	259.12
63000	359.21	349.49	340.64	332.54	300.77	278.95	263.30
64000	364.92	355.04	346.04	337.82	305.55	283.38	267.48
65000	370.62	360.59	351.45	343.09	310.32	287.80	271.66
70000	399.13	388.33	378.48	369.49	334.19	309.94	292.56
75000	427.64	416.06	405.52	395.88	358.06	332.08	313.45
80000	456.14	443.80	432.55	422.27	381.93	354.22	334.35
85000	484.65	471.54	459.59	448.66	405.80	376.36	355.25
90000	513.16	499.28	486.62	475.05	429.67	398.50	376.14
95000	541.67	527.01	513.66	501.44	453.54	420.64	397.04
100000	570.18	554.75	540.69	527.84	477.42	442.77	417.94
105000	598.69	582.49	567.73	554.23	501.29	464.91	438.84
110000	627.20	610.23	594.76	580.62	525.16	487.05	459.73
120000	684.22	665.70	648.83	633.40	572.90	531.33	501.53
130000	741.24	721.18	702.90	686.19	620.64	575.61	543.32
140000	798.25	776.65	756.97	738.97	668.38	619.88	585.11
150000	855.27	832.13	811.04	791.76	716.12	664.16	626.91
160000	912.29	887.60	865.11	844.54	763.86	708.44	668.70
175000	997.82	970.81	946.21	923.71	835.48	774.86	731.39
200000	1140.36	1109.50	1081.38	1055.67	954.83	885.55	835.88
250000	1425.45	1386.88	1351.73	1319.59	1193.54	1106.94	1044.85
500000	2850.91	2773.75	2703.45	2639.18	2387.08	2213.87	2089.69
1000000	5701.81	5547.50	5406.91	5278.37	4774.15	4427.75	4179.38

4.25%   MONTHLY PAYMENTS

AMOUNT	1 YEAR	2 YEARS	3 YEARS	4 YEARS	5 YEARS	6 YEARS	7 YEARS
100	8.53	4.35	2.96	2.27	1.85	1.58	1.38
200	17.05	8.71	5.93	4.54	3.71	3.15	2.76
500	42.63	21.77	14.82	11.35	9.26	7.88	6.89
1000	85.26	43.54	29.64	22.69	18.53	15.76	13.78
2000	170.53	87.07	59.27	45.38	37.06	31.52	27.57
3000	255.79	130.61	88.91	68.07	55.59	47.28	41.35
4000	341.06	174.15	118.54	90.76	74.12	63.04	55.14
5000	426.32	217.68	148.18	113.46	92.65	78.80	68.92
6000	511.59	261.22	177.81	136.15	111.18	94.56	82.71
7000	596.85	304.75	207.45	158.84	129.71	110.32	96.49
8000	682.11	348.29	237.08	181.53	148.24	126.07	110.27
9000	767.38	391.83	266.72	204.22	166.77	141.83	124.06
10000	852.64	435.36	296.35	226.91	185.30	157.59	137.84
11000	937.91	478.90	325.99	249.60	203.83	173.35	151.63
12000	1023.17	522.44	355.62	272.29	222.35	189.11	165.41
13000	1108.43	565.97	385.26	294.98	240.88	204.87	179.19
14000	1193.70	609.51	414.89	317.68	259.41	220.63	192.98
15000	1278.96	653.04	444.53	340.37	277.94	236.39	206.76
20000	1705.28	870.73	592.71	453.82	370.59	315.19	275.68
25000	2131.60	1088.41	740.88	567.28	463.24	393.98	344.60
30000	2557.93	1306.09	889.06	680.73	555.89	472.78	413.53
35000	2984.25	1523.77	1037.24	794.19	648.53	551.58	482.45
40000	3410.57	1741.45	1185.41	907.64	741.18	630.37	551.37
45000	3836.89	1959.13	1333.59	1021.10	833.83	709.17	620.29
50000	4263.21	2176.81	1481.77	1134.55	926.48	787.97	689.21
55000	4689.53	2394.50	1629.94	1248.01	1019.13	866.76	758.13
56000	4774.79	2438.03	1659.58	1270.70	1037.66	882.52	771.91
57000	4860.06	2481.57	1689.21	1293.39	1056.18	898.28	785.70
58000	4945.32	2525.10	1718.85	1316.08	1074.71	914.04	799.48
59000	5030.59	2568.64	1748.48	1338.77	1093.24	929.80	813.27
60000	5115.85	2612.18	1778.12	1361.47	1111.77	945.56	827.05
61000	5201.11	2655.71	1807.75	1384.16	1130.30	961.32	840.84
62000	5286.38	2699.25	1837.39	1406.85	1148.83	977.08	854.62
63000	5371.64	2742.79	1867.03	1429.54	1167.36	992.84	868.40
64000	5456.91	2786.32	1896.66	1452.23	1185.89	1008.60	882.19
65000	5542.17	2829.86	1926.30	1474.92	1204.42	1024.36	895.97
70000	5968.49	3047.54	2074.47	1588.38	1297.07	1103.15	964.89
75000	6394.81	3265.22	2222.65	1701.83	1389.72	1181.95	1033.81
80000	6821.13	3482.90	2370.83	1815.29	1482.36	1260.75	1102.73
85000	7247.45	3700.58	2519.00	1928.74	1575.01	1339.54	1171.66
90000	7673.78	3918.27	2667.18	2042.20	1667.66	1418.34	1240.58
95000	8100.10	4135.95	2815.36	2155.65	1760.31	1497.14	1309.50
100000	8526.42	4353.63	2963.53	2269.11	1852.96	1575.93	1378.42
105000	8952.74	4571.31	3111.71	2382.57	1945.60	1654.73	1447.34
110000	9379.06	4788.99	3259.89	2496.02	2038.25	1733.53	1516.26
120000	10231.70	5224.35	3556.24	2722.93	2223.55	1891.12	1654.10
130000	11084.34	5659.72	3852.59	2949.84	2408.84	2048.72	1791.94
140000	11936.98	6095.08	4148.95	3176.75	2594.14	2206.31	1929.79
150000	12789.63	6530.44	4445.30	3403.66	2779.43	2363.90	2067.63
160000	13642.27	6965.80	4741.65	3630.58	2964.73	2521.50	2205.47
175000	14921.23	7618.85	5186.18	3970.94	3242.67	2757.89	2412.23
200000	17052.83	8707.26	5927.07	4538.22	3705.91	3151.87	2756.84
250000	21316.04	10884.07	7408.83	5672.77	4632.39	3939.84	3446.05
500000	42632.09	21768.14	14817.66	11345.55	9264.78	7879.67	6892.09
1000000	85264.17	43536.28	29635.33	22691.10	18529.56	15759.35	13784.18

MONTHLY PAYMENTS 4.25%

AMOUNT	8 YEARS	9 YEARS	10 YEARS	11 YEARS	12 YEARS	13 YEARS	14 YEARS
100	1.23	1.12	1.02	0.95	0.89	0.84	0.79
200	2.46	2.23	2.05	1.90	1.78	1.67	1.58
500	6.15	5.58	5.12	4.75	4.44	4.18	3.95
1000	12.31	11.16	10.24	9.50	8.88	8.35	7.91
2000	24.61	22.32	20.49	18.99	17.75	16.71	15.82
3000	36.92	33.48	30.73	28.49	26.63	25.06	23.72
4000	49.22	44.64	40.98	37.99	35.51	33.42	31.63
5000	61.53	55.79	51.22	47.49	44.39	41.77	39.54
6000	73.84	66.95	61.46	56.98	53.26	50.13	47.45
7000	86.14	78.11	71.71	66.48	62.14	58.48	55.36
8000	98.45	89.27	81.95	75.98	71.02	66.84	63.26
9000	110.75	100.43	92.19	85.48	79.89	75.19	71.17
10000	123.06	111.59	102.44	94.97	88.77	83.54	79.08
11000	135.37	122.75	112.68	104.47	97.65	91.90	86.99
12000	147.67	133.91	122.93	113.97	106.53	100.25	94.90
13000	159.98	145.07	133.17	123.46	115.40	108.61	102.80
14000	172.28	156.22	143.41	132.96	124.28	116.96	110.71
15000	184.59	167.38	153.66	142.46	133.16	125.32	118.62
20000	246.12	223.18	204.88	189.94	177.54	167.09	158.16
25000	307.65	278.97	256.09	237.43	221.93	208.86	197.70
30000	369.18	334.77	307.31	284.92	266.32	250.63	237.24
35000	430.71	390.56	358.53	332.40	310.70	292.40	276.78
40000	492.24	446.36	409.75	379.89	355.09	334.18	316.32
45000	553.77	502.15	460.97	427.38	399.47	375.95	355.86
50000	615.30	557.94	512.19	474.86	443.86	417.72	395.40
55000	676.83	613.74	563.41	522.35	488.24	459.49	434.94
56000	689.13	624.90	573.65	531.85	497.12	467.85	442.85
57000	701.44	636.06	583.89	541.34	506.00	476.20	450.76
58000	713.74	647.22	594.14	550.84	514.88	484.55	458.67
59000	726.05	658.37	604.38	560.34	523.75	492.91	466.57
60000	738.35	669.53	614.63	569.83	532.63	501.26	474.48
61000	750.66	680.69	624.87	579.33	541.51	509.62	482.39
62000	762.97	691.85	635.11	588.83	550.39	517.97	490.30
63000	775.27	703.01	645.36	598.33	559.26	526.33	498.21
64000	787.58	714.17	655.60	607.82	568.14	534.68	506.11
65000	799.88	725.33	665.84	617.32	577.02	543.04	514.02
70000	861.41	781.12	717.06	664.81	621.40	584.81	553.56
75000	922.94	836.92	768.28	712.29	665.79	626.58	593.10
80000	984.47	892.71	819.50	759.78	710.17	668.35	632.64
85000	1046.00	948.51	870.72	807.26	754.56	710.12	672.18
90000	1107.53	1004.30	921.94	854.75	798.95	751.90	711.72
95000	1169.06	1060.10	973.16	902.24	843.33	793.67	751.26
100000	1230.59	1115.89	1024.38	949.72	887.72	835.44	790.80
105000	1292.12	1171.68	1075.59	997.21	932.10	877.21	830.34
110000	1353.65	1227.48	1126.81	1044.70	976.49	918.98	869.88
120000	1476.71	1339.07	1229.25	1139.67	1065.26	1002.53	948.96
130000	1599.77	1450.66	1331.69	1234.64	1154.03	1086.07	1028.04
140000	1722.83	1562.25	1434.13	1329.61	1242.80	1169.61	1107.12
150000	1845.89	1673.83	1536.56	1424.59	1331.58	1253.16	1186.20
160000	1968.95	1785.42	1639.00	1519.56	1420.35	1336.70	1265.28
175000	2153.53	1952.81	1792.66	1662.02	1553.51	1462.02	1383.90
200000	2461.18	2231.78	2048.75	1899.45	1775.44	1670.88	1581.60
250000	3076.48	2789.72	2560.94	2374.31	2219.29	2088.60	1977.01
500000	6152.96	5579.45	5121.88	4748.62	4438.59	4177.20	3954.01
1000000	12305.91	11158.90	10243.75	9497.23	8877.18	8354.39	7908.02

4.25%   MONTHLY PAYMENTS

AMOUNT	15 YEARS	16 YEARS	17 YEARS	18 YEARS	19 YEARS	20 YEARS	21 YEARS
100	0.75	0.72	0.69	0.66	0.64	0.62	0.60
200	1.50	1.44	1.38	1.33	1.28	1.24	1.20
500	3.76	3.59	3.45	3.32	3.20	3.10	3.00
1000	7.52	7.19	6.89	6.63	6.40	6.19	6.01
2000	15.05	14.37	13.79	13.26	12.80	12.38	12.01
3000	22.57	21.56	20.68	19.90	19.20	18.58	18.02
4000	30.09	28.75	27.57	26.53	25.60	24.77	24.02
5000	37.61	35.94	34.46	33.16	32.00	30.96	30.03
6000	45.14	43.12	41.36	39.79	38.40	37.15	36.03
7000	52.66	50.31	48.25	46.42	44.80	43.35	42.04
8000	60.18	57.50	55.14	53.06	51.20	49.54	48.05
9000	67.71	64.68	62.03	59.69	57.60	55.73	54.05
10000	75.23	71.87	68.93	66.32	64.00	61.92	60.06
11000	82.75	79.06	75.82	72.95	70.40	68.12	66.06
12000	90.27	86.25	82.71	79.58	76.80	74.31	72.07
13000	97.80	93.43	89.60	86.21	83.20	80.50	78.07
14000	105.32	100.62	96.50	92.85	89.60	86.69	84.08
15000	112.84	107.81	103.39	99.48	96.00	92.89	90.08
20000	150.46	143.74	137.85	132.64	128.00	123.85	120.11
25000	188.07	179.68	172.31	165.80	160.00	154.81	150.14
30000	225.68	215.62	206.78	198.96	192.00	185.77	180.17
35000	263.30	251.55	241.24	232.12	224.00	216.73	210.20
40000	300.91	287.49	275.70	265.28	256.00	247.69	240.23
45000	338.53	323.42	310.16	298.43	288.00	278.66	270.25
50000	376.14	359.36	344.63	331.59	320.00	309.62	300.28
55000	413.75	395.30	379.09	364.75	352.00	340.58	330.31
56000	421.28	402.48	385.98	371.39	358.40	346.77	336.32
57000	428.80	409.67	392.87	378.02	364.80	352.96	342.32
58000	436.32	416.86	399.77	384.65	371.20	359.16	348.33
59000	443.84	424.04	406.66	391.28	377.60	365.35	354.33
60000	451.37	431.23	413.55	397.91	384.00	371.54	360.34
61000	458.89	438.42	420.44	404.54	390.40	377.73	366.34
62000	466.41	445.61	427.34	411.18	396.80	383.93	372.35
63000	473.94	452.79	434.23	417.81	403.20	390.12	378.36
64000	481.46	459.98	441.12	424.44	409.60	396.31	384.36
65000	488.98	467.17	448.01	431.07	416.00	402.50	390.37
70000	526.59	503.10	482.48	464.23	447.99	433.46	420.39
75000	564.21	539.04	516.94	497.39	479.99	464.43	450.42
80000	601.82	574.98	551.40	530.55	511.99	495.39	480.45
85000	639.44	610.91	585.86	563.71	543.99	526.35	510.48
90000	677.05	646.85	620.33	596.87	575.99	557.31	540.51
95000	714.66	682.78	654.79	630.03	607.99	588.27	570.54
100000	752.28	718.72	689.25	663.19	639.99	619.23	600.56
105000	789.89	754.66	723.71	696.35	671.99	650.20	630.59
110000	827.51	790.59	758.18	729.51	703.99	681.16	660.62
120000	902.73	862.46	827.10	795.83	767.99	743.08	720.68
130000	977.96	934.34	896.03	862.14	831.99	805.00	780.73
140000	1053.19	1006.21	964.95	928.46	895.99	866.93	840.79
150000	1128.42	1078.08	1033.88	994.78	959.99	928.85	900.85
160000	1203.65	1149.95	1102.80	1061.10	1023.99	990.78	960.90
175000	1316.49	1257.76	1206.19	1160.58	1119.99	1083.66	1050.99
200000	1504.56	1437.44	1378.50	1326.38	1279.99	1238.47	1201.13
250000	1880.70	1796.80	1723.13	1657.97	1599.98	1548.09	1501.41
500000	3761.39	3593.60	3446.25	3315.94	3199.96	3096.17	3002.82
1000000	7522.78	7187.20	6892.51	6631.88	6399.93	6192.34	6005.64

MONTHLY PAYMENTS 4.25%

AMOUNT	22 YEARS	23 YEARS	24 YEARS	25 YEARS	30 YEARS	35 YEARS	40 YEARS
100	0.58	0.57	0.55	0.54	0.49	0.46	0.43
200	1.17	1.14	1.11	1.08	0.98	0.92	0.87
500	2.92	2.84	2.77	2.71	2.46	2.29	2.17
1000	5.84	5.68	5.54	5.42	4.92	4.58	4.34
2000	11.67	11.37	11.09	10.83	9.84	9.16	8.67
3000	17.51	17.05	16.63	16.25	14.76	13.74	13.01
4000	23.35	22.74	22.18	21.67	19.68	18.32	17.34
5000	29.18	28.42	27.72	27.09	24.60	22.89	21.68
6000	35.02	34.10	33.27	32.50	29.52	27.47	26.02
7000	40.86	39.79	38.81	37.92	34.44	32.05	30.35
8000	46.70	45.47	44.36	43.34	39.36	36.63	34.69
9000	52.53	51.16	49.90	48.76	44.27	41.21	39.03
10000	58.37	56.84	55.45	54.17	49.19	45.79	43.36
11000	64.21	62.52	60.99	59.59	54.11	50.37	47.70
12000	70.04	68.21	66.54	65.01	59.03	54.95	52.03
13000	75.88	73.89	72.08	70.43	63.95	59.53	56.37
14000	81.72	79.58	77.63	75.84	68.87	64.11	60.71
15000	87.55	85.26	83.17	81.26	73.79	68.68	65.04
20000	116.74	113.68	110.89	108.35	98.39	91.58	86.72
25000	145.92	142.10	138.62	135.43	122.98	114.47	108.41
30000	175.11	170.52	166.34	162.52	147.58	137.37	130.09
35000	204.29	198.94	194.06	189.61	172.18	160.26	151.77
40000	233.48	227.36	221.79	216.70	196.78	183.16	173.45
45000	262.66	255.78	249.51	243.78	221.37	206.05	195.13
50000	291.85	284.20	277.23	270.87	245.97	228.95	216.81
55000	321.03	312.62	304.96	297.96	270.57	251.84	238.49
56000	326.87	318.30	310.50	303.37	275.49	256.42	242.83
57000	332.71	323.99	316.04	308.79	280.41	261.00	247.16
58000	338.54	329.67	321.59	314.21	285.33	265.58	251.50
59000	344.38	335.35	327.13	319.63	290.24	270.16	255.84
60000	350.22	341.04	332.68	325.04	295.16	274.74	260.17
61000	356.05	346.72	338.22	330.46	300.08	279.32	264.51
62000	361.89	352.41	343.77	335.88	305.00	283.89	268.84
63000	367.73	358.09	349.31	341.30	309.92	288.47	273.18
64000	373.57	363.77	354.86	346.71	314.84	293.05	277.52
65000	379.40	369.46	360.40	352.13	319.76	297.63	281.85
70000	408.59	397.88	388.13	379.22	344.36	320.53	303.53
75000	437.77	426.30	415.85	406.30	368.95	343.42	325.22
80000	466.96	454.72	443.57	433.39	393.55	366.32	346.90
85000	496.14	483.14	471.29	460.48	418.15	389.21	368.58
90000	525.33	511.56	499.02	487.56	442.75	412.10	390.26
95000	554.51	539.98	526.74	514.65	467.34	435.00	411.94
100000	583.70	568.40	554.46	541.74	491.94	457.89	433.62
105000	612.88	596.82	582.19	568.83	516.54	480.79	455.30
110000	642.07	625.23	609.91	595.91	541.13	503.68	476.98
120000	700.44	682.07	665.36	650.09	590.33	549.47	520.34
130000	758.81	738.91	720.80	704.26	639.52	595.26	563.71
140000	817.18	795.75	776.25	758.43	688.72	641.05	607.07
150000	875.54	852.59	831.70	812.61	737.91	686.84	650.43
160000	933.91	909.43	887.14	866.78	787.10	732.63	693.79
175000	1021.47	994.69	970.31	948.04	860.89	801.31	758.84
200000	1167.39	1136.79	1108.93	1083.48	983.88	915.79	867.24
250000	1459.24	1420.99	1386.16	1354.35	1229.85	1144.73	1084.05
500000	2918.48	2841.98	2772.32	2708.69	2459.70	2289.47	2168.10
1000000	5836.96	5683.95	5544.64	5417.38	4919.40	4578.94	4336.20

4.50%   MONTHLY PAYMENTS

AMOUNT	1 YEAR	2 YEARS	3 YEARS	4 YEARS	5 YEARS	6 YEARS	7 YEARS
100	8.54	4.36	2.97	2.28	1.86	1.59	1.39
200	17.08	8.73	5.95	4.56	3.73	3.17	2.78
500	42.69	21.82	14.87	11.40	9.32	7.94	6.95
1000	85.38	43.65	29.75	22.80	18.64	15.87	13.90
2000	170.76	87.30	59.49	45.61	37.29	31.75	27.80
3000	256.14	130.94	89.24	68.41	55.93	47.62	41.70
4000	341.51	174.59	118.99	91.21	74.57	63.50	55.60
5000	426.89	218.24	148.73	114.02	93.22	79.37	69.50
6000	512.27	261.89	178.48	136.82	111.86	95.24	83.40
7000	597.65	305.53	208.23	159.62	130.50	111.12	97.30
8000	683.03	349.18	237.98	182.43	149.14	126.99	111.20
9000	768.41	392.83	267.72	205.23	167.79	142.87	125.10
10000	853.79	436.48	297.47	228.03	186.43	158.74	139.00
11000	939.16	480.13	327.22	250.84	205.07	174.61	152.90
12000	1024.54	523.77	356.96	273.64	223.72	190.49	166.80
13000	1109.92	567.42	386.71	296.45	242.36	206.36	180.70
14000	1195.30	611.07	416.46	319.25	261.00	222.24	194.60
15000	1280.68	654.72	446.20	342.05	279.65	238.11	208.50
20000	1707.57	872.96	594.94	456.07	372.86	317.48	278.00
25000	2134.46	1091.20	743.67	570.09	466.08	396.85	347.50
30000	2561.36	1309.43	892.41	684.10	559.29	476.22	417.00
35000	2988.25	1527.67	1041.14	798.12	652.51	555.59	486.51
40000	3415.14	1745.91	1189.88	912.14	745.72	634.96	556.01
45000	3842.03	1964.15	1338.61	1026.16	838.94	714.33	625.51
50000	4268.93	2182.39	1487.35	1140.17	932.15	793.70	695.01
55000	4695.82	2400.63	1636.08	1254.19	1025.37	873.07	764.51
56000	4781.20	2444.28	1665.83	1277.00	1044.01	888.95	778.41
57000	4866.58	2487.93	1695.57	1299.80	1062.65	904.82	792.31
58000	4951.95	2531.57	1725.32	1322.60	1081.30	920.69	806.21
59000	5037.33	2575.22	1755.07	1345.41	1099.94	936.57	820.11
60000	5122.71	2618.87	1784.82	1368.21	1118.58	952.44	834.01
61000	5208.09	2662.52	1814.56	1391.01	1137.22	968.32	847.91
62000	5293.47	2706.16	1844.31	1413.82	1155.87	984.19	861.81
63000	5378.85	2749.81	1874.06	1436.62	1174.51	1000.06	875.71
64000	5464.23	2793.46	1903.80	1459.42	1193.15	1015.94	889.61
65000	5549.60	2837.11	1933.55	1482.23	1211.80	1031.81	903.51
70000	5976.50	3055.35	2082.28	1596.24	1305.01	1111.18	973.01
75000	6403.39	3273.59	2231.02	1710.26	1398.23	1190.55	1042.51
80000	6830.28	3491.82	2379.75	1824.28	1491.44	1269.92	1112.01
85000	7257.17	3710.06	2528.49	1938.30	1584.66	1349.29	1181.51
90000	7684.07	3928.30	2677.22	2052.31	1677.87	1428.66	1251.01
95000	8110.96	4146.54	2825.96	2166.33	1771.09	1508.03	1320.52
100000	8537.85	4364.78	2974.69	2280.35	1864.30	1587.40	1390.02
105000	8964.74	4583.02	3123.43	2394.37	1957.52	1666.77	1459.52
110000	9391.64	4801.26	3272.16	2508.38	2050.73	1746.14	1529.02
120000	10245.42	5237.74	3569.63	2736.42	2237.16	1904.88	1668.02
130000	11099.21	5674.22	3867.10	2964.45	2423.59	2063.62	1807.02
140000	11952.99	6110.69	4164.57	3192.49	2610.02	2222.36	1946.02
150000	12806.78	6547.17	4462.04	3420.52	2796.45	2381.10	2085.02
160000	13660.56	6983.65	4759.51	3648.56	2982.88	2539.84	2224.03
175000	14941.24	7638.37	5205.71	3990.61	3262.53	2777.96	2432.53
200000	17075.70	8729.56	5949.38	4560.70	3728.60	3174.81	2780.03
250000	21344.63	10911.95	7436.73	5700.87	4660.75	3968.51	3475.04
500000	42689.26	21823.91	14873.46	11401.74	9321.51	7937.01	6950.08
1000000	85378.52	43647.81	29746.92	22803.49	18643.02	15874.03	13900.16

MONTHLY PAYMENTS 4.50%

AMOUNT	8 YEARS	9 YEARS	10 YEARS	11 YEARS	12 YEARS	13 YEARS	14 YEARS
100	1.24	1.13	1.04	0.96	0.90	0.85	0.80
200	2.48	2.26	2.07	1.92	1.80	1.70	1.61
500	6.21	5.64	5.18	4.81	4.50	4.24	4.02
1000	12.42	11.28	10.36	9.62	9.00	8.48	8.03
2000	24.85	22.56	20.73	19.24	18.00	16.96	16.07
3000	37.27	33.83	31.09	28.86	27.00	25.44	24.10
4000	49.69	45.11	41.46	38.47	36.00	33.91	32.14
5000	62.12	56.39	51.82	48.09	45.00	42.39	40.17
6000	74.54	67.67	62.18	57.71	54.00	50.87	48.20
7000	86.96	78.94	72.55	67.33	63.00	59.35	56.24
8000	99.39	90.22	82.91	76.95	72.00	67.83	64.27
9000	111.81	101.50	93.27	86.57	81.00	76.31	72.30
10000	124.23	112.78	103.64	96.19	90.00	84.79	80.34
11000	136.66	124.05	114.00	105.81	99.00	93.27	88.37
12000	149.08	135.33	124.37	115.42	108.00	101.74	96.41
13000	161.50	146.61	134.73	125.04	117.00	110.22	104.44
14000	173.93	157.89	145.09	134.66	126.00	118.70	112.47
15000	186.35	169.16	155.46	144.28	135.00	127.18	120.51
20000	248.46	225.55	207.28	192.37	180.00	169.57	160.68
25000	310.58	281.94	259.10	240.47	225.00	211.97	200.84
30000	372.70	338.33	310.92	288.56	270.00	254.36	241.01
35000	434.81	394.72	362.73	336.66	315.00	296.75	281.18
40000	496.93	451.10	414.55	384.75	360.00	339.15	321.35
45000	559.05	507.49	466.37	432.84	405.00	381.54	361.52
50000	621.16	563.88	518.19	480.94	450.00	423.94	401.69
55000	683.28	620.27	570.01	529.03	495.00	466.33	441.86
56000	695.70	631.55	580.38	538.65	504.00	474.81	449.89
57000	708.12	642.82	590.74	548.27	513.00	483.29	457.92
58000	720.55	654.10	601.10	557.89	522.00	491.77	465.96
59000	732.97	665.38	611.47	567.50	531.00	500.24	473.99
60000	745.39	676.66	621.83	577.12	540.00	508.72	482.03
61000	757.82	687.93	632.19	586.74	549.00	517.20	490.06
62000	770.24	699.21	642.56	596.36	558.01	525.68	498.09
63000	782.66	710.49	652.92	605.98	567.01	534.16	506.13
64000	795.09	721.77	663.29	615.60	576.01	542.64	514.16
65000	807.51	733.04	673.65	625.22	585.01	551.12	522.19
70000	869.63	789.43	725.47	673.31	630.01	593.51	562.36
75000	931.74	845.82	777.29	721.40	675.01	635.90	602.53
80000	993.86	902.21	829.11	769.50	720.01	678.30	642.70
85000	1055.97	958.60	880.93	817.59	765.01	720.69	682.87
90000	1118.09	1014.98	932.75	865.69	810.01	763.08	723.04
95000	1180.21	1071.37	984.56	913.78	855.01	805.48	763.21
100000	1242.32	1127.76	1036.38	961.87	900.01	847.87	803.38
105000	1304.44	1184.15	1088.20	1009.97	945.01	890.26	843.54
110000	1366.56	1240.54	1140.02	1058.06	990.01	932.66	883.71
120000	1490.79	1353.31	1243.66	1154.25	1080.01	1017.45	964.05
130000	1615.02	1466.09	1347.30	1250.43	1170.01	1102.23	1044.39
140000	1739.25	1578.86	1450.94	1346.62	1260.01	1187.02	1124.73
150000	1863.49	1691.64	1554.58	1442.81	1350.01	1271.81	1205.06
160000	1987.72	1804.41	1658.21	1539.00	1440.01	1356.59	1285.40
175000	2174.07	1973.58	1813.67	1683.28	1575.01	1483.77	1405.91
200000	2484.65	2255.52	2072.77	1923.75	1800.02	1695.75	1606.75
250000	3105.81	2819.40	2590.96	2404.68	2250.02	2119.68	2008.44
500000	6211.62	5638.80	5181.92	4809.36	4500.04	4239.36	4016.88
1000000	12423.23	11277.59	10363.84	9618.73	9000.08	8478.71	8033.76

4.50%　　　MONTHLY PAYMENTS

AMOUNT	15 YEARS	16 YEARS	17 YEARS	18 YEARS	19 YEARS	20 YEARS	21 YEARS
100	0.76	0.73	0.70	0.68	0.65	0.63	0.61
200	1.53	1.46	1.40	1.35	1.31	1.27	1.23
500	3.82	3.66	3.51	3.38	3.27	3.16	3.07
1000	7.65	7.32	7.02	6.76	6.53	6.33	6.14
2000	15.30	14.63	14.04	13.53	13.07	12.65	12.28
3000	22.95	21.95	21.07	20.29	19.60	18.98	18.42
4000	30.60	29.26	28.09	27.05	26.13	25.31	24.56
5000	38.25	36.58	35.11	33.82	32.66	31.63	30.71
6000	45.90	43.89	42.13	40.58	39.20	37.96	36.85
7000	53.55	51.21	49.16	47.34	45.73	44.29	42.99
8000	61.20	58.53	56.18	54.11	52.26	50.61	49.13
9000	68.85	65.84	63.20	60.87	58.79	56.94	55.27
10000	76.50	73.16	70.22	67.63	65.33	63.26	61.41
11000	84.15	80.47	77.25	74.40	71.86	69.59	67.55
12000	91.80	87.79	84.27	81.16	78.39	75.92	73.69
13000	99.45	95.10	91.29	87.92	84.92	82.24	79.84
14000	107.10	102.42	98.31	94.69	91.46	88.57	85.98
15000	114.75	109.74	105.34	101.45	97.99	94.90	92.12
20000	153.00	146.32	140.45	135.26	130.65	126.53	122.82
25000	191.25	182.89	175.56	169.08	163.32	158.16	153.53
30000	229.50	219.47	210.67	202.90	195.98	189.79	184.24
35000	267.75	256.05	245.79	236.71	228.64	221.43	214.94
40000	306.00	292.63	280.90	270.53	261.31	253.06	245.65
45000	344.25	329.21	316.01	304.35	293.97	284.69	276.35
50000	382.50	365.79	351.12	338.16	326.63	316.32	307.06
55000	420.75	402.37	386.24	371.98	359.30	347.96	337.76
56000	428.40	409.68	393.26	378.74	365.83	354.28	343.91
57000	436.05	417.00	400.28	385.51	372.36	360.61	350.05
58000	443.70	424.31	407.30	392.27	378.90	366.94	356.19
59000	451.35	431.63	414.33	399.03	385.43	373.26	362.33
60000	459.00	438.95	421.35	405.79	391.96	379.59	368.47
61000	466.65	446.26	428.37	412.56	398.49	385.92	374.61
62000	474.30	453.58	435.39	419.32	405.03	392.24	380.75
63000	481.95	460.89	442.42	426.08	411.56	398.57	386.89
64000	489.60	468.21	449.44	432.85	418.09	404.90	393.03
65000	497.25	475.52	456.46	439.61	424.62	411.22	399.18
70000	535.50	512.10	491.57	473.43	457.29	442.85	429.88
75000	573.74	548.68	526.69	507.24	489.95	474.49	460.59
80000	611.99	585.26	561.80	541.06	522.62	506.12	491.29
85000	650.24	621.84	596.91	574.88	555.28	537.75	522.00
90000	688.49	658.42	632.02	608.69	587.94	569.38	552.71
95000	726.74	695.00	667.14	642.51	620.61	601.02	583.41
100000	764.99	731.58	702.25	676.32	653.27	632.65	614.12
105000	803.24	768.16	737.36	710.14	685.93	664.28	644.82
110000	841.49	804.73	772.47	743.96	718.60	695.91	675.53
120000	917.99	877.89	842.70	811.59	783.92	759.18	736.94
130000	994.49	951.05	912.92	879.22	849.25	822.44	798.35
140000	1070.99	1024.21	983.15	946.85	914.58	885.71	859.76
150000	1147.49	1097.36	1053.37	1014.49	979.90	948.97	921.18
160000	1223.99	1170.52	1123.60	1082.12	1045.23	1012.24	982.59
175000	1338.74	1280.26	1228.93	1183.57	1143.22	1107.14	1074.70
200000	1529.99	1463.15	1404.49	1352.65	1306.54	1265.30	1228.23
250000	1912.48	1828.94	1755.62	1690.81	1633.17	1581.62	1535.29
500000	3824.97	3657.88	3511.24	3381.62	3266.34	3163.25	3070.58
1000000	7649.93	7315.76	7022.47	6763.25	6532.69	6326.49	6141.17

MONTHLY PAYMENTS   4.50%

AMOUNT	22 YEARS	23 YEARS	24 YEARS	25 YEARS	30 YEARS	35 YEARS	40 YEARS
100	0.60	0.58	0.57	0.56	0.51	0.47	0.45
200	1.19	1.16	1.14	1.11	1.01	0.95	0.90
500	2.99	2.91	2.84	2.78	2.53	2.37	2.25
1000	5.97	5.82	5.68	5.56	5.07	4.73	4.50
2000	11.95	11.64	11.37	11.12	10.13	9.47	8.99
3000	17.92	17.47	17.05	16.67	15.20	14.20	13.49
4000	23.90	23.29	22.74	22.23	20.27	18.93	17.98
5000	29.87	29.11	28.42	27.79	25.33	23.66	22.48
6000	35.84	34.93	34.11	33.35	30.40	28.40	26.97
7000	41.82	40.76	39.79	38.91	35.47	33.13	31.47
8000	47.79	46.58	45.47	44.47	40.53	37.86	35.97
9000	53.76	52.40	51.16	50.02	45.60	42.59	40.46
10000	59.74	58.22	56.84	55.58	50.67	47.33	44.96
11000	65.71	64.04	62.53	61.14	55.74	52.06	49.45
12000	71.69	69.87	68.21	66.70	60.80	56.79	53.95
13000	77.66	75.69	73.90	72.26	65.87	61.52	58.44
14000	83.63	81.51	79.58	77.82	70.94	66.26	62.94
15000	89.61	87.33	85.26	83.37	76.00	70.99	67.43
20000	119.48	116.44	113.68	111.17	101.34	94.65	89.91
25000	149.35	145.56	142.11	138.96	126.67	118.31	112.39
30000	179.22	174.67	170.53	166.75	152.01	141.98	134.87
35000	209.09	203.78	198.95	194.54	177.34	165.64	157.35
40000	238.95	232.89	227.37	222.33	202.67	189.30	179.83
45000	268.82	262.00	255.79	250.12	228.01	212.97	202.30
50000	298.69	291.11	284.21	277.92	253.34	236.63	224.78
55000	328.56	320.22	312.63	305.71	278.68	260.29	247.26
56000	334.54	326.04	318.32	311.27	283.74	265.02	251.76
57000	340.51	331.87	324.00	316.82	288.81	269.76	256.25
58000	346.48	337.69	329.69	322.38	293.88	274.49	260.75
59000	352.46	343.51	335.37	327.94	298.94	279.22	265.24
60000	358.43	349.33	341.05	333.50	304.01	283.95	269.74
61000	364.41	355.15	346.74	339.06	309.08	288.69	274.23
62000	370.38	360.98	352.42	344.62	314.14	293.42	278.73
63000	376.35	366.80	358.11	350.17	319.21	298.15	283.22
64000	382.33	372.62	363.79	355.73	324.28	302.88	287.72
65000	388.30	378.44	369.48	361.29	329.35	307.62	292.22
70000	418.17	407.55	397.90	389.08	354.68	331.28	314.69
75000	448.04	436.67	426.32	416.87	380.01	354.94	337.17
80000	477.91	465.78	454.74	444.67	405.35	378.61	359.65
85000	507.78	494.89	483.16	472.46	430.68	402.27	382.13
90000	537.65	524.00	511.58	500.25	456.02	425.93	404.61
95000	567.52	553.11	540.00	528.04	481.35	449.59	427.08
100000	597.39	582.22	568.42	555.83	506.69	473.26	449.56
105000	627.26	611.33	596.85	583.62	532.02	496.92	472.04
110000	657.12	640.44	625.27	611.42	557.35	520.58	494.52
120000	716.86	698.67	682.11	667.00	608.02	567.91	539.48
130000	776.60	756.89	738.95	722.58	658.69	615.23	584.43
140000	836.34	815.11	795.79	778.17	709.36	662.56	629.39
150000	896.08	873.33	852.64	833.75	760.03	709.89	674.34
160000	955.82	931.55	909.48	889.33	810.70	757.21	719.30
175000	1045.43	1018.89	994.74	972.71	886.70	828.20	786.73
200000	1194.77	1164.44	1136.85	1111.66	1013.37	946.51	899.13
250000	1493.47	1455.55	1421.06	1389.58	1266.71	1183.14	1123.91
500000	2986.93	2911.11	2842.12	2779.16	2533.43	2366.28	2247.81
1000000	5973.86	5822.21	5684.25	5558.32	5066.85	4732.57	4495.63

4.75% MONTHLY PAYMENTS

AMOUNT	1 YEAR	2 YEARS	3 YEARS	4 YEARS	5 YEARS	6 YEARS	7 YEARS
100	8.55	4.38	2.99	2.29	1.88	1.60	1.40
200	17.10	8.75	5.97	4.58	3.75	3.20	2.80
500	42.75	21.88	14.93	11.46	9.38	7.99	7.01
1000	85.49	43.76	29.86	22.92	18.76	15.99	14.02
2000	170.99	87.52	59.72	45.83	37.51	31.98	28.03
3000	256.48	131.28	89.58	68.75	56.27	47.97	42.05
4000	341.97	175.04	119.44	91.66	75.03	63.96	56.07
5000	427.46	218.80	149.29	114.58	93.78	79.95	70.08
6000	512.96	262.56	179.15	137.50	112.54	95.94	84.10
7000	598.45	306.32	209.01	160.41	131.30	111.92	98.12
8000	683.94	350.08	238.87	183.33	150.06	127.91	112.13
9000	769.44	393.84	268.73	206.25	168.81	143.90	126.15
10000	854.93	437.60	298.59	229.16	187.57	159.89	140.17
11000	940.42	481.35	328.45	252.08	206.33	175.88	154.18
12000	1025.92	525.11	358.31	274.99	225.08	191.87	168.20
13000	1111.41	568.87	388.16	297.91	243.84	207.86	182.22
14000	1196.90	612.63	418.02	320.83	262.60	223.85	196.23
15000	1282.39	656.39	447.88	343.74	281.35	239.84	210.25
20000	1709.86	875.19	597.18	458.32	375.14	319.78	280.33
25000	2137.32	1093.99	746.47	572.91	468.92	399.73	350.42
30000	2564.79	1312.79	895.76	687.49	562.71	479.68	420.50
35000	2992.25	1531.58	1045.06	802.07	656.49	559.62	490.59
40000	3419.72	1750.38	1194.35	916.65	750.28	639.57	560.67
45000	3847.18	1969.18	1343.65	1031.23	844.06	719.52	630.75
50000	4274.65	2187.98	1492.94	1145.81	937.85	799.46	700.84
55000	4702.11	2406.77	1642.23	1260.39	1031.63	879.41	770.92
56000	4787.61	2450.53	1672.09	1283.31	1050.39	895.40	784.94
57000	4873.10	2494.29	1701.95	1306.22	1069.14	911.39	798.95
58000	4958.59	2538.05	1731.81	1329.14	1087.90	927.38	812.97
59000	5044.08	2581.81	1761.67	1352.06	1106.66	943.36	826.99
60000	5129.58	2625.57	1791.53	1374.97	1125.41	959.35	841.00
61000	5215.07	2669.33	1821.39	1397.89	1144.17	975.34	855.02
62000	5300.56	2713.09	1851.24	1420.81	1162.93	991.33	869.04
63000	5386.06	2756.85	1881.10	1443.72	1181.69	1007.32	883.05
64000	5471.55	2800.61	1910.96	1466.64	1200.44	1023.31	897.07
65000	5557.04	2844.37	1940.82	1489.55	1219.20	1039.30	911.09
70000	5984.51	3063.17	2090.11	1604.14	1312.98	1119.25	981.17
75000	6411.97	3281.96	2239.41	1718.72	1406.77	1199.19	1051.26
80000	6839.44	3500.76	2388.70	1833.30	1500.55	1279.14	1121.34
85000	7266.90	3719.56	2538.00	1947.88	1594.34	1359.08	1191.42
90000	7694.37	3938.36	2687.29	2062.46	1688.12	1439.03	1261.51
95000	8121.83	4157.15	2836.58	2177.04	1781.91	1518.98	1331.59
100000	8549.30	4375.95	2985.88	2291.62	1875.69	1598.92	1401.67
105000	8976.76	4594.75	3135.17	2406.20	1969.48	1678.87	1471.76
110000	9404.23	4813.55	3284.47	2520.78	2063.26	1758.81	1541.84
120000	10259.16	5251.14	3583.05	2749.95	2250.83	1918.71	1682.01
130000	11114.08	5688.74	3881.64	2979.11	2438.40	2078.60	1822.18
140000	11969.01	6126.33	4180.23	3208.27	2625.97	2238.49	1962.34
150000	12823.94	6563.93	4478.82	3437.43	2813.54	2398.38	2102.51
160000	13678.87	7001.52	4777.41	3666.59	3001.11	2558.28	2242.68
175000	14961.27	7657.92	5225.29	4010.34	3282.46	2798.11	2452.93
200000	17098.59	8751.90	5971.76	4583.24	3751.38	3197.84	2803.35
250000	21373.24	10939.88	7464.70	5729.05	4689.23	3997.31	3504.18
500000	42746.48	21879.76	14929.39	11458.11	9378.46	7994.61	7008.37
1000000	85492.96	43759.51	29858.78	22916.22	18756.91	15989.22	14016.74

MONTHLY PAYMENTS 4.75%

AMOUNT	8 YEARS	9 YEARS	10 YEARS	11 YEARS	12 YEARS	13 YEARS	14 YEARS
100	1.25	1.14	1.05	0.97	0.91	0.86	0.82
200	2.51	2.28	2.10	1.95	1.82	1.72	1.63
500	6.27	5.70	5.24	4.87	4.56	4.30	4.08
1000	12.54	11.40	10.48	9.74	9.12	8.60	8.16
2000	25.08	22.79	20.97	19.48	18.25	17.21	16.32
3000	37.62	34.19	31.45	29.22	27.37	25.81	24.48
4000	50.16	45.59	41.94	38.96	36.50	34.42	32.64
5000	62.71	56.99	52.42	48.71	45.62	43.02	40.80
6000	75.25	68.38	62.91	58.45	54.74	51.62	48.96
7000	87.79	79.78	73.39	68.19	63.87	60.23	57.12
8000	100.33	91.18	83.88	77.93	72.99	68.83	65.29
9000	112.87	102.57	94.36	87.67	82.12	77.44	73.45
10000	125.41	113.97	104.85	97.41	91.24	86.04	81.61
11000	137.95	125.37	115.33	107.15	100.36	94.65	89.77
12000	150.49	136.76	125.82	116.89	109.49	103.25	97.93
13000	163.04	148.16	136.30	126.63	118.61	111.85	106.09
14000	175.58	159.56	146.79	136.38	127.74	120.46	114.25
15000	188.12	170.96	157.27	146.12	136.86	129.06	122.41
20000	250.82	227.94	209.70	194.82	182.48	172.08	163.21
25000	313.53	284.93	262.12	243.53	228.10	215.10	204.02
30000	376.24	341.91	314.54	292.23	273.72	258.12	244.82
35000	438.94	398.90	366.97	340.94	319.34	301.14	285.62
40000	501.65	455.88	419.39	389.65	364.96	344.16	326.43
45000	564.36	512.87	471.81	438.35	410.58	387.19	367.23
50000	627.06	569.85	524.24	487.06	456.20	430.21	408.03
55000	689.77	626.84	576.66	535.76	501.82	473.23	448.84
56000	702.31	638.23	587.15	545.50	510.94	481.83	457.00
57000	714.85	649.63	597.63	555.25	520.07	490.43	465.16
58000	727.39	661.03	608.12	564.99	529.19	499.04	473.32
59000	739.93	672.43	618.60	574.73	538.32	507.64	481.48
60000	752.47	683.82	629.09	584.47	547.44	516.25	489.64
61000	765.02	695.22	639.57	594.21	556.56	524.85	497.80
62000	777.56	706.62	650.06	603.95	565.69	533.46	505.96
63000	790.10	718.01	660.54	613.69	574.81	542.06	514.12
64000	802.64	729.41	671.03	623.43	583.94	550.66	522.28
65000	815.18	740.81	681.51	633.17	593.06	559.27	530.44
70000	877.89	797.79	733.93	681.88	638.68	602.29	571.25
75000	940.59	854.78	786.36	730.59	684.30	645.31	612.05
80000	1003.30	911.76	838.78	779.29	729.92	688.33	652.85
85000	1066.01	968.75	891.21	828.00	775.54	731.35	693.66
90000	1128.71	1025.73	943.63	876.70	821.16	774.37	734.46
95000	1191.42	1082.72	996.05	925.41	866.78	817.39	775.26
100000	1254.12	1139.71	1048.48	974.11	912.40	860.41	816.07
105000	1316.83	1196.69	1100.90	1022.82	958.02	903.43	856.87
110000	1379.54	1253.68	1153.33	1071.53	1003.64	946.45	897.67
120000	1504.95	1367.65	1258.17	1168.94	1094.88	1032.49	979.28
130000	1630.36	1481.62	1363.02	1266.35	1186.12	1118.53	1060.89
140000	1755.77	1595.59	1467.87	1363.76	1277.36	1204.58	1142.49
150000	1881.19	1709.56	1572.72	1461.17	1368.60	1290.62	1224.10
160000	2006.60	1823.53	1677.56	1558.58	1459.84	1376.66	1305.70
175000	2194.72	1994.48	1834.84	1704.70	1596.70	1505.72	1428.11
200000	2508.25	2279.41	2096.95	1948.23	1824.80	1720.82	1632.13
250000	3135.31	2849.26	2621.19	2435.29	2281.00	2151.03	2040.16
500000	6270.62	5698.53	5242.39	4870.57	4562.00	4302.06	4080.33
1000000	12541.24	11397.05	10484.77	9741.15	9123.99	8604.11	8160.65

4.75% MONTHLY PAYMENTS

AMOUNT	15 YEARS	16 YEARS	17 YEARS	18 YEARS	19 YEARS	20 YEARS	21 YEARS
100	0.78	0.74	0.72	0.69	0.67	0.65	0.63
200	1.56	1.49	1.43	1.38	1.33	1.29	1.26
500	3.89	3.72	3.58	3.45	3.33	3.23	3.14
1000	7.78	7.45	7.15	6.90	6.67	6.46	6.28
2000	15.56	14.89	14.31	13.79	13.33	12.92	12.56
3000	23.33	22.34	21.46	20.69	20.00	19.39	18.84
4000	31.11	29.78	28.62	27.58	26.67	25.85	25.11
5000	38.89	37.23	35.77	34.48	33.33	32.31	31.39
6000	46.67	44.67	42.92	41.38	40.00	38.77	37.67
7000	54.45	52.12	50.08	48.27	46.67	45.24	43.95
8000	62.23	59.57	57.23	55.17	53.34	51.70	50.23
9000	70.00	67.01	64.38	62.06	60.00	58.16	56.51
10000	77.78	74.46	71.54	68.96	66.67	64.62	62.78
11000	85.56	81.90	78.69	75.86	73.34	71.08	69.06
12000	93.34	89.35	85.85	82.75	80.00	77.55	75.34
13000	101.12	96.79	93.00	89.65	86.67	84.01	81.62
14000	108.90	104.24	100.15	96.54	93.34	90.47	87.90
15000	116.67	111.68	107.31	103.44	100.00	96.93	94.18
20000	155.57	148.91	143.08	137.92	133.34	129.24	125.57
25000	194.46	186.14	178.85	172.40	166.67	161.56	156.96
30000	233.35	223.37	214.61	206.88	200.01	193.87	188.35
35000	272.24	260.60	250.38	241.36	233.34	226.18	219.74
40000	311.13	297.83	286.15	275.84	266.68	258.49	251.13
45000	350.02	335.05	321.92	310.32	300.01	290.80	282.53
50000	388.92	372.28	357.69	344.80	333.35	323.11	313.92
55000	427.81	409.51	393.46	379.28	366.68	355.42	345.31
56000	435.59	416.96	400.61	386.18	373.35	361.89	351.59
57000	443.36	424.40	407.77	393.08	380.02	368.35	357.87
58000	451.14	431.85	414.92	399.97	386.68	374.81	364.14
59000	458.92	439.29	422.08	406.87	393.35	381.27	370.42
60000	466.70	446.74	429.23	413.76	400.02	387.73	376.70
61000	474.48	454.18	436.38	420.66	406.69	394.20	382.98
62000	482.26	461.63	443.54	427.56	413.35	400.66	389.26
63000	490.03	469.07	450.69	434.45	420.02	407.12	395.54
64000	497.81	476.52	457.84	441.35	426.69	413.58	401.81
65000	505.59	483.97	465.00	448.24	433.35	420.05	408.09
70000	544.48	521.19	500.77	482.72	466.69	452.36	439.48
75000	583.37	558.42	536.54	517.21	500.02	484.67	470.88
80000	622.27	595.65	572.31	551.69	533.36	516.98	502.27
85000	661.16	632.88	608.08	586.17	566.69	549.29	533.66
90000	700.05	670.11	643.84	620.65	600.03	581.60	565.05
95000	738.94	707.34	679.61	655.13	633.36	613.91	596.44
100000	777.83	744.56	715.38	689.61	666.70	646.22	627.84
105000	816.72	781.79	751.15	724.09	700.03	678.53	659.23
110000	855.62	819.02	786.92	758.57	733.37	710.85	690.62
120000	933.40	893.48	858.46	827.53	800.04	775.47	753.40
130000	1011.18	967.93	930.00	896.49	866.71	840.09	816.19
140000	1088.96	1042.39	1001.54	965.45	933.38	904.71	878.97
150000	1166.75	1116.85	1073.07	1034.41	1000.05	969.34	941.75
160000	1244.53	1191.30	1144.61	1103.37	1066.72	1033.96	1004.54
175000	1361.21	1302.99	1251.92	1206.81	1166.72	1130.89	1098.71
200000	1555.66	1489.13	1430.77	1379.21	1333.40	1292.45	1255.67
250000	1944.58	1861.41	1788.46	1724.02	1666.74	1615.56	1569.59
500000	3889.16	3722.82	3576.91	3448.03	3333.49	3231.12	3139.18
1000000	7778.32	7445.63	7153.83	6896.07	6666.98	6462.24	6278.36

MONTHLY PAYMENTS 4.75%

AMOUNT	22 YEARS	23 YEARS	24 YEARS	25 YEARS	30 YEARS	35 YEARS	40 YEARS
100	0.61	0.60	0.58	0.57	0.52	0.49	0.47
200	1.22	1.19	1.17	1.14	1.04	0.98	0.93
500	3.06	2.98	2.91	2.85	2.61	2.44	2.33
1000	6.11	5.96	5.83	5.70	5.22	4.89	4.66
2000	12.22	11.92	11.65	11.40	10.43	9.78	9.32
3000	18.34	17.89	17.48	17.10	15.65	14.67	13.97
4000	24.45	23.85	23.30	22.80	20.87	19.55	18.63
5000	30.56	29.81	29.13	28.51	26.08	24.44	23.29
6000	36.67	35.77	34.95	34.21	31.30	29.33	27.95
7000	42.79	41.74	40.78	39.91	36.52	34.22	32.60
8000	48.90	47.70	46.61	45.61	41.73	39.11	37.26
9000	55.01	53.66	52.43	51.31	46.95	44.00	41.92
10000	61.12	59.62	58.26	57.01	52.16	48.89	46.58
11000	67.24	65.58	64.08	62.71	57.38	53.77	51.23
12000	73.35	71.55	69.91	68.41	62.60	58.66	55.89
13000	79.46	77.51	75.73	74.12	67.81	63.55	60.55
14000	85.57	83.47	81.56	79.82	73.03	68.44	65.21
15000	91.69	89.43	87.39	85.52	78.25	73.33	69.86
20000	122.25	119.25	116.51	114.02	104.33	97.77	93.15
25000	152.81	149.06	145.64	142.53	130.41	122.21	116.44
30000	183.37	178.87	174.77	171.04	156.49	146.66	139.73
35000	213.94	208.68	203.90	199.54	182.58	171.10	163.02
40000	244.50	238.49	233.03	228.05	208.66	195.54	186.30
45000	275.06	268.30	262.16	256.55	234.74	219.99	209.59
50000	305.62	298.11	291.29	285.06	260.82	244.43	232.88
55000	336.19	327.92	320.41	313.56	286.91	268.87	256.17
56000	342.30	333.89	326.24	319.27	292.12	273.76	260.82
57000	348.41	339.85	332.06	324.97	297.34	278.65	265.48
58000	354.52	345.81	337.89	330.67	302.56	283.54	270.14
59000	360.64	351.77	343.72	336.37	307.77	288.43	274.80
60000	366.75	357.74	349.54	342.07	312.99	293.31	279.45
61000	372.86	363.70	355.37	347.77	318.20	298.20	284.11
62000	378.97	369.66	361.19	353.47	323.42	303.09	288.77
63000	385.09	375.62	367.02	359.17	328.64	307.98	293.43
64000	391.20	381.58	372.84	364.88	333.85	312.87	298.09
65000	397.31	387.55	378.67	370.58	339.07	317.76	302.74
70000	427.87	417.36	407.80	399.08	365.15	342.20	326.03
75000	458.44	447.17	436.93	427.59	391.24	366.64	349.32
80000	489.00	476.98	466.06	456.09	417.32	391.09	372.61
85000	519.56	506.79	495.18	484.60	443.40	415.53	395.89
90000	550.12	536.60	524.31	513.11	469.48	439.97	419.18
95000	580.69	566.41	553.44	541.61	495.56	464.41	442.47
100000	611.25	596.23	582.57	570.12	521.65	488.86	465.76
105000	641.81	626.04	611.70	598.62	547.73	513.30	489.05
110000	672.37	655.85	640.83	627.13	573.81	537.74	512.33
120000	733.50	715.47	699.08	684.14	625.98	586.63	558.91
130000	794.62	775.09	757.34	741.15	678.14	635.51	605.49
140000	855.75	834.72	815.60	798.16	730.31	684.40	652.06
150000	916.87	894.34	873.86	855.18	782.47	733.29	698.64
160000	978.00	953.96	932.11	912.19	834.64	782.17	745.21
175000	1069.68	1043.39	1019.50	997.71	912.88	855.50	815.08
200000	1222.50	1192.45	1165.14	1140.23	1043.29	977.71	931.52
250000	1528.12	1490.56	1456.43	1425.29	1304.12	1222.14	1164.39
500000	3056.24	2981.13	2912.85	2850.59	2608.24	2444.28	2328.79
1000000	6112.48	5962.25	5825.70	5701.17	5216.47	4888.57	4657.58

5.00%   MONTHLY PAYMENTS

AMOUNT	1 YEAR	2 YEARS	3 YEARS	4 YEARS	5 YEARS	6 YEARS	7 YEARS
100	8.56	4.39	3.00	2.30	1.89	1.61	1.41
200	17.12	8.77	5.99	4.61	3.77	3.22	2.83
500	42.80	21.94	14.99	11.51	9.44	8.05	7.07
1000	85.61	43.87	29.97	23.03	18.87	16.10	14.13
2000	171.21	87.74	59.94	46.06	37.74	32.21	28.27
3000	256.82	131.61	89.91	69.09	56.61	48.31	42.40
4000	342.43	175.49	119.88	92.12	75.48	64.42	56.54
5000	428.04	219.36	149.85	115.15	94.36	80.52	70.67
6000	513.64	263.23	179.83	138.18	113.23	96.63	84.80
7000	599.25	307.10	209.80	161.21	132.10	112.73	98.94
8000	684.86	350.97	239.77	184.23	150.97	128.84	113.07
9000	770.47	394.84	269.74	207.26	169.84	144.94	127.21
10000	856.07	438.71	299.71	230.29	188.71	161.05	141.34
11000	941.68	482.59	329.68	253.32	207.58	177.15	155.47
12000	1027.29	526.46	359.65	276.35	226.45	193.26	169.61
13000	1112.90	570.33	389.62	299.38	245.33	209.36	183.74
14000	1198.50	614.20	419.59	322.41	264.20	225.47	197.87
15000	1284.11	658.07	449.56	345.44	283.07	241.57	212.01
20000	1712.15	877.43	599.42	460.59	377.42	322.10	282.68
25000	2140.19	1096.78	749.27	575.73	471.78	402.62	353.35
30000	2568.22	1316.14	899.13	690.88	566.14	483.15	424.02
35000	2996.26	1535.50	1048.98	806.03	660.49	563.67	494.69
40000	3424.30	1754.86	1198.84	921.17	754.85	644.20	565.36
45000	3852.34	1974.21	1348.69	1036.32	849.21	724.72	636.03
50000	4280.37	2193.57	1498.54	1151.46	943.56	805.25	706.70
55000	4708.41	2412.93	1648.40	1266.61	1037.92	885.77	777.36
56000	4794.02	2456.80	1678.37	1289.64	1056.79	901.88	791.50
57000	4879.62	2500.67	1708.34	1312.67	1075.66	917.98	805.63
58000	4965.23	2544.54	1738.31	1335.70	1094.53	934.09	819.77
59000	5050.84	2588.41	1768.28	1358.73	1113.40	950.19	833.90
60000	5136.45	2632.28	1798.25	1381.76	1132.27	966.30	848.03
61000	5222.06	2676.15	1828.22	1404.79	1151.15	982.40	862.17
62000	5307.66	2720.03	1858.20	1427.82	1170.02	998.51	876.30
63000	5393.27	2763.90	1888.17	1450.85	1188.89	1014.61	890.44
64000	5478.88	2807.77	1918.14	1473.87	1207.76	1030.72	904.57
65000	5564.49	2851.64	1948.11	1496.90	1226.63	1046.82	918.70
70000	5992.52	3071.00	2097.96	1612.05	1320.99	1127.35	989.37
75000	6420.56	3290.35	2247.82	1727.20	1415.34	1207.87	1060.04
80000	6848.60	3509.71	2397.67	1842.34	1509.70	1288.39	1130.71
85000	7276.64	3729.07	2547.53	1957.49	1604.05	1368.92	1201.38
90000	7704.67	3948.43	2697.38	2072.64	1698.41	1449.44	1272.05
95000	8132.71	4167.78	2847.24	2187.78	1792.77	1529.97	1342.72
100000	8560.75	4387.14	2997.09	2302.93	1887.12	1610.49	1413.39
105000	8988.79	4606.50	3146.94	2418.08	1981.48	1691.02	1484.06
110000	9416.82	4825.85	3296.80	2533.22	2075.84	1771.54	1554.73
120000	10272.90	5264.57	3596.51	2763.52	2264.55	1932.59	1696.07
130000	11128.97	5703.28	3896.22	2993.81	2453.26	2093.64	1837.41
140000	11985.05	6141.99	4195.93	3224.11	2641.97	2254.69	1978.75
150000	12841.12	6580.71	4495.63	3454.39	2830.69	2415.74	2120.09
160000	13697.20	7019.42	4795.34	3684.69	3019.40	2576.79	2261.43
175000	14981.31	7677.49	5244.91	4030.13	3302.47	2818.36	2473.43
200000	17121.50	8774.28	5994.18	4605.86	3774.25	3220.99	2826.78
250000	21401.87	10967.85	7492.72	5757.32	4717.81	4026.23	3533.48
500000	42803.74	21935.69	14985.45	11514.65	9435.62	8052.47	7066.95
1000000	85607.48	43871.39	29970.90	23029.29	18871.23	16104.93	14133.91

MONTHLY PAYMENTS   5.00%

AMOUNT	8 YEARS	9 YEARS	10 YEARS	11 YEARS	12 YEARS	13 YEARS	14 YEARS
100	1.27	1.15	1.06	0.99	0.92	0.87	0.83
200	2.53	2.30	2.12	1.97	1.85	1.75	1.66
500	6.33	5.76	5.30	4.93	4.62	4.37	4.14
1000	12.66	11.52	10.61	9.86	9.25	8.73	8.29
2000	25.32	23.03	21.21	19.73	18.50	17.46	16.58
3000	37.98	34.55	31.82	29.59	27.75	26.19	24.87
4000	50.64	46.07	42.43	39.46	37.00	34.92	33.15
5000	63.30	57.59	53.03	49.32	46.24	43.65	41.44
6000	75.96	69.10	63.64	59.19	55.49	52.38	49.73
7000	88.62	80.62	74.25	69.05	64.74	61.11	58.02
8000	101.28	92.14	84.85	78.92	73.99	69.84	66.31
9000	113.94	103.66	95.46	88.78	83.24	78.58	74.60
10000	126.60	115.17	106.07	98.64	92.49	87.31	82.89
11000	139.26	126.69	116.67	108.51	101.74	96.04	91.18
12000	151.92	138.21	127.28	118.37	110.99	104.77	99.46
13000	164.58	149.72	137.89	128.24	120.24	113.50	107.75
14000	177.24	161.24	148.49	138.10	129.48	122.23	116.04
15000	189.90	172.76	159.10	147.97	138.73	130.96	124.33
20000	253.20	230.35	212.13	197.29	184.98	174.61	165.77
25000	316.50	287.93	265.16	246.61	231.22	218.26	207.22
30000	379.80	345.52	318.20	295.93	277.47	261.92	248.66
35000	443.10	403.10	371.23	345.26	323.71	305.57	290.10
40000	506.40	460.69	424.26	394.58	369.96	349.22	331.55
45000	569.70	518.28	477.29	443.90	416.20	392.88	372.99
50000	633.00	575.86	530.33	493.22	462.45	436.53	414.44
55000	696.30	633.45	583.36	542.55	508.69	480.18	455.88
56000	708.96	644.97	593.97	552.41	517.94	488.91	464.17
57000	721.62	656.48	604.57	562.28	527.19	497.64	472.46
58000	734.28	668.00	615.18	572.14	536.44	506.37	480.75
59000	746.94	679.52	625.79	582.00	545.69	515.11	489.03
60000	759.60	691.04	636.39	591.87	554.93	523.84	497.32
61000	772.26	702.55	647.00	601.73	564.18	532.57	505.61
62000	784.92	714.07	657.61	611.60	573.43	541.30	513.90
63000	797.57	725.59	668.21	621.46	582.68	550.03	522.19
64000	810.23	737.11	678.82	631.33	591.93	558.76	530.48
65000	822.89	748.62	689.43	641.19	601.18	567.49	538.77
70000	886.19	806.21	742.46	690.51	647.42	611.14	580.21
75000	949.49	863.80	795.49	739.84	693.67	654.79	621.65
80000	1012.79	921.38	848.52	789.16	739.91	698.45	663.10
85000	1076.09	978.97	901.56	838.48	786.16	742.10	704.54
90000	1139.39	1036.55	954.59	887.80	832.40	785.75	745.98
95000	1202.69	1094.14	1007.62	937.13	878.65	829.41	787.43
100000	1265.99	1151.73	1060.66	986.45	924.89	873.06	828.87
105000	1329.29	1209.31	1113.69	1035.77	971.13	916.71	870.31
110000	1392.59	1266.90	1166.72	1085.09	1017.38	960.37	911.76
120000	1519.19	1382.07	1272.79	1183.74	1109.87	1047.67	994.64
130000	1645.79	1497.25	1378.85	1282.38	1202.36	1134.98	1077.53
140000	1772.39	1612.42	1484.92	1381.03	1294.85	1222.28	1160.42
150000	1898.99	1727.59	1590.98	1479.67	1387.34	1309.59	1243.31
160000	2025.59	1842.76	1697.05	1578.32	1479.82	1396.90	1326.19
175000	2215.49	2015.52	1856.15	1726.29	1618.56	1527.85	1450.52
200000	2531.98	2303.45	2121.31	1972.90	1849.78	1746.12	1657.74
250000	3164.98	2879.32	2651.64	2466.12	2312.23	2182.65	2072.18
500000	6329.96	5758.64	5303.28	4932.24	4624.45	4365.30	4144.35
1000000	12659.92	11517.27	10606.55	9864.49	9248.90	8730.60	8288.71

5.00% MONTHLY PAYMENTS

AMOUNT	15 YEARS	16 YEARS	17 YEARS	18 YEARS	19 YEARS	20 YEARS	21 YEARS
100	0.79	0.76	0.73	0.70	0.68	0.66	0.64
200	1.58	1.52	1.46	1.41	1.36	1.32	1.28
500	3.95	3.79	3.64	3.52	3.40	3.30	3.21
1000	7.91	7.58	7.29	7.03	6.80	6.60	6.42
2000	15.82	15.15	14.57	14.06	13.61	13.20	12.83
3000	23.72	22.73	21.86	21.09	20.41	19.80	19.25
4000	31.63	30.31	29.15	28.12	27.21	26.40	25.67
5000	39.54	37.88	36.43	35.15	34.01	33.00	32.09
6000	47.45	45.46	43.72	42.18	40.82	39.60	38.50
7000	55.36	53.04	51.01	49.21	47.62	46.20	44.92
8000	63.26	60.61	58.29	56.24	54.42	52.80	51.34
9000	71.17	68.19	65.58	63.27	61.22	59.40	57.75
10000	79.08	75.77	72.87	70.30	68.03	66.00	64.17
11000	86.99	83.34	80.15	77.33	74.83	72.60	70.59
12000	94.90	90.92	87.44	84.36	81.63	79.19	77.01
13000	102.80	98.50	94.73	91.39	88.44	85.79	83.42
14000	110.71	106.08	102.01	98.42	95.24	92.39	89.84
15000	118.62	113.65	109.30	105.46	102.04	98.99	96.26
20000	158.16	151.54	145.73	140.61	136.06	131.99	128.34
25000	197.70	189.42	182.16	175.76	170.07	164.99	160.43
30000	237.24	227.30	218.60	210.91	204.08	197.99	192.52
35000	276.78	265.19	255.03	246.06	238.10	230.98	224.60
40000	316.32	303.07	291.46	281.21	272.11	263.98	256.69
45000	355.86	340.96	327.89	316.37	306.12	296.98	288.77
50000	395.40	378.84	364.33	351.52	340.14	329.98	320.86
55000	434.94	416.72	400.76	386.67	374.15	362.98	352.95
56000	442.84	424.30	408.05	393.70	380.96	369.58	359.36
57000	450.75	431.88	415.33	400.73	387.76	376.17	365.78
58000	458.66	439.45	422.62	407.76	394.56	382.77	372.20
59000	466.57	447.03	429.91	414.79	401.36	389.37	378.61
60000	474.48	454.61	437.19	421.82	408.17	395.97	385.03
61000	482.38	462.19	444.48	428.85	414.97	402.57	391.45
62000	490.29	469.76	451.77	435.88	421.77	409.17	397.87
63000	498.20	477.34	459.05	442.91	428.57	415.77	404.28
64000	506.11	484.92	466.34	449.94	435.38	422.37	410.70
65000	514.02	492.49	473.63	456.97	442.18	428.97	417.12
70000	553.56	530.38	510.06	492.12	476.19	461.97	449.20
75000	593.10	568.26	546.49	527.28	510.21	494.97	481.29
80000	632.63	606.14	582.92	562.43	544.22	527.96	513.37
85000	672.17	644.03	619.36	597.58	578.24	560.96	545.46
90000	711.71	681.91	655.79	632.73	612.25	593.96	577.55
95000	751.25	719.80	692.22	667.88	646.26	626.96	609.63
100000	790.79	757.68	728.66	703.03	680.28	659.96	641.72
105000	830.33	795.57	765.09	738.19	714.29	692.95	673.80
110000	869.87	833.45	801.52	773.34	748.31	725.95	705.89
120000	948.95	909.22	874.39	843.64	816.33	791.95	770.06
130000	1028.03	984.99	947.25	913.94	884.36	857.94	834.23
140000	1107.11	1060.75	1020.12	984.25	952.39	923.94	898.41
150000	1186.19	1136.52	1092.98	1054.55	1020.42	989.93	962.58
160000	1265.27	1212.29	1165.85	1124.85	1088.44	1055.93	1026.75
175000	1383.89	1325.94	1275.15	1230.31	1190.49	1154.92	1123.01
200000	1581.59	1515.36	1457.31	1406.07	1360.56	1319.91	1283.44
250000	1976.98	1894.20	1821.64	1757.58	1700.69	1649.89	1604.30
500000	3953.97	3788.40	3643.28	3515.17	3401.39	3299.78	3208.59
1000000	7907.94	7576.81	7286.55	7030.34	6802.78	6599.56	6417.19

MONTHLY PAYMENTS 5.00%

AMOUNT	22 YEARS	23 YEARS	24 YEARS	25 YEARS	30 YEARS	35 YEARS	40 YEARS
100	0.63	0.61	0.60	0.58	0.54	0.50	0.48
200	1.25	1.22	1.19	1.17	1.07	1.01	0.96
500	3.13	3.05	2.98	2.92	2.68	2.52	2.41
1000	6.25	6.10	5.97	5.85	5.37	5.05	4.82
2000	12.51	12.21	11.94	11.69	10.74	10.09	9.64
3000	18.76	18.31	17.91	17.54	16.10	15.14	14.47
4000	25.01	24.42	23.88	23.38	21.47	20.19	19.29
5000	31.26	30.52	29.84	29.23	26.84	25.23	24.11
6000	37.52	36.62	35.81	35.08	32.21	30.28	28.93
7000	43.77	42.73	41.78	40.92	37.58	35.33	33.75
8000	50.02	48.83	47.75	46.77	42.95	40.38	38.58
9000	56.28	54.94	53.72	52.61	48.31	45.42	43.40
10000	62.53	61.04	59.69	58.46	53.68	50.47	48.22
11000	68.78	67.14	65.66	64.30	59.05	55.52	53.04
12000	75.03	73.25	71.63	70.15	64.42	60.56	57.86
13000	81.29	79.35	77.60	76.00	69.79	65.61	62.69
14000	87.54	85.46	83.57	81.84	75.16	70.66	67.51
15000	93.79	91.56	89.53	87.69	80.52	75.70	72.33
20000	125.06	122.08	119.38	116.92	107.36	100.94	96.44
25000	156.32	152.60	149.22	146.15	134.21	126.17	120.55
30000	187.58	183.12	179.07	175.38	161.05	151.41	144.66
35000	218.85	213.64	208.91	204.61	187.89	176.64	168.77
40000	250.11	244.16	238.76	233.84	214.73	201.88	192.88
45000	281.38	274.68	268.60	263.07	241.57	227.11	216.99
50000	312.64	305.20	298.45	292.30	268.41	252.34	241.10
55000	343.90	335.72	328.29	321.52	295.25	277.58	265.21
56000	350.16	341.83	334.26	327.37	300.62	282.63	270.03
57000	356.41	347.93	340.23	333.22	305.99	287.67	274.85
58000	362.66	354.04	346.20	339.06	311.36	292.72	279.67
59000	368.92	360.14	352.17	344.91	316.72	297.77	284.50
60000	375.17	366.24	358.14	350.75	322.09	302.81	289.32
61000	381.42	372.35	364.11	356.60	327.46	307.86	294.14
62000	387.67	378.45	370.08	362.45	332.83	312.91	298.96
63000	393.93	384.56	376.05	368.29	338.20	317.95	303.78
64000	400.18	390.66	382.01	374.14	343.57	323.00	308.61
65000	406.43	396.76	387.98	379.98	348.93	328.05	313.43
70000	437.70	427.28	417.83	409.21	375.78	353.28	337.54
75000	468.96	457.80	447.67	438.44	402.62	378.52	361.65
80000	500.22	488.32	477.52	467.67	429.46	403.75	385.76
85000	531.49	518.85	507.36	496.90	456.30	428.98	409.87
90000	562.75	549.37	537.21	526.13	483.14	454.22	433.98
95000	594.02	579.89	567.05	555.36	509.98	479.45	458.09
100000	625.28	610.41	596.90	584.59	536.82	504.69	482.20
105000	656.54	640.93	626.74	613.82	563.66	529.92	506.31
110000	687.81	671.45	656.59	643.05	590.50	555.16	530.42
120000	750.34	732.49	716.28	701.51	644.19	605.63	578.64
130000	812.86	793.53	775.97	759.97	697.87	656.09	626.86
140000	875.39	854.57	835.66	818.43	751.55	706.56	675.08
150000	937.92	915.61	895.35	876.89	805.23	757.03	723.29
160000	1000.45	976.65	955.04	935.34	858.91	807.50	771.51
175000	1094.24	1068.21	1044.57	1023.03	939.44	883.20	843.84
200000	1250.56	1220.81	1193.80	1169.18	1073.64	1009.38	964.39
250000	1563.20	1526.01	1492.24	1461.48	1342.05	1261.72	1205.49
500000	3126.40	3052.03	2984.49	2922.95	2684.11	2523.44	2410.98
1000000	6252.81	6104.06	5968.98	5845.90	5368.22	5046.88	4821.97

5.25%　　　　MONTHLY PAYMENTS

AMOUNT	1 YEAR	2 YEARS	3 YEARS	4 YEARS	5 YEARS	6 YEARS	7 YEARS
100	8.57	4.40	3.01	2.31	1.90	1.62	1.43
200	17.14	8.80	6.02	4.63	3.80	3.24	2.85
500	42.86	21.99	15.04	11.57	9.49	8.11	7.13
1000	85.72	43.98	30.08	23.14	18.99	16.22	14.25
2000	171.44	87.97	60.17	46.29	37.97	32.44	28.50
3000	257.17	131.95	90.25	69.43	56.96	48.66	42.76
4000	342.89	175.93	120.33	92.57	75.94	64.88	57.01
5000	428.61	219.92	150.42	115.71	94.93	81.11	71.26
6000	514.33	263.90	180.50	138.86	113.92	97.33	85.51
7000	600.05	307.88	210.58	162.00	132.90	113.55	99.76
8000	685.78	351.87	240.67	185.14	151.89	129.77	114.01
9000	771.50	395.85	270.75	208.28	170.87	145.99	128.27
10000	857.22	439.83	300.83	231.43	189.86	162.21	142.52
11000	942.94	483.82	330.92	254.57	208.85	178.43	156.77
12000	1028.67	527.80	361.00	277.71	227.83	194.65	171.02
13000	1114.39	571.78	391.08	300.86	246.82	210.87	185.27
14000	1200.11	615.77	421.17	324.00	265.80	227.10	199.52
15000	1285.83	659.75	451.25	347.14	284.79	243.32	213.78
20000	1714.44	879.67	601.67	462.85	379.72	324.42	285.03
25000	2143.05	1099.59	752.08	578.57	474.65	405.53	356.29
30000	2571.66	1319.50	902.50	694.28	569.58	486.63	427.55
35000	3000.27	1539.42	1052.91	809.99	664.51	567.7ˣ	498.81
40000	3428.88	1759.34	1203.33	925.71	759.44	648.85	570.07
45000	3857.49	1979.25	1353.75	1041.42	854.37	729.95	641.33
50000	4286.10	2199.17	1504.16	1157.14	949.30	811.06	712.58
55000	4714.71	2419.09	1654.58	1272.85	1044.23	892.16	783.84
56000	4800.44	2463.07	1684.66	1295.99	1063.22	908.38	798.09
57000	4886.16	2507.06	1714.75	1319.13	1082.20	924.61	812.35
58000	4971.88	2551.04	1744.83	1342.28	1101.19	940.83	826.60
59000	5057.60	2595.02	1774.91	1365.42	1120.17	957.05	840.85
60000	5143.33	2639.01	1805.00	1388.56	1139.16	973.27	855.10
61000	5229.05	2682.99	1835.08	1411.71	1158.15	989.49	869.35
62000	5314.77	2726.97	1865.16	1434.85	1177.13	1005.71	883.60
63000	5400.49	2770.96	1895.25	1457.99	1196.12	1021.93	897.86
64000	5486.21	2814.94	1925.33	1481.13	1215.10	1038.15	912.11
65000	5571.94	2858.92	1955.41	1504.28	1234.09	1054.37	926.36
70000	6000.55	3078.84	2105.83	1619.99	1329.02	1135.48	997.62
75000	6429.16	3298.76	2256.25	1735.70	1423.95	1216.59	1068.88
80000	6857.77	3518.67	2406.66	1851.42	1518.88	1297.69	1140.13
85000	7286.38	3738.59	2557.08	1967.13	1613.81	1378.80	1211.39
90000	7714.99	3958.51	2707.49	2082.84	1708.74	1459.90	1282.65
95000	8143.60	4178.43	2857.91	2198.56	1803.67	1541.01	1353.91
100000	8572.21	4398.34	3008.33	2314.27	1898.60	1622.12	1425.17
105000	9000.82	4618.26	3158.74	2429.98	1993.53	1703.22	1496.43
110000	9429.43	4838.18	3309.16	2545.70	2088.46	1784.33	1567.68
120000	10286.65	5278.01	3609.99	2777.13	2278.32	1946.54	1710.20
130000	11143.87	5717.85	3910.83	3008.55	2468.18	2108.75	1852.72
140000	12001.09	6157.68	4211.66	3239.98	2658.04	2270.96	1995.23
150000	12858.31	6597.52	4512.49	3471.41	2847.90	2433.17	2137.75
160000	13715.53	7037.35	4813.32	3702.83	3037.76	2595.38	2280.27
175000	15001.37	7697.10	5264.57	4049.97	3322.55	2838.70	2494.04
200000	17144.42	8796.69	6016.65	4628.54	3797.20	3244.23	2850.34
250000	21430.52	10995.86	7520.82	5785.68	4746.50	4055.29	3562.92
500000	42861.05	21991.72	15041.64	11571.36	9492.99	8110.58	7125.84
1000000	85722.09	43983.44	30083.27	23142.71	18985.98	16221.15	14251.68

MONTHLY PAYMENTS 5.25%

AMOUNT	8 YEARS	9 YEARS	10 YEARS	11 YEARS	12 YEARS	13 YEARS	14 YEARS
100	1.28	1.16	1.07	1.00	0.94	0.89	0.84
200	2.56	2.33	2.15	2.00	1.87	1.77	1.68
500	6.39	5.82	5.36	4.99	4.69	4.43	4.21
1000	12.78	11.64	10.73	9.99	9.37	8.86	8.42
2000	25.56	23.28	21.46	19.98	18.75	17.72	16.84
3000	38.34	34.91	32.19	29.97	28.12	26.57	25.25
4000	51.12	46.55	42.92	39.96	37.50	35.43	33.67
5000	63.90	58.19	53.65	49.94	46.87	44.29	42.09
6000	76.68	69.83	64.38	59.93	56.25	53.15	50.51
7000	89.45	81.47	75.10	69.92	65.62	62.01	58.93
8000	102.23	93.11	85.83	79.91	75.00	70.87	67.34
9000	115.01	104.74	96.56	89.90	84.37	79.72	75.76
10000	127.79	116.38	107.29	99.89	93.75	88.58	84.18
11000	140.57	128.02	118.02	109.88	103.12	97.44	92.60
12000	153.35	139.66	128.75	119.87	112.50	106.30	101.01
13000	166.13	151.30	139.48	129.85	121.87	115.16	109.43
14000	178.91	162.94	150.21	139.84	131.25	124.01	117.85
15000	191.69	174.57	160.94	149.83	140.62	132.87	126.27
20000	255.59	232.77	214.58	199.78	187.50	177.16	168.36
25000	319.48	290.96	268.23	249.72	234.37	221.45	210.45
30000	383.38	349.16	321.88	299.66	281.24	265.74	252.54
35000	447.27	407.34	375.52	349.61	328.12	310.04	294.63
40000	511.17	465.53	429.17	399.55	374.99	354.33	336.72
45000	575.07	523.72	482.81	449.49	421.87	398.62	378.81
50000	638.96	581.91	536.46	499.44	468.74	442.91	420.90
55000	702.86	640.10	590.10	549.38	515.61	487.20	462.99
56000	715.64	651.74	600.83	559.37	524.99	496.06	471.40
57000	728.42	663.38	611.56	569.36	534.36	504.91	479.82
58000	741.20	675.02	622.29	579.35	543.74	513.77	488.24
59000	753.98	686.66	633.02	589.34	553.11	522.63	496.66
60000	766.76	698.30	643.75	599.33	562.49	531.49	505.07
61000	779.54	709.93	654.48	609.31	571.86	540.35	513.49
62000	792.32	721.57	665.21	619.30	581.24	549.21	521.91
63000	805.09	733.21	675.94	629.29	590.61	558.06	530.33
64000	817.87	744.85	686.67	639.28	599.99	566.92	538.75
65000	830.65	756.49	697.40	649.27	609.36	575.78	547.16
70000	894.55	814.68	751.04	699.21	656.24	620.07	589.25
75000	958.45	872.87	804.69	749.16	703.11	664.36	631.34
80000	1022.34	931.06	858.33	799.10	749.99	708.65	673.43
85000	1086.24	989.25	911.98	849.04	796.86	752.94	715.52
90000	1150.14	1047.44	965.63	898.99	843.73	797.23	757.61
95000	1214.03	1105.63	1019.27	948.93	890.61	841.52	799.70
100000	1277.93	1163.83	1072.92	998.88	937.48	885.82	841.79
105000	1341.82	1222.02	1126.56	1048.82	984.36	930.11	883.88
110000	1405.72	1280.21	1180.21	1098.76	1031.23	974.40	925.97
120000	1533.51	1396.59	1287.50	1198.65	1124.98	1062.98	1010.15
130000	1661.31	1512.97	1394.79	1298.54	1218.73	1151.56	1094.33
140000	1789.10	1629.36	1502.08	1398.43	1312.47	1240.14	1178.51
150000	1916.89	1745.74	1609.38	1498.31	1406.22	1328.72	1262.69
160000	2044.69	1862.12	1716.67	1598.20	1499.97	1417.30	1346.87
175000	2236.37	2036.69	1877.60	1748.03	1640.59	1550.18	1473.13
200000	2555.86	2327.65	2145.83	1997.76	1874.96	1771.63	1683.58
250000	3194.82	2909.56	2682.29	2497.19	2343.70	2214.54	2104.48
500000	6389.64	5819.13	5364.59	4994.38	4687.41	4429.08	4208.95
1000000	12779.28	11638.26	10729.17	9988.75	9374.82	8858.16	8417.91

5.25% MONTHLY PAYMENTS

AMOUNT	15 YEARS	16 YEARS	17 YEARS	18 YEARS	19 YEARS	20 YEARS	21 YEARS
100	0.80	0.77	0.74	0.72	0.69	0.67	0.66
200	1.61	1.54	1.48	1.43	1.39	1.35	1.31
500	4.02	3.85	3.71	3.58	3.47	3.37	3.28
1000	8.04	7.71	7.42	7.17	6.94	6.74	6.56
2000	16.08	15.42	14.84	14.33	13.88	13.48	13.12
3000	24.12	23.13	22.26	21.50	20.82	20.22	19.67
4000	32.16	30.84	29.68	28.66	27.76	26.95	26.23
5000	40.19	38.55	37.10	35.83	34.70	33.69	32.79
6000	48.23	46.26	44.52	43.00	41.64	40.43	39.35
7000	56.27	53.96	51.94	50.16	48.58	47.17	45.90
8000	64.31	61.67	59.37	57.33	55.52	53.91	52.46
9000	72.35	69.38	66.79	64.49	62.46	60.65	59.02
10000	80.39	77.09	74.21	71.66	69.40	67.38	65.58
11000	88.43	84.80	81.63	78.83	76.34	74.12	72.13
12000	96.47	92.51	89.05	85.99	83.28	80.86	78.69
13000	104.50	100.22	96.47	93.16	90.22	87.60	85.25
14000	112.54	107.93	103.89	100.32	97.16	94.34	91.81
15000	120.58	115.64	111.31	107.49	104.10	101.08	98.36
20000	160.78	154.19	148.41	143.32	138.80	134.77	131.15
25000	200.97	192.73	185.52	179.15	173.50	168.46	163.94
30000	241.16	231.28	222.62	214.98	208.20	202.15	196.73
35000	281.36	269.82	259.72	250.81	242.90	235.85	229.52
40000	321.55	308.37	296.83	286.64	277.60	269.54	262.31
45000	361.74	346.92	333.93	322.47	312.30	303.23	295.09
50000	401.94	385.46	371.03	358.30	347.00	336.92	327.88
55000	442.13	424.01	408.14	394.13	381.70	370.61	360.67
56000	450.17	431.72	415.56	401.30	388.64	377.35	367.23
57000	458.21	439.43	422.98	408.46	395.58	384.09	373.79
58000	466.25	447.14	430.40	415.63	402.52	390.83	380.34
59000	474.29	454.85	437.82	422.80	409.46	397.57	386.90
60000	482.33	462.56	445.24	429.96	416.40	404.31	393.46
61000	490.37	470.27	452.66	437.13	423.34	411.04	400.02
62000	498.40	477.98	460.08	444.29	430.28	417.78	406.57
63000	506.44	485.68	467.50	451.46	437.22	424.52	413.13
64000	514.48	493.39	474.92	458.63	444.16	431.26	419.69
65000	522.52	501.10	482.34	465.79	451.11	438.00	426.25
70000	562.71	539.65	519.45	501.62	485.81	471.69	459.03
75000	602.91	578.20	556.55	537.45	520.51	505.38	491.82
80000	643.10	616.74	593.65	573.28	555.21	539.08	524.61
85000	683.30	655.29	630.75	609.11	589.91	572.77	557.40
90000	723.49	693.84	667.86	644.94	624.61	606.46	590.19
95000	763.68	732.38	704.96	680.77	659.31	640.15	622.98
100000	803.88	770.93	742.06	716.60	694.01	673.84	655.76
105000	844.07	809.47	779.17	752.43	728.71	707.54	688.55
110000	884.27	848.02	816.27	788.26	763.41	741.23	721.34
120000	964.65	925.11	890.48	859.92	832.81	808.61	786.92
130000	1045.04	1002.21	964.68	931.59	902.21	876.00	852.49
140000	1125.43	1079.30	1038.89	1003.25	971.61	943.38	918.07
150000	1205.82	1156.39	1113.10	1074.91	1041.01	1010.77	983.65
160000	1286.20	1233.48	1187.30	1146.57	1110.41	1078.15	1049.22
175000	1406.79	1349.12	1298.61	1254.06	1214.51	1179.23	1147.59
200000	1607.76	1541.86	1484.13	1433.21	1388.02	1347.69	1311.53
250000	2009.69	1927.32	1855.16	1791.51	1735.02	1684.61	1639.41
500000	4019.39	3854.64	3710.32	3583.02	3470.04	3369.22	3278.82
1000000	8038.78	7709.28	7420.64	7166.04	6940.08	6738.44	6557.64

MONTHLY PAYMENTS 5.25%

AMOUNT	22 YEARS	23 YEARS	24 YEARS	25 YEARS	30 YEARS	35 YEARS	40 YEARS
100	0.64	0.62	0.61	0.60	0.55	0.52	0.50
200	1.28	1.25	1.22	1.20	1.10	1.04	1.00
500	3.20	3.12	3.06	3.00	2.76	2.60	2.49
1000	6.39	6.25	6.11	5.99	5.52	5.21	4.99
2000	12.79	12.50	12.23	11.98	11.04	10.41	9.98
3000	19.18	18.74	18.34	17.98	16.57	15.62	14.97
4000	25.58	24.99	24.46	23.97	22.09	20.83	19.95
5000	31.97	31.24	30.57	29.96	27.61	26.04	24.94
6000	38.37	37.49	36.68	35.95	33.13	31.24	29.93
7000	44.76	43.73	42.80	41.95	38.65	36.45	34.92
8000	51.16	49.98	48.91	47.94	44.18	41.66	39.91
9000	57.55	56.23	55.03	53.93	49.70	46.87	44.90
10000	63.95	62.48	61.14	59.92	55.22	52.07	49.89
11000	70.34	68.72	67.25	65.92	60.74	57.28	54.88
12000	76.74	74.97	73.37	71.91	66.26	62.49	59.86
13000	83.13	81.22	79.48	77.90	71.79	67.70	64.85
14000	89.53	87.47	85.60	83.89	77.31	72.90	69.84
15000	95.92	93.71	91.71	89.89	82.83	78.11	74.83
20000	127.90	124.95	122.28	119.85	110.44	104.15	99.77
25000	159.87	156.19	152.85	149.81	138.05	130.19	124.72
30000	191.84	187.43	183.42	179.77	165.66	156.22	149.66
35000	223.82	218.67	213.99	209.74	193.27	182.26	174.60
40000	255.79	249.90	244.56	239.70	220.88	208.30	199.55
45000	287.77	281.14	275.13	269.66	248.49	234.33	224.49
50000	319.74	312.38	305.70	299.62	276.10	260.37	249.44
55000	351.71	343.62	336.27	329.59	303.71	286.41	274.38
56000	358.11	349.87	342.39	335.58	309.23	291.62	279.37
57000	364.50	356.11	348.50	341.57	314.76	296.82	284.36
58000	370.90	362.36	354.61	347.56	320.28	302.03	289.34
59000	377.29	368.61	360.73	353.56	325.80	307.24	294.33
60000	383.69	374.86	366.84	359.55	331.32	312.45	299.32
61000	390.08	381.10	372.96	365.54	336.84	317.65	304.31
62000	396.48	387.35	379.07	371.53	342.37	322.86	309.30
63000	402.87	393.60	385.18	377.53	347.89	328.07	314.29
64000	409.27	399.85	391.30	383.52	353.41	333.28	319.28
65000	415.66	406.09	397.41	389.51	358.93	338.48	324.27
70000	447.64	437.33	427.98	419.47	386.54	364.52	349.21
75000	479.61	468.57	458.55	449.44	414.15	390.56	374.15
80000	511.59	499.81	489.12	479.40	441.76	416.59	399.10
85000	543.56	531.05	519.69	509.36	469.37	442.63	424.04
90000	575.53	562.28	550.26	539.32	496.98	468.67	448.98
95000	607.51	593.52	580.83	569.29	524.59	494.71	473.93
100000	639.48	624.76	611.40	599.25	552.20	520.74	498.87
105000	671.46	656.00	641.97	629.21	579.81	546.78	523.81
110000	703.43	687.24	672.55	659.17	607.42	572.82	548.76
120000	767.38	749.71	733.69	719.10	662.64	624.89	598.64
130000	831.33	812.19	794.83	779.02	717.86	676.97	648.53
140000	895.27	874.67	855.97	838.95	773.09	729.04	698.42
150000	959.22	937.14	917.11	898.87	828.31	781.11	748.31
160000	1023.17	999.62	978.25	958.80	883.53	833.19	798.19
175000	1119.09	1093.33	1069.96	1048.68	966.36	911.30	873.02
200000	1278.96	1249.52	1222.81	1198.50	1104.41	1041.49	997.74
250000	1598.70	1561.90	1528.51	1498.12	1380.51	1301.86	1247.18
500000	3197.41	3123.80	3057.02	2996.24	2761.02	2603.72	2494.35
1000000	6394.82	6247.61	6114.05	5992.48	5522.04	5207.43	4988.70

5.50%   MONTHLY PAYMENTS

AMOUNT	1 YEAR	2 YEARS	3 YEARS	4 YEARS	5 YEARS	6 YEARS	7 YEARS
100	8.58	4.41	3.02	2.33	1.91	1.63	1.44
200	17.17	8.82	6.04	4.65	3.82	3.27	2.87
500	42.92	22.05	15.10	11.63	9.55	8.17	7.19
1000	85.84	44.10	30.20	23.26	19.10	16.34	14.37
2000	171.67	88.19	60.39	46.51	38.20	32.68	28.74
3000	257.51	132.29	90.59	69.77	57.30	49.01	43.11
4000	343.35	176.38	120.78	93.03	76.40	65.35	57.48
5000	429.18	220.48	150.98	116.28	95.51	81.69	71.85
6000	515.02	264.57	181.18	139.54	114.61	98.03	86.22
7000	600.86	308.67	211.37	162.80	133.71	114.37	100.59
8000	686.69	352.77	241.57	186.05	152.81	130.70	114.96
9000	772.53	396.86	271.76	209.31	171.91	147.04	129.33
10000	858.37	440.96	301.96	232.56	191.01	163.38	143.70
11000	944.20	485.05	332.15	255.82	210.11	179.72	158.07
12000	1030.04	529.15	362.35	279.08	229.21	196.05	172.44
13000	1115.88	573.24	392.55	302.33	248.32	212.39	186.81
14000	1201.71	617.34	422.74	325.59	267.42	228.73	201.18
15000	1287.55	661.43	452.94	348.85	286.52	245.07	215.55
20000	1716.74	881.91	603.92	465.13	382.02	326.76	287.40
25000	2145.92	1102.39	754.90	581.41	477.53	408.45	359.25
30000	2575.01	1322.87	905.88	697.69	573.03	490.14	431.10
35000	3004.29	1543.35	1056.86	813.98	668.54	571.83	502.95
40000	3433.47	1763.83	1207.84	930.26	764.05	653.52	574.80
45000	3862.66	1984.30	1358.82	1046.54	859.55	735.20	646.65
50000	4291.84	2204.78	1509.80	1162.82	955.06	816.89	718.50
55000	4721.02	2425.26	1660.77	1279.11	1050.56	898.58	790.35
56000	4806.86	2469.36	1690.97	1302.36	1069.67	914.92	804.72
57000	4892.70	2513.45	1721.17	1325.62	1088.77	931.26	819.09
58000	4978.53	2557.55	1751.36	1348.88	1107.87	947.60	833.46
59000	5064.37	2601.64	1781.56	1372.13	1126.97	963.94	847.83
60000	5150.21	2645.74	1811.75	1395.39	1146.07	980.27	862.20
61000	5236.04	2689.84	1841.95	1418.64	1165.17	996.61	876.57
62000	5321.88	2733.93	1872.15	1441.90	1184.27	1012.95	890.94
63000	5407.72	2778.03	1902.34	1465.16	1203.37	1029.29	905.31
64000	5493.55	2822.12	1932.54	1488.41	1222.47	1045.62	919.68
65000	5579.39	2866.22	1962.73	1511.67	1241.58	1061.96	934.05
70000	6008.57	3086.70	2113.71	1627.95	1337.08	1143.65	1005.90
75000	6437.76	3307.17	2264.69	1744.24	1432.59	1225.34	1077.75
80000	6866.94	3527.65	2415.67	1860.52	1528.09	1307.03	1149.60
85000	7296.13	3748.13	2566.65	1976.80	1623.60	1388.72	1221.45
90000	7725.31	3968.61	2717.63	2093.08	1719.10	1470.41	1293.30
95000	8154.49	4189.09	2868.61	2209.37	1814.61	1552.10	1365.15
100000	8583.68	4409.57	3019.59	2325.65	1910.12	1633.79	1437.00
105000	9012.86	4630.04	3170.57	2441.93	2005.62	1715.48	1508.85
110000	9442.05	4850.52	3321.55	2558.21	2101.13	1797.17	1580.70
120000	10300.41	5291.48	3623.51	2790.78	2292.14	1960.55	1724.41
130000	11158.78	5732.44	3925.47	3023.34	2483.15	2123.93	1868.11
140000	12017.15	6173.39	4227.43	3255.91	2674.16	2287.30	2011.81
150000	12875.52	6614.35	4529.39	3488.47	2865.17	2450.68	2155.51
160000	13733.89	7055.30	4831.34	3721.04	3056.19	2614.06	2299.21
175000	15021.44	7716.74	5284.28	4069.88	3342.70	2859.13	2514.76
200000	17167.36	8819.13	6039.18	4651.30	3820.23	3267.58	2874.01
250000	21459.20	11023.91	7548.98	5814.12	4775.29	4084.47	3592.51
500000	42918.39	22047.83	15097.95	11628.24	9550.58	8168.94	7185.02
1000000	85836.78	44095.66	30195.90	23256.48	19101.16	16337.89	14370.04

MONTHLY PAYMENTS 5.50%

AMOUNT	8 YEARS	9 YEARS	10 YEARS	11 YEARS	12 YEARS	13 YEARS	14 YEARS
100	1.29	1.18	1.09	1.01	0.95	0.90	0.85
200	2.58	2.35	2.17	2.02	1.90	1.80	1.71
500	6.45	5.88	5.43	5.06	4.75	4.49	4.27
1000	12.90	11.76	10.85	10.11	9.50	8.99	8.55
2000	25.80	23.52	21.71	20.23	19.00	17.97	17.10
3000	38.70	35.28	32.56	30.34	28.51	26.96	25.64
4000	51.60	47.04	43.41	40.46	38.01	35.95	34.19
5000	64.50	58.80	54.26	50.57	47.51	44.93	42.74
6000	77.40	70.56	65.12	60.68	57.01	53.92	51.29
7000	90.30	82.32	75.97	70.80	66.51	62.91	59.84
8000	103.19	94.08	86.82	80.91	76.01	71.89	68.39
9000	116.09	105.84	97.67	91.03	85.52	80.88	76.93
10000	128.99	117.60	108.53	101.14	95.02	89.87	85.48
11000	141.89	129.36	119.38	111.25	104.52	98.85	94.03
12000	154.79	141.12	130.23	121.37	114.02	107.84	102.58
13000	167.69	152.88	141.08	131.48	123.52	116.83	111.13
14000	180.59	164.64	151.94	141.60	133.02	125.81	119.68
15000	193.49	176.40	162.79	151.71	142.53	134.80	128.22
20000	257.99	235.20	217.05	202.28	190.03	179.74	170.97
25000	322.48	294.00	271.32	252.85	237.54	224.67	213.71
30000	386.98	352.80	325.58	303.42	285.05	269.60	256.45
35000	451.48	411.60	379.84	353.99	332.56	314.54	299.19
40000	515.97	470.40	434.11	404.56	380.07	359.47	341.93
45000	580.47	529.20	488.37	455.13	427.58	404.41	384.67
50000	644.97	588.00	542.63	505.70	475.09	449.34	427.41
55000	709.46	646.80	596.89	556.27	522.59	494.27	470.15
56000	722.36	658.56	607.75	566.38	532.10	503.26	478.70
57000	735.26	670.32	618.60	576.49	541.60	512.25	487.25
58000	748.16	682.08	629.45	586.61	551.10	521.23	495.80
59000	761.06	693.84	640.31	596.72	560.60	530.22	504.35
60000	773.96	705.60	651.16	606.84	570.10	539.21	512.90
61000	786.86	717.36	662.01	616.95	579.61	548.19	521.44
62000	799.76	729.12	672.86	627.06	589.11	557.18	529.99
63000	812.66	740.88	683.72	637.18	598.61	566.17	538.54
64000	825.56	752.64	694.57	647.29	608.11	575.15	547.09
65000	838.46	764.40	705.42	657.41	617.61	584.14	555.64
70000	902.95	823.20	759.68	707.98	665.12	629.07	598.38
75000	967.45	882.00	813.95	758.54	712.63	674.01	641.12
80000	1031.95	940.80	868.21	809.11	760.14	718.94	683.86
85000	1096.44	999.60	922.47	859.68	807.65	763.88	726.60
90000	1160.94	1058.40	976.74	910.25	855.15	808.81	769.34
95000	1225.44	1117.20	1031.00	960.82	902.66	853.74	812.08
100000	1289.93	1176.00	1085.26	1011.39	950.17	898.68	854.83
105000	1354.43	1234.80	1139.53	1061.96	997.68	943.61	897.57
110000	1418.93	1293.60	1193.79	1112.53	1045.19	988.55	940.31
120000	1547.92	1411.20	1302.32	1213.67	1140.21	1078.41	1025.79
130000	1676.91	1528.80	1410.84	1314.81	1235.22	1168.28	1111.27
140000	1805.91	1646.40	1519.37	1415.95	1330.24	1258.15	1196.76
150000	1934.90	1764.00	1627.89	1517.09	1425.26	1348.02	1282.24
160000	2063.89	1881.60	1736.42	1618.23	1520.28	1437.89	1367.72
175000	2257.38	2058.00	1899.21	1769.94	1662.80	1572.69	1495.94
200000	2579.86	2352.00	2170.53	2022.79	1900.34	1797.36	1709.65
250000	3224.83	2940.00	2713.16	2528.48	2375.43	2246.70	2137.06
500000	6449.66	5880.00	5426.31	5056.97	4750.86	4493.39	4274.13
1000000	12899.32	11760.00	10852.63	10113.93	9501.72	8986.79	8548.26

5.50%　　　MONTHLY PAYMENTS

AMOUNT	15 YEAR	16 YEARS	17 YEARS	18 YEARS	19 YEARS	20 YEARS	21 YEARS
100	0.82	0.78	0.76	0.73	0.71	0.69	0.67
200	1.63	1.57	1.51	1.46	1.42	1.38	1.34
500	4.09	3.92	3.78	3.65	3.54	3.44	3.35
1000	8.17	7.84	7.56	7.30	7.08	6.88	6.70
2000	16.34	15.69	15.11	14.61	14.16	13.76	13.40
3000	24.51	23.53	22.67	21.91	21.24	20.64	20.10
4000	32.68	31.37	30.22	29.21	28.32	27.52	26.80
5000	40.85	39.22	37.78	36.52	35.39	34.39	33.50
6000	49.03	47.06	45.34	43.82	42.47	41.27	40.20
7000	57.20	54.90	52.89	51.12	49.55	48.15	46.90
8000	65.37	62.74	60.45	58.43	56.63	55.03	53.60
9000	73.54	70.59	68.00	65.73	63.71	61.91	60.30
10000	81.71	78.43	75.56	73.03	70.79	68.79	67.00
11000	89.88	86.27	83.12	80.33	77.87	75.67	73.70
12000	98.05	94.12	90.67	87.64	84.95	82.55	80.40
13000	106.22	101.96	98.23	94.94	92.03	89.43	87.10
14000	114.39	109.80	105.79	102.24	99.10	96.30	93.80
15000	122.56	117.65	113.34	109.55	106.18	103.18	100.50
20000	163.42	156.86	151.12	146.06	141.58	137.58	133.99
25000	204.27	196.08	188.90	182.58	176.97	171.97	167.49
30000	245.13	235.29	226.68	219.09	212.37	206.37	200.99
35000	285.98	274.51	264.46	255.61	247.76	240.76	234.49
40000	326.83	313.72	302.24	292.13	283.15	275.15	267.99
45000	367.69	352.94	340.02	328.64	318.55	309.55	301.49
50000	408.54	392.15	377.80	365.16	353.94	343.94	334.99
55000	449.40	431.37	415.59	401.67	389.34	378.34	368.48
56000	457.57	439.21	423.14	408.98	396.42	385.22	375.18
57000	465.74	447.05	430.70	416.28	403.50	392.10	381.88
58000	473.91	454.90	438.25	423.58	410.57	398.97	388.58
59000	482.08	462.74	445.81	430.89	417.65	405.85	395.28
60000	490.25	470.58	453.37	438.19	424.73	412.73	401.98
61000	498.42	478.43	460.92	445.49	431.81	419.61	408.68
62000	506.59	486.27	468.48	452.80	438.89	426.49	415.38
63000	514.76	494.11	476.03	460.10	445.97	433.37	422.08
64000	522.93	501.95	483.59	467.40	453.05	440.25	428.78
65000	531.10	509.80	491.15	474.71	460.13	447.13	435.48
70000	571.96	549.01	528.93	511.22	495.52	481.52	468.98
75000	612.81	588.23	566.71	547.74	530.91	515.92	502.48
80000	653.67	627.44	604.49	584.25	566.31	550.31	535.98
85000	694.52	666.66	642.27	620.77	601.70	584.70	569.47
90000	735.38	705.87	680.05	657.28	637.10	619.10	602.97
95000	776.23	745.09	717.83	693.80	672.49	653.49	636.47
100000	817.08	784.30	755.61	730.32	707.89	687.89	669.97
105000	857.94	823.52	793.39	766.83	743.28	722.28	703.47
110000	898.79	862.73	831.17	803.35	778.67	756.68	736.97
120000	980.50	941.16	906.73	876.38	849.46	825.46	803.96
130000	1062.21	1019.60	982.29	949.41	920.25	894.25	870.96
140000	1143.92	1098.03	1057.85	1022.44	991.04	963.04	937.96
150000	1225.63	1176.46	1133.41	1095.47	1061.83	1031.83	1004.96
160000	1307.33	1254.89	1208.97	1168.51	1132.62	1100.62	1071.95
175000	1429.90	1372.53	1322.32	1278.05	1238.80	1203.80	1172.45
200000	1634.17	1568.61	1511.22	1460.63	1415.77	1375.77	1339.94
250000	2042.71	1960.76	1889.02	1825.79	1769.72	1719.72	1674.93
500000	4085.42	3921.52	3778.05	3651.58	3539.43	3439.44	3349.85
1000000	8170.83	7843.04	7556.09	7303.16	7078.86	6878.87	6699.70

MONTHLY PAYMENTS 5.50%

AMOUNT	22 YEARS	23 YEARS	24 YEARS	25 YEARS	30 YEARS	35 YEARS	40 YEARS
100	0.65	0.64	0.63	0.61	0.57	0.54	0.52
200	1.31	1.28	1.25	1.23	1.14	1.07	1.03
500	3.27	3.20	3.13	3.07	2.84	2.69	2.58
1000	6.54	6.39	6.26	6.14	5.68	5.37	5.16
2000	13.08	12.79	12.52	12.28	11.36	10.74	10.32
3000	19.62	19.18	18.78	18.42	17.03	16.11	15.47
4000	26.15	25.57	25.04	24.56	22.71	21.48	20.63
5000	32.69	31.96	31.30	30.70	28.39	26.85	25.79
6000	39.23	38.36	37.57	36.85	34.07	32.22	30.95
7000	45.77	44.75	43.83	42.99	39.75	37.59	36.10
8000	52.31	51.14	50.09	49.13	45.42	42.96	41.26
9000	58.85	57.54	56.35	55.27	51.10	48.33	46.42
10000	65.38	63.93	62.61	61.41	56.78	53.70	51.58
11000	71.92	70.32	68.87	67.55	62.46	59.07	56.73
12000	78.46	76.71	75.13	73.69	68.13	64.44	61.89
13000	85.00	83.11	81.39	79.83	73.81	69.81	67.05
14000	91.54	89.50	87.65	85.97	79.49	75.18	72.21
15000	98.08	95.89	93.91	92.11	85.17	80.55	77.37
20000	130.77	127.86	125.22	122.82	113.56	107.40	103.15
25000	163.46	159.82	156.52	153.52	141.95	134.25	128.94
30000	196.15	191.79	187.83	184.23	170.34	161.10	154.73
35000	228.85	223.75	219.13	214.93	198.73	187.96	180.52
40000	261.54	255.72	250.44	245.63	227.12	214.81	206.31
45000	294.23	287.68	281.74	276.34	255.51	241.66	232.10
50000	326.92	319.64	313.04	307.04	283.89	268.51	257.89
55000	359.62	351.61	344.35	337.75	312.28	295.36	283.67
56000	366.16	358.00	350.61	343.89	317.96	300.73	288.83
57000	372.69	364.39	356.87	350.03	323.64	306.10	293.99
58000	379.23	370.79	363.13	356.17	329.32	311.47	299.15
59000	385.77	377.18	369.39	362.31	335.00	316.84	304.30
60000	392.31	383.57	375.65	368.45	340.67	322.21	309.46
61000	398.85	389.97	381.91	374.59	346.35	327.58	314.62
62000	405.39	396.36	388.18	380.73	352.03	332.95	319.78
63000	411.92	402.75	394.44	386.88	357.71	338.32	324.94
64000	418.46	409.14	400.70	393.02	363.38	343.69	330.09
65000	425.00	415.54	406.96	399.16	369.06	349.06	335.25
70000	457.69	447.50	438.26	429.86	397.45	375.91	361.04
75000	490.39	479.47	469.57	460.57	425.84	402.76	386.83
80000	523.08	511.43	500.87	491.27	454.23	429.61	412.62
85000	555.77	543.39	532.18	521.97	482.62	456.46	438.40
90000	588.46	575.36	563.48	552.68	511.01	483.31	464.19
95000	621.16	607.32	594.78	583.38	539.40	510.17	489.98
100000	653.85	639.29	626.09	614.09	567.79	537.02	515.77
105000	686.54	671.25	657.39	644.79	596.18	563.87	541.56
110000	719.23	703.22	688.70	675.50	624.57	590.72	567.35
120000	784.62	767.15	751.31	736.90	681.35	644.42	618.92
130000	850.00	831.07	813.92	798.31	738.13	698.12	670.50
140000	915.39	895.00	876.52	859.72	794.90	751.82	722.08
150000	980.77	958.93	939.13	921.13	851.68	805.52	773.66
160000	1046.16	1022.86	1001.74	982.54	908.46	859.23	825.23
175000	1144.24	1118.75	1095.66	1074.65	993.63	939.78	902.60
200000	1307.70	1278.58	1252.18	1228.17	1135.58	1074.03	1031.54
250000	1634.62	1598.22	1565.22	1535.22	1419.47	1342.54	1289.43
500000	3269.25	3196.44	3130.44	3070.44	2838.95	2685.08	2578.85
1000000	6538.49	6392.88	6260.89	6140.87	5677.89	5370.16	5157.70

5.75%   MONTHLY PAYMENTS

AMOUNT	1 YEAR	2 YEARS	3 YEARS	4 YEARS	5 YEARS	6 YEARS	7 YEARS
100	8.60	4.42	3.03	2.34	1.92	1.65	1.45
200	17.19	8.84	6.06	4.67	3.84	3.29	2.90
500	42.98	22.10	15.15	11.69	9.61	8.23	7.24
1000	85.95	44.21	30.31	23.37	19.22	16.46	14.49
2000	171.90	88.42	60.62	46.74	38.43	32.91	28.98
3000	257.85	132.62	90.93	70.11	57.65	49.37	43.47
4000	343.81	176.83	121.24	93.48	76.87	65.82	57.96
5000	429.76	221.04	151.54	116.85	96.08	82.28	72.45
6000	515.71	265.25	181.85	140.22	115.30	98.73	86.93
7000	601.66	309.46	212.16	163.59	134.52	115.19	101.42
8000	687.61	353.66	242.47	186.96	153.73	131.64	115.91
9000	773.56	397.87	272.78	210.34	172.95	148.10	130.40
10000	859.52	442.08	303.09	233.71	192.17	164.55	144.89
11000	945.47	486.29	333.40	257.08	211.38	181.01	159.38
12000	1031.42	530.50	363.71	280.45	230.60	197.46	173.87
13000	1117.37	574.70	394.01	303.82	249.82	213.92	188.36
14000	1203.32	618.91	424.32	327.19	269.03	230.37	202.85
15000	1289.27	663.12	454.63	350.56	288.25	246.83	217.34
20000	1719.03	884.16	606.18	467.41	384.34	329.10	289.78
25000	2148.79	1105.20	757.72	584.26	480.42	411.38	362.23
30000	2578.55	1326.24	909.26	701.12	576.50	493.65	434.67
35000	3008.30	1547.28	1060.81	817.97	672.59	575.93	507.12
40000	3438.06	1768.32	1212.35	934.82	768.67	658.21	579.56
45000	3867.82	1989.36	1363.90	1051.68	864.75	740.48	652.01
50000	4297.58	2210.40	1515.44	1168.53	960.84	822.76	724.45
55000	4727.34	2431.44	1666.98	1285.38	1056.92	905.03	796.90
56000	4813.29	2475.65	1697.29	1308.75	1076.14	921.49	811.38
57000	4899.24	2519.86	1727.60	1332.12	1095.36	937.94	825.87
58000	4985.19	2564.07	1757.91	1355.49	1114.57	954.40	840.36
59000	5071.14	2608.27	1788.22	1378.86	1133.79	970.85	854.85
60000	5157.09	2652.48	1818.53	1402.23	1153.01	987.31	869.34
61000	5243.05	2696.69	1848.84	1425.61	1172.22	1003.76	883.83
62000	5329.00	2740.90	1879.15	1448.98	1191.44	1020.22	898.32
63000	5414.95	2785.11	1909.45	1472.35	1210.66	1036.67	912.81
64000	5500.90	2829.32	1939.76	1495.72	1229.87	1053.13	927.30
65000	5586.85	2873.52	1970.07	1519.09	1249.09	1069.58	941.79
70000	6016.61	3094.56	2121.62	1635.94	1345.17	1151.86	1014.23
75000	6446.37	3315.60	2273.16	1752.79	1441.26	1234.13	1086.68
80000	6876.13	3536.64	2424.70	1869.65	1537.34	1316.41	1159.12
85000	7305.88	3757.68	2576.25	1986.50	1633.43	1398.69	1231.57
90000	7735.64	3978.72	2727.79	2103.35	1729.51	1480.96	1304.01
95000	8165.40	4199.76	2879.34	2220.21	1825.59	1563.24	1376.46
100000	8595.16	4420.80	3030.88	2337.06	1921.68	1645.51	1448.90
105000	9024.91	4641.84	3182.42	2453.91	2017.76	1727.79	1521.35
110000	9454.67	4862.89	3333.97	2570.76	2113.84	1810.06	1593.79
120000	10314.19	5304.97	3637.05	2804.47	2306.01	1974.62	1738.68
130000	11173.70	5747.05	3940.14	3038.18	2498.18	2139.17	1883.57
140000	12033.22	6189.13	4243.23	3271.88	2690.35	2303.72	2028.46
150000	12892.73	6631.21	4546.32	3505.59	2882.52	2468.27	2173.35
160000	13752.25	7073.29	4849.41	3739.29	3074.68	2632.82	2318.24
175000	15041.52	7736.41	5304.04	4089.85	3362.93	2879.65	2535.58
200000	17190.31	8841.61	6061.76	4674.12	3843.35	3291.03	2897.80
250000	21487.89	11052.01	7577.20	5842.65	4804.19	4113.78	3622.25
500000	42975.78	22104.02	15154.40	11685.29	9608.38	8227.57	7244.50
1000000	85951.56	44208.05	30308.79	23370.58	19216.77	16455.13	14489.00

MONTHLY PAYMENTS 5.75%

AMOUNT	8 YEARS	9 YEARS	10 YEARS	11 YEARS	12 YEARS	13 YEARS	14 YEARS
100	1.30	1.19	1.10	1.02	0.96	0.91	0.87
200	2.60	2.38	2.20	2.05	1.93	1.82	1.74
500	6.51	5.94	5.49	5.12	4.81	4.56	4.34
1000	13.02	11.88	10.98	10.24	9.63	9.12	8.68
2000	26.04	23.76	21.95	20.48	19.26	18.23	17.36
3000	39.06	35.65	32.93	30.72	28.89	27.35	26.04
4000	52.08	47.53	43.91	40.96	38.52	36.47	34.72
5000	65.10	59.41	54.88	51.20	48.15	45.58	43.40
6000	78.12	71.29	65.86	61.44	57.78	54.70	52.08
7000	91.14	83.18	76.84	71.68	67.41	63.82	60.76
8000	104.16	95.06	87.82	81.92	77.04	72.93	69.44
9000	117.18	106.94	98.79	92.16	86.67	82.05	78.12
10000	130.20	118.82	109.77	102.40	96.30	91.16	86.80
11000	143.22	130.71	120.75	112.64	105.93	100.28	95.48
12000	156.24	142.59	131.72	122.88	115.56	109.40	104.16
13000	169.26	154.47	142.70	133.12	125.19	118.51	112.84
14000	182.28	166.35	153.68	143.36	134.81	127.63	121.52
15000	195.30	178.24	164.65	153.60	144.44	136.75	130.20
20000	260.40	237.65	219.54	204.80	192.59	182.33	173.59
25000	325.50	297.06	274.42	256.00	240.74	227.91	216.99
30000	390.60	356.47	329.31	307.20	288.89	273.49	260.39
35000	455.70	415.89	384.19	358.40	337.04	319.08	303.79
40000	520.80	475.30	439.08	409.60	385.18	364.66	347.19
45000	585.90	534.71	493.96	460.80	433.33	410.24	390.59
50000	651.00	594.12	548.85	512.00	481.48	455.82	433.99
55000	716.10	653.54	603.73	563.20	529.63	501.41	477.39
56000	729.12	665.42	614.71	573.44	539.26	510.52	486.07
57000	742.14	677.30	625.68	583.68	548.89	519.64	494.75
58000	755.16	689.18	636.66	593.92	558.52	528.76	503.43
59000	768.18	701.07	647.64	604.16	568.15	537.87	512.10
60000	781.20	712.95	658.62	614.40	577.78	546.99	520.78
61000	794.22	724.83	669.59	624.64	587.41	556.11	529.46
62000	807.24	736.71	680.57	634.88	597.04	565.22	538.14
63000	820.26	748.60	691.55	645.12	606.67	574.34	546.82
64000	833.28	760.48	702.52	655.36	616.30	583.45	555.50
65000	846.30	772.36	713.50	665.60	625.93	592.57	564.18
70000	911.40	831.77	768.38	716.80	674.07	638.15	607.58
75000	976.50	891.19	823.27	768.00	722.22	683.74	650.98
80000	1041.60	950.60	878.15	819.20	770.37	729.32	694.38
85000	1106.70	1010.01	933.04	870.40	818.52	774.90	737.78
90000	1171.80	1069.42	987.92	921.60	866.67	820.48	781.18
95000	1236.90	1128.84	1042.81	972.80	914.81	866.07	824.58
100000	1302.00	1188.25	1097.69	1024.00	962.96	911.65	867.97
105000	1367.10	1247.66	1152.58	1075.20	1011.11	957.23	911.37
110000	1432.20	1307.07	1207.46	1126.40	1059.26	1002.81	954.77
120000	1562.40	1425.90	1317.23	1228.80	1155.55	1093.98	1041.57
130000	1692.61	1544.72	1427.00	1331.20	1251.85	1185.14	1128.37
140000	1822.81	1663.55	1536.77	1433.60	1348.15	1276.31	1215.16
150000	1953.01	1782.37	1646.54	1536.00	1444.44	1367.47	1301.96
160000	2083.21	1901.20	1756.31	1638.40	1540.74	1458.64	1388.76
175000	2278.51	2079.44	1920.96	1792.00	1685.18	1595.38	1518.95
200000	2604.01	2376.50	2195.38	2048.01	1925.92	1823.30	1735.95
250000	3255.01	2970.62	2744.23	2560.01	2407.40	2279.12	2169.94
500000	6510.02	5941.25	5488.46	5120.01	4814.81	4558.24	4339.87
1000000	13020.04	11882.50	10976.92	10240.03	9629.62	9116.48	8679.74

5.75% MONTHLY PAYMENTS

AMOUNT	15 YEARS	16 YEARS	17 YEARS	18 YEARS	19 YEARS	20 YEARS	21 YEARS
100	0.83	0.80	0.77	0.74	0.72	0.70	0.68
200	1.66	1.60	1.54	1.49	1.44	1.40	1.37
500	4.15	3.99	3.85	3.72	3.61	3.51	3.42
1000	8.30	7.98	7.69	7.44	7.22	7.02	6.84
2000	16.61	15.96	15.39	14.88	14.44	14.04	13.69
3000	24.91	23.93	23.08	22.33	21.66	21.06	20.53
4000	33.22	31.91	30.77	29.77	28.88	28.08	27.37
5000	41.52	39.89	38.46	37.21	36.10	35.10	34.22
6000	49.82	47.87	46.16	44.65	43.31	42.13	41.06
7000	58.13	55.85	53.85	52.09	50.53	49.15	47.90
8000	66.43	63.82	61.54	59.53	57.75	56.17	54.75
9000	74.74	71.80	69.24	66.98	64.97	63.19	61.59
10000	83.04	79.78	76.93	74.42	72.19	70.21	68.43
11000	91.35	87.76	84.62	81.86	79.41	77.23	75.28
12000	99.65	95.74	92.31	89.30	86.63	84.25	82.12
13000	107.95	103.71	100.01	96.74	93.85	91.27	88.96
14000	116.26	111.69	107.70	104.18	101.07	98.29	95.81
15000	124.56	119.67	115.39	111.63	108.29	105.31	102.65
20000	166.08	159.56	153.86	148.83	144.38	140.42	136.87
25000	207.60	199.45	192.32	186.04	180.48	175.52	171.08
30000	249.12	239.34	230.79	223.25	216.57	210.63	205.30
35000	290.64	279.23	269.25	260.46	252.67	245.73	239.52
40000	332.16	319.12	307.72	297.67	288.76	280.83	273.73
45000	373.68	359.01	346.18	334.88	324.86	315.94	307.95
50000	415.21	398.90	384.64	372.08	360.96	351.04	342.17
55000	456.73	438.79	423.11	409.29	397.05	386.15	376.38
56000	465.03	446.77	430.80	416.73	404.27	393.17	383.23
57000	473.33	454.75	438.49	424.18	411.49	400.19	390.07
58000	481.64	462.73	446.19	431.62	418.71	407.21	396.91
59000	489.94	470.71	453.88	439.06	425.93	414.23	403.76
60000	498.25	478.68	461.57	446.50	433.15	421.25	410.60
61000	506.55	486.66	469.27	453.94	440.37	428.27	417.44
62000	514.85	494.64	476.96	461.39	447.59	435.29	424.29
63000	523.16	502.62	484.65	468.83	454.80	442.31	431.13
64000	531.46	510.60	492.34	476.27	462.02	449.33	437.97
65000	539.77	518.57	500.04	483.71	469.24	456.35	444.82
70000	581.29	558.47	538.50	520.92	505.34	491.46	479.03
75000	622.81	598.36	576.97	558.13	541.43	526.56	513.25
80000	664.33	638.25	615.43	595.34	577.53	561.67	547.47
85000	705.85	678.14	653.90	632.54	613.63	596.77	581.68
90000	747.37	718.03	692.36	669.75	649.72	631.88	615.90
95000	788.89	757.92	730.82	706.96	685.82	666.98	650.12
100000	830.41	797.81	769.29	744.17	721.91	702.08	684.34
105000	871.93	837.70	807.75	781.38	758.01	737.19	718.55
110000	913.45	877.59	846.22	818.59	794.10	772.29	752.77
120000	996.49	957.37	923.15	893.00	866.29	842.50	821.20
130000	1079.53	1037.15	1000.07	967.42	938.49	912.71	889.64
140000	1162.57	1116.93	1077.00	1041.84	1010.68	982.92	958.07
150000	1245.62	1196.71	1153.93	1116.25	1082.87	1053.13	1026.50
160000	1328.66	1276.49	1230.86	1190.67	1155.06	1123.33	1094.94
175000	1453.22	1396.16	1346.25	1302.30	1263.35	1228.65	1197.59
200000	1660.82	1595.61	1538.58	1488.34	1443.82	1404.17	1368.67
250000	2076.03	1994.52	1923.22	1860.42	1804.78	1755.21	1710.84
500000	4152.05	3989.04	3846.44	3720.85	3609.56	3510.42	3421.68
1000000	8304.10	7978.07	7692.88	7441.70	7219.12	7020.84	6843.35

MONTHLY PAYMENTS

5.75%

AMOUNT	22 YEARS	23 YEARS	24 YEARS	25 YEARS	30 YEARS	35 YEARS	40 YEARS
100	0.67	0.65	0.64	0.63	0.58	0.55	0.53
200	1.34	1.31	1.28	1.26	1.17	1.11	1.07
500	3.34	3.27	3.20	3.15	2.92	2.77	2.66
1000	6.68	6.54	6.41	6.29	5.84	5.54	5.33
2000	13.37	13.08	12.82	12.58	11.67	11.07	10.66
3000	20.05	19.62	19.23	18.87	17.51	16.61	15.99
4000	26.74	26.16	25.64	25.16	23.34	22.14	21.32
5000	33.42	32.70	32.05	31.46	29.18	27.68	26.64
6000	40.10	39.24	38.46	37.75	35.01	33.21	31.97
7000	46.79	45.78	44.87	44.04	40.85	38.75	37.30
8000	53.47	52.32	51.28	50.33	46.69	44.28	42.63
9000	60.15	58.86	57.69	56.62	52.52	49.82	47.96
10000	66.84	65.40	64.09	62.91	58.36	55.35	53.29
11000	73.52	71.94	70.50	69.20	64.19	60.89	58.62
12000	80.21	78.48	76.91	75.49	70.03	66.42	63.95
13000	86.89	85.02	83.32	81.78	75.86	71.96	69.28
14000	93.57	91.56	89.73	88.07	81.70	77.49	74.60
15000	100.26	98.10	96.14	94.37	87.54	83.03	79.93
20000	133.68	130.80	128.19	125.82	116.71	110.70	106.58
25000	167.10	163.50	160.24	157.28	145.89	138.38	133.22
30000	200.51	196.20	192.28	188.73	175.07	166.05	159.87
35000	233.93	228.89	224.33	220.19	204.25	193.73	186.51
40000	267.35	261.59	256.38	251.64	233.43	221.40	213.16
45000	300.77	294.29	288.43	283.10	262.61	249.08	239.80
50000	334.19	326.99	320.47	314.55	291.79	276.75	266.44
55000	367.61	359.69	352.52	346.01	320.97	304.43	293.09
56000	374.29	366.23	358.93	352.30	326.80	309.96	298.42
57000	380.98	372.77	365.34	358.59	332.64	315.50	303.75
58000	387.66	379.31	371.75	364.88	338.47	321.03	309.07
59000	394.34	385.85	378.16	371.17	344.31	326.57	314.40
60000	401.03	392.39	384.57	377.46	350.14	332.10	319.73
61000	407.71	398.93	390.98	383.75	355.98	337.64	325.06
62000	414.40	405.47	397.39	390.05	361.82	343.17	330.39
63000	421.08	412.01	403.80	396.34	367.65	348.71	335.72
64000	427.76	418.55	410.21	402.63	373.49	354.24	341.05
65000	434.45	425.09	416.62	408.92	379.32	359.78	346.38
70000	467.87	457.79	448.66	440.37	408.50	387.45	373.02
75000	501.29	490.49	480.71	471.83	437.68	415.13	399.67
80000	534.70	523.19	512.76	503.29	466.86	442.80	426.31
85000	568.12	555.89	544.81	534.74	496.04	470.48	452.95
90000	601.54	588.59	576.85	566.20	525.22	498.15	479.60
95000	634.96	621.28	608.90	597.65	554.39	525.83	506.24
100000	668.38	653.98	640.95	629.11	583.57	553.50	532.89
105000	701.80	686.68	673.00	660.56	612.75	581.18	559.53
110000	735.22	719.38	705.04	692.02	641.93	608.85	586.18
120000	802.06	784.78	769.14	754.93	700.29	664.20	639.47
130000	868.89	850.18	833.23	817.84	758.64	719.55	692.75
140000	935.73	915.58	897.33	880.75	817.00	774.90	746.04
150000	1002.57	980.98	961.42	943.66	875.36	830.25	799.33
160000	1069.41	1046.37	1025.52	1006.57	933.72	885.60	852.62
175000	1169.67	1144.47	1121.68	1100.94	1021.25	968.63	932.55
200000	1336.76	1307.97	1281.90	1258.21	1167.15	1107.00	1065.78
250000	1670.95	1634.96	1602.37	1572.77	1458.93	1383.75	1332.22
500000	3341.90	3269.92	3204.74	3145.53	2917.86	2767.50	2664.44
1000000	6683.81	6539.84	6409.48	6291.06	5835.73	5535.01	5328.88

6.00%　　　MONTHLY PAYMENTS

AMOUNT	1 YEAR	2 YEARS	3 YEARS	4 YEARS	5 YEARS	6 YEARS	7 YEARS
100	8.61	4.43	3.04	2.35	1.93	1.66	1.46
200	17.21	8.86	6.08	4.70	3.87	3.31	2.92
500	43.03	22.16	15.21	11.74	9.67	8.29	7.30
1000	86.07	44.32	30.42	23.49	19.33	16.57	14.61
2000	172.13	88.64	60.84	46.97	38.67	33.15	29.22
3000	258.20	132.96	91.27	70.46	58.00	49.72	43.83
4000	344.27	177.28	121.69	93.94	77.33	66.29	58.43
5000	430.33	221.60	152.11	117.43	96.66	82.86	73.04
6000	516.40	265.92	182.53	140.91	116.00	99.44	87.65
7000	602.47	310.24	212.95	164.40	135.33	116.01	102.26
8000	688.53	354.56	243.38	187.88	154.66	132.58	116.87
9000	774.60	398.89	273.80	211.37	174.00	149.16	131.48
10000	860.66	443.21	304.22	234.85	193.33	165.73	146.09
11000	946.73	487.53	334.64	258.34	212.66	182.30	160.69
12000	1032.80	531.85	365.06	281.82	231.99	198.87	175.30
13000	1118.86	576.17	395.49	305.31	251.33	215.45	189.91
14000	1204.93	620.49	425.91	328.79	270.66	232.02	204.52
15000	1291.00	664.81	456.33	352.28	289.99	248.59	219.13
20000	1721.33	886.41	608.44	469.70	386.66	331.46	292.17
25000	2151.66	1108.02	760.55	587.13	483.32	414.32	365.21
30000	2581.99	1329.62	912.66	704.55	579.98	497.19	438.26
35000	3012.33	1551.22	1064.77	821.98	676.65	580.05	511.30
40000	3442.66	1772.82	1216.88	939.40	773.31	662.92	584.34
45000	3872.99	1994.43	1368.99	1056.83	869.98	745.78	657.38
50000	4303.32	2216.03	1521.10	1174.25	966.64	828.64	730.43
55000	4733.65	2437.63	1673.21	1291.68	1063.30	911.51	803.47
56000	4819.72	2481.95	1703.63	1315.16	1082.64	928.08	818.08
57000	4905.79	2526.27	1734.05	1338.65	1101.97	944.65	832.69
58000	4991.85	2570.60	1764.47	1362.13	1121.30	961.23	847.30
59000	5077.92	2614.92	1794.89	1385.62	1140.64	977.80	861.90
60000	5163.99	2659.24	1825.32	1409.10	1159.97	994.37	876.51
61000	5250.05	2703.56	1855.74	1432.59	1179.30	1010.95	891.12
62000	5336.12	2747.88	1886.16	1456.07	1198.63	1027.52	905.73
63000	5422.19	2792.20	1916.58	1479.56	1217.97	1044.09	920.34
64000	5508.25	2836.52	1947.00	1503.04	1237.30	1060.66	934.95
65000	5594.32	2880.84	1977.43	1526.53	1256.63	1077.24	949.56
70000	6024.65	3102.44	2129.54	1643.95	1353.30	1160.10	1022.60
75000	6454.98	3324.05	2281.65	1761.38	1449.96	1242.97	1095.64
80000	6885.31	3545.65	2433.75	1878.80	1546.62	1325.83	1168.68
85000	7315.65	3767.25	2585.86	1996.23	1643.29	1408.70	1241.73
90000	7745.98	3988.85	2737.97	2113.65	1739.95	1491.56	1314.77
95000	8176.31	4210.46	2890.08	2231.08	1836.62	1574.42	1387.81
100000	8606.64	4432.06	3042.19	2348.50	1933.28	1657.29	1460.86
105000	9036.98	4653.66	3194.30	2465.93	2029.94	1740.15	1533.90
110000	9467.31	4875.27	3346.41	2583.35	2126.61	1823.02	1606.94
120000	10327.97	5318.47	3650.63	2818.20	2319.94	1988.75	1753.03
130000	11188.64	5761.68	3954.85	3053.05	2513.26	2154.48	1899.11
140000	12049.30	6204.89	4259.07	3287.90	2706.59	2320.20	2045.20
150000	12909.96	6648.09	4563.29	3522.75	2899.92	2485.93	2191.28
160000	13770.63	7091.30	4867.51	3757.60	3093.25	2651.66	2337.37
175000	15061.63	7756.11	5323.84	4109.88	3383.24	2900.26	2556.50
200000	17213.29	8864.12	6084.39	4697.01	3866.56	3314.58	2921.71
250000	21516.61	11080.15	7605.48	5871.26	4833.20	4143.22	3652.14
500000	43033.21	22160.31	15210.97	11742.51	9666.40	8286.44	7304.28
1000000	86066.43	44320.61	30421.94	23485.03	19332.80	16572.89	14608.55

MONTHLY PAYMENTS 6.00%

AMOUNT	8 YEARS	9 YEARS	10 YEARS	11 YEARS	12 YEARS	13 YEARS	14 YEARS
100	1.31	1.20	1.11	1.04	0.98	0.92	0.88
200	2.63	2.40	2.22	2.07	1.95	1.85	1.76
500	6.57	6.00	5.55	5.18	4.88	4.62	4.41
1000	13.14	12.01	11.10	10.37	9.76	9.25	8.81
2000	26.28	24.01	22.20	20.73	19.52	18.49	17.62
3000	39.42	36.02	33.31	31.10	29.28	27.74	26.44
4000	52.57	48.02	44.41	41.47	39.03	36.99	35.25
5000	65.71	60.03	55.51	51.84	48.79	46.24	44.06
6000	78.85	72.03	66.61	62.20	58.55	55.48	52.87
7000	91.99	84.04	77.71	72.57	68.31	64.73	61.69
8000	105.13	96.05	88.82	82.94	78.07	73.98	70.50
9000	118.27	108.05	99.92	93.30	87.83	83.23	79.31
10000	131.41	120.06	111.02	103.67	97.59	92.47	88.12
11000	144.56	132.06	122.12	114.04	107.34	101.72	96.94
12000	157.70	144.07	133.22	124.40	117.10	110.97	105.75
13000	170.84	156.07	144.33	134.77	126.86	120.21	114.56
14000	183.98	168.08	155.43	145.14	136.62	129.46	123.37
15000	197.12	180.09	166.53	155.51	146.38	138.71	132.19
20000	262.83	240.11	222.04	207.34	195.17	184.94	176.25
25000	328.54	300.14	277.55	259.18	243.96	231.18	220.31
30000	394.24	360.17	333.06	311.01	292.76	277.42	264.37
35000	459.95	420.20	388.57	362.85	341.55	323.65	308.43
40000	525.66	480.23	444.08	414.68	390.34	369.89	352.49
45000	591.36	540.26	499.59	466.52	439.13	416.13	396.56
50000	657.07	600.29	555.10	518.35	487.93	462.36	440.62
55000	722.78	660.32	610.61	570.19	536.72	508.60	484.68
56000	735.92	672.32	621.71	580.55	546.48	517.85	493.49
57000	749.06	684.33	632.82	590.92	556.23	527.09	502.30
58000	762.20	696.33	643.92	601.29	565.99	536.34	511.12
59000	775.34	708.34	655.02	611.66	575.75	545.59	519.93
60000	788.49	720.34	666.12	622.02	585.51	554.83	528.74
61000	801.63	732.35	677.23	632.39	595.27	564.08	537.55
62000	814.77	744.36	688.33	642.76	605.03	573.33	546.37
63000	827.91	756.36	699.43	653.12	614.79	582.58	555.18
64000	841.05	768.37	710.53	663.49	624.54	591.82	563.99
65000	854.19	780.37	721.63	673.86	634.30	601.07	572.80
70000	919.90	840.40	777.14	725.69	683.10	647.31	616.87
75000	985.61	900.43	832.65	777.53	731.89	693.54	660.93
80000	1051.31	960.46	888.16	829.36	780.68	739.78	704.99
85000	1117.02	1020.49	943.67	881.20	829.47	786.01	749.05
90000	1182.73	1080.52	999.18	933.03	878.27	832.25	793.11
95000	1248.44	1140.55	1054.69	984.87	927.06	878.49	837.17
100000	1314.14	1200.57	1110.21	1036.70	975.85	924.72	881.24
105000	1379.85	1260.60	1165.72	1088.54	1024.64	970.96	925.30
110000	1445.56	1320.63	1221.23	1140.37	1073.44	1017.20	969.36
120000	1576.97	1440.69	1332.25	1244.04	1171.02	1109.67	1057.48
130000	1708.39	1560.75	1443.27	1347.71	1268.61	1202.14	1145.61
140000	1839.80	1680.80	1554.29	1451.38	1366.19	1294.61	1233.73
150000	1971.21	1800.86	1665.31	1555.06	1463.78	1387.09	1321.85
160000	2102.63	1920.92	1776.33	1658.73	1561.36	1479.56	1409.98
175000	2299.75	2101.01	1942.86	1814.23	1707.74	1618.27	1542.16
200000	2628.29	2401.15	2220.41	2073.41	1951.70	1849.45	1762.47
250000	3285.36	3001.44	2775.51	2591.76	2439.63	2311.81	2203.09
500000	6570.72	6002.87	5551.03	5183.52	4879.25	4623.62	4406.18
1000000	13141.43	12005.75	11102.05	10367.03	9758.50	9247.23	8812.36

6.00%

MONTHLY PAYMENTS

AMOUNT	15 YEARS	16 YEARS	17 YEARS	18 YEARS	19 YEARS	20 YEARS	21 YEARS
100	0.84	0.81	0.78	0.76	0.74	0.72	0.70
200	1.69	1.62	1.57	1.52	1.47	1.43	1.40
500	4.22	4.06	3.92	3.79	3.68	3.58	3.49
1000	8.44	8.11	7.83	7.58	7.36	7.16	6.99
2000	16.88	16.23	15.66	15.16	14.72	14.33	13.98
3000	25.32	24.34	23.49	22.74	22.08	21.49	20.97
4000	33.75	32.46	31.32	30.33	29.44	28.66	27.95
5000	42.19	40.57	39.16	37.91	36.80	35.82	34.94
6000	50.63	48.69	46.99	45.49	44.16	42.99	41.93
7000	59.07	56.80	54.82	53.07	51.53	50.15	48.92
8000	67.51	64.92	62.65	60.65	58.89	57.31	55.91
9000	75.95	73.03	70.48	68.23	66.25	64.48	62.90
10000	84.39	81.14	78.31	75.82	73.61	71.64	69.89
11000	92.82	89.26	86.14	83.40	80.97	78.81	76.87
12000	101.26	97.37	93.97	90.98	88.33	85.97	83.86
13000	109.70	105.49	101.80	98.56	95.69	93.14	90.85
14000	118.14	113.60	109.63	106.14	103.05	100.30	97.84
15000	126.58	121.72	117.47	113.72	110.41	107.46	104.83
20000	168.77	162.29	156.62	151.63	147.22	143.29	139.77
25000	210.96	202.86	195.78	189.54	184.02	179.11	174.71
30000	253.16	243.43	234.93	227.45	220.82	214.93	209.66
35000	295.35	284.00	274.09	265.36	257.63	250.75	244.60
40000	337.54	324.58	313.24	303.26	294.43	286.57	279.54
45000	379.74	365.15	352.40	341.17	331.24	322.39	314.49
50000	421.93	405.72	391.55	379.08	368.04	358.22	349.43
55000	464.12	446.29	430.71	416.99	404.85	394.04	384.37
56000	472.56	454.41	438.54	424.57	412.21	401.20	391.36
57000	481.00	462.52	446.37	432.15	419.57	408.37	398.35
58000	489.44	470.63	454.20	439.73	426.93	415.53	405.34
59000	497.88	478.75	462.03	447.32	434.29	422.69	412.33
60000	506.31	486.86	469.86	454.90	441.65	429.86	419.31
61000	514.75	494.98	477.69	462.48	449.01	437.02	426.30
62000	523.19	503.09	485.52	470.06	456.37	444.19	433.29
63000	531.63	511.21	493.35	477.64	463.73	451.35	440.28
64000	540.07	519.32	501.18	485.22	471.09	458.52	447.27
65000	548.51	527.43	509.02	492.81	478.45	465.68	454.26
70000	590.70	568.01	548.17	530.71	515.26	501.50	489.20
75000	632.89	608.58	587.33	568.62	552.06	537.32	524.14
80000	675.09	649.15	626.48	606.53	588.87	573.14	559.09
85000	717.28	689.72	665.64	644.44	625.67	608.97	594.03
90000	759.47	730.29	704.79	682.35	662.47	644.79	628.97
95000	801.66	770.87	743.95	720.25	699.28	680.61	663.91
100000	843.86	811.44	783.10	758.16	736.08	716.43	698.86
105000	886.05	852.01	822.26	796.07	772.89	752.25	733.80
110000	928.24	892.58	861.41	833.98	809.69	788.07	768.74
120000	1012.63	973.73	939.72	909.79	883.30	859.72	838.63
130000	1097.01	1054.87	1018.03	985.61	956.91	931.36	908.51
140000	1181.40	1136.01	1096.34	1061.43	1030.52	1003.00	978.40
150000	1265.79	1217.16	1174.65	1137.24	1104.12	1074.65	1048.29
160000	1350.17	1298.30	1252.96	1213.06	1177.73	1146.29	1118.17
175000	1476.75	1420.02	1370.43	1326.78	1288.15	1253.75	1223.00
200000	1687.71	1622.88	1566.20	1516.32	1472.17	1432.86	1397.71
250000	2109.64	2028.59	1957.75	1895.41	1840.21	1791.08	1747.14
500000	4219.28	4057.19	3915.50	3790.81	3680.41	3582.16	3494.28
1000000	8438.57	8114.38	7831.01	7581.62	7360.83	7164.31	6988.57

MONTHLY PAYMENTS 6.00%

AMOUNT	22 YEARS	23 YEARS	24 YEARS	25 YEARS	30 YEARS	35 YEARS	40 YEARS
100	0.68	0.67	0.66	0.64	0.60	0.57	0.55
200	1.37	1.34	1.31	1.29	1.20	1.14	1.10
500	3.42	3.34	3.28	3.22	3.00	2.85	2.75
1000	6.83	6.69	6.56	6.44	6.00	5.70	5.50
2000	13.66	13.38	13.12	12.89	11.99	11.40	11.00
3000	20.49	20.07	19.68	19.33	17.99	17.11	16.51
4000	27.32	26.75	26.24	25.77	23.98	22.81	22.01
5000	34.15	33.44	32.80	32.22	29.98	28.51	27.51
6000	40.98	40.13	39.36	38.66	35.97	34.21	33.01
7000	47.82	46.82	45.92	45.10	41.97	39.91	38.51
8000	54.65	53.51	52.48	51.54	47.96	45.62	44.02
9000	61.48	60.20	59.04	57.99	53.96	51.32	49.52
10000	68.31	66.88	65.60	64.43	59.96	57.02	55.02
11000	75.14	73.57	72.16	70.87	65.95	62.72	60.52
12000	81.97	80.26	78.72	77.32	71.95	68.42	66.03
13000	88.80	86.95	85.28	83.76	77.94	74.12	71.53
14000	95.63	93.64	91.84	90.20	83.94	79.83	77.03
15000	102.46	100.33	98.40	96.65	89.93	85.53	82.53
20000	136.61	133.77	131.20	128.86	119.91	114.04	110.04
25000	170.77	167.21	163.99	161.08	149.89	142.55	137.55
30000	204.92	200.65	196.79	193.29	179.87	171.06	165.06
35000	239.08	234.10	229.59	225.51	209.84	199.57	192.57
40000	273.23	267.54	262.39	257.72	239.82	228.08	220.09
45000	307.38	300.98	295.19	289.94	269.80	256.59	247.60
50000	341.54	334.42	327.99	322.15	299.78	285.09	275.11
55000	375.69	367.87	360.79	354.37	329.75	313.60	302.62
56000	382.52	374.55	367.35	360.81	335.75	319.31	308.12
57000	389.35	381.24	373.91	367.25	341.74	325.01	313.62
58000	396.18	387.93	380.47	373.69	347.74	330.71	319.12
59000	403.01	394.62	387.03	380.14	353.73	336.41	324.63
60000	409.84	401.31	393.59	386.58	359.73	342.11	330.13
61000	416.68	408.00	400.15	393.02	365.73	347.82	335.63
62000	423.51	414.69	406.71	399.47	371.72	353.52	341.13
63000	430.34	421.37	413.27	405.91	377.72	359.22	346.63
64000	437.17	428.06	419.83	412.35	383.71	364.92	352.14
65000	444.00	434.75	426.39	418.80	389.71	370.62	357.64
70000	478.15	468.19	459.18	451.01	419.69	399.13	385.15
75000	512.31	501.64	491.98	483.23	449.66	427.64	412.66
80000	546.46	535.08	524.78	515.44	479.64	456.15	440.17
85000	580.61	568.52	557.58	547.66	509.62	484.66	467.68
90000	614.77	601.96	590.38	579.87	539.60	513.17	495.19
95000	648.92	635.40	623.18	612.09	569.57	541.68	522.70
100000	683.07	668.85	655.98	644.30	599.55	570.19	550.21
105000	717.23	702.29	688.78	676.52	629.53	598.70	577.72
110000	751.38	735.73	721.58	708.73	659.51	627.21	605.24
120000	819.69	802.62	787.17	773.16	719.46	684.23	660.26
130000	888.00	869.50	852.77	837.59	779.42	741.25	715.28
140000	956.30	936.39	918.37	902.02	839.37	798.27	770.30
150000	1024.61	1003.27	983.97	966.45	899.33	855.28	825.32
160000	1092.92	1070.16	1049.56	1030.88	959.28	912.30	880.34
175000	1195.38	1170.48	1147.96	1127.53	1049.21	997.83	962.87
200000	1366.15	1337.69	1311.96	1288.60	1199.10	1140.38	1100.43
250000	1707.69	1672.12	1639.95	1610.75	1498.88	1425.47	1375.53
500000	3415.37	3344.24	3279.89	3221.51	2997.75	2850.95	2751.07
1000000	6830.74	6688.47	6559.78	6443.01	5995.51	5701.90	5502.14

6.25% MONTHLY PAYMENTS

AMOUNT	1 YEAR	2 YEARS	3 YEARS	4 YEARS	5 YEARS	6 YEARS	7 YEARS
100	8.62	4.44	3.05	2.36	1.94	1.67	1.47
200	17.24	8.89	6.11	4.72	3.89	3.34	2.95
500	43.09	22.22	15.27	11.80	9.72	8.35	7.36
1000	86.18	44.43	30.54	23.60	19.45	16.69	14.73
2000	172.36	88.87	61.07	47.20	38.90	33.38	29.46
3000	258.54	133.30	91.61	70.80	58.35	50.07	44.19
4000	344.73	177.73	122.14	94.40	77.80	66.76	58.91
5000	430.91	222.17	152.68	118.00	97.25	83.46	73.64
6000	517.09	266.60	183.21	141.60	116.70	100.15	88.37
7000	603.27	311.03	213.75	165.20	136.14	116.84	103.10
8000	689.45	355.47	244.28	188.80	155.59	133.53	117.83
9000	775.63	399.90	274.82	212.40	175.04	150.22	132.56
10000	861.81	444.33	305.35	236.00	194.49	166.91	147.29
11000	948.00	488.77	335.89	259.60	213.94	183.60	162.02
12000	1034.18	533.20	366.42	283.20	233.39	200.29	176.74
13000	1120.36	577.63	396.96	306.80	252.84	216.99	191.47
14000	1206.54	622.07	427.49	330.40	272.29	233.68	206.20
15000	1292.72	666.50	458.03	354.00	291.74	250.37	220.93
20000	1723.63	888.67	610.71	472.00	388.99	333.82	294.57
25000	2154.53	1110.83	763.38	590.00	486.23	417.28	368.22
30000	2585.44	1333.00	916.06	707.99	583.48	500.73	441.86
35000	3016.35	1555.17	1068.74	825.99	680.72	584.19	515.50
40000	3447.26	1777.33	1221.41	943.99	777.97	667.65	589.15
45000	3878.16	1999.50	1374.09	1061.99	875.22	751.10	662.79
50000	4309.07	2221.67	1526.77	1179.99	972.46	834.56	736.43
55000	4739.98	2443.83	1679.44	1297.99	1069.71	918.01	810.08
56000	4826.16	2488.27	1709.98	1321.59	1089.16	934.70	824.81
57000	4912.34	2532.70	1740.51	1345.19	1108.61	951.40	839.54
58000	4998.52	2577.13	1771.05	1368.79	1128.06	968.09	854.26
59000	5084.70	2621.57	1801.59	1392.39	1147.51	984.78	868.99
60000	5170.88	2666.00	1832.12	1415.99	1166.96	1001.47	883.72
61000	5257.06	2710.43	1862.66	1439.59	1186.40	1018.16	898.45
62000	5343.25	2754.87	1893.19	1463.19	1205.85	1034.85	913.18
63000	5429.43	2799.30	1923.73	1486.79	1225.30	1051.54	927.91
64000	5515.61	2843.73	1954.26	1510.39	1244.75	1068.23	942.64
65000	5601.79	2888.17	1984.80	1533.99	1264.20	1084.93	957.37
70000	6032.70	3110.33	2137.47	1651.99	1361.45	1168.38	1031.01
75000	6463.60	3332.50	2290.15	1769.99	1458.69	1251.84	1104.65
80000	6894.51	3554.67	2442.83	1887.99	1555.94	1335.29	1178.30
85000	7325.42	3776.83	2595.50	2005.98	1653.19	1418.75	1251.94
90000	7756.32	3999.00	2748.18	2123.98	1750.43	1502.20	1325.58
95000	8187.23	4221.17	2900.86	2241.98	1847.68	1585.66	1399.23
100000	8618.14	4443.33	3053.53	2359.98	1944.93	1669.12	1472.87
105000	9049.04	4665.50	3206.21	2477.98	2042.17	1752.57	1546.51
110000	9479.95	4887.67	3358.89	2595.98	2139.42	1836.03	1620.16
120000	10341.77	5332.00	3664.24	2831.98	2333.91	2002.94	1767.44
130000	11203.58	5776.33	3969.59	3067.98	2528.40	2169.85	1914.73
140000	12065.39	6220.67	4274.95	3303.97	2722.90	2336.76	2062.02
150000	12927.21	6665.00	4580.30	3539.97	2917.39	2503.67	2209.30
160000	13789.02	7109.34	4885.65	3775.97	3111.88	2670.58	2356.59
175000	15081.74	7775.84	5343.68	4129.97	3403.62	2920.95	2577.52
200000	17236.28	8886.67	6107.07	4719.96	3889.85	3338.23	2945.74
250000	21545.35	11108.34	7633.84	5899.95	4862.32	4172.79	3682.17
500000	43090.69	22216.67	15267.67	11799.91	9724.63	8345.58	7364.35
1000000	86181.38	44433.34	30535.34	23599.82	19449.26	16691.15	14728.70

MONTHLY PAYMENTS 6.25%

AMOUNT	8 YEARS	9 YEARS	10 YEARS	11 YEARS	12 YEARS	13 YEARS	14 YEARS
100	1.33	1.21	1.12	1.05	0.99	0.94	0.89
200	2.65	2.43	2.25	2.10	1.98	1.88	1.79
500	6.63	6.06	5.61	5.25	4.94	4.69	4.47
1000	13.26	12.13	11.23	10.49	9.89	9.38	8.95
2000	26.53	24.26	22.46	20.99	19.78	18.76	17.89
3000	39.79	36.39	33.68	31.48	29.67	28.14	26.84
4000	53.05	48.52	44.91	41.98	39.55	37.52	35.78
5000	66.32	60.65	56.14	52.47	49.44	46.90	44.73
6000	79.58	72.78	67.37	62.97	59.33	56.27	53.68
7000	92.84	84.91	78.60	73.46	69.22	65.65	62.62
8000	106.11	97.04	89.82	83.96	79.11	75.03	71.57
9000	119.37	109.17	101.05	94.45	89.00	84.41	80.51
10000	132.63	121.30	112.28	104.95	98.88	93.79	89.46
11000	145.90	133.43	123.51	115.44	108.77	103.17	98.41
12000	159.16	145.56	134.74	125.94	118.66	112.55	107.35
13000	172.43	157.69	145.96	136.43	128.55	121.93	116.30
14000	185.69	169.82	157.19	146.93	138.44	131.31	125.25
15000	198.95	181.95	168.42	157.42	148.33	140.69	134.19
20000	265.27	242.60	224.56	209.90	197.77	187.58	178.92
25000	331.59	303.24	280.70	262.37	247.21	234.48	223.65
30000	397.90	363.89	336.84	314.85	296.65	281.37	268.38
35000	464.22	424.54	392.98	367.32	346.09	328.27	313.11
40000	530.54	485.19	449.12	419.80	395.53	375.16	357.84
45000	596.86	545.84	505.26	472.27	444.98	422.06	402.57
50000	663.17	606.49	561.40	524.75	494.42	468.95	447.31
55000	729.49	667.14	617.54	577.22	543.86	515.85	492.04
56000	742.76	679.27	628.77	587.72	553.75	525.23	500.98
57000	756.02	691.40	640.00	598.21	563.64	534.61	509.93
58000	769.28	703.53	651.22	608.71	573.53	543.98	518.87
59000	782.55	715.66	662.45	619.20	583.41	553.36	527.82
60000	795.81	727.79	673.68	629.70	593.30	562.74	536.77
61000	809.07	739.92	684.91	640.19	603.19	572.12	545.71
62000	822.34	752.04	696.14	650.69	613.08	581.50	554.66
63000	835.60	764.17	707.36	661.18	622.97	590.88	563.60
64000	848.86	776.30	718.59	671.68	632.86	600.26	572.55
65000	862.13	788.43	729.82	682.17	642.74	609.64	581.50
70000	928.44	849.08	785.96	734.65	692.19	656.53	626.23
75000	994.76	909.73	842.10	787.12	741.63	703.43	670.96
80000	1061.08	970.38	898.24	839.60	791.07	750.32	715.69
85000	1127.40	1031.03	954.38	892.07	840.51	797.22	760.42
90000	1193.71	1091.68	1010.52	944.55	889.95	844.11	805.15
95000	1260.03	1152.33	1066.66	997.02	939.39	891.01	849.88
100000	1326.35	1212.98	1122.80	1049.49	988.84	937.90	894.61
105000	1392.67	1273.62	1178.94	1101.97	1038.28	984.80	939.34
110000	1458.98	1334.27	1235.08	1154.44	1087.72	1031.69	984.07
120000	1591.62	1455.57	1347.36	1259.39	1186.60	1125.49	1073.53
130000	1724.25	1576.87	1459.64	1364.34	1285.49	1219.28	1162.99
140000	1856.89	1698.17	1571.92	1469.29	1384.37	1313.07	1252.45
150000	1989.52	1819.46	1684.20	1574.24	1483.26	1406.86	1341.92
160000	2122.16	1940.76	1796.48	1679.19	1582.14	1500.65	1431.38
175000	2321.11	2122.71	1964.90	1836.62	1730.46	1641.33	1565.57
200000	2652.70	2425.95	2245.60	2098.99	1977.67	1875.81	1789.22
250000	3315.87	3032.44	2807.00	2623.74	2472.09	2344.76	2236.53
500000	6631.75	6064.88	5614.00	5247.47	4944.18	4689.52	4473.05
1000000	13263.50	12129.76	11228.01	10494.95	9888.37	9379.04	8946.10

6.25%   MONTHLY PAYMENTS

AMOUNT	15 YEARS	16 YEARS	17 YEARS	18 YEARS	19 YEARS	20 YEARS	21 YEARS
100	0.86	0.83	0.80	0.77	0.75	0.73	0.71
200	1.71	1.65	1.59	1.54	1.50	1.46	1.43
500	4.29	4.13	3.99	3.86	3.75	3.65	3.57
1000	8.57	8.25	7.97	7.72	7.50	7.31	7.14
2000	17.15	16.50	15.94	15.45	15.01	14.62	14.27
3000	25.72	24.76	23.91	23.17	22.51	21.93	21.41
4000	34.30	33.01	31.88	30.89	30.02	29.24	28.54
5000	42.87	41.26	39.85	38.61	37.52	36.55	35.68
6000	51.45	49.51	47.82	46.34	45.02	43.86	42.81
7000	60.02	57.76	55.79	54.06	52.53	51.16	49.95
8000	68.59	66.02	63.76	61.78	60.03	58.47	57.08
9000	77.17	74.27	71.73	69.51	67.54	65.78	64.22
10000	85.74	82.52	79.70	77.23	75.04	73.09	71.35
11000	94.32	90.77	87.67	84.95	82.54	80.40	78.49
12000	102.89	99.02	95.65	92.68	90.05	87.71	85.62
13000	111.46	107.28	103.62	100.40	97.55	95.02	92.76
14000	120.04	115.53	111.59	108.12	105.06	102.33	99.89
15000	128.61	123.78	119.56	115.84	112.56	109.64	107.03
20000	171.48	165.04	159.41	154.46	150.08	146.19	142.71
25000	214.36	206.30	199.26	193.07	187.60	182.73	178.38
30000	257.23	247.56	239.11	231.69	225.12	219.28	214.06
35000	300.10	288.82	278.97	270.30	262.64	255.82	249.74
40000	342.97	330.08	318.82	308.92	300.16	292.37	285.41
45000	385.84	371.34	358.67	347.53	337.68	328.92	321.09
50000	428.71	412.60	398.52	386.15	375.20	365.46	356.77
55000	471.58	453.86	438.37	424.76	412.72	402.01	392.44
56000	480.16	462.11	446.35	432.48	420.22	409.32	399.58
57000	488.73	470.36	454.32	440.21	427.73	416.63	406.71
58000	497.31	478.61	462.29	447.93	435.23	423.94	413.85
59000	505.88	486.86	470.26	455.65	442.73	431.25	420.98
60000	514.45	495.12	478.23	463.38	450.24	438.56	428.12
61000	523.03	503.37	486.20	471.10	457.74	445.87	435.26
62000	531.60	511.62	494.17	478.82	465.25	453.18	442.39
63000	540.18	519.87	502.14	486.54	472.75	460.48	449.53
64000	548.75	528.12	510.11	494.27	480.25	467.79	456.66
65000	557.32	536.38	518.08	501.99	487.76	475.10	463.80
70000	600.20	577.64	557.93	540.61	525.28	511.65	499.47
75000	643.07	618.90	597.78	579.22	562.80	548.20	535.15
80000	685.94	660.16	637.64	617.83	600.32	584.74	570.83
85000	728.81	701.42	677.49	656.45	637.84	621.29	606.50
90000	771.68	742.67	717.34	695.06	675.36	657.84	642.18
95000	814.55	783.93	757.19	733.68	712.88	694.38	677.86
100000	857.42	825.19	797.05	772.29	750.40	730.93	713.53
105000	900.29	866.45	836.90	810.91	787.92	767.47	749.21
110000	943.17	907.71	876.75	849.52	825.44	804.02	784.89
120000	1028.91	990.23	956.45	926.75	900.48	877.11	856.24
130000	1114.65	1072.75	1036.16	1003.98	975.52	950.21	927.59
140000	1200.39	1155.27	1115.86	1081.21	1050.56	1023.30	998.95
150000	1286.13	1237.79	1195.57	1158.44	1125.60	1096.39	1070.30
160000	1371.88	1320.31	1275.27	1235.67	1200.64	1169.49	1141.65
175000	1500.49	1444.09	1394.83	1351.51	1313.20	1279.12	1248.68
200000	1714.85	1650.39	1594.09	1544.59	1500.80	1461.86	1427.07
250000	2143.56	2062.99	1992.61	1930.73	1876.00	1827.32	1783.83
500000	4287.11	4125.97	3985.23	3861.47	3751.99	3654.64	3567.67
1000000	8574.23	8251.94	7970.45	7722.93	7503.98	7309.28	7135.34

MONTHLY PAYMENTS 6.25%

AMOUNT	22 YEARS	23 YEARS	24 YEARS	25 YEARS	30 YEARS	35 YEARS	40 YEARS
100	0.70	0.68	0.67	0.66	0.62	0.59	0.57
200	1.40	1.37	1.34	1.32	1.23	1.17	1.14
500	3.49	3.42	3.36	3.30	3.08	2.94	2.84
1000	6.98	6.84	6.71	6.60	6.16	5.87	5.68
2000	13.96	13.68	13.42	13.19	12.31	11.74	11.35
3000	20.94	20.52	20.14	19.79	18.47	17.61	17.03
4000	27.92	27.35	26.85	26.39	24.63	23.48	22.71
5000	34.90	34.19	33.56	32.98	30.79	29.35	28.39
6000	41.88	41.03	40.27	39.58	36.94	35.22	34.06
7000	48.85	47.87	46.98	46.18	43.10	41.10	39.74
8000	55.83	54.71	53.69	52.77	49.26	46.97	45.42
9000	62.81	61.55	60.41	59.37	55.41	52.84	51.10
10000	69.79	68.39	67.12	65.97	61.57	58.71	56.77
11000	76.77	75.23	73.83	72.56	67.73	64.58	62.45
12000	83.75	82.06	80.54	79.16	73.89	70.45	68.13
13000	90.73	88.90	87.25	85.76	80.04	76.32	73.81
14000	97.71	95.74	93.96	92.35	86.20	82.19	79.48
15000	104.69	102.58	100.68	98.95	92.36	88.06	85.16
20000	139.59	136.77	134.24	131.93	123.14	117.42	113.55
25000	174.48	170.97	167.79	164.92	153.93	146.77	141.93
30000	209.38	205.16	201.35	197.90	184.72	176.12	170.32
35000	244.27	239.36	234.91	230.88	215.50	205.48	198.71
40000	279.17	273.55	268.47	263.87	246.29	234.83	227.10
45000	314.07	307.74	302.03	296.85	277.07	264.18	255.48
50000	348.96	341.94	335.59	329.83	307.86	293.54	283.87
55000	383.86	376.13	369.15	362.82	338.64	322.89	312.26
56000	390.84	382.97	375.86	369.41	344.80	328.76	317.93
57000	397.82	389.81	382.57	376.01	350.96	334.63	323.61
58000	404.80	396.65	389.28	382.61	357.12	340.50	329.29
59000	411.78	403.49	395.99	389.20	363.27	346.38	334.97
60000	418.76	410.32	402.71	395.80	369.43	352.25	340.64
61000	425.74	417.16	409.42	402.40	375.59	358.12	346.32
62000	432.72	424.00	416.13	409.00	381.74	363.99	352.00
63000	439.69	430.84	422.84	415.59	387.90	369.86	357.68
64000	446.67	437.68	429.55	422.19	394.06	375.73	363.35
65000	453.65	444.52	436.27	428.79	400.22	381.60	369.03
70000	488.55	478.71	469.82	461.77	431.00	410.95	397.42
75000	523.45	512.91	503.38	494.75	461.79	440.31	425.80
80000	558.34	547.10	536.94	527.74	492.57	469.66	454.19
85000	593.24	581.29	570.50	560.72	523.36	499.02	482.58
90000	628.14	615.49	604.06	593.70	554.15	528.37	510.97
95000	663.03	649.68	637.62	626.69	584.93	557.72	539.35
100000	697.93	683.87	671.18	659.67	615.72	587.08	567.74
105000	732.82	718.07	704.74	692.65	646.50	616.43	596.13
110000	767.72	752.26	738.30	725.64	677.29	645.78	624.51
120000	837.51	820.65	805.41	791.60	738.86	704.49	681.29
130000	907.31	889.04	872.53	857.57	800.43	763.20	738.06
140000	977.10	957.42	939.65	923.54	862.00	821.91	794.84
150000	1046.89	1025.81	1006.77	989.50	923.58	880.61	851.61
160000	1116.68	1094.20	1073.88	1055.47	985.15	939.32	908.38
175000	1221.37	1196.78	1174.56	1154.42	1077.51	1027.38	993.54
200000	1395.86	1367.73	1342.35	1319.34	1231.43	1174.15	1135.48
250000	1744.82	1709.69	1677.94	1649.17	1539.29	1467.69	1419.35
500000	3489.64	3419.37	3355.89	3298.35	3078.59	2935.38	2838.70
1000000	6979.28	6838.75	6711.77	6596.69	6157.17	5870.76	5677.40

6.50%   MONTHLY PAYMENTS

AMOUNT	1 YEAR	2 YEARS	3 YEARS	4 YEARS	5 YEARS	6 YEARS	7 YEARS
100	8.63	4.45	3.06	2.37	1.96	1.68	1.48
200	17.26	8.91	6.13	4.74	3.91	3.36	2.97
500	43.15	22.27	15.32	11.86	9.78	8.40	7.42
1000	86.30	44.55	30.65	23.71	19.57	16.81	14.85
2000	172.59	89.09	61.30	47.43	39.13	33.62	29.70
3000	258.89	133.64	91.95	71.14	58.70	50.43	44.55
4000	345.19	178.19	122.60	94.86	78.26	67.24	59.40
5000	431.48	222.73	153.25	118.57	97.83	84.05	74.25
6000	517.78	267.28	183.89	142.29	117.40	100.86	89.10
7000	604.07	311.82	214.54	166.00	136.96	117.67	103.95
8000	690.37	356.37	245.19	189.72	156.53	134.48	118.80
9000	776.67	400.92	275.84	213.43	176.10	151.29	133.64
10000	862.96	445.46	306.49	237.15	195.66	168.10	148.49
11000	949.26	490.01	337.14	260.86	215.23	184.91	163.34
12000	1035.56	534.56	367.79	284.58	234.79	201.72	178.19
13000	1121.85	579.10	398.44	308.29	254.36	218.53	193.04
14000	1208.15	623.65	429.09	332.01	273.93	235.34	207.89
15000	1294.45	668.19	459.74	355.72	293.49	252.15	222.74
20000	1725.93	890.93	612.98	474.30	391.32	336.20	296.99
25000	2157.41	1113.66	766.23	592.87	489.15	420.25	371.24
30000	2588.89	1336.39	919.47	711.45	586.98	504.30	445.48
35000	3020.37	1559.12	1072.72	830.02	684.82	588.35	519.73
40000	3451.86	1781.85	1225.96	948.60	782.65	672.40	593.98
45000	3883.34	2004.58	1379.21	1067.17	880.48	756.45	668.22
50000	4314.82	2227.31	1532.45	1185.75	978.31	840.50	742.47
55000	4746.30	2450.04	1685.70	1304.32	1076.14	924.55	816.72
56000	4832.60	2494.59	1716.34	1328.04	1095.70	941.36	831.57
57000	4918.90	2539.14	1746.99	1351.75	1115.27	958.17	846.42
58000	5005.19	2583.68	1777.64	1375.47	1134.84	974.98	861.27
59000	5091.49	2628.23	1808.29	1399.18	1154.40	991.79	876.12
60000	5177.79	2672.78	1838.94	1422.90	1173.97	1008.60	890.97
61000	5264.08	2717.32	1869.59	1446.61	1193.54	1025.41	905.82
62000	5350.38	2761.87	1900.24	1470.33	1213.10	1042.22	920.67
63000	5436.67	2806.41	1930.89	1494.04	1232.67	1059.03	935.51
64000	5522.97	2850.96	1961.54	1517.76	1252.23	1075.84	950.36
65000	5609.27	2895.51	1992.19	1541.47	1271.80	1092.65	965.21
70000	6040.75	3118.24	2145.43	1660.05	1369.63	1176.70	1039.46
75000	6472.23	3340.97	2298.68	1778.62	1467.46	1260.74	1113.71
80000	6903.71	3563.70	2451.92	1897.20	1565.29	1344.79	1187.95
85000	7335.20	3786.43	2605.17	2015.77	1663.12	1428.84	1262.20
90000	7766.68	4009.16	2758.41	2134.35	1760.95	1512.89	1336.45
95000	8198.16	4231.89	2911.66	2252.92	1858.78	1596.94	1410.70
100000	8629.64	4454.63	3064.90	2371.50	1956.61	1680.99	1484.94
105000	9061.12	4677.36	3218.15	2490.07	2054.45	1765.04	1559.19
110000	9492.61	4900.09	3371.39	2608.64	2152.28	1849.09	1633.44
120000	10355.57	5345.55	3677.88	2845.79	2347.94	2017.19	1781.93
130000	11218.53	5791.01	3984.37	3082.94	2543.60	2185.29	1930.43
140000	12081.50	6236.48	4290.86	3320.09	2739.26	2353.39	2078.92
150000	12944.46	6681.94	4597.35	3557.24	2934.92	2521.49	2227.42
160000	13807.43	7127.40	4903.84	3794.39	3130.58	2689.59	2375.91
175000	15101.87	7795.59	5363.58	4150.12	3424.08	2941.74	2598.65
200000	17259.28	8909.25	6129.80	4742.99	3913.23	3361.99	2969.89
250000	21574.10	11136.56	7662.25	5928.74	4891.54	4202.48	3712.36
500000	43148.21	22273.13	15324.50	11857.48	9783.07	8404.96	7424.72
1000000	86296.42	44546.25	30649.00	23714.95	19566.15	16809.93	14849.44

MONTHLY PAYMENTS 6.50%

AMOUNT	8 YEARS	9 YEARS	10 YEARS	11 YEARS	12 YEARS	13 YEARS	14 YEARS
100	1.34	1.23	1.14	1.06	1.00	0.95	0.91
200	2.68	2.45	2.27	2.12	2.00	1.90	1.82
500	6.69	6.13	5.68	5.31	5.01	4.76	4.54
1000	13.39	12.25	11.35	10.62	10.02	9.51	9.08
2000	26.77	24.51	22.71	21.25	20.04	19.02	18.16
3000	40.16	36.76	34.06	31.87	30.06	28.54	27.24
4000	53.54	49.02	45.42	42.50	40.08	38.05	36.32
5000	66.93	61.27	56.77	53.12	50.10	47.56	45.40
6000	80.32	73.53	68.13	63.74	60.12	57.07	54.49
7000	93.70	85.78	79.48	74.37	70.13	66.58	63.57
8000	107.09	98.04	90.84	84.99	80.15	76.10	72.65
9000	120.48	110.29	102.19	95.61	90.17	85.61	81.73
10000	133.86	122.55	113.55	106.24	100.19	95.12	90.81
11000	147.25	134.80	124.90	116.86	110.21	104.63	99.89
12000	160.63	147.05	136.26	127.49	120.23	114.14	108.97
13000	174.02	159.31	147.61	138.11	130.25	123.65	118.05
14000	187.41	171.56	158.97	148.73	140.27	133.17	127.13
15000	200.79	183.82	170.32	159.36	150.29	142.68	136.21
20000	267.72	245.09	227.10	212.48	200.38	190.24	181.62
25000	334.66	306.36	283.87	265.59	250.48	237.80	227.02
30000	401.59	367.64	340.64	318.71	300.58	285.36	272.43
35000	468.52	428.91	397.42	371.83	350.67	332.92	317.83
40000	535.45	490.18	454.19	424.95	400.77	380.48	363.24
45000	602.38	551.45	510.97	478.07	450.86	428.04	408.64
50000	669.31	612.73	567.74	531.19	500.96	475.60	454.05
55000	736.24	674.00	624.51	584.31	551.06	523.15	499.45
56000	749.63	686.25	635.87	594.93	561.08	532.67	508.53
57000	763.02	698.51	647.22	605.55	571.10	542.18	517.61
58000	776.40	710.76	658.58	616.18	581.11	551.69	526.70
59000	789.79	723.02	669.93	626.80	591.13	561.20	535.78
60000	803.17	735.27	681.29	637.43	601.15	570.71	544.86
61000	816.56	747.53	692.64	648.05	611.17	580.23	553.94
62000	829.95	759.78	704.00	658.67	621.19	589.74	563.02
63000	843.33	772.03	715.35	669.30	631.21	599.25	572.10
64000	856.72	784.29	726.71	679.92	641.23	608.76	581.18
65000	870.11	796.54	738.06	690.54	651.25	618.27	590.26
70000	937.04	857.82	794.84	743.66	701.34	665.83	635.67
75000	1003.97	919.09	851.61	796.78	751.44	713.39	681.07
80000	1070.90	980.36	908.38	849.90	801.54	760.95	726.48
85000	1137.83	1041.63	965.16	903.02	851.63	808.51	771.88
90000	1204.76	1102.91	1021.93	956.14	901.73	856.07	817.29
95000	1271.69	1164.18	1078.71	1009.26	951.83	903.63	862.69
100000	1338.62	1225.45	1135.48	1062.38	1001.92	951.19	908.10
105000	1405.55	1286.72	1192.25	1115.50	1052.02	998.75	953.50
110000	1472.49	1348.00	1249.03	1168.61	1102.11	1046.31	998.91
120000	1606.35	1470.54	1362.58	1274.85	1202.31	1141.43	1089.72
130000	1740.21	1593.09	1476.12	1381.09	1302.50	1236.55	1180.52
140000	1874.07	1715.63	1589.67	1487.33	1402.69	1331.67	1271.33
150000	2007.93	1838.18	1703.22	1593.57	1502.88	1426.79	1362.14
160000	2141.80	1960.72	1816.77	1699.80	1603.07	1521.90	1452.95
175000	2342.59	2144.54	1987.09	1859.16	1753.36	1664.58	1589.17
200000	2677.25	2450.90	2270.96	2124.75	2003.84	1902.38	1816.19
250000	3346.56	3063.63	2838.70	2655.94	2504.80	2377.98	2270.24
500000	6693.12	6127.26	5677.40	5311.88	5009.61	4755.95	4540.48
1000000	13386.23	12254.52	11354.80	10623.77	10019.21	9511.90	9080.96

6.50%

MONTHLY PAYMENTS

AMOUNT	15 YEARS	16 YEARS	17 YEARS	18 YEARS	19 YEARS	20 YEARS	21 YEARS
100	0.87	0.84	0.81	0.79	0.76	0.75	0.73
200	1.74	1.68	1.62	1.57	1.53	1.49	1.46
500	4.36	4.20	4.06	3.93	3.82	3.73	3.64
1000	8.71	8.39	8.11	7.87	7.65	7.46	7.28
2000	17.42	16.78	16.22	15.73	15.30	14.91	14.57
3000	26.13	25.17	24.33	23.60	22.95	22.37	21.85
4000	34.84	33.56	32.44	31.46	30.59	29.82	29.13
5000	43.56	41.95	40.56	39.33	38.24	37.28	36.42
6000	52.27	50.34	48.67	47.19	45.89	44.73	43.70
7000	60.98	58.74	56.78	55.06	53.54	52.19	50.99
8000	69.69	67.13	64.89	62.92	61.19	59.65	58.27
9000	78.40	75.52	73.00	70.79	68.84	67.10	65.55
10000	87.11	83.91	81.11	78.66	76.49	74.56	72.84
11000	95.82	92.30	89.22	86.52	84.13	82.01	80.12
12000	104.53	100.69	97.33	94.39	91.78	89.47	87.40
13000	113.24	109.08	105.45	102.25	99.43	96.92	94.69
14000	121.96	117.47	113.56	110.12	107.08	104.38	101.97
15000	130.67	125.86	121.67	117.98	114.73	111.84	109.25
20000	174.22	167.82	162.22	157.31	152.97	149.11	145.67
25000	217.78	209.77	202.78	196.64	191.21	186.39	182.09
30000	261.33	251.72	243.34	235.97	229.46	223.67	218.51
35000	304.89	293.68	283.89	275.30	267.70	260.95	254.93
40000	348.45	335.63	324.45	314.62	305.94	298.23	291.35
45000	392.00	377.58	365.00	353.95	344.19	335.51	327.76
50000	435.55	419.54	405.56	393.28	382.43	372.79	364.18
55000	479.11	461.49	446.12	432.61	420.67	410.07	400.60
56000	487.82	469.88	454.23	440.47	428.32	417.52	407.88
57000	496.53	478.27	462.34	448.34	435.97	424.98	415.17
58000	505.24	486.66	470.45	456.21	443.62	432.43	422.45
59000	513.95	495.05	478.56	464.07	451.27	439.89	429.73
60000	522.66	503.45	486.67	471.94	458.91	447.34	437.02
61000	531.38	511.84	494.78	479.80	466.56	454.80	444.30
62000	540.09	520.23	502.90	487.67	474.21	462.26	451.59
63000	548.80	528.62	511.01	495.53	481.86	469.71	458.87
64000	557.51	537.01	519.12	503.40	489.51	477.17	466.15
65000	566.22	545.40	527.23	511.26	497.16	484.62	473.44
70000	609.78	587.35	567.78	550.59	535.40	521.90	509.85
75000	653.33	629.31	608.34	589.92	573.64	559.18	546.27
80000	696.89	671.26	648.90	629.25	611.88	596.46	582.69
85000	740.44	713.21	689.45	668.58	650.13	633.74	619.11
90000	784.00	755.17	730.01	707.91	688.37	671.02	655.53
95000	827.55	797.12	770.57	747.23	726.61	708.29	691.94
100000	871.11	839.08	811.12	786.56	764.86	745.57	728.36
105000	914.66	881.03	851.68	825.89	803.10	782.85	764.78
110000	958.22	922.98	892.23	865.22	841.34	820.13	801.20
120000	1045.33	1006.89	973.35	943.87	917.83	894.69	874.04
130000	1132.44	1090.80	1054.46	1022.53	994.31	969.25	946.87
140000	1219.55	1174.71	1135.57	1101.19	1070.80	1043.80	1019.71
150000	1306.66	1258.61	1216.68	1179.84	1147.28	1118.36	1092.54
160000	1393.77	1342.52	1297.79	1258.50	1223.77	1192.92	1165.38
175000	1524.44	1468.38	1419.46	1376.48	1338.50	1304.75	1274.64
200000	1742.21	1678.15	1622.24	1573.12	1529.71	1491.15	1456.73
250000	2177.77	2097.69	2027.80	1966.40	1912.14	1863.93	1820.91
500000	4355.54	4195.38	4055.61	3932.81	3824.28	3727.87	3641.81
1000000	8711.07	8390.75	8111.21	7865.61	7648.56	7455.73	7283.63

MONTHLY PAYMENTS 6.50%

AMOUNT	22 YEARS	23 YEARS	24 YEARS	25 YEARS	30 YEARS	35 YEARS	40 YEARS
100	0.71	0.70	0.69	0.68	0.63	0.60	0.59
200	1.43	1.40	1.37	1.35	1.26	1.21	1.17
500	3.56	3.50	3.43	3.38	3.16	3.02	2.93
1000	7.13	6.99	6.87	6.75	6.32	6.04	5.85
2000	14.26	13.98	13.73	13.50	12.64	12.08	11.71
3000	21.39	20.97	20.60	20.26	18.96	18.12	17.56
4000	28.52	27.96	27.46	27.01	25.28	24.17	23.42
5000	35.65	34.95	34.33	33.76	31.60	30.21	29.27
6000	42.78	41.94	41.19	40.51	37.92	36.25	35.13
7000	49.91	48.93	48.06	47.26	44.24	42.29	40.98
8000	57.04	55.93	54.92	54.02	50.57	48.33	46.84
9000	64.16	62.92	61.79	60.77	56.89	54.37	52.69
10000	71.29	69.91	68.65	67.52	63.21	60.42	58.55
11000	78.42	76.90	75.52	74.27	69.53	66.46	64.40
12000	85.55	83.89	82.39	81.02	75.85	72.50	70.25
13000	92.68	90.88	89.25	87.78	82.17	78.54	76.11
14000	99.81	97.87	96.12	94.53	88.49	84.58	81.96
15000	106.94	104.86	102.98	101.28	94.81	90.62	87.82
20000	142.59	139.81	137.31	135.04	126.41	120.83	117.09
25000	178.23	174.77	171.64	168.80	158.02	151.04	146.36
30000	213.88	209.72	205.96	202.56	189.62	181.25	175.64
35000	249.53	244.67	240.29	236.32	221.22	211.45	204.91
40000	285.18	279.63	274.62	270.08	252.83	241.66	234.18
45000	320.82	314.58	308.94	303.84	284.43	271.87	263.46
50000	356.47	349.53	343.27	337.60	316.03	302.08	292.73
55000	392.12	384.49	377.60	371.36	347.64	332.28	322.00
56000	399.25	391.48	384.46	378.12	353.96	338.33	327.86
57000	406.38	398.47	391.33	384.87	360.28	344.37	333.71
58000	413.50	405.46	398.19	391.62	366.60	350.41	339.56
59000	420.63	412.45	405.06	398.37	372.92	356.45	345.42
60000	427.76	419.44	411.93	405.12	379.24	362.49	351.27
61000	434.89	426.43	418.79	411.88	385.56	368.53	357.13
62000	442.02	433.42	425.66	418.63	391.88	374.58	362.98
63000	449.15	440.41	432.52	425.38	398.20	380.62	368.84
64000	456.28	447.40	439.39	432.13	404.52	386.66	374.69
65000	463.41	454.39	446.25	438.88	410.84	392.70	380.55
70000	499.06	489.35	480.58	472.65	442.45	422.91	409.82
75000	534.70	524.30	514.91	506.41	474.05	453.12	439.09
80000	570.35	559.25	549.23	540.17	505.65	483.32	468.37
85000	606.00	594.20	583.56	573.93	537.26	513.53	497.64
90000	641.65	629.16	617.89	607.69	568.86	543.74	526.91
95000	677.29	664.11	652.22	641.45	600.46	573.95	556.18
100000	712.94	699.06	686.54	675.21	632.07	604.15	585.46
105000	748.59	734.02	720.87	708.97	663.67	634.36	614.73
110000	784.23	768.97	755.20	742.73	695.27	664.57	644.00
120000	855.53	838.88	823.85	810.25	758.48	724.99	702.55
130000	926.82	908.78	892.51	877.77	821.69	785.40	761.09
140000	998.11	978.69	961.16	945.29	884.90	845.82	819.64
150000	1069.41	1048.60	1029.81	1012.81	948.10	906.23	878.19
160000	1140.70	1118.50	1098.47	1080.33	1011.31	966.65	936.73
175000	1247.64	1223.36	1201.45	1181.61	1106.12	1057.27	1024.55
200000	1425.88	1398.13	1373.09	1350.41	1264.14	1208.31	1170.91
250000	1782.35	1747.66	1716.36	1688.02	1580.17	1510.39	1463.64
500000	3564.69	3495.32	3432.71	3376.04	3160.34	3020.77	2927.28
1000000	7129.39	6990.65	6865.43	6752.07	6320.68	6041.54	5854.57

6.75% MONTHLY PAYMENTS

AMOUNT	1 YEAR	2 YEARS	3 YEARS	4 YEARS	5 YEARS	6 YEARS	7 YEARS
100	8.64	4.47	3.08	2.38	1.97	1.69	1.50
200	17.28	8.93	6.15	4.77	3.94	3.39	2.99
500	43.21	22.33	15.38	11.92	9.84	8.46	7.49
1000	86.41	44.66	30.76	23.83	19.68	16.93	14.97
2000	172.82	89.32	61.53	47.66	39.37	33.86	29.94
3000	259.23	133.98	92.29	71.49	59.05	50.79	44.91
4000	345.65	178.64	123.05	95.32	78.73	67.72	59.88
5000	432.06	223.30	153.81	119.15	98.42	84.65	74.85
6000	518.47	267.96	184.58	142.98	118.10	101.58	89.82
7000	604.88	312.62	215.34	166.81	137.78	118.50	104.80
8000	691.29	357.27	246.10	190.64	157.47	135.43	119.77
9000	777.70	401.93	276.87	214.47	177.15	152.36	134.74
10000	864.12	446.59	307.63	238.30	196.83	169.29	149.71
11000	950.53	491.25	338.39	262.13	216.52	186.22	164.68
12000	1036.94	535.91	369.16	285.97	236.20	203.15	179.65
13000	1123.35	580.57	399.92	309.80	255.88	220.08	194.62
14000	1209.76	625.23	430.68	333.63	275.57	237.01	209.59
15000	1296.17	669.89	461.44	357.46	295.25	253.94	224.56
20000	1728.23	893.19	615.26	476.61	393.67	338.58	299.42
25000	2160.29	1116.48	769.07	595.76	492.09	423.23	374.27
30000	2592.35	1339.78	922.89	714.91	590.50	507.88	449.12
35000	3024.40	1563.08	1076.70	834.06	688.92	592.52	523.98
40000	3456.46	1786.37	1230.52	953.22	787.34	677.17	598.83
45000	3888.52	2009.67	1384.33	1072.37	885.76	761.81	673.68
50000	4320.58	2232.97	1538.15	1191.52	984.17	846.46	748.54
55000	4752.63	2456.26	1691.96	1310.67	1082.59	931.11	823.39
56000	4839.05	2500.92	1722.72	1334.50	1102.27	948.04	838.36
57000	4925.46	2545.58	1753.49	1358.33	1121.96	964.97	853.33
58000	5011.87	2590.24	1784.25	1382.16	1141.64	981.89	868.30
59000	5098.28	2634.90	1815.01	1406.00	1161.32	998.82	883.28
60000	5184.69	2679.56	1845.78	1429.83	1181.01	1015.75	898.25
61000	5271.10	2724.22	1876.54	1453.66	1200.69	1032.68	913.22
62000	5357.52	2768.88	1907.30	1477.49	1220.37	1049.61	928.19
63000	5443.93	2813.54	1938.06	1501.32	1240.06	1066.54	943.16
64000	5530.34	2858.20	1968.83	1525.15	1259.74	1083.47	958.13
65000	5616.75	2902.86	1999.59	1548.98	1279.42	1100.40	973.10
70000	6048.81	3126.16	2153.40	1668.13	1377.84	1185.04	1047.95
75000	6480.87	3349.45	2307.22	1787.28	1476.26	1269.69	1122.81
80000	6912.92	3572.75	2461.03	1906.43	1574.68	1354.34	1197.66
85000	7344.98	3796.04	2614.85	2025.59	1673.09	1438.98	1272.51
90000	7777.04	4019.34	2768.66	2144.74	1771.51	1523.63	1347.37
95000	8209.10	4242.64	2922.48	2263.89	1869.93	1608.28	1422.22
100000	8641.15	4465.93	3076.29	2383.04	1968.35	1692.92	1497.08
105000	9073.21	4689.23	3230.11	2502.19	2066.76	1777.57	1571.93
110000	9505.27	4912.53	3383.92	2621.35	2165.18	1862.21	1646.78
120000	10369.38	5359.12	3691.55	2859.65	2362.02	2031.51	1796.49
130000	11233.50	5805.71	3999.18	3097.96	2558.85	2200.80	1946.20
140000	12097.62	6252.31	4306.81	3336.26	2755.68	2370.09	2095.91
150000	12961.73	6698.90	4614.44	3574.56	2952.52	2539.38	2245.61
160000	13825.85	7145.49	4922.07	3812.87	3149.35	2708.67	2395.32
175000	15122.02	7815.38	5383.51	4170.32	3444.61	2962.61	2619.88
200000	17282.31	8931.87	6152.58	4766.09	3936.69	3385.84	2994.15
250000	21602.88	11164.83	7690.73	5957.61	4920.87	4232.30	3742.69
500000	43205.77	22329.66	15381.46	11915.21	9841.73	8464.61	7485.38
1000000	86411.54	44659.33	30762.92	23830.43	19683.46	16929.21	14970.76

MONTHLY PAYMENTS   6.75%

AMOUNT	8 YEARS	9 YEARS	10 YEARS	11 YEARS	12 YEARS	13 YEARS	14 YEARS
100	1.35	1.24	1.15	1.08	1.02	0.96	0.92
200	2.70	2.48	2.30	2.15	2.03	1.93	1.84
500	6.75	6.19	5.74	5.38	5.08	4.82	4.61
1000	13.51	12.38	11.48	10.75	10.15	9.65	9.22
2000	27.02	24.76	22.96	21.51	20.30	19.29	18.43
3000	40.53	37.14	34.45	32.26	30.45	28.94	27.65
4000	54.04	49.52	45.93	43.01	40.60	38.58	36.87
5000	67.55	61.90	57.41	53.77	50.76	48.23	46.08
6000	81.06	74.28	68.89	64.52	60.91	57.87	55.30
7000	94.57	86.66	80.38	75.27	71.06	67.52	64.52
8000	108.08	99.04	91.86	86.03	81.21	77.17	73.74
9000	121.59	111.42	103.34	96.78	91.36	86.81	82.95
10000	135.10	123.80	114.82	107.53	101.51	96.46	92.17
11000	148.61	136.18	126.31	118.29	111.66	106.10	101.39
12000	162.12	148.56	137.79	129.04	121.81	115.75	110.60
13000	175.63	160.94	149.27	139.80	131.96	125.40	119.82
14000	189.13	173.32	160.75	150.55	142.11	135.04	129.04
15000	202.64	185.70	172.24	161.30	152.27	144.69	138.25
20000	270.19	247.60	229.65	215.07	203.02	192.92	184.34
25000	337.74	309.50	287.06	268.84	253.78	241.15	230.42
30000	405.29	371.40	344.47	322.60	304.53	289.37	276.51
35000	472.84	433.30	401.88	376.37	355.29	337.60	322.59
40000	540.39	495.20	459.30	430.14	406.04	385.83	368.68
45000	607.93	557.10	516.71	483.91	456.80	434.06	414.76
50000	675.48	619.00	574.12	537.67	507.55	482.29	460.85
55000	743.03	680.90	631.53	591.44	558.31	530.52	506.93
56000	756.54	693.28	643.02	602.20	568.46	540.16	516.15
57000	770.05	705.66	654.50	612.95	578.61	549.81	525.37
58000	783.56	718.04	665.98	623.70	588.76	559.46	534.58
59000	797.07	730.42	677.46	634.46	598.91	569.10	543.80
60000	810.58	742.80	688.94	645.21	609.06	578.75	553.02
61000	824.09	755.18	700.43	655.96	619.21	588.39	562.23
62000	837.60	767.56	711.91	666.72	629.36	598.04	571.45
63000	851.11	779.94	723.39	677.47	639.51	607.69	580.67
64000	864.62	792.32	734.87	688.22	649.67	617.33	589.88
65000	878.13	804.70	746.36	698.98	659.82	626.98	599.10
70000	945.67	866.60	803.77	752.74	710.57	675.21	645.19
75000	1013.22	928.50	861.18	806.51	761.33	723.44	691.27
80000	1080.77	990.40	918.59	860.28	812.08	771.66	737.35
85000	1148.32	1052.30	976.00	914.05	862.84	819.89	783.44
90000	1215.87	1114.20	1033.42	967.81	913.59	868.12	829.52
95000	1283.42	1176.10	1090.83	1021.58	964.35	916.35	875.61
100000	1350.96	1238.00	1148.24	1075.35	1015.10	964.58	921.69
105000	1418.51	1299.90	1205.65	1129.12	1065.86	1012.81	967.78
110000	1486.06	1361.80	1263.07	1182.88	1116.61	1061.04	1013.86
120000	1621.16	1485.60	1377.89	1290.42	1218.12	1157.50	1106.03
130000	1756.25	1609.40	1492.71	1397.95	1319.63	1253.95	1198.20
140000	1891.35	1733.20	1607.54	1505.49	1421.14	1350.41	1290.37
150000	2026.45	1857.00	1722.36	1613.02	1522.65	1446.87	1382.54
160000	2161.54	1980.80	1837.19	1720.56	1624.16	1543.33	1474.71
175000	2364.19	2166.50	2009.42	1881.86	1776.43	1688.02	1612.96
200000	2701.93	2476.00	2296.48	2150.70	2030.21	1929.16	1843.39
250000	3377.41	3095.01	2870.60	2688.37	2537.76	2411.45	2304.23
500000	6754.82	6190.01	5741.21	5376.74	5075.51	4822.90	4608.47
1000000	13509.64	12380.02	11482.41	10753.49	10151.03	9645.80	9216.93

6.75% — MONTHLY PAYMENTS

AMOUNT	15 YEARS	16 YEARS	17 YEARS	18 YEARS	19 YEARS	20 YEARS	21 YEARS
100	0.88	0.85	0.83	0.80	0.78	0.76	0.74
200	1.77	1.71	1.65	1.60	1.56	1.52	1.49
500	4.42	4.27	4.13	4.00	3.90	3.80	3.72
1000	8.85	8.53	8.25	8.01	7.79	7.60	7.43
2000	17.70	17.06	16.51	16.02	15.59	15.21	14.87
3000	26.55	25.59	24.76	24.03	23.38	22.81	22.30
4000	35.40	34.12	33.01	32.04	31.18	30.41	29.73
5000	44.25	42.65	41.27	40.05	38.97	38.02	37.17
6000	53.09	51.18	49.52	48.06	46.77	45.62	44.60
7000	61.94	59.72	57.77	56.07	54.56	53.23	52.03
8000	70.79	68.25	66.03	64.08	62.36	60.83	59.47
9000	79.64	76.78	74.28	72.09	70.15	68.43	66.90
10000	88.49	85.31	82.53	80.10	77.95	76.04	74.33
11000	97.34	93.84	90.79	88.11	85.74	83.64	81.77
12000	106.19	102.37	99.04	96.12	93.53	91.24	89.20
13000	115.04	110.90	107.29	104.13	101.33	98.85	96.63
14000	123.89	119.43	115.55	112.14	109.12	106.45	104.07
15000	132.74	127.96	123.80	120.14	116.92	114.05	111.50
20000	176.98	170.62	165.07	160.19	155.89	152.07	148.67
25000	221.23	213.27	206.33	200.24	194.86	190.09	185.84
30000	265.47	255.92	247.60	240.29	233.84	228.11	223.00
35000	309.72	298.58	288.86	280.34	272.81	266.13	260.17
40000	353.96	341.23	330.13	320.39	311.78	304.15	297.34
45000	398.21	383.89	371.40	360.43	350.75	342.16	334.50
50000	442.45	426.54	412.66	400.48	389.73	380.18	371.67
55000	486.70	469.19	453.93	440.53	428.70	418.20	408.84
56000	495.55	477.72	462.18	448.54	436.49	425.80	416.27
57000	504.40	486.26	470.44	456.55	444.29	433.41	423.71
58000	513.25	494.79	478.69	464.56	452.08	441.01	431.14
59000	522.10	503.32	486.94	472.57	459.88	448.61	438.57
60000	530.95	511.85	495.20	480.58	467.67	456.22	446.01
61000	539.79	520.38	503.45	488.59	475.47	463.82	453.44
62000	548.64	528.91	511.70	496.60	483.26	471.43	460.87
63000	557.49	537.44	519.96	504.61	491.06	479.03	468.31
64000	566.34	545.97	528.21	512.62	498.85	486.63	475.74
65000	575.19	554.50	536.46	520.63	506.65	494.24	483.17
70000	619.44	597.16	577.73	560.68	545.62	532.25	520.34
75000	663.68	639.81	618.99	600.72	584.59	570.27	557.51
80000	707.93	682.46	660.26	640.77	623.56	608.29	594.67
85000	752.17	725.12	701.53	680.82	662.54	646.31	631.84
90000	796.42	767.77	742.79	720.87	701.51	684.33	669.01
95000	840.66	810.43	784.06	760.92	740.48	722.35	706.18
100000	884.91	853.08	825.33	800.96	779.45	760.36	743.34
105000	929.15	895.73	866.59	841.01	818.43	798.38	780.51
110000	973.40	938.39	907.86	881.06	857.40	836.40	817.68
120000	1061.89	1023.70	990.39	961.16	935.35	912.44	892.01
130000	1150.38	1109.00	1072.92	1041.25	1013.29	988.47	966.35
140000	1238.87	1194.31	1155.46	1121.35	1091.24	1064.51	1040.68
150000	1327.36	1279.62	1237.99	1201.45	1169.18	1140.55	1115.01
160000	1415.86	1364.93	1320.52	1281.54	1247.13	1216.58	1189.35
175000	1548.59	1492.89	1444.32	1401.69	1364.05	1330.64	1300.85
200000	1769.82	1706.16	1650.65	1601.93	1558.91	1520.73	1486.69
250000	2212.27	2132.70	2063.32	2002.41	1948.64	1900.91	1858.36
500000	4424.55	4265.40	4126.63	4004.82	3897.27	3801.82	3716.72
1000000	8849.09	8530.80	8253.27	8009.65	7794.55	7603.64	7433.43

MONTHLY PAYMENTS 6.75%

AMOUNT	22 YEARS	23 YEARS	24 YEARS	25 YEARS	30 YEARS	35 YEARS	40 YEARS
100	0.73	0.71	0.70	0.69	0.65	0.62	0.60
200	1.46	1.43	1.40	1.38	1.30	1.24	1.21
500	3.64	3.57	3.51	3.45	3.24	3.11	3.02
1000	7.28	7.14	7.02	6.91	6.49	6.21	6.03
2000	14.56	14.29	14.04	13.82	12.97	12.43	12.07
3000	21.84	21.43	21.06	20.73	19.46	18.64	18.10
4000	29.12	28.58	28.08	27.64	25.94	24.86	24.13
5000	36.41	35.72	35.10	34.55	32.43	31.07	30.17
6000	43.69	42.86	42.12	41.45	38.92	37.28	36.20
7000	50.97	50.01	49.14	48.36	45.40	43.50	42.23
8000	58.25	57.15	56.17	55.27	51.89	49.71	48.27
9000	65.53	64.30	63.19	62.18	58.37	55.93	54.30
10000	72.81	71.44	70.21	69.09	64.86	62.14	60.34
11000	80.09	78.59	77.23	76.00	71.35	68.36	66.37
12000	87.37	85.73	84.25	82.91	77.83	74.57	72.40
13000	94.65	92.87	91.27	89.82	84.32	80.78	78.44
14000	101.93	100.02	98.29	96.73	90.80	87.00	84.47
15000	109.22	107.16	105.31	103.64	97.29	93.21	90.50
20000	145.62	142.88	140.41	138.18	129.72	124.28	120.67
25000	182.03	178.60	175.52	172.73	162.15	155.35	150.84
30000	218.43	214.32	210.62	207.27	194.58	186.42	181.01
35000	254.84	250.04	245.72	241.82	227.01	217.50	211.17
40000	291.24	285.77	280.83	276.36	259.44	248.57	241.34
45000	327.65	321.49	315.93	310.91	291.87	279.64	271.51
50000	364.05	357.21	351.04	345.46	324.30	310.71	301.68
55000	400.46	392.93	386.14	380.00	356.73	341.78	331.85
56000	407.74	400.07	393.16	386.91	363.21	347.99	337.88
57000	415.02	407.22	400.18	393.82	369.70	354.21	343.91
58000	422.30	414.36	407.20	400.73	376.19	360.42	349.95
59000	429.58	421.50	414.22	407.64	382.67	366.64	355.98
60000	436.86	428.65	421.24	414.55	389.16	372.85	362.01
61000	444.14	435.79	428.26	421.46	395.64	379.06	368.05
62000	451.43	442.94	435.28	428.37	402.13	385.28	374.08
63000	458.71	450.08	442.30	435.27	408.62	391.49	380.11
64000	465.99	457.22	449.33	442.18	415.10	397.71	386.15
65000	473.27	464.37	456.35	449.09	421.59	403.92	392.18
70000	509.67	500.09	491.46	483.64	454.02	434.99	422.35
75000	546.08	535.81	526.55	518.18	486.45	466.06	452.52
80000	582.48	571.53	561.66	552.73	518.88	497.13	482.69
85000	618.89	607.25	596.76	587.27	551.31	528.20	512.85
90000	655.29	642.97	631.86	621.82	583.74	559.27	543.02
95000	691.70	678.69	666.97	656.37	616.17	590.35	573.19
100000	728.11	714.41	702.07	690.91	648.60	621.42	603.36
105000	764.51	750.13	737.17	725.46	681.03	652.49	633.52
110000	800.92	785.86	772.28	760.00	713.46	683.56	663.69
120000	873.73	857.30	842.49	829.09	778.32	745.70	724.03
130000	946.54	928.74	912.69	898.18	843.18	807.84	784.36
140000	1019.35	1000.18	982.90	967.28	908.04	869.98	844.70
150000	1092.16	1071.62	1053.11	1036.37	972.90	932.12	905.04
160000	1164.97	1143.06	1123.31	1105.46	1037.76	994.27	965.37
175000	1274.18	1250.22	1228.62	1209.10	1135.05	1087.48	1055.87
200000	1456.21	1428.83	1404.14	1381.82	1297.20	1242.83	1206.71
250000	1820.26	1786.03	1755.18	1727.28	1621.50	1553.54	1508.39
500000	3640.53	3572.07	3510.36	3454.56	3242.99	3107.08	3016.78
1000000	7281.05	7144.14	7020.71	6909.12	6485.98	6214.17	6033.57

7.00%   MONTHLY PAYMENTS

AMOUNT	1 YEAR	2 YEARS	3 YEARS	4 YEARS	5 YEARS	6 YEARS	7 YEARS
100	8.65	4.48	3.09	2.39	1.98	1.70	1.51
200	17.31	8.95	6.18	4.79	3.96	3.41	3.02
500	43.26	22.39	15.44	11.97	9.90	8.52	7.55
1000	86.53	44.77	30.88	23.95	19.80	17.05	15.09
2000	173.05	89.55	61.75	47.89	39.60	34.10	30.19
3000	259.58	134.32	92.63	71.84	59.40	51.15	45.28
4000	346.11	179.09	123.51	95.78	79.20	68.20	60.37
5000	432.63	223.86	154.39	119.73	99.01	85.25	75.46
6000	519.16	268.64	185.26	143.68	118.81	102.29	90.56
7000	605.69	313.41	216.14	167.62	138.61	119.34	105.65
8000	692.21	358.18	247.02	191.57	158.41	136.39	120.74
9000	778.74	402.95	277.89	215.52	178.21	153.44	135.83
10000	865.27	447.73	308.77	239.46	198.01	170.49	150.93
11000	951.79	492.50	339.65	263.41	217.81	187.54	166.02
12000	1038.32	537.27	370.53	287.35	237.61	204.59	181.11
13000	1124.85	582.04	401.40	311.30	257.42	221.64	196.20
14000	1211.37	626.82	432.28	335.25	277.22	238.69	211.30
15000	1297.90	671.59	463.16	359.19	297.02	255.74	226.39
20000	1730.53	895.45	617.54	478.92	396.02	340.98	301.85
25000	2163.17	1119.31	771.93	598.66	495.03	426.23	377.32
30000	2595.80	1343.18	926.31	718.39	594.04	511.47	452.78
35000	3028.44	1567.04	1080.70	838.12	693.04	596.72	528.24
40000	3461.07	1790.90	1235.08	957.85	792.05	681.96	603.71
45000	3893.70	2014.77	1389.47	1077.58	891.05	767.21	679.17
50000	4326.34	2238.63	1543.85	1197.31	990.06	852.45	754.63
55000	4758.97	2462.49	1698.24	1317.04	1089.07	937.70	830.10
56000	4845.50	2507.26	1729.12	1340.99	1108.87	954.74	845.19
57000	4932.02	2552.04	1759.99	1364.94	1128.67	971.79	860.28
58000	5018.55	2596.81	1790.87	1388.88	1148.47	988.84	875.38
59000	5105.08	2641.58	1821.75	1412.83	1168.27	1005.89	890.47
60000	5191.60	2686.35	1852.63	1436.77	1188.07	1022.94	905.56
61000	5278.13	2731.13	1883.50	1460.72	1207.87	1039.99	920.65
62000	5364.66	2775.90	1914.38	1484.67	1227.67	1057.04	935.75
63000	5451.19	2820.67	1945.26	1508.61	1247.48	1074.09	950.84
64000	5537.71	2865.45	1976.13	1532.56	1267.28	1091.14	965.93
65000	5624.24	2910.22	2007.01	1556.51	1287.08	1108.19	981.02
70000	6056.87	3134.08	2161.40	1676.24	1386.08	1193.43	1056.49
75000	6489.51	3357.94	2315.78	1795.97	1485.09	1278.68	1131.95
80000	6922.14	3581.81	2470.17	1915.70	1584.10	1363.92	1207.41
85000	7354.77	3805.67	2624.55	2035.43	1683.10	1449.17	1282.88
90000	7787.41	4029.53	2778.94	2155.16	1782.11	1534.41	1358.34
95000	8220.04	4253.40	2933.32	2274.89	1881.11	1619.66	1433.80
100000	8652.67	4477.26	3087.71	2394.62	1980.12	1704.90	1509.27
105000	9085.31	4701.12	3242.10	2514.36	2079.13	1790.15	1584.73
110000	9517.94	4924.98	3396.48	2634.09	2178.13	1875.39	1660.19
120000	10383.21	5372.71	3705.25	2873.55	2376.14	2045.88	1811.12
130000	11248.48	5820.44	4014.02	3113.01	2574.16	2216.37	1962.05
140000	12113.74	6268.16	4322.79	3352.47	2772.17	2386.86	2112.98
150000	12979.01	6715.89	4631.56	3591.94	2970.18	2557.35	2263.90
160000	13844.28	7163.61	4940.34	3831.40	3168.19	2727.84	2414.83
175000	15142.18	7835.20	5403.49	4190.59	3465.21	2983.58	2641.22
200000	17305.35	8954.52	6175.42	4789.25	3960.24	3409.80	3018.54
250000	21631.69	11193.14	7719.27	5986.56	4950.30	4262.25	3773.17
500000	43263.37	22386.29	15438.55	11973.12	9900.60	8524.50	7546.34
1000000	86526.75	44772.58	30877.10	23946.24	19801.20	17049.01	15092.68

MONTHLY PAYMENTS 7.00%

AMOUNT	8 YEARS	9 YEARS	10 YEARS	11 YEARS	12 YEARS	13 YEARS	14 YEARS
100	1.36	1.25	1.16	1.09	1.03	0.98	0.94
200	2.73	2.50	2.32	2.18	2.06	1.96	1.87
500	6.82	6.25	5.81	5.44	5.14	4.89	4.68
1000	13.63	12.51	11.61	10.88	10.28	9.78	9.35
2000	27.27	25.01	23.22	21.77	20.57	19.56	18.71
3000	40.90	37.52	34.83	32.65	30.85	29.34	28.06
4000	54.53	50.03	46.44	43.54	41.14	39.12	37.42
5000	68.17	62.53	58.05	54.42	51.42	48.90	46.77
6000	81.80	75.04	69.67	65.30	61.70	58.68	56.12
7000	95.44	87.54	81.28	76.19	71.99	68.47	65.48
8000	109.07	100.05	92.89	87.07	82.27	78.25	74.83
9000	122.70	112.56	104.50	97.96	92.55	88.03	84.19
10000	136.34	125.06	116.11	108.84	102.84	97.81	93.54
11000	149.97	137.57	127.72	119.73	113.12	107.59	102.89
12000	163.60	150.08	139.33	130.61	123.41	117.37	112.25
13000	177.24	162.58	150.94	141.49	133.69	127.15	121.60
14000	190.87	175.09	162.55	152.38	143.97	136.93	130.96
15000	204.51	187.59	174.16	163.26	154.26	146.71	140.31
20000	272.67	250.13	232.22	217.68	205.68	195.61	187.08
25000	340.84	312.66	290.27	272.10	257.10	244.52	233.85
30000	409.01	375.19	348.33	326.52	308.51	293.42	280.62
35000	477.18	437.72	406.38	380.94	359.93	342.33	327.39
40000	545.35	500.25	464.43	435.36	411.35	391.23	374.16
45000	613.52	562.78	522.49	489.78	462.77	440.13	420.93
50000	681.69	625.31	580.54	544.21	514.19	489.04	467.70
55000	749.85	687.85	638.60	598.63	565.61	537.94	514.47
56000	763.49	700.35	650.21	609.51	575.89	547.72	523.82
57000	777.12	712.86	661.82	620.39	586.18	557.50	533.18
58000	790.76	725.36	673.43	631.28	596.46	567.28	542.53
59000	804.39	737.87	685.04	642.16	606.74	577.06	551.89
60000	818.02	750.38	696.65	653.05	617.03	586.84	561.24
61000	831.66	762.88	708.26	663.93	627.31	596.63	570.59
62000	845.29	775.39	719.87	674.81	637.60	606.41	579.95
63000	858.92	787.90	731.48	685.70	647.88	616.19	589.30
64000	872.56	800.40	743.09	696.58	658.16	625.97	598.66
65000	886.19	812.91	754.71	707.47	668.45	635.75	608.01
70000	954.36	875.44	812.76	761.89	719.87	684.65	654.78
75000	1022.53	937.97	870.81	816.31	771.29	733.56	701.55
80000	1090.70	1000.50	928.87	870.73	822.70	782.46	748.32
85000	1158.87	1063.03	986.92	925.15	874.12	831.36	795.09
90000	1227.03	1125.56	1044.98	979.57	925.54	880.27	841.86
95000	1295.20	1188.10	1103.03	1033.99	976.96	929.17	888.63
100000	1363.37	1250.63	1161.08	1088.41	1028.38	978.07	935.40
105000	1431.54	1313.16	1219.14	1142.83	1079.80	1026.98	982.17
110000	1499.71	1375.69	1277.19	1197.25	1131.22	1075.88	1028.94
120000	1636.05	1500.75	1393.30	1306.09	1234.06	1173.69	1122.48
130000	1772.38	1625.82	1509.41	1414.93	1336.90	1271.50	1216.02
140000	1908.72	1750.88	1625.52	1523.77	1439.73	1369.30	1309.56
150000	2045.06	1875.94	1741.63	1632.62	1542.57	1467.11	1403.10
160000	2181.39	2001.00	1857.74	1741.46	1645.41	1564.92	1496.64
175000	2385.90	2188.60	2031.90	1904.72	1799.67	1711.63	1636.95
200000	2726.74	2501.26	2322.17	2176.82	2056.76	1956.15	1870.80
250000	3408.43	3126.57	2902.71	2721.03	2570.95	2445.19	2338.50
500000	6816.86	6253.14	5805.42	5442.05	5141.91	4890.37	4677.00
1000000	13633.72	12506.28	11610.85	10884.10	10283.81	9780.74	9354.01

7.00%　　　　　　MONTHLY PAYMENTS

AMOUNT	15 YEARS	16 YEARS	17 YEARS	18 YEARS	19 YEARS	20 YEARS	21 YEARS
100	0.90	0.87	0.84	0.82	0.79	0.78	0.76
200	1.80	1.73	1.68	1.63	1.59	1.55	1.52
500	4.49	4.34	4.20	4.08	3.97	3.88	3.79
1000	8.99	8.67	8.40	8.16	7.94	7.75	7.58
2000	17.98	17.34	16.79	16.31	15.88	15.51	15.17
3000	26.96	26.02	25.19	24.47	23.83	23.26	22.75
4000	35.95	34.69	33.59	32.62	31.77	31.01	30.34
5000	44.94	43.36	41.98	40.78	39.71	38.76	37.92
6000	53.93	52.03	50.38	48.93	47.65	46.52	45.51
7000	62.92	60.70	58.78	57.09	55.59	54.27	53.09
8000	71.91	69.38	67.17	65.24	63.54	62.02	60.68
9000	80.89	78.05	75.57	73.40	71.48	69.78	68.26
10000	89.88	86.72	83.97	81.55	79.42	77.53	75.85
11000	98.87	95.39	92.36	89.71	87.36	85.28	83.43
12000	107.86	104.06	100.76	97.86	95.30	93.04	91.02
13000	116.85	112.74	109.16	106.02	103.25	100.79	98.60
14000	125.84	121.41	117.55	114.17	111.19	108.54	106.19
15000	134.82	130.08	125.95	122.33	119.13	116.29	113.77
20000	179.77	173.44	167.93	163.10	158.84	155.06	151.69
25000	224.71	216.80	209.92	203.88	198.55	193.82	189.62
30000	269.65	260.16	251.90	244.65	238.26	232.59	227.54
35000	314.59	303.52	293.88	285.43	277.97	271.35	265.47
40000	359.53	346.88	335.86	326.20	317.68	310.12	303.39
45000	404.47	390.24	377.85	366.98	357.39	348.88	341.31
50000	449.41	433.60	419.83	407.75	397.10	387.65	379.24
55000	494.36	476.96	461.81	448.53	436.81	426.41	417.16
56000	503.34	485.64	470.21	456.68	444.75	434.17	424.74
57000	512.33	494.31	478.61	464.84	452.69	441.92	432.33
58000	521.32	502.98	487.00	472.99	460.63	449.67	439.91
59000	530.31	511.65	495.40	481.15	468.57	457.43	447.50
60000	539.30	520.32	503.80	489.30	476.52	465.18	455.08
61000	548.29	529.00	512.19	497.46	484.46	472.93	462.67
62000	557.27	537.67	520.59	505.61	492.40	480.69	470.25
63000	566.26	546.34	528.99	513.77	500.34	488.44	477.84
64000	575.25	555.01	537.38	521.92	508.28	496.19	485.42
65000	584.24	563.69	545.78	530.08	516.23	503.94	493.01
70000	629.18	607.05	587.76	570.85	555.93	542.71	530.93
75000	674.12	650.41	629.75	611.63	595.64	581.47	568.85
80000	719.06	693.77	671.73	652.40	635.35	620.24	606.78
85000	764.00	737.13	713.71	693.18	675.06	659.00	644.70
90000	808.95	780.49	755.69	733.95	714.77	697.77	682.62
95000	853.89	823.85	797.68	774.73	754.48	736.53	720.55
100000	898.83	867.21	839.66	815.50	794.19	775.30	758.47
105000	943.77	910.57	881.64	856.28	833.90	814.06	796.40
110000	988.71	953.93	923.63	897.05	873.61	852.83	834.32
120000	1078.59	1040.65	1007.59	978.60	953.03	930.36	910.17
130000	1168.48	1127.37	1091.56	1060.15	1032.45	1007.89	986.01
140000	1258.36	1214.09	1175.52	1141.70	1111.87	1085.42	1061.86
150000	1348.24	1300.81	1259.49	1223.25	1191.29	1162.95	1137.71
160000	1438.13	1387.53	1343.46	1304.80	1270.71	1240.48	1213.55
175000	1572.95	1517.61	1469.41	1427.13	1389.84	1356.77	1327.33
200000	1797.66	1734.42	1679.32	1631.00	1588.38	1550.60	1516.94
250000	2247.07	2168.02	2099.15	2038.76	1985.48	1938.25	1896.18
500000	4494.14	4336.04	4198.30	4077.51	3970.96	3876.49	3792.36
1000000	8988.28	8672.08	8396.61	8155.02	7941.92	7752.99	7584.72

MONTHLY PAYMENTS 7.00%

AMOUNT	22 YEARS	23 YEARS	24 YEARS	25 YEARS	30 YEARS	35 YEARS	40 YEARS
100	0.74	0.73	0.72	0.71	0.67	0.64	0.62
200	1.49	1.46	1.44	1.41	1.33	1.28	1.24
500	3.72	3.65	3.59	3.53	3.33	3.19	3.11
1000	7.43	7.30	7.18	7.07	6.65	6.39	6.21
2000	14.87	14.60	14.36	14.14	13.31	12.78	12.43
3000	22.30	21.90	21.53	21.20	19.96	19.17	18.64
4000	29.74	29.20	28.71	28.27	26.61	25.55	24.86
5000	37.17	36.50	35.89	35.34	33.27	31.94	31.07
6000	44.61	43.80	43.07	42.41	39.92	38.33	37.29
7000	52.04	51.09	50.24	49.47	46.57	44.72	43.50
8000	59.47	58.39	57.42	56.54	53.22	51.11	49.71
9000	66.91	65.69	64.60	63.61	59.88	57.50	55.93
10000	74.34	72.99	71.78	70.68	66.53	63.89	62.14
11000	81.78	80.29	78.95	77.75	73.18	70.27	68.36
12000	89.21	87.59	86.13	84.81	79.84	76.66	74.57
13000	96.65	94.89	93.31	91.88	86.49	83.05	80.79
14000	104.08	102.19	100.49	98.95	93.14	89.44	87.00
15000	111.51	109.49	107.66	106.02	99.80	95.83	93.21
20000	148.68	145.98	143.55	141.36	133.06	127.77	124.29
25000	185.86	182.48	179.44	176.69	166.33	159.71	155.36
30000	223.03	218.98	215.33	212.03	199.59	191.66	186.43
35000	260.20	255.47	251.22	247.37	232.86	223.60	217.50
40000	297.37	291.97	287.10	282.71	266.12	255.54	248.57
45000	334.54	328.46	322.99	318.05	299.39	287.49	279.64
50000	371.71	364.96	358.88	353.39	332.65	319.43	310.72
55000	408.88	401.46	394.77	388.73	365.92	351.37	341.79
56000	416.32	408.75	401.95	395.80	372.57	357.76	348.00
57000	423.75	416.05	409.12	402.86	379.22	364.15	354.22
58000	431.19	423.35	416.30	409.93	385.88	370.54	360.43
59000	438.62	430.65	423.48	417.00	392.53	376.93	366.64
60000	446.05	437.95	430.66	424.07	399.18	383.31	372.86
61000	453.49	445.25	437.83	431.14	405.83	389.70	379.07
62000	460.92	452.55	445.01	438.20	412.49	396.09	385.29
63000	468.36	459.85	452.19	445.27	419.14	402.48	391.50
64000	475.79	467.15	459.37	452.34	425.79	408.87	397.72
65000	483.23	474.45	466.54	459.41	432.45	415.26	403.93
70000	520.40	510.94	502.43	494.75	465.71	447.20	435.00
75000	557.57	547.44	538.32	530.08	498.98	479.14	466.07
80000	594.74	583.94	574.21	565.42	532.24	511.09	497.15
85000	631.91	620.43	610.10	600.76	565.51	543.03	528.22
90000	669.08	656.93	645.98	636.10	598.77	574.97	559.29
95000	706.25	693.42	681.87	671.44	632.04	606.91	590.36
100000	743.42	729.92	717.76	706.78	665.30	638.86	621.43
105000	780.60	766.42	753.65	742.12	698.57	670.80	652.50
110000	817.77	802.91	789.54	777.46	731.83	702.74	683.57
120000	892.11	875.90	861.31	848.14	798.36	766.63	745.72
130000	966.45	948.89	933.09	918.81	864.89	830.51	807.86
140000	1040.79	1021.89	1004.86	989.49	931.42	894.40	870.00
150000	1115.14	1094.88	1076.64	1060.17	997.95	958.28	932.15
160000	1189.48	1167.87	1148.42	1130.85	1064.48	1022.17	994.29
175000	1300.99	1277.36	1256.08	1236.86	1164.28	1118.00	1087.50
200000	1486.85	1459.84	1435.52	1413.56	1330.60	1277.71	1242.86
250000	1858.56	1824.80	1794.40	1766.95	1663.26	1597.14	1553.58
500000	3717.12	3649.60	3588.80	3533.90	3326.51	3194.28	3107.16
1000000	7434.24	7299.19	7177.60	7067.79	6653.02	6388.56	6214.31

7.25% MONTHLY PAYMENTS

AMOUNT	1 YEAR	2 YEARS	3 YEARS	4 YEARS	5 YEARS	6 YEARS	7 YEARS
100	8.66	4.49	3.10	2.41	1.99	1.72	1.52
200	17.33	8.98	6.20	4.81	3.98	3.43	3.04
500	43.32	22.44	15.50	12.03	9.96	8.58	7.61
1000	86.64	44.89	30.99	24.06	19.92	17.17	15.22
2000	173.28	89.77	61.98	48.12	39.84	34.34	30.43
3000	259.93	134.66	92.97	72.19	59.76	51.51	45.65
4000	346.57	179.54	123.97	96.25	79.68	68.68	60.86
5000	433.21	224.43	154.96	120.31	99.60	85.85	76.08
6000	519.85	269.32	185.95	144.37	119.52	103.02	91.29
7000	606.49	314.20	216.94	168.44	139.44	120.19	106.51
8000	693.14	359.09	247.93	192.50	159.35	137.35	121.72
9000	779.78	403.97	278.92	216.56	179.27	154.52	136.94
10000	866.42	448.86	309.92	240.62	199.19	171.69	152.15
11000	953.06	493.75	340.91	264.69	219.11	188.86	167.37
12000	1039.70	538.63	371.90	288.75	239.03	206.03	182.58
13000	1126.35	583.52	402.89	312.81	258.95	223.20	197.80
14000	1212.99	628.40	433.88	336.87	278.87	240.37	213.01
15000	1299.63	673.29	464.87	360.94	298.79	257.54	228.23
20000	1732.84	897.72	619.83	481.25	398.39	343.39	304.30
25000	2166.05	1122.15	774.79	601.56	497.98	429.23	380.38
30000	2599.26	1346.58	929.75	721.87	597.58	515.08	456.46
35000	3032.47	1571.01	1084.70	842.18	697.18	600.93	532.53
40000	3465.68	1795.44	1239.66	962.50	796.77	686.77	608.61
45000	3898.89	2019.87	1394.62	1082.81	896.37	772.62	684.68
50000	4332.10	2244.30	1549.58	1203.12	995.97	858.47	760.76
55000	4765.31	2468.73	1704.53	1323.43	1095.56	944.31	836.84
56000	4851.95	2513.62	1735.53	1347.49	1115.48	961.48	852.05
57000	4938.60	2558.50	1766.52	1371.56	1135.40	978.65	867.27
58000	5025.24	2603.39	1797.51	1395.62	1155.32	995.82	882.48
59000	5111.88	2648.27	1828.50	1419.68	1175.24	1012.99	897.70
60000	5198.52	2693.16	1859.49	1443.74	1195.16	1030.16	912.91
61000	5285.16	2738.05	1890.48	1467.81	1215.08	1047.33	928.13
62000	5371.81	2782.93	1921.47	1491.87	1235.00	1064.50	943.34
63000	5458.45	2827.82	1952.47	1515.93	1254.92	1081.67	958.56
64000	5545.09	2872.70	1983.46	1539.99	1274.84	1098.84	973.77
65000	5631.73	2917.59	2014.45	1564.06	1294.76	1116.00	988.99
70000	6064.94	3142.02	2169.41	1684.37	1394.36	1201.85	1065.06
75000	6498.15	3366.45	2324.36	1804.68	1493.95	1287.70	1141.14
80000	6931.36	3590.88	2479.32	1924.99	1593.55	1373.54	1217.21
85000	7364.57	3815.31	2634.28	2045.30	1693.15	1459.39	1293.29
90000	7797.78	4039.74	2789.24	2165.62	1792.74	1545.24	1369.37
95000	8230.99	4264.17	2944.20	2285.93	1892.34	1631.08	1445.44
100000	8664.20	4488.60	3099.15	2406.24	1991.94	1716.93	1521.52
105000	9097.41	4713.03	3254.11	2526.55	2091.53	1802.78	1597.59
110000	9530.62	4937.46	3409.07	2646.86	2191.13	1888.62	1673.67
120000	10397.04	5386.32	3718.98	2887.49	2390.32	2060.32	1825.82
130000	11263.47	5835.18	4028.90	3128.11	2589.52	2232.01	1977.97
140000	12129.89	6284.04	4338.81	3368.74	2788.71	2403.70	2130.13
150000	12996.31	6732.90	4648.73	3609.36	2987.90	2575.40	2282.28
160000	13862.73	7181.76	4958.64	3849.98	3187.10	2747.09	2434.43
175000	15162.36	7855.05	5423.52	4210.92	3485.89	3004.63	2662.66
200000	17328.41	8977.20	6198.31	4812.48	3983.87	3433.86	3043.04
250000	21660.51	11221.50	7747.88	6015.60	4979.84	4292.33	3803.80
500000	43321.02	22443.00	15495.76	12031.20	9959.68	8584.65	7607.59
1000000	86642.04	44886.00	30991.53	24062.40	19919.36	17169.31	15215.18

MONTHLY PAYMENTS 7.25%

AMOUNT	8 YEARS	9 YEARS	10 YEARS	11 YEARS	12 YEARS	13 YEARS	14 YEARS
100	1.38	1.26	1.17	1.10	1.04	0.99	0.95
200	2.75	2.53	2.35	2.20	2.08	1.98	1.90
500	6.88	6.32	5.87	5.51	5.21	4.96	4.75
1000	13.76	12.63	11.74	11.02	10.42	9.92	9.49
2000	27.52	25.27	23.48	22.03	20.84	19.83	18.98
3000	41.28	37.90	35.22	33.05	31.25	29.75	28.48
4000	55.03	50.53	46.96	44.06	41.67	39.67	37.97
5000	68.79	63.17	58.70	55.08	52.09	49.58	47.46
6000	82.55	75.80	70.44	66.09	62.51	59.50	56.95
7000	96.31	88.43	82.18	77.11	72.92	69.42	66.45
8000	110.07	101.07	93.92	88.12	83.34	79.33	75.94
9000	123.83	113.70	105.66	99.14	93.76	89.25	85.43
10000	137.58	126.33	117.40	110.16	104.18	99.17	94.92
11000	151.34	138.97	129.14	121.17	114.59	109.08	104.41
12000	165.10	151.60	140.88	132.19	125.01	119.00	113.91
13000	178.86	164.23	152.62	143.20	135.43	128.92	123.40
14000	192.62	176.87	164.36	154.22	145.85	138.83	132.89
15000	206.38	189.50	176.10	165.23	156.26	148.75	142.38
20000	275.17	252.67	234.80	220.31	208.35	198.33	189.84
25000	343.96	315.83	293.50	275.39	260.44	247.92	237.30
30000	412.75	379.00	352.20	330.47	312.53	297.50	284.77
35000	481.55	442.16	410.90	385.55	364.61	347.08	332.23
40000	550.34	505.33	469.60	440.62	416.70	396.67	379.69
45000	619.13	568.50	528.30	495.70	468.79	446.25	427.15
50000	687.92	631.66	587.01	550.78	520.88	495.84	474.61
55000	756.72	694.83	645.71	605.86	572.97	545.42	522.07
56000	770.47	707.46	657.45	616.87	583.38	555.34	531.56
57000	784.23	720.10	669.19	627.89	593.80	565.25	541.05
58000	797.99	732.73	680.93	638.91	604.22	575.17	550.55
59000	811.75	745.36	692.67	649.92	614.64	585.09	560.04
60000	825.51	758.00	704.41	660.94	625.05	595.00	569.53
61000	839.27	770.63	716.15	671.95	635.47	604.92	579.02
62000	853.02	783.26	727.89	682.97	645.89	614.84	588.51
63000	866.78	795.90	739.63	693.98	656.31	624.75	598.01
64000	880.54	808.53	751.37	705.00	666.72	634.67	607.50
65000	894.30	821.16	763.11	716.01	677.14	644.59	616.99
70000	963.09	884.33	821.81	771.09	729.23	694.17	664.45
75000	1031.88	947.50	880.51	826.17	781.32	743.75	711.91
80000	1100.68	1010.66	939.21	881.25	833.40	793.34	759.37
85000	1169.47	1073.83	997.91	936.33	885.49	842.92	806.83
90000	1238.26	1136.99	1056.61	991.40	937.58	892.50	854.30
95000	1307.05	1200.16	1115.31	1046.48	989.67	942.09	901.76
100000	1375.85	1263.33	1174.01	1101.56	1041.76	991.67	949.22
105000	1444.64	1326.49	1232.71	1156.64	1093.84	1041.25	996.68
110000	1513.43	1389.66	1291.41	1211.72	1145.93	1090.84	1044.14
120000	1651.02	1515.99	1408.81	1321.87	1250.11	1190.01	1139.06
130000	1788.60	1642.33	1526.21	1432.03	1354.28	1289.17	1233.98
140000	1926.18	1768.66	1643.61	1542.19	1458.46	1388.34	1328.90
150000	2063.77	1894.99	1761.02	1652.34	1562.63	1487.51	1423.83
160000	2201.35	2021.32	1878.42	1762.50	1666.81	1586.67	1518.75
175000	2407.73	2210.82	2054.52	1927.73	1823.07	1735.42	1661.13
200000	2751.69	2526.66	2348.02	2203.12	2083.51	1983.34	1898.44
250000	3439.62	3158.32	2935.03	2753.90	2604.39	2479.18	2373.04
500000	6879.23	6316.64	5870.05	5507.80	5208.78	4958.36	4746.09
1000000	13758.46	12633.28	11740.10	11015.61	10417.56	9916.71	9492.18

7.25%　　　　MONTHLY PAYMENTS

AMOUNT	15 YEARS	16 YEARS	17 YEARS	18 YEARS	19 YEARS	20 YEARS	21 YEARS
100	0.91	0.88	0.85	0.83	0.81	0.79	0.77
200	1.83	1.76	1.71	1.66	1.62	1.58	1.55
500	4.56	4.41	4.27	4.15	4.05	3.95	3.87
1000	9.13	8.81	8.54	8.30	8.09	7.90	7.74
2000	18.26	17.63	17.08	16.60	16.18	15.81	15.47
3000	27.39	26.44	25.62	24.91	24.27	23.71	23.21
4000	36.51	35.26	34.16	33.21	32.36	31.62	30.95
5000	45.64	44.07	42.71	41.51	40.45	39.52	38.69
6000	54.77	52.89	51.25	49.81	48.54	47.42	46.42
7000	63.90	61.70	59.79	58.11	56.63	55.33	54.16
8000	73.03	70.52	68.33	66.41	64.73	63.23	61.90
9000	82.16	79.33	76.87	74.72	72.82	71.13	69.64
10000	91.29	88.15	85.41	83.02	80.91	79.04	77.37
11000	100.41	96.96	93.95	91.32	89.00	86.94	85.11
12000	109.54	105.77	102.49	99.62	97.09	94.85	92.85
13000	118.67	114.59	111.04	107.92	105.18	102.75	100.59
14000	127.80	123.40	119.58	116.22	113.27	110.65	108.32
15000	136.93	132.22	128.12	124.53	121.36	118.56	116.06
20000	182.57	176.29	170.82	166.03	161.81	158.08	154.75
25000	228.22	220.36	213.53	207.54	202.27	197.59	193.44
30000	273.86	264.44	256.24	249.05	242.72	237.11	232.12
35000	319.50	308.51	298.94	290.56	283.17	276.63	270.81
40000	365.15	352.58	341.65	332.07	323.63	316.15	309.50
45000	410.79	396.66	384.35	373.58	364.08	355.67	348.19
50000	456.43	440.73	427.06	415.09	404.53	395.19	386.87
55000	502.07	484.80	469.77	456.59	444.99	434.71	425.56
56000	511.20	493.62	478.31	464.90	453.08	442.61	433.30
57000	520.33	502.43	486.85	473.20	461.17	450.51	441.04
58000	529.46	511.25	495.39	481.50	469.26	458.42	448.77
59000	538.59	520.06	503.93	489.80	477.35	466.32	456.51
60000	547.72	528.87	512.47	498.10	485.44	474.23	464.25
61000	556.85	537.69	521.01	506.41	493.53	482.13	471.99
62000	565.97	546.50	529.56	514.71	501.62	490.03	479.72
63000	575.10	555.32	538.10	523.01	509.71	497.94	487.46
64000	584.23	564.13	546.64	531.31	517.80	505.84	495.20
65000	593.36	572.95	555.18	539.61	525.89	513.74	502.94
70000	639.00	617.02	597.89	581.12	566.35	553.26	541.62
75000	684.65	661.09	640.59	622.63	606.80	592.78	580.31
80000	730.29	705.17	683.30	664.14	647.25	632.30	619.00
85000	775.93	749.24	726.00	705.65	687.71	671.82	657.68
90000	821.58	793.31	768.71	747.15	728.16	711.34	696.37
95000	867.22	837.38	811.42	788.66	768.61	750.86	735.06
100000	912.86	881.46	854.12	830.17	809.07	790.38	773.75
105000	958.51	925.53	896.83	871.68	849.52	829.89	812.43
110000	1004.15	969.60	939.53	913.19	889.97	869.41	851.12
120000	1095.44	1057.75	1024.95	996.21	970.88	948.45	928.50
130000	1186.72	1145.89	1110.36	1079.22	1051.79	1027.49	1005.87
140000	1278.01	1234.04	1195.77	1162.24	1132.69	1106.53	1083.25
150000	1369.29	1322.19	1281.18	1245.26	1213.60	1185.56	1160.62
160000	1460.58	1410.33	1366.60	1328.28	1294.51	1264.60	1237.99
175000	1597.51	1542.55	1494.71	1452.80	1415.87	1383.16	1354.06
200000	1825.73	1762.92	1708.24	1660.34	1618.14	1580.75	1547.49
250000	2282.16	2203.64	2135.31	2075.43	2022.67	1975.94	1934.37
500000	4564.31	4407.29	4270.61	4150.86	4045.34	3951.88	3868.73
1000000	9128.63	8814.58	8541.22	8301.72	8090.68	7903.76	7737.47

MONTHLY PAYMENTS

7.25%

AMOUNT	22 YEARS	23 YEARS	24 YEARS	25 YEARS	30 YEARS	35 YEARS	40 YEARS
100	0.76	0.75	0.73	0.72	0.68	0.66	0.64
200	1.52	1.49	1.47	1.45	1.36	1.31	1.28
500	3.79	3.73	3.67	3.61	3.41	3.28	3.20
1000	7.59	7.46	7.34	7.23	6.82	6.56	6.40
2000	15.18	14.91	14.67	14.46	13.64	13.13	12.79
3000	22.77	22.37	22.01	21.68	20.47	19.69	19.19
4000	30.36	29.82	29.34	28.91	27.29	26.26	25.59
5000	37.94	37.28	36.68	36.14	34.11	32.82	31.98
6000	45.53	44.73	44.02	43.37	40.93	39.39	38.38
7000	53.12	52.19	51.35	50.60	47.75	45.95	44.78
8000	60.71	59.65	58.69	57.82	54.57	52.52	51.17
9000	68.30	67.10	66.02	65.05	61.40	59.08	57.57
10000	75.89	74.56	73.36	72.28	68.22	65.65	63.97
11000	83.48	82.01	80.70	79.51	75.04	72.21	70.36
12000	91.07	89.47	88.03	86.74	81.86	78.78	76.76
13000	98.66	96.93	95.37	93.96	88.68	85.34	83.16
14000	106.25	104.38	102.70	101.19	95.50	91.91	89.55
15000	113.83	111.84	110.04	108.42	102.33	98.47	95.95
20000	151.78	149.12	146.72	144.56	136.44	131.29	127.93
25000	189.72	186.39	183.40	180.70	170.54	164.12	159.92
30000	227.67	223.67	220.08	216.84	204.65	196.94	191.90
35000	265.61	260.95	256.76	252.98	238.76	229.76	223.89
40000	303.56	298.23	293.44	289.12	272.87	262.59	255.87
45000	341.50	335.51	330.12	325.26	306.98	295.41	287.85
50000	379.45	372.79	366.80	361.40	341.09	328.23	319.84
55000	417.39	410.07	403.48	397.54	375.20	361.06	351.82
56000	424.98	417.52	410.82	404.77	382.02	367.62	358.22
57000	432.57	424.98	418.15	412.00	388.84	374.19	364.61
58000	440.16	432.44	425.49	419.23	395.66	380.75	371.01
59000	447.75	439.89	432.83	426.46	402.48	387.32	377.41
60000	455.34	447.35	440.16	433.68	409.31	393.88	383.80
61000	462.92	454.80	447.50	440.91	416.13	400.45	390.20
62000	470.51	462.26	454.84	448.14	422.95	407.01	396.60
63000	478.10	469.71	462.17	455.37	429.77	413.57	402.99
64000	485.69	477.17	469.51	462.60	436.59	420.14	409.39
65000	493.28	484.63	476.84	469.82	443.41	426.70	415.79
70000	531.23	521.91	513.52	505.96	477.52	459.53	447.77
75000	569.17	559.18	550.20	542.11	511.63	492.35	479.75
80000	607.11	596.46	586.88	578.25	545.74	525.17	511.74
85000	645.06	633.74	623.56	614.39	579.85	558.00	543.72
90000	683.00	671.02	660.24	650.53	613.96	590.82	575.70
95000	720.95	708.30	696.92	686.67	648.07	623.64	607.69
100000	758.89	745.58	733.61	722.81	682.18	656.47	639.67
105000	796.84	782.86	770.29	758.95	716.29	689.29	671.66
110000	834.78	820.14	806.97	795.09	750.39	722.11	703.64
120000	910.67	894.69	880.33	867.37	818.61	787.76	767.61
130000	986.56	969.25	953.69	939.65	886.83	853.41	831.57
140000	1062.45	1043.81	1027.05	1011.93	955.05	919.05	895.54
150000	1138.34	1118.37	1100.41	1084.21	1023.26	984.70	959.51
160000	1214.23	1192.93	1173.77	1156.49	1091.48	1050.35	1023.48
175000	1328.06	1304.76	1283.81	1264.91	1193.81	1148.82	1119.43
200000	1517.79	1491.16	1467.21	1445.61	1364.35	1312.93	1279.34
250000	1897.23	1863.95	1834.01	1807.02	1705.44	1641.17	1599.18
500000	3794.47	3727.89	3668.03	3614.03	3410.88	3282.34	3198.36
1000000	7588.93	7455.79	7336.05	7228.07	6821.76	6564.67	6396.72

7.50%   MONTHLY PAYMENTS

AMOUNT	1 YEAR	2 YEARS	3 YEARS	4 YEARS	5 YEARS	6 YEARS	7 YEARS
100	8.68	4.50	3.11	2.42	2.00	1.73	1.53
200	17.35	9.00	6.22	4.84	4.01	3.46	3.07
500	43.38	22.50	15.55	12.09	10.02	8.65	7.67
1000	86.76	45.00	31.11	24.18	20.04	17.29	15.34
2000	173.51	90.00	62.21	48.36	40.08	34.58	30.68
3000	260.27	135.00	93.32	72.54	60.11	51.87	46.01
4000	347.03	180.00	124.42	96.72	80.15	69.16	61.35
5000	433.79	225.00	155.53	120.89	100.19	86.45	76.69
6000	520.54	270.00	186.64	145.07	120.23	103.74	92.03
7000	607.30	315.00	217.74	169.25	140.27	121.03	107.37
8000	694.06	360.00	248.85	193.43	160.30	138.32	122.71
9000	780.82	405.00	279.96	217.61	180.34	155.61	138.04
10000	867.57	450.00	311.06	241.79	200.38	172.90	153.38
11000	954.33	495.00	342.17	265.97	220.42	190.19	168.72
12000	1041.09	540.00	373.27	290.15	240.46	207.48	184.06
13000	1127.85	584.99	404.38	314.33	260.49	224.77	199.40
14000	1214.60	629.99	435.49	338.52	280.53	242.06	214.74
15000	1301.36	674.99	466.59	362.68	300.57	259.35	230.07
20000	1735.15	899.99	622.12	483.58	400.76	345.80	306.77
25000	2168.94	1124.99	777.66	604.47	500.95	432.25	383.46
30000	2602.72	1349.99	933.19	725.37	601.14	518.70	460.15
35000	3036.51	1574.99	1088.72	846.26	701.33	605.15	536.84
40000	3470.30	1799.98	1244.25	967.16	801.52	691.60	613.53
45000	3904.08	2024.98	1399.78	1088.05	901.71	778.06	690.22
50000	4337.87	2249.98	1555.31	1208.95	1001.90	864.51	766.91
55000	4771.66	2474.98	1710.84	1329.84	1102.09	950.96	843.61
56000	4858.42	2519.98	1741.95	1354.02	1122.13	968.25	858.94
57000	4945.17	2564.98	1773.05	1378.20	1142.16	985.54	874.28
58000	5031.93	2609.98	1804.16	1402.38	1162.20	1002.83	889.62
59000	5118.69	2654.98	1835.27	1426.56	1182.24	1020.12	904.96
60000	5205.45	2699.98	1866.37	1450.73	1202.28	1037.41	920.30
61000	5292.20	2744.98	1897.48	1474.91	1222.31	1054.70	935.63
62000	5378.96	2789.97	1928.59	1499.09	1242.35	1071.99	950.97
63000	5465.72	2834.97	1959.69	1523.27	1262.39	1089.28	966.31
64000	5552.47	2879.97	1990.80	1547.45	1282.43	1106.57	981.65
65000	5639.26	2924.97	2021.90	1571.63	1302.47	1123.86	996.99
70000	6073.02	3149.97	2177.44	1692.52	1402.66	1210.31	1073.68
75000	6506.81	3374.97	2332.97	1813.42	1502.85	1296.76	1150.37
80000	6940.59	3599.97	2488.50	1934.31	1603.04	1383.21	1227.06
85000	7374.38	3824.97	2644.03	2055.21	1703.23	1469.66	1303.75
90000	7808.17	4049.96	2799.56	2176.10	1803.42	1556.11	1380.44
95000	8241.95	4274.96	2955.09	2297.00	1903.61	1642.56	1457.14
100000	8675.74	4499.96	3110.62	2417.89	2003.79	1729.01	1533.83
105000	9109.53	4724.96	3266.15	2538.78	2103.98	1815.46	1610.52
110000	9543.32	4949.96	3421.68	2659.68	2204.17	1901.91	1687.21
120000	10410.89	5399.95	3732.75	2901.47	2404.55	2074.81	1840.59
130000	11278.46	5849.95	4043.81	3143.26	2604.93	2247.71	1993.98
140000	12146.04	6299.94	4354.87	3385.05	2805.31	2420.62	2147.36
150000	13013.61	6749.94	4665.93	3626.84	3005.69	2593.52	2300.74
160000	13881.19	7199.93	4976.99	3868.62	3206.07	2766.42	2454.12
175000	15182.55	7874.93	5443.59	4231.31	3506.64	3025.77	2684.20
200000	17351.48	8999.92	6221.24	4835.78	4007.59	3458.02	3067.66
250000	21689.35	11249.90	7776.55	6044.73	5009.49	4322.53	3834.57
500000	43378.71	22499.80	15553.11	12089.45	10018.97	8645.06	7669.14
1000000	86757.42	44999.59	31106.22	24178.90	20037.95	17290.11	15338.28

MONTHLY PAYMENTS   7.50%

AMOUNT	8 YEARS	9 YEARS	10 YEARS	11 YEARS	12 YEARS	13 YEARS	14 YEARS
100	1.39	1.28	1.19	1.11	1.06	1.01	0.96
200	2.78	2.55	2.37	2.23	2.11	2.01	1.93
500	6.94	6.38	5.94	5.57	5.28	5.03	4.82
1000	13.88	12.76	11.87	11.15	10.55	10.05	9.63
2000	27.77	25.52	23.74	22.30	21.10	20.11	19.26
3000	41.65	38.28	35.61	33.44	31.66	30.16	28.89
4000	55.54	51.04	47.48	44.59	42.21	40.21	38.53
5000	69.42	63.81	59.35	55.74	52.76	50.27	48.16
6000	83.30	76.57	71.22	66.89	63.31	60.32	57.79
7000	97.19	89.33	83.09	78.04	73.87	70.38	67.42
8000	111.07	102.09	94.96	89.18	84.42	80.43	77.05
9000	124.95	114.85	106.83	100.33	94.97	90.48	86.68
10000	138.84	127.61	118.70	111.48	105.52	100.54	96.31
11000	152.72	140.37	130.57	122.63	116.07	110.59	105.95
12000	166.61	153.13	142.44	133.78	126.63	120.64	115.58
13000	180.49	165.89	154.31	144.92	137.18	130.70	125.21
14000	194.37	178.65	166.18	156.07	147.73	140.75	134.84
15000	208.26	191.42	178.05	167.22	158.28	150.81	144.47
20000	277.68	255.22	237.40	222.96	211.05	201.07	192.63
25000	347.10	319.03	296.75	278.70	263.81	251.34	240.79
30000	416.52	382.83	356.11	334.44	316.57	301.61	288.94
35000	485.94	446.64	415.46	390.18	369.33	351.88	337.10
40000	555.35	510.44	474.81	445.92	422.09	402.15	385.26
45000	624.77	574.25	534.16	501.66	474.85	452.42	433.41
50000	694.19	638.05	593.51	557.40	527.61	502.69	481.57
55000	763.61	701.86	652.86	613.14	580.37	552.95	529.73
56000	777.50	714.62	664.73	624.29	590.93	563.01	539.36
57000	791.38	727.38	676.60	635.44	601.48	573.06	548.99
58000	805.26	740.14	688.47	646.58	612.03	583.11	558.62
59000	819.15	752.90	700.34	657.73	622.58	593.17	568.25
60000	833.03	765.66	712.21	668.88	633.14	603.22	577.89
61000	846.92	778.42	724.08	680.03	643.69	613.28	587.52
62000	860.80	791.18	735.95	691.18	654.24	623.33	597.15
63000	874.68	803.94	747.82	702.32	664.79	633.38	606.78
64000	888.57	816.71	759.69	713.47	675.34	643.44	616.41
65000	902.45	829.47	771.56	724.62	685.90	653.49	626.04
70000	971.87	893.27	830.91	780.36	738.66	703.76	674.20
75000	1041.29	957.08	890.26	836.10	791.42	754.03	722.36
80000	1110.71	1020.88	949.61	891.84	844.18	804.30	770.51
85000	1180.13	1084.69	1008.97	947.58	896.94	854.56	818.67
90000	1249.55	1148.49	1068.32	1003.32	949.70	904.83	866.83
95000	1318.97	1212.30	1127.67	1059.06	1002.46	955.10	914.99
100000	1388.39	1276.10	1187.02	1114.80	1055.23	1005.37	963.14
105000	1457.81	1339.91	1246.37	1170.54	1107.99	1055.64	1011.30
110000	1527.23	1403.71	1305.72	1226.28	1160.75	1105.91	1059.46
120000	1666.06	1531.32	1424.42	1337.76	1266.27	1206.44	1155.77
130000	1804.90	1658.93	1543.12	1449.24	1371.79	1306.98	1252.09
140000	1943.74	1786.54	1661.82	1560.72	1477.32	1407.52	1348.40
150000	2082.58	1914.15	1780.53	1672.20	1582.84	1508.06	1444.62
160000	2221.42	2041.76	1899.23	1783.68	1688.36	1608.59	1541.03
175000	2429.68	2233.18	2077.28	1950.90	1846.65	1759.40	1685.50
200000	2776.77	2552.20	2374.04	2229.60	2110.45	2010.74	1926.29
250000	3470.97	3190.25	2967.54	2787.00	2638.07	2513.43	2407.86
500000	6941.94	6380.51	5935.09	5574.00	5276.13	5026.85	4815.72
1000000	13883.87	12761.02	11870.18	11148.01	10552.26	10053.70	9631.43

7.50% MONTHLY PAYMENTS

AMOUNT	15 YEARS	16 YEARS	17 YEARS	18 YEARS	19 YEARS	20 YEARS	21 YEARS
100	0.93	0.90	0.87	0.84	0.82	0.81	0.79
200	1.85	1.79	1.74	1.69	1.65	1.61	1.58
500	4.64	4.48	4.34	4.22	4.12	4.03	3.95
1000	9.27	8.96	8.69	8.45	8.24	8.06	7.89
2000	18.54	17.92	17.37	16.90	16.48	16.11	15.78
3000	27.81	26.87	26.06	25.35	24.72	24.17	23.67
4000	37.08	35.83	34.75	33.80	32.96	32.22	31.57
5000	46.35	44.79	43.44	42.25	41.20	40.28	39.46
6000	55.62	53.75	52.12	50.70	49.44	48.34	47.35
7000	64.89	62.71	60.81	59.15	57.69	56.39	55.24
8000	74.16	71.67	69.50	67.60	65.93	64.45	63.13
9000	83.43	80.62	78.18	76.05	74.17	72.50	71.02
10000	92.70	89.58	86.87	84.50	82.41	80.56	78.92
11000	101.97	98.54	95.56	92.95	90.65	88.62	86.81
12000	111.24	107.50	104.25	101.40	98.89	96.67	94.70
13000	120.51	116.46	112.93	109.85	107.13	104.73	102.59
14000	129.78	125.42	121.62	118.30	115.37	112.78	110.48
15000	139.05	134.37	130.31	126.75	123.61	120.84	118.37
20000	185.40	179.17	173.74	168.99	164.82	161.12	157.83
25000	231.75	223.96	217.18	211.24	206.02	201.40	197.29
30000	278.10	268.75	260.61	253.49	247.22	241.68	236.75
35000	324.45	313.54	304.05	295.74	288.43	281.96	276.21
40000	370.80	358.33	347.48	337.99	329.63	322.24	315.67
45000	417.16	403.12	390.92	380.24	370.84	362.52	355.12
50000	463.51	447.91	434.35	422.49	412.04	402.80	394.58
55000	509.86	492.71	477.79	464.74	453.24	443.08	434.04
56000	519.13	501.66	486.48	473.19	461.48	451.13	441.93
57000	528.40	510.62	495.16	481.63	469.72	459.19	449.82
58000	537.67	519.58	503.85	490.08	477.97	467.24	457.72
59000	546.94	528.54	512.54	498.53	486.21	475.30	465.61
60000	556.21	537.50	521.23	506.98	494.45	483.36	473.50
61000	565.48	546.45	529.91	515.43	502.69	491.41	481.39
62000	574.75	555.41	538.60	523.88	510.93	499.47	489.28
63000	584.02	564.37	547.29	532.33	519.17	507.52	497.17
64000	593.29	573.33	555.97	540.78	527.41	515.58	505.07
65000	602.56	582.29	564.66	549.23	535.65	523.64	512.96
70000	648.91	627.08	608.10	591.48	576.86	563.92	552.42
75000	695.26	671.87	651.53	633.73	618.06	604.19	591.87
80000	741.61	716.66	694.97	675.98	659.26	644.47	631.33
85000	787.96	761.45	738.40	718.23	700.47	684.75	670.79
90000	834.31	806.24	781.84	760.48	741.67	725.03	710.25
95000	880.66	851.04	825.27	802.72	782.87	765.31	749.71
100000	927.01	895.83	868.71	844.97	824.08	805.59	789.17
105000	973.36	940.62	912.14	887.22	865.28	845.87	828.62
110000	1019.71	985.41	955.58	929.47	906.49	886.15	868.08
120000	1112.41	1074.99	1042.45	1013.97	988.89	966.71	947.00
130000	1205.12	1164.58	1129.32	1098.47	1071.30	1047.27	1025.92
140000	1297.82	1254.16	1216.19	1182.96	1153.71	1127.83	1104.83
150000	1390.52	1343.74	1303.06	1267.46	1236.12	1208.39	1183.75
160000	1483.22	1433.32	1389.94	1351.96	1318.53	1288.95	1262.67
175000	1622.27	1567.70	1520.24	1478.70	1442.14	1409.79	1381.04
200000	1854.02	1791.66	1737.42	1689.95	1648.16	1611.19	1578.33
250000	2317.53	2239.57	2171.77	2112.43	2060.20	2013.98	1972.92
500000	4635.06	4479.14	4343.55	4224.87	4120.39	4027.97	3945.83
1000000	9270.12	8958.28	8687.09	8449.73	8240.79	8055.93	7891.66

MONTHLY PAYMENTS 7.50%

AMOUNT	22 YEARS	23 YEARS	24 YEARS	25 YEARS	30 YEARS	35 YEARS	40 YEARS
100	0.77	0.76	0.75	0.74	0.70	0.67	0.66
200	1.55	1.52	1.50	1.48	1.40	1.35	1.32
500	3.87	3.81	3.75	3.69	3.50	3.37	3.29
1000	7.75	7.61	7.50	7.39	6.99	6.74	6.58
2000	15.49	15.23	14.99	14.78	13.98	13.48	13.16
3000	23.24	22.84	22.49	22.17	20.98	20.23	19.74
4000	30.98	30.46	29.98	29.56	27.97	26.97	26.32
5000	38.73	38.07	37.48	36.95	34.96	33.71	32.90
6000	46.47	45.68	44.98	44.34	41.95	40.45	39.48
7000	54.22	53.30	52.47	51.73	48.95	47.20	46.06
8000	61.96	60.91	59.97	59.12	55.94	53.94	52.65
9000	69.71	68.53	67.46	66.51	62.93	60.68	59.23
10000	77.45	76.14	74.96	73.90	69.92	67.42	65.81
11000	85.20	83.75	82.46	81.29	76.91	74.17	72.39
12000	92.94	91.37	89.95	88.68	83.91	80.91	78.97
13000	100.69	98.98	97.45	96.07	90.90	87.65	85.55
14000	108.43	106.59	104.94	103.46	97.89	94.39	92.13
15000	116.18	114.21	112.44	110.85	104.88	101.14	98.71
20000	154.90	152.28	149.92	147.80	139.84	134.85	131.61
25000	193.63	190.35	187.40	184.75	174.80	168.56	164.52
30000	232.35	228.42	224.88	221.70	209.76	202.27	197.42
35000	271.08	266.49	262.36	258.65	244.73	235.98	230.32
40000	309.80	304.56	299.84	295.60	279.69	269.70	263.23
45000	348.53	342.63	337.32	332.55	314.65	303.41	296.13
50000	387.26	380.69	374.80	369.50	349.61	337.12	329.04
55000	425.98	418.76	412.28	406.45	384.57	370.83	361.94
56000	433.73	426.38	419.78	413.84	391.56	377.58	368.52
57000	441.47	433.99	427.27	421.22	398.55	384.32	375.10
58000	449.22	441.61	434.77	428.61	405.54	391.06	381.68
59000	456.96	449.22	442.27	436.00	412.54	397.80	388.26
60000	464.71	456.83	449.76	443.39	419.53	404.55	394.84
61000	472.45	464.45	457.26	450.78	426.52	411.29	401.42
62000	480.20	472.06	464.76	458.17	433.51	418.03	408.00
63000	487.94	479.68	472.25	465.56	440.51	424.77	414.58
64000	495.69	487.29	479.75	472.95	447.50	431.52	421.17
65000	503.43	494.90	487.24	480.34	454.49	438.26	427.75
70000	542.16	532.97	524.72	517.29	489.45	471.97	460.65
75000	580.88	571.04	562.20	554.24	524.41	505.68	493.55
80000	619.61	609.11	599.68	591.19	559.37	539.39	526.46
85000	658.33	647.18	637.16	628.14	594.33	573.11	559.36
90000	697.06	685.25	674.64	665.09	629.29	606.82	592.26
95000	735.78	723.32	712.12	702.04	664.25	640.53	625.17
100000	774.51	761.39	749.60	738.99	699.21	674.24	658.07
105000	813.24	799.46	787.09	775.94	734.18	707.95	690.97
110000	851.96	837.53	824.57	812.89	769.14	741.67	723.88
120000	929.41	913.67	899.53	886.79	839.06	809.09	789.68
130000	1006.86	989.81	974.49	960.69	908.98	876.52	855.49
140000	1084.31	1065.94	1049.45	1034.59	978.90	943.94	921.30
150000	1161.77	1142.08	1124.41	1108.49	1048.82	1011.36	987.11
160000	1239.22	1218.22	1199.37	1182.39	1118.74	1078.79	1052.91
175000	1355.39	1332.43	1311.81	1293.23	1223.63	1179.92	1151.62
200000	1549.02	1522.78	1499.21	1477.98	1398.43	1348.49	1316.14
250000	1936.28	1903.47	1874.01	1847.48	1748.04	1685.61	1645.18
500000	3872.55	3806.95	3748.02	3694.96	3496.07	3371.21	3290.35
1000000	7745.10	7613.89	7496.05	7389.91	6992.15	6742.43	6580.71

7.75% MONTHLY PAYMENTS

AMOUNT	1 YEAR	2 YEARS	3 YEARS	4 YEARS	5 YEARS	6 YEARS	7 YEARS
100	8.69	4.51	3.12	2.43	2.02	1.74	1.55
200	17.37	9.02	6.24	4.86	4.03	3.48	3.09
500	43.44	22.56	15.61	12.15	10.08	8.71	7.73
1000	86.87	45.11	31.22	24.30	20.16	17.41	15.46
2000	173.75	90.23	62.44	48.59	40.31	34.82	30.92
3000	260.62	135.34	93.66	72.89	60.47	52.23	46.39
4000	347.49	180.45	124.88	97.18	80.63	69.65	61.85
5000	434.36	225.57	156.11	121.48	100.78	87.06	77.31
6000	521.24	270.68	187.33	145.77	120.94	104.47	92.77
7000	608.11	315.79	218.55	170.07	141.10	121.88	108.23
8000	694.98	360.91	249.77	194.37	161.26	139.29	123.70
9000	781.86	406.02	280.99	218.66	181.41	156.70	139.16
10000	868.73	451.13	312.21	242.96	201.57	174.11	154.62
11000	955.60	496.25	343.43	267.25	221.73	191.53	170.08
12000	1042.47	541.36	374.65	291.55	241.88	208.94	185.54
13000	1129.35	586.47	405.88	315.84	262.04	226.35	201.01
14000	1216.22	631.59	437.10	340.14	282.20	243.76	216.47
15000	1303.09	676.70	468.32	364.44	302.35	261.17	231.93
20000	1737.46	902.27	624.42	485.91	403.14	348.23	309.24
25000	2171.82	1127.83	780.53	607.39	503.92	435.29	386.55
30000	2606.19	1353.40	936.63	728.87	604.71	522.34	463.86
35000	3040.55	1578.97	1092.74	850.35	705.49	609.40	541.17
40000	3474.92	1804.53	1248.85	971.83	806.28	696.46	618.48
45000	3909.28	2030.10	1404.95	1093.31	907.06	783.51	695.79
50000	4343.64	2255.67	1561.06	1214.79	1007.85	870.57	773.10
55000	4778.01	2481.23	1717.16	1336.27	1108.63	957.63	850.41
56000	4864.88	2526.35	1748.39	1360.56	1128.79	975.04	865.87
57000	4951.75	2571.46	1779.61	1384.86	1148.95	992.45	881.33
58000	5038.63	2616.57	1810.83	1409.15	1169.10	1009.86	896.79
59000	5125.50	2661.69	1842.05	1433.45	1189.26	1027.27	912.26
60000	5212.37	2706.80	1873.27	1457.74	1209.42	1044.69	927.72
61000	5299.25	2751.91	1904.49	1482.04	1229.57	1062.10	943.18
62000	5386.12	2797.03	1935.71	1506.34	1249.73	1079.51	958.64
63000	5472.99	2842.14	1966.93	1530.63	1269.89	1096.92	974.10
64000	5559.86	2887.25	1998.15	1554.93	1290.05	1114.33	989.56
65000	5646.74	2932.37	2029.38	1579.22	1310.20	1131.74	1005.03
70000	6081.10	3157.93	2185.48	1700.70	1410.99	1218.80	1082.34
75000	6515.47	3383.50	2341.59	1822.18	1511.77	1305.86	1159.65
80000	6949.83	3609.07	2497.69	1943.66	1612.56	1392.91	1236.96
85000	7384.19	3834.64	2653.80	2065.14	1713.34	1479.97	1314.27
90000	7818.56	4060.20	2809.90	2186.62	1814.13	1567.03	1391.58
95000	8252.92	4285.77	2966.01	2308.10	1914.91	1654.09	1468.89
100000	8687.29	4511.34	3122.12	2429.57	2015.70	1741.14	1546.20
105000	9121.65	4736.90	3278.22	2551.05	2116.48	1828.20	1623.51
110000	9556.02	4962.47	3434.33	2672.53	2217.27	1915.26	1700.81
120000	10424.75	5413.60	3746.54	2915.49	2418.84	2089.37	1855.43
130000	11293.47	5864.74	4058.75	3158.45	2620.40	2263.49	2010.05
140000	12162.20	6315.87	4370.96	3401.40	2821.97	2437.60	2164.67
150000	13030.93	6767.00	4683.17	3644.36	3023.54	2611.71	2319.29
160000	13899.66	7218.14	4995.39	3887.32	3225.11	2785.83	2473.91
175000	15202.75	7894.84	5463.70	4251.75	3527.47	3047.00	2705.84
200000	17374.58	9022.67	6244.23	4859.15	4031.39	3482.28	3092.39
250000	21718.22	11278.34	7805.29	6073.94	5039.24	4352.86	3865.49
500000	43436.44	22556.68	15610.58	12147.87	10078.48	8705.71	7730.98
1000000	86872.88	45113.36	31221.16	24295.74	20156.96	17411.42	15461.95

MONTHLY PAYMENTS 7.75%

AMOUNT	8 YEARS	9 YEARS	10 YEARS	11 YEARS	12 YEARS	13 YEARS	14 YEARS
100	1.40	1.29	1.20	1.13	1.07	1.02	0.98
200	2.80	2.58	2.40	2.26	2.14	2.04	1.95
500	7.00	6.44	6.00	5.64	5.34	5.10	4.89
1000	14.01	12.89	12.00	11.28	10.69	10.19	9.77
2000	28.02	25.78	24.00	22.56	21.38	20.38	19.54
3000	42.03	38.67	36.00	33.84	32.06	30.58	29.32
4000	56.04	51.56	48.00	45.13	42.75	40.77	39.09
5000	70.05	64.45	60.01	56.41	53.44	50.96	48.86
6000	84.06	77.34	72.01	67.69	64.13	61.15	58.63
7000	98.07	90.23	84.01	78.97	74.82	71.34	68.40
8000	112.08	103.12	96.01	90.25	85.50	81.53	78.17
9000	126.09	116.01	108.01	101.53	96.19	91.73	87.95
10000	140.10	128.89	120.01	112.81	106.88	101.92	97.72
11000	154.11	141.78	132.01	124.09	117.57	112.11	107.49
12000	168.12	154.67	144.01	135.38	128.26	122.30	117.26
13000	182.13	167.56	156.01	146.66	138.94	132.49	127.03
14000	196.14	180.45	168.01	157.94	149.63	142.68	136.80
15000	210.15	193.34	180.02	169.22	160.32	152.88	146.58
20000	280.20	257.79	240.02	225.63	213.76	203.83	195.44
25000	350.25	322.24	300.03	282.03	267.20	254.79	244.29
30000	420.30	386.68	360.03	338.44	320.64	305.75	293.15
35000	490.35	451.13	420.04	394.85	374.08	356.71	342.01
40000	560.40	515.58	480.04	451.25	427.52	407.67	390.87
45000	630.45	580.03	540.05	507.66	480.96	458.63	439.73
50000	700.50	644.47	600.05	564.06	534.40	509.59	488.59
55000	770.55	708.92	660.06	620.47	587.84	560.54	537.45
56000	784.56	721.81	672.06	631.75	598.52	570.74	547.22
57000	798.57	734.70	684.06	643.03	609.21	580.93	556.99
58000	812.58	747.59	696.06	654.31	619.90	591.12	566.76
59000	826.59	760.48	708.06	665.60	630.59	601.31	576.53
60000	840.60	773.37	720.06	676.88	641.28	611.50	586.31
61000	854.61	786.26	732.06	688.16	651.96	621.69	596.08
62000	868.62	799.15	744.07	699.44	662.65	631.89	605.85
63000	882.63	812.04	756.07	710.72	673.34	642.08	615.62
64000	896.64	824.93	768.07	722.00	684.03	652.27	625.39
65000	910.65	837.82	780.07	733.28	694.71	662.46	635.17
70000	980.70	902.26	840.07	789.69	748.15	713.42	684.02
75000	1050.75	966.71	900.08	846.10	801.59	764.38	732.88
80000	1120.80	1031.16	960.09	902.50	855.03	815.34	781.74
85000	1190.85	1095.61	1020.09	958.91	908.47	866.30	830.60
90000	1260.89	1160.05	1080.10	1015.32	961.91	917.25	879.46
95000	1330.94	1224.50	1140.10	1071.72	1015.35	968.21	928.32
100000	1400.99	1288.95	1200.11	1128.13	1068.79	1019.17	977.18
105000	1471.04	1353.40	1260.11	1184.54	1122.23	1070.13	1026.04
110000	1541.09	1417.84	1320.12	1240.94	1175.67	1121.09	1074.89
120000	1681.19	1546.74	1440.13	1353.75	1282.55	1223.01	1172.61
130000	1821.29	1675.63	1560.14	1466.57	1389.43	1324.92	1270.33
140000	1961.39	1804.53	1680.15	1579.38	1496.31	1426.84	1368.05
150000	2101.49	1933.42	1800.16	1692.19	1603.19	1528.76	1465.77
160000	2241.59	2062.32	1920.17	1805.01	1710.07	1630.67	1563.48
175000	2451.74	2255.66	2100.19	1974.23	1870.39	1783.55	1710.06
200000	2801.99	2577.90	2400.21	2256.26	2137.58	2038.34	1954.35
250000	3502.49	3222.37	3000.27	2820.32	2671.98	2547.93	2442.94
500000	7004.97	6444.75	6000.53	5640.64	5343.96	5095.86	4885.89
1000000	14009.94	12889.50	12001.06	11281.29	10687.92	10191.72	9771.77

7.75% MONTHLY PAYMENTS

AMOUNT	15 YEARS	16 YEARS	17 YEARS	18 YEARS	19 YEARS	20 YEARS	21 YEARS
100	0.94	0.91	0.88	0.86	0.84	0.82	0.80
200	1.88	1.82	1.77	1.72	1.68	1.64	1.61
500	4.71	4.55	4.42	4.30	4.20	4.10	4.02
1000	9.41	9.10	8.83	8.60	8.39	8.21	8.05
2000	18.83	18.21	17.67	17.20	16.78	16.42	16.09
3000	28.24	27.31	26.50	25.80	25.18	24.63	24.14
4000	37.65	36.41	35.34	34.40	33.57	32.84	32.19
5000	47.06	45.52	44.17	43.00	41.96	41.05	40.24
6000	56.48	54.62	53.01	51.59	50.35	49.26	48.28
7000	65.89	63.72	61.84	60.19	58.75	57.47	56.33
8000	75.30	72.83	70.67	68.79	67.14	65.68	64.38
9000	84.71	81.93	79.51	77.39	75.53	73.89	72.43
10000	94.13	91.03	88.34	85.99	83.92	82.09	80.47
11000	103.54	100.13	97.18	94.59	92.31	90.30	88.52
12000	112.95	109.24	106.01	103.19	100.71	98.51	96.57
13000	122.37	118.34	114.84	111.79	109.10	106.72	104.61
14000	131.78	127.44	123.68	120.39	117.49	114.93	112.66
15000	141.19	136.55	132.51	128.99	125.88	123.14	120.71
20000	188.26	182.06	176.68	171.98	167.84	164.19	160.95
25000	235.32	227.58	220.86	214.98	209.81	205.24	201.18
30000	282.38	273.10	265.03	257.97	251.77	246.28	241.42
35000	329.45	318.61	309.20	300.97	293.73	287.33	281.65
40000	376.51	364.13	353.37	343.96	335.69	328.38	321.89
45000	423.57	409.64	397.54	386.96	377.65	369.43	362.13
50000	470.64	455.16	441.71	429.95	419.61	410.47	402.36
55000	517.70	500.67	485.88	472.95	461.57	451.52	442.60
56000	527.11	509.78	494.72	481.55	469.97	459.73	450.65
57000	536.53	518.88	503.55	490.15	478.36	467.94	458.69
58000	545.94	527.98	512.38	498.74	486.75	476.15	466.74
59000	555.35	537.09	521.22	507.34	495.14	484.36	474.79
60000	564.77	546.19	530.05	515.94	503.53	492.57	482.84
61000	574.18	555.29	538.89	524.54	511.93	500.78	490.88
62000	583.59	564.40	547.72	533.14	520.32	508.99	498.93
63000	593.00	573.50	556.56	541.74	528.71	517.20	506.98
64000	602.42	582.60	565.39	550.34	537.10	525.41	515.03
65000	611.83	591.71	574.22	558.94	545.50	533.62	523.07
70000	658.89	637.22	618.40	601.93	587.46	574.66	563.31
75000	705.96	682.74	662.57	644.93	629.42	615.71	603.55
80000	753.02	728.25	706.74	687.92	671.38	656.76	643.78
85000	800.08	773.77	750.91	730.92	713.34	697.81	684.02
90000	847.15	819.29	795.08	773.91	755.30	738.85	724.25
95000	894.21	864.80	839.25	816.91	797.26	779.90	764.49
100000	941.28	910.32	883.42	859.90	839.22	820.95	804.73
105000	988.34	955.83	927.59	902.90	881.19	862.00	844.96
110000	1035.40	1001.35	971.76	945.89	923.15	903.04	885.20
120000	1129.53	1092.38	1060.11	1031.88	1007.07	985.14	965.67
130000	1223.66	1183.41	1148.45	1117.88	1090.99	1067.23	1046.15
140000	1317.79	1274.44	1236.79	1203.87	1174.91	1149.33	1126.62
150000	1411.91	1365.48	1325.13	1289.86	1258.84	1231.42	1207.09
160000	1506.04	1456.51	1413.47	1375.85	1342.76	1313.52	1287.56
175000	1647.23	1593.06	1545.99	1504.83	1468.64	1436.66	1408.27
200000	1882.55	1820.63	1766.84	1719.81	1678.45	1641.90	1609.45
250000	2353.19	2275.79	2208.55	2149.76	2098.06	2052.37	2011.82
500000	4706.38	4551.59	4417.11	4299.52	4196.12	4104.74	4023.64
1000000	9412.76	9103.17	8834.21	8599.04	8392.24	8209.49	8047.27

MONTHLY PAYMENTS

7.75%

AMOUNT	22 YEARS	23 YEARS	24 YEARS	25 YEARS	30 YEARS	35 YEARS	40 YEARS
100	0.79	0.78	0.77	0.76	0.72	0.69	0.68
200	1.58	1.55	1.53	1.51	1.43	1.38	1.35
500	3.95	3.89	3.83	3.78	3.58	3.46	3.38
1000	7.90	7.77	7.66	7.55	7.16	6.92	6.77
2000	15.81	15.55	15.32	15.11	14.33	13.84	13.53
3000	23.71	23.32	22.97	22.66	21.49	20.77	20.30
4000	31.61	31.09	30.63	30.21	28.66	27.69	27.06
5000	39.51	38.87	38.29	37.77	35.82	34.61	33.83
6000	47.42	46.64	45.95	45.32	42.98	41.53	40.60
7000	55.32	54.41	53.60	52.87	50.15	48.45	47.36
8000	63.22	62.19	61.26	60.43	57.31	55.37	54.13
9000	71.12	69.96	68.92	67.98	64.48	62.30	60.90
10000	79.03	77.73	76.58	75.53	71.64	69.22	67.66
11000	86.93	85.51	84.23	83.09	78.81	76.14	74.43
12000	94.83	93.28	91.89	90.64	85.97	83.06	81.19
13000	102.74	101.06	99.55	98.19	93.13	89.98	87.96
14000	110.64	108.83	107.21	105.75	100.30	96.90	94.73
15000	118.54	116.60	114.86	113.30	107.46	103.83	101.49
20000	158.05	155.47	153.15	151.07	143.28	138.44	135.32
25000	197.57	194.34	191.44	188.83	179.10	173.04	169.15
30000	237.08	233.20	229.73	226.60	214.92	207.65	202.99
35000	276.60	272.07	268.01	264.37	250.74	242.26	236.82
40000	316.11	310.94	306.30	302.13	286.56	276.87	270.65
45000	355.62	349.81	344.59	339.90	322.39	311.48	304.48
50000	395.14	388.67	382.88	377.66	358.21	346.09	338.31
55000	434.65	427.54	421.17	415.43	394.03	380.70	372.14
56000	442.55	435.31	428.82	422.98	401.19	387.62	378.91
57000	450.46	443.09	436.48	430.54	408.35	394.54	385.67
58000	458.36	450.86	444.14	438.09	415.52	401.46	392.44
59000	466.26	458.64	451.80	445.64	422.68	408.38	399.21
60000	474.16	466.41	459.45	453.20	429.85	415.31	405.97
61000	482.07	474.18	467.11	460.75	437.01	422.23	412.74
62000	489.97	481.96	474.77	468.30	444.18	429.15	419.50
63000	497.87	489.73	482.43	475.86	451.34	436.07	426.27
64000	505.77	497.50	490.08	483.41	458.50	442.99	433.04
65000	513.68	505.28	497.74	490.96	465.67	449.91	439.80
70000	553.19	544.14	536.03	528.73	501.49	484.52	473.63
75000	592.70	583.01	574.32	566.50	537.31	519.13	507.46
80000	632.22	621.88	612.60	604.26	573.13	553.74	541.30
85000	671.73	660.75	650.89	642.03	608.95	588.35	575.13
90000	711.25	699.61	689.18	679.80	644.77	622.96	608.96
95000	750.76	738.48	727.47	717.56	680.59	657.57	642.79
100000	790.27	777.35	765.76	755.33	716.41	692.18	676.62
105000	829.79	816.22	804.04	793.10	752.23	726.78	710.45
110000	869.30	855.08	842.33	830.86	788.05	761.39	744.28
120000	948.33	932.82	918.91	906.39	859.69	830.61	811.94
130000	1027.35	1010.55	995.48	981.93	931.34	899.83	879.61
140000	1106.38	1088.29	1072.06	1057.46	1002.98	969.05	947.27
150000	1185.41	1166.02	1148.63	1132.99	1074.62	1038.26	1014.93
160000	1264.44	1243.76	1225.21	1208.53	1146.26	1107.48	1082.59
175000	1382.98	1360.36	1340.07	1321.83	1253.72	1211.31	1184.08
200000	1580.55	1554.70	1531.51	1510.66	1432.82	1384.35	1353.24
250000	1975.68	1943.37	1914.39	1888.32	1791.03	1730.44	1691.55
500000	3951.36	3886.74	3828.78	3776.64	3582.06	3460.88	3383.10
1000000	7902.73	7773.48	7657.56	7553.29	7164.12	6921.76	6766.20

8.00%   MONTHLY PAYMENTS

AMOUNT	1 YEAR	2 YEARS	3 YEARS	4 YEARS	5 YEARS	6 YEARS	7 YEARS
100	8.70	4.52	3.13	2.44	2.03	1.75	1.56
200	17.40	9.05	6.27	4.88	4.06	3.51	3.12
500	43.49	22.61	15.67	12.21	10.14	8.77	7.79
1000	86.99	45.23	31.34	24.41	20.28	17.53	15.59
2000	173.98	90.45	62.67	48.83	40.55	35.07	31.17
3000	260.97	135.68	94.01	73.24	60.83	52.60	46.76
4000	347.95	180.91	125.35	97.65	81.11	70.13	62.34
5000	434.94	226.14	156.68	122.06	101.38	87.67	77.93
6000	521.93	271.36	188.02	146.48	121.66	105.20	93.52
7000	608.92	316.59	219.35	170.89	141.93	122.73	109.10
8000	695.91	361.82	250.69	195.30	162.21	140.27	124.69
9000	782.90	407.05	282.03	219.72	182.49	157.80	140.28
10000	869.88	452.27	313.36	244.13	202.76	175.33	155.86
11000	956.87	497.50	344.70	268.54	223.04	192.87	171.45
12000	1043.86	542.73	376.04	292.96	243.32	210.40	187.03
13000	1130.85	587.95	407.37	317.37	263.59	227.93	202.62
14000	1217.84	633.18	438.71	341.78	283.87	245.47	218.21
15000	1304.83	678.41	470.05	366.19	304.15	263.00	233.79
20000	1739.77	904.55	626.73	488.26	405.53	350.66	311.72
25000	2174.71	1130.68	783.41	610.32	506.91	438.33	389.66
30000	2609.65	1356.82	940.09	732.39	608.29	526.00	467.59
35000	3044.60	1582.96	1096.77	854.45	709.67	613.66	545.52
40000	3479.54	1809.09	1253.45	976.52	811.06	701.33	623.45
45000	3914.48	2035.23	1410.14	1098.58	912.44	789.00	701.38
50000	4349.42	2261.36	1566.82	1220.65	1013.82	876.66	779.31
55000	4784.36	2487.50	1723.50	1342.71	1115.20	964.33	857.24
56000	4871.35	2532.73	1754.84	1367.12	1135.48	981.86	872.83
57000	4958.34	2577.96	1786.17	1391.54	1155.75	999.39	888.41
58000	5045.33	2623.18	1817.51	1415.95	1176.03	1016.93	904.00
59000	5132.32	2668.41	1848.85	1440.36	1196.31	1034.46	919.59
60000	5219.31	2713.64	1880.18	1464.78	1216.58	1051.99	935.17
61000	5306.29	2758.86	1911.52	1489.19	1236.86	1069.53	950.76
62000	5393.28	2804.09	1942.85	1513.60	1257.14	1087.06	966.35
63000	5480.27	2849.32	1974.19	1538.01	1277.41	1104.59	981.93
64000	5567.26	2894.55	2005.53	1562.43	1297.69	1122.13	997.52
65000	5654.25	2939.77	2036.86	1586.84	1317.97	1139.66	1013.10
70000	6089.19	3165.91	2193.55	1708.90	1419.35	1227.33	1091.04
75000	6524.13	3392.05	2350.23	1830.97	1520.73	1314.99	1168.97
80000	6959.07	3618.18	2506.91	1953.03	1622.11	1402.66	1246.90
85000	7394.02	3844.32	2663.59	2075.10	1723.49	1490.33	1324.83
90000	7828.96	4070.46	2820.27	2197.16	1824.88	1577.99	1402.76
95000	8263.90	4296.59	2976.95	2319.23	1926.26	1665.66	1480.69
100000	8698.84	4522.73	3133.64	2441.29	2027.64	1753.32	1558.62
105000	9133.79	4748.87	3290.32	2563.36	2129.02	1840.99	1636.55
110000	9568.73	4975.00	3447.00	2685.42	2230.40	1928.66	1714.48
120000	10438.61	5427.27	3760.36	2929.55	2433.17	2103.99	1870.35
130000	11308.50	5879.55	4073.73	3173.68	2635.93	2279.32	2026.21
140000	12178.38	6331.82	4387.09	3417.81	2838.70	2454.65	2182.07
150000	13048.26	6784.09	4700.45	3661.94	3041.46	2629.99	2337.93
160000	13918.15	7236.37	5013.82	3906.07	3244.22	2805.32	2493.79
175000	15222.98	7914.78	5483.86	4272.26	3548.37	3068.32	2727.59
200000	17397.69	9045.46	6267.27	4882.57	4055.28	3506.65	3117.24
250000	21747.11	11306.82	7834.09	6103.23	5069.10	4383.31	3896.55
500000	43494.21	22613.65	15668.18	12206.46	10138.20	8766.62	7793.11
1000000	86988.43	45227.29	31336.37	24412.92	20276.39	17533.24	15586.21

MONTHLY PAYMENTS 8.00%

AMOUNT	8 YEARS	9 YEARS	10 YEARS	11 YEARS	12 YEARS	13 YEARS	14 YEARS
100	1.41	1.30	1.21	1.14	1.08	1.03	0.99
200	2.83	2.60	2.43	2.28	2.16	2.07	1.98
500	7.07	6.51	6.07	5.71	5.41	5.17	4.96
1000	14.14	13.02	12.13	11.42	10.82	10.33	9.91
2000	28.27	26.04	24.27	22.83	21.65	20.66	19.83
3000	42.41	39.06	36.40	34.25	32.47	30.99	29.74
4000	56.55	52.07	48.53	45.66	43.30	41.32	39.65
5000	70.68	65.09	60.66	57.08	54.12	51.65	49.57
6000	84.82	78.11	72.80	68.49	64.95	61.98	59.48
7000	98.96	91.13	84.93	79.91	75.77	72.32	69.39
8000	113.09	104.15	97.06	91.32	86.60	82.65	79.31
9000	127.23	117.17	109.19	102.74	97.42	92.98	89.22
10000	141.37	130.19	121.33	114.15	108.25	103.31	99.13
11000	155.50	143.21	133.46	125.57	119.07	113.64	109.05
12000	169.64	156.22	145.59	136.99	129.89	123.97	118.96
13000	183.78	169.24	157.73	148.40	140.72	134.30	128.87
14000	197.91	182.26	169.86	159.82	151.54	144.63	138.78
15000	212.05	195.28	181.99	171.23	162.37	154.96	148.70
20000	282.73	260.37	242.66	228.31	216.49	206.61	198.26
25000	353.42	325.47	303.32	285.39	270.61	258.27	247.83
30000	424.10	390.56	363.98	342.46	324.74	309.92	297.40
35000	494.78	455.66	424.65	399.54	378.86	361.58	346.96
40000	565.47	520.75	485.31	456.62	432.98	413.23	396.53
45000	636.15	585.84	545.97	513.70	487.10	464.88	446.09
50000	706.83	650.94	606.64	570.77	541.23	516.54	495.66
55000	777.52	716.03	667.30	627.85	595.35	568.19	545.23
56000	791.65	729.05	679.43	639.27	606.17	578.52	555.14
57000	805.79	742.07	691.57	650.68	617.00	588.85	565.05
58000	819.93	755.09	703.70	662.10	627.82	599.18	574.96
59000	834.06	768.10	715.83	673.51	638.65	609.51	584.88
60000	848.20	781.12	727.97	684.93	649.47	619.84	594.79
61000	862.34	794.14	740.10	696.34	660.30	630.18	604.70
62000	876.47	807.16	752.23	707.76	671.12	640.51	614.62
63000	890.61	820.18	764.36	719.17	681.95	650.84	624.53
64000	904.75	833.20	776.50	730.59	692.77	661.17	634.44
65000	918.88	846.22	788.63	742.00	703.59	671.50	644.36
70000	989.57	911.31	849.29	799.08	757.72	723.15	693.92
75000	1060.25	976.40	909.96	856.16	811.84	774.81	743.49
80000	1130.93	1041.50	970.62	913.24	865.96	826.46	793.05
85000	1201.62	1106.59	1031.28	970.31	920.08	878.11	842.62
90000	1272.30	1171.68	1091.95	1027.39	974.21	929.77	892.19
95000	1342.98	1236.78	1152.61	1084.47	1028.33	981.42	941.75
100000	1413.67	1301.87	1213.28	1141.54	1082.45	1033.07	991.32
105000	1484.35	1366.97	1273.94	1198.62	1136.58	1084.73	1040.88
110000	1555.03	1432.06	1334.60	1255.70	1190.70	1136.38	1090.45
120000	1696.40	1562.25	1455.93	1369.85	1298.94	1239.69	1189.58
130000	1837.77	1692.43	1577.26	1484.01	1407.19	1343.00	1288.71
140000	1979.14	1822.62	1698.59	1598.16	1515.43	1446.30	1387.85
150000	2120.50	1952.81	1819.91	1712.32	1623.68	1549.61	1486.98
160000	2261.87	2082.99	1941.24	1826.47	1731.92	1652.92	1586.11
175000	2473.92	2278.28	2123.23	1997.70	1894.29	1807.88	1734.81
200000	2827.34	2603.74	2426.55	2283.09	2164.91	2066.15	1982.64
250000	3534.17	3254.68	3033.19	2853.86	2706.13	2582.68	2478.30
500000	7068.34	6509.36	6066.38	5707.72	5412.26	5165.37	4956.59
1000000	14136.68	13018.71	12132.76	11415.45	10824.53	10330.74	9913.18

8.00%   MONTHLY PAYMENTS

AMOUNT	15 YEARS	16 YEARS	17 YEARS	18 YEARS	19 YEARS	20 YEARS	21 YEARS
100	0.96	0.92	0.90	0.87	0.85	0.84	0.82
200	1.91	1.85	1.80	1.75	1.71	1.67	1.64
500	4.78	4.62	4.49	4.37	4.27	4.18	4.10
1000	9.56	9.25	8.98	8.75	8.55	8.36	8.20
2000	19.11	18.50	17.97	17.50	17.09	16.73	16.41
3000	28.67	27.75	26.95	26.25	25.64	25.09	24.61
4000	38.23	37.00	35.93	35.00	34.18	33.46	32.82
5000	47.78	46.25	44.91	43.75	42.73	41.82	41.02
6000	57.34	55.50	53.90	52.50	51.27	50.19	49.23
7000	66.90	64.74	62.88	61.25	59.82	58.55	57.43
8000	76.45	73.99	71.86	70.00	68.36	66.92	65.63
9000	86.01	83.24	80.84	78.75	76.91	75.28	73.84
10000	95.57	92.49	89.83	87.50	85.45	83.64	82.04
11000	105.12	101.74	98.81	96.25	94.00	92.01	90.25
12000	114.68	110.99	107.79	105.00	102.54	100.37	98.45
13000	124.23	120.24	116.77	113.75	111.09	108.74	106.66
14000	133.79	129.49	125.76	122.49	119.63	117.10	114.86
15000	143.35	138.74	134.74	131.24	128.18	125.47	123.06
20000	191.13	184.99	179.65	174.99	170.90	167.29	164.09
25000	238.91	231.23	224.56	218.74	213.63	209.11	205.11
30000	286.70	277.48	269.48	262.49	256.35	250.93	246.13
35000	334.48	323.72	314.39	306.24	299.08	292.75	287.15
40000	382.26	369.97	359.30	349.99	341.80	334.58	328.17
45000	430.04	416.22	404.22	393.73	384.53	376.40	369.19
50000	477.83	462.46	449.13	437.48	427.25	418.22	410.21
55000	525.61	508.71	494.04	481.23	469.98	460.04	451.24
56000	535.17	517.96	503.02	489.98	478.52	468.41	459.44
57000	544.72	527.21	512.01	498.73	487.07	476.77	467.64
58000	554.28	536.46	520.99	507.48	495.61	485.14	475.85
59000	563.83	545.71	529.97	516.23	504.16	493.50	484.05
60000	573.39	554.96	538.95	524.98	512.70	501.86	492.26
61000	582.95	564.20	547.94	533.73	521.25	510.23	500.46
62000	592.50	573.45	556.92	542.48	529.79	518.59	508.67
63000	602.06	582.70	565.90	551.23	538.34	526.96	516.87
64000	611.62	591.95	574.88	559.98	546.88	535.32	525.07
65000	621.17	601.20	583.87	568.73	555.43	543.69	533.28
70000	668.96	647.45	628.78	612.47	598.15	585.51	574.30
75000	716.74	693.69	673.69	656.22	640.88	627.33	615.32
80000	764.52	739.94	718.61	699.97	683.60	669.15	656.34
85000	812.30	786.19	763.52	743.72	726.33	710.97	697.36
90000	860.09	832.43	808.43	787.47	769.05	752.80	738.39
95000	907.87	878.68	853.34	831.21	811.78	794.62	779.41
100000	955.65	924.93	898.26	874.96	854.50	836.44	820.43
105000	1003.43	971.17	943.17	918.71	897.23	878.26	861.45
110000	1051.22	1017.42	988.08	962.46	939.95	920.08	902.47
120000	1146.78	1109.91	1077.91	1049.96	1025.40	1003.73	984.51
130000	1242.35	1202.40	1167.73	1137.45	1110.85	1087.37	1066.56
140000	1337.91	1294.90	1257.56	1224.95	1196.30	1171.02	1148.60
150000	1433.48	1387.39	1347.39	1312.44	1281.75	1254.66	1230.64
160000	1529.04	1479.88	1437.21	1399.94	1367.20	1338.30	1312.68
175000	1672.39	1618.62	1571.95	1531.18	1495.38	1463.77	1435.75
200000	1911.30	1849.85	1796.51	1749.93	1709.00	1672.88	1640.86
250000	2389.13	2312.31	2245.64	2187.41	2136.25	2091.10	2051.07
500000	4778.26	4624.63	4491.28	4374.81	4272.51	4182.20	4102.14
1000000	9556.52	9249.25	8982.57	8749.63	8545.01	8364.40	8204.28

MONTHLY PAYMENTS 8.00%

AMOUNT	22 YEARS	23 YEARS	24 YEARS	25 YEARS	30 YEARS	35 YEARS	40 YEARS
100	0.81	0.79	0.78	0.77	0.73	0.71	0.70
200	1.61	1.59	1.56	1.54	1.47	1.42	1.39
500	4.03	3.97	3.91	3.86	3.67	3.55	3.48
1000	8.06	7.93	7.82	7.72	7.34	7.10	6.95
2000	16.12	15.87	15.64	15.44	14.68	14.21	13.91
3000	24.19	23.80	23.46	23.15	22.01	21.31	20.86
4000	32.25	31.74	31.28	30.87	29.35	28.41	27.81
5000	40.31	39.67	39.10	38.59	36.69	35.51	34.77
6000	48.37	47.61	46.92	46.31	44.03	42.62	41.72
7000	56.43	55.54	54.74	54.03	51.36	49.72	48.67
8000	64.49	63.48	62.56	61.75	58.70	56.82	55.62
9000	72.56	71.41	70.38	69.46	66.04	63.92	62.58
10000	80.62	79.35	78.21	77.18	73.38	71.03	69.53
11000	88.68	87.28	86.03	84.90	80.71	78.13	76.48
12000	96.74	95.21	93.85	92.62	88.05	85.23	83.44
13000	104.80	103.15	101.67	100.34	95.39	92.33	90.39
14000	112.86	111.08	109.49	108.05	102.73	99.44	97.34
15000	120.93	119.02	117.31	115.77	110.06	106.54	104.30
20000	161.24	158.69	156.41	154.36	146.75	142.05	139.06
25000	201.54	198.36	195.51	192.95	183.44	177.57	173.83
30000	241.85	238.04	234.62	231.54	220.13	213.08	208.59
35000	282.16	277.71	273.72	270.14	256.82	248.59	243.36
40000	322.47	317.38	312.82	308.73	293.51	284.10	278.12
45000	362.78	357.05	351.92	347.32	330.19	319.62	312.89
50000	403.09	396.73	391.03	385.91	366.88	355.13	347.66
55000	443.40	436.40	430.13	424.50	403.57	390.64	382.42
56000	451.46	444.33	437.95	432.22	410.91	397.75	389.37
57000	459.52	452.27	445.77	439.94	418.25	404.85	396.33
58000	467.58	460.20	453.59	447.65	425.58	411.95	403.28
59000	475.64	468.14	461.41	455.37	432.92	419.05	410.23
60000	483.71	476.07	469.23	463.09	440.26	426.16	417.19
61000	491.77	484.01	477.05	470.81	447.60	433.26	424.14
62000	499.83	491.94	484.87	478.53	454.93	440.36	431.09
63000	507.89	499.88	492.69	486.24	462.27	447.46	438.05
64000	515.95	507.81	500.51	493.96	469.61	454.57	445.00
65000	524.02	515.74	508.34	501.68	476.95	461.67	451.95
70000	564.32	555.42	547.44	540.27	513.64	497.18	486.72
75000	604.63	595.09	586.54	578.86	550.32	532.70	521.48
80000	644.94	634.76	625.64	617.45	587.01	568.21	556.25
85000	685.25	674.43	664.75	656.04	623.70	603.72	591.01
90000	725.56	714.11	703.85	694.63	660.39	639.23	625.78
95000	765.87	753.78	742.95	733.23	697.08	674.75	660.55
100000	806.18	793.45	782.05	771.82	733.76	710.26	695.31
105000	846.49	833.13	821.16	810.41	770.45	745.77	730.08
110000	886.80	872.80	860.26	849.00	807.14	781.29	764.84
120000	967.41	952.14	938.46	926.18	880.52	852.31	834.37
130000	1048.03	1031.49	1016.67	1003.36	953.89	923.34	903.91
140000	1128.65	1110.83	1094.88	1080.54	1027.27	994.37	973.44
150000	1209.27	1190.18	1173.08	1157.72	1100.65	1065.39	1042.97
160000	1289.88	1269.52	1251.29	1234.91	1174.02	1136.42	1112.50
175000	1410.81	1388.54	1368.59	1350.68	1284.09	1242.96	1216.80
200000	1612.36	1586.91	1564.11	1543.63	1467.53	1420.52	1390.62
250000	2015.44	1983.63	1955.14	1929.54	1834.41	1775.65	1738.28
500000	4030.89	3967.26	3910.27	3859.08	3668.82	3551.30	3476.56
1000000	8061.78	7934.53	7820.54	7718.16	7337.65	7102.61	6953.12

8.25% MONTHLY PAYMENTS

AMOUNT	1 YEAR	2 YEARS	3 YEARS	4 YEARS	5 YEARS	6 YEARS	7 YEARS
100	8.71	4.53	3.15	2.45	2.04	1.77	1.57
200	17.42	9.07	6.29	4.91	4.08	3.53	3.14
500	43.55	22.67	15.73	12.27	10.20	8.83	7.86
1000	87.10	45.34	31.45	24.53	20.40	17.66	15.71
2000	174.21	90.68	62.90	49.06	40.79	35.31	31.42
3000	261.31	136.02	94.36	73.59	61.19	52.97	47.13
4000	348.42	181.37	125.81	98.12	81.59	70.62	62.84
5000	435.52	226.71	157.26	122.65	101.98	88.28	78.56
6000	522.62	272.05	188.71	147.18	122.38	105.93	94.27
7000	609.73	317.39	220.16	171.71	142.77	123.59	109.98
8000	696.83	362.73	251.61	196.24	163.17	141.24	125.69
9000	783.94	408.07	283.07	220.77	183.57	158.90	141.40
10000	871.04	453.41	314.52	245.30	203.96	176.56	157.11
11000	958.14	498.76	345.97	269.83	224.36	194.21	172.82
12000	1045.25	544.10	377.42	294.37	244.76	211.87	188.53
13000	1132.35	589.44	408.87	318.90	265.15	229.52	204.24
14000	1219.46	634.78	440.33	343.43	285.55	247.18	219.95
15000	1306.56	680.12	471.78	367.96	305.94	264.83	235.67
20000	1742.08	906.83	629.04	490.61	407.93	353.11	314.22
25000	2177.60	1133.53	786.30	613.26	509.91	441.39	392.78
30000	2613.12	1360.24	943.55	735.91	611.89	529.67	471.33
35000	3048.64	1586.95	1100.81	858.57	713.87	617.94	549.89
40000	3484.16	1813.66	1258.07	981.22	815.85	706.22	628.44
45000	3919.68	2040.36	1415.33	1103.87	917.83	794.50	707.00
50000	4355.20	2267.07	1572.59	1226.52	1019.81	882.78	785.55
55000	4790.72	2493.78	1729.85	1349.17	1121.79	971.06	864.11
56000	4877.83	2539.12	1761.30	1373.70	1142.19	988.71	879.82
57000	4964.93	2584.46	1792.75	1398.24	1162.59	1006.37	895.53
58000	5052.04	2629.80	1824.21	1422.77	1182.98	1024.02	911.24
59000	5139.14	2675.14	1855.66	1447.30	1203.38	1041.68	926.95
60000	5226.24	2720.48	1887.11	1471.83	1223.78	1059.33	942.66
61000	5313.35	2765.83	1918.56	1496.36	1244.17	1076.99	958.37
62000	5400.45	2811.17	1950.01	1520.89	1264.57	1094.64	974.09
63000	5487.56	2856.51	1981.46	1545.42	1284.96	1112.30	989.80
64000	5574.66	2901.85	2012.92	1569.95	1305.36	1129.96	1005.51
65000	5661.76	2947.19	2044.37	1594.48	1325.76	1147.61	1021.22
70000	6097.28	3173.90	2201.63	1717.13	1427.74	1235.89	1099.77
75000	6532.80	3400.60	2358.89	1839.78	1529.72	1324.17	1178.33
80000	6968.33	3627.31	2516.15	1962.44	1631.70	1412.44	1256.88
85000	7403.85	3854.02	2673.40	2085.09	1733.68	1500.72	1335.44
90000	7839.37	4080.73	2830.66	2207.74	1835.66	1589.00	1414.00
95000	8274.89	4307.43	2987.92	2330.39	1937.64	1677.28	1492.55
100000	8710.41	4534.14	3145.18	2453.04	2039.63	1765.56	1571.11
105000	9145.93	4760.85	3302.44	2575.70	2141.61	1853.83	1649.66
110000	9581.45	4987.55	3459.70	2698.35	2243.59	1942.11	1728.22
120000	10452.49	5440.97	3774.22	2943.65	2447.55	2118.67	1885.33
130000	11323.53	5894.38	4088.74	3188.96	2651.51	2295.22	2042.44
140000	12194.57	6347.80	4403.26	3434.26	2855.48	2471.78	2199.55
150000	13065.61	6801.21	4717.77	3679.57	3059.44	2648.33	2356.66
160000	13936.65	7254.62	5032.29	3924.87	3263.40	2824.89	2513.77
175000	15243.21	7934.74	5504.07	4292.83	3569.34	3089.72	2749.44
200000	17420.81	9068.28	6290.36	4906.09	4079.25	3531.11	3142.21
250000	21776.02	11335.35	7862.96	6132.61	5099.06	4413.89	3927.76
500000	43552.03	22670.70	15725.91	12265.22	10198.13	8827.78	7855.53
1000000	87104.06	45341.40	31451.82	24530.44	20396.25	17655.56	15711.06

MONTHLY PAYMENTS 8.25%

AMOUNT	8 YEARS	9 YEARS	10 YEARS	11 YEARS	12 YEARS	13 YEARS	14 YEARS
100	1.43	1.31	1.23	1.16	1.10	1.05	1.01
200	2.85	2.63	2.45	2.31	2.19	2.09	2.01
500	7.13	6.57	6.13	5.78	5.48	5.24	5.03
1000	14.26	13.15	12.27	11.55	10.96	10.47	10.06
2000	28.53	26.30	24.53	23.10	21.92	20.94	20.11
3000	42.79	39.45	36.80	34.65	32.89	31.41	30.17
4000	57.06	52.59	49.06	46.20	43.85	41.88	40.22
5000	71.32	65.74	61.33	57.75	54.81	52.35	50.28
6000	85.58	78.89	73.59	69.30	65.77	62.82	60.33
7000	99.85	92.04	85.86	80.85	76.73	73.30	70.39
8000	114.11	105.19	98.12	92.40	87.70	83.77	80.45
9000	128.38	118.34	110.39	103.95	98.66	94.24	90.50
10000	142.64	131.49	122.65	115.50	109.62	104.71	100.56
11000	156.90	144.64	134.92	127.06	120.58	115.18	110.61
12000	171.17	157.78	147.18	138.61	131.54	125.65	120.67
13000	185.43	170.93	159.45	150.16	142.51	136.12	130.72
14000	199.70	184.08	171.71	161.71	153.47	146.59	140.78
15000	213.96	197.23	183.98	173.26	164.43	157.06	150.83
20000	285.28	262.97	245.31	231.01	219.24	209.42	201.11
25000	356.60	328.72	306.63	288.76	274.05	261.77	251.39
30000	427.92	394.46	367.96	346.51	328.86	314.12	301.67
35000	499.24	460.20	429.28	404.27	383.67	366.48	351.95
40000	570.56	525.95	490.61	462.02	438.48	418.83	402.23
45000	641.88	591.69	551.94	519.77	493.29	471.18	452.50
50000	713.20	657.43	613.26	577.52	548.10	523.54	502.78
55000	784.52	723.18	674.59	635.28	602.91	575.89	553.06
56000	798.79	736.33	686.85	646.83	613.88	586.36	563.12
57000	813.05	749.47	699.12	658.38	624.84	596.83	573.17
58000	827.32	762.62	711.39	669.93	635.80	607.30	583.23
59000	841.58	775.77	723.65	681.48	646.76	617.78	593.28
60000	855.84	788.92	735.92	693.03	657.72	628.25	603.34
61000	870.11	802.07	748.18	704.58	668.69	638.72	613.40
62000	884.37	815.22	760.45	716.13	679.65	649.19	623.45
63000	898.64	828.37	772.71	727.68	690.61	659.66	633.51
64000	912.90	841.51	784.98	739.23	701.57	670.13	643.56
65000	927.16	854.66	797.24	750.78	712.53	680.60	653.62
70000	998.49	920.41	858.57	808.53	767.35	732.95	703.90
75000	1069.81	986.15	919.89	866.29	822.16	785.31	754.17
80000	1141.13	1051.89	981.22	924.04	876.97	837.66	804.45
85000	1212.45	1117.64	1042.55	981.79	931.78	890.02	854.73
90000	1283.77	1183.38	1103.87	1039.54	986.59	942.37	905.01
95000	1355.09	1249.12	1165.20	1097.30	1041.40	994.72	955.29
100000	1426.41	1314.87	1226.53	1155.05	1096.21	1047.08	1005.57
105000	1497.73	1380.61	1287.85	1212.80	1151.02	1099.43	1055.84
110000	1569.05	1446.35	1349.18	1270.55	1205.83	1151.78	1106.12
120000	1711.69	1577.84	1471.83	1386.06	1315.45	1256.49	1206.68
130000	1854.33	1709.33	1594.48	1501.56	1425.07	1361.20	1307.24
140000	1996.97	1840.81	1717.14	1617.07	1534.69	1465.91	1407.79
150000	2139.61	1972.30	1839.79	1732.57	1644.31	1570.61	1508.35
160000	2282.25	2103.79	1962.44	1848.08	1753.93	1675.32	1608.90
175000	2496.21	2301.02	2146.42	2021.33	1918.36	1832.38	1759.74
200000	2852.81	2629.73	2453.05	2310.10	2192.41	2094.15	2011.13
250000	3566.02	3287.17	3066.32	2887.62	2740.52	2617.69	2513.91
500000	7132.04	6574.33	6132.63	5775.24	5481.04	5235.38	5027.83
1000000	14264.07	13148.67	12265.26	11550.48	10962.07	10470.77	10055.66

8.25% MONTHLY PAYMENTS

AMOUNT	15 YEARS	16 YEARS	17 YEARS	18 YEARS	19 YEARS	20 YEARS	21 YEARS
100	0.97	0.94	0.91	0.89	0.87	0.85	0.84
200	1.94	1.88	1.83	1.78	1.74	1.70	1.67
500	4.85	4.70	4.57	4.45	4.35	4.26	4.18
1000	9.70	9.40	9.13	8.90	8.70	8.52	8.36
2000	19.40	18.79	18.26	17.80	17.40	17.04	16.73
3000	29.10	28.19	27.40	26.70	26.10	25.56	25.09
4000	38.81	37.59	36.53	35.61	34.80	34.08	33.45
5000	48.51	46.98	45.66	44.51	43.50	42.60	41.81
6000	58.21	56.38	54.79	53.41	52.19	51.12	50.18
7000	67.91	65.78	63.92	62.31	60.89	59.64	58.54
8000	77.61	75.17	73.06	71.21	69.59	68.17	66.90
9000	87.31	84.57	82.19	80.11	78.29	76.69	75.26
10000	97.01	93.97	91.32	89.01	86.99	85.21	83.63
11000	106.72	103.36	100.45	97.92	95.69	93.73	91.99
12000	116.42	112.76	109.59	106.82	104.39	102.25	100.35
13000	126.12	122.15	118.72	115.72	113.09	110.77	108.71
14000	135.82	131.55	127.85	124.62	121.79	119.29	117.08
15000	145.52	140.95	136.98	133.52	130.49	127.81	125.44
20000	194.03	187.93	182.64	178.03	173.98	170.41	167.25
25000	242.54	234.91	228.30	222.54	217.48	213.02	209.07
30000	291.04	281.90	273.96	267.04	260.97	255.62	250.88
35000	339.55	328.88	319.62	311.55	304.47	298.22	292.69
40000	388.06	375.86	365.29	356.06	347.96	340.83	334.51
45000	436.56	422.84	410.95	400.57	391.46	383.43	376.32
50000	485.07	469.83	456.61	445.07	434.95	426.03	418.13
55000	533.58	516.81	502.27	489.58	478.45	468.64	459.95
56000	543.28	526.20	511.40	498.48	487.15	477.16	468.31
57000	552.98	535.60	520.53	507.38	495.85	485.68	476.67
58000	562.68	545.00	529.66	516.29	504.55	494.20	485.03
59000	572.38	554.39	538.80	525.19	513.25	502.72	493.40
60000	582.08	563.79	547.93	534.09	521.95	511.24	501.76
61000	591.79	573.19	557.06	542.99	530.64	519.76	510.12
62000	601.49	582.58	566.19	551.89	539.34	528.28	518.48
63000	611.19	591.98	575.32	560.79	548.04	536.80	526.85
64000	620.89	601.38	584.46	569.69	556.74	545.32	535.21
65000	630.59	610.77	593.59	578.60	565.44	553.84	543.57
70000	679.10	657.76	639.25	623.10	608.94	596.45	585.39
75000	727.61	704.74	684.91	667.61	652.43	639.05	627.20
80000	776.11	751.72	730.57	712.12	695.93	681.65	669.01
85000	824.62	798.70	776.23	756.63	739.42	724.26	710.83
90000	873.13	845.69	821.89	801.13	782.92	766.86	752.64
95000	921.63	892.67	867.55	845.64	826.41	809.46	794.45
100000	970.14	939.65	913.21	890.15	869.91	852.07	836.27
105000	1018.65	986.63	958.87	934.66	913.40	894.67	878.08
110000	1067.15	1033.62	1004.54	979.16	956.90	937.27	919.89
120000	1164.17	1127.58	1095.86	1068.18	1043.89	1022.48	1003.52
130000	1261.18	1221.55	1187.18	1157.19	1130.88	1107.69	1087.15
140000	1358.20	1315.51	1278.50	1246.21	1217.87	1192.89	1170.77
150000	1455.21	1409.48	1369.82	1335.22	1304.86	1278.10	1254.40
160000	1552.22	1503.44	1461.14	1424.24	1391.85	1363.31	1338.03
175000	1697.75	1644.39	1598.12	1557.76	1522.34	1491.11	1463.47
200000	1940.28	1879.30	1826.43	1780.30	1739.82	1704.13	1672.54
250000	2425.35	2349.13	2283.04	2225.37	2174.77	2130.16	2090.67
500000	4850.70	4698.25	4566.07	4450.74	4349.55	4260.33	4181.33
1000000	9701.40	9396.50	9132.14	8901.48	8699.09	8520.66	8362.66

MONTHLY PAYMENTS   8.25%

AMOUNT	22 YEARS	23 YEARS	24 YEARS	25 YEARS	30 YEARS	35 YEARS	40 YEARS
100	0.82	0.81	0.80	0.79	0.75	0.73	0.71
200	1.64	1.62	1.60	1.58	1.50	1.46	1.43
500	4.11	4.05	3.99	3.94	3.76	3.64	3.57
1000	8.22	8.10	7.98	7.88	7.51	7.28	7.14
2000	16.44	16.19	15.97	15.77	15.03	14.57	14.28
3000	24.67	24.29	23.95	23.65	22.54	21.85	21.42
4000	32.89	32.39	31.94	31.54	30.05	29.14	28.57
5000	41.11	40.48	39.92	39.42	37.56	36.42	35.71
6000	49.33	48.58	47.91	47.31	45.08	43.71	42.85
7000	57.56	56.68	55.89	55.19	52.59	50.99	49.99
8000	65.78	64.78	63.88	63.08	60.10	58.28	57.13
9000	74.00	72.87	71.86	70.96	67.61	65.56	64.27
10000	82.22	80.97	79.85	78.85	75.13	72.85	71.41
11000	90.44	89.07	87.83	86.73	82.64	80.13	78.56
12000	98.67	97.16	95.82	94.61	90.15	87.42	85.70
13000	106.89	105.26	103.80	102.50	97.66	94.70	92.84
14000	115.11	113.36	111.79	110.38	105.18	101.99	99.98
15000	123.33	121.45	119.77	118.27	112.69	109.27	107.12
20000	164.44	161.94	159.70	157.69	150.25	145.70	142.83
25000	205.56	202.42	199.62	197.11	187.82	182.12	178.53
30000	246.67	242.91	239.55	236.54	225.38	218.55	214.24
35000	287.78	283.39	279.47	275.96	262.94	254.97	249.95
40000	328.89	323.88	319.40	315.38	300.51	291.40	285.66
45000	370.00	364.36	359.32	354.80	338.07	327.82	321.36
50000	411.11	404.85	399.25	394.23	375.63	364.25	357.07
55000	452.22	445.33	439.17	433.65	413.20	400.67	392.78
56000	460.45	453.43	447.16	441.53	420.71	407.96	399.92
57000	468.67	461.53	455.14	449.42	428.22	415.24	407.06
58000	476.89	469.63	463.13	457.30	435.73	422.52	414.20
59000	485.11	477.72	471.11	465.19	443.25	429.81	421.34
60000	493.33	485.82	479.10	473.07	450.76	437.09	428.48
61000	501.56	493.92	487.08	480.95	458.27	444.38	435.62
62000	509.78	502.01	495.07	488.84	465.79	451.66	442.77
63000	518.00	510.11	503.05	496.72	473.30	458.95	449.91
64000	526.22	518.21	511.04	504.61	480.81	466.23	457.05
65000	534.45	526.30	519.02	512.49	488.32	473.52	464.19
70000	575.56	566.79	558.95	551.92	525.89	509.94	499.90
75000	616.67	607.27	598.87	591.34	563.45	546.37	535.60
80000	657.78	647.76	638.80	630.76	601.01	582.79	571.31
85000	698.89	688.24	678.72	670.18	638.58	619.22	607.02
90000	740.00	728.73	718.65	709.61	676.14	655.64	642.72
95000	781.11	769.21	758.57	749.03	713.70	692.07	678.43
100000	822.22	809.70	798.50	788.45	751.27	728.49	714.14
105000	863.33	850.18	838.42	827.87	788.83	764.92	749.85
110000	904.45	890.67	878.35	867.30	826.39	801.34	785.55
120000	986.67	971.64	958.20	946.14	901.52	874.19	856.97
130000	1068.89	1052.61	1038.05	1024.99	976.65	947.04	928.38
140000	1151.11	1133.58	1117.90	1103.83	1051.77	1019.89	999.79
150000	1233.33	1214.55	1197.75	1182.68	1126.90	1092.74	1071.21
160000	1315.56	1295.52	1277.60	1261.52	1202.03	1165.59	1142.62
175000	1438.89	1416.97	1397.37	1379.79	1314.72	1274.86	1249.74
200000	1644.45	1619.40	1596.99	1576.90	1502.53	1456.98	1428.28
250000	2055.56	2024.25	1996.24	1971.13	1878.17	1821.23	1785.35
500000	4111.12	4048.50	3992.49	3942.25	3756.33	3642.46	3570.69
1000000	8222.23	8097.00	7984.97	7884.50	7512.67	7284.91	7141.39

8.50%　　　　MONTHLY PAYMENTS

AMOUNT	1 YEAR	2 YEARS	3 YEARS	4 YEARS	5 YEARS	6 YEARS	7 YEARS
100	8.72	4.55	3.16	2.46	2.05	1.78	1.58
200	17.44	9.09	6.31	4.93	4.10	3.56	3.17
500	43.61	22.73	15.78	12.32	10.26	8.89	7.92
1000	87.22	45.46	31.57	24.65	20.52	17.78	15.84
2000	174.44	90.91	63.14	49.30	41.03	35.56	31.67
3000	261.66	136.37	94.70	73.94	61.55	53.34	47.51
4000	348.88	181.82	126.27	98.59	82.07	71.11	63.35
5000	436.10	227.28	157.84	123.24	102.58	88.89	79.18
6000	523.32	272.73	189.41	147.89	123.10	106.67	95.02
7000	610.54	318.19	220.97	172.54	143.62	124.45	110.86
8000	697.76	363.65	252.54	197.19	164.13	142.23	126.69
9000	784.98	409.10	284.11	221.83	184.65	160.01	142.53
10000	872.20	454.56	315.68	246.48	205.17	177.78	158.36
11000	959.42	500.01	347.24	271.13	225.68	195.56	174.20
12000	1046.64	545.47	378.81	295.78	246.20	213.34	190.04
13000	1133.86	590.92	410.38	320.43	266.71	231.12	205.87
14000	1221.08	636.38	441.95	345.08	287.23	248.90	221.71
15000	1308.30	681.84	473.51	369.72	307.75	266.68	237.55
20000	1744.40	909.11	631.35	492.97	410.33	355.57	316.73
25000	2180.49	1136.39	789.19	616.21	512.91	444.46	395.91
30000	2616.59	1363.67	947.03	739.45	615.50	533.35	475.09
35000	3052.69	1590.95	1104.86	862.69	718.08	622.24	554.28
40000	3488.79	1818.23	1262.70	985.93	820.66	711.14	633.46
45000	3924.89	2045.51	1420.54	1109.17	923.24	800.03	712.64
50000	4360.99	2272.78	1578.38	1232.42	1025.83	888.92	791.82
55000	4797.09	2500.06	1736.21	1355.66	1128.41	977.81	871.01
56000	4884.31	2545.52	1767.78	1380.30	1148.93	995.59	886.84
57000	4971.53	2590.97	1799.35	1404.95	1169.44	1013.37	902.68
58000	5058.75	2636.43	1830.92	1429.60	1189.96	1031.15	918.52
59000	5145.97	2681.88	1862.48	1454.25	1210.48	1048.92	934.35
60000	5233.19	2727.34	1894.05	1478.90	1230.99	1066.70	950.19
61000	5320.41	2772.80	1925.62	1503.55	1251.51	1084.48	966.03
62000	5407.63	2818.25	1957.19	1528.19	1272.02	1102.26	981.86
63000	5494.85	2863.71	1988.75	1552.84	1292.54	1120.04	997.70
64000	5582.07	2909.16	2020.32	1577.49	1313.06	1137.82	1013.54
65000	5669.29	2954.62	2051.89	1602.14	1333.57	1155.59	1029.37
70000	6105.38	3181.90	2209.73	1725.38	1436.16	1244.49	1108.55
75000	6541.48	3409.18	2367.57	1848.62	1538.74	1333.38	1187.74
80000	6977.58	3636.45	2525.40	1971.86	1641.32	1422.27	1266.92
85000	7413.68	3863.73	2683.24	2095.11	1743.91	1511.16	1346.10
90000	7849.78	4091.01	2841.08	2218.35	1846.49	1600.05	1425.28
95000	8285.88	4318.29	2998.92	2341.59	1949.07	1688.95	1504.47
100000	8721.98	4545.57	3156.75	2464.83	2051.65	1777.84	1583.65
105000	9158.08	4772.85	3314.59	2588.07	2154.24	1866.73	1662.83
110000	9594.18	5000.12	3472.43	2711.31	2256.82	1955.62	1742.01
120000	10466.37	5454.68	3788.10	2957.80	2461.98	2133.41	1900.38
130000	11338.57	5909.24	4103.78	3204.28	2667.15	2311.19	2058.74
140000	12210.77	6363.79	4419.46	3450.76	2872.31	2488.97	2217.11
150000	13082.97	6818.35	4735.13	3697.25	3077.48	2666.76	2375.47
160000	13955.17	7272.91	5050.81	3943.73	3282.65	2844.54	2533.84
175000	15263.46	7954.74	5524.32	4313.45	3590.39	3111.22	2771.38
200000	17443.96	9091.13	6313.51	4929.66	4103.31	3555.68	3167.30
250000	21804.95	11363.92	7891.88	6162.08	5129.13	4444.60	3959.12
500000	43609.89	22727.84	15783.77	12324.15	10258.27	8889.19	7918.24
1000000	87219.78	45455.67	31567.54	24648.30	20516.53	17778.38	15836.49

MONTHLY PAYMENTS 8.50%

AMOUNT	8 YEARS	9 YEARS	10 YEARS	11 YEARS	12 YEARS	13 YEARS	14 YEARS
100	1.44	1.33	1.24	1.17	1.11	1.06	1.02
200	2.88	2.66	2.48	2.34	2.22	2.12	2.04
500	7.20	6.64	6.20	5.84	5.55	5.31	5.10
1000	14.39	13.28	12.40	11.69	11.10	10.61	10.20
2000	28.78	26.56	24.80	23.37	22.20	21.22	20.40
3000	43.18	39.84	37.20	35.06	33.30	31.84	30.60
4000	57.57	53.12	49.59	46.75	44.40	42.45	40.80
5000	71.96	66.40	61.99	58.43	55.50	53.06	51.00
6000	86.35	79.68	74.39	70.12	66.60	63.67	61.20
7000	100.74	92.96	86.79	81.80	77.70	74.28	71.39
8000	115.14	106.23	99.19	93.49	88.80	84.89	81.59
9000	129.53	119.51	111.59	105.18	99.91	95.51	91.79
10000	143.92	132.79	123.99	116.86	111.01	106.12	101.99
11000	158.31	146.07	136.38	128.55	122.11	116.73	112.19
12000	172.71	159.35	148.78	140.24	133.21	127.34	122.39
13000	187.10	172.63	161.18	151.92	144.31	137.95	132.59
14000	201.49	185.91	173.58	163.61	155.41	148.57	142.79
15000	215.88	199.19	185.98	175.30	166.51	159.18	152.99
20000	287.84	265.59	247.97	233.73	222.01	212.24	203.98
25000	359.80	331.98	309.96	292.16	277.51	265.29	254.98
30000	431.76	398.38	371.96	350.59	333.02	318.35	305.98
35000	503.72	464.78	433.95	409.02	388.52	371.41	356.97
40000	575.69	531.17	495.94	467.46	444.02	424.47	407.97
45000	647.65	597.57	557.94	525.89	499.53	477.53	458.96
50000	719.61	663.97	619.93	584.32	555.03	530.59	509.96
55000	791.57	730.36	681.92	642.75	610.53	583.65	560.96
56000	805.96	743.64	694.32	654.44	621.63	594.26	571.15
57000	820.35	756.92	706.72	666.12	632.73	604.87	581.35
58000	834.74	770.20	719.12	677.81	643.83	615.48	591.55
59000	849.14	783.48	731.52	689.50	654.93	626.10	601.75
60000	863.53	796.76	743.91	701.18	666.03	636.71	611.95
61000	877.92	810.04	756.31	712.87	677.13	647.32	622.15
62000	892.31	823.32	768.71	724.56	688.23	657.93	632.35
63000	906.70	836.60	781.11	736.24	699.34	668.54	642.55
64000	921.10	849.88	793.51	747.93	710.44	679.15	652.75
65000	935.49	863.16	805.91	759.62	721.54	689.77	662.95
70000	1007.45	929.55	867.90	818.05	777.04	742.83	713.94
75000	1079.41	995.95	929.89	876.48	832.54	795.88	764.94
80000	1151.37	1062.35	991.89	934.91	888.04	848.94	815.93
85000	1223.33	1128.74	1053.88	993.34	943.55	902.00	866.93
90000	1295.29	1195.14	1115.87	1051.78	999.05	955.06	917.93
95000	1367.25	1261.54	1177.86	1110.21	1054.55	1008.12	968.92
100000	1439.21	1327.94	1239.86	1168.64	1110.06	1061.18	1019.92
105000	1511.17	1394.33	1301.85	1227.07	1165.56	1114.24	1070.91
110000	1583.13	1460.73	1363.84	1285.50	1221.06	1167.30	1121.91
120000	1727.06	1593.52	1487.83	1402.37	1332.07	1273.41	1223.90
130000	1870.98	1726.32	1611.81	1519.23	1443.07	1379.53	1325.89
140000	2014.90	1859.11	1735.80	1636.09	1554.08	1485.65	1427.89
150000	2158.82	1991.90	1859.79	1752.96	1665.08	1591.77	1529.88
160000	2302.74	2124.70	1983.77	1869.82	1776.09	1697.89	1631.87
175000	2518.62	2323.89	2169.75	2045.12	1942.60	1857.06	1784.86
200000	2878.43	2655.87	2479.71	2337.28	2220.11	2122.36	2039.84
250000	3598.03	3319.84	3099.64	2921.60	2775.14	2652.95	2549.80
500000	7196.06	6639.68	6199.28	5843.20	5550.28	5305.90	5099.59
1000000	14392.13	13279.35	12398.57	11686.39	11100.56	10611.79	10199.19

8.50%   MONTHLY PAYMENTS

AMOUNT	15 YEARS	16 YEARS	17 YEARS	18 YEARS	19 YEARS	20 YEARS	21 YEARS
100	0.98	0.95	0.93	0.91	0.89	0.87	0.85
200	1.97	1.91	1.86	1.81	1.77	1.74	1.70
500	4.92	4.77	4.64	4.53	4.43	4.34	4.26
1000	9.85	9.54	9.28	9.05	8.85	8.68	8.52
2000	19.69	19.09	18.57	18.11	17.71	17.36	17.04
3000	29.54	28.63	27.85	27.16	26.56	26.03	25.57
4000	39.39	38.18	37.13	36.22	35.42	34.71	34.09
5000	49.24	47.72	46.41	45.27	44.27	43.39	42.61
6000	59.08	57.27	55.70	54.33	53.13	52.07	51.13
7000	68.93	66.81	64.98	63.38	61.98	60.75	59.66
8000	78.78	76.36	74.26	72.44	70.84	69.43	68.18
9000	88.63	85.90	83.55	81.49	79.69	78.10	76.70
10000	98.47	95.45	92.83	90.55	88.54	86.78	85.22
11000	108.32	104.99	102.11	99.60	97.40	95.46	93.75
12000	118.17	114.54	111.40	108.65	106.25	104.14	102.27
13000	128.02	124.08	120.68	117.71	115.11	112.82	110.79
14000	137.86	133.63	129.96	126.76	123.96	121.50	119.31
15000	147.71	143.17	139.24	135.82	132.82	130.17	127.84
20000	196.95	190.90	185.66	181.09	177.09	173.56	170.45
25000	246.18	238.62	232.07	226.36	221.36	216.96	213.06
30000	295.42	286.35	278.49	271.64	265.63	260.35	255.67
35000	344.66	334.07	324.90	316.91	309.91	303.74	298.28
40000	393.90	381.80	371.32	362.18	354.18	347.13	340.90
45000	443.13	429.52	417.73	407.46	398.45	390.52	383.51
50000	492.37	477.25	464.15	452.73	442.72	433.91	426.12
55000	541.61	524.97	510.56	498.00	487.00	477.30	468.73
56000	551.45	534.51	519.84	507.06	495.85	485.98	477.25
57000	561.30	544.06	529.13	516.11	504.70	494.66	485.78
58000	571.15	553.60	538.41	525.17	513.56	503.34	494.30
59000	581.00	563.15	547.69	534.22	522.41	512.02	502.82
60000	590.84	572.69	556.98	543.27	531.27	520.69	511.34
61000	600.69	582.24	566.26	552.33	540.12	529.37	519.87
62000	610.54	591.78	575.54	561.38	548.98	538.05	528.39
63000	620.39	601.33	584.82	570.44	557.83	546.73	536.91
64000	630.23	610.87	594.11	579.49	566.69	555.41	545.43
65000	640.08	620.42	603.39	588.55	575.54	564.09	553.96
70000	689.32	668.14	649.80	633.82	619.81	607.48	596.57
75000	738.55	715.87	696.22	679.09	664.08	650.87	639.18
80000	787.79	763.59	742.63	724.37	708.36	694.26	681.79
85000	837.03	811.32	789.05	769.64	752.63	737.65	724.40
90000	886.27	859.04	835.46	814.91	796.90	781.04	767.02
95000	935.50	906.77	881.88	860.18	841.17	824.43	809.63
100000	984.74	954.49	928.29	905.46	885.45	867.82	852.24
105000	1033.98	1002.22	974.71	950.73	929.72	911.21	894.85
110000	1083.21	1049.94	1021.12	996.00	973.99	954.61	937.46
120000	1181.69	1145.39	1113.95	1086.55	1062.53	1041.39	1022.69
130000	1280.16	1240.84	1206.78	1177.09	1151.08	1128.17	1107.91
140000	1378.64	1336.29	1299.61	1267.64	1239.62	1214.95	1193.13
150000	1477.11	1431.74	1392.44	1358.19	1328.17	1301.73	1278.36
160000	1575.58	1527.19	1485.27	1448.73	1416.71	1388.52	1363.58
175000	1723.29	1670.36	1624.51	1584.55	1549.53	1518.69	1491.42
200000	1969.48	1908.98	1856.58	1810.91	1770.89	1735.65	1704.48
250000	2461.85	2386.23	2320.73	2263.64	2213.61	2169.56	2130.60
500000	4923.70	4772.46	4641.46	4527.29	4427.23	4339.12	4261.20
1000000	9847.40	9544.91	9282.92	9054.57	8854.46	8678.23	8522.39

MONTHLY PAYMENTS 8.50%

AMOUNT	22 YEARS	23 YEARS	24 YEARS	25 YEARS	30 YEARS	35 YEARS	40 YEARS
100	0.84	0.83	0.82	0.81	0.77	0.75	0.73
200	1.68	1.65	1.63	1.61	1.54	1.49	1.47
500	4.19	4.13	4.08	4.03	3.84	3.73	3.67
1000	8.38	8.26	8.15	8.05	7.69	7.47	7.33
2000	16.77	16.52	16.30	16.10	15.38	14.94	14.66
3000	25.15	24.78	24.45	24.16	23.07	22.41	21.99
4000	33.54	33.04	32.60	32.21	30.76	29.87	29.32
5000	41.92	41.30	40.75	40.26	38.45	37.34	36.65
6000	50.30	49.57	48.90	48.31	46.13	44.81	43.99
7000	58.69	57.83	57.06	56.37	53.82	52.28	51.32
8000	67.07	66.09	65.21	64.42	61.51	59.75	58.65
9000	75.46	74.35	73.36	72.47	69.20	67.22	65.98
10000	83.84	82.61	81.51	80.52	76.89	74.69	73.31
11000	92.22	90.87	89.66	88.57	84.58	82.15	80.64
12000	100.61	99.13	97.81	96.63	92.27	89.62	87.97
13000	108.99	107.39	105.96	104.68	99.96	97.09	95.30
14000	117.38	115.65	114.11	112.73	107.65	104.56	102.63
15000	125.76	123.91	122.26	120.78	115.34	112.03	109.96
20000	167.68	165.22	163.02	161.05	153.78	149.37	146.62
25000	209.60	206.52	203.77	201.31	192.23	186.72	183.27
30000	251.52	247.83	244.52	241.57	230.67	224.06	219.93
35000	293.44	289.13	285.28	281.83	269.12	261.40	256.58
40000	335.36	330.43	326.03	322.09	307.57	298.74	293.24
45000	377.28	371.74	366.79	362.35	346.01	336.09	329.89
50000	419.20	413.04	407.54	402.61	384.46	373.43	366.55
55000	461.12	454.35	448.30	442.87	422.90	410.77	403.20
56000	469.51	462.61	456.45	450.93	430.59	418.24	410.53
57000	477.89	470.87	464.60	458.98	438.28	425.71	417.86
58000	486.28	479.13	472.75	467.03	445.97	433.18	425.19
59000	494.66	487.39	480.90	475.08	453.66	440.65	432.53
60000	503.04	495.65	489.05	483.14	461.35	448.12	439.86
61000	511.43	503.91	497.20	491.19	469.04	455.58	447.19
62000	519.81	512.17	505.35	499.24	476.73	463.05	454.52
63000	528.20	520.43	513.50	507.29	484.42	470.52	461.85
64000	536.58	528.70	521.65	515.35	492.10	477.99	469.18
65000	544.96	536.96	529.80	523.40	499.79	485.46	476.51
70000	586.88	578.26	570.56	563.66	538.24	522.80	513.17
75000	628.80	619.56	611.31	603.92	576.69	560.15	549.82
80000	670.72	660.87	652.07	644.18	615.13	597.49	586.48
85000	712.65	702.17	692.82	684.44	653.58	634.83	623.13
90000	754.57	743.48	733.57	724.70	692.02	672.17	659.78
95000	796.49	784.78	774.33	764.97	730.47	709.52	696.44
100000	838.41	826.09	815.08	805.23	768.91	746.86	733.09
105000	880.33	867.39	855.84	845.49	807.36	784.20	769.75
110000	922.25	908.70	896.59	885.75	845.80	821.55	806.40
120000	1006.09	991.30	978.10	966.27	922.70	896.23	879.71
130000	1089.93	1073.91	1059.61	1046.80	999.59	970.92	953.02
140000	1173.77	1156.52	1141.12	1127.32	1076.48	1045.60	1026.33
150000	1257.61	1239.13	1222.62	1207.84	1153.37	1120.29	1099.64
160000	1341.45	1321.73	1304.13	1288.36	1230.26	1194.98	1172.95
175000	1467.21	1445.65	1426.39	1409.15	1345.60	1307.01	1282.91
200000	1676.81	1652.17	1630.16	1610.45	1537.83	1493.72	1466.19
250000	2096.02	2065.22	2037.71	2013.07	1922.28	1867.15	1832.74
500000	4192.03	4130.43	4075.41	4026.14	3844.57	3734.30	3665.47
1000000	8384.06	8260.87	8150.82	8052.27	7689.13	7468.61	7330.94

8.75%   MONTHLY PAYMENTS

AMOUNT	1 YEAR	2 YEARS	3 YEARS	4 YEARS	5 YEARS	6 YEARS	7 YEARS
100	8.73	4.56	3.17	2.48	2.06	1.79	1.60
200	17.47	9.11	6.34	4.95	4.13	3.58	3.19
500	43.67	22.79	15.84	12.38	10.32	8.95	7.98
1000	87.34	45.57	31.68	24.77	20.64	17.90	15.96
2000	174.67	91.14	63.37	49.53	41.27	35.80	31.92
3000	262.01	136.71	95.05	74.30	61.91	53.71	47.89
4000	349.34	182.28	126.73	99.07	82.55	71.61	63.85
5000	436.68	227.85	158.42	123.83	103.19	89.51	79.81
6000	524.01	273.42	190.10	148.60	123.82	107.41	95.77
7000	611.35	318.99	221.78	173.37	144.46	125.31	111.74
8000	698.68	364.56	253.47	198.13	165.10	143.21	127.70
9000	786.02	410.13	285.15	222.90	185.74	161.12	143.66
10000	873.36	455.70	316.84	247.67	206.37	179.02	159.62
11000	960.69	501.27	348.52	272.43	227.01	196.92	175.59
12000	1048.03	546.84	380.20	297.20	247.65	214.82	191.55
13000	1135.36	592.41	411.89	321.96	268.28	232.72	207.51
14000	1222.70	637.98	443.57	346.73	288.92	250.62	223.47
15000	1310.03	683.55	475.25	371.50	309.56	268.53	239.44
20000	1746.71	911.40	633.67	495.33	412.74	358.03	319.25
25000	2183.39	1139.25	792.09	619.16	515.93	447.54	399.06
30000	2620.07	1367.10	950.51	743.00	619.12	537.05	478.87
35000	3056.75	1594.95	1108.92	866.83	722.30	626.56	558.69
40000	3493.42	1822.80	1267.34	990.66	825.49	716.07	638.50
45000	3930.10	2050.66	1425.76	1114.49	928.68	805.58	718.31
50000	4366.78	2278.51	1584.18	1238.33	1031.86	895.09	798.12
55000	4803.46	2506.36	1742.59	1362.16	1135.05	984.59	877.94
56000	4890.79	2551.93	1774.28	1386.92	1155.69	1002.50	893.90
57000	4978.13	2597.50	1805.96	1411.69	1176.32	1020.40	909.86
58000	5065.46	2643.07	1837.64	1436.46	1196.96	1038.30	925.82
59000	5152.80	2688.64	1869.33	1461.22	1217.60	1056.20	941.79
60000	5240.14	2734.21	1901.01	1485.99	1238.23	1074.10	957.75
61000	5327.47	2779.78	1932.69	1510.76	1258.87	1092.00	973.71
62000	5414.81	2825.35	1964.38	1535.52	1279.51	1109.91	989.67
63000	5502.14	2870.92	1996.06	1560.29	1300.15	1127.81	1005.64
64000	5589.48	2916.49	2027.74	1585.06	1320.78	1145.71	1021.60
65000	5676.81	2962.06	2059.43	1609.82	1341.42	1163.61	1037.56
70000	6113.49	3189.91	2217.85	1733.66	1444.61	1253.12	1117.37
75000	6550.17	3417.76	2376.26	1857.49	1547.79	1342.63	1197.19
80000	6986.85	3645.61	2534.68	1981.32	1650.98	1432.14	1277.00
85000	7423.52	3873.46	2693.10	2105.15	1754.16	1521.65	1356.81
90000	7860.20	4101.31	2851.52	2228.99	1857.35	1611.15	1436.62
95000	8296.88	4329.16	3009.93	2352.82	1960.54	1700.66	1516.44
100000	8733.56	4557.01	3168.35	2476.65	2063.72	1790.17	1596.25
105000	9170.24	4784.86	3326.77	2600.48	2166.91	1879.68	1676.06
110000	9606.91	5012.71	3485.19	2724.32	2270.10	1969.19	1755.87
120000	10480.27	5468.41	3802.02	2971.98	2476.47	2148.21	1915.50
130000	11353.63	5924.12	4118.86	3219.65	2682.84	2327.22	2075.12
140000	12226.98	6379.82	4435.69	3467.31	2889.21	2506.24	2234.75
150000	13100.34	6835.52	4752.53	3714.98	3095.58	2685.26	2394.37
160000	13973.69	7291.22	5069.36	3962.64	3301.96	2864.27	2554.00
175000	15283.73	7974.77	5544.61	4334.14	3611.52	3132.80	2793.44
200000	17467.12	9114.02	6336.70	4953.30	4127.45	3580.34	3192.50
250000	21833.90	11392.53	7920.88	6191.63	5159.31	4475.43	3990.62
500000	43667.79	22785.06	15841.75	12383.25	10318.62	8950.86	7981.25
1000000	87335.59	45570.12	31683.51	24766.50	20637.23	17901.71	15962.49

MONTHLY PAYMENTS 8.75%

AMOUNT	8 YEARS	9 YEARS	10 YEARS	11 YEARS	12 YEARS	13 YEARS	14 YEARS
100	1.45	1.34	1.25	1.18	1.12	1.08	1.03
200	2.90	2.68	2.51	2.36	2.25	2.15	2.07
500	7.26	6.71	6.27	5.91	5.62	5.38	5.17
1000	14.52	13.41	12.53	11.82	11.24	10.75	10.34
2000	29.04	26.82	25.07	23.65	22.48	21.51	20.69
3000	43.56	40.23	37.60	35.47	33.72	32.26	31.03
4000	58.08	53.64	50.13	47.29	44.96	43.02	41.38
5000	72.60	67.05	62.66	59.12	56.20	53.77	51.72
6000	87.13	80.46	75.20	70.94	67.44	64.52	62.06
7000	101.65	93.88	87.73	82.76	78.68	75.28	72.41
8000	116.17	107.29	100.26	94.59	89.92	86.03	82.75
9000	130.69	120.70	112.79	106.41	101.16	96.78	93.09
10000	145.21	134.11	125.33	118.23	112.40	107.54	103.44
11000	159.73	147.52	137.86	130.05	123.64	118.29	113.78
12000	174.25	160.93	150.39	141.88	134.88	129.05	124.13
13000	188.77	174.34	162.92	153.70	146.12	139.80	134.47
14000	203.29	187.75	175.46	165.52	157.36	150.55	144.81
15000	217.81	201.16	187.99	177.35	168.60	161.31	155.16
20000	290.42	268.22	250.65	236.46	224.80	215.08	206.88
25000	363.02	335.27	313.32	295.58	281.00	268.85	258.59
30000	435.63	402.32	375.98	354.70	337.20	322.61	310.31
35000	508.23	469.38	438.64	413.81	393.40	376.38	362.03
40000	580.83	536.43	501.31	472.93	449.60	430.15	413.75
45000	653.44	603.48	563.97	532.04	505.80	483.92	465.47
50000	726.04	670.54	626.63	591.16	562.00	537.69	517.19
55000	798.65	737.59	689.30	650.27	618.20	591.46	568.91
56000	813.17	751.00	701.83	662.10	629.44	602.21	579.25
57000	827.69	764.41	714.36	673.92	640.68	612.97	589.59
58000	842.21	777.82	726.90	685.74	651.92	623.72	599.94
59000	856.73	791.24	739.43	697.57	663.16	634.47	610.28
60000	871.25	804.65	751.96	709.39	674.40	645.23	620.63
61000	885.77	818.06	764.49	721.21	685.64	655.98	630.97
62000	900.29	831.47	777.03	733.04	696.88	666.74	641.31
63000	914.81	844.88	789.56	744.86	708.12	677.49	651.66
64000	929.33	858.29	802.09	756.68	719.36	688.24	662.00
65000	943.85	871.70	814.62	768.51	730.60	699.00	672.34
70000	1016.46	938.75	877.29	827.62	786.80	752.77	724.06
75000	1089.06	1005.81	939.95	886.74	843.00	806.54	775.78
80000	1161.67	1072.86	1002.61	945.85	899.20	860.30	827.50
85000	1234.27	1139.92	1065.28	1004.97	955.40	914.07	879.22
90000	1306.88	1206.97	1127.94	1064.09	1011.60	967.84	930.94
95000	1379.48	1274.02	1190.60	1123.20	1067.80	1021.61	982.66
100000	1452.08	1341.08	1253.27	1182.32	1124.00	1075.38	1034.38
105000	1524.69	1408.13	1315.93	1241.43	1180.20	1129.15	1086.09
110000	1597.29	1475.18	1378.59	1300.55	1236.40	1182.92	1137.81
120000	1742.50	1609.29	1503.92	1418.78	1348.80	1290.46	1241.25
130000	1887.71	1743.40	1629.25	1537.01	1461.20	1397.99	1344.69
140000	2032.92	1877.51	1754.57	1655.24	1573.60	1505.53	1448.13
150000	2178.13	2011.62	1879.90	1773.48	1686.00	1613.07	1551.56
160000	2323.33	2145.72	2005.23	1891.71	1798.40	1720.61	1655.00
175000	2541.15	2346.88	2193.22	2069.05	1966.99	1881.92	1810.16
200000	2904.17	2682.15	2506.54	2364.63	2247.99	2150.76	2068.75
250000	3630.21	3352.69	3133.17	2955.79	2809.99	2688.45	2585.94
500000	7260.42	6705.38	6266.34	5911.58	5619.98	5376.90	5171.88
1000000	14520.84	13410.77	12532.68	11823.17	11239.97	10753.81	10343.76

8.75%　　　　　MONTHLY PAYMENTS

AMOUNT	15 YEARS	16 YEARS	17 YEARS	18 YEARS	19 YEARS	20 YEARS	21 YEARS
100	1.00	0.97	0.94	0.92	0.90	0.88	0.87
200	2.00	1.94	1.89	1.84	1.80	1.77	1.74
500	5.00	4.85	4.72	4.60	4.51	4.42	4.34
1000	9.99	9.69	9.43	9.21	9.01	8.84	8.68
2000	19.99	19.39	18.87	18.42	18.02	17.67	17.37
3000	29.98	29.08	28.30	27.63	27.03	26.51	26.05
4000	39.98	38.78	37.74	36.84	36.04	35.35	34.73
5000	49.97	48.47	47.17	46.04	45.06	44.19	43.42
6000	59.97	58.17	56.61	55.25	54.07	53.02	52.10
7000	69.96	67.86	66.04	64.46	63.08	61.86	60.78
8000	79.96	77.56	75.48	73.67	72.09	70.70	69.47
9000	89.95	87.25	84.91	82.88	81.10	79.53	78.15
10000	99.94	96.94	94.35	92.09	90.11	88.37	86.83
11000	109.94	106.64	103.78	101.30	99.12	97.21	95.52
12000	119.93	116.33	113.22	110.51	108.13	106.05	104.20
13000	129.93	126.03	122.65	119.72	117.14	114.88	112.88
14000	139.92	135.72	132.09	128.92	126.16	123.72	121.57
15000	149.92	145.42	141.52	138.13	135.17	132.56	130.25
20000	199.89	193.89	188.70	184.18	180.22	176.74	173.67
25000	249.86	242.36	235.87	230.22	225.28	220.93	217.09
30000	299.83	290.83	283.05	276.27	270.33	265.11	260.50
35000	349.81	339.31	330.22	322.31	315.39	309.30	303.92
40000	399.78	387.78	377.40	368.36	360.44	353.48	347.34
45000	449.75	436.25	424.57	414.40	405.50	397.67	390.76
50000	499.72	484.72	471.74	460.45	450.55	441.86	434.17
55000	549.70	533.20	518.92	506.49	495.61	486.04	477.59
56000	559.69	542.89	528.35	515.70	504.62	494.88	486.27
57000	569.69	552.58	537.79	524.91	513.63	503.72	494.96
58000	579.68	562.28	547.22	534.12	522.64	512.55	503.64
59000	589.67	571.97	556.66	543.33	531.65	521.39	512.32
60000	599.67	581.67	566.09	552.53	540.67	530.23	521.01
61000	609.66	591.36	575.53	561.74	549.68	539.06	529.69
62000	619.66	601.06	584.96	570.95	558.69	547.90	538.37
63000	629.65	610.75	594.40	580.16	567.70	556.74	547.06
64000	639.65	620.45	603.83	589.37	576.71	565.57	555.74
65000	649.64	630.14	613.27	598.58	585.72	574.41	564.42
70000	699.61	678.61	660.44	644.62	630.78	618.60	607.84
75000	749.59	727.09	707.62	690.67	675.83	662.78	651.26
80000	799.56	775.56	754.79	736.71	720.89	706.97	694.68
85000	849.53	824.03	801.97	782.76	765.94	751.15	738.09
90000	899.50	872.50	849.14	828.80	811.00	795.34	781.51
95000	949.48	920.97	896.31	874.85	856.05	839.53	824.93
100000	999.45	969.45	943.49	920.89	901.11	883.71	868.34
105000	1049.42	1017.92	990.66	966.93	946.16	927.90	911.76
110000	1099.39	1066.39	1037.84	1012.98	991.22	972.08	955.18
120000	1199.34	1163.34	1132.19	1105.07	1081.33	1060.45	1042.01
130000	1299.28	1260.28	1226.54	1197.16	1171.44	1148.82	1128.85
140000	1399.23	1357.23	1320.88	1289.25	1261.55	1237.19	1215.68
150000	1499.17	1454.17	1415.23	1381.34	1351.66	1325.57	1302.52
160000	1599.12	1551.11	1509.58	1473.42	1441.77	1413.94	1389.35
175000	1749.04	1696.53	1651.11	1611.56	1576.94	1546.49	1519.60
200000	1998.90	1938.89	1886.98	1841.78	1802.22	1767.42	1736.69
250000	2498.62	2423.62	2358.72	2302.23	2252.77	2209.28	2170.86
500000	4997.24	4847.23	4717.45	4604.45	4505.54	4418.55	4341.72
1000000	9994.49	9694.47	9434.89	9208.90	9011.09	8837.11	8683.45

MONTHLY PAYMENTS 8.75%

AMOUNT	22 YEARS	23 YEARS	24 YEARS	25 YEARS	30 YEARS	35 YEARS	40 YEARS
100	0.85	0.84	0.83	0.82	0.79	0.77	0.75
200	1.71	1.69	1.66	1.64	1.57	1.53	1.50
500	4.27	4.21	4.16	4.11	3.93	3.83	3.76
1000	8.55	8.43	8.32	8.22	7.87	7.65	7.52
2000	17.09	16.85	16.64	16.44	15.73	15.31	15.04
3000	25.64	25.28	24.95	24.66	23.60	22.96	22.57
4000	34.19	33.70	33.27	32.89	31.47	30.61	30.09
5000	42.74	42.13	41.59	41.11	39.34	38.27	37.61
6000	51.28	50.56	49.91	49.33	47.20	45.92	45.13
7000	59.83	58.98	58.23	57.55	55.07	53.58	52.65
8000	68.38	67.41	66.54	65.77	62.94	61.23	60.17
9000	76.93	75.83	74.86	73.99	70.80	68.88	67.70
10000	85.47	84.26	83.18	82.21	78.67	76.54	75.22
11000	94.02	92.69	91.50	90.44	86.54	84.19	82.74
12000	102.57	101.11	99.82	98.66	94.40	91.84	90.26
13000	111.11	109.54	108.13	106.88	102.27	99.50	97.78
14000	119.66	117.97	116.45	115.10	110.14	107.15	105.30
15000	128.21	126.39	124.77	123.32	118.01	114.80	112.83
20000	170.94	168.52	166.36	164.43	157.34	153.07	150.43
25000	213.68	210.65	207.95	205.54	196.68	191.34	188.04
30000	256.42	252.78	249.54	246.64	236.01	229.61	225.65
35000	299.15	294.91	291.13	287.75	275.35	267.88	263.26
40000	341.89	337.04	332.72	328.86	314.68	306.15	300.87
45000	384.63	379.17	374.31	369.96	354.02	344.41	338.48
50000	427.36	421.31	415.90	411.07	393.35	382.68	376.09
55000	470.10	463.44	457.49	452.18	432.69	420.95	413.69
56000	478.65	471.86	465.81	460.40	440.55	428.60	421.22
57000	487.19	480.29	474.13	468.62	448.42	436.26	428.74
58000	495.74	488.71	482.45	476.84	456.29	443.91	436.26
59000	504.29	497.14	490.77	485.06	464.15	451.56	443.78
60000	512.83	505.57	499.08	493.29	472.02	459.22	451.30
61000	521.38	513.99	507.40	501.51	479.89	466.87	458.82
62000	529.93	522.42	515.72	509.73	487.75	474.53	466.35
63000	538.48	530.84	524.04	517.95	495.62	482.18	473.87
64000	547.02	539.27	532.36	526.17	503.49	489.83	481.39
65000	555.57	547.70	540.67	534.39	511.36	497.49	488.91
70000	598.31	589.83	582.26	575.50	550.69	535.75	526.52
75000	641.04	631.96	623.85	616.61	590.03	574.02	564.13
80000	683.78	674.09	665.44	657.71	629.36	612.29	601.74
85000	726.52	716.22	707.03	698.82	668.70	650.56	639.34
90000	769.25	758.35	748.63	739.93	708.03	688.83	676.95
95000	811.99	800.48	790.22	781.04	747.37	727.09	714.56
100000	854.72	842.61	831.81	822.14	786.70	765.36	752.17
105000	897.46	884.74	873.40	863.25	826.04	803.63	789.78
110000	940.20	926.87	914.99	904.36	865.37	841.90	827.39
120000	1025.67	1011.13	998.17	986.57	944.04	918.44	902.60
130000	1111.14	1095.39	1081.35	1068.79	1022.71	994.97	977.82
140000	1196.61	1179.65	1164.53	1151.00	1101.38	1071.51	1053.04
150000	1282.09	1263.92	1247.71	1233.22	1180.05	1148.04	1128.26
160000	1367.56	1348.18	1330.89	1315.43	1258.72	1224.58	1203.47
175000	1495.77	1474.57	1455.66	1438.75	1376.73	1339.39	1316.30
200000	1709.45	1685.22	1663.61	1644.29	1573.40	1530.73	1504.34
250000	2136.81	2106.53	2079.51	2055.36	1966.75	1913.41	1880.43
500000	4273.62	4213.05	4159.03	4110.72	3933.50	3826.82	3760.85
1000000	8547.24	8426.10	8318.06	8221.44	7867.00	7653.63	7521.71

9.00%　　　　MONTHLY PAYMENTS

AMOUNT	1 YEAR	2 YEARS	3 YEARS	4 YEARS	5 YEARS	6 YEARS	7 YEARS
100	8.75	4.57	3.18	2.49	2.08	1.80	1.61
200	17.49	9.14	6.36	4.98	4.15	3.61	3.22
500	43.73	22.84	15.90	12.44	10.38	9.01	8.04
1000	87.45	45.68	31.80	24.89	20.76	18.03	16.09
2000	174.90	91.37	63.60	49.77	41.52	36.05	32.18
3000	262.35	137.05	95.40	74.66	62.28	54.08	48.27
4000	349.81	182.74	127.20	99.54	83.03	72.10	64.36
5000	437.26	228.42	159.00	124.43	103.79	90.13	80.45
6000	524.71	274.11	190.80	149.31	124.55	108.15	96.53
7000	612.16	319.79	222.60	174.20	145.31	126.18	112.62
8000	699.61	365.48	254.40	199.08	166.07	144.20	128.71
9000	787.06	411.16	286.20	223.97	186.83	162.23	144.80
10000	874.51	456.85	318.00	248.85	207.58	180.26	160.89
11000	961.97	502.53	349.80	273.74	228.34	198.28	176.98
12000	1049.42	548.22	381.60	298.62	249.10	216.31	193.07
13000	1136.87	593.90	413.40	323.51	269.86	234.33	209.16
14000	1224.32	639.59	445.20	348.39	290.62	252.36	225.25
15000	1311.77	685.27	477.00	373.28	311.38	270.38	241.34
20000	1749.03	913.69	635.99	497.70	415.17	360.51	321.78
25000	2186.29	1142.12	794.99	622.13	518.96	450.64	402.23
30000	2623.54	1370.54	953.99	746.55	622.75	540.77	482.67
35000	3060.80	1598.97	1112.99	870.98	726.54	630.89	563.12
40000	3498.06	1827.39	1271.99	995.40	830.33	721.02	643.56
45000	3935.32	2055.81	1430.99	1119.83	934.13	811.15	724.01
50000	4372.57	2284.24	1589.99	1244.25	1037.92	901.28	804.45
55000	4809.83	2512.66	1748.98	1368.68	1141.71	991.40	884.90
56000	4897.28	2558.35	1780.79	1393.56	1162.47	1009.43	900.99
57000	4984.73	2604.03	1812.58	1418.45	1183.23	1027.46	917.08
58000	5072.19	2649.72	1844.38	1443.33	1203.98	1045.48	933.17
59000	5159.64	2695.40	1876.18	1468.22	1224.74	1063.51	949.26
60000	5247.09	2741.08	1907.98	1493.10	1245.50	1081.53	965.34
61000	5334.54	2786.77	1939.78	1517.99	1266.26	1099.56	981.43
62000	5421.99	2832.45	1971.58	1542.87	1287.02	1117.58	997.52
63000	5509.44	2878.14	2003.38	1567.76	1307.78	1135.61	1013.61
64000	5596.89	2923.82	2035.18	1592.64	1328.53	1153.63	1029.70
65000	5684.35	2969.51	2066.98	1617.53	1349.29	1171.66	1045.79
70000	6121.60	3197.63	2225.98	1741.95	1453.08	1261.79	1126.24
75000	6558.86	3426.36	2384.98	1866.38	1556.88	1351.92	1206.68
80000	6996.12	3654.78	2543.98	1990.80	1660.67	1442.04	1287.13
85000	7433.38	3883.20	2702.98	2115.23	1764.46	1532.17	1367.57
90000	7870.63	4111.63	2861.98	2239.65	1868.25	1622.30	1448.02
95000	8307.89	4340.05	3020.97	2364.08	1972.04	1712.43	1528.46
100000	8745.15	4568.47	3179.97	2488.50	2075.84	1802.55	1608.91
105000	9182.41	4796.90	3338.97	2612.93	2179.63	1892.68	1689.35
110000	9619.66	5025.32	3497.97	2737.35	2283.42	1982.81	1769.80
120000	10494.18	5482.17	3815.97	2986.21	2491.00	2163.06	1930.69
130000	11368.69	5939.02	4133.97	3235.06	2698.59	2343.32	2091.58
140000	12243.21	6395.86	4451.96	3483.91	2906.17	2523.58	2252.47
150000	13117.72	6852.71	4769.96	3732.76	3113.75	2703.83	2413.36
160000	13992.24	7309.56	5087.96	3981.61	3321.34	2884.09	2574.25
175000	15304.01	7994.83	5564.95	4354.88	3632.71	3154.47	2815.59
200000	17490.30	9136.95	6359.95	4977.01	4151.67	3605.11	3217.82
250000	21862.87	11421.19	7949.93	6221.26	5189.59	4506.38	4022.27
500000	43725.74	22842.37	15899.87	12442.52	10379.18	9012.77	8044.54
1000000	87451.48	45684.74	31799.73	24885.04	20758.36	18025.54	16089.08

MONTHLY PAYMENTS   9.00%

AMOUNT	8 YEARS	9 YEARS	10 YEARS	11 YEARS	12 YEARS	13 YEARS	14 YEARS
100	1.47	1.35	1.27	1.20	1.14	1.09	1.05
200	2.93	2.71	2.53	2.39	2.28	2.18	2.10
500	7.33	6.77	6.33	5.98	5.69	5.45	5.24
1000	14.65	13.54	12.67	11.96	11.38	10.90	10.49
2000	29.30	27.09	25.34	23.92	22.76	21.79	20.98
3000	43.95	40.63	38.00	35.88	34.14	32.69	31.47
4000	58.60	54.17	50.67	47.84	45.52	43.59	41.96
5000	73.25	67.71	63.34	59.80	56.90	54.48	52.45
6000	87.90	81.26	76.01	71.76	68.28	65.38	62.94
7000	102.55	94.80	88.67	83.73	79.66	76.28	73.43
8000	117.20	108.34	101.34	95.69	91.04	87.17	83.92
9000	131.85	121.89	114.01	107.65	102.42	98.07	94.40
10000	146.50	135.43	126.68	119.61	113.80	108.97	104.89
11000	161.15	148.97	139.34	131.57	125.18	119.86	115.38
12000	175.80	162.51	152.01	143.53	136.56	130.76	125.87
13000	190.45	176.06	164.68	155.49	147.94	141.66	136.36
14000	205.10	189.60	177.35	167.45	159.32	152.56	146.85
15000	219.75	203.14	190.01	179.41	170.70	163.45	157.34
20000	293.00	270.86	253.35	239.22	227.61	217.94	209.79
25000	366.26	338.57	316.69	299.02	284.51	272.42	262.23
30000	439.51	406.29	380.03	358.82	341.41	326.90	314.68
35000	512.76	474.00	443.37	418.63	398.31	381.39	367.13
40000	586.01	541.72	506.70	478.43	455.21	435.87	419.58
45000	659.26	609.43	570.04	538.24	512.11	490.36	472.02
50000	732.51	677.15	633.38	598.04	569.02	544.84	524.47
55000	805.76	744.86	696.72	657.84	625.92	599.32	576.92
56000	820.41	758.40	709.38	669.81	637.30	610.22	587.41
57000	835.06	771.95	722.05	681.77	648.68	621.12	597.89
58000	849.71	785.49	734.72	693.73	660.06	632.01	608.38
59000	864.36	799.03	747.39	705.69	671.44	642.91	618.87
60000	879.01	812.57	760.05	717.65	682.82	653.81	629.36
61000	893.66	826.12	772.72	729.61	694.20	664.71	639.85
62000	908.31	839.66	785.39	741.57	705.58	675.60	650.34
63000	922.96	853.20	798.06	753.53	716.96	686.50	660.83
64000	937.61	866.75	810.72	765.49	728.34	697.40	671.32
65000	952.26	880.29	823.39	777.45	739.72	708.29	681.81
70000	1025.51	948.00	886.73	837.26	796.62	762.78	734.26
75000	1098.77	1015.72	950.07	897.06	853.52	817.26	786.70
80000	1172.02	1083.43	1013.41	956.86	910.42	871.74	839.15
85000	1245.27	1151.15	1076.74	1016.67	967.33	926.23	891.60
90000	1318.52	1218.86	1140.08	1076.47	1024.23	980.71	944.04
95000	1391.77	1286.58	1203.42	1136.28	1081.13	1035.20	996.49
100000	1465.02	1354.29	1266.76	1196.08	1138.03	1089.68	1048.94
105000	1538.27	1422.01	1330.10	1255.88	1194.93	1144.16	1101.38
110000	1611.52	1489.72	1393.43	1315.69	1251.83	1198.65	1153.83
120000	1758.02	1625.15	1520.11	1435.30	1365.64	1307.62	1258.73
130000	1904.53	1760.58	1646.79	1554.90	1479.44	1416.58	1363.62
140000	2051.03	1896.01	1773.46	1674.51	1593.24	1525.55	1468.51
150000	2197.53	2031.44	1900.14	1794.12	1707.05	1634.52	1573.41
160000	2344.03	2166.87	2026.81	1913.73	1820.85	1743.49	1678.30
175000	2563.79	2370.01	2216.83	2093.14	1991.55	1906.94	1835.64
200000	2930.04	2708.58	2533.52	2392.16	2276.06	2179.36	2097.88
250000	3662.55	3385.73	3166.89	2990.20	2845.08	2724.20	2622.34
500000	7325.10	6771.45	6333.79	5980.40	5690.15	5448.40	5244.69
1000000	14650.20	13542.91	12667.58	11960.80	11380.31	10896.81	10489.38

9.00%   MONTHLY PAYMENTS

AMOUNT	15 YEARS	16 YEARS	17 YEARS	18 YEARS	19 YEARS	20 YEARS	21 YEARS
100	1.01	0.98	0.96	0.94	0.92	0.90	0.88
200	2.03	1.97	1.92	1.87	1.83	1.80	1.77
500	5.07	4.92	4.79	4.68	4.58	4.50	4.42
1000	10.14	9.85	9.59	9.36	9.17	9.00	8.85
2000	20.29	19.69	19.18	18.73	18.34	17.99	17.69
3000	30.43	29.54	28.76	28.09	27.51	26.99	26.54
4000	40.57	39.38	38.35	37.46	36.68	35.99	35.38
5000	50.71	49.23	47.94	46.82	45.84	44.99	44.23
6000	60.86	59.07	57.53	56.19	55.01	53.98	53.07
7000	71.00	68.92	67.12	65.55	64.18	62.98	61.92
8000	81.14	78.76	76.70	74.92	73.35	71.98	70.77
9000	91.28	88.61	86.29	84.28	82.52	80.98	79.61
10000	101.43	98.45	95.88	93.64	91.69	89.97	88.46
11000	111.57	108.30	105.47	103.01	100.86	98.97	97.30
12000	121.71	118.14	115.06	112.37	110.03	107.97	106.15
13000	131.85	127.99	124.64	121.74	119.20	116.96	115.00
14000	142.00	137.83	134.23	131.10	128.37	125.96	123.84
15000	152.14	147.68	143.82	140.47	137.53	134.96	132.69
20000	202.85	196.90	191.76	187.29	183.38	179.95	176.92
25000	253.57	246.13	239.70	234.11	229.22	224.93	221.15
30000	304.28	295.35	287.64	280.93	275.07	269.92	265.37
35000	354.99	344.58	335.58	327.76	320.91	314.90	309.60
40000	405.71	393.81	383.52	374.58	366.76	359.89	353.83
45000	456.42	443.03	431.46	421.40	412.60	404.88	398.06
50000	507.13	492.26	479.40	468.22	458.45	449.86	442.29
55000	557.85	541.48	527.34	515.04	504.29	494.85	486.52
56000	567.99	551.33	536.93	524.41	513.46	503.85	495.37
57000	578.13	561.17	546.52	533.77	522.63	512.84	504.21
58000	588.27	571.02	556.11	543.14	531.80	521.84	513.06
59000	598.42	580.86	565.69	552.50	540.97	530.84	521.90
60000	608.56	590.71	575.28	561.87	550.14	539.84	530.75
61000	618.70	600.55	584.87	571.23	559.31	548.83	539.59
62000	628.85	610.40	594.46	580.60	568.48	557.83	548.44
63000	638.99	620.24	604.05	589.96	577.64	566.83	557.29
64000	649.13	630.09	613.63	599.32	586.81	575.82	566.13
65000	659.27	639.94	623.22	608.69	595.98	584.82	574.98
70000	709.99	689.16	671.16	655.51	641.83	629.81	619.21
75000	760.70	738.39	719.10	702.33	687.67	674.79	663.44
80000	811.41	787.61	767.04	749.16	733.52	719.78	707.66
85000	862.13	836.84	814.98	795.98	779.36	764.77	751.89
90000	912.84	886.06	862.92	842.80	825.21	809.75	796.12
95000	963.55	935.29	910.86	889.62	871.05	854.74	840.35
100000	1014.27	984.52	958.80	936.44	916.90	899.73	884.58
105000	1064.98	1033.74	1006.74	983.27	962.74	944.71	928.81
110000	1115.69	1082.97	1054.68	1030.09	1008.59	989.70	973.04
120000	1217.12	1181.42	1150.56	1123.73	1100.28	1079.67	1061.50
130000	1318.55	1279.87	1246.45	1217.38	1191.97	1169.64	1149.96
140000	1419.97	1378.32	1342.33	1311.02	1283.66	1259.62	1238.41
150000	1521.40	1476.77	1438.21	1404.67	1375.35	1349.59	1326.87
160000	1622.83	1575.23	1534.09	1498.31	1467.03	1439.56	1415.33
175000	1774.97	1722.90	1677.91	1638.78	1604.57	1574.52	1548.02
200000	2028.53	1969.03	1917.61	1872.89	1833.79	1799.45	1769.16
250000	2535.67	2461.29	2397.01	2341.11	2292.24	2249.31	2211.45
500000	5071.33	4922.58	4794.02	4682.22	4584.48	4498.63	4422.91
1000000	10142.67	9845.16	9588.04	9364.45	9168.97	8997.26	8845.81

MONTHLY PAYMENTS   9.00%

AMOUNT	22 YEARS	23 YEARS	24 YEARS	25 YEARS	30 YEARS	35 YEARS	40 YEARS
100	0.87	0.86	0.85	0.84	0.80	0.78	0.77
200	1.74	1.72	1.70	1.68	1.61	1.57	1.54
500	4.36	4.30	4.24	4.20	4.02	3.92	3.86
1000	8.71	8.59	8.49	8.39	8.05	7.84	7.71
2000	17.42	17.19	16.97	16.78	16.09	15.68	15.43
3000	26.14	25.78	25.46	25.18	24.14	23.52	23.14
4000	34.85	34.37	33.95	33.57	32.18	31.36	30.85
5000	43.56	42.96	42.43	41.96	40.23	39.20	38.57
6000	52.27	51.56	50.92	50.35	48.28	47.04	46.28
7000	60.98	60.15	59.41	58.74	56.32	54.88	54.00
8000	69.69	68.74	67.89	67.14	64.37	62.72	61.71
9000	78.41	77.33	76.38	75.53	72.42	70.56	69.42
10000	87.12	85.93	84.87	83.92	80.46	78.40	77.14
11000	95.83	94.52	93.35	92.31	88.51	86.24	84.85
12000	104.54	103.11	101.84	100.70	96.55	94.08	92.56
13000	113.25	111.70	110.33	109.10	104.60	101.92	100.28
14000	121.96	120.30	118.81	117.49	112.65	109.76	107.99
15000	130.68	128.89	127.30	125.88	120.69	117.60	115.70
20000	174.23	171.85	169.73	167.84	160.92	156.80	154.27
25000	217.79	214.82	212.17	209.80	201.16	196.00	192.84
30000	261.35	257.78	254.60	251.76	241.39	235.20	231.41
35000	304.91	300.74	297.03	293.72	281.62	274.40	269.98
40000	348.47	343.71	339.47	335.68	321.85	313.60	308.54
45000	392.03	386.67	381.90	377.64	362.08	352.80	347.11
50000	435.59	429.63	424.33	419.60	402.31	392.00	385.68
55000	479.15	472.60	466.77	461.56	442.54	431.20	424.25
56000	487.86	481.19	475.25	469.95	450.59	439.04	431.96
57000	496.57	489.78	483.74	478.34	458.63	446.88	439.68
58000	505.28	498.38	492.23	486.73	466.68	454.72	447.39
59000	513.99	506.97	500.71	495.13	474.73	462.56	455.10
60000	522.70	515.56	509.20	503.52	482.77	470.40	462.82
61000	531.42	524.15	517.69	511.91	490.82	478.24	470.53
62000	540.13	532.75	526.17	520.30	498.87	486.08	478.24
63000	548.84	541.34	534.66	528.69	506.91	493.92	485.96
64000	557.55	549.93	543.15	537.09	514.96	501.76	493.67
65000	566.26	558.52	551.63	545.48	523.00	509.60	501.38
70000	609.82	601.49	594.07	587.44	563.24	548.80	539.95
75000	653.38	644.45	636.50	629.40	603.47	587.99	578.52
80000	696.94	687.41	678.93	671.36	643.70	627.19	617.09
85000	740.50	730.38	721.36	713.32	683.93	666.39	655.66
90000	784.06	773.34	763.80	755.28	724.16	705.59	694.23
95000	827.62	816.30	806.23	797.24	764.39	744.79	732.79
100000	871.17	859.27	848.66	839.20	804.62	783.99	771.36
105000	914.73	902.23	891.10	881.16	844.85	823.19	809.93
110000	958.29	945.19	933.53	923.12	885.08	862.39	848.50
120000	1045.41	1031.12	1018.40	1007.04	965.55	940.79	925.63
130000	1132.53	1117.05	1103.26	1090.96	1046.01	1019.19	1002.77
140000	1219.64	1202.98	1188.13	1174.87	1126.47	1097.59	1079.91
150000	1306.76	1288.90	1273.00	1258.79	1206.93	1175.99	1157.04
160000	1393.88	1374.83	1357.86	1342.71	1287.40	1254.39	1234.18
175000	1524.56	1503.72	1485.16	1468.59	1408.09	1371.99	1349.88
200000	1742.35	1718.54	1697.33	1678.39	1609.25	1567.99	1542.72
250000	2177.94	2148.17	2121.66	2097.99	2011.56	1959.98	1928.40
500000	4355.87	4296.34	4243.32	4195.98	4023.11	3919.96	3856.81
1000000	8711.74	8592.68	8486.64	8391.96	8046.23	7839.93	7713.61

9.25%   MONTHLY PAYMENTS

AMOUNT	1 YEAR	2 YEARS	3 YEARS	4 YEARS	5 YEARS	6 YEARS	7 YEARS
100	8.76	4.58	3.19	2.50	2.09	1.81	1.62
200	17.51	9.16	6.38	5.00	4.18	3.63	3.24
500	43.78	22.90	15.96	12.50	10.44	9.07	8.11
1000	87.57	45.80	31.92	25.00	20.88	18.15	16.22
2000	175.13	91.60	63.83	50.01	41.76	36.30	32.43
3000	262.70	137.40	95.75	75.01	62.64	54.45	48.65
4000	350.27	183.20	127.66	100.02	83.52	72.60	64.86
5000	437.84	229.00	159.58	125.02	104.40	90.75	81.08
6000	525.40	274.80	191.50	150.02	125.28	108.90	97.30
7000	612.97	320.60	223.41	175.03	146.16	127.05	113.51
8000	700.54	366.40	255.33	200.03	167.04	145.20	129.73
9000	788.11	412.20	287.25	225.04	187.92	163.35	145.95
10000	875.67	458.00	319.16	250.04	208.80	181.50	162.16
11000	963.24	503.79	351.08	275.04	229.68	199.65	178.38
12000	1050.81	549.59	382.99	300.05	250.56	217.80	194.59
13000	1138.38	595.39	414.91	325.05	271.44	235.95	210.81
14000	1225.94	641.19	446.83	350.05	292.32	254.10	227.03
15000	1313.51	686.99	478.74	375.06	313.20	272.25	243.24
20000	1751.35	915.99	638.32	500.08	417.60	363.00	324.32
25000	2189.19	1144.99	797.91	625.10	522.00	453.75	405.41
30000	2627.02	1373.99	957.49	750.12	626.40	544.50	486.49
35000	3064.86	1602.98	1117.07	875.14	730.80	635.25	567.57
40000	3502.70	1831.98	1276.65	1000.16	835.20	725.99	648.65
45000	3940.54	2060.98	1436.23	1125.18	939.60	816.74	729.73
50000	4378.37	2289.98	1595.81	1250.20	1043.99	907.49	810.81
55000	4816.21	2518.97	1755.39	1375.22	1148.39	998.24	891.89
56000	4903.78	2564.77	1787.31	1400.22	1169.27	1016.39	908.11
57000	4991.34	2610.57	1819.22	1425.22	1190.15	1034.54	924.33
58000	5078.91	2656.37	1851.14	1450.23	1211.03	1052.69	940.54
59000	5166.48	2702.17	1883.06	1475.23	1231.91	1070.84	956.76
60000	5254.05	2747.97	1914.97	1500.24	1252.79	1088.99	972.97
61000	5341.61	2793.77	1946.89	1525.24	1273.67	1107.14	989.19
62000	5429.18	2839.57	1978.81	1550.24	1294.55	1125.29	1005.41
63000	5516.75	2885.37	2010.72	1575.25	1315.43	1143.44	1021.62
64000	5604.32	2931.17	2042.64	1600.25	1336.31	1161.59	1037.84
65000	5691.88	2976.97	2074.55	1625.25	1357.19	1179.74	1054.06
70000	6129.72	3205.97	2234.13	1750.27	1461.59	1270.49	1135.14
75000	6567.56	3434.96	2393.72	1875.29	1565.99	1361.24	1216.22
80000	7005.40	3663.96	2553.30	2000.31	1670.39	1451.99	1297.30
85000	7443.23	3892.96	2712.88	2125.33	1774.79	1542.74	1378.38
90000	7881.07	4121.96	2872.46	2250.35	1879.19	1633.49	1459.46
95000	8318.91	4350.96	3032.04	2375.37	1983.59	1724.24	1540.54
100000	8756.75	4579.95	3191.62	2500.39	2087.99	1814.99	1621.62
105000	9194.58	4808.95	3351.20	2625.41	2192.39	1905.74	1702.71
110000	9632.42	5037.95	3510.78	2750.43	2296.79	1996.49	1783.79
120000	10508.09	5495.94	3829.95	3000.47	2505.59	2177.98	1945.95
130000	11383.77	5953.94	4149.11	3250.51	2714.39	2359.48	2108.11
140000	12259.44	6411.93	4468.27	3500.55	2923.19	2540.98	2270.27
150000	13135.12	6869.93	4787.43	3750.59	3131.98	2722.48	2432.44
160000	14010.79	7327.93	5106.59	4000.63	3340.78	2903.98	2594.60
175000	15324.30	8014.92	5585.34	4375.69	3653.98	3176.23	2837.84
200000	17513.49	9159.91	6383.24	5000.78	4175.98	3629.97	3243.25
250000	21891.86	11449.88	7979.05	6250.98	5219.97	4537.47	4054.06
500000	43783.73	22899.77	15958.11	12501.96	10439.95	9074.93	8108.12
1000000	87567.45	45799.53	31916.21	25003.92	20879.90	18149.86	16216.24

MONTHLY PAYMENTS 9.25%

AMOUNT	8 YEARS	9 YEARS	10 YEARS	11 YEARS	12 YEARS	13 YEARS	14 YEARS
100	1.48	1.37	1.28	1.21	1.15	1.10	1.06
200	2.96	2.74	2.56	2.42	2.30	2.21	2.13
500	7.39	6.84	6.40	6.05	5.76	5.52	5.32
1000	14.78	13.68	12.80	12.10	11.52	11.04	10.64
2000	29.56	27.35	25.61	24.20	23.04	22.08	21.27
3000	44.34	41.03	38.41	36.30	34.56	33.12	31.91
4000	59.12	54.70	51.21	48.40	46.09	44.16	42.54
5000	73.90	68.38	64.02	60.50	57.61	55.20	53.18
6000	88.68	82.05	76.82	72.60	69.13	66.24	63.82
7000	103.46	95.73	89.62	84.70	80.65	77.29	74.45
8000	118.24	109.41	102.43	96.79	92.17	88.33	85.09
9000	133.02	123.08	115.23	108.89	103.69	99.37	95.72
10000	147.80	136.76	128.03	120.99	115.22	110.41	106.36
11000	162.58	150.43	140.84	133.09	126.74	121.45	117.00
12000	177.36	164.11	153.64	145.19	138.26	132.49	127.63
13000	192.14	177.79	166.44	157.29	149.78	143.53	138.27
14000	206.92	191.46	179.25	169.39	161.30	154.57	148.90
15000	221.70	205.14	192.05	181.49	172.82	165.61	159.54
20000	295.60	273.52	256.07	241.99	230.43	220.82	212.72
25000	369.51	341.89	320.08	302.48	288.04	276.02	265.90
30000	443.41	410.27	384.10	362.98	345.65	331.22	319.08
35000	517.31	478.65	448.11	423.48	403.25	386.43	372.26
40000	591.21	547.03	512.13	483.97	460.86	441.63	425.44
45000	665.11	615.41	576.15	544.47	518.47	496.84	478.62
50000	739.01	683.79	640.16	604.96	576.08	552.04	531.80
55000	812.91	752.17	704.18	665.46	633.69	607.24	584.98
56000	827.69	765.84	716.98	677.56	645.21	618.28	595.62
57000	842.47	779.52	729.79	689.66	656.73	629.32	606.25
58000	857.25	793.19	742.59	701.76	668.25	640.37	616.89
59000	872.03	806.87	755.39	713.86	679.77	651.41	627.53
60000	886.81	820.55	768.20	725.96	691.29	662.45	638.16
61000	901.59	834.22	781.00	738.06	702.82	673.49	648.80
62000	916.37	847.90	793.80	750.16	714.34	684.53	659.43
63000	931.15	861.57	806.61	762.26	725.86	695.57	670.07
64000	945.93	875.25	819.41	774.36	737.38	706.61	680.71
65000	960.71	888.93	832.21	786.45	748.90	717.65	691.34
70000	1034.62	957.30	896.23	846.95	806.51	772.85	744.52
75000	1108.52	1025.68	960.25	907.45	864.12	828.06	797.70
80000	1182.42	1094.06	1024.26	967.94	921.73	883.26	850.88
85000	1256.32	1162.44	1088.28	1028.44	979.33	938.47	904.06
90000	1330.22	1230.82	1152.29	1088.94	1036.94	993.67	957.24
95000	1404.12	1299.20	1216.31	1149.43	1094.55	1048.87	1010.42
100000	1478.02	1367.58	1280.33	1209.93	1152.16	1104.08	1063.60
105000	1551.92	1435.96	1344.34	1270.43	1209.76	1159.28	1116.78
110000	1625.82	1504.34	1408.36	1330.92	1267.37	1214.49	1169.96
120000	1773.63	1641.09	1536.39	1451.92	1382.59	1324.89	1276.32
130000	1921.43	1777.85	1664.43	1572.91	1497.80	1435.30	1382.68
140000	2069.23	1914.61	1792.46	1693.90	1613.02	1545.71	1489.04
150000	2217.03	2051.37	1920.49	1814.89	1728.23	1656.12	1595.40
160000	2364.84	2188.12	2048.52	1935.89	1843.45	1766.52	1701.76
175000	2586.54	2393.26	2240.57	2117.38	2016.27	1932.14	1861.30
200000	2956.04	2735.15	2560.65	2419.86	2304.31	2208.16	2127.20
250000	3695.06	3418.94	3200.82	3024.82	2880.39	2760.19	2659.00
500000	7390.11	6837.89	6401.64	6049.65	5760.78	5520.39	5318.01
1000000	14780.22	13675.77	12803.27	12099.30	11521.56	11040.78	10636.02

9.25% MONTHLY PAYMENTS

AMOUNT	15 YEARS	16 YEARS	17 YEARS	18 YEARS	19 YEARS	20 YEARS	21 YEARS
100	1.03	1.00	0.97	0.95	0.93	0.92	0.90
200	2.06	2.00	1.95	1.90	1.87	1.83	1.80
500	5.15	5.00	4.87	4.76	4.66	4.58	4.50
1000	10.29	10.00	9.74	9.52	9.33	9.16	9.01
2000	20.58	19.99	19.48	19.04	18.66	18.32	18.02
3000	30.88	29.99	29.23	28.56	27.98	27.48	27.03
4000	41.17	39.99	38.97	38.08	37.31	36.63	36.04
5000	51.46	49.98	48.71	47.61	46.64	45.79	45.05
6000	61.75	59.98	58.45	57.13	55.97	54.95	54.06
7000	72.04	69.98	68.20	66.65	65.30	64.11	63.07
8000	82.34	79.98	77.94	76.17	74.62	73.27	72.08
9000	92.63	89.97	87.68	85.69	83.95	82.43	81.09
10000	102.92	99.97	97.42	95.21	93.28	91.59	90.09
11000	113.21	109.97	107.17	104.73	102.61	100.75	99.10
12000	123.50	119.96	116.91	114.25	111.94	109.90	108.11
13000	133.79	129.96	126.65	123.78	121.27	119.06	117.12
14000	144.09	139.96	136.39	133.30	130.59	128.22	126.13
15000	154.38	149.95	146.14	142.82	139.92	137.38	135.14
20000	205.84	199.94	194.85	190.42	186.56	183.17	180.19
25000	257.30	249.92	243.56	238.03	233.20	228.97	225.24
30000	308.76	299.91	292.27	285.64	279.84	274.76	270.28
35000	360.22	349.89	340.98	333.24	326.48	320.55	315.33
40000	411.68	399.88	389.69	380.85	373.12	366.35	360.38
45000	463.14	449.86	438.41	428.45	419.76	412.14	405.43
50000	514.60	499.85	487.12	476.06	466.40	457.93	450.47
55000	566.06	549.83	535.83	523.67	513.04	503.73	495.52
56000	576.35	559.83	545.57	533.19	522.37	512.89	504.53
57000	586.64	569.83	555.31	542.71	531.70	522.04	513.54
58000	596.93	579.82	565.06	552.23	541.03	531.20	522.55
59000	607.22	589.82	574.80	561.75	550.36	540.36	531.56
60000	617.52	599.82	584.54	571.27	559.68	549.52	540.57
61000	627.81	609.82	594.28	580.79	569.01	558.68	549.58
62000	638.10	619.81	604.03	590.31	578.34	567.84	558.59
63000	648.39	629.81	613.77	599.84	587.67	577.00	567.60
64000	658.68	639.81	623.51	609.36	597.00	586.15	576.60
65000	668.97	649.80	633.25	618.88	606.33	595.31	585.61
70000	720.43	699.79	681.96	666.48	652.97	641.11	630.66
75000	771.89	749.77	730.68	714.09	699.61	686.90	675.71
80000	823.35	799.76	779.39	761.70	746.25	732.69	720.76
85000	874.81	849.74	828.10	809.30	792.89	778.49	765.80
90000	926.27	899.73	876.81	856.91	839.53	824.28	810.85
95000	977.73	949.71	925.52	904.51	886.17	870.07	855.90
100000	1029.19	999.70	974.23	952.12	932.81	915.87	900.94
105000	1080.65	1049.68	1022.95	999.73	979.45	961.66	945.99
110000	1132.11	1099.67	1071.66	1047.33	1026.09	1007.45	991.04
120000	1235.03	1199.64	1169.08	1142.54	1119.37	1099.04	1081.13
130000	1337.95	1299.61	1266.51	1237.75	1212.65	1190.63	1171.23
140000	1440.87	1399.58	1363.93	1332.97	1305.93	1282.21	1261.32
150000	1543.79	1499.55	1461.35	1428.18	1399.21	1373.80	1351.42
160000	1646.71	1599.52	1558.78	1523.39	1492.49	1465.39	1441.51
175000	1801.09	1749.47	1704.91	1666.21	1632.41	1602.77	1576.65
200000	2058.38	1999.39	1948.47	1904.24	1865.62	1831.73	1801.89
250000	2572.98	2499.24	2435.59	2380.30	2332.02	2289.67	2252.36
500000	5145.96	4998.49	4871.17	4760.60	4664.04	4579.33	4504.72
1000000	10291.92	9996.97	9742.35	9521.19	9328.08	9158.67	9009.45

MONTHLY PAYMENTS 9.25%

AMOUNT	22 YEARS	23 YEARS	24 YEARS	25 YEARS	30 YEARS	35 YEARS	40 YEARS
100	0.89	0.88	0.87	0.86	0.82	0.80	0.79
200	1.78	1.75	1.73	1.71	1.65	1.61	1.58
500	4.44	4.38	4.33	4.28	4.11	4.01	3.95
1000	8.88	8.76	8.66	8.56	8.23	8.03	7.91
2000	17.76	17.52	17.31	17.13	16.45	16.05	15.81
3000	26.63	26.28	25.97	25.69	24.68	24.08	23.72
4000	35.51	35.04	34.63	34.26	32.91	32.11	31.63
5000	44.39	43.80	43.28	42.82	41.13	40.14	39.53
6000	53.27	52.56	51.94	51.38	49.36	48.16	47.44
7000	62.14	61.32	60.60	59.95	57.59	56.19	55.35
8000	71.02	70.08	69.25	68.51	65.81	64.22	63.25
9000	79.90	78.85	77.91	77.07	74.04	72.25	71.16
10000	88.78	87.61	86.57	85.64	82.27	80.27	79.07
11000	97.65	96.37	95.22	94.20	90.49	88.30	86.97
12000	106.53	105.13	103.88	102.77	98.72	96.33	94.88
13000	115.41	113.89	112.54	111.33	106.95	104.36	102.79
14000	124.29	122.65	121.19	119.89	115.17	112.38	110.69
15000	133.16	131.41	129.85	128.46	123.40	120.41	118.60
20000	177.55	175.21	173.13	171.28	164.54	160.55	158.13
25000	221.94	219.01	216.41	214.10	205.67	200.69	197.67
30000	266.33	262.82	259.70	256.91	246.80	240.82	237.20
35000	310.71	306.62	302.98	299.73	287.94	280.96	276.73
40000	355.10	350.42	346.26	342.55	329.07	321.10	316.26
45000	399.49	394.23	389.54	385.37	370.20	361.23	355.80
50000	443.88	438.03	432.83	428.19	411.34	401.37	395.33
55000	488.26	481.83	476.11	471.01	452.47	441.51	434.86
56000	497.14	490.59	484.77	479.57	460.70	449.54	442.77
57000	506.02	499.35	493.42	488.14	468.92	457.56	450.68
58000	514.90	508.11	502.08	496.70	477.15	465.59	458.58
59000	523.78	516.87	510.74	505.27	485.38	473.62	466.49
60000	532.65	525.63	519.39	513.83	493.61	481.65	474.40
61000	541.53	534.39	528.05	522.39	501.83	489.67	482.30
62000	550.41	543.16	536.71	530.96	510.06	497.70	490.21
63000	559.29	551.92	545.36	539.52	518.29	505.73	498.12
64000	568.16	560.68	554.02	548.08	526.51	513.76	506.02
65000	577.04	569.44	562.68	556.65	534.74	521.78	513.93
70000	621.43	613.24	605.96	599.47	575.87	561.92	553.46
75000	665.82	657.04	649.24	642.29	617.01	602.06	593.00
80000	710.20	700.85	692.52	685.11	658.14	642.20	632.53
85000	754.59	744.65	735.81	727.92	699.27	682.33	672.06
90000	798.98	788.45	779.09	770.74	740.41	722.47	711.59
95000	843.37	832.25	822.37	813.56	781.54	762.61	751.13
100000	887.75	876.06	865.66	856.38	822.68	802.74	790.66
105000	932.14	919.86	908.94	899.20	863.81	842.88	830.19
110000	976.53	963.66	952.22	942.02	904.94	883.02	869.73
120000	1065.31	1051.27	1038.79	1027.66	987.21	963.29	948.79
130000	1154.08	1138.87	1125.35	1113.30	1069.48	1043.57	1027.86
140000	1242.86	1226.48	1211.92	1198.93	1151.75	1123.84	1106.92
150000	1331.63	1314.09	1298.48	1284.57	1234.01	1204.12	1185.99
160000	1420.41	1401.69	1385.05	1370.21	1316.28	1284.39	1265.06
175000	1553.57	1533.10	1514.90	1498.67	1439.68	1404.80	1383.66
200000	1775.51	1752.11	1731.31	1712.76	1645.35	1605.49	1581.32
250000	2219.39	2190.14	2164.14	2140.95	2056.69	2006.86	1976.65
500000	4438.77	4380.29	4328.28	4281.91	4113.38	4013.72	3953.30
1000000	8877.54	8760.57	8656.55	8563.82	8226.75	8027.44	7906.61

9.50%   MONTHLY PAYMENTS

AMOUNT	1 YEAR	2 YEARS	3 YEARS	4 YEARS	5 YEARS	6 YEARS	7 YEARS
100	8.77	4.59	3.20	2.51	2.10	1.83	1.63
200	17.54	9.18	6.41	5.02	4.20	3.65	3.27
500	43.84	22.96	16.02	12.56	10.50	9.14	8.17
1000	87.68	45.91	32.03	25.12	21.00	18.27	16.34
2000	175.37	91.83	64.07	50.25	42.00	36.55	32.69
3000	263.05	137.74	96.10	75.37	63.01	54.82	49.03
4000	350.73	183.66	128.13	100.49	84.01	73.10	65.38
5000	438.42	229.57	160.16	125.62	105.01	91.37	81.72
6000	526.10	275.49	192.20	150.74	126.01	109.65	98.06
7000	613.78	321.40	224.23	175.86	147.01	127.92	114.41
8000	701.47	367.32	256.26	200.99	168.01	146.20	130.75
9000	789.15	413.23	288.30	226.11	189.02	164.47	147.10
10000	876.84	459.14	320.33	251.23	210.02	182.75	163.44
11000	964.52	505.06	352.36	276.35	231.02	201.02	179.78
12000	1052.20	550.97	384.40	301.48	252.02	219.30	196.13
13000	1139.89	596.89	416.43	326.60	273.02	237.57	212.47
14000	1227.57	642.80	448.46	351.72	294.03	255.85	228.82
15000	1315.25	688.72	480.49	376.85	315.03	274.12	245.16
20000	1753.67	918.29	640.66	502.46	420.04	365.49	326.88
25000	2192.09	1147.86	800.82	628.08	525.05	456.87	408.60
30000	2630.51	1377.43	960.99	753.69	630.06	548.24	490.32
35000	3068.92	1607.01	1121.15	879.31	735.07	639.61	572.04
40000	3507.34	1836.58	1281.32	1004.93	840.07	730.99	653.76
45000	3945.76	2066.15	1441.48	1130.54	945.08	822.36	735.48
50000	4384.18	2295.72	1601.65	1256.16	1050.09	913.73	817.20
55000	4822.59	2525.30	1761.81	1381.77	1155.10	1005.11	898.92
56000	4910.28	2571.21	1793.85	1406.90	1176.10	1023.38	915.26
57000	4997.96	2617.13	1825.88	1432.02	1197.11	1041.66	931.61
58000	5085.64	2663.04	1857.91	1457.14	1218.11	1059.93	947.95
59000	5173.33	2708.96	1889.94	1482.27	1239.11	1078.21	964.29
60000	5261.01	2754.87	1921.98	1507.39	1260.11	1096.48	980.64
61000	5348.69	2800.78	1954.01	1532.51	1281.11	1114.76	996.98
62000	5436.38	2846.70	1986.04	1557.63	1302.12	1133.03	1013.33
63000	5524.06	2892.61	2018.08	1582.76	1323.12	1151.31	1029.67
64000	5611.74	2938.53	2050.11	1607.88	1344.12	1169.58	1046.01
65000	5699.43	2984.44	2082.14	1633.00	1365.12	1187.85	1062.36
70000	6137.85	3214.01	2242.31	1758.62	1470.13	1279.23	1144.08
75000	6576.26	3443.59	2402.47	1884.24	1575.14	1370.60	1225.80
80000	7014.68	3673.16	2562.64	2009.85	1680.15	1461.98	1307.52
85000	7453.10	3902.73	2722.80	2135.47	1785.16	1553.35	1389.24
90000	7891.52	4132.30	2882.97	2261.08	1890.17	1644.72	1470.96
95000	8329.93	4361.88	3043.13	2386.70	1995.18	1736.10	1552.68
100000	8768.35	4591.45	3203.29	2512.31	2100.19	1827.47	1634.40
105000	9206.77	4821.02	3363.46	2637.93	2205.20	1918.84	1716.12
110000	9645.19	5050.59	3523.62	2763.55	2310.20	2010.22	1797.84
120000	10522.02	5509.74	3843.95	3014.78	2520.22	2192.96	1961.28
130000	11398.86	5968.88	4164.28	3266.01	2730.24	2375.71	2124.72
140000	12275.69	6428.03	4484.61	3517.24	2940.26	2558.46	2288.16
150000	13152.53	6887.17	4804.94	3768.47	3150.28	2741.20	2451.60
160000	14029.36	7346.32	5125.27	4019.70	3360.30	2923.95	2615.04
175000	15344.61	8035.04	5605.77	4396.55	3675.33	3198.07	2860.20
200000	17536.70	9182.90	6406.59	5024.63	4200.37	3654.94	3268.80
250000	21920.88	11478.62	8008.24	6280.78	5250.47	4568.67	4086.00
500000	43841.76	22957.25	16016.47	12561.57	10500.93	9137.35	8171.99
1000000	87683.51	45914.49	32032.95	25123.14	21001.86	18274.69	16343.98

MONTHLY PAYMENTS 9.50%

AMOUNT	8 YEARS	9 YEARS	10 YEARS	11 YEARS	12 YEARS	13 YEARS	14 YEARS
100	1.49	1.38	1.29	1.22	1.17	1.12	1.08
200	2.98	2.76	2.59	2.45	2.33	2.24	2.16
500	7.46	6.90	6.47	6.12	5.83	5.59	5.39
1000	14.91	13.81	12.94	12.24	11.66	11.19	10.78
2000	29.82	27.62	25.88	24.48	23.33	22.37	21.57
3000	44.73	41.43	38.82	36.72	34.99	33.56	32.35
4000	59.64	55.24	51.76	48.95	46.65	44.74	43.13
5000	74.55	69.05	64.70	61.19	58.32	55.93	53.92
6000	89.47	82.86	77.64	73.43	69.98	67.11	64.70
7000	104.38	96.67	90.58	85.67	81.65	78.30	75.49
8000	119.29	110.47	103.52	97.91	93.31	89.49	86.27
9000	134.20	124.28	116.46	110.15	104.97	100.67	97.05
10000	149.11	138.09	129.40	122.39	116.64	111.86	107.84
11000	164.02	151.90	142.34	134.63	128.30	123.04	118.62
12000	178.93	165.71	155.28	146.86	139.96	134.23	129.40
13000	193.84	179.52	168.22	159.10	151.63	145.41	140.19
14000	208.75	193.33	181.16	171.34	163.29	156.60	150.97
15000	223.66	207.14	194.10	183.58	174.96	167.79	161.76
20000	298.22	276.19	258.80	244.77	233.27	223.71	215.67
25000	372.77	345.23	323.49	305.97	291.59	279.64	269.59
30000	447.33	414.28	388.19	367.16	349.91	335.57	323.51
35000	521.88	483.33	452.89	428.35	408.23	391.50	377.43
40000	596.44	552.37	517.59	489.55	466.55	447.43	431.35
45000	670.99	621.42	582.29	550.74	524.87	503.36	485.27
50000	745.54	690.47	646.99	611.93	583.19	559.29	539.18
55000	820.10	759.51	711.69	673.13	641.51	615.21	593.10
56000	835.01	773.32	724.63	685.36	653.17	626.40	603.89
57000	849.92	787.13	737.57	697.60	664.83	637.59	614.67
58000	864.83	800.94	750.51	709.84	676.50	648.77	625.45
59000	879.74	814.75	763.45	722.08	688.16	659.96	636.24
60000	894.65	828.56	776.39	734.32	699.82	671.14	647.02
61000	909.56	842.37	789.33	746.56	711.49	682.33	657.80
62000	924.48	856.18	802.26	758.80	723.15	693.51	668.59
63000	939.39	869.99	815.20	771.03	734.82	704.70	679.37
64000	954.30	883.80	828.14	783.27	746.48	715.89	690.16
65000	969.21	897.61	841.08	795.51	758.14	727.07	700.94
70000	1043.76	966.66	905.78	856.71	816.46	783.00	754.86
75000	1118.32	1035.70	970.48	917.90	874.78	838.93	808.78
80000	1192.87	1104.75	1035.18	979.09	933.10	894.86	862.69
85000	1267.43	1173.80	1099.88	1040.28	991.42	950.79	916.61
90000	1341.98	1242.84	1164.58	1101.48	1049.74	1006.71	970.53
95000	1416.53	1311.89	1229.28	1162.67	1108.05	1062.64	1024.45
100000	1491.09	1380.94	1293.98	1223.86	1166.37	1118.57	1078.37
105000	1565.64	1449.98	1358.67	1285.06	1224.69	1174.50	1132.29
110000	1640.20	1519.03	1423.37	1346.25	1283.01	1230.43	1186.20
120000	1789.31	1657.12	1552.77	1468.64	1399.65	1342.29	1294.04
130000	1938.42	1795.22	1682.17	1591.02	1516.29	1454.14	1401.88
140000	2087.52	1933.31	1811.57	1713.41	1632.92	1566.00	1509.72
150000	2236.63	2071.40	1940.96	1835.80	1749.56	1677.86	1617.55
160000	2385.74	2209.50	2070.36	1958.18	1866.20	1789.72	1725.39
175000	2609.41	2416.64	2264.46	2141.76	2041.15	1957.50	1887.14
200000	2982.18	2761.87	2587.95	2447.73	2332.75	2237.14	2156.74
250000	3727.72	3452.34	3234.94	3059.66	2915.93	2796.43	2695.92
500000	7455.44	6904.68	6469.88	6119.32	5831.87	5592.86	5391.84
1000000	14910.89	13809.36	12939.76	12238.65	11663.73	11185.72	10783.68

9.50%　　　MONTHLY PAYMENTS

AMOUNT	15 YEARS	16 YEARS	17 YEARS	18 YEARS	19 YEARS	20 YEARS	21 YEARS
100	1.04	1.01	0.99	0.97	0.95	0.93	0.92
200	2.09	2.03	1.98	1.94	1.90	1.86	1.83
500	5.22	5.07	4.95	4.84	4.74	4.66	4.59
1000	10.44	10.15	9.90	9.68	9.49	9.32	9.17
2000	20.88	20.30	19.80	19.36	18.98	18.64	18.35
3000	31.33	30.45	29.69	29.04	28.47	27.96	27.52
4000	41.77	40.60	39.59	38.72	37.95	37.29	36.70
5000	52.21	50.75	49.49	48.40	47.44	46.61	45.87
6000	62.65	60.90	59.39	58.07	56.93	55.93	55.05
7000	73.10	71.05	69.28	67.75	66.42	65.25	64.22
8000	83.54	81.20	79.18	77.43	75.91	74.57	73.39
9000	93.98	91.35	89.08	87.11	85.40	83.89	82.57
10000	104.42	101.50	98.98	96.79	94.88	93.21	91.74
11000	114.86	111.65	108.88	106.47	104.37	102.53	100.92
12000	125.31	121.80	118.77	116.15	113.86	111.86	110.09
13000	135.75	131.95	128.67	125.83	123.35	121.18	119.27
14000	146.19	142.10	138.57	135.51	132.84	130.50	128.44
15000	156.63	152.25	148.47	145.19	142.33	139.82	137.62
20000	208.84	203.00	197.96	193.58	189.77	186.43	183.49
25000	261.06	253.75	247.45	241.98	237.21	233.03	229.36
30000	313.27	304.50	296.93	290.37	284.65	279.64	275.23
35000	365.48	355.25	346.42	338.77	332.09	326.25	321.10
40000	417.69	406.00	395.91	387.16	379.54	372.85	366.97
45000	469.90	456.75	445.40	435.56	426.98	419.46	412.85
50000	522.11	507.49	494.89	483.96	474.42	466.07	458.72
55000	574.32	558.24	544.38	532.35	521.86	512.67	504.59
56000	584.77	568.39	554.28	542.03	531.35	521.99	513.76
57000	595.21	578.54	564.17	551.71	540.84	531.31	522.94
58000	605.65	588.69	574.07	561.39	550.33	540.64	532.11
59000	616.09	598.84	583.97	571.07	559.82	549.96	541.29
60000	626.53	608.99	593.87	580.75	569.30	559.28	550.46
61000	636.98	619.14	603.77	590.43	578.79	568.60	559.63
62000	647.42	629.29	613.66	600.11	588.28	577.92	568.81
63000	657.86	639.44	623.56	609.78	597.77	587.24	577.98
64000	668.30	649.59	633.46	619.46	607.26	596.56	587.16
65000	678.75	659.74	643.36	629.14	616.75	605.89	596.33
70000	730.96	710.49	692.85	677.54	664.19	652.49	642.20
75000	783.17	761.24	742.34	725.93	711.63	699.10	688.08
80000	835.38	811.99	791.82	774.33	759.07	745.70	733.95
85000	887.59	862.74	841.31	822.72	806.51	792.31	779.82
90000	939.80	913.49	890.80	871.12	853.96	838.92	825.69
95000	992.01	964.24	940.29	919.52	901.40	885.52	871.56
100000	1044.22	1014.99	989.78	967.91	948.84	932.13	917.43
105000	1096.44	1065.74	1039.27	1016.31	996.28	978.74	963.31
110000	1148.65	1116.49	1088.76	1064.70	1043.72	1025.34	1009.18
120000	1253.07	1217.99	1187.74	1161.49	1138.61	1118.56	1100.92
130000	1357.49	1319.49	1286.71	1258.28	1233.49	1211.77	1192.66
140000	1461.91	1420.99	1385.69	1355.08	1328.38	1304.98	1284.41
150000	1566.34	1522.48	1484.67	1451.87	1423.26	1398.20	1376.15
160000	1670.76	1623.98	1583.65	1548.66	1518.14	1491.41	1467.89
175000	1827.39	1776.23	1732.12	1693.85	1660.47	1631.23	1605.51
200000	2088.45	2029.98	1979.56	1935.82	1897.68	1864.26	1834.87
250000	2610.56	2537.47	2474.45	2419.78	2372.10	2330.33	2293.59
500000	5221.12	5074.95	4948.90	4839.56	4744.20	4660.66	4587.17
1000000	10442.25	10149.90	9897.81	9679.11	9488.40	9321.31	9174.34

MONTHLY PAYMENTS 9.50%

AMOUNT	22 YEARS	23 YEARS	24 YEARS	25 YEARS	30 YEARS	35 YEARS	40 YEARS
100	0.90	0.89	0.88	0.87	0.84	0.82	0.81
200	1.81	1.79	1.77	1.75	1.68	1.64	1.62
500	4.52	4.46	4.41	4.37	4.20	4.11	4.05
1000	9.04	8.93	8.83	8.74	8.41	8.22	8.10
2000	18.09	17.86	17.66	17.47	16.82	16.43	16.20
3000	27.13	26.79	26.48	26.21	25.23	24.65	24.30
4000	36.18	35.72	35.31	34.95	33.63	32.86	32.40
5000	45.22	44.65	44.14	43.68	42.04	41.08	40.50
6000	54.27	53.58	52.97	52.42	50.45	49.30	48.60
7000	63.31	62.51	61.79	61.16	58.86	57.51	56.70
8000	72.36	71.44	70.62	69.90	67.27	65.73	64.80
9000	81.40	80.37	79.45	78.63	75.68	73.95	72.91
10000	90.45	89.30	88.28	87.37	84.09	82.16	81.01
11000	99.49	98.23	97.11	96.11	92.49	90.38	89.11
12000	108.54	107.16	105.93	104.84	100.90	98.59	97.21
13000	117.58	116.09	114.76	113.58	109.31	106.81	105.31
14000	126.62	125.02	123.59	122.32	117.72	115.03	113.41
15000	135.67	133.95	132.42	131.05	126.13	123.24	121.51
20000	180.89	178.59	176.55	174.74	168.17	164.32	162.01
25000	226.12	223.24	220.69	218.42	210.21	205.40	202.52
30000	271.34	267.89	264.83	262.11	252.26	246.48	243.02
35000	316.56	312.54	308.97	305.79	294.30	287.56	283.52
40000	361.78	357.19	353.11	349.48	336.34	328.64	324.02
45000	407.01	401.84	397.25	393.16	378.38	369.73	364.53
50000	452.23	446.49	441.39	436.85	420.43	410.81	405.03
55000	497.45	491.14	485.53	480.53	462.47	451.89	445.53
56000	506.50	500.07	494.35	489.27	470.88	460.10	453.63
57000	515.54	509.00	503.18	498.01	479.29	468.32	461.74
58000	524.59	517.93	512.01	506.74	487.70	476.53	469.84
59000	533.63	526.85	520.84	515.48	496.10	484.75	477.94
60000	542.68	535.78	529.66	524.22	504.51	492.97	486.04
61000	551.72	544.71	538.49	532.95	512.92	501.18	494.14
62000	560.77	553.64	547.32	541.69	521.33	509.40	502.24
63000	569.81	562.57	556.15	550.43	529.74	517.62	510.34
64000	578.86	571.50	564.98	559.17	538.15	525.83	518.44
65000	587.90	580.43	573.80	567.90	546.56	534.05	526.54
70000	633.12	625.08	617.94	611.59	588.60	575.13	567.04
75000	678.35	669.73	662.08	655.27	630.64	616.21	607.55
80000	723.57	714.38	706.22	698.96	672.68	657.29	648.05
85000	768.79	759.03	750.36	742.64	714.73	698.37	688.55
90000	814.02	803.68	794.50	786.33	756.77	739.45	729.06
95000	859.24	848.33	838.64	830.01	798.81	780.53	769.56
100000	904.46	892.97	882.77	873.70	840.85	821.61	810.06
105000	949.68	937.62	926.91	917.38	882.90	862.69	850.56
110000	994.91	982.27	971.05	961.07	924.94	903.77	891.07
120000	1085.35	1071.57	1059.33	1048.44	1009.03	985.93	972.07
130000	1175.80	1160.87	1147.61	1135.81	1093.11	1068.10	1053.08
140000	1266.25	1250.16	1235.88	1223.18	1177.20	1150.26	1134.09
150000	1356.69	1339.46	1324.16	1310.54	1261.28	1232.42	1215.09
160000	1447.14	1428.76	1412.44	1397.91	1345.37	1314.58	1296.10
175000	1582.81	1562.70	1544.86	1528.97	1471.49	1437.82	1417.61
200000	1808.92	1785.95	1765.55	1747.39	1681.71	1643.22	1620.12
250000	2261.15	2232.44	2206.94	2184.24	2102.14	2054.03	2025.15
500000	4522.31	4464.87	4413.87	4368.48	4204.27	4108.06	4050.31
1000000	9044.61	8929.74	8827.75	8736.97	8408.54	8216.12	8100.62

9.75%   MONTHLY PAYMENTS

AMOUNT	1 YEAR	2 YEARS	3 YEARS	4 YEARS	5 YEARS	6 YEARS	7 YEARS
100	8.78	4.60	3.21	2.52	2.11	1.84	1.65
200	17.56	9.21	6.43	5.05	4.22	3.68	3.29
500	43.90	23.01	16.07	12.62	10.56	9.20	8.24
1000	87.80	46.03	32.15	25.24	21.12	18.40	16.47
2000	175.60	92.06	64.30	50.49	42.25	36.80	32.94
3000	263.40	138.09	96.45	75.73	63.37	55.20	49.42
4000	351.20	184.12	128.60	100.97	84.50	73.60	65.89
5000	439.00	230.15	160.75	126.21	105.62	92.00	82.36
6000	526.80	276.18	192.90	151.46	126.75	110.40	98.83
7000	614.60	322.21	225.05	176.70	147.87	128.80	115.31
8000	702.40	368.24	257.20	201.94	168.99	147.20	131.78
9000	790.20	414.27	289.35	227.18	190.12	165.60	148.25
10000	878.00	460.30	321.50	252.43	211.24	184.00	164.72
11000	965.80	506.33	353.65	277.67	232.37	202.40	181.20
12000	1053.60	552.36	385.80	302.91	253.49	220.80	197.67
13000	1141.40	598.39	417.95	328.15	274.62	239.20	214.14
14000	1229.20	644.41	450.10	353.40	295.74	257.60	230.61
15000	1316.99	690.44	482.25	378.64	316.86	276.00	247.08
20000	1755.99	920.59	643.00	504.85	422.48	368.00	329.45
25000	2194.99	1150.74	803.75	631.07	528.11	460.00	411.81
30000	2633.99	1380.89	964.50	757.28	633.73	552.00	494.17
35000	3072.99	1611.04	1125.25	883.49	739.35	644.00	576.53
40000	3511.99	1841.18	1286.00	1009.71	844.97	736.00	658.89
45000	3950.98	2071.33	1446.75	1135.92	950.59	828.00	741.25
50000	4389.98	2301.48	1607.50	1262.13	1056.21	920.00	823.61
55000	4828.98	2531.63	1768.25	1388.35	1161.83	1012.00	905.98
56000	4916.78	2577.66	1800.40	1413.59	1182.96	1030.40	922.45
57000	5004.58	2623.69	1832.55	1438.83	1204.08	1048.80	938.92
58000	5092.38	2669.72	1864.70	1464.08	1225.21	1067.20	955.39
59000	5180.18	2715.75	1896.85	1489.32	1246.33	1085.60	971.87
60000	5267.98	2761.78	1929.00	1514.56	1267.45	1104.00	988.34
61000	5355.78	2807.81	1961.15	1539.80	1288.58	1122.40	1004.81
62000	5443.58	2853.84	1993.30	1565.05	1309.70	1140.80	1021.28
63000	5531.38	2899.87	2025.45	1590.29	1330.83	1159.20	1037.75
64000	5619.18	2945.90	2057.60	1615.53	1351.95	1177.60	1054.23
65000	5706.98	2991.93	2089.75	1640.77	1373.08	1196.00	1070.70
70000	6145.98	3222.07	2250.50	1766.99	1478.70	1288.00	1153.06
75000	6584.97	3452.22	2411.25	1893.20	1584.32	1380.00	1235.42
80000	7023.97	3682.37	2572.00	2019.42	1689.94	1472.00	1317.78
85000	7462.97	3912.52	2732.74	2145.63	1795.56	1564.00	1400.15
90000	7901.97	4142.67	2893.49	2271.84	1901.18	1656.00	1482.51
95000	8340.97	4372.81	3054.24	2398.06	2006.80	1748.00	1564.87
100000	8779.97	4602.96	3214.99	2524.27	2112.42	1840.00	1647.23
105000	9218.96	4833.11	3375.74	2650.48	2218.05	1932.00	1729.59
110000	9657.96	5063.26	3536.49	2776.70	2323.67	2024.00	1811.95
120000	10535.96	5523.55	3857.99	3029.12	2534.91	2208.00	1976.68
130000	11413.96	5983.85	4179.49	3281.55	2746.15	2392.00	2141.40
140000	12291.95	6444.15	4500.99	3533.98	2957.39	2576.00	2306.12
150000	13169.95	6904.44	4822.49	3786.40	3168.64	2760.00	2470.84
160000	14047.95	7364.74	5143.99	4038.83	3379.88	2944.00	2635.57
175000	15364.94	8055.18	5626.24	4417.47	3696.74	3220.00	2882.65
200000	17559.93	9205.92	6429.99	5048.54	4224.85	3680.00	3294.46
250000	21949.91	11507.41	8037.49	6310.67	5281.06	4600.00	4118.07
500000	43899.83	23014.81	16074.97	12621.35	10562.12	9200.01	8236.15
1000000	87799.66	46029.62	32149.94	25242.69	21124.24	18400.02	16472.30

MONTHLY PAYMENTS 9.75%

AMOUNT	8 YEARS	9 YEARS	10 YEARS	11 YEARS	12 YEARS	13 YEARS	14 YEARS
100	1.50	1.39	1.31	1.24	1.18	1.13	1.09
200	3.01	2.79	2.62	2.48	2.36	2.27	2.19
500	7.52	6.97	6.54	6.19	5.90	5.67	5.47
1000	15.04	13.94	13.08	12.38	11.81	11.33	10.93
2000	30.08	27.89	26.15	24.76	23.61	22.66	21.86
3000	45.13	41.83	39.23	37.14	35.42	33.99	32.80
4000	60.17	55.77	52.31	49.52	47.23	45.33	43.73
5000	75.21	69.72	65.39	61.89	59.03	56.66	54.66
6000	90.25	83.66	78.46	74.27	70.84	67.99	65.59
7000	105.30	97.61	91.54	86.65	82.65	79.32	76.53
8000	120.34	111.55	104.62	99.03	94.45	90.65	87.46
9000	135.38	125.49	117.69	111.41	106.26	101.98	98.39
10000	150.42	139.44	130.77	123.79	118.07	113.32	109.32
11000	165.46	153.38	143.85	136.17	129.87	124.65	120.26
12000	180.51	167.32	156.92	148.55	141.68	135.98	131.19
13000	195.55	181.27	170.00	160.92	153.49	147.31	142.12
14000	210.59	195.21	183.08	173.30	165.30	158.64	153.05
15000	225.63	209.15	196.16	185.68	177.10	169.97	163.99
20000	300.84	278.87	261.54	247.58	236.14	226.63	218.65
25000	376.06	348.59	326.93	309.47	295.17	283.29	273.31
30000	451.27	418.31	392.31	371.37	354.20	339.95	327.97
35000	526.48	488.03	457.70	433.26	413.24	396.61	382.63
40000	601.69	557.75	523.08	495.15	472.27	453.27	437.29
45000	676.90	627.46	588.47	557.05	531.31	509.92	491.96
50000	752.11	697.18	653.85	618.94	590.34	566.58	546.62
55000	827.32	766.90	719.24	680.84	649.37	623.24	601.28
56000	842.36	780.85	732.31	693.22	661.18	634.57	612.21
57000	857.41	794.79	745.39	705.59	672.99	645.90	623.14
58000	872.45	808.73	758.47	717.97	684.79	657.23	634.08
59000	887.49	822.68	771.54	730.35	696.60	668.57	645.01
60000	902.53	836.62	784.62	742.73	708.41	679.90	655.94
61000	917.57	850.56	797.70	755.11	720.22	691.23	666.87
62000	932.62	864.51	810.78	767.49	732.02	702.56	677.81
63000	947.66	878.45	823.85	779.87	743.83	713.89	688.74
64000	962.70	892.39	836.93	792.25	755.64	725.22	699.67
65000	977.74	906.34	850.01	804.62	767.44	736.56	710.60
70000	1052.95	976.06	915.39	866.52	826.48	793.21	765.26
75000	1128.17	1045.77	980.78	928.41	885.51	849.87	819.93
80000	1203.38	1115.49	1046.16	990.31	944.54	906.53	874.59
85000	1278.59	1185.21	1111.55	1052.20	1003.58	963.19	929.25
90000	1353.80	1254.93	1176.93	1114.10	1062.61	1019.85	983.91
95000	1429.01	1324.65	1242.32	1175.99	1121.65	1076.50	1038.57
100000	1504.22	1394.37	1307.70	1237.88	1180.68	1133.16	1093.24
105000	1579.43	1464.08	1373.09	1299.78	1239.71	1189.82	1147.90
110000	1654.64	1533.80	1438.47	1361.67	1298.75	1246.48	1202.56
120000	1805.06	1673.24	1569.24	1485.46	1416.82	1359.80	1311.88
130000	1955.49	1812.68	1700.01	1609.25	1534.88	1473.11	1421.21
140000	2105.91	1952.11	1830.78	1733.04	1652.95	1586.43	1530.53
150000	2256.33	2091.55	1961.55	1856.83	1771.02	1699.74	1639.85
160000	2406.75	2230.99	2092.32	1980.61	1889.09	1813.06	1749.18
175000	2632.39	2440.14	2288.48	2166.30	2066.19	1983.03	1913.16
200000	3008.44	2788.73	2615.40	2475.77	2361.36	2266.33	2186.47
250000	3760.55	3485.92	3269.26	3094.71	2951.70	2832.91	2733.09
500000	7521.10	6971.83	6538.51	6189.42	5903.40	5665.81	5466.18
1000000	15042.20	13943.67	13077.02	12378.84	11806.81	11331.63	10932.35

9.75% MONTHLY PAYMENTS

AMOUNT	15 YEARS	16 YEARS	17 YEARS	18 YEARS	19 YEARS	20 YEARS	21 YEARS
100	1.06	1.03	1.01	0.98	0.96	0.95	0.93
200	2.12	2.06	2.01	1.97	1.93	1.90	1.87
500	5.30	5.15	5.03	4.92	4.82	4.74	4.67
1000	10.59	10.30	10.05	9.84	9.65	9.49	9.34
2000	21.19	20.61	20.11	19.68	19.30	18.97	18.68
3000	31.78	30.91	30.16	29.51	28.95	28.46	28.02
4000	42.37	41.22	40.22	39.35	38.60	37.94	37.36
5000	52.97	51.52	50.27	49.19	48.25	47.43	46.70
6000	63.56	61.82	60.33	59.03	57.90	56.91	56.04
7000	74.16	72.13	70.38	68.87	67.55	66.40	65.38
8000	84.75	82.43	80.44	78.71	77.20	75.88	74.72
9000	95.34	92.74	90.49	88.54	86.85	85.37	84.06
10000	105.94	103.04	100.54	98.38	96.50	94.85	93.40
11000	116.53	113.34	110.60	108.22	106.15	104.34	102.75
12000	127.12	123.65	120.65	118.06	115.80	113.82	112.09
13000	137.72	133.95	130.71	127.90	125.45	123.31	121.43
14000	148.31	144.25	140.76	137.73	135.10	132.79	130.77
15000	158.90	154.56	150.82	147.57	144.75	142.28	140.11
20000	211.87	206.08	201.09	196.76	193.00	189.70	186.81
25000	264.84	257.60	251.36	245.96	241.25	237.13	233.51
30000	317.81	309.12	301.63	295.15	289.50	284.56	280.21
35000	370.78	360.64	351.90	344.34	337.75	331.98	326.92
40000	423.75	412.16	402.18	393.53	386.00	379.41	373.62
45000	476.71	463.68	452.45	442.72	434.25	426.83	420.32
50000	529.68	515.20	502.72	491.91	482.50	474.26	467.02
55000	582.65	566.72	552.99	541.10	530.74	521.68	513.73
56000	593.24	577.02	563.05	550.94	540.39	531.17	523.07
57000	603.84	587.32	573.10	560.78	550.04	540.65	532.41
58000	614.43	597.63	583.16	570.62	559.69	550.14	541.75
59000	625.02	607.93	593.21	580.45	569.34	559.62	551.09
60000	635.62	618.23	603.26	590.29	578.99	569.11	560.43
61000	646.21	628.54	613.32	600.13	588.64	578.60	569.77
62000	656.80	638.84	623.37	609.97	598.29	588.08	579.11
63000	667.40	649.15	633.43	619.81	607.94	597.57	588.45
64000	677.99	659.45	643.48	629.64	617.59	607.05	597.79
65000	688.59	669.75	653.54	639.48	627.24	616.54	607.13
70000	741.55	721.27	703.81	688.67	675.49	663.96	653.83
75000	794.52	772.79	754.08	737.87	723.74	711.39	700.54
80000	847.49	824.31	804.35	787.06	771.99	758.81	747.24
85000	900.46	875.83	854.62	836.25	820.24	806.24	793.94
90000	953.43	927.35	904.90	885.44	868.49	853.67	840.64
95000	1006.39	978.87	955.17	934.63	916.74	901.09	887.34
100000	1059.36	1030.39	1005.44	983.82	964.99	948.52	934.05
105000	1112.33	1081.91	1055.71	1033.01	1013.24	995.94	980.75
110000	1165.30	1133.43	1105.98	1082.20	1061.49	1043.37	1027.45
120000	1271.24	1236.47	1206.53	1180.58	1157.99	1138.22	1120.86
130000	1377.17	1339.51	1307.07	1278.97	1254.49	1233.07	1214.26
140000	1483.11	1442.55	1407.62	1377.35	1350.99	1327.92	1307.67
150000	1589.04	1545.59	1508.16	1475.73	1447.49	1422.78	1401.07
160000	1694.98	1648.63	1608.70	1574.11	1543.99	1517.63	1494.47
175000	1853.88	1803.19	1759.52	1721.69	1688.73	1659.90	1634.58
200000	2118.73	2060.78	2010.88	1967.64	1929.98	1897.03	1868.09
250000	2648.41	2575.98	2513.60	2459.55	2412.48	2371.29	2335.12
500000	5296.81	5151.96	5027.20	4919.10	4824.95	4742.58	4670.23
1000000	10593.63	10303.92	10054.40	9838.20	9649.91	9485.17	9340.47

MONTHLY PAYMENTS 9.75%

AMOUNT	22 YEARS	23 YEARS	24 YEARS	25 YEARS	30 YEARS	35 YEARS	40 YEARS
100	0.92	0.91	0.90	0.89	0.86	0.84	0.83
200	1.84	1.82	1.80	1.78	1.72	1.68	1.66
500	4.61	4.55	4.50	4.46	4.30	4.20	4.15
1000	9.21	9.10	9.00	8.91	8.59	8.41	8.30
2000	18.43	18.20	18.00	17.82	17.18	16.81	16.59
3000	27.64	27.30	27.00	26.73	25.77	25.22	24.89
4000	36.85	36.40	36.00	35.65	34.37	33.62	33.18
5000	46.06	45.50	45.00	44.56	42.96	42.03	41.48
6000	55.28	54.60	54.00	53.47	51.55	50.44	49.77
7000	64.49	63.70	63.00	62.38	60.14	58.84	58.07
8000	73.70	72.80	72.00	71.29	68.73	67.25	66.36
9000	82.92	81.90	81.00	80.20	77.32	75.65	74.66
10000	92.13	91.00	90.00	89.11	85.92	84.06	82.96
11000	101.34	100.10	99.00	98.03	94.51	92.46	91.25
12000	110.56	109.20	108.00	106.94	103.10	100.87	99.55
13000	119.77	118.30	117.00	115.85	111.69	109.28	107.84
14000	128.98	127.40	126.00	124.76	120.28	117.68	116.14
15000	138.19	136.50	135.00	133.67	128.87	126.09	124.43
20000	184.26	182.00	180.00	178.23	171.83	168.12	165.91
25000	230.32	227.50	225.01	222.78	214.79	210.15	207.39
30000	276.39	273.01	270.01	267.34	257.75	252.18	248.87
35000	322.45	318.51	315.01	311.90	300.70	294.21	290.35
40000	368.52	364.01	360.01	356.45	343.66	336.24	331.82
45000	414.58	409.51	405.01	401.01	386.62	378.27	373.30
50000	460.65	455.01	450.01	445.57	429.58	420.29	414.78
55000	506.71	500.51	495.01	490.13	472.53	462.32	456.26
56000	515.92	509.61	504.01	499.04	481.13	470.73	464.55
57000	525.14	518.71	513.01	507.95	489.72	479.14	472.85
58000	534.35	527.81	522.01	516.86	498.31	487.54	481.14
59000	543.56	536.91	531.01	525.77	506.90	495.95	489.44
60000	552.78	546.01	540.01	534.68	515.49	504.35	497.74
61000	561.99	555.11	549.01	543.59	524.08	512.76	506.03
62000	571.20	564.21	558.01	552.51	532.68	521.17	514.33
63000	580.41	573.31	567.01	561.42	541.27	529.57	522.62
64000	589.63	582.41	576.01	570.33	549.86	537.98	530.92
65000	598.84	591.51	585.01	579.24	558.45	546.38	539.21
70000	644.90	637.01	630.01	623.80	601.41	588.41	580.69
75000	690.97	682.51	675.02	668.35	644.37	630.44	622.17
80000	737.03	728.01	720.02	712.91	687.32	672.47	663.65
85000	783.10	773.51	765.02	757.47	730.28	714.50	705.12
90000	829.16	819.02	810.02	802.02	773.24	756.53	746.60
95000	875.23	864.52	855.02	846.58	816.20	798.56	788.08
100000	921.29	910.02	900.02	891.14	859.15	840.59	829.56
105000	967.36	955.52	945.02	935.69	902.11	882.62	871.04
110000	1013.42	1001.02	990.02	980.25	945.07	924.65	912.51
120000	1105.55	1092.02	1080.02	1069.36	1030.99	1008.71	995.47
130000	1197.68	1183.02	1170.03	1158.48	1116.90	1092.77	1078.43
140000	1289.81	1274.02	1260.03	1247.59	1202.82	1176.83	1161.38
150000	1381.94	1365.03	1350.03	1336.71	1288.73	1260.88	1244.34
160000	1474.07	1456.03	1440.03	1425.82	1374.65	1344.94	1327.29
175000	1612.26	1592.53	1575.04	1559.49	1503.52	1471.03	1451.73
200000	1842.59	1820.03	1800.04	1782.27	1718.31	1681.18	1659.12
250000	2303.23	2275.04	2250.05	2227.84	2147.89	2101.47	2073.90
500000	4606.46	4550.08	4500.10	4455.69	4295.77	4202.95	4147.79
1000000	9212.93	9100.17	9000.20	8911.37	8591.54	8405.89	8295.59

10.00% MONTHLY PAYMENTS

AMOUNT	1 YEAR	2 YEARS	3 YEARS	4 YEARS	5 YEARS	6 YEARS	7 YEARS
100	8.79	4.61	3.23	2.54	2.12	1.85	1.66
200	17.58	9.23	6.45	5.07	4.25	3.71	3.32
500	43.96	23.07	16.13	12.68	10.62	9.26	8.30
1000	87.92	46.14	32.27	25.36	21.25	18.53	16.60
2000	175.83	92.29	64.53	50.73	42.49	37.05	33.20
3000	263.75	138.43	96.80	76.09	63.74	55.58	49.80
4000	351.66	184.58	129.07	101.45	84.99	74.10	66.40
5000	439.58	230.72	161.34	126.81	106.24	92.63	83.01
6000	527.50	276.87	193.60	152.18	127.48	111.16	99.61
7000	615.41	323.01	225.87	177.54	148.73	129.68	116.21
8000	703.33	369.16	258.14	202.90	169.98	148.21	132.81
9000	791.24	415.30	290.40	228.26	191.22	166.73	149.41
10000	879.16	461.45	322.67	253.63	212.47	185.26	166.01
11000	967.07	507.59	354.94	278.99	233.72	203.78	182.61
12000	1054.99	553.74	387.21	304.35	254.96	222.31	199.21
13000	1142.91	599.88	419.47	329.71	276.21	240.84	215.82
14000	1230.82	646.03	451.74	355.08	297.46	259.36	232.42
15000	1318.74	692.17	484.01	380.44	318.71	277.89	249.02
20000	1758.32	922.90	645.34	507.25	424.94	370.52	332.02
25000	2197.90	1153.62	806.68	634.06	531.18	463.15	415.03
30000	2637.48	1384.35	968.02	760.88	637.41	555.78	498.04
35000	3077.06	1615.07	1129.35	887.69	743.65	648.40	581.04
40000	3516.64	1845.80	1290.69	1014.50	849.88	741.03	664.05
45000	3956.21	2076.52	1452.02	1141.32	956.12	833.66	747.05
50000	4395.79	2307.25	1613.36	1268.13	1062.35	926.29	830.06
55000	4835.37	2537.97	1774.70	1394.94	1168.59	1018.92	913.07
56000	4923.29	2584.12	1806.96	1420.30	1189.83	1037.45	929.67
57000	5011.21	2630.26	1839.23	1445.67	1211.08	1055.97	946.27
58000	5099.12	2676.41	1871.50	1471.03	1232.33	1074.50	962.87
59000	5187.04	2722.55	1903.76	1496.39	1253.58	1093.02	979.47
60000	5274.95	2768.70	1936.03	1521.76	1274.82	1111.55	996.07
61000	5362.87	2814.84	1968.30	1547.12	1296.07	1130.08	1012.67
62000	5450.79	2860.99	2000.57	1572.48	1317.32	1148.60	1029.27
63000	5538.70	2907.13	2032.83	1597.84	1338.56	1167.13	1045.87
64000	5626.62	2953.28	2065.10	1623.21	1359.81	1185.65	1062.48
65000	5714.53	2999.42	2097.37	1648.57	1381.06	1204.18	1079.08
70000	6154.11	3230.14	2258.70	1775.38	1487.29	1296.81	1162.08
75000	6593.69	3460.87	2420.04	1902.19	1593.53	1389.44	1245.09
80000	7033.27	3691.59	2581.37	2029.01	1699.76	1482.07	1328.09
85000	7472.85	3922.32	2742.71	2155.82	1806.00	1574.70	1411.10
90000	7912.43	4153.04	2904.05	2282.63	1912.23	1667.33	1494.11
95000	8352.01	4383.77	3065.38	2409.45	2018.47	1759.95	1577.11
100000	8791.59	4614.49	3226.72	2536.26	2124.70	1852.58	1660.12
105000	9231.17	4845.22	3388.05	2663.07	2230.94	1945.21	1743.12
110000	9670.75	5075.94	3549.39	2789.88	2337.17	2037.84	1826.13
120000	10549.91	5537.39	3872.06	3043.51	2549.65	2223.10	1992.14
130000	11429.07	5998.84	4194.73	3297.14	2762.12	2408.36	2158.15
140000	12308.22	6460.29	4517.41	3550.76	2974.59	2593.62	2324.17
150000	13187.38	6921.74	4840.08	3804.39	3187.06	2778.88	2490.18
160000	14066.54	7383.19	5162.75	4058.01	3399.53	2964.13	2656.19
175000	15385.28	8075.36	5646.76	4438.45	3718.23	3242.02	2905.21
200000	17583.18	9228.99	6453.44	5072.52	4249.41	3705.17	3320.24
250000	21978.97	11536.23	8066.80	6340.65	5311.76	4631.46	4150.30
500000	43957.94	23072.46	16133.59	12681.29	10623.52	9262.92	8300.59
1000000	87915.89	46144.93	32267.19	25362.58	21247.04	18525.84	16601.18

MONTHLY PAYMENTS   10.00%

AMOUNT	8 YEARS	9 YEARS	10 YEARS	11 YEARS	12 YEARS	13 YEARS	14 YEARS
100	1.52	1.41	1.32	1.25	1.20	1.15	1.11
200	3.03	2.82	2.64	2.50	2.39	2.30	2.22
500	7.59	7.04	6.61	6.26	5.98	5.74	5.54
1000	15.17	14.08	13.22	12.52	11.95	11.48	11.08
2000	30.35	28.16	26.43	25.04	23.90	22.96	22.16
3000	45.52	42.24	39.65	37.56	35.85	34.44	33.25
4000	60.70	56.31	52.86	50.08	47.80	45.91	44.33
5000	75.87	70.39	66.08	62.60	59.75	57.39	55.41
6000	91.04	84.47	79.29	75.12	71.70	68.87	66.49
7000	106.22	98.55	92.51	87.64	83.66	80.35	77.57
8000	121.39	112.63	105.72	100.16	95.61	91.83	88.66
9000	136.57	126.71	118.94	112.68	107.56	103.31	99.74
10000	151.74	140.79	132.15	125.20	119.51	114.78	110.82
11000	166.92	154.87	145.37	137.72	131.46	126.26	121.90
12000	182.09	168.94	158.58	150.24	143.41	137.74	132.98
13000	197.26	183.02	171.80	162.76	155.36	149.22	144.07
14000	212.44	197.10	185.01	175.28	167.31	160.70	155.15
15000	227.61	211.18	198.23	187.80	179.26	172.18	166.23
20000	303.48	281.57	264.30	250.40	239.02	229.57	221.64
25000	379.35	351.97	330.38	313.00	298.77	286.96	277.05
30000	455.22	422.36	396.45	375.60	358.52	344.35	332.46
35000	531.10	492.75	462.53	438.20	418.28	401.75	387.87
40000	606.97	563.15	528.60	500.80	478.03	459.14	443.28
45000	682.84	633.54	594.68	563.39	537.79	516.53	498.69
50000	758.71	703.93	660.75	625.99	597.54	573.92	554.10
55000	834.58	774.33	726.83	688.59	657.29	631.32	609.51
56000	849.75	788.41	740.04	701.11	669.24	642.79	620.59
57000	864.93	802.49	753.26	713.63	681.19	654.27	631.68
58000	880.10	816.56	766.47	726.15	693.15	665.75	642.76
59000	895.28	830.64	779.69	738.67	705.10	677.23	653.84
60000	910.45	844.72	792.90	751.19	717.05	688.71	664.92
61000	925.62	858.80	806.12	763.71	729.00	700.19	676.00
62000	940.80	872.88	819.33	776.23	740.95	711.67	687.09
63000	955.97	886.96	832.55	788.75	752.90	723.14	698.17
64000	971.15	901.04	845.76	801.27	764.85	734.62	709.25
65000	986.32	915.11	858.98	813.79	776.80	746.10	720.33
70000	1062.19	985.51	925.06	876.39	836.55	803.49	775.74
75000	1138.06	1055.90	991.13	938.99	896.31	860.89	831.15
80000	1213.93	1126.29	1057.21	1001.59	956.06	918.28	886.56
85000	1289.80	1196.69	1123.28	1064.19	1015.82	975.67	941.97
90000	1365.67	1267.08	1189.36	1126.79	1075.57	1033.06	997.38
95000	1441.55	1337.48	1255.43	1189.39	1135.32	1090.46	1052.79
100000	1517.42	1407.87	1321.51	1251.99	1195.08	1147.85	1108.20
105000	1593.29	1478.26	1387.58	1314.59	1254.83	1205.24	1163.61
110000	1669.16	1548.66	1453.66	1377.19	1314.59	1262.63	1219.02
120000	1820.90	1689.44	1585.81	1502.39	1434.09	1377.42	1329.84
130000	1972.64	1830.23	1717.96	1627.58	1553.60	1492.20	1440.66
140000	2124.38	1971.02	1850.11	1752.78	1673.11	1606.99	1551.48
150000	2276.12	2111.80	1982.26	1877.98	1792.62	1721.77	1662.30
160000	2427.87	2252.59	2114.41	2003.18	1912.13	1836.56	1773.12
175000	2655.48	2463.77	2312.64	2190.98	2091.39	2008.73	1939.35
200000	3034.83	2815.74	2643.01	2503.98	2390.16	2295.70	2216.41
250000	3793.54	3519.67	3303.77	3129.97	2987.70	2869.62	2770.51
500000	7587.08	7039.34	6607.54	6259.94	5975.39	5739.24	5541.01
1000000	15174.16	14078.69	13215.07	12519.88	11950.78	11478.48	11082.03

10.00%   MONTHLY PAYMENTS

AMOUNT	15 YEARS	16 YEARS	17 YEARS	18 YEARS	19 YEARS	20 YEARS	21 YEARS
100	1.07	1.05	1.02	1.00	0.98	0.97	0.95
200	2.15	2.09	2.04	2.00	1.96	1.93	1.90
500	5.37	5.23	5.11	5.00	4.91	4.83	4.75
1000	10.75	10.46	10.21	10.00	9.81	9.65	9.51
2000	21.49	20.92	20.42	20.00	19.63	19.30	19.02
3000	32.24	31.38	30.64	30.00	29.44	28.95	28.52
4000	42.98	41.84	40.85	39.99	39.25	38.60	38.03
5000	53.73	52.30	51.06	49.99	49.06	48.25	47.54
6000	64.48	62.75	61.27	59.99	58.88	57.90	57.05
7000	75.22	73.21	71.48	69.99	68.69	67.55	66.55
8000	85.97	83.67	81.70	79.99	78.50	77.20	76.06
9000	96.71	94.13	91.91	89.99	88.31	86.85	85.57
10000	107.46	104.59	102.12	99.98	98.13	96.50	95.08
11000	118.21	115.05	112.33	109.98	107.94	106.15	104.59
12000	128.95	125.51	122.55	119.98	117.75	115.80	114.09
13000	139.70	135.97	132.76	129.98	127.56	125.45	123.60
14000	150.44	146.43	142.97	139.98	137.38	135.10	133.11
15000	161.19	156.89	153.18	149.98	147.19	144.75	142.62
20000	214.92	209.18	204.24	199.97	196.25	193.00	190.16
25000	268.65	261.48	255.30	249.96	245.31	241.26	237.70
30000	322.38	313.77	306.36	299.95	294.38	289.51	285.23
35000	376.11	366.07	357.42	349.95	343.44	337.76	332.77
40000	429.84	418.36	408.48	399.94	392.50	386.01	380.31
45000	483.57	470.66	459.54	449.93	441.57	434.26	427.85
50000	537.30	522.95	510.61	499.92	490.63	482.51	475.39
55000	591.03	575.25	561.67	549.91	539.69	530.76	522.93
56000	601.78	585.71	571.88	559.91	549.50	540.41	532.44
57000	612.52	596.16	582.09	569.91	559.32	550.06	541.94
58000	623.27	606.62	592.30	579.91	569.13	559.71	551.45
59000	634.02	617.08	602.51	589.91	578.94	569.36	560.96
60000	644.76	627.54	612.73	599.91	588.76	579.01	570.47
61000	655.51	638.00	622.94	609.90	598.57	588.66	579.98
62000	666.26	648.46	633.15	619.90	608.38	598.31	589.48
63000	677.00	658.92	643.36	629.90	618.19	607.96	598.99
64000	687.75	669.38	653.57	639.90	628.01	617.61	608.50
65000	698.49	679.84	663.79	649.90	637.82	627.26	618.01
70000	752.22	732.13	714.85	699.89	686.88	675.52	665.55
75000	805.95	784.43	765.91	749.88	735.94	723.77	713.09
80000	859.68	836.72	816.97	799.87	785.01	772.02	760.62
85000	913.41	889.02	868.03	849.87	834.07	820.27	808.16
90000	967.14	941.31	919.09	899.86	883.13	868.52	855.70
95000	1020.87	993.61	970.15	949.85	932.20	916.77	903.24
100000	1074.61	1045.90	1021.21	999.84	981.26	965.02	950.78
105000	1128.34	1098.20	1072.27	1049.84	1030.32	1013.27	998.32
110000	1182.07	1150.49	1123.33	1099.83	1079.38	1061.52	1045.86
120000	1289.53	1255.08	1225.45	1199.81	1177.51	1158.03	1140.94
130000	1396.99	1359.67	1327.57	1299.80	1275.64	1254.53	1236.01
140000	1504.45	1464.26	1429.69	1399.78	1373.76	1351.03	1331.09
150000	1611.91	1568.85	1531.82	1499.77	1471.89	1447.53	1426.17
160000	1719.37	1673.44	1633.94	1599.75	1570.01	1544.03	1521.25
175000	1880.56	1830.33	1787.12	1749.73	1717.20	1688.79	1663.87
200000	2149.21	2091.80	2042.42	1999.69	1962.52	1930.04	1901.56
250000	2686.51	2614.75	2553.03	2499.61	2453.15	2412.55	2376.95
500000	5373.03	5229.51	5106.05	4999.22	4906.29	4825.11	4753.90
1000000	10746.05	10459.02	10212.10	9998.44	9812.59	9650.22	9507.80

MONTHLY PAYMENTS 10.00%

AMOUNT	22 YEARS	23 YEARS	24 YEARS	25 YEARS	30 YEARS	35 YEARS	40 YEARS
100	0.94	0.93	0.92	0.91	0.88	0.86	0.85
200	1.88	1.85	1.83	1.82	1.76	1.72	1.70
500	4.69	4.64	4.59	4.54	4.39	4.30	4.25
1000	9.38	9.27	9.17	9.09	8.78	8.60	8.49
2000	18.76	18.54	18.35	18.17	17.55	17.19	16.98
3000	28.15	27.82	27.52	27.26	26.33	25.79	25.47
4000	37.53	37.09	36.70	36.35	35.10	34.39	33.97
5000	46.91	46.36	45.87	45.44	43.88	42.98	42.46
6000	56.29	55.63	55.04	54.52	52.65	51.58	50.95
7000	65.68	64.90	64.22	63.61	61.43	60.18	59.44
8000	75.06	74.17	73.39	72.70	70.21	68.77	67.93
9000	84.44	83.45	82.56	81.78	78.98	77.37	76.42
10000	93.82	92.72	91.74	90.87	87.76	85.97	84.91
11000	103.21	101.99	100.91	99.96	96.53	94.56	93.41
12000	112.59	111.26	110.09	109.04	105.31	103.16	101.90
13000	121.97	120.53	119.26	118.13	114.08	111.76	110.39
14000	131.35	129.81	128.43	127.22	122.86	120.35	118.88
15000	140.74	139.08	137.61	136.31	131.64	128.95	127.37
20000	187.65	185.44	183.48	181.74	175.51	171.93	169.83
25000	234.56	231.80	229.35	227.18	219.39	214.92	212.29
30000	281.47	278.15	275.22	272.61	263.27	257.90	254.74
35000	328.39	324.51	321.09	318.05	307.15	300.89	297.20
40000	375.30	370.87	366.96	363.48	351.03	343.87	339.66
45000	422.21	417.23	412.82	408.92	394.91	386.85	382.12
50000	469.12	463.59	458.69	454.35	438.79	429.84	424.57
55000	516.04	509.95	504.56	499.79	482.66	472.82	467.03
56000	525.42	519.22	513.74	508.87	491.44	481.42	475.52
57000	534.80	528.49	522.91	517.96	500.22	490.01	484.01
58000	544.18	537.77	532.09	527.05	508.99	498.61	492.50
59000	553.57	547.04	541.26	536.13	517.77	507.21	501.00
60000	562.95	556.31	550.43	545.22	526.54	515.80	509.49
61000	572.33	565.58	559.61	554.31	535.32	524.40	517.98
62000	581.71	574.85	568.78	563.39	544.09	533.00	526.47
63000	591.09	584.12	577.95	572.48	552.87	541.59	534.96
64000	600.48	593.40	587.13	581.57	561.65	550.19	543.45
65000	609.86	602.67	596.30	590.66	570.42	558.79	551.94
70000	656.77	649.03	642.17	636.09	614.30	601.77	594.40
75000	703.68	695.39	688.04	681.53	658.18	644.75	636.86
80000	750.60	741.75	733.91	726.96	702.06	687.74	679.32
85000	797.51	788.10	779.78	772.40	745.94	730.72	721.77
90000	844.42	834.46	825.65	817.83	789.81	773.71	764.23
95000	891.33	880.82	871.52	863.27	833.69	816.69	806.69
100000	938.25	927.18	917.39	908.70	877.57	859.67	849.15
105000	985.16	973.54	963.26	954.14	921.45	902.66	891.60
110000	1032.07	1019.90	1009.13	999.57	965.33	945.64	934.06
120000	1125.90	1112.62	1100.87	1090.44	1053.09	1031.61	1018.98
130000	1219.72	1205.34	1192.61	1181.31	1140.84	1117.57	1103.89
140000	1313.54	1298.05	1284.34	1272.18	1228.60	1203.54	1188.80
150000	1407.37	1390.77	1376.08	1363.05	1316.36	1289.51	1273.72
160000	1501.19	1483.49	1467.82	1453.92	1404.11	1375.48	1358.63
175000	1641.93	1622.57	1605.43	1590.23	1535.75	1504.43	1486.01
200000	1876.49	1854.36	1834.78	1817.40	1755.14	1719.34	1698.29
250000	2345.61	2317.95	2293.47	2271.75	2193.93	2149.18	2122.86
500000	4691.23	4635.91	4586.94	4543.50	4387.86	4298.36	4245.73
1000000	9382.46	9271.82	9173.89	9087.01	8775.72	8596.72	8491.46

10.25% MONTHLY PAYMENTS

AMOUNT	1 YEAR	2 YEARS	3 YEARS	4 YEARS	5 YEARS	6 YEARS	7 YEARS
100	8.80	4.63	3.24	2.55	2.14	1.87	1.67
200	17.61	9.25	6.48	5.10	4.27	3.73	3.35
500	44.02	23.13	16.19	12.74	10.69	9.33	8.37
1000	88.03	46.26	32.38	25.48	21.37	18.65	16.73
2000	176.06	92.52	64.77	50.97	42.74	37.30	33.46
3000	264.10	138.78	97.15	76.45	64.11	55.96	50.19
4000	352.13	185.04	129.54	101.93	85.48	74.61	66.92
5000	440.16	231.30	161.92	127.41	106.85	93.26	83.65
6000	528.19	277.56	194.31	152.90	128.22	111.91	100.38
7000	616.23	323.82	226.69	178.38	149.59	130.57	117.11
8000	704.26	370.08	259.08	203.86	170.96	149.22	133.85
9000	792.29	416.34	291.46	229.35	192.33	167.87	150.58
10000	880.32	462.60	323.85	254.83	213.70	186.52	167.31
11000	968.35	508.86	356.23	280.31	235.07	205.17	184.04
12000	1056.39	555.12	388.62	305.79	256.44	223.83	200.77
13000	1144.42	601.39	421.00	331.28	277.81	242.48	217.50
14000	1232.45	647.65	453.39	356.76	299.18	261.13	234.23
15000	1320.48	693.91	485.77	382.24	320.55	279.78	250.96
20000	1760.64	925.21	647.69	509.66	427.41	373.04	334.61
25000	2200.81	1156.51	809.62	637.07	534.26	466.30	418.27
30000	2640.97	1387.81	971.54	764.48	641.11	559.56	501.92
35000	3081.13	1619.11	1133.46	891.90	747.96	652.83	585.57
40000	3521.29	1850.42	1295.39	1019.31	854.81	746.09	669.23
45000	3961.45	2081.72	1457.31	1146.73	961.66	839.35	752.88
50000	4401.61	2313.02	1619.23	1274.14	1068.51	932.61	836.53
55000	4841.77	2544.32	1781.16	1401.55	1175.36	1025.87	920.19
56000	4929.80	2590.58	1813.54	1427.04	1196.73	1044.52	936.92
57000	5017.84	2636.84	1845.93	1452.52	1218.11	1063.17	953.65
58000	5105.87	2683.10	1878.31	1478.00	1239.48	1081.83	970.38
59000	5193.90	2729.36	1910.70	1503.49	1260.85	1100.48	987.11
60000	5281.93	2775.62	1943.08	1528.97	1282.22	1119.13	1003.84
61000	5369.96	2821.88	1975.47	1554.45	1303.59	1137.78	1020.57
62000	5458.00	2868.14	2007.85	1579.93	1324.96	1156.43	1037.30
63000	5546.03	2914.41	2040.24	1605.42	1346.33	1175.09	1054.03
64000	5634.06	2960.67	2072.62	1630.90	1367.70	1193.74	1070.76
65000	5722.09	3006.93	2105.00	1656.38	1389.07	1212.39	1087.49
70000	6162.25	3238.23	2266.93	1783.80	1495.92	1305.65	1171.15
75000	6602.42	3469.53	2428.85	1911.21	1602.77	1398.91	1254.80
80000	7042.58	3700.83	2590.78	2038.63	1709.62	1492.17	1338.45
85000	7482.74	3932.13	2752.70	2166.04	1816.47	1585.43	1422.10
90000	7922.90	4163.44	2914.62	2293.45	1923.32	1678.69	1505.76
95000	8363.06	4394.74	3076.55	2420.87	2030.18	1771.95	1589.41
100000	8803.22	4626.04	3238.47	2548.28	2137.03	1865.22	1673.06
105000	9243.38	4857.34	3400.39	2675.70	2243.88	1958.48	1756.72
110000	9683.54	5088.64	3562.32	2803.11	2350.73	2051.74	1840.37
120000	10563.86	5551.25	3886.16	3057.94	2564.43	2238.26	2007.68
130000	11444.19	6013.85	4210.01	3312.77	2778.13	2424.78	2174.98
140000	12324.51	6476.46	4533.86	3567.59	2991.84	2611.30	2342.29
150000	13204.83	6939.06	4857.70	3822.42	3205.54	2797.82	2509.60
160000	14085.15	7401.66	5181.55	4077.25	3419.24	2984.34	2676.90
175000	15405.64	8095.57	5667.32	4459.49	3739.80	3264.13	2927.86
200000	17606.44	9252.08	6476.94	5096.56	4274.05	3730.43	3346.13
250000	22008.05	11565.10	8096.17	6370.70	5342.57	4663.04	4182.66
500000	44016.10	23130.20	16192.34	12741.41	10685.13	9326.08	8365.32
1000000	88032.20	46260.40	32384.69	25482.81	21370.26	18652.16	16730.64

MONTHLY PAYMENTS 10.25%

AMOUNT	8 YEARS	9 YEARS	10 YEARS	11 YEARS	12 YEARS	13 YEARS	14 YEARS
100	1.53	1.42	1.34	1.27	1.21	1.16	1.12
200	3.06	2.84	2.67	2.53	2.42	2.33	2.25
500	7.65	7.11	6.68	6.33	6.05	5.81	5.62
1000	15.31	14.21	13.35	12.66	12.10	11.63	11.23
2000	30.61	28.43	26.71	25.32	24.19	23.25	22.47
3000	45.92	42.64	40.06	37.99	36.29	34.88	33.70
4000	61.23	56.86	53.42	50.65	48.38	46.51	44.93
5000	76.53	71.07	66.77	63.31	60.48	58.13	56.16
6000	91.84	85.29	80.12	75.97	72.57	69.76	67.40
7000	107.15	99.50	93.48	88.63	84.67	81.38	78.63
8000	122.45	113.72	106.83	101.29	96.77	93.01	89.86
9000	137.76	127.93	120.19	113.96	108.86	104.64	101.09
10000	153.07	142.14	133.54	126.62	120.96	116.26	112.33
11000	168.37	156.36	146.89	139.28	133.05	127.89	123.56
12000	183.68	170.57	160.25	151.94	145.15	139.52	134.79
13000	198.99	184.79	173.60	164.60	157.24	151.14	146.03
14000	214.29	199.00	186.95	177.26	169.34	162.77	157.26
15000	229.60	213.22	200.31	189.93	181.43	174.39	168.49
20000	306.14	284.29	267.08	253.24	241.91	232.53	224.65
25000	382.67	355.36	333.85	316.54	302.39	290.66	280.82
30000	459.20	426.43	400.62	379.85	362.87	348.79	336.98
35000	535.74	497.50	467.39	443.16	423.35	406.92	393.14
40000	612.27	568.58	534.16	506.47	483.83	465.05	449.31
45000	688.80	639.65	600.93	569.78	544.30	523.18	505.47
50000	765.34	710.72	667.70	633.09	604.78	581.31	561.63
55000	841.87	781.79	734.46	696.40	665.26	639.45	617.80
56000	857.18	796.01	747.82	709.06	677.36	651.07	629.03
57000	872.49	810.22	761.17	721.72	689.45	662.70	640.26
58000	887.79	824.44	774.53	734.38	701.55	674.32	651.50
59000	903.10	838.65	787.88	747.04	713.64	685.95	662.73
60000	918.41	852.87	801.23	759.71	725.74	697.58	673.96
61000	933.71	867.08	814.59	772.37	737.83	709.20	685.19
62000	949.02	881.29	827.94	785.03	749.93	720.83	696.43
63000	964.33	895.51	841.30	797.69	762.03	732.46	707.66
64000	979.63	909.72	854.65	810.35	774.12	744.08	718.89
65000	994.94	923.94	868.00	823.01	786.22	755.71	730.13
70000	1071.47	995.01	934.77	886.32	846.70	813.84	786.29
75000	1148.01	1066.08	1001.54	949.63	907.17	871.97	842.45
80000	1224.54	1137.15	1068.31	1012.94	967.65	930.10	898.62
85000	1301.08	1208.23	1135.08	1076.25	1028.13	988.23	954.78
90000	1377.61	1279.30	1201.85	1139.56	1088.61	1046.37	1010.94
95000	1454.14	1350.37	1268.62	1202.87	1149.09	1104.50	1067.11
100000	1530.68	1421.44	1335.39	1266.18	1209.57	1162.63	1123.27
105000	1607.21	1492.51	1402.16	1329.48	1270.04	1220.76	1179.43
110000	1683.74	1563.59	1468.93	1392.79	1330.52	1278.89	1235.60
120000	1836.81	1705.73	1602.47	1519.41	1451.48	1395.15	1347.92
130000	1989.88	1847.87	1736.01	1646.03	1572.43	1511.42	1460.25
140000	2142.95	1990.02	1869.55	1772.65	1693.39	1627.68	1572.58
150000	2296.02	2132.16	2003.09	1899.26	1814.35	1743.94	1684.90
160000	2449.08	2274.31	2136.62	2025.88	1935.30	1860.21	1797.23
175000	2678.68	2487.52	2336.93	2215.81	2116.74	2034.60	1965.72
200000	3061.35	2842.88	2670.78	2532.35	2419.13	2325.26	2246.54
250000	3826.69	3553.60	3338.48	3165.44	3023.91	2906.57	2808.17
500000	7653.38	7107.21	6676.95	6330.88	6047.83	5813.14	5616.35
1000000	15306.77	14214.42	13353.90	12661.75	12095.65	11626.28	11232.69

10.25% MONTHLY PAYMENTS

AMOUNT	15 YEARS	16 YEARS	17 YEARS	18 YEARS	19 YEARS	20 YEARS	21 YEARS
100	1.09	1.06	1.04	1.02	1.00	0.98	0.97
200	2.18	2.12	2.07	2.03	2.00	1.96	1.94
500	5.45	5.31	5.19	5.08	4.99	4.91	4.84
1000	10.90	10.62	10.37	10.16	9.98	9.82	9.68
2000	21.80	21.23	20.74	20.32	19.95	19.63	19.35
3000	32.70	31.85	31.11	30.48	29.93	29.45	29.03
4000	43.60	42.46	41.48	40.64	39.91	39.27	38.71
5000	54.50	53.08	51.85	50.80	49.88	49.08	48.38
6000	65.40	63.69	62.23	60.96	59.86	58.90	58.06
7000	76.30	74.31	72.60	71.12	69.83	68.72	67.73
8000	87.20	84.92	82.97	81.28	79.81	78.53	77.41
9000	98.10	95.54	93.34	91.44	89.79	88.35	87.09
10000	109.00	106.15	103.71	101.60	99.76	98.16	96.76
11000	119.89	116.77	114.08	111.76	109.74	107.98	106.44
12000	130.79	127.38	124.45	121.92	119.72	117.80	116.12
13000	141.69	138.00	134.82	132.08	129.69	127.61	125.79
14000	152.59	148.61	145.19	142.24	139.67	137.43	135.47
15000	163.49	159.23	155.56	152.40	149.65	147.25	145.14
20000	217.99	212.30	207.42	203.20	199.53	196.33	193.53
25000	272.49	265.38	259.27	254.00	249.41	245.41	241.91
30000	326.99	318.46	311.13	304.79	299.29	294.49	290.29
35000	381.48	371.53	362.98	355.59	349.17	343.58	338.67
40000	435.98	424.61	414.84	406.39	399.06	392.66	387.05
45000	490.48	477.68	466.69	457.19	448.94	441.74	435.43
50000	544.98	530.76	518.55	507.99	498.82	490.82	483.82
55000	599.47	583.84	570.40	558.79	548.70	539.90	532.20
56000	610.37	594.45	580.77	568.95	558.68	549.72	541.87
57000	621.27	605.07	591.14	579.11	568.66	559.54	551.55
58000	632.17	615.68	601.51	589.27	578.63	569.35	561.23
59000	643.07	626.30	611.88	599.43	588.61	579.17	570.90
60000	653.97	636.91	622.25	609.59	598.59	588.99	580.58
61000	664.87	647.53	632.63	619.75	608.56	598.80	590.26
62000	675.77	658.14	643.00	629.91	618.54	608.62	599.93
63000	686.67	668.76	653.37	640.07	628.51	618.44	609.61
64000	697.57	679.37	663.74	650.23	638.49	628.25	619.28
65000	708.47	689.99	674.11	660.39	648.47	638.07	628.96
70000	762.97	743.06	725.96	711.19	698.35	687.15	677.34
75000	817.46	796.14	777.82	761.99	748.23	736.23	725.72
80000	871.96	849.22	829.67	812.78	798.11	785.31	774.11
85000	926.46	902.29	881.53	863.58	848.00	834.40	822.49
90000	980.96	955.37	933.38	914.38	897.88	883.48	870.87
95000	1035.45	1008.44	985.24	965.18	947.76	932.56	919.25
100000	1089.95	1061.52	1037.09	1015.98	997.64	981.64	967.63
105000	1144.45	1114.60	1088.95	1066.78	1047.52	1030.73	1016.01
110000	1198.95	1167.67	1140.80	1117.58	1097.41	1079.81	1064.39
120000	1307.94	1273.82	1244.51	1219.18	1197.17	1177.97	1161.16
130000	1416.94	1379.98	1348.22	1320.77	1296.93	1276.14	1257.92
140000	1525.93	1486.13	1451.93	1422.37	1396.70	1374.30	1354.68
150000	1634.93	1592.28	1555.64	1523.97	1496.46	1472.47	1451.45
160000	1743.92	1698.43	1659.35	1625.57	1596.23	1570.63	1548.21
175000	1907.41	1857.66	1814.91	1777.97	1745.87	1717.88	1693.35
200000	2179.90	2123.04	2074.18	2031.96	1995.28	1963.29	1935.26
250000	2724.88	2653.80	2592.73	2539.95	2494.11	2454.11	2419.08
500000	5449.75	5307.60	5185.46	5079.90	4988.21	4908.22	4838.16
1000000	10899.51	10615.19	10370.91	10159.80	9976.42	9816.43	9676.31

MONTHLY PAYMENTS   10.25%

AMOUNT	22 YEARS	23 YEARS	24 YEARS	25 YEARS	30 YEARS	35 YEARS	40 YEARS
100	0.96	0.94	0.93	0.93	0.90	0.88	0.87
200	1.91	1.89	1.87	1.85	1.79	1.76	1.74
500	4.78	4.72	4.67	4.63	4.48	4.39	4.34
1000	9.55	9.44	9.35	9.26	8.96	8.79	8.69
2000	19.11	18.89	18.70	18.53	17.92	17.58	17.38
3000	28.66	28.33	28.05	27.79	26.88	26.37	26.06
4000	38.21	37.78	37.40	37.06	35.84	35.15	34.75
5000	47.77	47.22	46.74	46.32	44.81	43.94	43.44
6000	57.32	56.67	56.09	55.58	53.77	52.73	52.13
7000	66.87	66.11	65.44	64.85	62.73	61.52	60.82
8000	76.43	75.56	74.79	74.11	71.69	70.31	69.51
9000	85.98	85.00	84.14	83.37	80.65	79.10	78.19
10000	95.53	94.45	93.49	92.64	89.61	87.89	86.88
11000	105.09	103.89	102.84	101.90	98.57	96.67	95.57
12000	114.64	113.34	112.19	111.17	107.53	105.46	104.26
13000	124.19	122.78	121.53	120.43	116.49	114.25	112.95
14000	133.74	132.23	130.88	129.69	125.45	123.04	121.63
15000	143.30	141.67	140.23	138.96	134.42	131.83	130.32
20000	191.06	188.89	186.98	185.28	179.22	175.77	173.76
25000	238.83	236.12	233.72	231.60	224.03	219.71	217.20
30000	286.60	283.34	280.46	277.91	268.83	263.66	260.65
35000	334.36	330.56	327.21	324.23	313.64	307.60	304.09
40000	382.13	377.79	373.95	370.55	358.44	351.54	347.53
45000	429.89	425.01	420.69	416.87	403.25	395.49	390.97
50000	477.66	472.23	467.44	463.19	448.05	439.43	434.41
55000	525.43	519.46	514.18	509.51	492.86	483.37	477.85
56000	534.98	528.90	523.53	518.77	501.82	492.16	486.54
57000	544.53	538.35	532.88	528.04	510.78	500.95	495.23
58000	554.08	547.79	542.23	537.30	519.74	509.74	503.91
59000	563.64	557.24	551.58	546.57	528.70	518.52	512.60
60000	573.19	566.68	560.93	555.83	537.66	527.31	521.29
61000	582.74	576.12	570.27	565.09	546.62	536.10	529.98
62000	592.30	585.57	579.62	574.36	555.58	544.89	538.67
63000	601.85	595.01	588.97	583.62	564.54	553.68	547.36
64000	611.40	604.46	598.32	592.89	573.50	562.47	556.04
65000	620.96	613.90	607.67	602.15	582.47	571.26	564.73
70000	668.72	661.13	654.41	648.47	627.27	615.20	608.17
75000	716.49	708.35	701.16	694.79	672.08	659.14	651.61
80000	764.25	755.57	747.90	741.11	716.88	703.08	695.05
85000	812.02	802.80	794.65	787.43	761.69	747.03	738.50
90000	859.79	850.02	841.39	833.74	806.49	790.97	781.94
95000	907.55	897.24	888.13	880.06	851.30	834.91	825.38
100000	955.32	944.47	934.88	926.38	896.10	878.86	868.82
105000	1003.08	991.69	981.62	972.70	940.91	922.80	912.26
110000	1050.85	1038.91	1028.36	1019.02	985.71	966.74	955.70
120000	1146.38	1133.36	1121.85	1111.66	1075.32	1054.63	1042.58
130000	1241.91	1227.81	1215.34	1204.30	1164.93	1142.51	1129.46
140000	1337.45	1322.25	1308.83	1296.94	1254.54	1230.40	1216.35
150000	1432.98	1416.70	1402.31	1389.57	1344.15	1318.28	1303.23
160000	1528.51	1511.15	1495.80	1482.21	1433.76	1406.17	1390.11
175000	1671.81	1652.82	1636.03	1621.17	1568.18	1538.00	1520.43
200000	1910.64	1888.93	1869.75	1852.77	1792.20	1757.71	1737.64
250000	2388.30	2361.17	2337.19	2315.96	2240.25	2197.14	2172.05
500000	4776.59	4722.33	4674.38	4631.92	4480.51	4394.28	4344.09
1000000	9553.18	9444.66	9348.77	9263.83	8961.01	8788.56	8688.18

10.50%   MONTHLY PAYMENTS

AMOUNT	1 YEAR	2 YEARS	3 YEARS	4 YEARS	5 YEARS	6 YEARS	7 YEARS
100	8.81	4.64	3.25	2.56	2.15	1.88	1.69
200	17.63	9.28	6.50	5.12	4.30	3.76	3.37
500	44.07	23.19	16.25	12.80	10.75	9.39	8.43
1000	88.15	46.38	32.50	25.60	21.49	18.78	16.86
2000	176.30	92.75	65.00	51.21	42.99	37.56	33.72
3000	264.45	139.13	97.51	76.81	64.48	56.34	50.58
4000	352.59	185.50	130.01	102.41	85.98	75.12	67.44
5000	440.74	231.88	162.51	128.02	107.47	93.89	84.30
6000	528.89	278.26	195.01	153.62	128.96	112.67	101.16
7000	617.04	324.63	227.52	179.22	150.46	131.45	118.02
8000	705.19	371.01	260.02	204.83	171.95	150.23	134.89
9000	793.34	417.38	292.52	230.43	193.45	169.01	151.75
10000	881.49	463.76	325.02	256.03	214.94	187.79	168.61
11000	969.63	510.14	357.53	281.64	236.43	206.57	185.47
12000	1057.78	556.51	390.03	307.24	257.93	225.35	202.33
13000	1145.93	602.89	422.53	332.84	279.42	244.13	219.19
14000	1234.08	649.26	455.03	358.45	300.91	262.91	236.05
15000	1322.23	695.64	487.54	384.05	322.41	281.68	252.91
20000	1762.97	927.52	650.05	512.07	429.88	375.58	337.21
25000	2203.72	1159.40	812.56	640.08	537.35	469.47	421.52
30000	2644.46	1391.28	975.07	768.10	644.82	563.37	505.82
35000	3085.20	1623.16	1137.59	896.12	752.29	657.26	590.12
40000	3525.94	1855.04	1300.10	1024.14	859.76	751.16	674.43
45000	3966.69	2086.92	1462.61	1152.15	967.23	845.05	758.73
50000	4407.43	2318.80	1625.12	1280.17	1074.70	938.95	843.03
55000	4848.17	2550.68	1787.63	1408.19	1182.16	1032.84	927.34
56000	4936.32	2597.06	1820.14	1433.79	1203.66	1051.62	944.20
57000	5024.47	2643.43	1852.64	1459.39	1225.15	1070.40	961.06
58000	5112.62	2689.81	1885.14	1485.00	1246.65	1089.18	977.92
59000	5200.77	2736.19	1917.64	1510.60	1268.14	1107.96	994.78
60000	5288.92	2782.56	1950.15	1536.20	1289.63	1126.74	1011.64
61000	5377.06	2828.94	1982.65	1561.81	1311.13	1145.52	1028.50
62000	5465.21	2875.31	2015.15	1587.41	1332.62	1164.30	1045.36
63000	5553.36	2921.69	2047.65	1613.01	1354.12	1183.08	1062.22
64000	5641.51	2968.07	2080.16	1638.62	1375.61	1201.85	1079.08
65000	5729.66	3014.44	2112.66	1664.22	1397.10	1220.63	1095.94
70000	6170.40	3246.32	2275.17	1792.24	1504.57	1314.53	1180.25
75000	6611.15	3478.20	2437.68	1920.25	1612.04	1408.42	1264.55
80000	7051.89	3710.08	2600.20	2048.27	1719.51	1502.32	1348.85
85000	7492.63	3941.96	2762.71	2176.29	1826.98	1596.21	1433.16
90000	7933.37	4173.84	2925.22	2304.30	1934.45	1690.11	1517.46
95000	8374.12	4405.72	3087.73	2432.32	2041.92	1784.00	1601.76
100000	8814.86	4637.60	3250.24	2560.34	2149.39	1877.90	1686.07
105000	9255.60	4869.48	3412.76	2688.35	2256.86	1971.79	1770.37
110000	9696.35	5101.36	3575.27	2816.37	2364.33	2065.69	1854.67
120000	10577.83	5565.12	3900.29	3072.41	2579.27	2253.48	2023.28
130000	11459.32	6028.89	4225.32	3328.44	2794.21	2441.27	2191.89
140000	12340.80	6492.65	4550.34	3584.47	3009.15	2629.06	2360.49
150000	13222.29	6956.41	4875.37	3840.51	3224.09	2816.85	2529.10
160000	14103.78	7420.17	5200.39	4096.54	3439.02	3004.64	2697.71
175000	15426.01	8115.81	5687.93	4480.59	3761.43	3286.32	2950.62
200000	17629.72	9275.21	6500.49	5120.68	4298.78	3755.79	3372.13
250000	22037.15	11594.01	8125.61	6400.84	5373.48	4694.74	4215.17
500000	44074.30	23188.02	16251.22	12801.69	10746.95	9389.48	8430.34
1000000	88148.60	46376.04	32502.44	25603.38	21493.90	18778.97	16860.67

MONTHLY PAYMENTS 10.50%

AMOUNT	8 YEARS	9 YEARS	10 YEARS	11 YEARS	12 YEARS	13 YEARS	14 YEARS
100	1.54	1.44	1.35	1.28	1.22	1.18	1.14
200	3.09	2.87	2.70	2.56	2.45	2.36	2.28
500	7.72	7.18	6.75	6.40	6.12	5.89	5.69
1000	15.44	14.35	13.49	12.80	12.24	11.78	11.38
2000	30.88	28.70	26.99	25.61	24.48	23.55	22.77
3000	46.32	43.05	40.48	38.41	36.72	35.33	34.15
4000	61.76	57.40	53.97	51.22	48.97	47.10	45.54
5000	77.20	71.75	67.47	64.02	61.21	58.88	56.92
6000	92.64	86.11	80.96	76.83	73.45	70.65	68.31
7000	108.08	100.46	94.45	89.63	85.69	82.43	79.69
8000	123.52	114.81	107.95	102.44	97.93	94.20	91.07
9000	138.96	129.16	121.44	115.24	110.17	105.98	102.46
10000	154.40	143.51	134.93	128.04	122.41	117.75	113.84
11000	169.84	157.86	148.43	140.85	134.66	129.53	125.23
12000	185.28	172.21	161.92	153.65	146.90	141.30	136.61
13000	200.72	186.56	175.42	166.46	159.14	153.08	148.00
14000	216.16	200.91	188.91	179.26	171.38	164.85	159.38
15000	231.60	215.26	202.40	192.07	183.62	176.63	170.77
20000	308.80	287.02	269.87	256.09	244.83	235.50	227.69
25000	386.00	358.77	337.34	320.11	306.04	294.38	284.61
30000	463.20	430.53	404.80	384.13	367.24	353.25	341.53
35000	540.40	502.28	472.27	448.16	428.45	412.13	398.45
40000	617.60	574.03	539.74	512.18	489.66	471.00	455.37
45000	694.80	645.79	607.21	576.20	550.86	529.88	512.30
50000	772.00	717.54	674.67	640.22	612.07	588.75	569.22
55000	849.20	789.30	742.14	704.25	673.28	647.63	626.14
56000	864.64	803.65	755.64	717.05	685.52	659.40	637.52
57000	880.08	818.00	769.13	729.85	697.76	671.18	648.91
58000	895.52	832.35	782.62	742.66	710.00	682.95	660.29
59000	910.96	846.70	796.12	755.46	722.24	694.73	671.68
60000	926.40	861.05	809.61	768.27	734.48	706.50	683.06
61000	941.84	875.40	823.10	781.07	746.73	718.28	694.44
62000	957.28	889.75	836.60	793.88	758.97	730.05	705.83
63000	972.72	904.10	850.09	806.68	771.21	741.83	717.21
64000	988.16	918.46	863.58	819.49	783.45	753.60	728.60
65000	1003.60	932.81	877.08	832.29	795.69	765.38	739.98
70000	1080.80	1004.56	944.54	896.31	856.90	824.25	796.90
75000	1158.00	1076.31	1012.01	960.33	918.11	883.13	853.83
80000	1235.20	1148.07	1079.48	1024.36	979.31	942.00	910.75
85000	1312.40	1219.82	1146.95	1088.38	1040.52	1000.88	967.67
90000	1389.60	1291.58	1214.41	1152.40	1101.73	1059.75	1024.59
95000	1466.80	1363.33	1281.88	1216.42	1162.93	1118.63	1081.51
100000	1544.00	1435.09	1349.35	1280.45	1224.14	1177.50	1138.43
105000	1621.20	1506.84	1416.82	1344.47	1285.35	1236.38	1195.36
110000	1698.40	1578.59	1484.28	1408.49	1346.55	1295.25	1252.28
120000	1852.80	1722.10	1619.22	1536.54	1468.97	1413.00	1366.12
130000	2007.20	1865.61	1754.15	1664.58	1591.38	1530.75	1479.96
140000	2161.60	2009.12	1889.09	1792.62	1713.80	1648.50	1593.81
150000	2316.00	2152.63	2024.02	1920.67	1836.21	1766.25	1707.65
160000	2470.40	2296.14	2158.96	2048.71	1958.63	1884.00	1821.49
175000	2702.00	2511.40	2361.36	2240.78	2142.25	2060.63	1992.26
200000	3088.00	2870.17	2698.70	2560.89	2448.28	2355.00	2276.87
250000	3860.00	3587.72	3373.37	3201.11	3060.35	2943.75	2846.09
500000	7720.01	7175.43	6746.75	6402.23	6120.70	5887.51	5692.17
1000000	15440.02	14350.86	13493.50	12804.46	12241.41	11775.02	11384.34

10.50%　　MONTHLY PAYMENTS

AMOUNT	15 YEARS	16 YEARS	17 YEARS	18 YEARS	19 YEARS	20 YEARS	21 YEARS
100	1.11	1.08	1.05	1.03	1.01	1.00	0.98
200	2.21	2.15	2.11	2.06	2.03	2.00	1.97
500	5.53	5.39	5.27	5.16	5.07	4.99	4.92
1000	11.05	10.77	10.53	10.32	10.14	9.98	9.85
2000	22.11	21.54	21.06	20.64	20.28	19.97	19.69
3000	33.16	32.32	31.59	30.97	30.42	29.95	29.54
4000	44.22	43.09	42.12	41.29	40.57	39.94	39.38
5000	55.27	53.86	52.65	51.61	50.71	49.92	49.23
6000	66.32	64.63	63.18	61.93	60.85	59.90	59.08
7000	77.38	75.41	73.72	72.26	70.99	69.89	68.92
8000	88.43	86.18	84.25	82.58	81.13	79.87	78.77
9000	99.49	96.95	94.78	92.90	91.27	89.85	88.61
10000	110.54	107.72	105.31	103.22	101.41	99.84	98.46
11000	121.59	118.50	115.84	113.55	111.56	109.82	108.31
12000	132.65	129.27	126.37	123.87	121.70	119.81	118.15
13000	143.70	140.04	136.90	134.19	131.84	129.79	128.00
14000	154.76	150.81	147.43	144.51	141.98	139.77	137.84
15000	165.81	161.59	157.96	154.83	152.12	149.76	147.69
20000	221.08	215.45	210.62	206.45	202.83	199.68	196.92
25000	276.35	269.31	263.27	258.06	253.53	249.59	246.15
30000	331.62	323.17	315.92	309.67	304.24	299.51	295.38
35000	386.89	377.03	368.58	361.28	354.95	349.43	344.61
40000	442.16	430.90	421.23	412.89	405.66	399.35	393.84
45000	497.43	484.76	473.89	464.50	456.36	449.27	443.07
50000	552.70	538.62	526.54	516.11	507.07	499.19	492.30
55000	607.97	592.48	579.19	567.73	557.78	549.11	541.53
56000	619.02	603.26	589.73	578.05	567.92	559.09	551.38
57000	630.08	614.03	600.26	588.37	578.06	569.08	561.22
58000	641.13	624.80	610.79	598.69	588.20	579.06	571.07
59000	652.19	635.57	621.32	609.01	598.34	589.04	580.91
60000	663.24	646.35	631.85	619.34	608.48	599.03	590.76
61000	674.29	657.12	642.38	629.66	618.62	609.01	600.61
62000	685.35	667.89	652.91	639.98	628.77	619.00	610.45
63000	696.40	678.66	663.44	650.30	638.91	628.98	620.30
64000	707.46	689.44	673.97	660.63	649.05	638.96	630.14
65000	718.51	700.21	684.50	670.95	659.19	648.95	639.99
70000	773.78	754.07	737.16	722.56	709.90	698.87	689.22
75000	829.05	807.93	789.81	774.17	760.60	748.78	738.45
80000	884.32	861.79	842.46	825.78	811.31	798.70	787.68
85000	939.59	915.66	895.12	877.39	862.02	848.62	836.91
90000	994.86	969.52	947.77	929.00	912.73	898.54	886.14
95000	1050.13	1023.38	1000.43	980.62	963.43	948.46	935.37
100000	1105.40	1077.24	1053.08	1032.23	1014.14	998.38	984.60
105000	1160.67	1131.10	1105.74	1083.84	1064.85	1048.30	1033.83
110000	1215.94	1184.97	1158.39	1135.45	1115.55	1098.22	1083.06
120000	1326.48	1292.69	1263.70	1238.67	1216.97	1198.06	1181.52
130000	1437.02	1400.42	1369.01	1341.90	1318.38	1297.89	1279.98
140000	1547.56	1508.14	1474.31	1445.12	1419.79	1397.73	1378.44
150000	1658.10	1615.86	1579.62	1548.34	1521.21	1497.57	1476.90
160000	1768.64	1723.59	1684.93	1651.56	1622.62	1597.41	1575.36
175000	1934.45	1885.17	1842.89	1806.40	1774.74	1747.16	1723.05
200000	2210.80	2154.48	2106.16	2064.46	2028.28	1996.76	1969.20
250000	2763.50	2693.11	2632.70	2580.57	2535.35	2495.95	2461.50
500000	5526.99	5386.21	5265.41	5161.14	5070.69	4991.90	4922.99
1000000	11053.99	10772.42	10530.81	10322.28	10141.39	9983.80	9845.99

MONTHLY PAYMENTS 10.50%

AMOUNT	22 YEARS	23 YEARS	24 YEARS	25 YEARS	30 YEARS	35 YEARS	40 YEARS
100	0.97	0.96	0.95	0.94	0.91	0.90	0.89
200	1.95	1.92	1.90	1.89	1.83	1.80	1.78
500	4.86	4.81	4.76	4.72	4.57	4.49	4.44
1000	9.73	9.62	9.52	9.44	9.15	8.98	8.89
2000	19.45	19.24	19.05	18.88	18.29	17.96	17.77
3000	29.18	28.86	28.57	28.33	27.44	26.94	26.66
4000	38.90	38.47	38.10	37.77	36.59	35.93	35.54
5000	48.63	48.09	47.62	47.21	45.74	44.91	44.43
6000	58.35	57.71	57.15	56.65	54.88	53.89	53.31
7000	68.08	67.33	66.67	66.09	64.03	62.87	62.20
8000	77.80	76.95	76.20	75.53	73.18	71.85	71.09
9000	87.53	86.57	85.72	84.98	82.33	80.83	79.97
10000	97.25	96.19	95.25	94.42	91.47	89.81	88.86
11000	106.98	105.81	104.77	103.86	100.62	98.79	97.74
12000	116.70	115.42	114.30	113.30	109.77	107.78	106.63
13000	126.43	125.04	123.82	122.74	118.92	116.76	115.51
14000	136.15	134.66	133.35	132.19	128.06	125.74	124.40
15000	145.88	144.28	142.87	141.63	137.21	134.72	133.29
20000	194.50	192.37	190.50	188.84	182.95	179.63	177.71
25000	243.13	240.47	238.12	236.05	228.68	224.53	222.14
30000	291.75	288.56	285.74	283.25	274.42	269.44	266.57
35000	340.38	336.65	333.37	330.46	320.16	314.35	311.00
40000	389.00	384.75	380.99	377.67	365.90	359.25	355.43
45000	437.63	432.84	428.62	424.88	411.63	404.16	399.86
50000	486.25	480.93	476.24	472.09	457.37	449.07	444.29
55000	534.88	529.03	523.86	519.30	503.11	493.97	488.71
56000	544.60	538.65	533.39	528.74	512.25	502.96	497.60
57000	554.33	548.26	542.91	538.18	521.40	511.94	506.49
58000	564.05	557.88	552.44	547.63	530.55	520.92	515.37
59000	573.78	567.50	561.96	557.07	539.70	529.90	524.26
60000	583.50	577.12	571.49	566.51	548.84	538.88	533.14
61000	593.23	586.74	581.01	575.95	557.99	547.86	542.03
62000	602.95	596.36	590.54	585.39	567.14	556.84	550.91
63000	612.68	605.98	600.06	594.83	576.29	565.82	559.80
64000	622.40	615.60	609.59	604.28	585.43	574.81	568.68
65000	632.13	625.21	619.11	613.72	594.58	583.79	577.57
70000	680.75	673.31	666.74	660.93	640.32	628.69	622.00
75000	729.38	721.40	714.36	708.14	686.05	673.60	666.43
80000	778.01	769.49	761.98	755.35	731.79	718.51	710.86
85000	826.63	817.59	809.61	802.55	777.53	763.41	755.28
90000	875.26	865.68	857.23	849.76	823.27	808.32	799.71
95000	923.88	913.77	904.86	896.97	869.00	853.23	844.14
100000	972.51	961.87	952.48	944.18	914.74	898.13	888.57
105000	1021.13	1009.96	1000.10	991.39	960.48	943.04	933.00
110000	1069.76	1058.05	1047.73	1038.60	1006.21	987.95	977.43
120000	1167.01	1154.24	1142.98	1133.02	1097.69	1077.76	1066.28
130000	1264.26	1250.43	1238.23	1227.44	1189.16	1167.57	1155.14
140000	1361.51	1346.61	1333.47	1321.85	1280.64	1257.39	1244.00
150000	1458.76	1442.80	1428.72	1416.27	1372.11	1347.20	1332.86
160000	1556.01	1538.99	1523.97	1510.69	1463.58	1437.01	1421.71
175000	1701.89	1683.27	1666.84	1652.32	1600.79	1571.73	1555.00
200000	1945.01	1923.73	1904.96	1888.36	1829.48	1796.27	1777.14
250000	2431.27	2404.67	2381.20	2360.45	2286.85	2245.34	2221.43
500000	4862.54	4809.34	4762.40	4720.91	4573.70	4490.67	4442.85
1000000	9725.07	9618.67	9524.81	9441.82	9147.39	8981.34	8885.70

10.75% MONTHLY PAYMENTS

AMOUNT	1 YEAR	2 YEARS	3 YEARS	4 YEARS	5 YEARS	6 YEARS	7 YEARS
100	8.83	4.65	3.26	2.57	2.16	1.89	1.70
200	17.65	9.30	6.52	5.14	4.32	3.78	3.40
500	44.13	23.25	16.31	12.86	10.81	9.45	8.50
1000	88.27	46.49	32.62	25.72	21.62	18.91	16.99
2000	176.53	92.98	65.24	51.45	43.24	37.81	33.98
3000	264.80	139.48	97.86	77.17	64.85	56.72	50.97
4000	353.06	185.97	130.48	102.90	86.47	75.63	67.97
5000	441.33	232.46	163.10	128.62	108.09	94.53	84.96
6000	529.59	278.95	195.72	154.35	129.71	113.44	101.95
7000	617.86	325.44	228.34	180.07	151.33	132.34	118.94
8000	706.12	371.93	260.96	205.79	172.94	151.25	135.93
9000	794.39	418.43	293.58	231.52	194.56	170.16	152.92
10000	882.65	464.92	326.20	257.24	216.18	189.06	169.91
11000	970.92	511.41	358.82	282.97	237.80	207.97	186.90
12000	1059.18	557.90	391.45	308.69	259.42	226.88	203.90
13000	1147.45	604.39	424.07	334.42	281.03	245.78	220.89
14000	1235.71	650.89	456.69	360.14	302.65	264.69	237.88
15000	1323.98	697.38	489.31	385.86	324.27	283.59	254.87
20000	1765.30	929.84	652.41	514.49	432.36	378.13	339.83
25000	2206.63	1162.30	815.51	643.11	540.45	472.66	424.78
30000	2647.95	1394.76	978.61	771.73	648.54	567.19	509.74
35000	3089.28	1627.21	1141.72	900.35	756.63	661.72	594.69
40000	3530.60	1859.67	1304.82	1028.97	864.72	756.25	679.65
45000	3971.93	2092.13	1467.92	1157.59	972.81	850.78	764.61
50000	4413.25	2324.59	1631.02	1286.21	1080.90	945.31	849.56
55000	4854.58	2557.05	1794.12	1414.84	1188.99	1039.85	934.52
56000	4942.84	2603.54	1826.75	1440.56	1210.61	1058.75	951.51
57000	5031.11	2650.04	1859.37	1466.28	1232.22	1077.66	968.50
58000	5119.38	2696.53	1891.99	1492.01	1253.84	1096.56	985.49
59000	5207.64	2743.02	1924.61	1517.73	1275.46	1115.47	1002.49
60000	5295.91	2789.51	1957.23	1543.46	1297.08	1134.38	1019.48
61000	5384.17	2836.00	1989.85	1569.18	1318.70	1153.28	1036.47
62000	5472.44	2882.49	2022.47	1594.91	1340.31	1172.19	1053.46
63000	5560.70	2928.99	2055.09	1620.63	1361.93	1191.10	1070.45
64000	5648.97	2975.48	2087.71	1646.35	1383.55	1210.00	1087.44
65000	5737.23	3021.97	2120.33	1672.08	1405.17	1228.91	1104.43
70000	6178.56	3254.43	2283.43	1800.70	1513.26	1323.44	1189.39
75000	6619.88	3486.89	2446.53	1929.32	1621.35	1417.97	1274.35
80000	7061.21	3719.35	2609.64	2057.94	1729.44	1512.50	1359.30
85000	7502.53	3951.81	2772.74	2186.56	1837.53	1607.03	1444.26
90000	7943.86	4184.27	2935.84	2315.19	1945.62	1701.57	1529.21
95000	8385.18	4416.73	3098.94	2443.81	2053.71	1796.10	1614.17
100000	8826.51	4649.19	3262.05	2572.43	2161.80	1890.63	1699.13
105000	9267.83	4881.64	3425.15	2701.05	2269.89	1985.16	1784.08
110000	9709.16	5114.10	3588.25	2829.67	2377.97	2079.69	1869.04
120000	10591.81	5579.02	3914.45	3086.91	2594.15	2268.75	2038.95
130000	11474.46	6043.94	4240.66	3344.16	2810.33	2457.82	2208.87
140000	12357.11	6508.86	4566.86	3601.40	3026.51	2646.88	2378.78
150000	13239.76	6973.78	4893.07	3858.64	3242.69	2835.94	2548.69
160000	14122.41	7438.70	5219.27	4115.89	3458.87	3025.00	2718.60
175000	15446.39	8136.07	5708.58	4501.75	3783.14	3308.60	2973.47
200000	17653.02	9298.37	6524.09	5144.86	4323.59	3781.26	3398.25
250000	22066.27	11622.96	8155.11	6431.07	5404.49	4726.57	4247.82
500000	44132.54	23245.93	16310.23	12862.14	10808.98	9453.14	8495.64
1000000	88265.09	46491.85	32620.45	25724.28	21617.95	18906.28	16991.27

MONTHLY PAYMENTS 10.75%

AMOUNT	8 YEARS	9 YEARS	10 YEARS	11 YEARS	12 YEARS	13 YEARS	14 YEARS
100	1.56	1.45	1.36	1.29	1.24	1.19	1.15
200	3.11	2.90	2.73	2.59	2.48	2.38	2.31
500	7.79	7.24	6.82	6.47	6.19	5.96	5.77
1000	15.57	14.49	13.63	12.95	12.39	11.92	11.54
2000	31.15	28.98	27.27	25.90	24.78	23.85	23.07
3000	46.72	43.46	40.90	38.84	37.16	35.77	34.61
4000	62.30	57.95	54.54	51.79	49.55	47.70	46.15
5000	77.87	72.44	68.17	64.74	61.94	59.62	57.68
6000	93.44	86.93	81.80	77.69	74.33	71.55	69.22
7000	109.02	101.42	95.44	90.64	86.72	83.47	80.76
8000	124.59	115.90	109.07	103.58	99.10	95.40	92.30
9000	140.17	130.39	122.70	116.53	111.49	107.32	103.83
10000	155.74	144.88	136.34	129.48	123.88	119.25	115.37
11000	171.31	159.37	149.97	142.43	136.27	131.17	126.91
12000	186.89	173.86	163.61	155.38	148.66	143.10	138.44
13000	202.46	188.34	177.24	168.32	161.04	155.02	149.98
14000	218.03	202.83	190.87	181.27	173.43	166.95	161.52
15000	233.61	217.32	204.51	194.22	185.82	178.87	173.05
20000	311.48	289.76	272.68	258.96	247.76	238.49	230.74
25000	389.35	362.20	340.85	323.70	309.70	298.12	288.42
30000	467.22	434.64	409.02	388.44	371.64	357.74	346.11
35000	545.09	507.08	477.19	453.18	433.58	417.36	403.79
40000	622.96	579.52	545.35	517.92	495.52	476.99	461.48
45000	700.83	651.96	613.52	582.66	557.46	536.61	519.16
50000	778.70	724.40	681.69	647.40	619.40	596.23	576.85
55000	856.56	796.84	749.86	712.14	681.34	655.86	634.53
56000	872.14	811.33	763.50	725.09	693.73	667.78	646.07
57000	887.71	825.82	777.13	738.04	706.12	679.71	657.61
58000	903.29	840.30	790.76	750.98	718.51	691.63	669.14
59000	918.86	854.79	804.40	763.93	730.89	703.56	680.68
60000	934.43	869.28	818.03	776.88	743.28	715.48	692.22
61000	950.01	883.77	831.67	789.83	755.67	727.41	703.75
62000	965.58	898.26	845.30	802.78	768.06	739.33	715.29
63000	981.16	912.74	858.93	815.72	780.45	751.26	726.83
64000	996.73	927.23	872.57	828.67	792.83	763.18	738.37
65000	1012.30	941.72	886.20	841.62	805.22	775.10	749.90
70000	1090.17	1014.16	954.37	906.36	867.16	834.73	807.59
75000	1168.04	1086.60	1022.54	971.10	929.10	894.35	865.27
80000	1245.91	1159.04	1090.71	1035.84	991.04	953.97	922.96
85000	1323.78	1231.48	1158.88	1100.58	1052.98	1013.60	980.64
90000	1401.65	1303.92	1227.05	1165.32	1114.92	1073.22	1038.33
95000	1479.52	1376.36	1295.22	1230.06	1176.86	1132.85	1096.01
100000	1557.39	1448.80	1363.39	1294.80	1238.80	1192.47	1153.70
105000	1635.26	1521.24	1431.56	1359.54	1300.74	1252.09	1211.38
110000	1713.13	1593.68	1499.73	1424.28	1362.68	1311.72	1269.07
120000	1868.87	1738.56	1636.06	1553.76	1486.57	1430.96	1384.44
130000	2024.61	1883.44	1772.40	1683.24	1610.45	1550.21	1499.80
140000	2180.35	2028.32	1908.74	1812.72	1734.33	1669.46	1615.17
150000	2336.09	2173.20	2045.08	1942.20	1858.21	1788.70	1730.54
160000	2491.82	2318.08	2181.42	2071.68	1982.09	1907.95	1845.91
175000	2725.43	2535.40	2385.93	2265.90	2167.91	2086.82	2018.97
200000	3114.78	2897.60	2726.77	2589.60	2477.61	2384.94	2307.39
250000	3893.48	3622.00	3408.47	3237.00	3097.01	2981.17	2884.24
500000	7786.95	7244.00	6816.93	6474.00	6194.02	5962.34	5768.48
1000000	15573.90	14488.01	13633.87	12947.99	12388.04	11924.69	11536.96

10.75%

MONTHLY PAYMENTS

AMOUNT	15 YEARS	16 YEARS	17 YEARS	18 YEARS	19 YEARS	20 YEARS	21 YEARS
100	1.12	1.09	1.07	1.05	1.03	1.02	1.00
200	2.24	2.19	2.14	2.10	2.06	2.03	2.00
500	5.60	5.47	5.35	5.24	5.15	5.08	5.01
1000	11.21	10.93	10.69	10.49	10.31	10.15	10.02
2000	22.42	21.86	21.38	20.97	20.61	20.30	20.03
3000	33.63	32.79	32.08	31.46	30.92	30.46	30.05
4000	44.84	43.72	42.77	41.94	41.23	40.61	40.07
5000	56.05	54.65	53.46	52.43	51.54	50.76	50.08
6000	67.26	65.58	64.15	62.92	61.84	60.91	60.10
7000	78.47	76.51	74.84	73.40	72.15	71.07	70.12
8000	89.68	87.45	85.53	83.89	82.46	81.22	80.13
9000	100.89	98.38	96.23	94.37	92.77	91.37	90.15
10000	112.09	109.31	106.92	104.86	103.07	101.52	100.17
11000	123.30	120.24	117.61	115.34	113.38	111.68	110.18
12000	134.51	131.17	128.30	125.83	123.69	121.83	120.20
13000	145.72	142.10	138.99	136.32	134.00	131.98	130.22
14000	156.93	153.03	149.68	146.80	144.30	142.13	140.24
15000	168.14	163.96	160.38	157.29	154.61	152.28	150.25
20000	224.19	218.61	213.84	209.72	206.15	203.05	200.34
25000	280.24	273.27	267.29	262.15	257.69	253.81	250.42
30000	336.28	327.92	320.75	314.58	309.22	304.57	300.50
35000	392.33	382.57	374.21	367.00	360.76	355.33	350.59
40000	448.38	437.23	427.67	419.43	412.30	406.09	400.67
45000	504.43	491.88	481.13	471.86	463.84	456.85	450.76
50000	560.47	546.53	534.59	524.29	515.37	507.61	500.84
55000	616.52	601.19	588.05	576.72	566.91	558.38	550.92
56000	627.73	612.12	598.74	587.21	577.22	568.53	560.94
57000	638.94	623.05	609.43	597.69	587.53	578.68	570.96
58000	650.15	633.98	620.12	608.18	597.83	588.83	580.97
59000	661.36	644.91	630.82	618.67	608.14	598.99	590.99
60000	672.57	655.84	641.51	629.15	618.45	609.14	601.01
61000	683.78	666.77	652.20	639.64	628.76	619.29	611.02
62000	694.99	677.70	662.89	650.12	639.06	629.44	621.04
63000	706.20	688.63	673.58	660.61	649.37	639.59	631.06
64000	717.41	699.56	684.27	671.09	659.68	649.75	641.07
65000	728.62	710.50	694.97	681.58	669.99	659.90	651.09
70000	784.66	765.15	748.42	734.01	721.52	710.66	701.18
75000	840.71	819.80	801.88	786.44	773.06	761.42	751.26
80000	896.76	874.46	855.34	838.87	824.60	812.18	801.34
85000	952.81	929.11	908.80	891.30	876.13	862.94	851.43
90000	1008.85	983.76	962.26	943.73	927.67	913.71	901.51
95000	1064.90	1038.42	1015.72	996.16	979.21	964.47	951.60
100000	1120.95	1093.07	1069.18	1048.58	1030.75	1015.23	1001.68
105000	1177.00	1147.72	1122.64	1101.01	1082.28	1065.99	1051.76
110000	1233.04	1202.38	1176.10	1153.44	1133.82	1116.75	1101.85
120000	1345.14	1311.68	1283.01	1258.30	1236.90	1218.27	1202.02
130000	1457.23	1420.99	1389.93	1363.16	1339.97	1319.80	1302.18
140000	1569.33	1530.30	1496.85	1468.02	1443.05	1421.32	1402.35
150000	1681.42	1639.60	1603.77	1572.88	1546.12	1522.84	1502.52
160000	1793.52	1748.91	1710.69	1677.74	1649.19	1624.37	1602.69
175000	1961.66	1912.87	1871.06	1835.02	1803.81	1776.65	1752.94
200000	2241.90	2186.14	2138.36	2097.17	2061.49	2030.46	2003.36
250000	2802.37	2732.67	2672.95	2621.46	2576.87	2538.07	2504.20
500000	5604.74	5465.35	5345.89	5242.92	5153.73	5076.14	5008.40
1000000	11209.48	10930.70	10691.78	10485.85	10307.47	10152.29	10016.79

MONTHLY PAYMENTS 10.75%

AMOUNT	22 YEARS	23 YEARS	24 YEARS	25 YEARS	30 YEARS	35 YEARS	40 YEARS
100	0.99	0.98	0.97	0.96	0.93	0.92	0.91
200	1.98	1.96	1.94	1.92	1.87	1.84	1.82
500	4.95	4.90	4.85	4.81	4.67	4.59	4.54
1000	9.90	9.79	9.70	9.62	9.33	9.18	9.08
2000	19.80	19.59	19.40	19.24	18.67	18.35	18.17
3000	29.69	29.38	29.11	28.86	28.00	27.53	27.25
4000	39.59	39.18	38.81	38.48	37.34	36.70	36.34
5000	49.49	48.97	48.51	48.10	46.67	45.88	45.42
6000	59.39	58.76	58.21	57.73	56.01	55.05	54.50
7000	69.29	68.56	67.91	67.35	65.34	64.23	63.59
8000	79.18	78.35	77.62	76.97	74.68	73.40	72.67
9000	89.08	88.14	87.32	86.59	84.01	82.58	81.76
10000	98.98	97.94	97.02	96.21	93.35	91.75	90.84
11000	108.88	107.73	106.72	105.83	102.68	100.93	99.92
12000	118.78	117.53	116.42	115.45	112.02	110.10	109.01
13000	128.68	127.32	126.13	125.07	121.35	119.28	118.09
14000	138.57	137.11	135.83	134.69	130.69	128.45	127.18
15000	148.47	146.91	145.53	144.31	140.02	137.63	136.26
20000	197.96	195.88	194.04	192.42	186.70	183.50	181.68
25000	247.45	244.85	242.55	240.52	233.37	229.38	227.10
30000	296.94	293.81	291.06	288.63	280.04	275.25	272.52
35000	346.43	342.78	339.57	336.73	326.72	321.13	317.94
40000	395.92	391.75	388.08	384.84	373.39	367.00	363.36
45000	445.41	440.72	436.59	432.94	420.07	412.88	408.78
50000	494.90	489.69	485.10	481.05	466.74	458.75	454.20
55000	544.40	538.66	533.61	529.15	513.41	504.63	499.62
56000	554.29	548.45	543.31	538.77	522.75	513.80	508.70
57000	564.19	558.25	553.01	548.39	532.08	522.98	517.79
58000	574.09	568.04	562.72	558.01	541.42	532.15	526.87
59000	583.99	577.84	572.42	567.63	550.75	541.33	535.95
60000	593.89	587.63	582.12	577.26	560.09	550.50	545.04
61000	603.78	597.42	591.82	586.88	569.42	559.68	554.12
62000	613.68	607.22	601.52	596.50	578.76	568.85	563.21
63000	623.58	617.01	611.23	606.12	588.09	578.03	572.29
64000	633.48	626.80	620.93	615.74	597.43	587.20	581.37
65000	643.38	636.60	630.63	625.36	606.76	596.38	590.46
70000	692.87	685.57	679.14	673.46	653.44	642.25	635.88
75000	742.36	734.54	727.65	721.57	700.11	688.13	681.30
80000	791.85	783.51	776.16	769.67	746.79	734.00	726.72
85000	841.34	832.47	824.67	817.78	793.46	779.88	772.14
90000	890.83	881.44	873.18	865.88	840.13	825.75	817.56
95000	940.32	930.41	921.69	913.99	886.81	871.63	862.98
100000	989.81	979.38	970.20	962.09	933.48	917.50	908.40
105000	1039.30	1028.35	1018.71	1010.20	980.16	963.38	953.82
110000	1088.79	1077.32	1067.22	1058.30	1026.83	1009.25	999.24
120000	1187.77	1175.26	1164.24	1154.51	1120.18	1101.00	1090.08
130000	1286.75	1273.20	1261.26	1250.72	1213.53	1192.75	1180.92
140000	1385.73	1371.13	1358.28	1346.93	1306.87	1284.50	1271.76
150000	1484.71	1469.07	1455.30	1443.14	1400.22	1376.25	1362.60
160000	1583.70	1567.01	1552.32	1539.35	1493.57	1468.00	1453.44
175000	1732.17	1713.92	1697.85	1683.66	1633.59	1605.63	1589.70
200000	1979.62	1958.76	1940.40	1924.19	1866.96	1835.01	1816.79
250000	2474.52	2448.46	2425.50	2405.23	2333.70	2293.76	2270.99
500000	4949.05	4896.91	4850.99	4810.46	4667.41	4587.51	4541.99
1000000	9898.10	9793.82	9701.99	9620.93	9334.81	9175.03	9083.97

11.00%   MONTHLY PAYMENTS

AMOUNT	1 YEAR	2 YEARS	3 YEARS	4 YEARS	5 YEARS	6 YEARS	7 YEARS
100	8.84	4.66	3.27	2.58	2.17	1.90	1.71
200	17.68	9.32	6.55	5.17	4.35	3.81	3.42
500	44.19	23.30	16.37	12.92	10.87	9.52	8.56
1000	88.38	46.61	32.74	25.85	21.74	19.03	17.12
2000	176.76	93.22	65.48	51.69	43.48	38.07	34.24
3000	265.14	139.82	98.22	77.54	65.23	57.10	51.37
4000	353.53	186.43	130.95	103.38	86.97	76.14	68.49
5000	441.91	233.04	163.69	129.23	108.71	95.17	85.61
6000	530.29	279.65	196.43	155.07	130.45	114.20	102.73
7000	618.67	326.25	229.17	180.92	152.20	133.24	119.86
8000	707.05	372.86	261.91	206.76	173.94	152.27	136.98
9000	795.43	419.47	294.65	232.61	195.68	171.31	154.10
10000	883.82	466.08	327.39	258.46	217.42	190.34	171.22
11000	972.20	512.69	360.13	284.30	239.17	209.37	188.35
12000	1060.58	559.29	392.86	310.15	260.91	228.41	205.47
13000	1148.96	605.90	425.60	335.99	282.65	247.44	222.59
14000	1237.34	652.51	458.34	361.84	304.39	266.48	239.71
15000	1325.72	699.12	491.08	387.68	326.14	285.51	256.84
20000	1767.63	932.16	654.77	516.91	434.85	380.68	342.45
25000	2209.54	1165.20	818.47	646.14	543.56	475.85	428.06
30000	2651.45	1398.24	982.16	775.37	652.27	571.02	513.67
35000	3093.36	1631.27	1145.86	904.59	760.98	666.19	599.29
40000	3535.27	1864.31	1309.55	1033.82	869.70	761.36	684.90
45000	3977.17	2097.35	1473.24	1163.05	978.41	856.53	770.51
50000	4419.08	2330.39	1636.94	1292.28	1087.12	951.70	856.12
55000	4860.99	2563.43	1800.63	1421.50	1195.83	1046.87	941.73
56000	4949.37	2610.04	1833.37	1447.35	1217.58	1065.91	958.86
57000	5037.75	2656.65	1866.11	1473.19	1239.32	1084.94	975.98
58000	5126.14	2703.25	1898.85	1499.04	1261.06	1103.98	993.10
59000	5214.52	2749.86	1931.58	1524.89	1282.80	1123.01	1010.22
60000	5302.90	2796.47	1964.32	1550.73	1304.55	1142.04	1027.35
61000	5391.28	2843.08	1997.06	1576.58	1326.29	1161.08	1044.47
62000	5479.66	2889.69	2029.80	1602.42	1348.03	1180.11	1061.59
63000	5568.04	2936.29	2062.54	1628.27	1369.77	1199.15	1078.71
64000	5656.43	2982.90	2095.28	1654.11	1391.52	1218.18	1095.84
65000	5744.81	3029.51	2128.02	1679.96	1413.26	1237.22	1112.96
70000	6186.72	3262.55	2291.71	1809.19	1521.97	1332.39	1198.57
75000	6628.62	3495.59	2455.40	1938.41	1630.68	1427.56	1284.18
80000	7070.53	3728.63	2619.10	2067.64	1739.39	1522.73	1369.79
85000	7512.44	3961.67	2782.79	2196.87	1848.11	1617.90	1455.41
90000	7954.35	4194.71	2946.48	2326.10	1956.82	1713.07	1541.02
95000	8396.26	4427.74	3110.18	2455.32	2065.53	1808.24	1626.63
100000	8838.17	4660.78	3273.87	2584.55	2174.24	1903.41	1712.24
105000	9280.07	4893.82	3437.57	2713.78	2282.95	1998.58	1797.86
110000	9721.98	5126.86	3601.26	2843.01	2391.67	2093.75	1883.47
120000	10605.80	5592.94	3928.65	3101.46	2609.09	2284.09	2054.69
130000	11489.62	6059.02	4256.03	3359.92	2826.51	2474.43	2225.92
140000	12373.43	6525.10	4583.42	3618.37	3043.94	2664.77	2397.14
150000	13257.25	6991.18	4910.81	3876.83	3261.36	2855.11	2568.37
160000	14141.07	7457.25	5238.19	4135.28	3478.79	3045.45	2739.59
175000	15466.79	8156.37	5729.28	4522.97	3804.92	3330.96	2996.43
200000	17676.33	9321.57	6547.74	5169.10	4348.48	3806.82	3424.49
250000	22095.41	11651.96	8184.68	6461.38	5435.61	4758.52	4280.61
500000	44190.83	23303.92	16369.36	12922.76	10871.21	9517.04	8561.22
1000000	88381.66	46607.84	32738.72	25845.52	21742.42	19034.08	17122.44

MONTHLY PAYMENTS 11.00%

AMOUNT	8 YEARS	9 YEARS	10 YEARS	11 YEARS	12 YEARS	13 YEARS	14 YEARS
100	1.57	1.46	1.38	1.31	1.25	1.21	1.17
200	3.14	2.93	2.76	2.62	2.51	2.42	2.34
500	7.85	7.31	6.89	6.55	6.27	6.04	5.85
1000	15.71	14.63	13.78	13.09	12.54	12.08	11.69
2000	31.42	29.25	27.55	26.18	25.07	24.15	23.38
3000	47.13	43.88	41.33	39.28	37.61	36.23	35.07
4000	62.83	58.50	55.10	52.37	50.14	48.30	46.76
5000	78.54	73.13	68.88	65.46	62.68	60.38	58.45
6000	94.25	87.76	82.65	78.55	75.21	72.45	70.14
7000	109.96	102.38	96.43	91.65	87.75	84.53	81.83
8000	125.67	117.01	110.20	104.74	100.28	96.60	93.52
9000	141.38	131.63	123.98	117.83	112.82	108.68	105.21
10000	157.08	146.26	137.75	130.92	125.36	120.75	116.91
11000	172.79	160.88	151.53	144.02	137.89	132.83	128.60
12000	188.50	175.51	165.30	157.11	150.43	144.90	140.29
13000	204.21	190.14	179.08	170.20	162.96	156.98	151.98
14000	219.92	204.76	192.85	183.29	175.50	169.05	163.67
15000	235.63	219.39	206.63	196.39	188.03	181.13	175.36
20000	314.17	292.52	275.50	261.85	250.71	241.51	233.81
25000	392.71	365.65	344.38	327.31	313.39	301.88	292.26
30000	471.25	438.78	413.25	392.77	376.07	362.26	350.72
35000	549.79	511.91	482.13	458.23	438.74	422.63	409.17
40000	628.34	585.03	551.00	523.69	501.42	483.01	467.62
45000	706.88	658.16	619.88	589.16	564.10	543.39	526.07
50000	785.42	731.29	688.75	654.62	626.78	603.76	584.53
55000	863.96	804.42	757.63	720.08	689.46	664.14	642.98
56000	879.67	819.05	771.40	733.17	701.99	676.22	654.67
57000	895.38	833.67	785.18	746.26	714.53	688.29	666.36
58000	911.09	848.30	798.95	759.36	727.06	700.37	678.05
59000	926.80	862.93	812.73	772.45	739.60	712.44	689.74
60000	942.51	877.55	826.50	785.54	752.13	724.52	701.43
61000	958.21	892.18	840.28	798.63	764.67	736.59	713.12
62000	973.92	906.80	854.05	811.73	777.20	748.67	724.81
63000	989.63	921.43	867.83	824.82	789.74	760.74	736.50
64000	1005.34	936.06	881.60	837.91	802.28	772.82	748.19
65000	1021.05	950.68	895.38	851.00	814.81	784.89	759.89
70000	1099.59	1023.81	964.25	916.46	877.49	845.27	818.34
75000	1178.13	1096.94	1033.13	981.93	940.17	905.65	876.79
80000	1256.67	1170.07	1102.00	1047.39	1002.84	966.02	935.24
85000	1335.22	1243.20	1170.88	1112.85	1065.52	1026.40	993.70
90000	1413.76	1316.33	1239.75	1178.31	1128.20	1086.77	1052.15
95000	1492.30	1389.46	1308.63	1243.77	1190.88	1147.15	1110.60
100000	1570.84	1462.59	1377.50	1309.23	1253.56	1207.53	1169.05
105000	1649.38	1535.72	1446.38	1374.70	1316.23	1267.90	1227.51
110000	1727.93	1608.84	1515.25	1440.16	1378.91	1328.28	1285.96
120000	1885.01	1755.10	1653.00	1571.08	1504.27	1449.03	1402.87
130000	2042.10	1901.36	1790.75	1702.01	1629.62	1569.79	1519.77
140000	2199.18	2047.62	1928.50	1832.93	1754.98	1690.54	1636.68
150000	2356.26	2193.88	2066.25	1963.85	1880.33	1811.29	1753.58
160000	2513.35	2340.14	2204.00	2094.78	2005.69	1932.04	1870.49
175000	2748.97	2559.53	2410.63	2291.16	2193.72	2113.17	2045.84
200000	3141.69	2925.17	2755.00	2618.47	2507.11	2415.05	2338.11
250000	3927.11	3656.47	3443.75	3273.09	3133.89	3018.82	2922.64
500000	7854.21	7312.93	6887.50	6546.17	6267.78	6037.64	5845.27
1000000	15708.43	14625.86	13775.00	13092.35	12535.55	12075.27	11690.54

11.00%　　　MONTHLY PAYMENTS

AMOUNT	15 YEARS	16 YEARS	17 YEARS	18 YEARS	19 YEARS	20 YEARS	21 YEARS
100	1.14	1.11	1.09	1.07	1.05	1.03	1.02
200	2.27	2.22	2.17	2.13	2.09	2.06	2.04
500	5.68	5.55	5.43	5.33	5.24	5.16	5.09
1000	11.37	11.09	10.85	10.65	10.47	10.32	10.19
2000	22.73	22.18	21.71	21.30	20.95	20.64	20.38
3000	34.10	33.27	32.56	31.95	31.42	30.97	30.57
4000	45.46	44.36	43.42	42.60	41.90	41.29	40.75
5000	56.83	55.45	54.27	53.25	52.37	51.61	50.94
6000	68.20	66.54	65.12	63.90	62.85	61.93	61.13
7000	79.56	77.63	75.98	74.55	73.32	72.25	71.32
8000	90.93	88.72	86.83	85.20	83.80	82.58	81.51
9000	102.29	99.81	97.68	95.85	94.27	92.90	91.70
10000	113.66	110.90	108.54	106.50	104.75	103.22	101.89
11000	125.03	121.99	119.39	117.16	115.22	113.54	112.08
12000	136.39	133.08	130.25	127.81	125.70	123.86	122.26
13000	147.76	144.17	141.10	138.46	136.17	134.18	132.45
14000	159.12	155.26	151.95	149.11	146.64	144.51	142.64
15000	170.49	166.35	162.81	159.76	157.12	154.83	152.83
20000	227.32	221.80	217.08	213.01	209.49	206.44	203.77
25000	284.15	277.25	271.35	266.26	261.87	258.05	254.72
30000	340.98	332.70	325.61	319.51	314.24	309.66	305.66
35000	397.81	388.15	379.88	372.77	366.61	361.27	356.60
40000	454.64	443.60	434.15	426.02	418.99	412.88	407.55
45000	511.47	499.05	488.42	479.27	471.36	464.48	458.49
50000	568.30	554.50	542.69	532.52	523.73	516.09	509.44
55000	625.13	609.95	596.96	585.78	576.11	567.70	560.38
56000	636.49	621.04	607.81	596.43	586.58	578.03	570.57
57000	647.86	632.13	618.67	607.08	597.05	588.35	580.76
58000	659.23	643.22	629.52	617.73	607.53	598.67	590.95
59000	670.59	654.31	640.37	628.38	618.00	608.99	601.13
60000	681.96	665.40	651.23	639.03	628.48	619.31	611.32
61000	693.32	676.49	662.08	649.68	638.95	629.63	621.51
62000	704.69	687.58	672.94	660.33	649.43	639.96	631.70
63000	716.06	698.67	683.79	670.98	659.90	650.28	641.89
64000	727.42	709.76	694.64	681.63	670.38	660.60	652.08
65000	738.79	720.85	705.50	692.28	680.85	670.92	662.27
70000	795.62	776.30	759.77	745.53	733.22	722.53	713.21
75000	852.45	831.75	814.04	798.79	785.60	774.14	764.15
80000	909.28	887.20	868.30	852.04	837.97	825.75	815.10
85000	966.11	942.65	922.57	905.29	890.34	877.36	866.04
90000	1022.94	998.10	976.84	958.54	942.72	928.97	916.98
95000	1079.77	1053.55	1031.11	1011.80	995.09	980.58	967.93
100000	1136.60	1109.00	1085.38	1065.05	1047.46	1032.19	1018.87
105000	1193.43	1164.45	1139.65	1118.30	1099.84	1083.80	1069.81
110000	1250.26	1219.90	1193.92	1171.55	1152.21	1135.41	1120.76
120000	1363.92	1330.80	1302.46	1278.06	1256.96	1238.63	1222.65
130000	1477.58	1441.70	1410.99	1384.56	1361.70	1341.84	1324.53
140000	1591.24	1552.60	1519.53	1491.07	1466.45	1445.06	1426.42
150000	1704.90	1663.50	1628.07	1597.57	1571.20	1548.28	1528.31
160000	1818.56	1774.40	1736.61	1704.08	1675.94	1651.50	1630.19
175000	1989.04	1940.75	1899.42	1863.84	1833.06	1806.33	1783.02
200000	2273.19	2218.00	2170.76	2130.10	2094.93	2064.38	2037.74
250000	2841.49	2772.50	2713.45	2662.62	2618.66	2580.47	2547.18
500000	5682.98	5545.00	5426.90	5325.25	5237.32	5160.94	5094.35
1000000	11365.97	11090.00	10853.81	10650.50	10474.64	10321.88	10188.71

MONTHLY PAYMENTS 11.00%

AMOUNT	22 YEARS	23 YEARS	24 YEARS	25 YEARS	30 YEARS	35 YEARS	40 YEARS
100	1.01	1.00	0.99	0.98	0.95	0.94	0.93
200	2.01	1.99	1.98	1.96	1.90	1.87	1.86
500	5.04	4.99	4.94	4.90	4.76	4.68	4.64
1000	10.07	9.97	9.88	9.80	9.52	9.37	9.28
2000	20.14	19.94	19.76	19.60	19.05	18.74	18.57
3000	30.22	29.91	29.64	29.40	28.57	28.11	27.85
4000	40.29	39.88	39.52	39.20	38.09	37.48	37.13
5000	50.36	49.85	49.40	49.01	47.62	46.85	46.41
6000	60.43	59.82	59.28	58.81	57.14	56.22	55.70
7000	70.51	69.79	69.16	68.61	66.66	65.59	64.98
8000	80.58	79.76	79.04	78.41	76.19	74.96	74.26
9000	90.65	89.73	88.92	88.21	85.71	84.33	83.55
10000	100.72	99.70	98.80	98.01	95.23	93.70	92.83
11000	110.79	109.67	108.68	107.81	104.76	103.07	102.11
12000	120.87	119.64	118.56	117.61	114.28	112.43	111.40
13000	130.94	129.61	128.44	127.41	123.80	121.80	120.68
14000	141.01	139.58	138.32	137.22	133.33	131.17	129.96
15000	151.08	149.55	148.20	147.02	142.85	140.54	139.24
20000	201.44	199.40	197.61	196.02	190.46	187.39	185.66
25000	251.81	249.25	247.01	245.03	238.08	234.24	232.07
30000	302.17	299.10	296.41	294.03	285.70	281.09	278.49
35000	352.53	348.95	345.81	343.04	333.31	327.94	324.90
40000	402.89	398.80	395.21	392.05	380.93	374.78	371.32
45000	453.25	448.65	444.61	441.05	428.55	421.63	417.73
50000	503.61	498.50	494.01	490.06	476.16	468.48	464.15
55000	553.97	548.35	543.41	539.06	523.78	515.33	510.56
56000	564.05	558.32	553.29	548.86	533.30	524.70	519.84
57000	574.12	568.29	563.18	558.66	542.82	534.07	529.13
58000	584.19	578.26	573.06	568.47	552.35	543.44	538.41
59000	594.26	588.23	582.94	578.27	561.87	552.81	547.69
60000	604.33	598.20	592.82	588.07	571.39	562.17	556.98
61000	614.41	608.17	602.70	597.87	580.92	571.54	566.26
62000	624.48	618.14	612.58	607.67	590.44	580.91	575.54
63000	634.55	628.12	622.46	617.47	599.96	590.28	584.83
64000	644.62	638.09	632.34	627.27	609.49	599.65	594.11
65000	654.70	648.06	642.22	637.07	619.01	609.02	603.39
70000	705.06	697.91	691.62	686.08	666.63	655.87	649.81
75000	755.42	747.76	741.02	735.08	714.24	702.72	696.22
80000	805.78	797.61	790.42	784.09	761.86	749.57	742.64
85000	856.14	847.46	839.82	833.10	809.47	796.41	789.05
90000	906.50	897.31	889.22	882.10	857.09	843.26	835.46
95000	956.86	947.16	938.63	931.11	904.71	890.11	881.88
100000	1007.22	997.01	988.03	980.11	952.32	936.96	928.29
105000	1057.58	1046.86	1037.43	1029.12	999.94	983.81	974.71
110000	1107.95	1096.71	1086.83	1078.12	1047.56	1030.65	1021.12
120000	1208.67	1196.41	1185.63	1176.14	1142.79	1124.35	1113.95
130000	1309.39	1296.11	1284.43	1274.15	1238.02	1218.04	1206.78
140000	1410.11	1395.81	1383.24	1372.16	1333.25	1311.74	1299.61
150000	1510.84	1495.51	1482.04	1470.17	1428.49	1405.44	1392.44
160000	1611.56	1595.21	1580.84	1568.18	1523.72	1499.13	1485.27
175000	1762.64	1744.76	1729.05	1715.20	1666.57	1639.68	1624.52
200000	2014.45	1994.02	1976.05	1960.23	1904.65	1873.92	1856.59
250000	2518.06	2492.52	2470.07	2450.28	2380.81	2342.39	2320.74
500000	5036.12	4985.04	4940.13	4900.57	4761.62	4684.79	4641.47
1000000	10072.23	9970.08	9880.27	9801.13	9523.23	9369.58	9282.94

11.25%   MONTHLY PAYMENTS

AMOUNT	1 YEAR	2 YEARS	3 YEARS	4 YEARS	5 YEARS	6 YEARS	7 YEARS
100	8.85	4.67	3.29	2.60	2.19	1.92	1.73
200	17.70	9.34	6.57	5.19	4.37	3.83	3.45
500	44.25	23.36	16.43	12.98	10.93	9.58	8.63
1000	88.50	46.72	32.86	25.97	21.87	19.16	17.25
2000	177.00	93.45	65.71	51.93	43.73	38.32	34.51
3000	265.49	140.17	98.57	77.90	65.60	57.49	51.76
4000	353.99	186.90	131.43	103.87	87.47	76.65	69.02
5000	442.49	233.62	164.29	129.84	109.34	95.81	86.27
6000	530.99	280.34	197.14	155.80	131.20	114.97	103.53
7000	619.49	327.07	230.00	181.77	153.07	134.14	120.78
8000	707.99	373.79	262.86	207.74	174.94	153.30	138.03
9000	796.48	420.52	295.72	233.70	196.81	172.46	155.29
10000	884.98	467.24	328.57	259.67	218.67	191.62	172.54
11000	973.48	513.96	361.43	285.64	240.54	210.79	189.80
12000	1061.98	560.69	394.29	311.61	262.41	229.95	207.05
13000	1150.48	607.41	427.14	337.57	284.28	249.11	224.30
14000	1238.98	654.14	460.00	363.54	306.14	268.27	241.56
15000	1327.47	700.86	492.86	389.51	328.01	287.44	258.81
20000	1769.97	934.48	657.14	519.34	437.35	383.25	345.08
25000	2212.46	1168.10	821.43	649.18	546.68	479.06	431.35
30000	2654.95	1401.72	985.72	779.01	656.02	574.87	517.63
35000	3097.44	1635.34	1150.00	908.85	765.36	670.68	603.90
40000	3539.93	1868.96	1314.29	1038.68	874.69	766.49	690.17
45000	3982.42	2102.58	1478.58	1168.52	984.03	862.31	776.44
50000	4424.92	2336.20	1642.86	1298.35	1093.37	958.12	862.71
55000	4867.41	2569.82	1807.15	1428.19	1202.70	1053.93	948.98
56000	4955.91	2616.54	1840.01	1454.16	1224.57	1073.09	966.23
57000	5044.40	2663.27	1872.86	1480.12	1246.44	1092.26	983.49
58000	5132.90	2709.99	1905.72	1506.09	1268.30	1111.42	1000.74
59000	5221.40	2756.72	1938.58	1532.06	1290.17	1130.58	1018.00
60000	5309.90	2803.44	1971.43	1558.03	1312.04	1149.74	1035.25
61000	5398.40	2850.16	2004.29	1583.99	1333.91	1168.90	1052.50
62000	5486.90	2896.89	2037.15	1609.96	1355.77	1188.07	1069.76
63000	5575.39	2943.61	2070.01	1635.93	1377.64	1207.23	1087.01
64000	5663.89	2990.34	2102.86	1661.89	1399.51	1226.39	1104.27
65000	5752.39	3037.06	2135.72	1687.86	1421.38	1245.55	1121.52
70000	6194.88	3270.68	2300.01	1817.70	1530.71	1341.37	1207.79
75000	6637.37	3504.30	2464.29	1947.53	1640.05	1437.18	1294.06
80000	7079.87	3737.92	2628.58	2077.37	1749.38	1532.99	1380.33
85000	7522.36	3971.54	2792.86	2207.20	1858.72	1628.80	1466.60
90000	7964.85	4205.16	2957.15	2337.04	1968.06	1724.61	1552.88
95000	8407.34	4438.78	3121.44	2466.87	2077.39	1820.43	1639.15
100000	8849.83	4672.40	3285.72	2596.71	2186.73	1916.24	1725.42
105000	9292.32	4906.02	3450.01	2726.55	2296.07	2012.05	1811.69
110000	9734.81	5139.64	3614.30	2856.38	2405.40	2107.86	1897.96
120000	10619.80	5606.88	3942.87	3116.05	2624.08	2299.48	2070.50
130000	11504.78	6074.12	4271.44	3375.72	2842.75	2491.11	2243.04
140000	12389.76	6541.36	4600.01	3635.39	3061.42	2682.73	2415.58
150000	13274.75	7008.60	4928.59	3895.06	3280.10	2874.36	2588.13
160000	14159.73	7475.84	5257.16	4154.74	3498.77	3065.98	2760.67
175000	15487.20	8176.70	5750.02	4544.24	3826.78	3353.42	3019.48
200000	17699.66	9344.80	6571.45	5193.42	4373.46	3832.47	3450.83
250000	22124.58	11681.00	8214.31	6491.77	5466.83	4790.59	4313.54
500000	44249.16	23362.00	16428.62	12983.55	10933.65	9581.19	8627.08
1000000	88498.31	46723.99	32857.23	25967.10	21867.31	19162.37	17254.17

MONTHLY PAYMENTS 11.25%

AMOUNT	8 YEARS	9 YEARS	10 YEARS	11 YEARS	12 YEARS	13 YEARS	14 YEARS
100	1.58	1.48	1.39	1.32	1.27	1.22	1.18
200	3.17	2.95	2.78	2.65	2.54	2.45	2.37
500	7.92	7.38	6.96	6.62	6.34	6.11	5.92
1000	15.84	14.76	13.92	13.24	12.68	12.23	11.85
2000	31.69	29.53	27.83	26.48	25.37	24.45	23.69
3000	47.53	44.29	41.75	39.71	38.05	36.68	35.54
4000	63.37	59.06	55.67	52.95	50.74	48.91	47.38
5000	79.22	73.82	69.58	66.19	63.42	61.13	59.23
6000	95.06	88.59	83.50	79.43	76.10	73.36	71.07
7000	110.91	103.35	97.42	92.66	88.79	85.59	82.92
8000	126.75	118.12	111.34	105.90	101.47	97.81	94.76
9000	142.59	132.88	125.25	119.14	114.16	110.04	106.61
10000	158.44	147.64	139.17	132.38	126.84	122.27	118.45
11000	174.28	162.41	153.09	145.61	139.52	134.49	130.30
12000	190.12	177.17	167.00	158.85	152.21	146.72	142.14
13000	205.97	191.94	180.92	172.09	164.89	158.95	153.99
14000	221.81	206.70	194.84	185.33	177.58	171.17	165.83
15000	237.65	221.47	208.75	198.56	190.26	183.40	177.68
20000	316.87	295.29	278.34	264.75	253.68	244.54	236.90
25000	396.09	369.11	347.92	330.94	317.10	305.67	296.13
30000	475.31	442.93	417.51	397.13	380.52	366.80	355.35
35000	554.53	516.75	487.09	463.31	443.94	427.94	414.58
40000	633.74	590.58	556.68	529.50	507.36	489.07	473.80
45000	712.96	664.40	626.26	595.69	570.78	550.20	533.03
50000	792.18	738.22	695.84	661.88	634.20	611.34	592.25
55000	871.40	812.04	765.43	728.06	697.62	672.47	651.48
56000	887.24	826.81	779.35	741.30	710.30	684.70	663.32
57000	903.08	841.57	793.26	754.54	722.98	696.93	675.17
58000	918.93	856.34	807.18	767.78	735.67	709.15	687.01
59000	934.77	871.10	821.10	781.01	748.35	721.38	698.86
60000	950.62	885.86	835.01	794.25	761.04	733.61	710.70
61000	966.46	900.63	848.93	807.49	773.72	745.83	722.55
62000	982.30	915.39	862.85	820.73	786.40	758.06	734.39
63000	998.15	930.16	876.76	833.96	799.09	770.29	746.24
64000	1013.99	944.92	890.68	847.20	811.77	782.51	758.08
65000	1029.83	959.69	904.60	860.44	824.46	794.74	769.93
70000	1109.05	1033.51	974.18	926.63	887.88	855.87	829.16
75000	1188.27	1107.33	1043.77	992.81	951.29	917.01	888.38
80000	1267.49	1181.15	1113.35	1059.00	1014.71	978.14	947.61
85000	1346.70	1254.98	1182.94	1125.19	1078.13	1039.28	1006.83
90000	1425.92	1328.80	1252.52	1191.38	1141.55	1100.41	1066.06
95000	1505.14	1402.62	1322.10	1257.56	1204.97	1161.54	1125.28
100000	1584.36	1476.44	1391.69	1323.75	1268.39	1222.68	1184.51
105000	1663.58	1550.26	1461.27	1389.94	1331.81	1283.81	1243.73
110000	1742.79	1624.09	1530.86	1456.13	1395.23	1344.95	1302.96
120000	1901.23	1771.73	1670.03	1588.50	1522.07	1467.21	1421.41
130000	2059.67	1919.37	1809.20	1720.88	1648.91	1589.48	1539.86
140000	2218.10	2067.02	1948.37	1853.25	1775.75	1711.75	1658.31
150000	2376.54	2214.66	2087.53	1985.63	1902.59	1834.02	1776.76
160000	2534.97	2362.31	2226.70	2118.00	2029.43	1956.28	1895.21
175000	2772.63	2583.77	2435.46	2316.57	2219.69	2139.69	2072.89
200000	3168.72	2952.88	2783.38	2647.50	2536.79	2445.35	2369.02
250000	3960.90	3691.10	3479.22	3309.38	3170.98	3056.69	2961.27
500000	7921.79	7382.21	6958.45	6618.76	6341.96	6113.39	5922.54
1000000	15843.58	14764.41	13916.89	13237.52	12683.93	12226.77	11845.08

11.25% MONTHLY PAYMENTS

AMOUNT	15 YEARS	16 YEARS	17 YEARS	18 YEARS	19 YEARS	20 YEARS	21 YEARS
100	1.15	1.13	1.10	1.08	1.06	1.05	1.04
200	2.30	2.25	2.20	2.16	2.13	2.10	2.07
500	5.76	5.63	5.51	5.41	5.32	5.25	5.18
1000	11.52	11.25	11.02	10.82	10.64	10.49	10.36
2000	23.05	22.50	22.03	21.63	21.29	20.99	20.72
3000	34.57	33.75	33.05	32.45	31.93	31.48	31.09
4000	46.09	45.00	44.07	43.26	42.57	41.97	41.45
5000	57.62	56.25	55.08	54.08	53.21	52.46	51.81
6000	69.14	67.50	66.10	64.90	63.86	62.96	62.17
7000	80.66	78.75	77.12	75.71	74.50	73.45	72.53
8000	92.19	90.00	88.13	86.53	85.14	83.94	82.89
9000	103.71	101.25	99.15	97.35	95.79	94.43	93.26
10000	115.23	112.50	110.17	108.16	106.43	104.93	103.62
11000	126.76	123.75	121.19	118.98	117.07	115.42	113.98
12000	138.28	135.00	132.20	129.79	127.71	125.91	124.34
13000	149.80	146.25	143.22	140.61	138.36	136.40	134.70
14000	161.33	157.50	154.24	151.43	149.00	146.90	145.06
15000	172.85	168.75	165.25	162.24	159.64	157.39	155.43
20000	230.47	225.01	220.34	216.32	212.86	209.85	207.23
25000	288.09	281.26	275.42	270.41	266.07	262.31	259.04
30000	345.70	337.51	330.51	324.49	319.29	314.78	310.85
35000	403.32	393.76	385.59	378.57	372.50	367.24	362.66
40000	460.94	450.01	440.67	432.65	425.72	419.70	414.47
45000	518.56	506.26	495.76	486.73	478.93	472.17	466.28
50000	576.17	562.52	550.84	540.81	532.14	524.63	518.09
55000	633.79	618.77	605.93	594.89	585.36	577.09	569.89
56000	645.31	630.02	616.94	605.71	596.00	587.58	580.26
57000	656.84	641.27	627.96	616.52	606.64	598.08	590.62
58000	668.36	652.52	638.98	627.34	617.29	608.57	600.98
59000	679.88	663.77	650.00	638.16	627.93	619.06	611.34
60000	691.41	675.02	661.01	648.97	638.57	629.55	621.70
61000	702.93	686.27	672.03	659.79	649.22	640.05	632.06
62000	714.45	697.52	683.05	670.60	659.86	650.54	642.43
63000	725.98	708.77	694.06	681.42	670.50	661.03	652.79
64000	737.50	720.02	705.08	692.24	681.14	671.52	663.15
65000	749.02	731.27	716.10	703.05	691.79	682.02	673.51
70000	806.64	787.52	771.18	757.13	745.00	734.48	725.32
75000	864.26	843.77	826.27	811.22	798.22	786.94	777.13
80000	921.88	900.03	881.35	865.30	851.43	839.40	828.94
85000	979.49	956.28	936.43	919.38	904.65	891.87	880.75
90000	1037.11	1012.53	991.52	973.46	957.86	944.33	932.55
95000	1094.73	1068.78	1046.60	1027.54	1011.07	996.79	984.36
100000	1152.34	1125.03	1101.69	1081.62	1064.29	1049.26	1036.17
105000	1209.96	1181.28	1156.77	1135.70	1117.50	1101.72	1087.98
110000	1267.58	1237.54	1211.86	1189.78	1170.72	1154.18	1139.79
120000	1382.81	1350.04	1322.02	1297.94	1277.15	1259.11	1243.41
130000	1498.05	1462.54	1432.19	1406.11	1383.57	1364.03	1347.02
140000	1613.28	1575.05	1542.36	1514.27	1490.00	1468.96	1450.64
150000	1728.52	1687.55	1652.53	1622.43	1596.43	1573.88	1554.26
160000	1843.75	1800.05	1762.70	1730.59	1702.86	1678.81	1657.87
175000	2016.60	1968.81	1927.95	1892.84	1862.50	1836.20	1813.30
200000	2304.69	2250.07	2203.37	2163.24	2128.58	2098.51	2072.34
250000	2880.86	2812.58	2754.22	2704.05	2660.72	2623.14	2590.43
500000	5761.72	5625.16	5508.44	5408.10	5321.44	5246.28	5180.86
1000000	11523.45	11250.33	11016.87	10816.20	10642.88	10492.56	10361.71

MONTHLY PAYMENTS 11.25%

AMOUNT	22 YEARS	23 YEARS	24 YEARS	25 YEARS	30 YEARS	35 YEARS	40 YEARS
100	1.02	1.01	1.01	1.00	0.97	0.96	0.95
200	2.05	2.03	2.01	2.00	1.94	1.91	1.90
500	5.12	5.07	5.03	4.99	4.86	4.78	4.74
1000	10.25	10.15	10.06	9.98	9.71	9.56	9.48
2000	20.49	20.29	20.12	19.96	19.43	19.13	18.97
3000	30.74	30.44	30.18	29.95	29.14	28.69	28.45
4000	40.99	40.59	40.24	39.93	38.85	38.26	37.93
5000	51.24	50.74	50.30	49.91	48.56	47.82	47.41
6000	61.48	60.88	60.36	59.89	58.28	57.39	56.90
7000	71.73	71.03	70.42	69.88	67.99	66.95	66.38
8000	81.98	81.18	80.48	79.86	77.70	76.52	75.86
9000	92.23	91.33	90.54	89.84	87.41	86.08	85.34
10000	102.47	101.47	100.60	99.82	97.13	95.65	94.83
11000	112.72	111.62	110.66	109.81	106.84	105.21	104.31
12000	122.97	121.77	120.72	119.79	116.55	114.78	113.79
13000	133.22	131.92	130.78	129.77	126.26	124.34	123.27
14000	143.46	142.06	140.83	139.75	135.98	133.91	132.76
15000	153.71	152.21	150.89	149.74	145.69	143.47	142.24
20000	204.95	202.95	201.19	199.65	194.25	191.30	189.65
25000	256.19	253.69	251.49	249.56	242.82	239.12	237.06
30000	307.42	304.42	301.79	299.47	291.38	286.95	284.48
35000	358.66	355.16	352.09	349.38	339.94	334.77	331.89
40000	409.90	405.90	402.38	399.30	388.50	382.60	379.30
45000	461.14	456.63	452.68	449.21	437.07	430.42	426.72
50000	512.37	507.37	502.98	499.12	485.63	478.25	474.13
55000	563.61	558.11	553.28	549.03	534.19	526.07	521.54
56000	573.86	568.26	563.34	559.01	543.91	535.64	531.02
57000	584.11	578.40	573.40	569.00	553.62	545.20	540.51
58000	594.35	588.55	583.46	578.98	563.33	554.77	549.99
59000	604.60	598.70	593.52	588.96	573.04	564.33	559.47
60000	614.85	608.85	603.58	598.94	582.76	573.90	568.95
61000	625.09	618.99	613.64	608.93	592.47	583.46	578.44
62000	635.34	629.14	623.70	618.91	602.18	593.03	587.92
63000	645.59	639.29	633.76	628.89	611.89	602.59	597.40
64000	655.84	649.43	643.82	638.87	621.61	612.16	606.88
65000	666.08	659.58	653.88	648.86	631.32	621.72	616.37
70000	717.32	710.32	704.17	698.77	679.88	669.55	663.78
75000	768.56	761.06	754.47	748.68	728.45	717.37	711.19
80000	819.80	811.79	804.77	798.59	777.01	765.20	758.61
85000	871.03	862.53	855.07	848.50	825.57	813.02	806.02
90000	922.27	913.27	905.37	898.42	874.14	860.84	853.43
95000	973.51	964.00	955.66	948.33	922.70	908.67	900.84
100000	1024.75	1014.74	1005.96	998.24	971.26	956.49	948.26
105000	1075.98	1065.48	1056.26	1048.15	1019.82	1004.32	995.67
110000	1127.22	1116.22	1106.56	1098.06	1068.39	1052.14	1043.08
120000	1229.69	1217.69	1207.15	1197.89	1165.51	1147.79	1137.91
130000	1332.17	1319.16	1307.75	1297.71	1262.64	1243.44	1232.73
140000	1434.64	1420.64	1408.35	1397.54	1359.77	1339.09	1327.56
150000	1537.12	1522.11	1508.94	1497.36	1456.89	1434.74	1422.39
160000	1639.59	1623.59	1609.54	1597.18	1554.02	1530.39	1517.21
175000	1793.31	1775.80	1760.43	1746.92	1699.71	1673.86	1659.45
200000	2049.49	2029.48	2011.92	1996.48	1942.52	1912.99	1896.51
250000	2561.86	2536.85	2514.90	2495.60	2428.15	2391.23	2370.64
500000	5123.73	5073.71	5029.81	4991.20	4856.31	4782.47	4741.29
1000000	10247.46	10147.42	10059.62	9982.40	9712.61	9564.94	9482.57

11.50%   MONTHLY PAYMENTS

AMOUNT	1 YEAR	2 YEARS	3 YEARS	4 YEARS	5 YEARS	6 YEARS	7 YEARS
100	8.86	4.68	3.30	2.61	2.20	1.93	1.74
200	17.72	9.37	6.60	5.22	4.40	3.86	3.48
500	44.31	23.42	16.49	13.04	11.00	9.65	8.69
1000	88.62	46.84	32.98	26.09	21.99	19.29	17.39
2000	177.23	93.68	65.95	52.18	43.99	38.58	34.77
3000	265.85	140.52	98.93	78.27	65.98	57.87	52.16
4000	354.46	187.36	131.90	104.36	87.97	77.16	69.55
5000	443.08	234.20	164.88	130.45	109.96	96.46	86.93
6000	531.69	281.04	197.86	156.53	131.96	115.75	104.32
7000	620.31	327.88	230.83	182.62	153.95	135.04	121.71
8000	708.92	374.72	263.81	208.71	175.94	154.33	139.09
9000	797.54	421.56	296.78	234.80	197.93	173.62	156.48
10000	886.15	468.40	329.76	260.89	219.93	192.91	173.86
11000	974.77	515.24	362.74	286.98	241.92	212.20	191.25
12000	1063.38	562.08	395.71	313.07	263.91	231.49	208.64
13000	1152.00	608.92	428.69	339.16	285.90	250.79	226.02
14000	1240.61	655.76	461.66	365.25	307.90	270.08	243.41
15000	1329.23	702.60	494.64	391.34	329.89	289.37	260.80
20000	1772.30	936.81	659.52	521.78	439.85	385.82	347.73
25000	2215.38	1171.01	824.40	652.23	549.82	482.28	434.66
30000	2658.45	1405.21	989.28	782.67	659.78	578.73	521.59
35000	3101.53	1639.41	1154.16	913.12	769.74	675.19	608.53
40000	3544.60	1873.61	1319.04	1043.56	879.70	771.65	695.46
45000	3987.68	2107.81	1483.92	1174.01	989.67	868.10	782.39
50000	4430.75	2342.02	1648.80	1304.45	1099.63	964.56	869.32
55000	4873.83	2576.22	1813.68	1434.90	1209.59	1061.01	956.26
56000	4962.44	2623.06	1846.66	1460.98	1231.59	1080.30	973.64
57000	5051.06	2669.90	1879.63	1487.07	1253.58	1099.60	991.03
58000	5139.67	2716.74	1912.61	1513.16	1275.57	1118.89	1008.41
59000	5228.29	2763.58	1945.58	1539.25	1297.56	1138.18	1025.80
60000	5316.90	2810.42	1978.56	1565.34	1319.56	1157.47	1043.19
61000	5405.52	2857.26	2011.54	1591.43	1341.55	1176.76	1060.57
62000	5494.13	2904.10	2044.51	1617.52	1363.54	1196.05	1077.96
63000	5582.75	2950.94	2077.49	1643.61	1385.53	1215.34	1095.35
64000	5671.36	2997.78	2110.46	1669.70	1407.53	1234.63	1112.73
65000	5759.98	3044.62	2143.44	1695.79	1429.52	1253.93	1130.12
70000	6203.05	3278.82	2308.32	1826.23	1539.48	1350.38	1217.05
75000	6646.13	3513.02	2473.20	1956.68	1649.45	1446.84	1303.98
80000	7089.20	3747.23	2638.08	2087.12	1759.41	1543.29	1390.92
85000	7532.28	3981.43	2802.96	2217.57	1869.37	1639.75	1477.85
90000	7975.35	4215.63	2967.84	2348.01	1979.33	1736.20	1564.78
95000	8418.43	4449.83	3132.72	2478.46	2089.30	1832.66	1651.71
100000	8861.51	4684.03	3297.60	2608.90	2199.26	1929.12	1738.65
105000	9304.58	4918.23	3462.48	2739.35	2309.22	2025.57	1825.58
110000	9747.66	5152.43	3627.36	2869.79	2419.19	2122.03	1912.51
120000	10633.81	5620.84	3957.12	3130.68	2639.11	2314.94	2086.38
130000	11519.96	6089.24	4286.88	3391.57	2859.04	2507.85	2260.24
140000	12406.11	6557.64	4616.64	3652.46	3078.97	2700.76	2434.10
150000	13292.26	7026.05	4946.40	3913.35	3298.89	2893.67	2607.97
160000	14178.41	7494.45	5276.16	4174.24	3518.82	3086.58	2781.83
175000	15507.63	8197.06	5770.80	4565.58	3848.71	3375.95	3042.63
200000	17723.01	9368.06	6595.20	5217.80	4398.52	3858.23	3477.29
250000	22153.76	11710.08	8244.00	6522.25	5498.15	4822.79	4346.62
500000	44307.53	23420.16	16488.00	13044.50	10996.30	9645.58	8693.23
1000000	88615.05	46840.32	32976.01	26089.01	21992.61	19291.16	17386.46

MONTHLY PAYMENTS 11.50%

AMOUNT	8 YEARS	9 YEARS	10 YEARS	11 YEARS	12 YEARS	13 YEARS	14 YEARS
100	1.60	1.49	1.41	1.34	1.28	1.24	1.20
200	3.20	2.98	2.81	2.68	2.57	2.48	2.40
500	7.99	7.45	7.03	6.69	6.42	6.19	6.00
1000	15.98	14.90	14.06	13.38	12.83	12.38	12.00
2000	31.96	29.81	28.12	26.77	25.67	24.76	24.00
3000	47.94	44.71	42.18	40.15	38.50	37.14	36.00
4000	63.92	59.61	56.24	53.53	51.33	49.52	48.00
5000	79.90	74.52	70.30	66.92	64.17	61.90	60.00
6000	95.88	89.42	84.36	80.30	77.00	74.28	72.00
7000	111.86	104.33	98.42	93.68	89.83	86.65	84.00
8000	127.83	119.23	112.48	107.07	102.67	99.03	96.00
9000	143.81	134.13	126.54	120.45	115.50	111.41	108.00
10000	159.79	149.04	140.60	133.84	128.33	123.79	120.01
11000	175.77	163.94	154.65	147.22	141.16	136.17	132.01
12000	191.75	178.84	168.71	160.60	154.00	148.55	144.01
13000	207.73	193.75	182.77	173.99	166.83	160.93	156.01
14000	223.71	208.65	196.83	187.37	179.66	173.31	168.01
15000	239.69	223.55	210.89	200.75	192.50	185.69	180.01
20000	319.59	298.07	281.19	267.67	256.66	247.58	240.01
25000	399.48	372.59	351.49	334.59	320.83	309.48	300.01
30000	479.38	447.11	421.79	401.51	384.99	371.38	360.02
35000	559.28	521.63	492.08	468.42	449.16	433.27	420.02
40000	639.17	596.15	562.38	535.34	513.33	495.17	480.02
45000	719.07	670.66	632.68	602.26	577.49	557.06	540.02
50000	798.97	745.18	702.98	669.18	641.66	618.96	600.03
55000	878.87	819.70	773.27	736.09	705.82	680.85	660.03
56000	894.84	834.60	787.33	749.48	718.66	693.23	672.03
57000	910.82	849.51	801.39	762.86	731.49	705.61	684.03
58000	926.80	864.41	815.45	776.24	744.32	717.99	696.03
59000	942.78	879.32	829.51	789.63	757.16	730.37	708.03
60000	958.76	894.22	843.57	803.01	769.99	742.75	720.03
61000	974.74	909.12	857.63	816.39	782.82	755.13	732.03
62000	990.72	924.03	871.69	829.78	795.66	767.51	744.03
63000	1006.70	938.93	885.75	843.16	808.49	779.89	756.03
64000	1022.68	953.83	899.81	856.54	821.32	792.27	768.04
65000	1038.66	968.74	913.87	869.93	834.16	804.65	780.04
70000	1118.56	1043.26	984.17	936.85	898.32	866.54	840.04
75000	1198.45	1117.77	1054.47	1003.76	962.49	928.44	900.04
80000	1278.35	1192.29	1124.76	1070.68	1026.65	990.33	960.04
85000	1358.25	1266.81	1195.06	1137.60	1090.82	1052.23	1020.05
90000	1438.14	1341.33	1265.36	1204.52	1154.98	1114.13	1080.05
95000	1518.04	1415.85	1335.66	1271.43	1219.15	1176.02	1140.05
100000	1597.94	1490.37	1405.95	1338.35	1283.32	1237.92	1200.06
105000	1677.83	1564.88	1476.25	1405.27	1347.48	1299.81	1260.06
110000	1757.73	1639.40	1546.55	1472.19	1411.65	1361.71	1320.06
120000	1917.52	1788.44	1687.15	1606.02	1539.98	1485.50	1440.07
130000	2077.32	1937.48	1827.74	1739.86	1668.31	1609.29	1560.07
140000	2237.11	2086.51	1968.34	1873.69	1796.64	1733.08	1680.08
150000	2396.91	2235.55	2108.93	2007.53	1924.97	1856.88	1800.08
160000	2556.70	2384.59	2249.53	2141.36	2053.31	1980.67	1920.09
175000	2796.39	2608.14	2460.42	2342.11	2245.80	2166.36	2100.10
200000	3195.87	2980.73	2811.91	2676.70	2566.63	2475.84	2400.11
250000	3994.84	3725.92	3514.89	3345.88	3208.29	3094.79	3000.14
500000	7989.69	7451.83	7029.77	6691.75	6416.58	6189.59	6000.28
1000000	15979.37	14903.66	14059.54	13383.50	12833.17	12379.18	12000.55

11.50%   MONTHLY PAYMENTS

AMOUNT	15 YEARS	16 YEARS	17 YEARS	18 YEARS	19 YEARS	20 YEARS	21 YEARS
100	1.17	1.14	1.12	1.10	1.08	1.07	1.05
200	2.34	2.28	2.24	2.20	2.16	2.13	2.11
500	5.84	5.71	5.59	5.49	5.41	5.33	5.27
1000	11.68	11.41	11.18	10.98	10.81	10.66	10.54
2000	23.36	22.82	22.36	21.97	21.62	21.33	21.07
3000	35.05	34.23	33.54	32.95	32.44	31.99	31.61
4000	46.73	45.65	44.72	43.93	43.25	42.66	42.14
5000	58.41	57.06	55.90	54.91	54.06	53.32	52.68
6000	70.09	68.47	67.09	65.90	64.87	63.99	63.21
7000	81.77	79.88	78.27	76.88	75.69	74.65	73.75
8000	93.46	91.29	89.45	87.86	86.50	85.31	84.29
9000	105.14	102.70	100.63	98.85	97.31	95.98	94.82
10000	116.82	114.12	111.81	109.83	108.12	106.64	105.36
11000	128.50	125.53	122.99	120.81	118.93	117.31	115.89
12000	140.18	136.94	134.17	131.80	129.75	127.97	126.43
13000	151.86	148.35	145.35	142.78	140.56	138.64	136.97
14000	163.55	159.76	156.53	153.76	151.37	149.30	147.50
15000	175.23	171.17	167.71	164.74	162.18	159.96	158.04
20000	233.64	228.23	223.62	219.66	216.24	213.29	210.72
25000	292.05	285.29	279.52	274.57	270.30	266.61	263.39
30000	350.46	342.35	335.43	329.49	324.37	319.93	316.07
35000	408.87	399.41	391.33	384.40	378.43	373.25	368.75
40000	467.28	456.47	447.24	439.32	432.49	426.57	421.43
45000	525.69	513.52	503.14	494.23	486.55	479.89	474.11
50000	584.09	570.58	559.05	549.15	540.61	533.21	526.79
55000	642.50	627.64	614.95	604.06	594.67	586.54	579.47
56000	654.19	639.05	626.13	615.05	605.48	597.20	590.00
57000	665.87	650.46	637.31	626.03	616.29	607.86	600.54
58000	677.55	661.88	648.50	637.01	627.11	618.53	611.08
59000	689.23	673.29	659.68	647.99	637.92	629.19	621.61
60000	700.91	684.70	670.86	658.98	648.73	639.86	632.15
61000	712.60	696.11	682.04	669.96	659.54	650.52	642.68
62000	724.28	707.52	693.22	680.94	670.36	661.19	653.22
63000	735.96	718.93	704.40	691.93	681.17	671.85	663.75
64000	747.64	730.35	715.58	702.91	691.98	682.51	674.29
65000	759.32	741.76	726.76	713.89	702.79	693.18	684.83
70000	817.73	798.82	782.67	768.81	756.85	746.50	737.50
75000	876.14	855.87	838.57	823.72	810.91	799.82	790.18
80000	934.55	912.93	894.48	878.64	864.97	853.14	842.86
85000	992.96	969.99	950.38	933.55	919.04	906.47	895.54
90000	1051.37	1027.05	1006.29	988.47	973.10	959.79	948.22
95000	1109.78	1084.11	1062.19	1043.38	1027.16	1013.11	1000.90
100000	1168.19	1141.16	1118.10	1098.30	1081.22	1066.43	1053.58
105000	1226.60	1198.22	1174.00	1153.21	1135.28	1119.75	1106.26
110000	1285.01	1255.28	1229.91	1208.12	1189.34	1173.07	1158.94
120000	1401.83	1369.40	1341.72	1317.95	1297.46	1279.72	1264.29
130000	1518.65	1483.51	1453.53	1427.78	1405.58	1386.36	1369.65
140000	1635.47	1597.63	1565.33	1537.61	1513.71	1493.00	1475.01
150000	1752.28	1711.75	1677.14	1647.44	1621.83	1599.64	1580.37
160000	1869.10	1825.86	1788.95	1757.27	1729.95	1706.29	1685.72
175000	2044.38	1997.04	1956.67	1922.02	1892.13	1866.25	1843.76
200000	2336.38	2282.33	2236.19	2196.59	2162.44	2132.86	2107.16
250000	2920.47	2852.91	2795.24	2745.74	2703.05	2666.07	2633.94
500000	5840.95	5705.82	5590.48	5491.48	5406.09	5332.15	5267.89
1000000	11681.90	11411.65	11180.96	10982.95	10812.18	10664.30	10535.78

MONTHLY PAYMENTS   11.50%

AMOUNT	22 YEARS	23 YEARS	24 YEARS	25 YEARS	30 YEARS	35 YEARS	40 YEARS
100	1.04	1.03	1.02	1.02	0.99	0.98	0.97
200	2.08	2.07	2.05	2.03	1.98	1.95	1.94
500	5.21	5.16	5.12	5.08	4.95	4.88	4.84
1000	10.42	10.33	10.24	10.16	9.90	9.76	9.68
2000	20.85	20.65	20.48	20.33	19.81	19.52	19.37
3000	31.27	30.98	30.72	30.49	29.71	29.28	29.05
4000	41.69	41.30	40.96	40.66	39.61	39.04	38.73
5000	52.12	51.63	51.20	50.82	49.51	48.81	48.41
6000	62.54	61.95	61.44	60.99	59.42	58.57	58.10
7000	72.97	72.28	71.68	71.15	69.32	68.33	67.78
8000	83.39	82.61	81.92	81.32	79.22	78.09	77.46
9000	93.81	92.93	92.16	91.48	89.13	87.85	87.15
10000	104.24	103.26	102.40	101.65	99.03	97.61	96.83
11000	114.66	113.58	112.64	111.81	108.93	107.37	106.51
12000	125.08	123.91	122.88	121.98	118.83	117.13	116.19
13000	135.51	134.24	133.12	132.14	128.74	126.89	125.88
14000	145.93	144.56	143.36	142.31	138.64	136.66	135.56
15000	156.36	154.89	153.60	152.47	148.54	146.42	145.24
20000	208.47	206.52	204.80	203.29	198.06	195.22	193.66
25000	260.59	258.15	256.00	254.12	247.57	244.03	242.07
30000	312.71	309.77	307.20	304.94	297.09	292.83	290.48
35000	364.83	361.40	358.40	355.76	346.60	341.64	338.90
40000	416.95	413.03	409.60	406.59	396.12	390.44	387.31
45000	469.07	464.66	460.80	457.41	445.63	439.25	435.73
50000	521.19	516.29	512.00	508.23	495.15	488.05	484.14
55000	573.31	567.92	563.20	559.06	544.66	536.86	532.56
56000	583.73	578.25	573.44	569.22	554.56	546.62	542.24
57000	594.57	588.57	583.68	579.39	564.47	556.38	551.92
58000	604.58	598.90	593.92	589.55	574.37	566.14	561.60
59000	615.00	609.22	604.16	599.72	584.27	575.90	571.29
60000	625.42	619.55	614.40	609.88	594.17	585.66	580.97
61000	635.85	629.87	624.64	620.05	604.08	595.43	590.65
62000	646.27	640.20	634.88	630.21	613.98	605.19	600.33
63000	656.70	650.53	645.12	640.38	623.88	614.95	610.02
64000	667.12	660.85	655.36	650.54	633.79	624.71	619.70
65000	677.54	671.18	665.60	660.70	643.69	634.47	629.38
70000	729.66	722.81	716.80	711.53	693.20	683.28	677.80
75000	781.78	774.44	768.00	762.35	742.72	732.08	726.21
80000	833.90	826.07	819.20	813.18	792.23	780.89	774.63
85000	886.02	877.69	870.40	864.00	841.75	829.69	823.04
90000	938.14	929.32	921.60	914.82	891.26	878.50	871.45
95000	990.26	980.95	972.80	965.65	940.78	927.30	919.87
100000	1042.37	1032.58	1024.00	1016.47	990.29	976.11	968.28
105000	1094.49	1084.21	1075.20	1067.29	1039.81	1024.91	1016.70
110000	1146.61	1135.84	1126.40	1118.12	1089.32	1073.72	1065.11
120000	1250.85	1239.10	1228.80	1219.76	1188.35	1171.33	1161.94
130000	1355.09	1342.36	1331.20	1321.41	1287.38	1268.94	1258.77
140000	1459.32	1445.61	1433.60	1423.06	1386.41	1366.55	1355.59
150000	1563.56	1548.87	1536.00	1524.70	1485.44	1464.16	1452.42
160000	1667.80	1652.13	1638.40	1626.35	1584.47	1561.77	1549.25
175000	1824.15	1807.02	1792.00	1778.82	1733.01	1708.19	1694.49
200000	2084.75	2065.16	2048.00	2032.94	1980.58	1952.21	1936.56
250000	2605.94	2581.45	2560.00	2541.17	2475.73	2440.27	2420.70
500000	5211.87	5162.91	5120.01	5082.34	4951.46	4880.54	4841.41
1000000	10423.74	10325.81	10240.02	10164.69	9902.91	9761.07	9682.82

11.75% MONTHLY PAYMENTS

AMOUNT	1 YEAR	2 YEARS	3 YEARS	4 YEARS	5 YEARS	6 YEARS	7 YEARS
100	8.87	4.70	3.31	2.62	2.21	1.94	1.75
200	17.75	9.39	6.62	5.24	4.42	3.88	3.50
500	44.37	23.48	16.55	13.11	11.06	9.71	8.76
1000	88.73	46.96	33.10	26.21	22.12	19.42	17.52
2000	177.46	93.91	66.19	52.42	44.24	38.84	35.04
3000	266.20	140.87	99.29	78.63	66.35	58.26	52.56
4000	354.93	187.83	132.38	104.85	88.47	77.68	70.08
5000	443.66	234.78	165.48	131.06	110.59	97.10	87.60
6000	532.39	281.74	198.57	157.27	132.71	116.52	105.12
7000	621.12	328.70	231.67	183.48	154.83	135.94	122.64
8000	709.86	375.65	264.76	209.69	176.95	155.36	140.15
9000	798.59	422.61	297.86	235.90	199.06	174.78	157.67
10000	887.32	469.57	330.95	262.11	221.18	194.20	175.19
11000	976.05	516.52	364.05	288.32	243.30	213.62	192.71
12000	1064.78	563.48	397.14	314.54	265.42	233.05	210.23
13000	1153.51	610.44	430.24	340.75	287.54	252.47	227.75
14000	1242.25	657.40	463.33	366.96	309.66	271.89	245.27
15000	1330.98	704.35	496.43	393.17	331.77	291.31	262.79
20000	1774.64	939.14	661.90	524.23	442.37	388.41	350.39
25000	2218.30	1173.92	827.38	655.28	552.96	485.51	437.98
30000	2661.96	1408.70	992.85	786.34	663.55	582.61	525.58
35000	3105.62	1643.49	1158.33	917.39	774.14	679.72	613.18
40000	3549.28	1878.27	1323.80	1048.45	884.73	776.82	700.77
45000	3992.93	2113.06	1489.28	1179.51	995.32	873.92	788.37
50000	4436.59	2347.84	1654.75	1310.56	1105.92	971.02	875.97
55000	4880.25	2582.62	1820.23	1441.62	1216.51	1068.12	963.56
56000	4968.99	2629.58	1853.32	1467.83	1238.63	1087.54	981.08
57000	5057.72	2676.54	1886.42	1494.04	1260.74	1106.96	998.60
58000	5146.45	2723.49	1919.51	1520.25	1282.86	1126.38	1016.12
59000	5235.18	2770.45	1952.61	1546.46	1304.98	1145.81	1033.64
60000	5323.91	2817.41	1985.70	1572.68	1327.10	1165.23	1051.16
61000	5412.64	2864.37	2018.80	1598.89	1349.22	1184.65	1068.68
62000	5501.38	2911.32	2051.89	1625.10	1371.34	1204.07	1086.20
63000	5590.11	2958.28	2084.99	1651.31	1393.45	1223.49	1103.72
64000	5678.84	3005.24	2118.08	1677.52	1415.57	1242.91	1121.24
65000	5767.57	3052.19	2151.18	1703.73	1437.69	1262.33	1138.76
70000	6211.23	3286.98	2316.65	1834.79	1548.28	1359.43	1226.35
75000	6654.89	3521.76	2482.13	1965.84	1658.87	1456.53	1313.95
80000	7098.55	3756.54	2647.60	2096.90	1769.47	1553.63	1401.55
85000	7542.21	3991.33	2813.08	2227.96	1880.06	1650.74	1489.14
90000	7985.87	4226.11	2978.55	2359.01	1990.65	1747.84	1576.74
95000	8429.53	4460.90	3144.03	2490.07	2101.24	1844.94	1664.34
100000	8873.19	4695.68	3309.50	2621.13	2211.83	1942.04	1751.93
105000	9316.85	4930.46	3474.98	2752.18	2322.42	2039.15	1839.53
110000	9760.51	5165.25	3640.45	2883.24	2433.02	2136.25	1927.12
120000	10647.83	5634.82	3971.40	3145.35	2654.20	2330.45	2102.32
130000	11535.14	6104.39	4302.35	3407.46	2875.38	2524.66	2277.51
140000	12422.46	6573.95	4633.30	3669.58	3096.56	2718.86	2452.70
150000	13309.78	7043.52	4964.25	3931.69	3317.75	2913.06	2627.90
160000	14197.10	7513.09	5295.21	4193.80	3538.93	3107.27	2803.09
175000	15528.08	8217.44	5791.63	4586.97	3870.71	3398.58	3065.88
200000	17746.38	9391.36	6619.01	5242.25	4423.66	3884.09	3503.86
250000	22182.97	11739.20	8273.76	6552.81	5529.58	4855.11	4379.83
500000	44365.94	23478.40	16547.52	13105.63	11059.16	9710.22	8759.66
1000000	88731.88	46956.81	33095.03	26211.25	22118.32	19420.43	17519.32

MONTHLY PAYMENTS 11.75%

AMOUNT	8 YEARS	9 YEARS	10 YEARS	11 YEARS	12 YEARS	13 YEARS	14 YEARS
100	1.61	1.50	1.42	1.35	1.30	1.25	1.22
200	3.22	3.01	2.84	2.71	2.60	2.51	2.43
500	8.06	7.52	7.10	6.77	6.49	6.27	6.08
1000	16.12	15.04	14.20	13.53	12.98	12.53	12.16
2000	32.23	30.09	28.41	27.06	25.97	25.06	24.31
3000	48.35	45.13	42.61	40.59	38.95	37.60	36.47
4000	64.46	60.17	56.81	54.12	51.93	50.13	48.63
5000	80.58	75.22	71.01	67.65	64.92	62.66	60.78
6000	96.69	90.26	85.22	81.18	77.90	75.19	72.94
7000	112.81	105.31	99.42	94.71	90.88	87.73	85.10
8000	128.93	120.35	113.62	108.24	103.87	100.26	97.26
9000	145.04	135.39	127.83	121.77	116.85	112.79	109.41
10000	161.16	150.44	142.03	135.30	129.83	125.32	121.57
11000	177.27	165.48	156.23	148.83	142.82	137.86	133.73
12000	193.39	180.52	170.44	162.36	155.80	150.39	145.88
13000	209.51	195.57	184.64	175.89	168.78	162.92	158.04
14000	225.62	210.61	198.84	189.42	181.77	175.45	170.20
15000	241.74	225.65	213.04	202.95	194.75	187.99	182.35
20000	322.32	300.87	284.06	270.61	259.67	250.65	243.14
25000	402.89	376.09	355.07	338.26	324.58	313.31	303.92
30000	483.47	451.31	426.09	405.91	389.50	375.97	364.71
35000	564.05	526.53	497.10	473.56	454.41	438.64	425.49
40000	644.63	601.74	568.12	541.21	519.33	501.30	486.28
45000	725.21	676.96	639.13	608.86	584.25	563.96	547.06
50000	805.79	752.18	710.15	676.51	649.16	626.62	607.85
55000	886.37	827.40	781.16	744.17	714.08	689.29	668.63
56000	902.48	842.44	795.36	757.70	727.06	701.82	680.79
57000	918.60	857.49	809.57	771.23	740.05	714.35	692.95
58000	934.72	872.53	823.77	784.76	753.03	726.88	705.10
59000	950.83	887.57	837.97	798.29	766.01	739.42	717.26
60000	966.95	902.62	852.18	811.82	779.00	751.95	729.42
61000	983.06	917.66	866.38	825.35	791.98	764.48	741.57
62000	999.18	932.70	880.58	838.88	804.96	777.01	753.73
63000	1015.30	947.75	894.79	852.41	817.95	789.55	765.89
64000	1031.41	962.79	908.99	865.94	830.93	802.08	778.05
65000	1047.53	977.83	923.19	879.47	843.91	814.61	790.20
70000	1128.11	1053.05	994.21	947.12	908.83	877.27	850.99
75000	1208.68	1128.27	1065.22	1014.77	973.74	939.94	911.77
80000	1289.26	1203.49	1136.24	1082.42	1038.66	1002.60	972.56
85000	1369.84	1278.71	1207.25	1150.07	1103.58	1065.26	1033.34
90000	1450.42	1353.92	1278.27	1217.73	1168.49	1127.92	1094.13
95000	1531.00	1429.14	1349.28	1285.38	1233.41	1190.59	1154.91
100000	1611.58	1504.36	1420.29	1353.03	1298.33	1253.25	1215.70
105000	1692.16	1579.58	1491.31	1420.68	1363.24	1315.91	1276.48
110000	1772.74	1654.80	1562.32	1488.33	1428.16	1378.57	1337.27
120000	1933.90	1805.23	1704.35	1623.63	1557.99	1503.90	1458.84
130000	2095.05	1955.67	1846.38	1758.94	1687.82	1629.22	1580.41
140000	2256.21	2106.10	1988.41	1894.24	1817.66	1754.55	1701.97
150000	2417.37	2256.54	2130.44	2029.54	1947.49	1879.87	1823.54
160000	2578.53	2406.98	2272.47	2164.85	2077.32	2005.20	1945.11
175000	2820.26	2632.63	2485.52	2367.80	2272.07	2193.18	2127.47
200000	3223.16	3008.72	2840.59	2706.06	2596.65	2506.50	2431.39
250000	4028.95	3760.90	3550.74	3382.57	3245.81	3133.12	3039.24
500000	8057.90	7521.80	7101.47	6765.15	6491.63	6266.24	6078.48
1000000	16115.79	15043.60	14202.95	13530.29	12983.26	12532.48	12156.96

11.75%   MONTHLY PAYMENTS

AMOUNT	15 YEARS	16 YEARS	17 YEARS	18 YEARS	19 YEARS	20 YEARS	21 YEARS
100	1.18	1.16	1.13	1.12	1.10	1.08	1.07
200	2.37	2.31	2.27	2.23	2.20	2.17	2.14
500	5.92	5.79	5.67	5.58	5.49	5.42	5.36
1000	11.84	11.57	11.35	11.15	10.98	10.84	10.71
2000	23.68	23.15	22.69	22.30	21.97	21.67	21.42
3000	35.52	34.72	34.04	33.45	32.95	32.51	32.13
4000	47.37	46.30	45.38	44.60	43.93	43.35	42.84
5000	59.21	57.87	56.73	55.75	54.91	54.19	53.55
6000	71.05	69.44	68.08	66.90	65.90	65.02	64.27
7000	82.89	81.02	79.42	78.06	76.88	75.86	74.98
8000	94.73	92.59	90.77	89.21	87.86	86.70	85.69
9000	106.57	104.17	102.11	100.36	98.84	97.53	96.40
10000	118.41	115.74	113.46	111.51	109.83	108.37	107.11
11000	130.25	127.31	124.81	122.66	120.81	119.21	117.82
12000	142.10	138.89	136.15	133.81	131.79	130.04	128.53
13000	153.94	150.46	147.50	144.96	142.77	140.88	139.24
14000	165.78	162.04	158.84	156.11	153.76	151.72	149.95
15000	177.62	173.61	170.19	167.26	164.74	162.56	160.66
20000	236.83	231.48	226.92	223.01	219.65	216.74	214.22
25000	296.03	289.35	283.65	278.77	274.56	270.93	267.77
30000	355.24	347.22	340.38	334.52	329.48	325.11	321.33
35000	414.45	405.09	397.11	390.28	384.39	379.30	374.88
40000	473.65	462.96	453.84	446.03	439.30	433.48	428.44
45000	532.86	520.83	510.57	501.78	494.21	487.67	481.99
50000	592.07	578.70	567.30	557.54	549.13	541.85	535.54
55000	651.27	636.57	624.03	613.29	604.04	596.04	589.10
56000	663.11	648.14	635.38	624.44	615.02	606.88	599.81
57000	674.95	659.72	646.73	635.59	626.00	617.71	610.52
58000	686.80	671.29	658.07	646.74	636.99	628.55	621.23
59000	698.64	682.86	669.42	657.89	647.97	639.39	631.94
60000	710.48	694.44	680.76	669.04	658.95	650.22	642.65
61000	722.32	706.01	692.11	680.19	669.93	661.06	653.36
62000	734.16	717.59	703.46	691.34	680.92	671.90	664.07
63000	746.00	729.16	714.80	702.50	691.90	682.74	674.79
64000	757.84	740.73	726.15	713.65	702.88	693.57	685.50
65000	769.69	752.31	737.49	724.80	713.86	704.41	696.21
70000	828.89	810.18	794.22	780.55	768.78	758.59	749.76
75000	888.10	868.05	850.95	836.30	823.69	812.78	803.32
80000	947.31	925.92	907.68	892.06	878.60	866.97	856.87
85000	1006.51	983.79	964.42	947.81	933.51	921.15	910.42
90000	1065.72	1041.66	1021.15	1003.57	988.43	975.34	963.98
95000	1124.92	1099.53	1077.88	1059.32	1043.34	1029.52	1017.53
100000	1184.13	1157.40	1134.61	1115.07	1098.25	1083.71	1071.09
105000	1243.34	1215.27	1191.34	1170.83	1153.16	1137.89	1124.64
110000	1302.54	1273.14	1248.07	1226.58	1208.08	1192.08	1178.20
120000	1420.96	1388.88	1361.53	1338.09	1317.90	1300.45	1285.31
130000	1539.37	1504.62	1474.99	1449.59	1427.73	1408.82	1392.41
140000	1657.78	1620.35	1588.45	1561.10	1537.55	1517.19	1499.52
150000	1776.20	1736.09	1701.91	1672.61	1647.38	1625.56	1606.63
160000	1894.61	1851.83	1815.37	1784.12	1757.20	1733.93	1713.74
175000	2072.23	2025.44	1985.56	1951.38	1921.94	1896.49	1874.40
200000	2368.26	2314.79	2269.21	2230.15	2196.50	2167.41	2142.18
250000	2960.33	2893.49	2836.52	2787.68	2745.63	2709.27	2677.72
500000	5920.66	5786.98	5673.03	5575.36	5491.26	5418.54	5355.44
1000000	11841.31	11573.96	11346.06	11150.73	10982.51	10837.07	10710.88

MONTHLY PAYMENTS   11.75%

AMOUNT	22 YEARS	23 YEARS	24 YEARS	25 YEARS	30 YEARS	35 YEARS	40 YEARS
100	1.06	1.05	1.04	1.03	1.01	1.00	0.99
200	2.12	2.10	2.08	2.07	2.02	1.99	1.98
500	5.30	5.25	5.21	5.17	5.05	4.98	4.94
1000	10.60	10.51	10.42	10.35	10.09	9.96	9.88
2000	21.20	21.01	20.84	20.70	20.19	19.92	19.77
3000	31.80	31.52	31.26	31.04	30.28	29.87	29.65
4000	42.40	42.02	41.69	41.39	40.38	39.83	39.53
5000	53.01	52.53	52.11	51.74	50.47	49.79	49.42
6000	63.61	63.03	62.53	62.09	60.56	59.75	59.30
7000	74.21	73.54	72.95	72.44	70.66	69.71	69.19
8000	84.81	84.04	83.37	82.78	80.75	79.66	79.07
9000	95.41	94.55	93.79	93.13	90.85	89.62	88.95
10000	106.01	105.05	104.21	103.48	100.94	99.58	98.84
11000	116.61	115.56	114.64	113.83	111.04	109.54	108.72
12000	127.21	126.06	125.06	124.18	121.13	119.50	118.60
13000	137.81	136.57	135.48	134.52	131.22	129.45	128.49
14000	148.41	147.07	145.90	144.87	141.32	139.41	138.37
15000	159.02	157.58	156.32	155.22	151.41	149.37	148.25
20000	212.02	210.10	208.43	206.96	201.88	199.16	197.67
25000	265.03	262.63	260.54	258.70	252.35	248.95	247.09
30000	318.03	315.16	312.64	310.44	302.82	298.74	296.51
35000	371.04	367.68	364.75	362.18	353.29	348.53	345.93
40000	424.04	420.21	416.86	413.92	403.76	398.32	395.35
45000	477.05	472.74	468.96	465.66	454.23	448.11	444.76
50000	530.05	525.26	521.07	517.40	504.70	497.90	494.18
55000	583.06	577.79	573.18	569.14	555.18	547.69	543.60
56000	593.66	588.29	583.60	579.49	565.27	557.64	553.48
57000	604.26	598.80	594.02	589.83	575.36	567.60	563.37
58000	614.86	609.30	604.44	600.18	585.46	577.56	573.25
59000	625.46	619.81	614.86	610.53	595.55	587.52	583.13
60000	636.06	630.31	625.29	620.88	605.65	597.48	593.02
61000	646.66	640.82	635.71	631.23	615.74	607.43	602.90
62000	657.27	651.32	646.13	641.57	625.83	617.39	612.79
63000	667.87	661.83	656.55	651.92	635.93	627.35	622.67
64000	678.47	672.33	666.97	662.27	646.02	637.31	632.55
65000	689.07	682.84	677.39	672.62	656.12	647.27	642.44
70000	742.07	735.37	729.50	724.36	706.59	697.06	691.85
75000	795.08	787.89	781.61	776.10	757.06	746.85	741.27
80000	848.08	840.42	833.71	827.84	807.53	796.64	790.69
85000	901.09	892.94	885.82	879.58	858.00	846.42	840.11
90000	954.10	945.47	937.93	931.32	908.47	896.21	889.53
95000	1007.10	998.00	990.04	983.06	958.94	946.00	938.95
100000	1060.11	1050.52	1042.14	1034.80	1009.41	995.79	988.36
105000	1113.11	1103.05	1094.25	1086.54	1059.88	1045.58	1037.78
110000	1166.12	1155.58	1146.36	1138.28	1110.35	1095.37	1087.20
120000	1272.13	1260.63	1250.57	1241.76	1211.29	1194.95	1186.04
130000	1378.14	1365.68	1354.79	1345.24	1312.23	1294.53	1284.87
140000	1484.15	1470.73	1459.00	1448.72	1413.17	1394.11	1383.71
150000	1590.16	1575.78	1563.21	1552.20	1514.11	1493.69	1482.55
160000	1696.17	1680.84	1667.43	1655.68	1615.06	1593.27	1581.38
175000	1855.19	1838.42	1823.75	1810.90	1766.47	1742.64	1729.64
200000	2120.21	2101.05	2084.28	2069.60	2018.82	1991.59	1976.73
250000	2650.26	2626.31	2605.36	2587.00	2523.52	2489.48	2470.91
500000	5300.53	5252.62	5210.71	5173.99	5047.05	4978.97	4941.82
1000000	10601.06	10505.23	10421.42	10347.98	10094.10	9957.94	9883.64

12.00% MONTHLY PAYMENTS

AMOUNT	1 YEAR	2 YEARS	3 YEARS	4 YEARS	5 YEARS	6 YEARS	7 YEARS
100	8.88	4.71	3.32	2.63	2.22	1.96	1.77
200	17.77	9.41	6.64	5.27	4.45	3.91	3.53
500	44.42	23.54	16.61	13.17	11.12	9.78	8.83
1000	88.85	47.07	33.21	26.33	22.24	19.55	17.65
2000	177.70	94.15	66.43	52.67	44.49	39.10	35.31
3000	266.55	141.22	99.64	79.00	66.73	58.65	52.96
4000	355.40	188.29	132.86	105.34	88.98	78.20	70.61
5000	444.24	235.37	166.07	131.67	111.22	97.75	88.26
6000	533.09	282.44	199.29	158.00	133.47	117.30	105.92
7000	621.94	329.51	232.50	184.34	155.71	136.85	123.57
8000	710.79	376.59	265.71	210.67	177.96	156.40	141.22
9000	799.64	423.66	298.93	237.00	200.20	175.95	158.87
10000	888.49	470.73	332.14	263.34	222.44	195.50	176.53
11000	977.34	517.81	365.36	289.67	244.69	215.05	194.18
12000	1066.19	564.88	398.57	316.01	266.93	234.60	211.83
13000	1155.03	611.96	431.79	342.34	289.18	254.15	229.49
14000	1243.88	659.03	465.00	368.67	311.42	273.70	247.14
15000	1332.73	706.10	498.21	395.01	333.67	293.25	264.79
20000	1776.98	941.47	664.29	526.68	444.89	391.00	353.05
25000	2221.22	1176.84	830.36	658.35	556.11	488.75	441.32
30000	2665.46	1412.20	996.43	790.02	667.33	586.51	529.58
35000	3109.71	1647.57	1162.50	921.68	778.56	684.26	617.85
40000	3553.95	1882.94	1328.57	1053.35	889.78	782.01	706.11
45000	3998.20	2118.31	1494.64	1185.02	1001.00	879.76	794.37
50000	4442.44	2353.67	1660.72	1316.69	1112.22	977.51	882.64
55000	4886.68	2589.04	1826.79	1448.36	1223.44	1075.26	970.90
56000	4975.53	2636.11	1860.00	1474.69	1245.69	1094.81	988.55
57000	5064.38	2683.19	1893.22	1501.03	1267.93	1114.36	1006.21
58000	5153.23	2730.26	1926.43	1527.36	1290.18	1133.91	1023.86
59000	5242.08	2777.33	1959.64	1553.70	1312.42	1153.46	1041.51
60000	5330.93	2824.41	1992.86	1580.03	1334.67	1173.01	1059.16
61000	5419.78	2871.48	2026.07	1606.36	1356.91	1192.56	1076.82
62000	5508.62	2918.56	2059.29	1632.70	1379.16	1212.11	1094.47
63000	5597.47	2965.63	2092.50	1659.03	1401.40	1231.66	1112.12
64000	5686.32	3012.70	2125.72	1685.37	1423.64	1251.21	1129.77
65000	5775.17	3059.78	2158.93	1711.70	1445.89	1270.76	1147.43
70000	6219.42	3295.14	2325.00	1843.37	1557.11	1368.51	1235.69
75000	6663.66	3530.51	2491.07	1975.04	1668.33	1466.26	1323.95
80000	7107.90	3765.88	2657.14	2106.71	1779.56	1564.02	1412.22
85000	7552.15	4001.25	2823.22	2238.38	1890.78	1661.77	1500.48
90000	7996.39	4236.61	2989.29	2370.05	2002.00	1759.52	1588.75
95000	8440.63	4471.98	3155.36	2501.71	2113.22	1857.27	1677.01
100000	8884.88	4707.35	3321.43	2633.38	2224.44	1955.02	1765.27
105000	9329.12	4942.71	3487.50	2765.05	2335.67	2052.77	1853.54
110000	9773.37	5178.08	3653.57	2896.72	2446.89	2150.52	1941.80
120000	10661.85	5648.82	3985.72	3160.06	2669.33	2346.02	2118.33
130000	11550.34	6119.55	4317.86	3423.40	2891.78	2541.53	2294.86
140000	12438.83	6590.29	4650.00	3686.74	3114.22	2737.03	2471.38
150000	13327.32	7061.02	4982.15	3950.08	3336.67	2932.53	2647.91
160000	14215.81	7531.76	5314.29	4213.41	3559.11	3128.03	2824.44
175000	15548.54	8237.86	5812.50	4608.42	3892.78	3421.28	3089.23
200000	17769.76	9414.69	6642.86	5266.77	4448.89	3910.04	3530.55
250000	22212.20	11768.37	8303.58	6583.46	5561.11	4887.55	4413.18
500000	44424.39	23536.74	16607.15	13166.92	11122.22	9775.10	8826.37
1000000	88848.79	47073.47	33214.31	26333.84	22244.45	19550.19	17652.73

MONTHLY PAYMENTS   12.00%

AMOUNT	8 YEARS	9 YEARS	10 YEARS	11 YEARS	12 YEARS	13 YEARS	14 YEARS
100	1.63	1.52	1.43	1.37	1.31	1.27	1.23
200	3.25	3.04	2.87	2.74	2.63	2.54	2.46
500	8.13	7.59	7.17	6.84	6.57	6.34	6.16
1000	16.25	15.18	14.35	13.68	13.13	12.69	12.31
2000	32.51	30.37	28.69	27.36	26.27	25.37	24.63
3000	48.76	45.55	43.04	41.03	39.40	38.06	36.94
4000	65.01	60.74	57.39	54.71	52.54	50.75	49.26
5000	81.26	75.92	71.74	68.39	65.67	63.43	61.57
6000	97.52	91.11	86.08	82.07	78.81	76.12	73.89
7000	113.77	106.29	100.43	95.75	91.94	88.81	86.20
8000	130.02	121.47	114.78	109.42	105.07	101.49	98.51
9000	146.28	136.66	129.12	123.10	118.21	114.18	110.83
10000	162.53	151.84	143.47	136.78	131.34	126.87	123.14
11000	178.78	167.03	157.82	150.46	144.48	139.55	135.46
12000	195.03	182.21	172.17	164.13	157.61	152.24	147.77
13000	211.29	197.40	186.51	177.81	170.74	164.93	160.09
14000	227.54	212.58	200.86	191.49	183.88	177.61	172.40
15000	243.79	227.76	215.21	205.17	197.01	190.30	184.71
20000	325.06	303.68	286.94	273.56	262.68	253.73	246.29
25000	406.32	379.61	358.68	341.95	328.35	317.17	307.86
30000	487.59	455.53	430.41	410.34	394.03	380.60	369.43
35000	568.85	531.45	502.15	478.73	459.70	444.03	431.00
40000	650.11	607.37	573.88	547.12	525.37	507.47	492.57
45000	731.38	683.29	645.62	615.50	591.04	570.90	554.14
50000	812.64	759.21	717.35	683.89	656.71	634.33	615.71
55000	893.91	835.13	789.09	752.28	722.38	697.77	677.29
56000	910.16	850.32	803.44	765.96	735.51	710.45	689.60
57000	926.41	865.50	817.78	779.64	748.65	723.14	701.91
58000	942.66	880.69	832.13	793.32	761.78	735.83	714.23
59000	958.92	895.87	846.48	806.99	774.92	748.51	726.54
60000	975.17	911.05	860.83	820.67	788.05	761.20	738.86
61000	991.42	926.24	875.17	834.35	801.19	773.89	751.17
62000	1007.68	941.42	889.52	848.03	814.32	786.57	763.49
63000	1023.93	956.61	903.87	861.71	827.45	799.26	775.80
64000	1040.18	971.79	918.21	875.38	840.59	811.95	788.11
65000	1056.43	986.98	932.56	889.06	853.72	824.63	800.43
70000	1137.70	1062.90	1004.30	957.45	919.39	888.07	862.00
75000	1218.96	1138.82	1076.03	1025.84	985.06	951.50	923.57
80000	1300.23	1214.74	1147.77	1094.23	1050.74	1014.93	985.14
85000	1381.49	1290.66	1219.50	1162.62	1116.41	1078.37	1046.72
90000	1462.76	1366.58	1291.24	1231.01	1182.08	1141.80	1108.29
95000	1544.02	1442.50	1362.97	1299.40	1247.75	1205.23	1169.86
100000	1625.28	1518.42	1434.71	1367.79	1313.42	1268.67	1231.43
105000	1706.55	1594.34	1506.44	1436.18	1379.09	1332.10	1293.00
110000	1787.81	1670.27	1578.18	1504.57	1444.76	1395.53	1354.57
120000	1950.34	1822.11	1721.65	1641.35	1576.10	1522.40	1477.72
130000	2112.87	1973.95	1865.12	1778.12	1707.44	1649.27	1600.86
140000	2275.40	2125.79	2008.59	1914.90	1838.79	1776.13	1724.00
150000	2437.93	2277.63	2152.06	2051.68	1970.13	1903.00	1847.14
160000	2600.45	2429.48	2295.54	2188.46	2101.47	2029.87	1970.29
175000	2844.25	2657.24	2510.74	2393.63	2298.48	2220.17	2155.00
200000	3250.57	3036.85	2869.42	2735.58	2626.84	2537.33	2462.86
250000	4063.21	3796.06	3586.77	3419.47	3283.55	3171.67	3078.57
500000	8126.42	7592.12	7173.55	6838.94	6567.10	6343.33	6157.15
1000000	16252.84	15184.23	14347.09	13677.88	13134.19	12686.66	12314.30

12.00%   MONTHLY PAYMENTS

AMOUNT	15 YEARS	16 YEARS	17 YEARS	18 YEARS	19 YEARS	20 YEARS	21 YEARS
100	1.20	1.17	1.15	1.13	1.12	1.10	1.09
200	2.40	2.35	2.30	2.26	2.23	2.20	2.18
500	6.00	5.87	5.76	5.66	5.58	5.51	5.44
1000	12.00	11.74	11.51	11.32	11.15	11.01	10.89
2000	24.00	23.47	23.02	22.64	22.31	22.02	21.77
3000	36.01	35.21	34.54	33.96	33.46	33.03	32.66
4000	48.01	46.95	46.05	45.28	44.62	44.04	43.55
5000	60.01	58.69	57.56	56.60	55.77	55.05	54.43
6000	72.01	70.42	69.07	67.92	66.92	66.07	65.32
7000	84.01	82.16	80.59	79.24	78.08	77.08	76.21
8000	96.01	93.90	92.10	90.56	89.23	88.09	87.10
9000	108.02	105.64	103.61	101.88	100.38	99.10	97.98
10000	120.02	117.37	115.12	113.20	111.54	110.11	108.87
11000	132.02	129.11	126.63	124.51	122.69	121.12	119.76
12000	144.02	140.85	138.15	135.83	133.85	132.13	130.64
13000	156.02	152.58	149.66	147.15	145.00	143.14	141.53
14000	168.02	164.32	161.17	158.47	156.15	154.15	152.42
15000	180.03	176.06	172.68	169.79	167.31	165.16	163.30
20000	240.03	234.75	230.24	226.39	223.08	220.22	217.74
25000	300.04	293.43	287.80	282.99	278.85	275.27	272.17
30000	360.05	352.12	345.36	339.59	334.62	330.33	326.61
35000	420.06	410.80	402.93	396.18	390.38	385.38	381.04
40000	480.07	469.49	460.49	452.78	446.15	440.43	435.48
45000	540.08	528.18	518.05	509.38	501.92	495.49	489.91
50000	600.08	586.86	575.61	565.98	557.69	550.54	544.35
55000	660.09	645.55	633.17	622.57	613.46	605.60	598.78
56000	672.09	657.29	644.68	633.89	624.62	616.61	609.67
57000	684.10	669.02	656.19	645.21	635.77	627.62	620.56
58000	696.10	680.76	667.71	656.53	646.92	638.63	631.45
59000	708.10	692.50	679.22	667.85	658.08	649.64	642.33
60000	720.10	704.24	690.73	679.17	669.23	660.65	653.22
61000	732.10	715.97	702.24	690.49	680.39	671.66	664.11
62000	744.10	727.71	713.75	701.81	691.54	682.67	674.99
63000	756.11	739.45	725.27	713.13	702.69	693.68	685.88
64000	768.11	751.18	736.78	724.45	713.85	704.70	696.77
65000	780.11	762.92	748.29	735.77	725.00	715.71	707.65
70000	840.12	821.61	805.85	792.37	780.77	770.76	762.09
75000	900.13	880.29	863.41	848.96	836.54	825.81	816.52
80000	960.13	938.98	920.97	905.56	892.31	880.87	870.96
85000	1020.14	997.67	978.53	962.16	948.08	935.92	925.39
90000	1080.15	1056.35	1036.09	1018.76	1003.85	990.98	979.83
95000	1140.16	1115.04	1093.65	1075.35	1059.62	1046.03	1034.26
100000	1200.17	1173.73	1151.22	1131.95	1115.39	1101.09	1088.70
105000	1260.18	1232.41	1208.78	1188.55	1171.15	1156.14	1143.13
110000	1320.18	1291.10	1266.34	1245.15	1226.92	1211.19	1197.57
120000	1440.20	1408.47	1381.46	1358.34	1338.46	1321.30	1306.44
130000	1560.22	1525.84	1496.58	1471.54	1450.00	1431.41	1415.31
140000	1680.24	1643.22	1611.70	1584.73	1561.54	1541.52	1524.18
150000	1800.25	1760.59	1726.82	1697.93	1673.08	1651.63	1633.05
160000	1920.27	1877.96	1841.94	1811.12	1784.62	1761.74	1741.92
175000	2100.29	2054.02	2014.63	1980.91	1951.92	1926.90	1905.22
200000	2400.34	2347.45	2302.43	2263.90	2230.77	2202.17	2177.40
250000	3000.42	2934.31	2878.04	2829.88	2788.46	2752.72	2721.75
500000	6000.84	5868.63	5756.08	5659.75	5576.93	5505.43	5443.50
1000000	12001.68	11737.25	11512.16	11319.50	11153.86	11010.86	10887.00

MONTHLY PAYMENTS   12.00%

AMOUNT	22 YEARS	23 YEARS	24 YEARS	25 YEARS	30 YEARS	35 YEARS	40 YEARS
100	1.08	1.07	1.06	1.05	1.03	1.02	1.01
200	2.16	2.14	2.12	2.11	2.06	2.03	2.02
500	5.39	5.34	5.30	5.27	5.14	5.08	5.04
1000	10.78	10.69	10.60	10.53	10.29	10.16	10.08
2000	21.56	21.37	21.21	21.06	20.57	20.31	20.17
3000	32.34	32.06	31.81	31.60	30.86	30.47	30.25
4000	43.12	42.74	42.42	42.13	41.14	40.62	40.34
5000	53.90	53.43	53.02	52.66	51.43	50.78	50.42
6000	64.68	64.11	63.62	63.19	61.72	60.93	60.51
7000	75.46	74.80	74.23	73.73	72.00	71.09	70.59
8000	86.24	85.49	84.83	84.26	82.29	81.24	80.68
9000	97.01	96.17	95.43	94.79	92.58	91.40	90.76
10000	107.79	106.86	106.04	105.32	102.86	101.55	100.85
11000	118.57	117.54	116.64	115.85	113.15	111.71	110.93
12000	129.35	128.23	127.25	126.39	123.43	121.87	121.02
13000	140.13	138.91	137.85	136.92	133.72	132.02	131.10
14000	150.91	149.60	148.45	147.45	144.01	142.18	141.19
15000	161.69	160.28	159.06	157.98	154.29	152.33	151.27
20000	215.59	213.71	212.08	210.64	205.72	203.11	201.70
25000	269.48	267.14	265.10	263.31	257.15	253.89	252.12
30000	323.38	320.57	318.11	315.97	308.58	304.66	302.55
35000	377.28	374.00	371.13	368.63	360.01	355.44	352.97
40000	431.18	427.43	424.15	421.29	411.45	406.22	403.40
45000	485.07	480.85	477.17	473.95	462.88	457.00	453.82
50000	538.97	534.28	530.19	526.61	514.31	507.77	504.25
55000	592.87	587.71	583.21	579.27	565.74	558.55	554.67
56000	603.65	598.40	593.81	589.81	576.02	568.71	564.76
57000	614.42	609.08	604.42	600.34	586.31	578.86	574.84
58000	625.20	619.77	615.02	610.87	596.60	589.02	584.93
59000	635.98	630.45	625.63	621.40	606.88	599.17	595.01
60000	646.76	641.14	636.23	631.93	617.17	609.33	605.10
61000	657.54	651.82	646.83	642.47	627.45	619.49	615.18
62000	668.32	662.51	657.44	653.00	637.74	629.64	625.27
63000	679.10	673.20	668.04	663.53	648.03	639.80	635.35
64000	689.88	683.88	678.64	674.06	658.31	649.95	645.44
65000	700.66	694.57	689.25	684.60	668.60	660.11	655.52
70000	754.56	748.00	742.27	737.26	720.03	710.88	705.95
75000	808.45	801.42	795.29	789.92	771.46	761.66	756.37
80000	862.35	854.85	848.31	842.58	822.89	812.44	806.80
85000	916.25	908.28	901.32	895.24	874.32	863.22	857.22
90000	970.14	961.71	954.34	947.90	925.75	913.99	907.65
95000	1024.04	1015.14	1007.36	1000.56	977.18	964.77	958.07
100000	1077.94	1068.56	1060.38	1053.22	1028.61	1015.55	1008.50
105000	1131.84	1121.99	1113.40	1105.89	1080.04	1066.33	1058.92
110000	1185.73	1175.42	1166.42	1158.55	1131.47	1117.10	1109.35
120000	1293.53	1282.28	1272.46	1263.87	1234.34	1218.66	1210.20
130000	1401.32	1389.13	1378.50	1369.19	1337.20	1320.21	1311.05
140000	1509.11	1495.99	1484.53	1474.51	1440.06	1421.77	1411.90
150000	1616.91	1602.85	1590.57	1579.84	1542.92	1523.32	1512.75
160000	1724.70	1709.70	1696.61	1685.16	1645.78	1624.88	1613.60
175000	1886.39	1869.99	1855.67	1843.14	1800.07	1777.21	1764.87
200000	2155.88	2137.13	2120.76	2106.45	2057.23	2031.10	2017.00
250000	2694.85	2671.41	2650.95	2633.06	2571.53	2538.87	2521.25
500000	5389.69	5342.82	5301.91	5266.12	5143.06	5077.75	5042.50
1000000	10779.38	10685.65	10603.82	10532.24	10286.13	10155.50	10085.00

12.25% MONTHLY PAYMENTS

AMOUNT	1 YEAR	2 YEARS	3 YEARS	4 YEARS	5 YEARS	6 YEARS	7 YEARS
100	8.90	4.72	3.33	2.65	2.24	1.97	1.78
200	17.79	9.44	6.67	5.29	4.47	3.94	3.56
500	44.48	23.60	16.67	13.23	11.19	9.84	8.89
1000	88.97	47.19	33.33	26.46	22.37	19.68	17.79
2000	177.93	94.38	66.67	52.91	44.74	39.36	35.57
3000	266.90	141.57	100.00	79.37	67.11	59.04	53.36
4000	355.86	188.76	133.34	105.83	89.48	78.72	71.15
5000	444.83	235.95	166.67	132.28	111.85	98.40	88.93
6000	533.79	283.14	200.00	158.74	134.23	118.08	106.72
7000	622.76	330.33	233.34	185.20	156.60	137.76	124.51
8000	711.73	377.52	266.67	211.65	178.97	157.44	142.29
9000	800.69	424.71	300.00	238.11	201.34	177.12	160.08
10000	889.66	471.90	333.34	264.57	223.71	196.80	177.87
11000	978.62	519.09	366.67	291.02	246.08	216.48	195.65
12000	1067.59	566.28	400.01	317.48	268.45	236.17	213.44
13000	1156.56	613.47	433.34	343.94	290.82	255.85	231.23
14000	1245.52	660.66	466.67	370.39	313.19	275.53	249.01
15000	1334.49	707.85	500.01	396.85	335.56	295.21	266.80
20000	1779.32	943.81	666.68	529.14	447.42	393.61	355.73
25000	2224.14	1179.76	833.35	661.42	559.27	492.01	444.67
30000	2668.97	1415.71	1000.02	793.70	671.13	590.41	533.60
35000	3113.80	1651.66	1166.68	925.99	782.98	688.82	622.53
40000	3558.63	1887.61	1333.35	1058.27	894.84	787.22	711.47
45000	4003.46	2123.56	1500.02	1190.55	1006.69	885.62	800.40
50000	4448.29	2359.52	1666.69	1322.84	1118.55	984.02	889.34
55000	4893.12	2595.47	1833.36	1455.12	1230.40	1082.42	978.27
56000	4982.08	2642.66	1866.70	1481.58	1252.78	1102.10	996.06
57000	5071.05	2689.85	1900.03	1508.03	1275.15	1121.79	1013.84
58000	5160.02	2737.04	1933.36	1534.49	1297.52	1141.47	1031.63
59000	5248.98	2784.23	1966.70	1560.95	1319.89	1161.15	1049.42
60000	5337.95	2831.42	2000.03	1587.41	1342.26	1180.83	1067.20
61000	5426.91	2878.61	2033.36	1613.86	1364.63	1200.51	1084.99
62000	5515.88	2925.80	2066.70	1640.32	1387.00	1220.19	1102.78
63000	5604.84	2972.99	2100.03	1666.78	1409.37	1239.87	1120.56
64000	5693.81	3020.18	2133.37	1693.23	1431.74	1259.55	1138.35
65000	5782.78	3067.37	2166.70	1719.69	1454.11	1279.23	1156.14
70000	6227.60	3303.32	2333.37	1851.97	1565.97	1377.63	1245.07
75000	6672.43	3539.27	2500.04	1984.26	1677.82	1476.03	1334.00
80000	7117.26	3775.22	2666.71	2116.54	1789.68	1574.44	1422.94
85000	7562.09	4011.18	2833.38	2248.82	1901.53	1672.84	1511.87
90000	8006.92	4247.13	3000.05	2381.11	2013.39	1771.24	1600.80
95000	8451.75	4483.08	3166.71	2513.39	2125.24	1869.64	1689.74
100000	8896.58	4719.03	3333.38	2645.68	2237.10	1968.04	1778.67
105000	9341.41	4954.98	3500.05	2777.96	2348.95	2066.45	1867.60
110000	9786.24	5190.93	3666.72	2910.24	2460.81	2164.85	1956.54
120000	10675.89	5662.84	4000.06	3174.81	2684.52	2361.65	2134.40
130000	11565.55	6134.74	4333.40	3439.38	2908.23	2558.46	2312.27
140000	12455.21	6606.64	4666.74	3703.95	3131.94	2755.26	2490.14
150000	13344.87	7078.55	5000.08	3968.51	3355.65	2952.07	2668.01
160000	14234.53	7550.45	5333.41	4233.08	3579.36	3148.87	2845.87
175000	15569.01	8258.30	5833.42	4629.93	3914.92	3444.08	3112.67
200000	17793.16	9438.06	6666.77	5291.35	4474.20	3936.09	3557.34
250000	22241.45	11797.58	8333.46	6614.19	5592.75	4920.11	4446.68
500000	44482.89	23595.15	16666.92	13228.38	11185.49	9840.22	8893.35
1000000	88965.78	47190.31	33333.84	26456.75	22370.99	19680.44	17786.71

MONTHLY PAYMENTS 12.25%

AMOUNT	8 YEARS	9 YEARS	10 YEARS	11 YEARS	12 YEARS	13 YEARS	14 YEARS
100	1.64	1.53	1.45	1.38	1.33	1.28	1.25
200	3.28	3.07	2.90	2.77	2.66	2.57	2.49
500	8.20	7.66	7.25	6.91	6.64	6.42	6.24
1000	16.39	15.33	14.49	13.83	13.29	12.84	12.47
2000	32.78	30.65	28.98	27.65	26.57	25.68	24.95
3000	49.17	45.98	43.48	41.48	39.86	38.53	37.42
4000	65.56	61.30	57.97	55.31	53.14	51.37	49.89
5000	81.95	76.63	72.46	69.13	66.43	64.21	62.36
6000	98.34	91.95	86.95	82.96	79.72	77.05	74.84
7000	114.73	107.28	101.44	96.78	93.00	89.89	87.31
8000	131.12	122.60	115.94	110.61	106.29	102.73	99.78
9000	147.51	137.93	130.43	124.44	119.57	115.58	112.25
10000	163.91	153.26	144.92	138.26	132.86	128.42	124.73
11000	180.30	168.58	159.41	152.09	146.15	141.26	137.20
12000	196.69	183.91	173.90	165.92	159.43	154.10	149.67
13000	213.08	199.23	188.40	179.74	172.72	166.94	162.14
14000	229.47	214.56	202.89	193.57	186.00	179.78	174.62
15000	245.86	229.88	217.38	207.39	199.29	192.63	187.09
20000	327.81	306.51	289.84	276.53	265.72	256.83	249.45
25000	409.76	383.14	362.30	345.66	332.15	321.04	311.81
30000	491.72	459.77	434.76	414.79	398.58	385.25	374.18
35000	573.67	536.39	507.22	483.92	465.01	449.46	436.54
40000	655.62	613.02	579.68	553.05	531.44	513.67	498.90
45000	737.57	689.65	652.14	622.18	597.87	577.88	561.26
50000	819.53	766.28	724.60	691.31	664.30	642.09	623.63
55000	901.48	842.91	797.06	760.44	730.73	706.29	685.99
56000	917.87	858.23	811.55	774.27	744.01	719.14	698.46
57000	934.26	873.56	826.04	788.10	757.30	731.98	710.93
58000	950.65	888.88	840.54	801.92	770.59	744.82	723.41
59000	967.04	904.21	855.03	815.75	783.87	757.66	735.88
60000	983.43	919.53	869.52	829.58	797.16	770.50	748.35
61000	999.82	934.86	884.01	843.40	810.44	783.35	760.82
62000	1016.21	950.18	898.50	857.23	823.73	796.19	773.30
63000	1032.60	965.51	913.00	871.05	837.02	809.03	785.77
64000	1048.99	980.84	927.49	884.88	850.30	821.87	798.24
65000	1065.38	996.16	941.98	898.71	863.59	834.71	810.72
70000	1147.34	1072.79	1014.44	967.84	930.02	898.92	873.08
75000	1229.29	1149.42	1086.90	1036.97	996.45	963.13	935.44
80000	1311.24	1226.04	1159.36	1106.10	1062.88	1027.34	997.80
85000	1393.19	1302.67	1231.82	1175.23	1129.31	1091.55	1060.17
90000	1475.15	1379.30	1304.28	1244.36	1195.74	1155.76	1122.53
95000	1557.10	1455.93	1376.74	1313.49	1262.17	1219.96	1184.89
100000	1639.05	1532.56	1449.20	1382.63	1328.60	1284.17	1247.25
105000	1721.00	1609.18	1521.66	1451.76	1395.03	1348.38	1309.62
110000	1802.96	1685.81	1594.12	1520.89	1461.46	1412.59	1371.98
120000	1966.86	1839.07	1739.04	1659.15	1594.32	1541.01	1496.70
130000	2130.77	1992.32	1883.96	1797.41	1727.18	1669.42	1621.43
140000	2294.67	2145.58	2028.88	1935.68	1860.04	1797.84	1746.16
150000	2458.58	2298.83	2173.80	2073.94	1992.89	1926.26	1870.88
160000	2622.48	2452.09	2318.72	2212.20	2125.75	2054.68	1995.61
175000	2868.34	2681.97	2536.10	2419.60	2325.04	2247.30	2182.69
200000	3278.10	3065.11	2898.40	2765.25	2657.19	2568.35	2494.51
250000	4097.63	3831.39	3623.00	3456.56	3321.49	3210.43	3118.13
500000	8195.26	7662.78	7245.99	6913.13	6642.98	6420.86	6236.27
1000000	16390.51	15325.55	14491.99	13826.26	13285.97	12841.73	12472.54

12.25% MONTHLY PAYMENTS

AMOUNT	15 YEARS	16 YEARS	17 YEARS	18 YEARS	19 YEARS	20 YEARS	21 YEARS
100	1.22	1.19	1.17	1.15	1.13	1.12	1.11
200	2.43	2.38	2.34	2.30	2.27	2.24	2.21
500	6.08	5.95	5.84	5.74	5.66	5.59	5.53
1000	12.16	11.90	11.68	11.49	11.33	11.19	11.06
2000	24.33	23.80	23.36	22.98	22.65	22.37	22.13
3000	36.49	35.70	35.04	34.47	33.98	33.56	33.19
4000	48.65	47.61	46.72	45.96	45.30	44.74	44.26
5000	60.81	59.51	58.40	57.45	56.63	55.93	55.32
6000	72.98	71.41	70.08	68.94	67.96	67.11	66.38
7000	85.14	83.31	81.75	80.42	79.28	78.30	77.45
8000	97.30	95.21	93.43	91.91	90.61	89.49	88.51
9000	109.47	107.11	105.11	103.40	101.94	100.67	99.58
10000	121.63	119.02	116.79	114.89	113.26	111.86	110.64
11000	133.79	130.92	128.47	126.38	124.59	123.04	121.71
12000	145.96	142.82	140.15	137.87	135.91	134.23	132.77
13000	158.12	154.72	151.83	149.36	147.24	145.41	143.83
14000	170.28	166.62	163.51	160.85	158.57	156.60	154.90
15000	182.44	178.52	175.19	172.34	169.89	167.78	165.96
20000	243.26	238.03	233.58	229.79	226.52	223.71	221.28
25000	304.07	297.54	291.98	287.23	283.15	279.64	276.60
30000	364.89	357.05	350.38	344.68	339.79	335.57	331.92
35000	425.70	416.55	408.77	402.12	396.42	391.50	387.24
40000	486.52	476.06	467.17	459.57	453.05	447.43	442.56
45000	547.33	535.57	525.57	517.02	509.68	503.35	497.88
50000	608.15	595.08	583.96	574.46	566.31	559.28	553.21
55000	668.96	654.58	642.36	631.91	622.94	615.21	608.53
56000	681.13	666.48	654.04	643.40	634.27	626.40	619.59
57000	693.29	678.39	665.72	654.89	645.59	637.58	630.65
58000	705.45	690.29	677.40	666.38	656.92	648.77	641.72
59000	717.62	702.19	689.07	677.87	668.25	659.95	652.78
60000	729.78	714.09	700.75	689.36	679.57	671.14	663.85
61000	741.94	725.99	712.43	700.85	690.90	682.32	674.91
62000	754.11	737.89	724.11	712.33	702.22	693.51	685.97
63000	766.27	749.79	735.79	723.82	713.55	704.70	697.04
64000	778.43	761.70	747.47	735.31	724.88	715.88	708.10
65000	790.59	773.60	759.15	746.80	736.20	727.07	719.17
70000	851.41	833.11	817.55	804.25	792.83	783.00	774.49
75000	912.22	892.61	875.94	861.70	849.46	838.92	829.81
80000	973.04	952.12	934.34	919.14	906.10	894.85	885.13
85000	1033.85	1011.63	992.73	976.59	962.73	950.78	940.45
90000	1094.67	1071.14	1051.13	1034.03	1019.36	1006.71	995.77
95000	1155.48	1130.64	1109.53	1091.48	1075.99	1062.64	1051.09
100000	1216.30	1190.15	1167.92	1148.93	1132.62	1118.56	1106.41
105000	1277.11	1249.66	1226.32	1206.37	1189.25	1174.49	1161.73
110000	1337.93	1309.17	1284.71	1263.82	1245.88	1230.42	1217.05
120000	1459.56	1428.18	1401.51	1378.71	1359.14	1342.28	1327.69
130000	1581.19	1547.20	1518.30	1493.61	1472.41	1454.13	1438.33
140000	1702.82	1666.21	1635.09	1608.50	1585.67	1565.99	1548.97
150000	1824.45	1785.23	1751.88	1723.39	1698.93	1677.85	1659.62
160000	1946.08	1904.24	1868.68	1838.29	1812.19	1789.70	1770.26
175000	2128.52	2082.76	2043.86	2010.62	1982.08	1957.49	1936.22
200000	2432.60	2380.30	2335.85	2297.85	2265.24	2237.13	2212.82
250000	3040.75	2975.38	2919.81	2872.32	2831.55	2796.41	2766.03
500000	6081.49	5950.75	5839.61	5744.64	5663.10	5592.82	5532.05
1000000	12162.99	11901.50	11679.23	11489.27	11326.20	11185.65	11064.10

MONTHLY PAYMENTS 12.25%

AMOUNT	22 YEARS	23 YEARS	24 YEARS	25 YEARS	30 YEARS	35 YEARS	40 YEARS
100	1.10	1.09	1.08	1.07	1.05	1.04	1.03
200	2.19	2.17	2.16	2.14	2.10	2.07	2.06
500	5.48	5.43	5.39	5.36	5.24	5.18	5.14
1000	10.96	10.87	10.79	10.72	10.48	10.35	10.29
2000	21.92	21.73	21.57	21.43	20.96	20.71	20.57
3000	32.88	32.60	32.36	32.15	31.44	31.06	30.86
4000	43.83	43.47	43.15	42.87	41.92	41.41	41.15
5000	54.79	54.34	53.94	53.59	52.39	51.77	51.43
6000	65.75	65.20	64.72	64.30	62.87	62.12	61.72
7000	76.71	76.07	75.51	75.02	73.35	72.48	72.01
8000	87.67	86.94	86.30	85.74	83.83	82.83	82.29
9000	98.63	97.80	97.08	96.46	94.31	93.18	92.58
10000	109.59	108.67	107.87	107.17	104.79	103.54	102.87
11000	120.55	119.54	118.66	117.89	115.27	113.89	113.16
12000	131.50	130.40	129.45	128.61	125.75	124.24	123.44
13000	142.46	141.27	140.23	139.33	136.23	134.60	133.73
14000	153.42	152.14	151.02	150.04	146.71	144.95	144.02
15000	164.38	163.01	161.81	160.76	157.18	155.31	154.30
20000	219.17	217.34	215.74	214.35	209.58	207.07	205.74
25000	273.97	271.68	269.68	267.94	261.97	258.84	257.17
30000	328.76	326.01	323.62	321.52	314.37	310.61	308.61
35000	383.55	380.35	377.55	375.11	366.76	362.38	360.04
40000	438.35	434.68	431 49	428.70	419.16	414.15	411.47
45000	493.14	489.02	485.42	482.28	471.55	465.92	462.91
50000	547.93	543.35	539.36	535.87	523.95	517.69	514.34
55000	602.73	597.69	593.29	589.46	576.34	569.45	565.78
56000	613.69	608.55	604.08	600.18	586.82	579.81	576.06
57000	624.65	619.42	614.87	610.89	597.30	590.16	586.35
58000	635.60	630.29	625.66	621.61	607.78	600.52	596.64
59000	646.56	641.16	636.44	632.33	618.26	610.87	606.92
60000	657.52	652.02	647.23	643.05	628.74	621.22	617.21
61000	668.48	662.89	658.02	653.76	639.22	631.58	627.50
62000	679.44	673.76	668.80	664.48	649.70	641.93	637.79
63000	690.40	684.62	679.59	675.20	660.17	652.28	648.07
64000	701.36	695.49	690.38	685.92	670.65	662.64	658.36
65000	712.31	706.36	701.17	696.63	681.13	672.99	668.65
70000	767.11	760.69	755.10	750.22	733.53	724.76	720.08
75000	821.90	815.03	809.04	803.81	785.92	776.53	771.51
80000	876.70	869.36	862.97	857.40	838.32	828.30	822.95
85000	931.49	923.70	916.91	910.98	890.71	880.07	874.38
90000	986.28	978.03	970.85	964.57	943.11	931.83	925.82
95000	1041.08	1032.37	1024.78	1018.16	995.50	983.60	977.25
100000	1095.87	1086.70	1078.72	1071.74	1047.90	1035.37	1028.69
105000	1150.66	1141.04	1132.65	1125.33	1100.29	1087.14	1080.12
110000	1205.46	1195.37	1186.59	1178.92	1152.69	1138.91	1131.55
120000	1315.04	1304.04	1294.46	1286.09	1257.48	1242.45	1234.42
130000	1424.63	1412.71	1402.33	1393.27	1362.27	1345.98	1337.29
140000	1534.22	1521.39	1510.20	1500.44	1467.06	1449.52	1440.16
150000	1643.80	1630.06	1618.08	1607.62	1571.84	1553.06	1543.03
160000	1753.39	1738.73	1725.95	1714.79	1676.63	1656.59	1645.90
175000	1917.77	1901.73	1887.75	1875.55	1833.82	1811.90	1800.20
200000	2191.74	2173.41	2157.43	2143.49	2095.79	2070.74	2057.37
250000	2739.67	2716.76	2696.79	2679.36	2619.74	2588.43	2571.72
500000	5479.35	5433.52	5393.58	5358.72	5239.48	5176.86	5143.43
1000000	10958.69	10867.04	10787.17	10717.44	10478.96	10353.71	10286.86

12.50% MONTHLY PAYMENTS

AMOUNT	1 YEAR	2 YEARS	3 YEARS	4 YEARS	5 YEARS	6 YEARS	7 YEARS
100	8.91	4.73	3.35	2.66	2.25	1.98	1.79
200	17.82	9.46	6.69	5.32	4.50	3.96	3.58
500	44.54	23.65	16.73	13.29	11.25	9.91	8.96
1000	89.08	47.31	33.45	26.58	22.50	19.81	17.92
2000	178.17	94.61	66.91	53.16	45.00	39.62	35.84
3000	267.25	141.92	100.36	79.74	67.49	59.43	53.76
4000	356.33	189.23	133.81	106.32	89.99	79.24	71.68
5000	445.41	236.54	167.27	132.90	112.49	99.06	89.61
6000	534.50	283.84	200.72	159.48	134.99	118.87	107.53
7000	623.58	331.15	234.18	186.06	157.49	138.68	125.45
8000	712.66	378.46	267.63	212.64	179.98	158.49	143.37
9000	801.75	425.77	301.08	239.22	202.48	178.30	161.29
10000	890.83	473.07	334.54	265.80	224.98	198.11	179.21
11000	979.91	520.38	367.99	292.38	247.48	217.92	197.13
12000	1068.99	567.69	401.44	318.96	269.98	237.73	215.05
13000	1158.08	615.00	434.90	345.54	292.47	257.55	232.98
14000	1247.16	662.30	468.35	372.12	314.97	277.36	250.90
15000	1336.24	709.61	501.80	398.70	337.47	297.17	268.82
20000	1781.66	946.15	669.07	531.60	449.96	396.22	358.42
25000	2227.07	1182.68	836.34	664.50	562.45	495.28	448.03
30000	2672.49	1419.22	1003.61	797.40	674.94	594.34	537.64
35000	3117.90	1655.76	1170.88	930.30	787.43	693.39	627.24
40000	3563.31	1892.29	1338.15	1063.20	899.92	792.45	716.85
45000	4008.73	2128.83	1505.41	1196.10	1012.41	891.50	806.46
50000	4454.14	2365.37	1672.68	1329.00	1124.90	990.56	896.06
55000	4899.56	2601.90	1839.95	1461.90	1237.39	1089.61	985.67
56000	4988.64	2649.21	1873.40	1488.48	1259.88	1109.43	1003.59
57000	5077.72	2696.52	1906.86	1515.06	1282.38	1129.24	1021.51
58000	5166.81	2743.82	1940.31	1541.64	1304.88	1149.05	1039.43
59000	5255.89	2791.13	1973.76	1568.22	1327.38	1168.86	1057.35
60000	5344.97	2838.44	2007.22	1594.80	1349.88	1188.67	1075.27
61000	5434.05	2885.75	2040.67	1621.38	1372.37	1208.48	1093.20
62000	5523.14	2933.05	2074.12	1647.96	1394.87	1228.29	1111.12
63000	5612.22	2980.36	2107.58	1674.54	1417.37	1248.10	1129.04
64000	5701.30	3027.67	2141.03	1701.12	1439.87	1267.92	1146.96
65000	5790.39	3074.98	2174.49	1727.70	1462.37	1287.73	1164.88
70000	6235.80	3311.51	2341.75	1860.60	1574.86	1386.78	1254.49
75000	6681.21	3548.05	2509.02	1993.50	1687.35	1485.84	1344.09
80000	7126.63	3784.58	2676.29	2126.40	1799.84	1584.89	1433.70
85000	7572.04	4021.12	2843.56	2259.30	1912.32	1683.95	1523.31
90000	8017.46	4257.66	3010.83	2392.20	2024.81	1783.01	1612.91
95000	8462.87	4494.19	3178.09	2525.10	2137.30	1882.06	1702.52
100000	8908.29	4730.73	3345.36	2658.00	2249.79	1981.12	1792.12
105000	9353.70	4967.27	3512.63	2790.90	2362.28	2080.17	1881.73
110000	9799.11	5203.80	3679.90	2923.80	2474.77	2179.23	1971.34
120000	10689.94	5676.88	4014.44	3189.60	2699.75	2377.34	2150.55
130000	11580.77	6149.95	4348.97	3455.40	2924.73	2575.45	2329.76
140000	12471.60	6623.02	4683.51	3721.20	3149.71	2773.57	2508.97
150000	13362.43	7096.10	5018.04	3987.00	3374.69	2971.68	2688.19
160000	14253.26	7569.17	5352.58	4252.80	3599.67	3169.79	2867.40
175000	15589.50	8278.78	5854.38	4651.50	3937.14	3466.96	3136.22
200000	17816.57	9461.46	6690.73	5316.00	4499.59	3962.24	3584.25
250000	22270.72	11826.83	8363.41	6645.00	5624.48	4952.79	4480.31
500000	44541.43	23653.65	16726.81	13290.00	11248.97	9905.59	8960.62
1000000	89082.86	47307.31	33453.63	26580.00	22497.94	19811.18	17921.24

MONTHLY PAYMENTS   12.50%

AMOUNT	8 YEARS	9 YEARS	10 YEARS	11 YEARS	12 YEARS	13 YEARS	14 YEARS
100	1.65	1.55	1.46	1.40	1.34	1.30	1.26
200	3.31	3.09	2.93	2.80	2.69	2.60	2.53
500	8.26	7.73	7.32	6.99	6.72	6.50	6.32
1000	16.53	15.47	14.64	13.98	13.44	13.00	12.63
2000	33.06	30.94	29.28	27.95	26.88	26.00	25.26
3000	49.59	46.40	43.91	41.93	40.32	38.99	37.90
4000	66.12	61.87	58.55	55.90	53.75	51.99	50.53
5000	82.64	77.34	73.19	69.88	67.19	64.99	63.16
6000	99.17	92.81	87.83	83.85	80.63	77.99	75.79
7000	115.70	108.27	102.46	97.83	94.07	90.98	88.42
8000	132.23	123.74	117.10	111.80	107.51	103.98	101.05
9000	148.76	139.21	131.74	125.78	120.95	116.98	113.69
10000	165.29	154.68	146.38	139.75	134.39	129.98	126.32
11000	181.82	170.14	161.01	153.73	147.82	142.97	138.95
12000	198.35	185.61	175.65	167.71	161.26	155.97	151.58
13000	214.87	201.08	190.29	181.68	174.70	168.97	164.21
14000	231.40	216.55	204.93	195.66	188.14	181.97	176.84
15000	247.93	232.01	219.56	209.63	201.58	194.96	189.48
20000	330.58	309.35	292.75	279.51	268.77	259.95	252.63
25000	413.22	386.69	365.94	349.39	335.96	324.94	315.79
30000	495.86	464.03	439.13	419.26	403.16	389.93	378.95
35000	578.51	541.36	512.32	489.14	470.35	454.92	442.11
40000	661.15	618.70	585.50	559.02	537.54	519.91	505.27
45000	743.80	696.04	658.69	628.89	604.74	584.89	568.43
50000	826.44	773.38	731.88	698.77	671.93	649.88	631.58
55000	909.08	850.72	805.07	768.65	739.12	714.87	694.74
56000	925.61	866.18	819.71	782.62	752.56	727.87	707.37
57000	942.14	881.65	834.34	796.60	766.00	740.87	720.01
58000	958.67	897.12	848.98	810.57	779.44	753.86	732.64
59000	975.20	912.59	863.62	824.55	792.88	766.86	745.27
60000	991.73	928.05	878.26	838.53	806.31	779.86	757.90
61000	1008.26	943.52	892.89	852.50	819.75	792.86	770.53
62000	1024.79	958.99	907.53	866.48	833.19	805.85	783.16
63000	1041.31	974.46	922.17	880.45	846.63	818.85	795.80
64000	1057.84	989.92	936.81	894.43	860.07	831.85	808.43
65000	1074.37	1005.39	951.45	908.40	873.51	844.85	821.06
70000	1157.02	1082.73	1024.63	978.28	940.70	909.84	884.22
75000	1239.66	1160.07	1097.82	1048.16	1007.89	974.82	947.38
80000	1322.30	1237.40	1171.01	1118.03	1075.09	1039.81	1010.53
85000	1404.95	1314.74	1244.20	1187.91	1142.28	1104.80	1073.69
90000	1487.59	1392.08	1317.39	1257.79	1209.47	1169.79	1136.85
95000	1570.24	1469.42	1390.57	1327.67	1276.66	1234.78	1200.01
100000	1652.88	1546.76	1463.76	1397.54	1343.86	1299.77	1263.17
105000	1735.52	1624.09	1536.95	1467.42	1411.05	1364.75	1326.33
110000	1818.17	1701.43	1610.14	1537.30	1478.24	1429.74	1389.49
120000	1983.46	1856.11	1756.51	1677.05	1612.63	1559.72	1515.80
130000	2148.75	2010.78	1902.89	1816.81	1747.01	1689.70	1642.12
140000	2314.03	2165.46	2049.27	1956.56	1881.40	1819.67	1768.44
150000	2479.32	2320.13	2195.64	2096.31	2015.79	1949.65	1894.75
160000	2644.61	2474.81	2342.02	2236.07	2150.17	2079.63	2021.07
175000	2892.54	2706.82	2561.58	2445.70	2351.75	2274.59	2210.54
200000	3305.76	3093.51	2927.52	2795.09	2687.71	2599.53	2526.34
250000	4132.20	3866.89	3659.40	3493.86	3359.64	3249.42	3157.92
500000	8264.40	7733.78	7318.81	6987.71	6719.29	6498.83	6315.84
1000000	16528.81	15467.55	14637.62	13975.43	13438.57	12997.66	12631.68

12.50% MONTHLY PAYMENTS

AMOUNT	15 YEARS	16 YEARS	17 YEARS	18 YEARS	19 YEARS	20 YEARS	21 YEARS
100	1.23	1.21	1.18	1.17	1.15	1.14	1.12
200	2.47	2.41	2.37	2.33	2.30	2.27	2.25
500	6.16	6.03	5.92	5.83	5.75	5.68	5.62
1000	12.33	12.07	11.85	11.66	11.50	11.36	11.24
2000	24.65	24.13	23.69	23.32	23.00	22.72	22.48
3000	36.98	36.20	35.54	34.98	34.50	34.08	33.73
4000	49.30	48.27	47.39	46.64	46.00	45.45	44.97
5000	61.63	60.33	59.24	58.30	57.50	56.81	56.21
6000	73.95	72.40	71.08	69.96	69.00	68.17	67.45
7000	86.28	84.47	82.93	81.62	80.50	79.53	78.70
8000	98.60	96.53	94.78	93.28	92.00	90.89	89.94
9000	110.93	108.60	106.63	104.94	103.50	102.25	101.18
10000	123.25	120.67	118.47	116.60	115.00	113.61	112.42
11000	135.58	132.73	130.32	128.26	126.49	124.98	123.66
12000	147.90	144.80	142.17	139.92	137.99	136.34	134.91
13000	160.23	156.87	154.01	151.58	149.49	147.70	146.15
14000	172.55	168.93	165.86	163.24	160.99	159.06	157.39
15000	184.88	181.00	177.71	174.90	172.49	170.42	168.63
20000	246.50	241.33	236.95	233.20	229.99	227.23	224.84
25000	308.13	301.67	296.18	291.50	287.49	284.04	281.05
30000	369.76	362.00	355.42	349.80	344.99	340.84	337.27
35000	431.38	422.33	414.65	408.10	402.48	397.65	393.48
40000	493.01	482.67	473.89	466.40	459.98	454.46	449.69
45000	554.63	543.00	533.13	524.70	517.48	511.26	505.90
50000	616.26	603.33	592.36	583.00	574.98	568.07	562.11
55000	677.89	663.67	651.60	641.30	632.47	624.88	618.32
56000	690.21	675.74	663.45	652.96	643.97	636.24	629.56
57000	702.54	687.80	675.29	664.62	655.47	647.60	640.80
58000	714.86	699.87	687.14	676.28	666.97	658.96	652.05
59000	727.19	711.94	698.99	687.94	678.47	670.32	663.29
60000	739.51	724.00	710.84	699.60	689.97	681.68	674.53
61000	751.84	736.07	722.68	711.26	701.47	693.05	685.77
62000	764.16	748.14	734.53	722.92	712.97	704.41	697.02
63000	776.49	760.20	746.38	734.58	724.47	715.77	708.26
64000	788.81	772.27	758.22	746.24	735.97	727.13	719.50
65000	801.14	784.34	770.07	757.90	747.47	738.49	730.74
70000	862.77	844.67	829.31	816.20	804.97	795.30	786.95
75000	924.39	905.00	888.54	874.50	862.46	852.11	843.16
80000	986.02	965.34	947.78	932.80	919.96	908.91	899.37
85000	1047.64	1025.67	1007.02	991.10	977.46	965.72	955.59
90000	1109.27	1086.00	1066.25	1049.40	1034.96	1022.53	1011.80
95000	1170.90	1146.34	1125.49	1107.70	1092.45	1079.33	1068.01
100000	1232.52	1206.67	1184.73	1166.00	1149.95	1136.14	1124.22
105000	1294.15	1267.00	1243.96	1224.30	1207.45	1192.95	1180.43
110000	1355.77	1327.34	1303.20	1282.60	1264.95	1249.75	1236.64
120000	1479.03	1448.00	1421.67	1399.20	1379.94	1363.37	1349.06
130000	1602.28	1568.67	1540.14	1515.80	1494.94	1476.98	1461.48
140000	1725.53	1689.34	1658.62	1632.40	1609.93	1590.60	1573.91
150000	1848.78	1810.00	1777.09	1749.00	1724.93	1704.21	1686.33
160000	1972.04	1930.67	1895.56	1865.60	1839.92	1817.82	1798.75
175000	2156.91	2111.67	2073.27	2040.50	2012.41	1988.25	1967.38
200000	2465.04	2413.34	2369.45	2332.00	2299.90	2272.28	2248.44
250000	3081.31	3016.67	2961.81	2915.00	2874.88	2840.35	2810.55
500000	6162.61	6033.35	5923.63	5830.00	5749.75	5680.70	5621.09
1000000	12325.22	12066.70	11847.26	11660.01	11499.51	11361.41	11242.18

MONTHLY PAYMENTS 12.50%

AMOUNT	22 YEARS	23 YEARS	24 YEARS	25 YEARS	30 YEARS	35 YEARS	40 YEARS
100	1.11	1.10	1.10	1.09	1.07	1.06	1.05
200	2.23	2.21	2.19	2.18	2.13	2.11	2.10
500	5.57	5.52	5.49	5.45	5.34	5.28	5.24
1000	11.14	11.05	10.97	10.90	10.67	10.55	10.49
2000	22.28	22.10	21.94	21.81	21.35	21.11	20.98
3000	33.42	33.15	32.91	32.71	32.02	31.66	31.47
4000	44.56	44.20	43.89	43.61	42.69	42.21	41.96
5000	55.69	55.25	54.86	54.52	53.36	52.76	52.45
6000	66.83	66.30	65.83	65.42	64.04	63.32	62.94
7000	77.97	77.35	76.80	76.32	74.71	73.87	73.42
8000	89.11	88.39	87.77	87.23	85.38	84.42	83.91
9000	100.25	99.44	98.74	98.13	96.05	94.97	94.40
10000	111.39	110.49	109.71	109.04	106.73	105.53	104.89
11000	122.53	121.54	120.69	119.94	117.40	116.08	115.38
12000	133.67	132.59	131.66	130.84	128.07	126.63	125.87
13000	144.81	143.64	142.63	141.75	138.74	137.18	136.36
14000	155.95	154.69	153.60	152.65	149.42	147.74	146.85
15000	167.08	165.74	164.57	163.55	160.09	158.29	157.34
20000	222.78	220.99	219.43	218.07	213.45	211.05	209.78
25000	278.47	276.23	274.29	272.59	266.81	263.81	262.23
30000	334.17	331.48	329.14	327.11	320.18	316.58	314.68
35000	389.86	386.73	384.00	381.62	373.54	369.34	367.12
40000	445.56	441.97	438.86	436.14	426.90	422.10	419.57
45000	501.25	497.22	493.72	490.66	480.27	474.86	472.01
50000	556.95	552.47	548.57	545.18	533.63	527.63	524.46
55000	612.64	607.72	603.43	599.69	586.99	580.39	576.91
56000	623.78	618.76	614.40	610.60	597.66	590.94	587.39
57000	634.92	629.81	625.37	621.50	608.34	601.50	597.88
58000	646.06	640.86	636.34	632.41	619.01	612.05	608.37
59000	657.20	651.91	647.32	643.31	629.68	622.60	618.86
60000	668.34	662.96	658.29	654.21	640.35	633.15	629.35
61000	679.48	674.01	669.26	665.12	651.03	643.71	639.84
62000	690.62	685.06	680.23	676.02	661.70	654.26	650.33
63000	701.75	696.11	691.20	686.92	672.37	664.81	660.82
64000	712.89	707.16	702.17	697.83	683.04	675.36	671.31
65000	724.03	718.21	713.14	708.73	693.72	685.92	681.80
70000	779.73	773.46	768.00	763.25	747.08	738.68	734.24
75000	835.42	828.70	822.86	817.77	800.44	791.44	786.69
80000	891.12	883.95	877.72	872.28	853.81	844.20	839.14
85000	946.81	939.20	932.57	926.80	907.17	896.97	891.58
90000	1002.51	994.44	987.43	981.32	960.53	949.73	944.03
95000	1058.20	1049.69	1042.29	1035.84	1013.89	1002.49	996.47
100000	1113.90	1104.94	1097.14	1090.35	1067.26	1055.25	1048.92
105000	1169.59	1160.18	1152.00	1144.87	1120.62	1108.02	1101.37
110000	1225.29	1215.43	1206.86	1199.39	1173.98	1160.78	1153.81
120000	1336.67	1325.92	1316.57	1308.42	1280.71	1266.31	1258.70
130000	1448.06	1436.42	1426.29	1417.46	1387.44	1371.83	1363.60
140000	1559.45	1546.91	1536.00	1526.50	1494.16	1477.36	1468.49
150000	1670.84	1657.41	1645.72	1635.53	1600.89	1582.88	1573.38
160000	1782.23	1767.90	1755.43	1744.57	1707.61	1688.41	1678.27
175000	1949.32	1933.64	1920.00	1908.12	1867.70	1846.70	1835.61
200000	2227.79	2209.87	2194.29	2180.71	2134.52	2110.51	2097.84
250000	2784.74	2762.34	2742.86	2725.89	2668.14	2638.14	2622.30
500000	5569.48	5524.68	5485.72	5451.77	5336.29	5276.27	5244.60
1000000	11138.96	11049.37	10971.44	10903.54	10672.58	10552.54	10489.19

12.75%   MONTHLY PAYMENTS

AMOUNT	1 YEAR	2 YEARS	3 YEARS	4 YEARS	5 YEARS	6 YEARS	7 YEARS
100	8.92	4.74	3.36	2.67	2.26	1.99	1.81
200	17.84	9.48	6.71	5.34	4.53	3.99	3.61
500	44.60	23.71	16.79	13.35	11.31	9.97	9.03
1000	89.20	47.42	33.57	26.70	22.63	19.94	18.06
2000	178.40	94.85	67.15	53.41	45.25	39.88	36.11
3000	267.60	142.27	100.72	80.11	67.88	59.83	54.17
4000	356.80	189.70	134.29	106.81	90.50	79.77	72.23
5000	446.00	237.12	167.87	133.52	113.13	99.71	90.28
6000	535.20	284.55	201.44	160.22	135.75	119.65	108.34
7000	624.40	331.97	235.02	186.93	158.38	139.60	126.39
8000	713.60	379.40	268.59	213.63	181.00	159.54	144.45
9000	802.80	426.82	302.16	240.33	203.63	179.48	162.51
10000	892.00	474.24	335.74	267.04	226.25	199.42	180.56
11000	981.20	521.67	369.31	293.74	248.88	219.37	198.62
12000	1070.40	569.09	402.88	320.44	271.50	239.31	216.68
13000	1159.60	616.52	436.46	347.15	294.13	259.25	234.73
14000	1248.80	663.94	470.03	373.85	316.75	279.19	252.79
15000	1338.00	711.37	503.60	400.55	339.38	299.14	270.84
20000	1784.00	948.49	671.47	534.07	452.51	398.85	361.13
25000	2230.00	1185.61	839.34	667.59	565.63	498.56	451.41
30000	2676.00	1422.73	1007.21	801.11	678.76	598.27	541.69
35000	3122.00	1659.86	1175.08	934.63	791.89	697.98	631.97
40000	3568.00	1896.98	1342.95	1068.14	905.01	797.70	722.25
45000	4014.00	2134.10	1510.81	1201.66	1018.14	897.41	812.53
50000	4460.00	2371.22	1678.68	1335.18	1131.27	997.12	902.82
55000	4906.00	2608.35	1846.55	1468.70	1244.39	1096.83	993.10
56000	4995.20	2655.77	1880.13	1495.40	1267.02	1116.77	1011.15
57000	5084.40	2703.20	1913.70	1522.10	1289.64	1136.72	1029.21
58000	5173.60	2750.62	1947.27	1548.81	1312.27	1156.66	1047.27
59000	5262.80	2798.04	1980.85	1575.51	1334.89	1176.60	1065.32
60000	5352.00	2845.47	2014.42	1602.21	1357.52	1196.54	1083.38
61000	5441.20	2892.89	2047.99	1628.92	1380.14	1216.49	1101.44
62000	5530.40	2940.32	2081.57	1655.62	1402.77	1236.43	1119.49
63000	5619.60	2987.74	2115.14	1682.33	1425.39	1256.37	1137.55
64000	5708.80	3035.17	2148.71	1709.03	1448.02	1276.31	1155.60
65000	5798.00	3082.59	2182.29	1735.73	1470.64	1296.26	1173.66
70000	6244.00	3319.71	2350.16	1869.25	1583.77	1395.97	1263.94
75000	6690.00	3556.84	2518.02	2002.77	1696.90	1495.68	1354.22
80000	7136.00	3793.96	2685.89	2136.29	1810.02	1595.39	1444.51
85000	7582.00	4031.08	2853.76	2269.80	1923.15	1695.10	1534.79
90000	8028.00	4268.20	3021.63	2403.32	2036.28	1794.82	1625.07
95000	8474.00	4505.33	3189.50	2536.84	2149.40	1894.53	1715.35
100000	8920.00	4742.45	3357.37	2670.36	2262.53	1994.24	1805.63
105000	9366.00	4979.57	3525.23	2803.88	2375.66	2093.95	1895.91
110000	9812.00	5216.69	3693.10	2937.39	2488.78	2193.66	1986.20
120000	10704.00	5690.94	4028.84	3204.43	2715.04	2393.09	2166.76
130000	11596.00	6165.18	4364.58	3471.47	2941.29	2592.51	2347.32
140000	12488.00	6639.43	4700.31	3738.50	3167.54	2791.94	2527.89
150000	13380.00	7113.67	5036.05	4005.54	3393.80	2991.36	2708.45
160000	14272.00	7587.92	5371.79	4272.57	3620.05	3190.78	2889.01
175000	15610.00	8299.28	5875.39	4673.13	3959.43	3489.92	3159.86
200000	17840.00	9484.90	6714.73	5340.72	4525.06	3988.48	3611.26
250000	22300.01	11856.12	8393.42	6675.90	5656.33	4985.60	4514.08
500000	44600.01	23712.24	16786.83	13351.79	11312.65	9971.20	9028.16
1000000	89200.03	47424.48	33573.66	26703.58	22625.30	19942.40	18056.32

MONTHLY PAYMENTS 12.75%

AMOUNT	8 YEARS	9 YEARS	10 YEARS	11 YEARS	12 YEARS	13 YEARS	14 YEARS
100	1.67	1.56	1.48	1.41	1.36	1.32	1.28
200	3.33	3.12	2.96	2.83	2.72	2.63	2.56
500	8.33	7.81	7.39	7.06	6.80	6.58	6.40
1000	16.67	15.61	14.78	14.13	13.59	13.15	12.79
2000	33.34	31.22	29.57	28.25	27.18	26.31	25.58
3000	50.00	46.83	44.35	42.38	40.78	39.46	38.38
4000	66.67	62.44	59.14	56.50	54.37	52.62	51.17
5000	83.34	78.05	73.92	70.63	67.96	65.77	63.96
6000	100.01	93.66	88.70	84.75	81.55	78.93	76.75
7000	116.67	109.27	103.49	98.88	95.14	92.08	89.54
8000	133.34	124.88	118.27	113.00	108.74	105.24	102.33
9000	150.01	140.49	133.06	127.13	122.33	118.39	115.13
10000	166.68	156.10	147.84	141.25	135.92	131.54	127.92
11000	183.34	171.71	162.62	155.38	149.51	144.70	140.71
12000	200.01	187.32	177.41	169.50	163.10	157.85	153.50
13000	216.68	202.93	192.19	183.63	176.70	171.01	166.29
14000	233.35	218.54	206.98	197.76	190.29	184.16	179.08
15000	250.02	234.15	221.76	211.88	203.88	197.32	191.88
20000	333.35	312.20	295.68	282.51	271.84	263.09	255.83
25000	416.69	390.26	369.60	353.13	339.80	328.86	319.79
30000	500.03	468.31	443.52	423.76	407.76	394.63	383.75
35000	583.37	546.36	517.44	494.39	475.72	460.41	447.71
40000	666.71	624.41	591.36	565.02	543.68	526.18	511.67
45000	750.05	702.46	665.28	635.64	611.64	591.95	575.63
50000	833.39	780.51	739.20	706.27	679.60	657.72	639.59
55000	916.72	858.56	813.12	776.90	747.56	723.50	703.54
56000	933.39	874.17	827.90	791.02	761.15	736.65	716.34
57000	950.06	889.78	842.69	805.15	774.74	749.80	729.13
58000	966.73	905.39	857.47	819.27	788.34	762.96	741.92
59000	983.40	921.00	872.25	833.40	801.93	776.11	754.71
60000	1000.00	936.61	887.04	847.52	815.52	789.27	767.50
61000	1016.73	952.22	901.82	861.65	829.11	802.42	780.29
62000	1033.40	967.83	916.61	875.77	842.70	815.58	793.09
63000	1050.07	983.44	931.39	889.90	856.30	828.73	805.88
64000	1066.73	999.05	946.17	904.02	869.89	841.89	818.67
65000	1083.40	1014.67	960.96	918.15	883.48	855.04	831.46
70000	1166.74	1092.72	1034.88	988.78	951.44	920.81	895.42
75000	1250.08	1170.77	1108.80	1059.40	1019.40	986.58	959.38
80000	1333.42	1248.82	1182.72	1130.03	1087.36	1052.36	1023.34
85000	1416.76	1326.87	1256.64	1200.66	1155.32	1118.13	1087.30
90000	1500.10	1404.92	1330.56	1271.28	1223.28	1183.90	1151.25
95000	1583.43	1482.97	1404.48	1341.91	1291.24	1249.67	1215.21
100000	1666.77	1561.02	1478.40	1412.54	1359.20	1315.45	1279.17
105000	1750.11	1639.07	1552.32	1483.16	1427.16	1381.22	1343.13
110000	1833.45	1717.13	1626.24	1553.79	1495.12	1446.99	1407.09
120000	2000.13	1873.23	1774.08	1695.05	1631.04	1578.53	1535.01
130000	2166.80	2029.33	1921.92	1836.30	1766.96	1710.08	1662.92
140000	2333.48	2185.43	2069.76	1977.55	1902.88	1841.62	1790.84
150000	2500.16	2341.53	2217.60	2118.81	2038.80	1973.17	1918.76
160000	2666.84	2497.64	2365.44	2260.06	2174.72	2104.71	2046.68
175000	2916.85	2731.79	2587.20	2471.94	2378.60	2302.03	2238.55
200000	3333.54	3122.05	2956.80	2825.08	2718.40	2630.89	2558.34
250000	4166.93	3902.56	3696.00	3531.35	3398.00	3288.61	3197.93
500000	8333.86	7805.12	7391.99	7062.69	6796.00	6577.23	6395.86
1000000	16667.72	15610.23	14783.98	14125.38	13592.00	13154.46	12791.72

12.75%　　MONTHLY PAYMENTS

AMOUNT	15 YEARS	16 YEARS	17 YEARS	18 YEARS	19 YEARS	20 YEARS	21 YEARS
100	1.25	1.22	1.20	1.18	1.17	1.15	1.14
200	2.50	2.45	2.40	2.37	2.33	2.31	2.28
500	6.24	6.12	6.01	5.92	5.84	5.77	5.71
1000	12.49	12.23	12.02	11.83	11.67	11.54	11.42
2000	24.98	24.47	24.03	23.66	23.35	23.08	22.84
3000	37.47	36.70	36.05	35.50	35.02	34.61	34.26
4000	49.95	48.93	48.06	47.33	46.70	46.15	45.68
5000	62.44	61.16	60.08	59.16	58.37	57.69	57.11
6000	74.93	73.40	72.10	70.99	70.04	69.23	68.53
7000	87.42	85.63	84.11	82.82	81.72	80.77	79.95
8000	99.91	97.86	96.13	94.65	93.39	92.30	91.37
9000	112.40	110.10	108.15	106.49	105.06	103.84	102.79
10000	124.88	122.33	120.16	118.32	116.74	115.38	114.21
11000	137.37	134.56	132.18	130.15	128.41	126.92	125.63
12000	149.86	146.79	144.19	141.98	140.09	138.46	137.05
13000	162.35	159.03	156.21	153.81	151.76	150.00	148.48
14000	174.84	171.26	168.23	165.64	163.43	161.53	159.90
15000	187.33	183.49	180.24	177.48	175.11	173.07	171.32
20000	249.77	244.66	240.32	236.63	233.48	230.76	228.42
25000	312.21	305.82	300.41	295.79	291.84	288.45	285.53
30000	374.65	366.98	360.49	354.95	350.21	346.14	342.64
35000	437.09	428.15	420.57	414.11	408.58	403.83	399.74
40000	499.53	489.31	480.65	473.27	466.95	461.52	456.85
45000	561.98	550.48	540.73	532.43	525.32	519.22	513.95
50000	624.42	611.64	600.81	591.58	583.69	576.91	571.06
55000	686.86	672.81	660.89	650.74	642.06	634.60	628.17
56000	699.35	685.04	672.91	662.58	653.73	646.13	639.59
57000	711.84	697.27	684.93	674.41	665.41	657.67	651.01
58000	724.33	709.50	696.94	686.24	677.08	669.21	662.43
59000	736.81	721.74	708.96	698.07	688.75	680.75	673.85
60000	749.30	733.97	720.97	709.90	700.43	692.29	685.27
61000	761.79	746.20	732.99	721.73	712.10	703.83	696.69
62000	774.28	758.44	745.01	733.57	723.77	715.36	708.11
63000	786.77	770.67	757.02	745.40	735.45	726.90	719.54
64000	799.26	782.90	769.04	757.23	747.12	738.44	730.96
65000	811.74	795.13	781.06	769.06	758.80	749.98	742.38
70000	874.19	856.30	841.14	828.22	817.16	807.67	799.48
75000	936.63	917.46	901.22	887.38	875.53	865.36	856.59
80000	999.07	978.63	961.30	946.54	933.90	923.05	913.70
85000	1061.51	1039.79	1021.38	1005.69	992.27	980.74	970.80
90000	1123.95	1100.95	1081.46	1064.85	1050.64	1038.43	1027.91
95000	1186.40	1162.12	1141.54	1124.01	1109.01	1096.12	1085.01
100000	1248.84	1223.28	1201.62	1183.17	1167.38	1153.81	1142.12
105000	1311.28	1284.45	1261.70	1242.33	1225.75	1211.50	1199.23
110000	1373.72	1345.61	1321.79	1301.49	1284.12	1269.19	1256.33
120000	1498.60	1467.94	1441.95	1419.80	1400.85	1384.57	1370.54
130000	1623.49	1590.27	1562.11	1538.12	1517.59	1499.96	1484.76
140000	1748.37	1712.60	1682.27	1656.44	1634.33	1615.34	1598.97
150000	1873.26	1834.92	1802.44	1774.75	1751.07	1730.72	1713.18
160000	1998.14	1957.25	1922.60	1893.07	1867.80	1846.10	1827.39
175000	2185.46	2140.74	2102.84	2070.55	2042.91	2019.17	1998.71
200000	2497.67	2446.57	2403.25	2366.34	2334.76	2307.62	2284.24
250000	3122.09	3058.21	3004.06	2957.92	2918.44	2884.53	2855.30
500000	6244.18	6116.41	6008.12	5915.85	5836.89	5769.06	5710.60
1000000	12488.37	12232.83	12016.24	11831.70	11673.78	11538.12	11421.20

MONTHLY PAYMENTS 12.75%

AMOUNT	22 YEARS	23 YEARS	24 YEARS	25 YEARS	30 YEARS	35 YEARS	40 YEARS
100	1.13	1.12	1.12	1.11	1.09	1.08	1.07
200	2.26	2.25	2.23	2.22	2.17	2.15	2.14
500	5.66	5.62	5.58	5.55	5.43	5.38	5.35
1000	11.32	11.23	11.16	11.09	10.87	10.75	10.69
2000	22.64	22.47	22.31	22.18	21.73	21.50	21.38
3000	33.96	33.70	33.47	33.27	32.60	32.26	32.08
4000	45.28	44.93	44.63	44.36	43.47	43.01	42.77
5000	56.60	56.16	55.78	55.45	54.33	53.76	53.46
6000	67.92	67.40	66.94	66.54	65.20	64.51	64.15
7000	79.24	78.63	78.10	77.63	76.07	75.26	74.84
8000	90.56	89.86	89.25	88.72	86.94	86.02	85.54
9000	101.88	101.09	100.41	99.81	97.80	96.77	96.23
10000	113.20	112.33	111.57	110.91	108.67	107.52	106.92
11000	124.52	123.56	122.72	122.00	119.54	118.27	117.61
12000	135.84	134.79	133.88	133.09	130.40	129.02	128.30
13000	147.16	146.02	145.04	144.18	141.27	139.78	139.00
14000	158.48	157.26	156.19	155.27	152.14	150.53	149.69
15000	169.80	168.49	167.35	166.36	163.00	161.28	160.38
20000	226.40	224.65	223.13	221.81	217.34	215.04	213.84
25000	283.00	280.82	278.92	277.26	271.67	268.80	267.30
30000	339.60	336.98	334.70	332.72	326.01	322.56	320.76
35000	396.21	393.14	390.48	388.17	380.34	376.32	374.22
40000	452.81	449.30	446.26	443.62	434.68	430.08	427.68
45000	509.41	505.47	502.05	499.07	489.01	483.84	481.14
50000	566.01	561.63	557.83	554.53	543.35	537.60	534.60
55000	622.61	617.79	613.61	609.98	597.68	591.36	588.06
56000	633.93	629.03	624.77	621.07	608.55	602.11	598.75
57000	645.25	640.26	635.93	632.16	619.42	612.86	609.44
58000	656.57	651.49	647.08	643.25	630.28	623.61	620.13
59000	667.89	662.72	658.24	654.34	641.15	634.37	630.83
60000	679.21	673.96	669.40	665.43	652.02	645.12	641.52
61000	690.53	685.19	680.55	676.52	662.88	655.87	652.21
62000	701.85	696.42	691.71	687.61	673.75	666.62	662.90
63000	713.17	707.65	702.87	698.70	684.62	677.37	673.59
64000	724.49	718.89	714.02	709.79	695.48	688.13	684.29
65000	735.81	730.12	725.18	720.88	706.35	698.88	694.98
70000	792.41	786.28	780.96	776.34	760.69	752.64	748.44
75000	849.01	842.45	836.75	831.79	815.02	806.40	801.90
80000	905.61	898.61	892.53	887.24	869.35	860.16	855.36
85000	962.21	954.77	948.31	942.69	923.69	913.92	908.82
90000	1018.81	1010.94	1004.10	998.15	978.02	967.68	962.28
95000	1075.41	1067.10	1059.88	1053.60	1032.36	1021.44	1015.74
100000	1132.02	1123.26	1115.66	1109.05	1086.69	1075.20	1069.20
105000	1188.62	1179.42	1171.45	1164.50	1141.03	1128.96	1122.66
110000	1245.22	1235.59	1227.23	1219.96	1195.36	1182.72	1176.12
120000	1358.42	1347.91	1338.79	1330.86	1304.03	1290.24	1283.04
130000	1471.62	1460.24	1450.36	1441.77	1412.70	1397.75	1389.96
140000	1584.82	1572.57	1561.93	1552.67	1521.37	1505.27	1496.87
150000	1698.02	1684.89	1673.49	1663.58	1630.04	1612.79	1603.79
160000	1811.23	1797.22	1785.06	1774.48	1738.71	1720.31	1710.71
175000	1981.03	1965.71	1952.41	1940.84	1901.71	1881.59	1871.09
200000	2264.03	2246.52	2231.32	2218.10	2173.39	2150.39	2138.39
250000	2830.04	2808.15	2789.16	2772.63	2716.73	2687.99	2672.99
500000	5660.08	5616.31	5578.31	5545.26	5433.47	5375.98	5345.98
1000000	11320.16	11232.62	11156.62	11090.52	10866.93	10751.96	10691.96

13.00%   MONTHLY PAYMENTS

AMOUNT	1 YEAR	2 YEARS	3 YEARS	4 YEARS	5 YEARS	6 YEARS	7 YEARS
100	8.93	4.75	3.37	2.68	2.28	2.01	1.82
200	17.86	9.51	6.74	5.37	4.55	4.01	3.64
500	44.66	23.77	16.85	13.41	11.38	10.04	9.10
1000	89.32	47.54	33.69	26.83	22.75	20.07	18.19
2000	178.63	95.08	67.39	53.65	45.51	40.15	36.38
3000	267.95	142.63	101.08	80.48	68.26	60.22	54.58
4000	357.27	190.17	134.78	107.31	91.01	80.30	72.77
5000	446.59	237.71	168.47	134.14	113.77	100.37	90.96
6000	535.90	285.25	202.16	160.96	136.52	120.44	109.15
7000	625.22	332.79	235.86	187.79	159.27	140.52	127.34
8000	714.54	380.33	269.55	214.62	182.02	160.59	145.54
9000	803.86	427.88	303.25	241.45	204.78	180.67	163.73
10000	893.17	475.42	336.94	268.27	227.53	200.74	181.92
11000	982.49	522.96	370.63	295.10	250.28	220.82	200.11
12000	1071.81	570.50	404.33	321.93	273.04	240.89	218.30
13000	1161.12	618.04	438.02	348.76	295.79	260.96	236.50
14000	1250.44	665.59	471.72	375.58	318.54	281.04	254.69
15000	1339.76	713.13	505.41	402.41	341.30	301.11	272.88
20000	1786.35	950.84	673.88	536.55	455.06	401.48	363.84
25000	2232.93	1188.55	842.35	670.69	568.83	501.85	454.80
30000	2679.52	1426.25	1010.82	804.82	682.59	602.22	545.76
35000	3126.10	1663.96	1179.29	938.96	796.36	702.59	636.72
40000	3572.69	1901.67	1347.76	1073.10	910.12	802.96	727.68
45000	4019.28	2139.38	1516.23	1207.24	1023.89	903.33	818.64
50000	4465.86	2377.09	1684.70	1341.37	1137.65	1003.71	909.60
55000	4912.45	2614.80	1853.17	1475.51	1251.42	1104.08	1000.56
56000	5001.77	2662.34	1886.86	1502.34	1274.17	1124.15	1018.75
57000	5091.08	2709.88	1920.56	1529.17	1296.93	1144.22	1036.94
58000	5180.40	2757.43	1954.25	1555.99	1319.68	1164.30	1055.13
59000	5269.72	2804.97	1987.94	1582.82	1342.43	1184.37	1073.33
60000	5359.04	2852.51	2021.64	1609.65	1365.18	1204.45	1091.52
61000	5448.35	2900.05	2055.33	1636.48	1387.94	1224.52	1109.71
62000	5537.67	2947.59	2089.03	1663.30	1410.69	1244.59	1127.90
63000	5626.99	2995.13	2122.72	1690.13	1433.44	1264.67	1146.09
64000	5716.31	3042.68	2156.41	1716.96	1456.20	1284.74	1164.29
65000	5805.62	3090.22	2190.11	1743.79	1478.95	1304.82	1182.48
70000	6252.21	3327.93	2358.58	1877.92	1592.72	1405.19	1273.44
75000	6698.80	3565.64	2527.05	✦ 2012.06	1706.48	1505.56	1364.40
80000	7145.38	3803.35	2695.52	2146.20	1820.25	1605.93	1455.36
85000	7591.97	4041.05	2863.99	2280.34	1934.01	1706.30	1546.32
90000	8038.55	4278.76	3032.46	2414.47	2047.78	1806.67	1637.28
95000	8485.14	4516.47	3200.93	2548.61	2161.54	1907.04	1728.24
100000	8931.73	4754.18	3369.40	2682.75	2275.31	2007.41	1819.20
105000	9378.31	4991.89	3537.86	2816.89	2389.07	2107.78	1910.16
110000	9824.90	5229.60	3706.33	2951.02	2502.84	2208.15	2001.12
120000	10718.07	5705.02	4043.27	3219.30	2730.37	2408.89	2183.04
130000	11611.25	6180.44	4380.21	3487.57	2957.90	2609.63	2364.96
140000	12504.42	6655.86	4717.15	3755.85	3185.43	2810.37	2546.87
150000	13397.59	7131.27	5054.09	4024.12	3412.96	3011.12	2728.79
160000	14290.76	7606.69	5391.03	4292.40	3640.49	3211.86	2910.71
175000	15630.52	8319.82	5896.44	4694.81	3981.79	3512.97	3183.59
200000	17863.46	9508.36	6738.79	5365.50	4550.61	4014.82	3638.39
250000	22329.32	11885.46	8423.49	6706.87	5688.27	5018.53	4547.99
500000	44658.64	23770.91	16846.98	13413.75	11376.54	10037.05	9095.98
1000000	89317.28	47541.82	33693.95	26827.50	22753.07	20074.11	18191.96

MONTHLY PAYMENTS 13.00%

AMOUNT	8 YEARS	9 YEARS	10 YEARS	11 YEARS	12 YEARS	13 YEARS	14 YEARS
100	1.68	1.58	1.49	1.43	1.37	1.33	1.30
200	3.36	3.15	2.99	2.86	2.75	2.66	2.59
500	8.40	7.88	7.47	7.14	6.87	6.66	6.48
1000	16.81	15.75	14.93	14.28	13.75	13.31	12.95
2000	33.61	31.51	29.86	28.55	27.49	26.62	25.91
3000	50.42	47.26	44.79	42.83	41.24	39.94	38.86
4000	67.23	63.01	59.72	57.10	54.99	53.25	51.81
5000	84.04	78.77	74.66	71.38	68.73	66.56	64.76
6000	100.84	94.52	89.59	85.66	82.48	79.87	77.72
7000	117.65	110.28	104.52	99.93	96.22	93.18	90.67
8000	134.46	126.03	119.45	114.21	109.97	106.50	103.62
9000	151.27	141.78	134.38	128.48	123.72	119.81	116.57
10000	168.07	157.54	149.31	142.76	137.46	133.12	129.53
11000	184.88	173.29	164.24	157.04	151.21	146.43	142.48
12000	201.69	189.04	179.17	171.31	164.96	159.75	155.43
13000	218.49	204.80	194.10	185.59	178.70	173.06	168.38
14000	235.30	220.55	209.04	199.87	192.45	186.37	181.34
15000	252.11	236.30	223.97	214.14	206.19	199.68	194.29
20000	336.15	315.07	298.62	285.52	274.93	266.24	259.05
25000	420.18	393.84	373.28	356.90	343.66	332.80	323.82
30000	504.22	472.61	447.93	428.28	412.39	399.36	388.58
35000	588.25	551.38	522.59	499.66	481.12	465.92	453.34
40000	672.29	630.14	597.24	571.04	549.85	532.48	518.11
45000	756.33	708.91	671.90	642.42	618.58	599.04	582.87
50000	840.36	787.68	746.55	713.81	687.31	665.61	647.63
55000	924.40	866.45	821.21	785.19	756.04	732.17	712.39
56000	941.21	882.20	836.14	799.46	769.79	745.48	725.35
57000	958.01	897.95	851.07	813.74	783.54	758.79	738.30
58000	974.82	913.71	866.00	828.01	797.28	772.10	751.25
59000	991.63	929.46	880.93	842.29	811.03	785.41	764.21
60000	1008.44	945.22	895.86	856.57	824.78	798.73	777.16
61000	1025.24	960.97	910.80	870.84	838.52	812.04	790.11
62000	1042.05	976.72	925.73	885.12	852.27	825.35	803.06
63000	1058.86	992.48	940.66	899.39	866.01	838.66	816.02
64000	1075.66	1008.23	955.59	913.67	879.76	851.97	828.97
65000	1092.47	1023.98	970.52	927.95	893.51	865.29	841.92
70000	1176.51	1102.75	1045.18	999.33	962.24	931.85	906.68
75000	1260.54	1181.52	1119.83	1070.71	1030.97	998.41	971.45
80000	1344.58	1260.29	1194.49	1142.09	1099.70	1064.97	1036.21
85000	1428.62	1339.05	1269.14	1213.47	1168.43	1131.53	1100.97
90000	1512.65	1417.82	1343.80	1284.85	1237.16	1198.09	1165.74
95000	1596.69	1496.59	1418.45	1356.23	1305.89	1264.65	1230.50
100000	1680.73	1575.36	1493.11	1427.61	1374.63	1331.21	1295.26
105000	1764.76	1654.13	1567.76	1498.99	1443.36	1397.77	1360.03
110000	1848.80	1732.89	1642.42	1570.37	1512.09	1464.33	1424.79
120000	2016.87	1890.43	1791.73	1713.13	1649.55	1597.45	1554.32
130000	2184.94	2047.97	1941.04	1855.89	1787.01	1730.57	1683.84
140000	2353.02	2205.50	2090.35	1998.66	1924.48	1863.69	1813.37
150000	2521.09	2363.04	2239.66	2141.42	2061.94	1996.82	1942.90
160000	2689.16	2520.57	2388.97	2284.18	2199.40	2129.94	2072.42
175000	2941.27	2756.88	2612.94	2498.32	2405.59	2329.62	2266.71
200000	3361.45	3150.72	2986.21	2855.22	2749.25	2662.42	2590.53
250000	4201.81	3938.40	3732.77	3569.03	3436.56	3328.03	3238.16
500000	8403.63	7876.79	7465.54	7138.05	6873.13	6656.05	6476.32
1000000	16807.26	15753.59	14931.07	14276.11	13746.25	13312.10	12952.64

13.00%   MONTHLY PAYMENTS

AMOUNT	15 YEARS	16 YEARS	17 YEARS	18 YEARS	19 YEARS	20 YEARS	21 YEARS
100	1.27	1.24	1.22	1.20	1.18	1.17	1.16
200	2.53	2.48	2.44	2.40	2.37	2.34	2.32
500	6.33	6.20	6.09	6.00	5.92	5.86	5.80
1000	12.65	12.40	12.19	12.00	11.85	11.72	11.60
2000	25.30	24.80	24.37	24.01	23.70	23.43	23.20
3000	37.96	37.20	36.56	36.01	35.55	35.15	34.80
4000	50.61	49.60	48.74	48.02	47.40	46.86	46.40
5000	63.26	62.00	60.93	60.02	59.24	58.58	58.01
6000	75.91	74.40	73.12	72.03	71.09	70.29	69.61
7000	88.57	86.80	85.30	84.03	82.94	82.01	81.21
8000	101.22	99.20	97.49	96.03	94.79	93.73	92.81
9000	113.87	111.60	109.68	108.04	106.64	105.44	104.41
10000	126.52	124.00	121.86	120.04	118.49	117.16	116.01
11000	139.18	136.40	134.05	132.05	130.34	128.87	127.61
12000	151.83	148.80	146.23	144.05	142.19	140.59	139.21
13000	164.48	161.20	158.42	156.06	154.04	152.30	150.81
14000	177.13	173.60	170.61	168.06	165.89	164.02	162.42
15000	189.79	186.00	182.79	180.06	177.73	175.74	174.02
20000	253.05	248.00	243.72	240.09	236.98	234.32	232.02
25000	316.31	310.00	304.65	300.11	296.22	292.89	290.03
30000	379.57	372.00	365.58	360.13	355.47	351.47	348.03
35000	442.83	434.00	426.52	420.15	414.71	410.05	406.04
40000	506.10	496.00	487.45	480.17	473.96	468.63	464.05
45000	569.36	557.99	548.38	540.19	533.20	527.21	522.05
50000	632.62	619.99	609.31	600.22	592.45	585.79	580.06
55000	695.88	681.99	670.24	660.24	651.69	644.37	638.06
56000	708.54	694.39	682.42	672.24	663.54	656.08	649.66
57000	721.19	706.79	694.61	684.25	675.39	667.80	661.27
58000	733.84	719.19	706.80	696.25	687.24	679.51	672.87
59000	746.49	731.59	718.98	708.26	699.09	691.23	684.47
60000	759.15	743.99	731.17	720.26	710.94	702.95	696.07
61000	771.80	756.39	743.35	732.26	722.79	714.66	707.67
62000	784.45	768.79	755.54	744.27	734.64	726.38	719.27
63000	797.10	781.19	767.73	756.27	746.49	738.09	730.87
64000	809.75	793.59	779.91	768.28	758.33	749.81	742.47
65000	822.41	805.99	792.10	780.28	770.18	761.52	754.07
70000	885.67	867.99	853.03	840.30	829.43	820.10	812.08
75000	948.93	929.99	913.96	900.32	888.67	878.68	870.09
80000	1012.19	991.99	974.89	960.35	947.92	937.26	928.09
85000	1075.46	1053.99	1035.82	1020.37	1007.16	995.84	986.10
90000	1138.72	1115.99	1096.75	1080.39	1066.41	1054.42	1044.10
95000	1201.98	1177.99	1157.68	1140.41	1125.65	1113.00	1102.11
100000	1265.24	1239.99	1218.61	1200.43	1184.90	1171.58	1160.11
105000	1328.50	1301.99	1279.55	1260.45	1244.14	1230.15	1218.12
110000	1391.77	1363.99	1340.48	1320.48	1303.39	1288.73	1276.13
120000	1518.29	1487.99	1462.34	1440.52	1421.88	1405.89	1392.14
130000	1644.81	1611.98	1584.20	1560.56	1540.37	1523.05	1508.15
140000	1771.34	1735.98	1706.06	1680.61	1658.86	1640.21	1624.16
150000	1897.86	1859.98	1827.92	1800.65	1777.35	1757.36	1740.17
160000	2024.39	1983.98	1949.78	1920.69	1895.84	1874.52	1856.18
175000	2214.17	2169.98	2132.58	2100.76	2073.57	2050.26	2030.20
200000	2530.48	2479.98	2437.23	2400.87	2369.80	2343.15	2320.23
250000	3163.11	3099.97	3046.54	3001.08	2962.24	2928.94	2900.29
500000	6326.21	6199.94	6093.07	6002.16	5924.49	5857.88	5800.57
1000000	12652.42	12399.88	12186.14	12004.33	11848.98	11715.76	11601.14

MONTHLY PAYMENTS

13.00%

AMOUNT	22 YEARS	23 YEARS	24 YEARS	25 YEARS	30 YEARS	35 YEARS	40 YEARS
100	1.15	1.14	1.13	1.13	1.11	1.10	1.09
200	2.30	2.28	2.27	2.26	2.21	2.19	2.18
500	5.75	5.71	5.67	5.64	5.53	5.48	5.45
1000	11.50	11.42	11.34	11.28	11.06	10.95	10.90
2000	23.00	22.83	22.69	22.56	22.12	21.90	21.79
3000	34.51	34.25	34.03	33.84	33.19	32.86	32.69
4000	46.01	45.67	45.37	45.11	44.25	43.81	43.58
5000	57.51	57.08	56.71	56.39	55.31	54.76	54.48
6000	69.01	68.50	68.06	67.67	66.37	65.71	65.37
7000	80.52	79.92	79.40	78.95	77.43	76.66	76.27
8000	92.02	91.33	90.74	90.23	88.50	87.62	87.16
9000	103.52	102.75	102.08	101.51	99.56	98.57	98.06
10000	115.02	114.17	113.43	112.78	110.62	109.52	108.95
11000	126.52	125.58	124.77	124.06	121.68	120.47	119.85
12000	138.03	137.00	136.11	135.34	132.74	131.42	130.74
13000	149.53	148.42	147.45	146.62	143.81	142.38	141.64
14000	161.03	159.83	158.80	157.90	154.87	153.33	152.53
15000	172.53	171.25	170.14	169.18	165.93	164.28	163.43
20000	230.05	228.34	226.85	225.57	221.24	219.04	217.90
25000	287.56	285.42	283.57	281.96	276.55	273.80	272.38
30000	345.07	342.50	340.28	338.35	331.86	328.56	326.85
35000	402.58	399.59	396.99	394.74	387.17	383.32	381.33
40000	460.09	456.67	453.71	451.13	442.48	438.08	435.81
45000	517.60	513.75	510.42	507.53	497.79	492.84	490.28
50000	575.11	570.84	567.13	563.92	553.10	547.60	544.76
55000	632.62	627.92	623.85	620.31	608.41	602.36	599.23
56000	644.13	639.34	635.19	631.59	619.47	613.31	610.13
57000	655.63	650.76	646.53	642.87	630.53	624.26	621.02
58000	667.13	662.17	657.87	654.14	641.60	635.21	631.92
59000	678.63	673.59	669.22	665.42	652.66	646.16	642.81
60000	690.14	685.01	680.56	676.70	663.72	657.12	653.71
61000	701.64	696.42	691.90	687.98	674.78	668.07	664.60
62000	713.14	707.84	703.25	699.26	685.84	679.02	675.50
63000	724.64	719.26	714.59	710.54	696.91	689.97	686.39
64000	736.14	730.67	725.93	721.81	707.97	700.92	697.29
65000	747.65	742.09	737.27	733.09	719.03	711.88	708.18
70000	805.16	799.17	793.99	789.48	774.34	766.64	762.66
75000	862.67	856.26	850.70	845.88	829.65	821.39	817.14
80000	920.18	913.34	907.41	902.27	884.96	876.15	871.61
85000	977.69	970.42	964.13	958.66	940.27	930.91	926.09
90000	1035.20	1027.51	1020.84	1015.05	995.58	985.67	980.56
95000	1092.72	1084.59	1077.55	1071.44	1050.89	1040.43	1035.04
100000	1150.23	1141.68	1134.27	1127.84	1106.20	1095.19	1089.51
105000	1207.74	1198.76	1190.98	1184.23	1161.51	1149.95	1143.99
110000	1265.25	1255.84	1247.69	1240.62	1216.82	1204.71	1198.47
120000	1380.27	1370.01	1361.12	1353.40	1327.44	1314.23	1307.42
130000	1495.29	1484.18	1474.55	1466.19	1438.05	1423.75	1416.37
140000	1610.32	1598.35	1587.97	1578.97	1548.68	1533.27	1525.32
150000	1725.34	1712.51	1701.40	1691.75	1659.30	1642.79	1634.27
160000	1840.36	1826.68	1814.83	1804.54	1769.92	1752.31	1743.22
175000	2012.90	1997.93	1984.97	1973.71	1935.85	1916.59	1906.65
200000	2300.45	2283.35	2268.53	2255.67	2212.40	2190.39	2179.03
250000	2875.57	2854.19	2835.67	2819.59	2765.50	2737.98	2723.79
500000	5751.13	5708.38	5671.33	5639.18	5531.00	5475.97	5447.57
1000000	11502.26	11416.76	11342.67	11278.35	11062.00	10951.93	10895.14

13.25%　　　　MONTHLY PAYMENTS

AMOUNT	1 YEAR	2 YEARS	3 YEARS	4 YEARS	5 YEARS	6 YEARS	7 YEARS
100	8.94	4.77	3.38	2.70	2.29	2.02	1.83
200	17.89	9.53	6.76	5.39	4.58	4.04	3.67
500	44.72	23.83	16.91	13.48	11.44	10.10	9.16
1000	89.43	47.66	33.81	26.95	22.88	20.21	18.33
2000	178.87	95.32	67.63	53.90	45.76	40.41	36.66
3000	268.30	142.98	101.44	80.86	68.64	60.62	54.98
4000	357.74	190.64	135.26	107.81	91.53	80.83	73.31
5000	447.17	238.30	169.07	134.76	114.41	101.03	91.64
6000	536.61	285.96	202.89	161.71	137.29	121.24	109.97
7000	626.04	333.62	236.70	188.66	160.17	141.44	128.30
8000	715.48	381.27	270.52	215.61	183.05	161.65	146.63
9000	804.91	428.93	304.33	242.57	205.93	181.86	164.95
10000	894.35	476.59	338.14	269.52	228.81	202.06	183.28
11000	983.78	524.25	371.96	296.47	251.69	222.27	201.61
12000	1073.22	571.91	405.77	323.42	274.58	242.48	219.94
13000	1162.65	619.57	439.59	350.37	297.46	262.68	238.27
14000	1252.08	667.23	473.40	377.32	320.34	282.89	256.59
15000	1341.52	714.89	507.22	404.28	343.22	303.09	274.92
20000	1788.69	953.19	676.29	539.03	457.63	404.13	366.56
25000	2235.87	1191.48	845.36	673.79	572.03	505.16	458.20
30000	2683.04	1429.78	1014.43	808.55	686.44	606.19	549.84
35000	3130.21	1668.08	1183.51	943.31	800.84	707.22	641.49
40000	3577.38	1906.37	1352.58	1078.07	915.25	808.25	733.13
45000	4024.56	2144.67	1521.65	1212.83	1029.66	909.28	824.77
50000	4471.73	2382.97	1690.72	1347.59	1144.06	1010.31	916.41
55000	4918.90	2621.26	1859.80	1482.35	1258.47	1111.35	1008.05
56000	5008.34	2668.92	1893.61	1509.30	1281.35	1131.55	1026.38
57000	5097.77	2716.58	1927.43	1536.25	1304.23	1151.76	1044.70
58000	5187.21	2764.24	1961.24	1563.20	1327.11	1171.96	1063.03
59000	5276.64	2811.90	1995.06	1590.15	1349.99	1192.17	1081.36
60000	5366.08	2859.56	2028.87	1617.10	1372.88	1212.38	1099.69
61000	5455.51	2907.22	2062.68	1644.06	1395.76	1232.58	1118.02
62000	5544.95	2954.88	2096.50	1671.01	1418.64	1252.79	1136.35
63000	5634.38	3002.54	2130.31	1697.96	1441.52	1273.00	1154.67
64000	5723.81	3050.20	2164.13	1724.91	1464.40	1293.20	1173.00
65000	5813.25	3097.86	2197.94	1751.86	1487.28	1313.41	1191.33
70000	6260.42	3336.15	2367.01	1886.62	1601.69	1414.44	1282.97
75000	6707.60	3574.45	2536.09	2021.38	1716.09	1515.47	1374.61
80000	7154.77	3812.75	2705.16	2156.14	1830.50	1616.50	1466.25
85000	7601.94	4051.04	2874.23	2290.90	1944.91	1717.53	1557.89
90000	8049.11	4289.34	3043.30	2425.66	2059.31	1818.57	1649.53
95000	8496.29	4527.64	3212.38	2560.42	2173.72	1919.60	1741.17
100000	8943.46	4765.93	3381.45	2695.17	2288.13	2020.63	1832.82
105000	9390.63	5004.23	3550.52	2829.93	2402.53	2121.66	1924.46
110000	9837.81	5242.53	3719.59	2964.69	2516.94	2222.69	2016.10
120000	10732.15	5719.12	4057.74	3234.21	2745.75	2424.76	2199.38
130000	11626.50	6195.71	4395.88	3503.73	2974.56	2626.82	2382.66
140000	12520.85	6672.31	4734.03	3773.24	3203.38	2828.88	2565.94
150000	13415.19	7148.90	5072.17	4042.76	3432.19	3030.94	2749.22
160000	14309.54	7625.49	5410.32	4312.28	3661.00	3233.01	2932.50
175000	15651.06	8340.38	5917.54	4716.56	4004.22	3536.10	3207.43
200000	17886.92	9531.87	6762.90	5390.35	4576.25	4041.26	3665.63
250000	22358.65	11914.83	8453.62	6737.94	5720.31	5051.57	4582.04
500000	44717.30	23829.67	16907.25	13475.87	11440.63	10103.15	9164.08
1000000	89434.61	47659.33	33814.49	26951.74	22881.26	20206.29	18328.15

MONTHLY PAYMENTS 13.25%

AMOUNT	8 YEARS	9 YEARS	10 YEARS	11 YEARS	12 YEARS	13 YEARS	14 YEARS
100	1.69	1.59	1.51	1.44	1.39	1.35	1.31
200	3.39	3.18	3.02	2.89	2.78	2.69	2.62
500	8.47	7.95	7.54	7.21	6.95	6.74	6.56
1000	16.95	15.90	15.08	14.43	13.90	13.47	13.11
2000	33.89	31.80	30.16	28.86	27.80	26.94	26.23
3000	50.84	47.69	45.24	43.28	41.70	40.41	39.34
4000	67.79	63.59	60.32	57.71	55.61	53.88	52.46
5000	84.74	79.49	75.39	72.14	69.51	67.35	65.57
6000	101.68	95.39	90.47	86.57	83.41	80.82	78.69
7000	118.63	111.28	105.55	100.99	97.31	94.29	91.80
8000	135.58	127.18	120.63	115.42	111.21	107.76	104.92
9000	152.53	143.08	135.71	129.85	125.11	121.24	118.03
10000	169.47	158.98	150.79	144.28	139.01	134.71	131.14
11000	186.42	174.87	165.87	158.70	152.91	148.18	144.26
12000	203.37	190.77	180.95	173.13	166.82	161.65	157.37
13000	220.32	206.67	196.03	187.56	180.72	175.12	170.49
14000	237.26	222.57	211.10	201.99	194.62	188.59	183.60
15000	254.21	238.46	226.18	216.41	208.52	202.06	196.72
20000	338.95	317.95	301.58	288.55	278.03	269.41	262.29
25000	423.69	397.44	376.97	360.69	347.53	336.76	327.86
30000	508.42	476.93	452.37	432.83	417.04	404.12	393.43
35000	593.16	556.42	527.76	504.97	486.55	471.47	459.00
40000	677.90	635.90	603.16	577.10	556.05	538.82	524.58
45000	762.63	715.39	678.55	649.24	625.56	606.18	590.15
50000	847.37	794.88	753.94	721.38	695.07	673.53	655.72
55000	932.11	874.37	829.34	793.52	764.57	740.88	721.29
56000	949.05	890.27	844.42	807.95	778.47	754.35	734.41
57000	966.00	906.16	859.50	822.37	792.37	767.82	747.52
58000	982.95	922.06	874.58	836.80	806.28	781.29	760.64
59000	999.90	937.96	889.65	851.23	820.18	794.76	773.75
60000	1016.84	953.86	904.73	865.66	834.08	808.24	786.87
61000	1033.79	969.75	919.81	880.08	847.98	821.71	799.98
62000	1050.74	985.65	934.89	894.51	861.88	835.18	813.09
63000	1067.69	1001.55	949.97	908.94	875.78	848.65	826.21
64000	1084.63	1017.45	965.05	923.37	889.68	862.12	839.32
65000	1101.58	1033.35	980.13	937.79	903.59	875.59	852.44
70000	1186.32	1112.83	1055.52	1009.93	973.09	942.94	918.01
75000	1271.06	1192.32	1130.92	1082.07	1042.60	1010.29	983.58
80000	1355.79	1271.81	1206.31	1154.21	1112.10	1077.65	1049.15
85000	1440.53	1351.30	1281.71	1226.35	1181.61	1145.00	1114.73
90000	1525.27	1430.79	1357.10	1298.48	1251.12	1212.35	1180.30
95000	1610.00	1510.27	1432.49	1370.62	1320.62	1279.71	1245.87
100000	1694.74	1589.76	1507.89	1442.76	1390.13	1347.06	1311.44
105000	1779.48	1669.25	1583.28	1514.90	1459.64	1414.41	1377.01
110000	1864.21	1748.74	1658.68	1587.04	1529.14	1481.77	1442.59
120000	2033.69	1907.71	1809.47	1731.31	1668.16	1616.47	1573.73
130000	2203.16	2066.69	1960.26	1875.59	1807.17	1751.18	1704.87
140000	2372.64	2225.67	2111.04	2019.86	1946.18	1885.88	1836.02
150000	2542.11	2384.64	2261.83	2164.14	2085.20	2020.59	1967.16
160000	2711.58	2543.62	2412.62	2308.42	2224.21	2155.29	2098.31
175000	2965.80	2782.08	2638.81	2524.83	2432.73	2357.35	2295.02
200000	3389.48	3179.52	3015.78	2885.52	2780.26	2694.12	2622.88
250000	4236.85	3974.40	3769.72	3606.90	3475.33	3367.65	3278.61
500000	8473.70	7948.81	7539.45	7213.80	6950.66	6735.30	6557.21
1000000	16947.40	15897.62	15078.89	14427.61	13901.31	13470.59	13114.42

13.25% MONTHLY PAYMENTS

AMOUNT	15 YEARS	16 YEARS	17 YEARS	18 YEARS	19 YEARS	20 YEARS	21 YEARS
100	1.28	1.26	1.24	1.22	1.20	1.19	1.18
200	2.56	2.51	2.47	2.44	2.41	2.38	2.36
500	6.41	6.28	6.18	6.09	6.01	5.95	5.89
1000	12.82	12.57	12.36	12.18	12.03	11.89	11.78
2000	25.63	25.14	24.71	24.36	24.05	23.79	23.56
3000	38.45	37.70	37.07	36.53	36.08	35.68	35.35
4000	51.27	50.27	49.43	48.71	48.10	47.58	47.13
5000	64.09	62.84	61.78	60.89	60.13	59.47	58.91
6000	76.90	75.41	74.14	73.07	72.15	71.37	70.69
7000	89.72	87.97	86.50	85.25	84.18	83.26	82.47
8000	102.54	100.54	98.86	97.42	96.20	95.15	94.26
9000	115.36	113.11	111.21	109.60	108.23	107.05	106.04
10000	128.17	125.68	123.57	121.78	120.25	118.94	117.82
11000	140.99	138.25	135.93	133.96	132.28	130.84	129.60
12000	153.81	150.81	148.28	146.13	144.30	142.73	141.38
13000	166.63	163.38	160.64	158.31	156.33	154.63	153.17
14000	179.44	175.95	173.00	170.49	168.35	166.52	164.95
15000	192.26	188.52	185.35	182.67	180.38	178.41	176.73
20000	256.35	251.36	247.14	243.56	240.50	237.89	235.64
25000	320.43	314.20	308.92	304.45	300.63	297.36	294.55
30000	384.52	377.04	370.71	365.34	360.75	356.83	353.46
35000	448.61	439.87	432.49	426.23	420.88	416.30	412.37
40000	512.69	502.71	494.28	487.11	481.00	475.77	471.28
45000	576.78	565.55	556.06	548.00	541.13	535.24	530.19
50000	640.87	628.39	617.85	608.89	601.25	594.72	589.10
55000	704.96	691.23	679.63	669.78	661.38	654.19	648.01
56000	717.77	703.80	691.99	681.96	673.41	666.08	659.79
57000	730.59	716.37	704.35	694.14	685.43	677.98	671.57
58000	743.41	728.93	716.70	706.32	697.46	689.87	683.35
59000	756.22	741.50	729.06	718.49	709.48	701.76	695.14
60000	769.04	754.07	741.42	730.67	721.51	713.66	706.92
61000	781.86	766.64	753.77	742.85	733.53	725.55	718.70
62000	794.68	779.21	766.13	755.03	745.56	737.45	730.48
63000	807.49	791.77	778.49	767.21	757.58	749.34	742.26
64000	820.31	804.34	790.85	779.38	769.61	761.24	754.05
65000	833.13	816.91	803.20	791.56	781.63	773.13	765.83
70000	897.22	879.75	864.99	852.45	841.76	832.60	824.74
75000	961.30	942.59	926.77	913.34	901.88	892.07	883.65
80000	1025.39	1005.43	988.56	974.23	962.01	951.54	942.56
85000	1089.48	1068.27	1050.34	1035.12	1022.13	1011.02	1001.47
90000	1153.56	1131.11	1112.13	1096.01	1082.26	1070.49	1060.38
95000	1217.65	1193.94	1173.91	1156.90	1142.38	1129.96	1119.29
100000	1281.74	1256.78	1235.70	1217.79	1202.51	1189.43	1178.20
105000	1345.82	1319.62	1297.48	1278.68	1262.64	1248.90	1237.11
110000	1409.91	1382.46	1359.27	1339.57	1322.76	1308.37	1296.02
120000	1538.08	1508.14	1482.84	1461.34	1443.01	1427.32	1413.84
130000	1666.26	1633.82	1606.41	1583.12	1563.26	1546.26	1531.66
140000	1794.43	1759.50	1729.98	1704.90	1683.51	1665.20	1649.48
150000	1922.60	1885.18	1853.55	1826.68	1803.76	1784.15	1767.30
160000	2050.78	2010.85	1977.11	1948.46	1924.02	1903.09	1885.12
175000	2243.04	2199.37	2162.47	2131.13	2104.39	2081.50	2061.85
200000	2563.47	2513.57	2471.39	2435.57	2405.02	2378.86	2356.40
250000	3204.34	3141.96	3089.24	3044.47	3006.27	2973.58	2945.50
500000	6408.68	6283.92	6178.48	6088.93	6012.55	5947.15	5890.99
1000000	12817.36	12567.83	12356.97	12177.87	12025.10	11894.31	11781.98

MONTHLY PAYMENTS   13.25%

AMOUNT	22 YEARS	23 YEARS	24 YEARS	25 YEARS	30 YEARS	35 YEARS	40 YEARS
100	1.17	1.16	1.15	1.15	1.13	1.12	1.11
200	2.34	2.32	2.31	2.29	2.25	2.23	2.22
500	5.84	5.80	5.76	5.73	5.63	5.58	5.55
1000	11.69	11.60	11.53	11.47	11.26	11.15	11.10
2000	23.37	23.20	23.06	22.93	22.52	22.30	22.20
3000	35.06	34.81	34.59	34.40	33.77	33.46	33.30
4000	46.74	46.41	46.12	45.87	45.03	44.61	44.39
5000	58.43	58.01	57.65	57.34	56.29	55.76	55.49
6000	70.11	69.61	69.18	68.80	67.55	66.91	66.59
7000	81.80	81.21	80.71	80.27	78.80	78.07	77.69
8000	93.48	92.81	92.24	91.74	90.06	89.22	88.79
9000	105.17	104.42	103.77	103.20	101.32	100.37	99.89
10000	116.85	116.02	115.30	114.67	112.58	111.52	110.99
11000	128.54	127.62	126.83	126.14	123.84	122.68	122.09
12000	140.22	139.22	138.35	137.60	135.09	133.83	133.18
13000	151.91	150.82	149.88	149.07	146.35	144.98	144.28
14000	163.59	162.42	161.41	160.54	157.61	156.13	155.38
15000	175.28	174.03	172.94	172.01	168.87	167.29	166.48
20000	233.71	232.04	230.59	229.34	225.15	223.05	221.97
25000	292.13	290.04	288.24	286.68	281.44	278.81	277.47
30000	350.56	348.05	345.89	344.01	337.73	334.57	332.96
35000	408.98	406.06	403.53	401.35	394.02	390.33	388.45
40000	467.41	464.07	461.18	458.68	450.31	446.10	443.95
45000	525.84	522.08	518.83	516.02	506.60	501.86	499.44
50000	584.26	580.09	576.48	573.35	562.89	557.62	554.93
55000	642.69	638.10	634.13	630.69	619.18	613.38	610.43
56000	654.37	649.70	645.66	642.15	630.43	624.54	621.53
57000	666.06	661.30	657.18	653.62	641.69	635.69	632.63
58000	677.74	672.90	668.71	665.09	652.95	646.84	643.72
59000	689.43	684.50	680.24	676.55	664.21	657.99	654.82
60000	701.12	696.11	691.77	688.02	675.46	669.15	665.92
61000	712.80	707.71	703.30	699.49	686.72	680.30	677.02
62000	724.49	719.31	714.83	710.95	697.98	691.45	688.12
63000	736.17	730.91	726.36	722.42	709.24	702.60	699.22
64000	747.86	742.51	737.89	733.89	720.50	713.76	710.32
65000	759.54	754.11	749.42	745.36	731.75	724.91	721.42
70000	817.97	812.12	807.07	802.69	788.04	780.67	776.91
75000	876.39	870.13	864.72	860.03	844.33	836.43	832.40
80000	934.82	928.14	922.36	917.36	900.62	892.19	887.90
85000	993.25	986.15	980.01	974.70	956.91	947.96	943.39
90000	1051.67	1044.16	1037.66	1032.03	1013.20	1003.72	998.88
95000	1110.10	1102.17	1095.31	1089.37	1069.48	1059.48	1054.38
100000	1168.53	1160.18	1152.96	1146.70	1125.77	1115.24	1109.87
105000	1226.95	1218.19	1210.60	1204.04	1182.06	1171.00	1165.36
110000	1285.38	1276.19	1268.25	1261.37	1238.35	1226.77	1220.86
120000	1402.23	1392.21	1383.55	1376.04	1350.93	1338.29	1331.84
130000	1519.08	1508.23	1498.84	1490.71	1463.51	1449.81	1442.83
140000	1635.94	1624.25	1614.14	1605.38	1576.08	1561.34	1553.82
150000	1752.79	1740.26	1729.43	1720.05	1688.66	1672.86	1664.80
160000	1869.64	1856.28	1844.73	1834.72	1801.24	1784.39	1775.79
175000	2044.92	2030.31	2017.67	2006.73	1970.10	1951.67	1942.27
200000	2337.05	2320.35	2305.91	2293.40	2251.55	2230.48	2219.74
250000	2921.31	2900.44	2882.39	2866.75	2814.43	2788.11	2774.67
500000	5842.63	5800.88	5764.78	5733.50	5628.87	5576.21	5549.35
1000000	11685.25	11601.77	11529.56	11467.00	11257.74	11152.42	11098.70

13.50% MONTHLY PAYMENTS

AMOUNT	1 YEAR	2 YEARS	3 YEARS	4 YEARS	5 YEARS	6 YEARS	7 YEARS
100	8.96	4.78	3.39	2.71	2.30	2.03	1.85
200	17.91	9.56	6.79	5.42	4.60	4.07	3.69
500	44.78	23.89	16.97	13.54	11.50	10.17	9.23
1000	89.55	47.78	33.94	27.08	23.01	20.34	18.46
2000	179.10	95.55	67.87	54.15	46.02	40.68	36.93
3000	268.66	143.33	101.81	81.23	69.03	61.02	55.39
4000	358.21	191.11	135.74	108.31	92.04	81.36	73.86
5000	447.76	238.89	169.68	135.38	115.05	101.69	92.32
6000	537.31	286.66	203.61	162.46	138.06	122.03	110.79
7000	626.86	334.44	237.55	189.53	161.07	142.37	129.25
8000	716.42	382.22	271.48	216.61	184.08	162.71	147.72
9000	805.97	429.99	305.42	243.69	207.09	183.05	166.18
10000	895.52	477.77	339.35	270.76	230.10	203.39	184.65
11000	985.07	525.55	373.29	297.84	253.11	223.73	203.11
12000	1074.62	573.32	407.22	324.92	276.12	244.07	221.58
13000	1164.18	621.10	441.16	351.99	299.13	264.41	240.04
14000	1253.73	668.88	475.09	379.07	322.14	284.75	258.51
15000	1343.28	716.66	509.03	406.14	345.15	305.08	276.97
20000	1791.04	955.54	678.71	541.53	460.20	406.78	369.30
25000	2238.80	1194.43	848.38	676.91	575.25	508.47	461.62
30000	2686.56	1433.31	1018.06	812.29	690.30	610.17	553.95
35000	3134.32	1672.20	1187.74	947.67	805.34	711.86	646.27
40000	3582.08	1911.08	1357.41	1083.05	920.39	813.56	738.60
45000	4029.84	2149.97	1527.09	1218.43	1035.44	915.25	830.92
50000	4477.60	2388.85	1696.76	1353.82	1150.49	1016.95	923.24
55000	4925.36	2627.74	1866.44	1489.20	1265.54	1118.64	1015.57
56000	5014.91	2675.51	1900.38	1516.27	1288.55	1138.98	1034.03
57000	5104.47	2723.29	1934.31	1543.35	1311.56	1159.32	1052.50
58000	5194.02	2771.07	1968.25	1570.43	1334.57	1179.66	1070.96
59000	5283.57	2818.84	2002.18	1597.50	1357.58	1200.00	1089.43
60000	5373.12	2866.62	2036.12	1624.58	1380.59	1220.34	1107.89
61000	5462.67	2914.40	2070.05	1651.66	1403.60	1240.68	1126.36
62000	5552.23	2962.17	2103.99	1678.73	1426.61	1261.02	1144.82
63000	5641.78	3009.95	2137.92	1705.81	1449.62	1281.35	1163.29
64000	5731.33	3057.73	2171.86	1732.88	1472.63	1301.69	1181.75
65000	5820.88	3105.51	2205.79	1759.96	1495.64	1322.03	1200.22
70000	6268.64	3344.39	2375.47	1895.34	1610.69	1423.73	1292.54
75000	6716.40	3583.28	2545.15	2030.72	1725.74	1525.42	1384.87
80000	7164.16	3822.16	2714.82	2166.11	1840.79	1627.12	1477.19
85000	7611.92	4061.05	2884.50	2301.49	1955.84	1728.81	1569.52
90000	8059.68	4299.93	3054.18	2436.87	2070.89	1830.51	1661.84
95000	8507.44	4538.82	3223.85	2572.25	2185.94	1932.20	1754.16
100000	8955.20	4777.70	3393.53	2707.63	2300.98	2033.90	1846.49
105000	9402.96	5016.59	3563.21	2843.01	2416.03	2135.59	1938.81
110000	9850.72	5255.47	3732.88	2978.40	2531.08	2237.29	2031.14
120000	10746.24	5733.24	4072.23	3249.16	2761.18	2440.68	2215.79
130000	11641.76	6211.01	4411.59	3519.92	2991.28	2644.07	2400.44
140000	12537.28	6688.78	4750.94	3790.69	3221.38	2847.45	2585.08
150000	13432.80	7166.55	5090.29	4061.45	3451.48	3050.84	2769.73
160000	14328.32	7644.32	5429.65	4332.21	3681.58	3254.23	2954.38
175000	15671.60	8360.98	5938.68	4738.36	4026.72	3559.32	3231.36
200000	17910.41	9555.40	6787.06	5415.26	4601.97	4067.79	3692.98
250000	22388.01	11944.25	8483.82	6769.08	5752.46	5084.74	4616.22
500000	44776.01	23888.51	16967.64	13538.16	11504.92	10169.48	9232.45
1000000	89552.03	47777.01	33935.29	27076.32	23009.85	20338.96	18464.89

MONTHLY PAYMENTS 13.50%

AMOUNT	8 YEARS	9 YEARS	10 YEARS	11 YEARS	12 YEARS	13 YEARS	14 YEARS
100	1.71	1.60	1.52	1.46	1.41	1.36	1.33
200	3.42	3.21	3.05	2.92	2.81	2.73	2.66
500	8.54	8.02	7.61	7.29	7.03	6.81	6.64
1000	17.09	16.04	15.23	14.58	14.06	13.63	13.28
2000	34.18	32.08	30.45	29.16	28.11	27.26	26.55
3000	51.26	48.13	45.68	43.74	42.17	40.89	39.83
4000	68.35	64.17	60.91	58.32	56.23	54.52	53.11
5000	85.44	80.21	76.14	72.90	70.29	68.15	66.39
6000	102.53	96.25	91.36	87.48	84.34	81.78	79.66
7000	119.62	112.30	106.59	102.06	98.40	95.41	92.94
8000	136.71	128.34	121.82	116.64	112.46	109.04	106.22
9000	153.79	144.38	137.05	131.22	126.51	122.67	119.49
10000	170.88	160.42	152.27	145.80	140.57	136.30	132.77
11000	187.97	176.47	167.50	160.38	154.63	149.93	146.05
12000	205.06	192.51	182.73	174.96	168.69	163.56	159.32
13000	222.15	208.55	197.96	189.54	182.74	177.19	172.60
14000	239.23	224.59	213.18	204.12	196.80	190.82	185.88
15000	256.32	240.63	228.41	218.70	210.86	204.45	199.16
20000	341.76	320.85	304.55	291.60	281.14	272.60	265.54
25000	427.20	401.06	380.69	364.50	351.43	340.75	331.93
30000	512.64	481.27	456.82	437.40	421.72	408.90	398.31
35000	598.09	561.48	532.96	510.30	492.00	477.05	464.70
40000	683.53	641.69	609.10	583.19	562.29	545.20	531.08
45000	768.97	721.90	685.23	656.09	632.57	613.35	597.47
50000	854.41	802.12	761.37	728.99	702.86	681.50	663.85
55000	939.85	882.33	837.51	801.89	773.14	749.65	730.24
56000	956.94	898.37	852.74	816.47	787.20	763.28	743.52
57000	974.03	914.41	867.96	831.05	801.26	776.91	756.79
58000	991.11	930.45	883.19	845.63	815.32	790.54	770.07
59000	1008.20	946.50	898.42	860.21	829.37	804.17	783.35
60000	1025.29	962.54	913.65	874.79	843.43	817.80	796.62
61000	1042.38	978.58	928.87	889.37	857.49	831.42	809.90
62000	1059.47	994.62	944.10	903.95	871.54	845.05	823.18
63000	1076.55	1010.67	959.33	918.53	885.60	858.68	836.46
64000	1093.64	1026.71	974.56	933.11	899.66	872.31	849.73
65000	1110.73	1042.75	989.78	947.69	913.72	885.94	863.01
70000	1196.17	1122.96	1065.92	1020.59	984.00	954.09	929.39
75000	1281.61	1203.17	1142.06	1093.49	1054.29	1022.24	995.78
80000	1367.05	1283.39	1218.19	1166.39	1124.57	1090.39	1062.17
85000	1452.49	1363.60	1294.33	1239.29	1194.86	1158.54	1128.55
90000	1537.93	1443.81	1370.47	1312.19	1265.15	1226.69	1194.94
95000	1623.38	1524.02	1446.61	1385.09	1335.43	1294.84	1261.32
100000	1708.82	1604.23	1522.74	1457.99	1405.72	1362.99	1327.71
105000	1794.26	1684.44	1598.88	1530.89	1476.00	1431.14	1394.09
110000	1879.70	1764.65	1675.02	1603.79	1546.29	1499.29	1460.48
120000	2050.58	1925.08	1827.29	1749.58	1686.86	1635.59	1593.25
130000	2221.46	2085.50	1979.57	1895.38	1827.43	1771.89	1726.02
140000	2392.34	2245.92	2131.84	2041.18	1968.00	1908.19	1858.79
150000	2563.22	2406.35	2284.11	2186.98	2108.58	2044.49	1991.56
160000	2734.11	2566.77	2436.39	2332.78	2249.15	2180.79	2124.33
175000	2990.43	2807.40	2664.80	2551.48	2460.01	2385.24	2323.49
200000	3417.63	3208.46	3045.49	2915.97	2811.43	2725.98	2655.41
250000	4272.04	4010.58	3806.86	3644.97	3514.29	3407.48	3319.27
500000	8544.08	8021.16	7613.71	7289.93	7028.59	6814.96	6638.53
1000000	17088.16	16042.31	15227.43	14579.87	14057.17	13629.92	13277.07

13.50% MONTHLY PAYMENTS

AMOUNT	15 YEARS	16 YEARS	17 YEARS	18 YEARS	19 YEARS	20 YEARS	21 YEARS
100	1.30	1.27	1.25	1.24	1.22	1.21	1.20
200	2.60	2.55	2.51	2.47	2.44	2.41	2.39
500	6.49	6.37	6.26	6.18	6.10	6.04	5.98
1000	12.98	12.74	12.53	12.35	12.20	12.07	11.96
2000	25.97	25.47	25.06	24.70	24.40	24.15	23.93
3000	38.95	38.21	37.59	37.06	36.61	36.22	35.89
4000	51.93	50.95	50.11	49.41	48.81	48.29	47.85
5000	64.92	63.68	62.64	61.76	61.01	60.37	59.82
6000	77.90	76.42	75.17	74.11	73.21	72.44	71.78
7000	90.88	89.16	87.70	86.47	85.41	84.52	83.75
8000	103.87	101.89	100.23	98.82	97.62	96.59	95.71
9000	116.85	114.63	112.76	111.17	109.82	108.66	107.67
10000	129.83	127.37	125.29	123.52	122.02	120.74	119.64
11000	142.82	140.10	137.82	135.88	134.22	132.81	131.60
12000	155.80	152.84	150.34	148.23	146.43	144.88	143.56
13000	168.78	165.58	162.87	160.58	158.63	156.96	155.53
14000	181.76	178.31	175.40	172.93	170.83	169.03	167.49
15000	194.75	191.05	187.93	185.28	183.03	181.11	179.46
20000	259.66	254.73	250.57	247.05	244.04	241.47	239.27
25000	324.58	318.42	313.22	308.81	305.05	301.84	299.09
30000	389.50	382.10	375.86	370.57	366.06	362.21	358.91
35000	454.41	445.78	438.50	432.33	427.07	422.58	418.73
40000	519.33	509.47	501.15	494.09	488.08	482.95	478.55
45000	584.24	573.15	563.79	555.85	549.10	543.32	538.37
50000	649.16	636.83	626.43	617.62	610.11	603.69	598.18
55000	714.08	700.52	689.08	679.38	671.12	664.06	658.00
56000	727.06	713.25	701.61	691.73	683.32	676.13	669.97
57000	740.04	725.99	714.14	704.08	695.52	688.20	681.93
58000	753.02	738.73	726.66	716.43	707.72	700.28	693.89
59000	766.01	751.46	739.19	728.79	719.92	712.35	705.86
60000	778.99	764.20	751.72	741.14	732.13	724.42	717.82
61000	791.97	776.94	764.25	753.49	744.33	736.50	729.79
62000	804.96	789.67	776.78	765.84	756.53	748.57	741.75
63000	817.94	802.41	789.31	778.20	768.73	760.65	753.71
64000	830.92	815.15	801.84	790.55	780.94	772.72	765.68
65000	843.91	827.88	814.36	802.90	793.14	784.79	777.64
70000	908.82	891.57	877.01	864.66	854.15	845.16	837.46
75000	973.74	955.25	939.65	926.42	915.16	905.53	897.28
80000	1038.65	1018.93	1002.30	988.19	976.17	965.90	957.10
85000	1103.57	1082.62	1064.94	1049.95	1037.18	1026.27	1016.91
90000	1168.49	1146.30	1127.58	1111.71	1098.19	1086.64	1076.73
95000	1233.40	1209.98	1190.23	1173.47	1159.20	1147.01	1136.55
100000	1298.32	1273.67	1252.87	1235.23	1220.21	1207.37	1196.37
105000	1363.23	1337.35	1315.51	1296.99	1281.22	1267.74	1256.19
110000	1428.15	1401.03	1378.16	1358.75	1342.23	1328.11	1316.01
120000	1557.98	1528.40	1503.44	1482.28	1464.25	1448.85	1435.64
130000	1687.81	1655.77	1628.73	1605.80	1586.27	1569.59	1555.28
140000	1817.65	1783.14	1754.02	1729.32	1708.30	1690.32	1674.92
150000	1947.48	1910.50	1879.30	1852.85	1830.32	1811.06	1794.55
160000	2077.31	2037.87	2004.59	1976.37	1952.34	1931.80	1914.19
175000	2272.06	2228.92	2192.52	2161.65	2135.37	2112.91	2093.65
200000	2596.64	2547.34	2505.74	2470.46	2440.42	2414.75	2392.74
250000	3245.80	3184.17	3132.17	3088.08	3050.53	3018.44	2990.92
500000	6491.59	6368.34	6264.34	6176.16	6101.06	6036.87	5981.85
1000000	12983.19	12736.68	12528.69	12352.31	12202.11	12073.75	11963.70

MONTHLY PAYMENTS 13.50%

AMOUNT	22 YEARS	23 YEARS	24 YEARS	25 YEARS	30 YEARS	35 YEARS	40 YEARS
100	1.19	1.18	1.17	1.17	1.15	1.14	1.13
200	2.37	2.36	2.34	2.33	2.29	2.27	2.26
500	5.93	5.89	5.86	5.83	5.73	5.68	5.65
1000	11.87	11.79	11.72	11.66	11.45	11.35	11.30
2000	23.74	23.58	23.43	23.31	22.91	22.71	22.61
3000	35.61	35.36	35.15	34.97	34.36	34.06	33.91
4000	47.48	47.15	46.87	46.63	45.82	45.41	45.21
5000	59.35	58.94	58.59	58.28	57.27	56.77	56.51
6000	71.21	70.73	70.30	69.94	68.72	68.12	67.82
7000	83.08	82.51	82.02	81.60	80.18	79.47	79.12
8000	94.95	94.30	93.74	93.25	91.63	90.83	90.42
9000	106.82	106.09	105.46	104.91	103.09	102.18	101.72
10000	118.69	117.88	117.17	116.56	114.54	113.53	113.03
11000	130.56	129.66	128.89	128.22	126.00	124.89	124.33
12000	142.43	141.45	140.61	139.88	137.45	136.24	135.63
13000	154.30	153.24	152.32	151.53	148.90	147.59	146.93
14000	166.17	165.03	164.04	163.19	160.36	158.95	158.24
15000	178.04	176.81	175.76	174.85	171.81	170.30	169.54
20000	237.38	235.75	234.35	233.13	229.08	227.07	226.05
25000	296.73	294.69	292.93	291.41	286.35	283.84	282.57
30000	356.07	353.63	351.52	349.69	343.62	340.60	339.08
35000	415.42	412.57	410.10	407.98	400.89	397.37	395.59
40000	474.76	471.50	468.69	466.26	458.16	454.14	452.10
45000	534.11	530.44	527.28	524.54	515.44	510.90	508.62
50000	593.46	589.38	585.86	582.82	572.71	567.67	565.13
55000	652.80	648.32	644.45	641.10	629.98	624.44	621.64
56000	664.67	660.11	656.17	652.76	641.43	635.79	632.95
57000	676.54	671.89	667.88	664.42	652.88	647.14	644.25
58000	688.41	683.68	679.60	676.07	664.34	658.50	655.55
59000	700.28	695.47	691.32	687.73	675.79	669.85	666.85
60000	712.15	707.26	703.04	699.39	687.25	681.20	678.16
61000	724.02	719.04	714.75	711.04	698.70	692.56	689.46
62000	735.88	730.83	726.47	722.70	710.16	703.91	700.76
63000	747.75	742.62	738.19	734.36	721.61	715.26	712.06
64000	759.62	754.41	749.91	746.01	733.06	726.62	723.37
65000	771.49	766.19	761.62	757.67	744.52	737.97	734.67
70000	830.84	825.13	820.21	815.95	801.79	794.74	791.18
75000	890.18	884.07	878.80	874.23	859.06	851.51	847.70
80000	949.53	943.01	937.38	932.52	916.33	908.27	904.21
85000	1008.87	1001.95	995.97	990.80	973.60	965.04	960.72
90000	1068.22	1060.89	1054.55	1049.08	1030.87	1021.81	1017.24
95000	1127.57	1119.82	1113.14	1107.36	1088.14	1078.57	1073.75
100000	1186.91	1178.76	1171.73	1165.64	1145.41	1135.34	1130.26
105000	1246.26	1237.70	1230.31	1223.93	1202.68	1192.11	1186.77
110000	1305.60	1296.64	1288.90	1282.21	1259.95	1248.87	1243.29
120000	1424.29	1414.51	1406.07	1398.77	1374.49	1362.41	1356.31
130000	1542.98	1532.39	1523.25	1515.34	1489.04	1475.94	1469.34
140000	1661.67	1650.27	1640.42	1631.90	1603.58	1589.48	1582.37
150000	1780.37	1768.14	1757.59	1748.47	1718.12	1703.01	1695.39
160000	1899.06	1886.02	1874.76	1865.03	1832.66	1816.54	1808.42
175000	2077.09	2062.83	2050.52	2039.88	2004.47	1986.85	1977.96
200000	2373.82	2357.52	2343.45	2331.29	2290.82	2270.68	2260.52
250000	2967.28	2946.90	2929.32	2914.11	2863.53	2838.35	2825.65
500000	5934.55	5893.81	5858.64	5828.22	5727.06	5676.70	5651.31
1000000	11869.11	11787.61	11717.27	11656.45	11454.12	11353.41	11302.61

13.75%   MONTHLY PAYMENTS

AMOUNT	1 YEAR	2 YEARS	3 YEARS	4 YEARS	5 YEARS	6 YEARS	7 YEARS
100	8.97	4.79	3.41	2.72	2.31	2.05	1.86
200	17.93	9.58	6.81	5.44	4.63	4.09	3.72
500	44.83	23.95	17.03	13.60	11.57	10.24	9.30
1000	89.67	47.89	34.06	27.20	23.14	20.47	18.60
2000	179.34	95.79	68.11	54.40	46.28	40.94	37.20
3000	269.01	143.68	102.17	81.60	69.42	61.42	55.81
4000	358.68	191.58	136.23	108.80	92.56	81.89	74.41
5000	448.35	239.47	170.28	136.01	115.69	102.36	93.01
6000	538.02	287.37	204.34	163.21	138.83	122.83	111.61
7000	627.69	335.26	238.39	190.41	161.97	143.30	130.22
8000	717.36	383.16	272.45	217.61	185.11	163.78	148.82
9000	807.03	431.05	306.51	244.81	208.25	184.25	167.42
10000	896.70	478.95	340.56	272.01	231.39	204.72	186.02
11000	986.36	526.84	374.62	299.21	254.53	225.19	204.62
12000	1076.03	574.74	408.68	326.41	277.67	245.67	223.23
13000	1165.70	622.63	442.73	353.62	300.80	266.14	241.83
14000	1255.37	670.53	476.79	380.82	323.94	286.61	260.43
15000	1345.04	718.42	510.84	408.02	347.08	307.08	279.03
20000	1793.39	957.90	681.13	544.02	462.78	409.44	372.04
25000	2241.74	1197.37	851.41	680.03	578.47	511.80	465.05
30000	2690.09	1436.85	1021.69	816.04	694.17	614.16	558.07
35000	3138.43	1676.32	1191.97	952.04	809.86	716.52	651.08
40000	3586.78	1915.79	1362.25	1088.05	925.55	818.88	744.09
45000	4035.13	2155.27	1532.53	1224.06	1041.25	921.25	837.10
50000	4483.48	2394.74	1702.82	1360.06	1156.94	1023.61	930.11
55000	4931.82	2634.22	1873.10	1496.07	1272.64	1125.97	1023.12
56000	5021.49	2682.11	1907.15	1523.27	1295.78	1146.44	1041.72
57000	5111.16	2730.01	1941.21	1550.47	1318.91	1166.91	1060.32
58000	5200.83	2777.90	1975.27	1577.67	1342.05	1187.38	1078.93
59000	5290.50	2825.80	2009.32	1604.87	1365.19	1207.85	1097.53
60000	5380.17	2873.69	2043.38	1632.07	1388.33	1228.33	1116.13
61000	5469.84	2921.59	2077.44	1659.28	1411.47	1248.80	1134.73
62000	5559.51	2969.48	2111.49	1686.48	1434.61	1269.27	1153.34
63000	5649.18	3017.38	2145.55	1713.68	1457.75	1289.74	1171.94
64000	5738.85	3065.27	2179.61	1740.88	1480.89	1310.22	1190.54
65000	5828.52	3113.17	2213.66	1768.08	1504.02	1330.69	1209.14
70000	6276.87	3352.64	2383.94	1904.09	1619.72	1433.05	1302.15
75000	6725.21	3592.11	2554.22	2040.09	1735.41	1535.41	1395.16
80000	7173.56	3831.59	2724.51	2176.10	1851.11	1637.77	1488.17
85000	7621.91	4071.06	2894.79	2312.10	1966.80	1740.13	1581.19
90000	8070.26	4310.54	3065.07	2448.11	2082.50	1842.49	1674.20
95000	8518.61	4550.01	3235.35	2584.12	2198.19	1944.85	1767.21
100000	8966.95	4789.49	3405.63	2720.12	2313.88	2047.21	1860.22
105000	9415.30	5028.96	3575.91	2856.13	2429.58	2149.57	1953.23
110000	9863.65	5268.44	3746.20	2992.14	2545.27	2251.93	2046.24
120000	10760.34	5747.38	4086.76	3264.15	2776.66	2456.65	2232.26
130000	11657.04	6226.33	4427.32	3536.16	3008.05	2661.37	2418.28
140000	12553.73	6705.28	4767.89	3808.17	3239.44	2866.10	2604.31
150000	13450.43	7184.23	5108.45	4080.19	3470.83	3070.82	2790.33
160000	14347.12	7663.18	5449.01	4352.20	3702.22	3275.54	2976.35
175000	15692.17	8381.60	5959.86	4760.22	4049.30	3582.62	3255.38
200000	17933.91	9578.97	6811.27	5440.25	4627.77	4094.42	3720.44
250000	22417.38	11973.72	8514.08	6800.31	5784.71	5118.03	4650.54
500000	44834.77	23947.43	17028.17	13600.62	11569.42	10236.06	9301.09
1000000	89669.53	47894.86	34056.33	27201.23	23138.84	20472.11	18602.18

MONTHLY PAYMENTS   13.75%

AMOUNT	8 YEARS	9 YEARS	10 YEARS	11 YEARS	12 YEARS	13 YEARS	14 YEARS
100	1.72	1.62	1.54	1.47	1.42	1.38	1.34
200	3.45	3.24	3.08	2.95	2.84	2.76	2.69
500	8.61	8.09	7.69	7.37	7.11	6.90	6.72
1000	17.23	16.19	15.38	14.73	14.21	13.79	13.44
2000	34.46	32.38	30.75	29.47	28.43	27.58	26.88
3000	51.69	48.56	46.13	44.20	42.64	41.37	40.32
4000	68.92	64.75	61.51	58.93	56.86	55.16	53.76
5000	86.15	80.94	76.88	73.66	71.07	68.95	67.20
6000	103.38	97.13	92.26	88.40	85.28	82.74	80.64
7000	120.61	113.31	107.64	103.13	99.50	96.53	94.08
8000	137.84	129.50	123.01	117.86	113.71	110.32	107.52
9000	155.07	145.69	138.39	132.60	127.92	124.11	120.97
10000	172.30	161.88	153.77	147.33	142.14	137.90	134.41
11000	189.52	178.06	169.14	162.06	156.35	151.69	147.85
12000	206.75	194.25	184.52	176.79	170.57	165.48	161.29
13000	223.98	210.44	199.90	191.53	184.78	179.27	174.73
14000	241.21	226.63	215.27	206.26	198.99	193.06	188.17
15000	258.44	242.82	230.65	220.99	213.21	206.85	201.61
20000	344.59	323.75	307.53	294.66	284.28	275.80	268.81
25000	430.74	404.69	384.42	368.32	355.35	344.75	336.01
30000	516.89	485.63	461.30	441.99	426.41	413.70	403.22
35000	603.03	566.57	538.18	515.65	497.48	482.65	470.42
40000	689.18	647.51	615.07	589.32	568.55	551.60	537.62
45000	775.33	728.45	691.95	662.98	639.62	620.55	604.83
50000	861.48	809.38	768.83	736.64	710.69	689.50	672.03
55000	947.62	890.32	845.72	810.31	781.76	758.45	739.23
56000	964.85	906.51	861.09	825.04	795.97	772.24	752.67
57000	982.08	922.70	876.47	839.77	810.19	786.03	766.11
58000	999.31	938.89	891.85	854.51	824.40	799.82	779.55
59000	1016.54	955.07	907.22	869.24	838.62	813.61	792.99
60000	1033.77	971.26	922.60	883.97	852.83	827.40	806.43
61000	1051.00	987.45	937.98	898.71	867.04	841.19	819.87
62000	1068.23	1003.64	953.35	913.44	881.26	854.98	833.31
63000	1085.46	1019.82	968.73	928.17	895.47	868.77	846.76
64000	1102.69	1036.01	984.11	942.90	909.68	882.56	860.20
65000	1119.92	1052.20	999.48	957.64	923.90	896.35	873.64
70000	1206.07	1133.14	1076.37	1031.30	994.97	965.30	940.84
75000	1292.21	1214.08	1153.25	1104.97	1066.04	1034.25	1008.04
80000	1378.36	1295.01	1230.13	1178.63	1137.11	1103.21	1075.25
85000	1464.51	1375.95	1307.02	1252.30	1208.18	1172.16	1142.45
90000	1550.66	1456.89	1383.90	1325.96	1279.24	1241.11	1209.65
95000	1636.81	1537.83	1460.78	1399.62	1350.31	1310.06	1276.85
100000	1722.95	1618.77	1537.67	1473.29	1421.38	1379.01	1344.06
105000	1809.10	1699.71	1614.55	1546.95	1492.45	1447.96	1411.26
110000	1895.25	1780.64	1691.43	1620.62	1563.52	1516.91	1478.46
120000	2067.54	1942.52	1845.20	1767.95	1705.66	1654.81	1612.87
130000	2239.84	2104.40	1998.97	1915.28	1847.80	1792.71	1747.27
140000	2412.13	2266.27	2152.74	2062.60	1989.94	1930.61	1881.68
150000	2584.43	2428.15	2306.50	2209.93	2132.07	2068.51	2016.08
160000	2756.72	2590.03	2460.27	2357.26	2274.21	2206.41	2150.49
175000	3015.17	2832.84	2690.92	2578.26	2487.42	2413.26	2352.10
200000	3445.91	3237.54	3075.34	2946.58	2842.77	2758.01	2688.11
250000	4307.38	4046.92	3844.17	3683.22	3553.46	3447.52	3360.14
500000	8614.76	8093.84	7688.34	7366.44	7106.91	6895.03	6720.28
1000000	17229.53	16187.68	15376.68	14732.89	14213.83	13790.07	13440.56

13.75% MONTHLY PAYMENTS

AMOUNT	15 YEARS	16 YEARS	17 YEARS	18 YEARS	19 YEARS	20 YEARS	21 YEARS
100	1.31	1.29	1.27	1.25	1.24	1.23	1.21
200	2.63	2.58	2.54	2.51	2.48	2.45	2.43
500	6.57	6.45	6.35	6.26	6.19	6.13	6.07
1000	13.15	12.91	12.70	12.53	12.38	12.25	12.15
2000	26.30	25.81	25.40	25.06	24.76	24.51	24.29
3000	39.45	38.72	38.10	37.58	37.14	36.76	36.44
4000	52.60	51.63	50.81	50.11	49.52	49.02	48.59
5000	65.75	64.53	63.51	62.64	61.90	61.27	60.73
6000	78.90	77.44	76.21	75.17	74.28	73.52	72.88
7000	92.05	90.34	88.91	87.69	86.66	85.78	85.02
8000	105.20	103.25	101.61	100.22	99.04	98.03	97.17
9000	118.35	116.16	114.31	112.75	111.42	110.29	109.32
10000	131.50	129.06	127.01	125.28	123.80	122.54	121.46
11000	144.65	141.97	139.71	137.80	136.18	134.79	133.61
12000	157.80	154.88	152.42	150.33	148.56	147.05	145.76
13000	170.95	167.78	165.12	162.86	160.94	159.30	157.90
14000	184.10	180.69	177.82	175.39	173.32	171.56	170.05
15000	197.25	193.60	190.52	187.91	185.70	183.81	182.19
20000	263.00	258.13	254.03	250.55	247.60	245.08	242.93
25000	328.75	322.66	317.53	313.19	309.50	306.35	303.66
30000	394.50	387.19	381.04	375.83	371.40	367.62	364.39
35000	460.25	451.72	444.55	438.47	433.30	428.89	425.12
40000	525.99	516.26	508.05	501.11	495.20	490.16	485.85
45000	591.74	580.79	571.56	563.74	557.10	551.43	546.58
50000	657.49	645.32	635.06	626.38	619.00	612.70	607.31
55000	723.24	709.85	698.57	689.02	680.90	673.97	668.04
56000	736.39	722.76	711.27	701.55	693.28	686.23	680.19
57000	749.54	735.67	723.97	714.08	705.66	698.48	692.34
58000	762.69	748.57	736.67	726.60	718.04	710.74	704.48
59000	775.84	761.48	749.38	739.13	730.42	722.99	716.63
60000	788.99	774.30	762.08	751.66	742.80	735.24	728.78
61000	802.14	787.29	774.78	764.19	755.18	747.50	740.92
62000	815.29	800.20	787.48	776.71	767.56	759.75	753.07
63000	828.44	813.10	800.18	789.24	779.94	772.01	765.21
64000	841.59	826.01	812.88	801.77	792.32	784.26	777.36
65000	854.74	838.92	825.58	814.30	804.70	796.51	789.51
70000	920.49	903.45	889.09	876.93	866.60	857.78	850.24
75000	986.24	967.98	952.60	939.57	928.50	919.05	910.97
80000	1051.99	1032.51	1016.10	1002.21	990.40	980.32	971.70
85000	1117.74	1097.04	1079.61	1064.85	1052.30	1041.59	1032.43
90000	1183.49	1161.58	1143.12	1127.49	1114.20	1102.86	1093.16
95000	1249.24	1226.11	1206.62	1190.13	1176.10	1164.14	1153.90
100000	1314.99	1290.64	1270.13	1252.76	1238.00	1225.41	1214.63
105000	1380.74	1355.17	1333.64	1315.40	1299.90	1286.68	1275.36
110000	1446.49	1419.70	1397.14	1378.04	1361.80	1347.95	1336.09
120000	1577.98	1548.77	1524.15	1503.32	1485.60	1470.49	1457.55
130000	1709.48	1677.83	1651.17	1628.59	1609.40	1593.03	1579.01
140000	1840.98	1806.90	1778.18	1753.87	1733.20	1715.57	1700.48
150000	1972.48	1935.96	1905.19	1879.15	1857.00	1838.11	1821.94
160000	2103.98	2065.02	2032.21	2004.42	1980.80	1960.65	1943.40
175000	2301.23	2258.62	2222.73	2192.34	2166.50	2144.46	2125.60
200000	2629.97	2581.28	2540.26	2505.53	2476.00	2450.81	2429.25
250000	3287.47	3226.60	3175.32	3131.91	3095.00	3063.51	3036.57
500000	6574.94	6453.20	6350.65	6263.82	6190.00	6127.03	6073.13
1000000	13149.87	12906.40	12701.29	12527.64	12380.01	12254.05	12146.27

MONTHLY PAYMENTS 13.75%

AMOUNT	22 YEARS	23 YEARS	24 YEARS	25 YEARS	30 YEARS	35 YEARS	40 YEARS
100	1.21	1.20	1.19	1.18	1.17	1.16	1.15
200	2.41	2.39	2.38	2.37	2.33	2.31	2.30
500	6.03	5.99	5.95	5.92	5.83	5.78	5.75
1000	12.05	11.97	11.91	11.85	11.65	11.55	11.51
2000	24.11	23.95	23.81	23.69	23.30	23.11	23.01
3000	36.16	35.92	35.72	35.54	34.95	34.66	34.52
4000	48.22	47.90	47.62	47.39	46.60	46.22	46.03
5000	60.27	59.87	59.53	59.23	58.26	57.77	57.53
6000	72.32	71.85	71.43	71.08	69.91	69.33	69.04
7000	84.38	83.82	83.34	82.93	81.56	80.88	80.55
8000	96.43	95.79	95.25	94.77	93.21	92.44	92.05
9000	108.48	107.77	107.15	106.62	104.86	103.99	103.56
10000	120.54	119.74	119.06	118.47	116.51	115.55	115.07
11000	132.59	131.72	130.96	130.31	128.16	127.10	126.58
12000	144.65	143.69	142.87	142.16	139.81	138.66	138.08
13000	156.70	155.67	154.78	154.01	151.46	150.21	149.59
14000	168.75	167.64	166.68	165.85	163.12	161.77	161.10
15000	180.81	179.61	178.59	177.70	174.77	173.32	172.60
20000	241.08	239.49	238.12	236.93	233.02	231.10	230.14
25000	301.34	299.36	297.64	296.17	291.28	288.87	287.67
30000	361.61	359.23	357.17	355.40	349.53	346.65	345.21
35000	421.88	419.10	416.70	414.63	407.79	404.42	402.74
40000	482.15	478.97	476.23	473.87	466.05	462.19	460.27
45000	542.42	538.84	535.76	533.10	524.30	519.97	517.81
50000	602.69	598.71	595.29	592.33	582.56	577.74	575.34
55000	662.96	658.59	654.82	651.57	640.81	635.52	632.88
56000	675.01	670.56	666.72	663.41	652.46	647.07	644.38
57000	687.07	682.53	678.63	675.26	664.11	658.63	655.89
58000	699.12	694.51	690.53	687.11	675.77	670.18	667.40
59000	711.17	706.48	702.44	698.95	687.42	681.74	678.90
60000	723.23	718.46	714.35	710.80	699.07	693.29	690.41
61000	735.28	730.43	726.25	722.65	710.72	704.85	701.92
62000	747.34	742.41	738.16	734.49	722.37	716.40	713.42
63000	759.39	754.38	750.06	746.34	734.02	727.96	724.93
64000	771.44	766.35	761.97	758.19	745.67	739.51	736.44
65000	783.50	778.33	773.88	770.03	757.32	751.07	747.95
70000	843.77	838.20	833.40	829.27	815.58	808.84	805.48
75000	904.03	898.07	892.93	888.50	873.83	866.61	863.01
80000	964.30	957.94	952.46	947.73	932.09	924.39	920.55
85000	1024.57	1017.81	1011.99	1006.97	990.35	982.16	978.08
90000	1084.84	1077.68	1071.52	1066.20	1048.60	1039.94	1035.62
95000	1145.11	1137.56	1131.05	1125.43	1106.86	1097.71	1093.15
100000	1205.38	1197.43	1190.58	1184.67	1165.11	1155.49	1150.69
105000	1265.65	1257.30	1250.11	1243.90	1223.37	1213.26	1208.22
110000	1325.92	1317.17	1309.64	1303.13	1281.62	1271.03	1265.75
120000	1446.46	1436.91	1428.69	1421.60	1398.14	1386.58	1380.82
130000	1566.99	1556.66	1547.75	1540.07	1514.65	1502.13	1495.89
140000	1687.53	1676.40	1666.81	1658.53	1631.16	1617.68	1610.96
150000	1808.07	1796.14	1785.87	1777.00	1747.67	1733.23	1726.03
160000	1928.61	1915.88	1904.92	1895.47	1864.18	1848.78	1841.10
175000	2109.41	2095.50	2083.51	2073.17	2038.95	2022.10	2013.70
200000	2410.76	2394.86	2381.15	2369.33	2330.23	2310.97	2301.37
250000	3013.45	2993.57	2976.44	2961.66	2912.78	2888.71	2876.71
500000	6026.90	5987.14	5952.89	5923.33	5825.56	5777.43	5753.43
1000000	12053.79	11974.28	11905.77	11846.66	11651.13	11554.85	11506.85

14.00%   MONTHLY PAYMENTS

AMOUNT	1 YEAR	2 YEARS	3 YEARS	4 YEARS	5 YEARS	6 YEARS	7 YEARS
100	8.98	4.80	3.42	2.73	2.33	2.06	1.87
200	17.96	9.60	6.84	5.47	4.65	4.12	3.75
500	44.89	24.01	17.09	13.66	11.63	10.30	9.37
1000	89.79	48.01	34.18	27.33	23.27	20.61	18.74
2000	179.57	96.03	68.36	54.65	46.54	41.21	37.48
3000	269.36	144.04	102.53	81.98	69.80	61.82	56.22
4000	359.15	192.05	136.71	109.31	93.07	82.42	74.96
5000	448.94	240.06	170.89	136.63	116.34	103.03	93.70
6000	538.72	288.08	205.07	163.96	139.61	123.63	112.44
7000	628.51	336.09	239.24	191.29	162.88	144.24	131.18
8000	718.30	384.10	273.42	218.61	186.15	164.85	149.92
9000	808.08	432.12	307.60	245.94	209.41	185.45	168.66
10000	897.87	480.13	341.78	273.26	232.68	206.06	187.40
11000	987.66	528.14	375.95	300.59	255.95	226.66	206.14
12000	1077.45	576.15	410.13	327.92	279.22	247.26	224.88
13000	1167.23	624.17	444.31	355.24	302.49	267.87	243.62
14000	1257.02	672.18	478.49	382.57	325.76	288.48	262.36
15000	1346.81	720.19	512.66	409.90	349.02	309.09	281.10
20000	1795.74	960.26	683.55	546.53	465.37	412.11	374.80
25000	2244.68	1200.32	854.44	683.16	581.71	515.14	468.50
30000	2693.61	1440.39	1025.33	819.79	698.05	618.17	562.20
35000	3142.55	1680.45	1196.22	956.43	814.39	721.20	655.90
40000	3591.48	1920.52	1367.11	1093.06	930.73	824.23	749.60
45000	4040.42	2160.58	1537.99	1229.69	1047.07	927.26	843.30
50000	4489.36	2400.64	1708.88	1366.32	1163.41	1030.29	937.00
55000	4938.29	2640.71	1879.77	1502.96	1279.75	1133.32	1030.70
56000	5028.08	2688.72	1913.95	1530.28	1303.02	1153.92	1049.44
57000	5117.87	2736.73	1948.12	1557.61	1326.29	1174.53	1068.18
58000	5207.65	2784.75	1982.30	1584.94	1349.56	1195.13	1086.92
59000	5297.44	2832.76	2016.48	1612.26	1372.83	1215.74	1105.66
60000	5387.23	2880.77	2050.66	1639.59	1396.10	1236.34	1124.40
61000	5477.01	2928.79	2084.84	1666.92	1419.36	1256.95	1143.14
62000	5566.80	2976.80	2119.01	1694.24	1442.63	1277.56	1161.88
63000	5656.59	3024.81	2153.19	1721.57	1465.90	1298.16	1180.62
64000	5746.38	3072.82	2187.37	1748.89	1489.17	1318.77	1199.36
65000	5836.16	3120.84	2221.55	1776.22	1512.44	1339.37	1218.10
70000	6285.10	3360.90	2392.43	1912.85	1628.78	1442.40	1311.80
75000	6734.03	3600.97	2563.32	2049.49	1745.12	1545.43	1405.50
80000	7182.97	3841.03	2734.21	2186.12	1861.46	1648.46	1499.20
85000	7631.90	4081.10	2905.10	2322.75	1977.80	1751.49	1592.90
90000	8080.84	4321.16	3075.99	2459.38	2094.14	1854.52	1686.60
95000	8529.78	4561.22	3246.87	2596.02	2210.48	1957.55	1780.30
100000	8978.71	4801.29	3417.76	2732.65	2326.83	2060.57	1874.00
105000	9427.65	5041.35	3588.65	2869.28	2443.17	2163.60	1967.70
110000	9876.58	5281.42	3759.54	3005.91	2559.51	2266.63	2061.40
120000	10774.45	5761.55	4101.32	3279.18	2792.19	2472.69	2248.80
130000	11672.33	6241.67	4443.09	3552.44	3024.87	2678.75	2436.20
140000	12570.20	6721.80	4784.87	3825.71	3257.56	2884.80	2623.60
150000	13468.07	7201.93	5126.64	4098.97	3490.24	3090.86	2811.00
160000	14365.94	7682.06	5468.42	4372.24	3722.92	3296.92	2998.40
175000	15712.75	8402.25	5981.09	4782.13	4071.94	3606.00	3279.50
200000	17957.42	9602.58	6835.53	5465.30	4653.65	4121.15	3748.00
250000	22446.78	12003.22	8544.41	6831.62	5817.06	5151.43	4685.00
500000	44893.56	24006.44	17088.81	13663.24	11634.13	10302.87	9370.01
1000000	89787.12	48012.88	34177.63	27326.48	23268.25	20605.74	18740.01

MONTHLY PAYMENTS 14.00%

AMOUNT	8 YEARS	9 YEARS	10 YEARS	11 YEARS	12 YEARS	13 YEARS	14 YEARS
100	1.74	1.63	1.55	1.49	1.44	1.40	1.36
200	3.47	3.27	3.11	2.98	2.87	2.79	2.72
500	8.69	8.17	7.76	7.44	7.19	6.98	6.80
1000	17.37	16.33	15.53	14.89	14.37	13.95	13.60
2000	34.74	32.67	31.05	29.77	28.74	27.90	27.21
3000	52.11	49.00	46.58	44.66	43.11	41.85	40.81
4000	69.49	65.33	62.11	59.55	57.49	55.80	54.42
5000	86.86	81.67	77.63	74.43	71.86	69.76	68.02
6000	104.23	98.00	93.16	89.32	86.23	83.71	81.63
7000	121.60	114.34	108.69	104.21	100.60	97.66	95.23
8000	138.97	130.67	124.21	119.09	114.97	111.61	108.84
9000	156.34	147.00	139.74	133.98	129.34	125.56	122.44
10000	173.72	163.34	155.27	148.87	143.71	139.51	136.05
11000	191.09	179.67	170.79	163.75	158.08	153.46	149.65
12000	208.46	196.00	186.32	178.64	172.46	167.41	163.26
13000	225.83	212.34	201.85	193.53	186.83	181.36	176.86
14000	243.20	228.67	217.37	208.41	201.20	195.31	190.47
15000	260.57	245.01	232.90	223.30	215.57	209.27	204.07
20000	347.43	326.67	310.53	297.73	287.43	279.02	272.10
25000	434.29	408.34	388.17	372.17	359.28	348.78	340.12
30000	521.15	490.01	465.80	446.60	431.14	418.53	408.15
35000	608.00	571.68	543.43	521.03	502.99	488.29	476.17
40000	694.86	653.35	621.07	595.47	574.85	558.04	544.20
45000	781.72	735.02	698.70	669.90	646.71	627.80	612.22
50000	868.58	816.69	776.33	744.33	718.56	697.55	680.24
55000	955.43	898.35	853.97	818.77	790.42	767.31	748.27
56000	972.80	914.69	869.49	833.65	804.79	781.26	761.87
57000	990.18	931.02	885.02	848.54	819.16	795.21	775.48
58000	1007.55	947.35	900.55	863.43	833.53	809.16	789.08
59000	1024.92	963.69	916.07	878.31	847.90	823.11	802.69
60000	1042.29	980.02	931.60	893.20	862.28	837.06	816.29
61000	1059.66	996.36	947.13	908.09	876.65	851.01	829.90
62000	1077.03	1012.69	962.65	922.97	891.02	864.96	843.50
63000	1094.40	1029.02	978.18	937.86	905.39	878.92	857.11
64000	1111.78	1045.36	993.71	952.75	919.76	892.87	870.71
65000	1129.15	1061.69	1009.23	967.63	934.13	906.82	884.32
70000	1216.01	1143.36	1086.87	1042.07	1005.99	976.57	952.34
75000	1302.86	1225.03	1164.50	1116.50	1077.85	1046.33	1020.37
80000	1389.72	1306.70	1242.13	1190.93	1149.70	1116.08	1088.39
85000	1476.58	1388.36	1319.76	1265.37	1221.56	1185.84	1156.42
90000	1563.44	1470.03	1397.40	1339.80	1293.41	1255.59	1224.44
95000	1650.29	1551.70	1475.03	1414.23	1365.27	1325.35	1292.47
100000	1737.15	1633.37	1552.66	1488.67	1437.13	1395.10	1360.49
105000	1824.01	1715.04	1630.30	1563.10	1508.98	1464.86	1428.51
110000	1910.87	1796.71	1707.93	1637.53	1580.84	1534.61	1496.54
120000	2084.58	1960.04	1863.20	1786.40	1724.55	1674.12	1632.59
130000	2258.30	2123.38	2018.46	1935.27	1868.27	1813.63	1768.64
140000	2432.01	2286.72	2173.73	2084.13	2011.98	1953.14	1904.69
150000	2605.73	2450.06	2329.00	2233.00	2155.69	2092.65	2040.73
160000	2779.44	2613.39	2484.26	2381.87	2299.40	2232.17	2176.78
175000	3040.01	2858.40	2717.16	2605.17	2514.97	2441.43	2380.86
200000	3474.30	3266.74	3105.33	2977.33	2874.25	2790.21	2720.98
250000	4342.88	4083.43	3881.66	3721.67	3592.82	3487.76	3401.22
500000	8685.75	8166.85	7763.32	7443.33	7185.64	6975.52	6802.45
1000000	17371.50	16333.70	15526.64	14886.66	14371.27	13951.03	13604.90

14.00% MONTHLY PAYMENTS

AMOUNT	15 YEARS	16 YEARS	17 YEARS	18 YEARS	19 YEARS	20 YEARS	21 YEARS
100	1.33	1.31	1.29	1.27	1.26	1.24	1.23
200	2.66	2.62	2.57	2.54	2.51	2.49	2.47
500	6.66	6.54	6.44	6.35	6.28	6.22	6.16
1000	13.32	13.08	12.87	12.70	12.56	12.44	12.33
2000	26.63	26.15	25.75	25.41	25.12	24.87	24.66
3000	39.95	39.23	38.62	38.11	37.68	37.31	36.99
4000	53.27	52.31	51.50	50.82	50.24	49.74	49.32
5000	66.59	65.38	64.37	63.52	62.79	62.18	61.65
6000	79.90	78.46	77.25	76.22	75.35	74.61	73.98
7000	93.22	91.54	90.12	88.93	87.91	87.05	86.31
8000	106.54	104.62	103.00	101.63	100.47	99.48	98.64
9000	119.86	117.69	115.87	114.33	113.03	111.92	110.97
10000	133.17	130.77	128.75	127.04	125.59	124.35	123.30
11000	146.49	143.85	141.62	139.74	138.15	136.79	135.63
12000	159.81	156.92	154.50	152.45	150.71	149.22	147.96
13000	173.13	170.00	167.37	165.15	163.26	161.66	160.29
14000	186.44	183.08	180.25	177.85	175.82	174.09	172.62
15000	199.76	196.15	193.12	190.56	188.38	186.53	184.95
20000	266.35	261.54	257.50	254.08	251.18	248.70	246.59
25000	332.94	326.92	321.87	317.60	313.97	310.88	308.24
30000	399.52	392.31	386.24	381.11	376.76	373.06	369.89
35000	466.11	457.69	450.62	444.63	439.56	435.23	431.54
40000	532.70	523.08	514.99	508.15	502.35	497.41	493.19
45000	599.28	588.46	579.36	571.67	565.14	559.58	554.84
50000	665.87	653.85	643.74	635.19	627.94	621.76	616.48
55000	732.46	719.23	708.11	698.71	690.73	683.94	678.13
56000	745.78	732.31	720.99	711.41	703.29	696.37	690.46
57000	759.09	745.39	733.86	724.12	715.85	708.81	702.79
58000	772.41	758.47	746.74	736.82	728.41	721.24	715.12
59000	785.73	771.54	759.61	749.53	740.97	733.68	727.45
60000	799.04	784.62	772.49	762.23	753.53	746.11	739.78
61000	812.36	797.70	785.36	774.93	766.08	758.55	752.11
62000	825.68	810.77	798.24	787.64	778.64	770.98	764.44
63000	839.00	823.85	811.11	800.34	791.20	783.42	776.77
64000	852.31	836.93	823.98	813.05	803.76	795.85	789.10
65000	865.63	850.00	836.86	825.75	816.32	808.29	801.43
70000	932.22	915.39	901.23	889.27	879.11	870.46	863.08
75000	998.81	980.77	965.61	952.79	941.91	932.64	924.73
80000	1065.39	1046.16	1029.98	1016.31	1004.70	994.82	986.37
85000	1131.98	1111.54	1094.35	1079.83	1067.49	1056.99	1048.02
90000	1198.57	1176.93	1158.73	1143.34	1130.29	1119.17	1109.67
95000	1265.15	1242.31	1223.10	1206.86	1193.08	1181.34	1171.32
100000	1331.74	1307.70	1287.48	1270.38	1255.88	1243.52	1232.97
105000	1398.33	1373.08	1351.85	1333.90	1318.67	1305.70	1294.62
110000	1464.92	1438.47	1416.22	1397.42	1381.46	1367.87	1356.26
120000	1598.09	1569.24	1544.97	1524.46	1507.05	1492.22	1479.56
130000	1731.26	1700.01	1673.72	1651.50	1632.64	1616.58	1602.86
140000	1864.44	1830.78	1802.47	1778.54	1758.23	1740.93	1726.15
150000	1997.61	1961.55	1931.21	1905.57	1883.81	1865.28	1849.45
160000	2130.79	2092.32	2059.96	2032.61	2009.40	1989.63	1972.75
175000	2330.55	2288.47	2253.08	2223.17	2197.78	2176.16	2157.69
200000	2663.48	2615.40	2574.95	2540.77	2511.75	2487.04	2465.93
250000	3329.35	3269.25	3218.69	3175.96	3139.69	3108.80	3082.42
500000	6658.71	6538.50	6437.38	6351.92	6279.38	6217.60	6164.84
1000000	13317.41	13076.99	12874.76	12703.83	12558.76	12435.21	12329.67

MONTHLY PAYMENTS 14.00%

AMOUNT	22 YEARS	23 YEARS	24 YEARS	25 YEARS	30 YEARS	35 YEARS	40 YEARS
100	1.22	1.22	1.21	1.20	1.18	1.18	1.17
200	2.45	2.43	2.42	2.41	2.37	2.35	2.34
500	6.12	6.08	6.05	6.02	5.92	5.88	5.86
1000	12.24	12.16	12.10	12.04	11.85	11.76	11.71
2000	24.48	24.32	24.19	24.08	23.70	23.51	23.42
3000	36.72	36.49	36.29	36.11	35.55	35.27	35.13
4000	48.96	48.65	48.38	48.15	47.39	47.03	46.85
5000	61.20	60.81	60.48	60.19	59.24	58.78	58.56
6000	73.44	72.97	72.57	72.23	71.09	70.54	70.27
7000	85.68	85.13	84.67	84.26	82.94	82.30	81.98
8000	97.91	97.29	96.76	96.30	94.79	94.05	93.69
9000	110.15	109.46	108.86	108.34	106.64	105.81	105.40
10000	122.39	121.62	120.95	120.38	118.49	117.57	117.11
11000	134.63	133.78	133.05	132.41	130.34	129.32	128.83
12000	146.87	145.94	145.14	144.45	142.18	141.08	140.54
13000	159.11	158.10	157.24	156.49	154.03	152.84	152.25
14000	171.35	170.26	169.33	168.53	165.88	164.59	163.96
15000	183.59	182.43	181.43	180.56	177.73	176.35	175.67
20000	244.79	243.23	241.90	240.75	236.97	235.13	234.23
25000	305.98	304.04	302.38	300.94	296.22	293.92	292.79
30000	367.18	364.85	362.85	361.13	355.46	352.70	351.34
35000	428.38	425.66	423.33	421.32	414.71	411.49	409.90
40000	489.57	486.47	483.80	481.50	473.95	470.27	468.46
45000	550.77	547.28	544.28	541.69	533.19	529.05	527.01
50000	611.96	608.09	604.75	601.88	592.44	587.84	585.57
55000	673.16	668.90	665.23	662.07	651.68	646.62	644.13
56000	685.40	681.06	677.32	674.11	663.53	658.38	655.84
57000	697.64	693.22	689.42	686.14	675.38	670.13	667.55
58000	709.88	705.38	701.51	698.18	687.23	681.89	679.26
59000	722.12	717.54	713.61	710.22	699.07	693.65	690.97
60000	734.36	729.70	725.70	722.26	710.92	705.40	702.68
61000	746.60	741.87	737.80	734.29	722.77	717.16	714.40
62000	758.84	754.03	749.89	746.33	734.62	728.92	726.11
63000	771.08	766.19	761.99	758.37	746.47	740.67	737.82
64000	783.31	778.35	774.08	770.41	758.32	752.43	749.53
65000	795.55	790.51	786.18	782.44	770.17	764.19	761.24
70000	856.75	851.32	846.65	842.63	829.41	822.97	819.80
75000	917.95	912.13	907.13	902.82	888.65	881.75	878.36
80000	979.14	972.94	967.60	963.01	947.90	940.54	936.91
85000	1040.34	1033.75	1028.08	1023.20	1007.14	999.32	995.47
90000	1101.54	1094.56	1088.55	1083.38	1066.38	1058.11	1054.03
95000	1162.73	1155.36	1149.03	1143.57	1125.63	1116.89	1112.58
100000	1223.93	1216.17	1209.50	1203.76	1184.87	1175.67	1171.14
105000	1285.13	1276.98	1269.98	1263.95	1244.12	1234.46	1229.70
110000	1346.32	1337.79	1330.45	1324.14	1303.36	1293.24	1288.25
120000	1468.72	1459.41	1451.41	1444.51	1421.85	1410.81	1405.37
130000	1591.11	1581.03	1572.36	1564.89	1540.33	1528.38	1522.48
140000	1713.50	1702.64	1693.31	1685.27	1658.82	1645.94	1639.60
150000	1835.89	1824.26	1814.26	1805.64	1777.31	1763.51	1756.71
160000	1958.29	1945.88	1935.21	1926.02	1895.79	1881.08	1873.82
175000	2141.88	2128.30	2116.63	2106.58	2073.53	2057.43	2049.50
200000	2447.86	2432.35	2419.01	2407.52	2369.74	2351.35	2342.28
250000	3059.82	3040.43	3023.76	3009.40	2962.18	2939.18	2927.85
500000	6119.65	6080.87	6047.52	6018.81	5924.36	5878.37	5855.70
1000000	12239.29	12161.73	12095.04	12037.61	11848.72	11756.73	11711.40

14.25% MONTHLY PAYMENTS

AMOUNT	1 YEAR	2 YEARS	3 YEARS	4 YEARS	5 YEARS	6 YEARS	7 YEARS
100	8.99	4.81	3.43	2.75	2.34	2.07	1.89
200	17.98	9.63	6.86	5.49	4.68	4.15	3.78
500	44.95	24.07	17.15	13.73	11.70	10.37	9.44
1000	89.90	48.13	34.30	27.45	23.40	20.74	18.88
2000	179.81	96.26	68.60	54.90	46.80	41.48	37.76
3000	269.71	144.39	102.90	82.36	70.19	62.22	56.64
4000	359.62	192.52	137.20	109.81	93.59	82.96	75.51
5000	449.52	240.66	171.50	137.26	116.99	103.70	94.39
6000	539.43	288.79	205.80	164.71	140.39	124.44	113.27
7000	629.33	336.92	240.09	192.16	163.79	145.18	132.15
8000	719.24	385.05	274.39	219.62	187.18	165.92	151.03
9000	809.14	433.18	308.69	247.07	210.58	186.66	169.91
10000	899.05	481.31	342.99	274.52	233.98	207.40	188.78
11000	988.95	529.44	377.29	301.97	257.38	228.14	207.66
12000	1078.86	577.57	411.59	329.42	280.78	248.88	226.54
13000	1168.76	625.70	445.89	356.88	304.17	269.62	245.42
14000	1258.67	673.83	480.19	384.33	327.57	290.36	264.30
15000	1348.57	721.97	514.49	411.78	350.97	311.10	283.18
20000	1798.10	962.62	685.98	549.04	467.96	414.80	377.57
25000	2247.62	1203.28	857.48	686.30	584.95	518.50	471.96
30000	2697.14	1443.93	1028.98	823.56	701.94	622.20	566.35
35000	3146.67	1684.59	1200.47	960.82	818.93	725.89	660.74
40000	3596.19	1925.24	1371.97	1098.08	935.92	829.59	755.14
45000	4045.72	2165.90	1543.46	1235.34	1052.91	933.29	849.53
50000	4495.24	2406.55	1714.96	1372.60	1169.90	1036.99	943.92
55000	4944.76	2647.21	1886.45	1509.86	1286.89	1140.69	1038.31
56000	5034.67	2695.34	1920.75	1537.31	1310.29	1161.43	1057.19
57000	5124.57	2743.47	1955.05	1564.77	1333.69	1182.17	1076.07
58000	5214.48	2791.60	1989.35	1592.22	1357.09	1202.91	1094.95
59000	5304.38	2839.73	2023.65	1619.67	1380.49	1223.65	1113.82
60000	5394.29	2887.86	2057.95	1647.12	1403.88	1244.39	1132.70
61000	5484.19	2936.00	2092.25	1674.58	1427.28	1265.13	1151.58
62000	5574.10	2984.13	2126.55	1702.03	1450.68	1285.87	1170.46
63000	5664.00	3032.26	2160.85	1729.48	1474.08	1306.61	1189.34
64000	5753.91	3080.39	2195.15	1756.93	1497.48	1327.35	1208.22
65000	5843.81	3128.52	2229.45	1784.38	1520.87	1348.09	1227.10
70000	6293.34	3369.17	2400.94	1921.64	1637.86	1451.79	1321.49
75000	6742.86	3609.83	2572.44	2058.90	1754.85	1555.49	1415.88
80000	7192.38	3850.49	2743.93	2196.16	1871.85	1659.19	1510.27
85000	7641.91	4091.14	2915.43	2333.42	1988.84	1762.89	1604.66
90000	8091.43	4331.80	3086.93	2470.68	2105.83	1866.59	1699.05
95000	8540.96	4572.45	3258.42	2607.94	2222.82	1970.29	1793.45
100000	8990.48	4813.11	3429.92	2745.20	2339.81	2073.98	1887.84
105000	9440.00	5053.76	3601.41	2882.47	2456.80	2177.68	1982.23
110000	9889.53	5294.42	3772.91	3019.73	2573.79	2281.38	2076.62
120000	10788.57	5775.73	4115.90	3294.25	2807.77	2488.78	2265.41
130000	11687.62	6257.04	4458.89	3568.77	3041.75	2696.18	2454.19
140000	12586.67	6738.35	4801.88	3843.29	3275.73	2903.58	2642.97
150000	13485.72	7219.66	5144.88	4117.81	3509.71	3110.98	2831.76
160000	14384.77	7700.97	5487.87	4392.33	3743.69	3318.38	3020.54
175000	15733.34	8422.94	6002.36	4804.11	4094.66	3629.47	3303.72
200000	17980.96	9626.21	6859.84	5490.41	4679.61	4147.97	3775.68
250000	22476.20	12032.77	8574.79	6863.01	5849.52	5184.96	4719.60
500000	44952.39	24065.54	17149.59	13726.02	11699.03	10369.92	9439.19
1000000	89904.79	48131.07	34299.18	27452.05	23398.06	20739.85	18878.39

MONTHLY PAYMENTS 14.25%

AMOUNT	8 YEARS	9 YEARS	10 YEARS	11 YEARS	12 YEARS	13 YEARS	14 YEARS
100	1.75	1.65	1.57	1.50	1.45	1.41	1.38
200	3.50	3.30	3.14	3.01	2.91	2.82	2.75
500	8.76	8.24	7.84	7.52	7.26	7.06	6.89
1000	17.51	16.48	15.68	15.04	14.53	14.11	13.77
2000	35.03	32.96	31.35	30.08	29.06	28.23	27.54
3000	52.54	49.44	47.03	45.12	43.59	42.34	41.31
4000	70.06	65.92	62.71	60.16	58.12	56.45	55.08
5000	87.57	82.40	78.39	75.21	72.65	70.56	68.85
6000	105.08	98.88	94.06	90.25	87.18	84.68	82.62
7000	122.60	115.36	109.74	105.29	101.71	98.79	96.39
8000	140.11	131.84	125.42	120.33	116.24	112.90	110.16
9000	157.63	148.32	141.10	135.37	130.77	127.02	123.93
10000	175.14	164.80	156.77	150.41	145.29	141.13	137.70
11000	192.65	181.28	172.45	165.45	159.82	155.24	151.47
12000	210.17	197.76	188.13	180.49	174.35	169.35	165.24
13000	227.68	214.24	203.81	195.54	188.88	183.47	179.01
14000	245.20	230.73	219.48	210.58	203.41	197.58	192.78
15000	262.71	247.21	235.16	225.62	217.94	211.69	206.55
20000	350.28	329.61	313.55	300.82	290.59	282.26	275.40
25000	437.85	412.01	391.93	376.03	363.24	352.82	344.25
30000	525.42	494.41	470.32	451.24	435.88	423.38	413.10
35000	612.99	576.81	548.71	526.44	508.53	493.95	481.95
40000	700.56	659.22	627.09	601.65	581.18	564.51	550.80
45000	788.13	741.62	705.48	676.85	653.83	635.08	619.65
50000	875.70	824.02	783.87	752.06	726.47	705.64	688.50
55000	963.27	906.42	862.25	827.26	799.12	776.20	757.35
56000	980.79	922.90	877.93	842.31	813.65	790.32	771.12
57000	998.30	939.38	893.61	857.35	828.18	804.43	784.89
58000	1015.82	955.86	909.28	872.39	842.71	818.54	798.66
59000	1033.33	972.34	924.96	887.43	857.24	832.66	812.43
60000	1050.84	988.82	940.64	902.47	871.77	846.77	826.20
61000	1068.36	1005.30	956.32	917.51	886.30	860.88	839.97
62000	1085.87	1021.78	971.99	932.55	900.83	874.99	853.74
63000	1103.39	1038.26	987.67	947.59	915.36	889.11	867.51
64000	1120.90	1054.74	1003.35	962.64	929.89	903.22	881.28
65000	1138.42	1071.22	1019.03	977.68	944.42	917.33	895.05
70000	1225.99	1153.63	1097.41	1052.88	1017.06	987.90	963.90
75000	1313.56	1236.03	1175.80	1128.09	1089.71	1058.46	1032.75
80000	1401.13	1318.43	1254.18	1203.29	1162.36	1129.02	1101.60
85000	1488.70	1400.83	1332.57	1278.50	1235.01	1199.59	1170.45
90000	1576.27	1483.23	1410.96	1353.71	1307.65	1270.15	1239.31
95000	1663.84	1565.64	1489.34	1428.91	1380.30	1340.72	1308.16
100000	1751.41	1648.04	1567.73	1504.12	1452.95	1411.28	1377.01
105000	1838.98	1730.44	1646.12	1579.32	1525.60	1481.84	1445.86
110000	1926.55	1812.84	1724.50	1654.53	1598.24	1552.41	1514.71
120000	2101.69	1977.65	1881.28	1804.94	1743.54	1693.54	1652.41
130000	2276.83	2142.45	2038.05	1955.35	1888.83	1834.66	1790.11
140000	2451.97	2307.25	2194.82	2105.77	2034.13	1975.79	1927.81
150000	2627.11	2472.06	2351.60	2256.18	2179.42	2116.92	2065.51
160000	2802.25	2636.86	2508.37	2406.59	2324.72	2258.05	2203.21
175000	3064.96	2884.07	2743.53	2632.21	2542.66	2469.74	2409.76
200000	3502.82	3296.08	3135.46	3008.24	2905.90	2822.56	2754.01
250000	4378.52	4120.10	3919.33	3760.29	3632.37	3528.20	3442.51
500000	8757.04	8240.19	7838.66	7520.59	7264.75	7056.40	6885.03
1000000	17514.08	16480.38	15677.31	15041.18	14529.49	14112.80	13770.06

14.25% MONTHLY PAYMENTS

AMOUNT	15 YEARS	16 YEARS	17 YEARS	18 YEARS	19 YEARS	20 YEARS	21 YEARS
100	1.35	1.32	1.30	1.29	1.27	1.26	1.25
200	2.70	2.65	2.61	2.58	2.55	2.52	2.50
500	6.74	6.62	6.52	6.44	6.37	6.31	6.26
1000	13.49	13.25	13.05	12.88	12.74	12.62	12.51
2000	26.97	26.50	26.10	25.76	25.48	25.23	25.03
3000	40.46	39.75	39.15	38.64	38.22	37.85	37.54
4000	53.94	52.99	52.20	51.52	50.95	50.47	50.06
5000	67.43	66.24	65.25	64.40	63.69	63.09	62.57
6000	80.91	79.49	78.29	77.29	76.43	75.70	75.08
7000	94.40	92.74	91.34	90.17	89.17	88.32	87.60
8000	107.89	105.99	104.39	103.05	101.91	100.94	100.11
9000	121.37	119.24	117.44	115.93	114.65	113.55	112.62
10000	134.86	132.48	130.49	128.81	127.38	126.17	125.14
11000	148.34	145.73	143.54	141.69	140.12	138.79	137.65
12000	161.83	158.98	156.59	154.57	152.86	151.41	150.17
13000	175.32	172.23	169.64	167.45	165.60	164.02	162.68
14000	188.80	185.48	182.69	180.33	178.34	176.64	175.19
15000	202.29	198.73	195.74	193.21	191.08	189.26	187.71
20000	269.72	264.97	260.98	257.62	254.77	252.34	250.28
25000	337.14	331.21	326.23	322.02	318.46	315.43	312.85
30000	404.57	397.45	391.47	386.43	382.15	378.52	375.42
35000	472.00	463.70	456.72	450.83	445.84	441.60	437.99
40000	539.43	529.94	521.96	515.23	509.53	504.69	500.56
45000	606.86	596.18	587.21	579.64	573.23	567.77	563.12
50000	674.29	662.42	652.45	644.04	636.92	630.86	625.69
55000	741.72	728.66	717.70	708.45	700.61	693.95	688.26
56000	755.20	741.91	730.75	721.33	713.35	706.56	700.78
57000	768.69	755.16	743.80	734.21	726.09	719.18	713.29
58000	782.18	768.41	756.85	747.09	738.82	731.80	725.81
59000	795.66	781.66	769.90	759.97	751.56	744.41	738.32
60000	809.15	794.91	782.95	772.85	764.30	757.03	750.83
61000	822.63	808.15	795.99	785.73	777.04	769.65	763.35
62000	836.12	821.40	809.04	798.61	789.78	782.27	775.86
63000	849.61	834.65	822.09	811.49	802.52	794.88	788.37
64000	863.09	847.90	835.14	824.38	815.25	807.50	800.89
65000	876.58	861.15	848.19	837.26	827.99	820.12	813.40
70000	944.01	927.39	913.44	901.66	891.68	883.20	875.97
75000	1011.43	993.63	978.68	966.07	955.38	946.29	938.54
80000	1078.86	1059.87	1043.93	1030.47	1019.07	1009.38	1001.11
85000	1146.29	1126.12	1109.17	1094.87	1082.76	1072.46	1063.68
90000	1213.72	1192.36	1174.42	1159.28	1146.45	1135.55	1126.25
95000	1281.15	1258.60	1239.66	1223.68	1210.14	1198.63	1188.82
100000	1348.58	1324.84	1304.91	1288.09	1273.84	1261.72	1251.39
105000	1416.01	1391.09	1370.15	1352.49	1337.53	1324.80	1313.96
110000	1483.44	1457.33	1435.40	1416.90	1401.22	1387.89	1376.53
120000	1618.30	1589.81	1565.89	1545.70	1528.60	1514.06	1501.67
130000	1753.15	1722.30	1696.38	1674.51	1655.99	1640.23	1626.80
140000	1888.01	1854.78	1826.87	1803.32	1783.37	1766.41	1751.94
150000	2022.87	1987.26	1957.36	1932.13	1910.75	1892.58	1877.08
160000	2157.73	2119.75	2087.85	2060.94	2038.14	2018.75	2002.22
175000	2360.01	2318.48	2283.59	2254.15	2229.21	2208.01	2189.93
200000	2697.16	2649.69	2609.82	2576.17	2547.67	2523.44	2502.78
250000	3371.45	3312.11	3262.27	3220.22	3184.59	3154.30	3128.47
500000	6742.90	6624.21	6524.54	6440.44	6369.18	6308.59	6256.94
1000000	13485.80	13248.43	13049.08	12880.87	12738.35	12617.19	12513.88

MONTHLY PAYMENTS 14.25%

AMOUNT	22 YEARS	23 YEARS	24 YEARS	25 YEARS	30 YEARS	35 YEARS	40 YEARS
100	1.24	1.23	1.23	1.22	1.20	1.20	1.19
200	2.49	2.47	2.46	2.45	2.41	2.39	2.38
500	6.21	6.17	6.14	6.11	6.02	5.98	5.96
1000	12.43	12.35	12.29	12.23	12.05	11.96	11.92
2000	24.85	24.70	24.57	24.46	24.09	23.92	23.83
3000	37.28	37.05	36.86	36.69	36.14	35.88	35.75
4000	49.70	49.40	49.14	48.92	48.19	47.84	47.66
5000	62.13	61.75	61.43	61.15	60.23	59.80	59.58
6000	74.55	74.10	73.71	73.38	72.28	71.75	71.50
7000	86.98	86.45	86.00	85.60	84.33	83.71	83.41
8000	99.40	98.80	98.28	97.83	96.37	95.67	95.33
9000	111.83	111.15	110.57	110.06	108.42	107.63	107.25
10000	124.26	123.50	122.85	122.29	120.47	119.59	119.16
11000	136.68	135.85	135.14	134.52	132.52	131.55	131.08
12000	149.11	148.20	147.42	146.75	144.56	143.51	142.99
13000	161.53	160.55	159.71	158.98	156.61	155.47	154.91
14000	173.96	172.90	171.99	171.21	168.66	167.43	166.83
15000	186.38	185.25	184.28	183.44	180.70	179.39	178.74
20000	248.51	247.00	245.70	244.59	240.94	239.18	238.32
25000	310.64	308.75	307.13	305.73	301.17	298.98	297.91
30000	372.77	370.50	368.55	366.88	361.41	358.77	357.49
35000	434.90	432.25	429.98	428.02	421.64	418.57	417.07
40000	497.02	494.00	491.40	489.17	481.87	478.36	476.65
45000	559.15	555.75	552.83	550.32	542.11	538.16	536.23
50000	621.28	617.50	614.25	611.46	602.34	597.95	595.81
55000	683.41	679.25	675.68	672.61	662.58	657.75	655.39
56000	695.83	691.60	687.96	684.84	674.62	669.71	667.31
57000	708.26	703.95	700.25	697.07	686.67	681.66	679.23
58000	720.68	716.30	712.53	709.30	698.72	693.62	691.14
59000	733.11	728.65	724.82	721.53	710.77	705.58	703.06
60000	745.54	741.00	737.10	733.76	722.81	717.54	714.97
61000	757.96	753.35	749.39	745.99	734.86	729.50	726.89
62000	770.39	765.70	761.67	758.22	746.91	741.46	738.81
63000	782.81	778.05	773.96	770.44	758.95	753.42	750.72
64000	795.24	790.40	786.24	782.67	771.00	765.38	762.64
65000	807.66	802.75	798.53	794.90	783.05	777.34	774.56
70000	869.79	864.50	859.95	856.05	843.28	837.13	834.14
75000	931.92	926.25	921.38	917.20	903.52	896.93	893.72
80000	994.05	988.00	982.80	978.34	963.75	956.72	953.30
85000	1056.17	1049.75	1044.23	1039.49	1023.98	1016.52	1012.88
90000	1118.30	1111.50	1105.65	1100.63	1084.22	1076.31	1072.46
95000	1180.43	1173.25	1167.08	1161.78	1144.45	1136.11	1132.04
100000	1242.56	1235.00	1228.51	1222.93	1204.69	1195.90	1191.62
105000	1304.69	1296.75	1289.93	1284.07	1264.92	1255.70	1251.20
110000	1366.81	1358.49	1351.36	1345.22	1325.16	1315.49	1310.79
120000	1491.07	1481.99	1474.21	1467.51	1445.62	1435.08	1429.95
130000	1615.33	1605.49	1597.06	1589.81	1566.09	1554.67	1549.11
140000	1739.58	1728.99	1719.91	1712.10	1686.56	1674.26	1668.27
150000	1863.84	1852.49	1842.76	1834.39	1807.03	1793.85	1787.43
160000	1988.09	1975.99	1965.61	1956.68	1927.50	1913.44	1906.60
175000	2174.48	2161.24	2149.88	2140.12	2108.20	2092.83	2085.34
200000	2485.12	2469.99	2457.01	2445.86	2409.37	2391.81	2383.25
250000	3106.40	3087.49	3071.26	3057.32	3011.72	2989.76	2979.06
500000	6212.79	6174.98	6142.53	6114.64	6023.44	5979.51	5958.12
1000000	12425.58	12349.95	12285.05	12229.28	12046.87	11959.03	11916.23

14.50%　　　　MONTHLY PAYMENTS

AMOUNT	1 YEAR	2 YEARS	3 YEARS	4 YEARS	5 YEARS	6 YEARS	7 YEARS
100	9.00	4.82	3.44	2.76	2.35	2.09	1.90
200	18.00	9.65	6.88	5.52	4.71	4.17	3.80
500	45.01	24.12	17.21	13.79	11.76	10.44	9.51
1000	90.02	48.25	34.42	27.58	23.53	20.87	19.02
2000	180.05	96.50	68.84	55.16	47.06	41.75	38.03
3000	270.07	144.75	103.26	82.73	70.58	62.62	57.05
4000	360.09	193.00	137.68	110.31	94.11	83.50	76.07
5000	450.11	241.25	172.10	137.89	117.64	104.37	95.09
6000	540.14	289.50	206.53	165.47	141.17	125.25	114.10
7000	630.16	337.75	240.95	193.05	164.70	146.12	133.12
8000	720.18	386.00	275.37	220.62	188.23	167.00	152.14
9000	810.20	434.24	309.79	248.20	211.75	187.87	171.16
10000	900.23	482.49	344.21	275.78	235.28	208.74	190.17
11000	990.25	530.74	378.63	303.36	258.81	229.62	209.19
12000	1080.27	578.99	413.05	330.94	282.34	250.49	228.21
13000	1170.29	627.24	447.47	358.51	305.87	271.37	247.22
14000	1260.32	675.49	481.89	386.09	329.40	292.24	266.24
15000	1350.34	723.73	516.31	413.67	352.92	313.12	285.26
20000	1800.45	964.99	688.42	551.56	470.57	417.49	380.35
25000	2250.56	1206.24	860.52	689.45	588.21	521.86	475.43
30000	2700.68	1447.48	1032.63	827.34	705.85	626.23	570.52
35000	3150.79	1688.73	1204.73	965.23	823.49	730.60	665.61
40000	3600.90	1929.98	1376.84	1103.12	941.13	834.98	760.69
45000	4051.01	2171.22	1548.94	1241.01	1058.77	939.35	855.78
50000	4501.13	2412.47	1721.05	1378.90	1176.41	1043.72	950.87
55000	4951.24	2653.72	1893.15	1516.79	1294.06	1148.09	1045.95
56000	5041.26	2701.97	1927.57	1544.37	1317.58	1168.97	1064.97
57000	5131.29	2750.22	1962.00	1571.94	1341.11	1189.84	1083.99
58000	5221.31	2798.47	1996.42	1599.52	1364.64	1210.72	1103.00
59000	5311.33	2846.72	2030.84	1627.10	1388.17	1231.59	1122.02
60000	5401.35	2894.97	2065.26	1654.68	1411.70	1252.47	1141.04
61000	5491.38	2943.22	2099.68	1682.26	1435.23	1273.34	1160.06
62000	5581.40	2991.46	2134.10	1709.83	1458.75	1294.21	1179.07
63000	5671.42	3039.71	2168.52	1737.41	1482.28	1315.09	1198.09
64000	5761.44	3087.96	2202.94	1764.99	1505.81	1335.96	1217.11
65000	5851.47	3136.21	2237.36	1792.57	1529.34	1356.84	1236.12
70000	6301.58	3377.46	2409.47	1930.46	1646.98	1461.21	1331.21
75000	6751.69	3618.71	2581.57	2068.35	1764.62	1565.58	1426.30
80000	7201.80	3859.95	2753.68	2206.24	1882.26	1669.95	1521.38
85000	7651.92	4101.20	2925.78	2344.13	1999.90	1774.33	1616.47
90000	8102.03	4342.45	3097.89	2482.02	2117.55	1878.70	1711.56
95000	8552.14	4583.70	3269.99	2619.91	2235.19	1983.07	1806.64
100000	9002.25	4824.94	3442.10	2757.80	2352.83	2087.44	1901.73
105000	9452.37	5066.19	3614.20	2895.69	2470.47	2191.81	1996.82
110000	9902.48	5307.44	3786.31	3033.57	2588.11	2296.19	2091.90
120000	10802.71	5789.93	4130.52	3309.35	2823.39	2504.93	2282.08
130000	11702.93	6272.43	4474.73	3585.13	3058.68	2713.68	2472.25
140000	12603.16	6754.92	4818.94	3860.91	3293.96	2922.42	2662.42
150000	13503.38	7237.41	5163.15	4136.69	3529.04	3131.16	2852.60
160000	14403.61	7719.91	5507.36	4412.47	3764.52	3339.91	3042.77
175000	15753.95	8443.65	6023.67	4826.14	4117.45	3653.02	3328.03
200000	18004.51	9649.89	6884.20	5515.59	4705.66	4174.89	3803.46
250000	22505.64	12062.36	8605.24	6894.49	5882.07	5218.61	4754.33
500000	45011.27	24124.71	17210.49	13788.98	11764.14	10437.21	9508.65
1000000	90022.55	48249.43	34420.98	27577.95	23528.28	20874.43	19017.30

MONTHLY PAYMENTS 14.50%

AMOUNT	8 YEARS	9 YEARS	10 YEARS	11 YEARS	12 YEARS	13 YEARS	14 YEARS
100	1.77	1.66	1.58	1.52	1.47	1.43	1.39
200	3.53	3.33	3.17	3.04	2.94	2.86	2.79
500	8.83	8.31	7.91	7.60	7.34	7.14	6.97
1000	17.66	16.63	15.83	15.20	14.69	14.28	13.94
2000	35.31	33.26	31.66	30.39	29.38	28.55	27.87
3000	52.97	49.88	47.49	45.59	44.07	42.83	41.81
4000	70.63	66.51	63.31	60.79	58.75	57.10	55.74
5000	88.29	83.14	79.14	75.98	73.44	71.38	69.68
6000	105.94	99.77	94.97	91.18	88.13	85.65	83.62
7000	123.60	116.39	110.80	106.38	102.82	99.93	97.55
8000	141.26	133.02	126.63	121.57	117.51	114.20	111.49
9000	158.92	149.65	142.46	136.77	132.20	128.48	125.42
10000	176.57	166.28	158.29	151.96	146.88	142.75	139.36
11000	194.23	182.90	174.12	167.16	161.57	157.03	153.30
12000	211.89	199.53	189.94	182.36	176.26	171.30	167.23
13000	229.54	216.16	205.77	197.55	190.95	185.58	181.17
14000	247.20	232.79	221.60	212.75	205.64	199.86	195.10
15000	264.86	249.42	237.43	227.95	220.33	214.13	209.04
20000	353.15	332.55	316.57	303.93	293.77	285.51	278.72
25000	441.43	415.69	395.72	379.91	367.21	356.88	348.40
30000	529.72	498.83	474.86	455.89	440.65	428.26	418.08
35000	618.00	581.97	554.00	531.88	514.10	499.64	487.76
40000	706.29	665.11	633.15	607.86	587.54	571.02	557.44
45000	794.58	748.25	712.29	683.84	660.98	642.39	627.12
50000	882.86	831.39	791.43	759.82	734.42	713.77	696.80
55000	971.15	914.52	870.58	835.80	807.87	785.15	766.48
56000	988.81	931.15	886.41	851.00	822.56	799.42	780.42
57000	1006.46	947.78	902.23	866.20	837.24	813.70	794.35
58000	1024.12	964.41	918.06	881.39	851.93	827.97	808.29
59000	1041.78	981.04	933.89	896.59	866.62	842.25	822.23
60000	1059.44	997.66	949.72	911.79	881.31	856.52	836.16
61000	1077.09	1014.29	965.55	926.98	896.00	870.80	850.10
62000	1094.75	1030.92	981.38	942.18	910.69	885.07	864.03
63000	1112.41	1047.55	997.21	957.38	925.37	899.35	877.97
64000	1130.06	1064.17	1013.04	972.57	940.06	913.62	891.91
65000	1147.72	1080.80	1028.86	987.77	954.75	927.90	905.84
70000	1236.01	1163.94	1108.01	1063.75	1028.19	999.28	975.52
75000	1324.29	1247.08	1187.15	1139.73	1101.64	1070.65	1045.20
80000	1412.58	1330.22	1266.29	1215.72	1175.08	1142.03	1114.88
85000	1500.87	1413.36	1345.44	1291.70	1248.52	1213.41	1184.56
90000	1589.15	1496.49	1424.58	1367.68	1321.96	1284.78	1254.24
95000	1677.44	1579.63	1503.72	1443.66	1395.41	1356.16	1323.92
100000	1765.73	1662.77	1582.87	1519.64	1468.85	1427.54	1393.60
105000	1854.01	1745.91	1662.01	1595.63	1542.29	1498.91	1463.28
110000	1942.30	1829.05	1741.15	1671.61	1615.73	1570.29	1532.96
120000	2118.87	1995.33	1899.44	1823.57	1762.62	1713.05	1672.32
130000	2295.44	2161.60	2057.73	1975.54	1909.50	1855.80	1811.68
140000	2472.02	2327.88	2216.02	2127.50	2056.39	1998.55	1951.04
150000	2648.59	2494.16	2374.30	2279.47	2203.27	2141.31	2090.41
160000	2825.16	2660.44	2532.59	2431.43	2350.16	2284.06	2229.77
175000	3090.02	2909.85	2770.02	2659.38	2570.49	2498.19	2438.81
200000	3531.45	3325.54	3165.74	3039.29	2937.70	2855.08	2787.21
250000	4414.31	4156.93	3957.17	3799.11	3672.12	3568.84	3484.01
500000	8828.63	8313.86	7914.34	7598.22	7344.24	7137.69	6968.02
1000000	17657.26	16627.72	15828.68	15196.44	14688.49	14275.38	13936.03

14.50% MONTHLY PAYMENTS

AMOUNT	15 YEARS	16 YEARS	17 YEARS	18 YEARS	19 YEARS	20 YEARS	21 YEARS
100	1.37	1.34	1.32	1.31	1.29	1.28	1.27
200	2.73	2.68	2.64	2.61	2.58	2.56	2.54
500	6.83	6.71	6.61	6.53	6.46	6.40	6.35
1000	13.66	13.42	13.22	13.06	12.92	12.80	12.70
2000	27.31	26.84	26.45	26.12	25.84	25.60	25.40
3000	40.97	40.26	39.67	39.18	38.76	38.40	38.10
4000	54.62	53.68	52.90	52.23	51.68	51.20	50.80
5000	68.28	67.10	66.12	65.29	64.59	64.00	63.49
6000	81.93	80.52	79.35	78.35	77.51	76.80	76.19
7000	95.59	93.94	92.57	91.41	90.43	89.60	88.89
8000	109.24	107.37	105.79	104.47	103.35	102.40	101.59
9000	122.90	120.79	119.02	117.53	116.27	115.20	114.29
10000	136.55	134.21	132.24	130.59	129.19	128.00	126.99
11000	150.21	147.63	145.47	143.65	142.11	140.80	139.69
12000	163.86	161.05	158.69	156.70	155.03	153.60	152.39
13000	177.52	174.47	171.92	169.76	167.94	166.40	165.09
14000	191.17	187.89	185.14	182.82	180.86	179.20	177.78
15000	204.83	201.31	198.36	195.88	193.78	192.00	190.48
20000	273.10	268.41	264.48	261.17	258.38	256.00	253.98
25000	341.38	335.52	330.61	326.47	322.97	320.00	317.47
30000	409.65	402.62	396.73	391.76	387.56	384.00	380.97
35000	477.93	469.72	462.85	457.06	452.16	448.00	444.46
40000	546.20	536.83	528.97	522.35	516.75	512.00	507.96
45000	614.48	603.93	595.09	587.64	581.34	576.00	571.45
50000	682.75	671.04	661.21	652.94	645.94	640.00	634.94
55000	751.03	738.14	727.33	718.23	710.53	704.00	698.44
56000	764.68	751.56	740.56	731.29	723.45	716.80	711.14
57000	778.34	764.98	753.78	744.35	736.37	729.60	723.84
58000	791.99	778.40	767.01	757.41	749.29	742.40	736.54
59000	805.65	791.82	780.23	770.47	762.21	755.20	749.23
60000	819.30	805.24	793.45	783.52	775.13	768.00	761.93
61000	832.96	818.66	806.68	796.58	788.04	780.80	774.63
62000	846.61	832.08	819.90	809.64	800.96	793.60	787.33
63000	860.27	845.50	833.13	822.70	813.88	806.40	800.03
64000	873.92	858.92	846.35	835.76	826.80	819.20	812.73
65000	887.58	872.35	859.58	848.82	839.72	832.00	825.43
70000	955.85	939.45	925.70	914.11	904.31	896.00	888.92
75000	1024.13	1006.55	991.82	979.41	968.91	960.00	952.42
80000	1092.40	1073.66	1057.94	1044.70	1033.50	1024.00	1015.91
85000	1160.68	1140.76	1124.06	1109.99	1098.09	1088.00	1079.41
90000	1228.95	1207.86	1190.18	1175.29	1162.69	1152.00	1142.90
95000	1297.23	1274.97	1256.30	1240.58	1227.28	1216.00	1206.39
100000	1365.50	1342.07	1322.42	1305.87	1291.88	1280.00	1269.89
105000	1433.78	1409.17	1388.55	1371.17	1356.47	1344.00	1333.38
110000	1502.05	1476.28	1454.67	1436.46	1421.06	1408.00	1396.88
120000	1638.60	1610.48	1586.91	1567.05	1550.25	1536.00	1523.87
130000	1775.15	1744.69	1719.15	1697.64	1679.44	1664.00	1650.86
140000	1911.70	1878.90	1851.39	1828.22	1808.63	1792.00	1777.84
150000	2048.25	2013.11	1983.64	1958.81	1937.81	1920.00	1904.83
160000	2184.80	2147.31	2115.88	2089.40	2067.00	2048.00	2031.82
175000	2389.63	2348.62	2314.24	2285.28	2260.78	2240.00	2222.30
200000	2731.00	2684.14	2644.85	2611.75	2583.75	2560.00	2539.78
250000	3413.75	3355.18	3306.06	3264.69	3229.69	3199.99	3174.72
500000	6827.50	6710.35	6612.12	6529.37	6459.38	6399.99	6349.44
1000000	13655.01	13420.70	13224.24	13058.74	12918.76	12799.98	12698.89

MONTHLY PAYMENTS 14.50%

AMOUNT	22 YEARS	23 YEARS	24 YEARS	25 YEARS	30 YEARS	35 YEARS	40 YEARS
100	1.26	1.25	1.25	1.24	1.22	1.22	1.21
200	2.52	2.51	2.50	2.48	2.45	2.43	2.42
500	6.31	6.27	6.24	6.21	6.12	6.08	6.06
1000	12.61	12.54	12.48	12.42	12.25	12.16	12.12
2000	25.23	25.08	24.95	24.84	24.49	24.32	24.24
3000	37.84	37.62	37.43	37.26	36.74	36.49	36.36
4000	50.45	50.16	49.90	49.69	48.98	48.65	48.49
5000	63.06	62.69	62.38	62.11	61.23	60.81	60.61
6000	75.68	75.23	74.85	74.53	73.47	72.97	72.73
7000	88.29	87.77	87.33	86.95	85.72	85.13	84.85
8000	100.90	100.31	99.81	99.37	97.96	97.29	96.97
9000	113.51	112.85	112.28	111.79	110.21	109.46	109.09
10000	126.13	125.39	124.76	124.22	122.46	121.62	121.21
11000	138.74	137.93	137.23	136.64	134.70	133.78	133.33
12000	151.35	150.47	149.71	149.06	146.95	145.94	145.46
13000	163.96	163.01	162.19	161.48	159.19	158.10	157.58
14000	176.58	175.54	174.66	173.90	171.44	170.26	169.70
15000	189.19	188.08	187.14	186.32	183.68	182.43	181.82
20000	252.25	250.78	249.52	248.43	244.91	243.23	242.43
25000	315.32	313.47	311.89	310.54	306.14	304.04	303.03
30000	378.38	376.17	374.27	372.65	367.37	364.85	363.64
35000	441.44	438.86	436.65	434.76	428.59	425.66	424.25
40000	504.51	501.56	499.03	496.87	489.82	486.47	484.85
45000	567.57	564.25	561.41	558.97	551.05	547.28	545.46
50000	630.63	626.95	623.79	621.08	612.28	608.09	606.07
55000	693.70	689.64	686.17	683.19	673.51	668.89	666.67
56000	706.31	702.18	698.64	695.61	685.75	681.06	678.79
57000	718.92	714.72	711.12	708.03	698.00	693.22	690.92
58000	731.53	727.26	723.60	720.45	710.24	705.38	703.04
59000	744.15	739.80	736.07	732.88	722.49	717.54	715.16
60000	756.76	752.34	748.55	745.30	734.73	729.70	727.28
61000	769.37	764.87	761.02	757.72	746.98	741.86	739.40
62000	781.98	777.41	773.50	770.14	759.22	754.03	751.52
63000	794.60	789.95	785.97	782.56	771.47	766.19	763.64
64000	807.21	802.49	798.45	794.98	783.72	778.35	775.77
65000	819.82	815.03	810.93	807.41	795.96	790.51	787.89
70000	882.89	877.72	873.30	869.51	857.19	851.32	848.49
75000	945.95	940.42	935.68	931.62	918.42	912.13	909.10
80000	1009.01	1003.11	998.06	993.73	979.64	972.94	969.71
85000	1072.07	1065.81	1060.44	1055.84	1040.87	1033.74	1030.31
90000	1135.14	1128.50	1122.82	1117.95	1102.10	1094.55	1090.92
95000	1198.20	1191.20	1185.20	1180.05	1163.33	1155.36	1151.53
100000	1261.26	1253.89	1247.58	1242.16	1224.56	1216.17	1212.13
105000	1324.33	1316.59	1309.96	1304.27	1285.78	1276.98	1272.74
110000	1387.39	1379.28	1372.34	1366.38	1347.01	1337.79	1333.35
120000	1513.52	1504.67	1497.09	1490.60	1469.47	1459.40	1454.56
130000	1639.64	1630.06	1621.85	1614.81	1591.92	1581.02	1575.77
140000	1765.77	1755.45	1746.61	1739.03	1714.38	1702.64	1696.99
150000	1891.90	1880.84	1871.37	1863.24	1836.83	1824.26	1818.20
160000	2018.02	2006.23	1996.12	1987.46	1959.29	1945.87	1939.41
175000	2207.21	2194.31	2183.26	2173.79	2142.97	2128.30	2121.23
200000	2522.53	2507.78	2495.16	2484.33	2449.11	2432.34	2424.27
250000	3153.16	3134.73	3118.95	3105.41	3061.39	3040.43	3030.33
500000	6306.32	6269.46	6237.89	6210.81	6122.78	6080.85	6060.66
1000000	12612.64	12538.92	12475.78	12421.63	12245.56	12161.71	12121.33

14.75%　　　　MONTHLY PAYMENTS

AMOUNT	1 YEAR	2 YEARS	3 YEARS	4 YEARS	5 YEARS	6 YEARS	7 YEARS
100	9.01	4.84	3.45	2.77	2.37	2.10	1.92
200	18.03	9.67	6.91	5.54	4.73	4.20	3.83
500	45.07	24.18	17.27	13.85	11.83	10.50	9.58
1000	90.14	48.37	34.54	27.70	23.66	21.01	19.16
2000	180.28	96.74	69.09	55.41	47.32	42.02	38.31
3000	270.42	145.10	103.63	83.11	70.98	63.03	57.47
4000	360.56	193.47	138.17	110.82	94.64	84.04	76.63
5000	450.70	241.84	172.72	138.52	118.29	105.05	95.78
6000	540.84	290.21	207.26	166.23	141.95	126.06	114.94
7000	630.98	338.58	241.80	193.93	165.61	147.07	134.10
8000	721.12	386.94	276.34	221.63	189.27	168.08	153.25
9000	811.26	435.31	310.89	249.34	212.93	189.09	172.41
10000	901.40	483.68	345.43	277.04	236.59	210.09	191.57
11000	991.54	532.05	379.97	304.75	260.25	231.10	210.72
12000	1081.68	580.42	414.52	332.45	283.91	252.11	229.88
13000	1171.83	628.78	449.06	360.15	307.57	273.12	249.04
14000	1261.97	677.15	483.60	387.86	331.22	294.13	268.19
15000	1352.11	725.52	518.15	415.56	354.88	315.14	287.35
20000	1802.81	967.36	690.86	554.08	473.18	420.19	383.14
25000	2253.51	1209.20	863.58	692.60	591.47	525.24	478.92
30000	2704.21	1451.04	1036.29	831.13	709.77	630.28	574.70
35000	3154.91	1692.88	1209.01	969.65	828.06	735.33	670.49
40000	3605.62	1934.72	1381.72	1108.17	946.36	840.38	766.27
45000	4056.32	2176.56	1554.44	1246.69	1064.65	945.43	862.05
50000	4507.02	2418.40	1727.15	1385.21	1182.95	1050.47	957.84
55000	4957.72	2660.24	1899.87	1523.73	1301.24	1155.52	1053.62
56000	5047.86	2708.61	1934.41	1551.43	1324.90	1176.53	1072.78
57000	5138.00	2756.97	1968.95	1579.14	1348.56	1197.54	1091.94
58000	5228.14	2805.34	2003.50	1606.84	1372.22	1218.55	1111.09
59000	5318.28	2853.71	2038.04	1634.55	1395.88	1239.56	1130.25
60000	5408.42	2902.08	2072.58	1662.25	1419.53	1260.57	1149.41
61000	5498.56	2950.45	2107.12	1689.96	1443.19	1281.58	1168.56
62000	5588.70	2998.81	2141.67	1717.66	1466.85	1302.59	1187.72
63000	5678.84	3047.18	2176.21	1745.36	1490.51	1323.60	1206.88
64000	5768.98	3095.55	2210.75	1773.07	1514.17	1344.61	1226.03
65000	5859.13	3143.92	2245.30	1800.77	1537.83	1365.62	1245.19
70000	6309.83	3385.26	2418.01	1939.29	1656.12	1470.66	1340.97
75000	6760.53	3627.60	2590.73	2077.81	1774.42	1575.71	1436.76
80000	7211.23	3869.44	2763.44	2216.33	1892.71	1680.76	1532.54
85000	7661.93	4111.28	2936.16	2354.86	2011.01	1785.81	1628.32
90000	8112.63	4353.12	3108.87	2493.38	2129.30	1890.85	1724.11
95000	8563.34	4594.96	3281.59	2631.90	2247.60	1995.90	1819.89
100000	9014.04	4836.80	3454.30	2770.42	2365.89	2100.95	1915.68
105000	9464.74	5078.64	3627.02	2908.94	2484.18	2206.00	2011.46
110000	9915.44	5320.47	3799.73	3047.46	2602.48	2311.04	2107.24
120000	10816.85	5804.15	4145.16	3324.50	2839.07	2521.14	2298.81
130000	11718.25	6287.83	4490.59	3601.54	3075.66	2731.23	2490.38
140000	12619.65	6771.51	4836.02	3878.59	3312.25	2941.33	2681.95
150000	13521.06	7255.19	5181.45	4155.63	3548.84	3151.42	2873.51
160000	14422.46	7738.87	5526.88	4432.67	3785.42	3361.52	3065.08
175000	15774.57	8464.39	6045.03	4848.23	4140.31	3676.66	3352.43
200000	18028.08	9673.59	6908.61	5540.84	4731.78	4201.90	3831.35
250000	22535.10	12091.99	8635.76	6926.05	5914.73	5252.37	4789.19
500000	45070.19	24183.98	17271.51	13852.09	11829.45	10504.74	9578.38
1000000	90140.39	48367.95	34543.03	27704.19	23658.90	21009.48	19156.76

MONTHLY PAYMENTS   14.75%

AMOUNT	8 YEARS	9 YEARS	10 YEARS	11 YEARS	12 YEARS	13 YEARS	14 YEARS
100	1.78	1.68	1.60	1.54	1.48	1.44	1.41
200	3.56	3.36	3.20	3.07	2.97	2.89	2.82
500	8.90	8.39	7.99	7.68	7.42	7.22	7.05
1000	17.80	16.78	15.98	15.35	14.85	14.44	14.10
2000	35.60	33.55	31.96	30.70	29.70	28.88	28.21
3000	53.40	50.33	47.94	46.06	44.54	43.32	42.31
4000	71.20	67.10	63.92	61.41	59.39	57.75	56.41
5000	89.01	83.88	79.90	76.76	74.24	72.19	70.51
6000	106.81	100.65	95.88	92.11	89.09	86.63	84.62
7000	124.61	117.43	111.87	107.47	103.94	101.07	98.72
8000	142.41	134.21	127.85	122.82	118.79	115.51	112.82
9000	160.21	150.98	143.83	138.17	133.63	129.95	126.93
10000	178.01	167.76	159.81	153.52	148.48	144.39	141.03
11000	195.81	184.53	175.79	168.88	163.33	158.83	155.13
12000	213.61	201.31	191.77	184.23	178.18	173.26	169.23
13000	231.41	218.08	207.75	199.58	193.03	187.70	183.34
14000	249.21	234.86	223.73	214.93	207.88	202.14	197.44
15000	267.02	251.64	239.71	230.29	222.72	216.58	211.54
20000	356.02	335.51	319.61	307.05	296.97	288.77	282.06
25000	445.03	419.39	399.52	383.81	371.21	360.97	352.57
30000	534.03	503.27	479.42	460.57	445.45	433.16	423.08
35000	623.04	587.15	559.33	537.34	519.69	505.36	493.60
40000	712.04	671.03	639.23	614.10	593.93	577.55	564.11
45000	801.05	754.91	719.13	690.86	668.17	649.74	634.63
50000	890.05	838.79	799.04	767.62	742.41	721.94	705.14
55000	979.06	922.66	878.94	844.38	816.65	794.13	775.65
56000	996.86	939.44	894.92	859.74	831.50	808.57	789.76
57000	1014.66	956.22	910.90	875.09	846.35	823.01	803.86
58000	1032.46	972.99	926.88	890.44	861.20	837.45	817.96
59000	1050.26	989.77	942.86	905.79	876.05	851.89	832.07
60000	1068.06	1006.54	958.84	921.15	890.90	866.32	846.17
61000	1085.86	1023.32	974.83	936.50	905.74	880.76	860.27
62000	1103.66	1040.09	990.81	951.85	920.59	895.20	874.37
63000	1121.47	1056.87	1006.79	967.20	935.44	909.64	888.48
64000	1139.27	1073.65	1022.77	982.56	950.29	924.08	902.58
65000	1157.07	1090.42	1038.75	997.91	965.14	938.52	916.68
70000	1246.07	1174.30	1118.65	1074.67	1039.38	1010.71	987.20
75000	1335.08	1258.18	1198.56	1151.43	1113.62	1082.91	1057.71
80000	1424.08	1342.06	1278.46	1228.19	1187.86	1155.10	1128.23
85000	1513.09	1425.93	1358.36	1304.96	1262.10	1227.29	1198.74
90000	1602.09	1509.81	1438.27	1381.72	1336.34	1299.49	1269.25
95000	1691.10	1593.69	1518.17	1458.48	1410.58	1371.68	1339.77
100000	1780.10	1677.57	1598.07	1535.24	1484.83	1443.87	1410.28
105000	1869.11	1761.45	1677.98	1612.01	1559.07	1516.07	1480.80
110000	1958.11	1845.33	1757.88	1688.77	1633.31	1588.26	1551.31
120000	2136.12	2013.08	1917.69	1842.29	1781.79	1732.65	1692.34
130000	2314.13	2180.84	2077.50	1995.82	1930.27	1877.04	1833.37
140000	2492.14	2348.60	2237.30	2149.34	2078.76	2021.42	1974.39
150000	2670.16	2516.36	2397.11	2302.86	2227.24	2165.81	2115.42
160000	2848.17	2684.11	2556.92	2456.39	2375.72	2310.20	2256.45
175000	3115.18	2935.75	2796.63	2686.68	2598.44	2526.78	2467.99
200000	3560.21	3355.14	3196.15	3070.49	2969.65	2887.75	2820.56
250000	4450.26	4193.93	3995.19	3838.11	3712.06	3609.68	3525.70
500000	8900.52	8387.85	7990.37	7676.22	7424.13	7219.37	7051.41
1000000	17801.03	16775.71	15980.74	15352.43	14848.25	14438.74	14102.82

14.75%　　　MONTHLY PAYMENTS

AMOUNT	15 YEARS	16 YEARS	17 YEARS	18 YEARS	19 YEARS	20 YEARS	21 YEARS
100	1.38	1.36	1.34	1.32	1.31	1.30	1.29
200	2.77	2.72	2.68	2.65	2.62	2.60	2.58
500	6.91	6.80	6.70	6.62	6.55	6.49	6.44
1000	13.83	13.59	13.40	13.24	13.10	12.98	12.88
2000	27.65	27.19	26.80	26.47	26.20	25.97	25.77
3000	41.48	40.78	40.20	39.71	39.30	38.95	38.65
4000	55.30	54.38	53.60	52.95	52.40	51.93	51.54
5000	69.13	67.97	67.00	66.19	65.50	64.92	64.42
6000	82.95	81.56	80.40	79.42	78.60	77.90	77.31
7000	96.78	95.16	93.80	92.66	91.70	90.88	90.19
8000	110.60	108.75	107.20	105.90	104.80	103.87	103.08
9000	124.43	122.34	120.60	119.14	117.90	116.85	115.96
10000	138.25	135.94	134.00	132.37	131.00	129.84	128.85
11000	152.08	149.53	147.40	145.61	144.10	142.82	141.73
12000	165.90	163.13	160.80	158.85	157.20	155.80	154.62
13000	179.73	176.72	174.20	172.09	170.30	168.79	167.50
14000	193.55	190.31	187.60	185.32	183.40	181.77	180.39
15000	207.38	203.91	201.00	198.56	196.50	194.75	193.27
20000	276.50	271.88	268.00	264.75	262.00	259.67	257.69
25000	345.63	339.84	335.01	330.94	327.50	324.59	322.12
30000	414.75	407.81	402.01	397.12	393.00	389.51	386.54
35000	483.88	475.78	469.01	463.31	458.50	454.42	450.96
40000	553.00	543.75	536.01	529.50	524.00	519.34	515.39
45000	622.13	611.72	603.01	595.68	589.50	584.26	579.81
50000	691.25	679.69	670.01	661.87	655.00	649.18	644.23
55000	760.38	747.66	737.01	728.06	720.50	714.10	708.66
56000	774.20	761.25	750.41	741.30	733.60	727.08	721.54
57000	788.03	774.85	763.81	754.53	746.70	740.06	734.43
58000	801.85	788.44	777.21	767.77	759.80	753.05	747.31
59000	815.68	802.03	790.61	781.01	772.90	766.03	760.19
60000	829.50	815.63	804.01	794.25	786.00	779.01	773.08
61000	843.33	829.22	817.41	807.48	799.10	792.00	785.96
62000	857.15	842.82	830.81	820.72	812.20	804.98	798.85
63000	870.98	856.41	844.21	833.96	825.30	817.96	811.73
64000	884.80	870.00	857.61	847.20	838.40	830.95	824.62
65000	898.63	883.60	871.01	860.43	851.50	843.93	837.50
70000	967.75	951.57	938.02	926.62	917.00	908.85	901.93
75000	1036.88	1019.53	1005.02	992.81	982.50	973.77	966.35
80000	1106.00	1087.50	1072.02	1058.99	1048.00	1038.68	1030.77
85000	1175.13	1155.47	1139.02	1125.18	1113.50	1103.60	1095.20
90000	1244.25	1223.44	1206.02	1191.37	1179.00	1168.52	1159.62
95000	1313.38	1291.41	1273.02	1257.56	1244.50	1233.44	1224.04
100000	1382.50	1359.38	1340.02	1323.74	1310.00	1298.36	1288.47
105000	1451.63	1427.35	1407.02	1389.93	1375.50	1363.27	1352.89
110000	1520.75	1495.32	1474.02	1456.12	1441.00	1428.19	1417.31
120000	1659.00	1631.26	1608.03	1588.49	1572.00	1558.03	1546.16
130000	1797.25	1767.19	1742.03	1720.87	1703.00	1687.86	1675.01
140000	1935.51	1903.13	1876.03	1853.24	1834.00	1817.70	1803.85
150000	2073.76	2039.07	2010.03	1985.61	1965.00	1947.53	1932.70
160000	2212.01	2175.01	2144.04	2117.99	2096.00	2077.37	2061.54
175000	2419.38	2378.91	2345.04	2316.55	2292.50	2272.12	2254.81
200000	2765.01	2718.76	2680.04	2647.49	2620.00	2596.71	2576.93
250000	3456.26	3398.45	3350.06	3309.36	3275.00	3245.89	3221.16
500000	6912.52	6796.90	6700.11	6618.71	6549.99	6491.78	6442.33
1000000	13825.04	13593.79	13400.22	13237.43	13099.98	12983.55	12884.65

MONTHLY PAYMENTS 14.75%

AMOUNT	22 YEARS	23 YEARS	24 YEARS	25 YEARS	30 YEARS	35 YEARS	40 YEARS
100	1.28	1.27	1.27	1.26	1.24	1.24	1.23
200	2.56	2.55	2.53	2.52	2.49	2.47	2.47
500	6.40	6.36	6.33	6.31	6.22	6.18	6.16
1000	12.80	12.73	12.67	12.61	12.44	12.36	12.33
2000	25.60	25.46	25.33	25.23	24.89	24.73	24.65
3000	38.40	38.19	38.00	37.84	37.33	37.09	36.98
4000	51.20	50.91	50.67	50.46	49.78	49.46	49.31
5000	64.00	63.64	63.34	63.07	62.22	61.82	61.63
6000	76.80	76.37	76.00	75.69	74.67	74.19	73.96
7000	89.60	89.10	88.67	88.30	87.11	86.55	86.29
8000	102.40	101.83	101.34	100.92	99.56	98.92	98.61
9000	115.20	114.56	114.00	113.53	112.00	111.28	110.94
10000	128.00	127.29	126.67	126.15	124.45	123.65	123.27
11000	140.80	140.01	139.34	138.76	136.89	136.01	135.59
12000	153.61	152.74	152.01	151.38	149.34	148.38	147.92
13000	166.41	165.47	164.67	163.99	161.78	160.74	160.25
14000	179.21	178.20	177.34	176.61	174.23	173.11	172.57
15000	192.01	190.93	190.01	189.22	186.67	185.47	184.90
20000	256.01	254.57	253.34	252.29	248.90	247.29	246.53
25000	320.01	318.22	316.68	315.37	311.12	309.12	308.17
30000	384.01	381.86	380.02	378.44	373.34	370.94	369.80
35000	448.02	445.50	443.35	441.51	435.57	432.77	431.43
40000	512.02	509.14	506.69	504.59	497.79	494.59	493.07
45000	576.02	572.79	570.02	567.66	560.01	556.41	554.70
50000	640.02	636.43	633.36	630.73	622.24	618.24	616.33
55000	704.02	700.07	696.70	693.81	684.46	680.06	677.97
56000	716.83	712.80	709.36	706.42	696.91	692.43	690.29
57000	729.63	725.53	722.03	719.03	709.35	704.79	702.62
58000	742.43	738.26	734.70	731.65	721.80	717.16	714.95
59000	755.23	750.99	747.36	744.26	734.24	729.52	727.27
60000	768.03	763.72	760.03	756.88	746.69	741.88	739.60
61000	780.83	776.44	772.70	769.49	759.13	754.25	751.93
62000	793.63	789.17	785.37	782.11	771.57	766.61	764.25
63000	806.43	801.90	798.03	794.72	784.02	778.98	776.58
64000	819.23	814.63	810.70	807.34	796.46	791.34	788.91
65000	832.03	827.36	823.37	819.95	808.91	803.71	801.23
70000	896.03	891.00	886.70	883.03	871.13	865.53	862.87
75000	960.03	954.65	950.04	946.10	933.36	927.36	924.50
80000	1024.04	1018.29	1013.38	1009.17	995.58	989.18	986.13
85000	1088.04	1081.93	1076.71	1072.25	1057.80	1051.00	1047.77
90000	1152.04	1145.57	1140.05	1135.32	1120.03	1112.83	1109.40
95000	1216.04	1209.22	1203.38	1198.39	1182.25	1174.65	1171.03
100000	1280.04	1272.86	1266.72	1261.46	1244.48	1236.47	1232.67
105000	1344.05	1336.50	1330.06	1324.54	1306.70	1298.30	1294.30
110000	1408.05	1400.15	1393.39	1387.61	1368.92	1360.12	1355.93
120000	1536.05	1527.43	1520.06	1513.76	1493.37	1483.77	1479.20
130000	1664.06	1654.72	1646.74	1639.90	1617.82	1607.42	1602.47
140000	1792.06	1782.00	1773.41	1766.05	1742.27	1731.06	1725.73
150000	1920.07	1909.29	1900.08	1892.20	1866.71	1854.71	1849.00
160000	2048.07	2036.58	2026.75	2018.34	1991.16	1978.36	1972.27
175000	2240.08	2227.51	2216.76	2207.56	2177.83	2163.83	2157.17
200000	2560.09	2545.72	2533.44	2522.93	2488.95	2472.95	2465.33
250000	3200.11	3182.15	3166.80	3153.66	3111.19	3091.19	3081.67
500000	6400.22	6364.30	6333.60	6307.32	6222.38	6182.37	6163.34
1000000	12800.45	12728.60	12667.20	12614.65	12444.76	12364.75	12326.67

15.00%   MONTHLY PAYMENTS

AMOUNT	1 YEAR	2 YEARS	3 YEARS	4 YEARS	5 YEARS	6 YEARS	7 YEARS
100	9.03	4.85	3.47	2.78	2.38	2.11	1.93
200	18.05	9.70	6.93	5.57	4.76	4.23	3.86
500	45.13	24.24	17.33	13.92	11.89	10.57	9.65
1000	90.26	48.49	34.67	27.83	23.79	21.15	19.30
2000	180.52	96.97	69.33	55.66	47.58	42.29	38.59
3000	270.77	145.46	104.00	83.49	71.37	63.44	57.89
4000	361.03	193.95	138.66	111.32	95.16	84.58	77.19
5000	451.29	242.43	173.33	139.15	118.95	105.73	96.48
6000	541.55	290.92	207.99	166.98	142.74	126.87	115.78
7000	631.81	339.41	242.66	194.82	166.53	148.02	135.08
8000	722.07	387.89	277.32	222.65	190.32	169.16	154.37
9000	812.32	436.38	311.99	250.48	214.11	190.31	173.67
10000	902.58	484.87	346.65	278.31	237.90	211.45	192.97
11000	992.84	533.35	381.32	306.14	261.69	232.60	212.26
12000	1083.10	581.84	415.98	333.97	285.48	253.74	231.56
13000	1173.36	630.33	450.65	361.80	309.27	274.89	250.86
14000	1263.62	678.81	485.31	389.63	333.06	296.03	270.15
15000	1353.87	727.30	519.98	417.46	356.85	317.18	289.45
20000	1805.17	969.73	693.31	556.61	475.80	422.90	385.94
25000	2256.46	1212.17	866.63	695.77	594.75	528.63	482.42
30000	2707.75	1454.60	1039.96	834.92	713.70	634.35	578.90
35000	3159.04	1697.03	1213.29	974.08	832.65	740.08	675.39
40000	3610.33	1939.47	1386.61	1113.23	951.60	845.80	771.87
45000	4061.62	2181.90	1559.94	1252.38	1070.55	951.53	868.35
50000	4512.92	2424.33	1733.27	1391.54	1189.50	1057.25	964.84
55000	4964.21	2666.77	1906.59	1530.69	1308.45	1162.98	1061.32
56000	5054.47	2715.25	1941.26	1558.52	1332.24	1184.12	1080.62
57000	5144.72	2763.74	1975.92	1586.35	1356.03	1205.27	1099.92
58000	5234.98	2812.23	2010.59	1614.18	1379.82	1226.41	1119.21
59000	5325.24	2860.71	2045.25	1642.01	1403.61	1247.56	1138.51
60000	5415.50	2909.20	2079.92	1669.84	1427.40	1268.70	1157.81
61000	5505.76	2957.69	2114.59	1697.68	1451.19	1289.85	1177.10
62000	5596.02	3006.17	2149.25	1725.51	1474.98	1310.99	1196.40
63000	5686.27	3054.66	2183.92	1753.34	1498.77	1332.14	1215.70
64000	5776.53	3103.15	2218.58	1781.17	1522.56	1353.28	1234.99
65000	5866.79	3151.63	2253.25	1809.00	1546.35	1374.43	1254.29
70000	6318.08	3394.07	2426.57	1948.15	1665.30	1480.15	1350.77
75000	6769.37	3636.50	2599.90	2087.31	1784.24	1585.88	1447.26
80000	7220.66	3878.93	2773.23	2226.46	1903.19	1691.60	1543.74
85000	7671.96	4121.37	2946.55	2365.61	2022.14	1797.33	1640.22
90000	8123.25	4363.80	3119.88	2504.77	2141.09	1903.05	1736.71
95000	8574.54	4606.23	3293.21	2643.92	2260.04	2008.78	1833.19
100000	9025.83	4848.66	3466.53	2783.07	2378.99	2114.50	1929.68
105000	9477.12	5091.10	3639.86	2922.23	2497.94	2220.23	2026.16
110000	9928.41	5333.53	3813.19	3061.38	2616.89	2325.95	2122.64
120000	10831.00	5818.40	4159.84	3339.69	2854.79	2537.40	2315.61
130000	11733.58	6303.26	4506.49	3618.00	3092.69	2748.85	2508.58
140000	12636.16	6788.13	4853.15	3896.30	3330.59	2960.30	2701.55
150000	13538.75	7273.00	5199.80	4174.61	3568.49	3171.75	2894.51
160000	14441.33	7757.86	5546.45	4452.92	3806.39	3383.20	3087.48
175000	15795.20	8485.16	6066.43	4870.38	4163.24	3700.38	3376.93
200000	18051.66	9697.33	6933.07	5566.15	4757.99	4229.00	3859.35
250000	22564.58	12121.66	8666.33	6957.69	5947.48	5286.25	4824.19
500000	45129.16	24243.32	17332.66	13915.37	11894.97	10572.51	9648.38
1000000	90258.31	48486.65	34665.33	27830.75	23789.93	21145.01	19296.75

MONTHLY PAYMENTS 15.00%

AMOUNT	8 YEARS	9 YEARS	10 YEARS	11 YEARS	12 YEARS	13 YEARS	14 YEARS
100	1.79	1.69	1.61	1.55	1.50	1.46	1.43
200	3.59	3.38	3.23	3.10	3.00	2.92	2.85
500	8.97	8.46	8.07	7.75	7.50	7.30	7.14
1000	17.95	16.92	16.13	15.51	15.01	14.60	14.27
2000	35.89	33.85	32.27	31.02	30.02	29.21	28.54
3000	53.84	50.77	48.40	46.53	45.03	43.81	42.81
4000	71.78	67.70	64.53	62.04	60.04	58.41	57.08
5000	89.73	84.62	80.67	77.55	75.04	73.01	71.35
6000	107.67	101.55	96.80	93.05	90.05	87.62	85.62
7000	125.62	118.47	112.93	108.56	105.06	102.22	99.89
8000	143.56	135.39	129.07	124.07	120.07	116.82	114.16
9000	161.51	152.32	145.20	139.58	135.08	131.43	128.43
10000	179.45	169.24	161.33	155.09	150.09	146.03	142.70
11000	197.40	186.17	177.47	170.60	165.10	160.63	156.97
12000	215.34	203.09	193.60	186.11	180.11	175.23	171.24
13000	233.29	220.02	209.74	201.62	195.11	189.84	185.52
14000	251.24	236.94	225.87	217.13	210.12	204.44	199.79
15000	269.18	253.87	242.00	232.64	225.13	219.04	214.06
20000	358.91	338.49	322.67	310.18	300.18	292.06	285.41
25000	448.64	423.11	403.34	387.73	375.22	365.07	356.76
30000	538.36	507.73	484.00	465.27	450.26	438.09	428.11
35000	628.09	592.35	564.67	542.82	525.31	511.10	499.46
40000	717.82	676.97	645.34	620.37	600.35	584.11	570.82
45000	807.54	761.60	726.01	697.91	675.39	657.13	642.17
50000	897.27	846.22	806.67	775.46	750.44	730.14	713.52
55000	987.00	930.84	887.34	853.00	825.48	803.16	784.87
56000	1004.94	947.76	903.48	868.51	840.49	817.76	799.14
57000	1022.89	964.69	919.61	884.02	855.50	832.36	813.41
58000	1040.83	981.61	935.74	899.53	870.51	846.97	827.68
59000	1058.78	998.54	951.88	915.04	885.52	861.57	841.95
60000	1076.72	1015.46	968.01	930.55	900.53	876.17	856.22
61000	1094.67	1032.38	984.14	946.06	915.53	890.78	870.49
62000	1112.62	1049.31	1000.28	961.57	930.54	905.38	884.76
63000	1130.56	1066.23	1016.41	977.08	945.55	919.98	899.04
64000	1148.51	1083.16	1032.54	992.59	960.56	934.58	913.31
65000	1166.45	1100.08	1048.68	1008.09	975.57	949.19	927.58
70000	1256.18	1184.70	1129.34	1085.64	1050.61	1022.20	998.93
75000	1345.91	1269.33	1210.01	1163.19	1125.66	1095.22	1070.28
80000	1435.63	1353.95	1290.68	1240.73	1200.70	1168.23	1141.63
85000	1525.36	1438.57	1371.35	1318.28	1275.75	1241.24	1212.98
90000	1615.09	1523.19	1452.01	1395.82	1350.79	1314.26	1284.34
95000	1704.81	1607.81	1532.68	1473.37	1425.83	1387.27	1355.69
100000	1794.54	1692.43	1613.35	1550.91	1500.88	1460.29	1427.04
105000	1884.27	1777.06	1694.02	1628.46	1575.92	1533.30	1498.39
110000	1973.99	1861.68	1774.68	1706.01	1650.96	1606.32	1569.74
120000	2153.45	2030.92	1936.02	1861.10	1801.05	1752.34	1712.45
130000	2332.90	2200.16	2097.35	2016.19	1951.14	1898.37	1855.15
140000	2512.36	2369.41	2258.69	2171.28	2101.23	2044.40	1997.86
150000	2691.81	2538.65	2420.02	2326.37	2251.32	2190.43	2140.56
160000	2871.26	2707.89	2581.36	2481.46	2401.40	2336.46	2283.26
175000	3140.45	2961.76	2823.36	2714.10	2626.53	2555.50	2497.32
200000	3589.08	3384.87	3226.70	3101.83	3001.75	2920.57	2854.08
250000	4486.35	4231.08	4033.37	3877.29	3752.19	3650.72	3567.60
500000	8972.70	8462.17	8066.75	7754.57	7504.38	7301.44	7135.20
1000000	17945.41	16924.34	16133.50	15509.15	15008.77	14602.87	14270.40

15.00%   MONTHLY PAYMENTS

AMOUNT	15 YEARS	16 YEARS	17 YEARS	18 YEARS	19 YEARS	20 YEARS	21 YEARS
100	1.40	1.38	1.36	1.34	1.33	1.32	1.31
200	2.80	2.75	2.72	2.68	2.66	2.63	2.61
500	7.00	6.88	6.79	6.71	6.64	6.58	6.54
1000	14.00	13.77	13.58	13.42	13.28	13.17	13.07
2000	27.99	27.54	27.15	26.83	26.56	26.34	26.14
3000	41.99	41.30	40.73	40.25	39.85	39.50	39.21
4000	55.98	55.07	54.31	53.67	53.13	52.67	52.28
5000	69.98	68.84	67.89	67.08	66.41	65.84	65.36
6000	83.98	82.61	81.46	80.50	79.69	79.01	78.43
7000	97.97	96.37	95.04	93.92	92.97	92.18	91.50
8000	111.97	110.14	108.62	107.34	106.26	105.34	104.57
9000	125.96	123.91	122.19	120.75	119.54	118.51	117.64
10000	139.96	137.68	135.77	134.17	132.82	131.68	130.71
11000	153.95	151.44	149.35	147.59	146.10	144.85	143.78
12000	167.95	165.21	162.92	161.00	159.38	158.01	156.85
13000	181.95	178.98	176.50	174.42	172.67	171.18	169.93
14000	195.94	192.75	190.08	187.84	185.95	184.35	183.00
15000	209.94	206.52	203.66	201.25	199.23	197.52	196.07
20000	279.92	275.35	271.54	268.34	265.64	263.36	261.42
25000	349.90	344.19	339.43	335.42	332.05	329.20	326.78
30000	419.88	413.03	407.31	402.51	398.46	395.04	392.14
35000	489.86	481.87	475.20	469.59	464.87	460.88	457.49
40000	559.83	550.71	543.08	536.68	531.28	526.72	522.85
45000	629.81	619.55	610.97	603.76	597.69	592.56	588.20
50000	699.79	688.38	678.85	670.85	664.10	658.39	653.56
55000	769.77	757.22	746.74	737.93	730.51	724.23	718.91
56000	783.77	770.99	760.31	751.35	743.79	737.40	731.99
57000	797.76	784.76	773.89	764.76	757.07	750.57	745.06
58000	811.76	798.53	787.47	778.18	770.35	763.74	758.13
59000	825.76	812.29	801.04	791.60	783.64	776.91	771.20
60000	839.75	826.06	814.62	805.01	796.92	790.07	784.27
61000	853.75	839.83	828.20	818.43	810.20	803.24	797.34
62000	867.74	853.60	841.77	831.85	823.48	816.41	810.41
63000	881.74	867.36	855.35	845.27	836.76	829.58	823.48
64000	895.74	881.13	868.93	858.68	850.05	842.75	836.55
65000	909.73	894.90	882.51	872.10	863.33	855.91	849.63
70000	979.71	963.74	950.39	939.18	929.74	921.75	914.98
75000	1049.69	1032.58	1018.28	1006.27	996.15	987.59	980.34
80000	1119.67	1101.42	1086.16	1073.35	1062.56	1053.43	1045.69
85000	1189.65	1170.25	1154.05	1140.44	1128.97	1119.27	1111.05
90000	1259.63	1239.09	1221.93	1207.52	1195.38	1185.11	1176.41
95000	1329.61	1307.93	1289.82	1274.61	1261.79	1250.95	1241.76
100000	1399.59	1376.77	1357.70	1341.69	1328.20	1316.79	1307.12
105000	1469.57	1445.61	1425.59	1408.78	1394.61	1382.63	1372.47
110000	1539.55	1514.45	1493.47	1475.86	1461.02	1448.47	1437.83
120000	1679.50	1652.12	1629.24	1610.03	1593.84	1580.15	1568.54
130000	1819.46	1789.80	1765.01	1744.20	1726.66	1711.83	1699.25
140000	1959.42	1927.48	1900.78	1878.37	1859.48	1843.51	1829.96
150000	2099.38	2065.15	2036.55	2012.54	1992.30	1975.18	1960.68
160000	2239.34	2202.83	2172.32	2146.71	2125.12	2106.86	2091.39
175000	2449.28	2409.35	2375.98	2347.96	2324.35	2304.38	2287.46
200000	2799.17	2753.54	2715.40	2683.38	2656.40	2633.58	2614.23
250000	3498.97	3441.92	3394.25	3354.23	3320.49	3291.97	3267.79
500000	6997.94	6883.85	6788.50	6708.45	6640.99	6583.95	6535.59
1000000	13995.87	13767.70	13577.00	13416.91	13281.98	13167.90	13071.17

MONTHLY PAYMENTS   15.00%

AMOUNT	22 YEARS	23 YEARS	24 YEARS	25 YEARS	30 YEARS	35 YEARS	40 YEARS
100	1.30	1.29	1.29	1.28	1.26	1.26	1.25
200	2.60	2.58	2.57	2.56	2.53	2.51	2.51
500	6.49	6.46	6.43	6.40	6.32	6.28	6.27
1000	12.99	12.92	12.86	12.81	12.64	12.57	12.53
2000	25.98	25.84	25.72	25.62	25.29	25.14	25.06
3000	38.97	38.76	38.58	38.42	37.93	37.70	37.60
4000	51.96	51.68	51.44	51.23	50.58	50.27	50.13
5000	64.94	64.59	64.30	64.04	63.22	62.84	62.66
6000	77.93	77.51	77.16	76.85	75.87	75.41	75.19
7000	90.92	90.43	90.02	89.66	88.51	87.98	87.73
8000	103.91	103.35	102.87	102.47	101.16	100.55	100.26
9000	116.90	116.27	115.73	115.27	113.80	113.11	112.79
10000	129.89	129.19	128.59	128.08	126.44	125.68	125.32
11000	142.88	142.11	141.45	140.89	139.09	138.25	137.85
12000	155.87	155.03	154.31	153.70	151.73	150.82	150.39
13000	168.86	167.95	167.17	166.51	164.38	163.39	162.92
14000	181.85	180.87	180.03	179.32	177.02	175.95	175.45
15000	194.83	193.78	192.89	192.12	189.67	188.52	187.98
20000	259.78	258.38	257.19	256.17	252.89	251.36	250.64
25000	324.72	322.97	321.48	320.21	316.11	314.20	313.31
30000	389.67	387.57	385.78	384.25	379.33	377.04	375.97
35000	454.61	452.16	450.08	448.29	442.56	439.88	438.63
40000	519.56	516.76	514.37	512.33	505.78	502.73	501.29
45000	584.50	581.35	578.67	576.37	569.00	565.57	563.95
50000	649.45	645.95	642.96	640.42	632.22	628.41	626.61
55000	714.39	710.54	707.26	704.46	695.44	691.25	689.27
56000	727.38	723.46	720.12	717.27	708.09	703.82	701.81
57000	740.37	736.38	732.98	730.07	720.73	716.38	714.34
58000	753.36	749.30	745.84	742.88	733.38	728.95	726.87
59000	766.35	762.22	758.70	755.69	746.02	741.52	739.40
60000	779.34	775.14	771.56	768.50	758.67	754.09	751.93
61000	792.33	788.06	784.42	781.31	771.31	766.66	764.47
62000	805.32	800.98	797.28	794.11	783.96	779.22	777.00
63000	818.31	813.90	810.14	806.92	796.60	791.79	789.53
64000	831.29	826.82	822.99	819.73	809.24	804.36	802.06
65000	844.28	839.73	835.85	832.54	821.89	816.93	814.60
70000	909.23	904.33	900.15	896.58	885.11	879.77	877.26
75000	974.17	968.92	964.45	960.62	948.33	942.61	939.92
80000	1039.12	1033.52	1028.74	1024.66	1011.56	1005.45	1002.58
85000	1104.06	1098.11	1093.04	1088.71	1074.78	1068.29	1065.24
90000	1169.01	1162.71	1157.34	1152.75	1138.00	1131.13	1127.90
95000	1233.95	1227.30	1221.63	1216.79	1201.22	1193.97	1190.56
100000	1298.90	1291.90	1285.93	1280.83	1264.44	1256.81	1253.22
105000	1363.84	1356.49	1350.23	1344.87	1327.67	1319.65	1315.89
110000	1428.79	1421.09	1414.52	1408.91	1390.89	1382.49	1378.55
120000	1558.68	1550.28	1543.12	1537.00	1517.33	1508.18	1503.87
130000	1688.57	1679.47	1671.71	1665.08	1643.78	1633.86	1629.19
140000	1818.46	1808.66	1800.30	1793.16	1770.22	1759.54	1754.51
150000	1948.35	1937.85	1928.89	1921.25	1896.67	1885.22	1879.84
160000	2078.24	2067.04	2057.49	2049.33	2023.11	2010.90	2005.16
175000	2273.07	2260.82	2250.38	2241.45	2212.78	2199.42	2193.14
200000	2597.79	2583.80	2571.86	2561.66	2528.89	2513.63	2506.45
250000	3247.24	3229.75	3214.82	3202.08	3161.11	3142.03	3133.06
500000	6494.49	6459.49	6429.65	6404.15	6322.22	6284.07	6266.12
1000000	12988.97	12918.99	12859.29	12808.31	12644.44	12568.13	12532.24

15.25%   MONTHLY PAYMENTS

AMOUNT	1 YEAR	2 YEARS	3 YEARS	4 YEARS	5 YEARS	6 YEARS	7 YEARS
100	9.04	4.86	3.48	2.80	2.39	2.13	1.94
200	18.08	9.72	6.96	5.59	4.78	4.26	3.89
500	45.19	24.30	17.39	13.98	11.96	10.64	9.72
1000	90.38	48.61	34.79	27.96	23.92	21.28	19.44
2000	180.75	97.21	69.58	55.92	47.84	42.56	38.87
3000	271.13	145.82	104.36	83.87	71.76	63.84	58.31
4000	361.51	194.42	139.15	111.83	95.69	85.12	77.75
5000	451.88	243.03	173.94	139.79	119.61	106.41	97.19
6000	542.26	291.63	208.73	167.75	143.53	127.69	116.62
7000	632.63	340.24	243.52	195.70	167.45	148.97	136.06
8000	723.01	388.84	278.30	223.66	191.37	170.25	155.50
9000	813.39	437.45	313.09	251.62	215.29	191.53	174.94
10000	903.76	486.06	347.88	279.58	239.21	212.81	194.37
11000	994.14	534.66	382.67	307.53	263.13	234.09	213.81
12000	1084.52	583.27	417.45	335.49	287.06	255.37	233.25
13000	1174.89	631.87	452.24	363.45	310.98	276.65	252.68
14000	1265.27	680.48	487.03	391.41	334.90	297.93	272.12
15000	1355.64	729.08	521.82	419.36	358.82	319.22	291.56
20000	1807.53	972.11	695.76	559.15	478.43	425.62	388.75
25000	2259.41	1215.14	869.70	698.94	598.03	532.03	485.93
30000	2711.29	1458.17	1043.64	838.73	717.64	638.43	583.12
35000	3163.17	1701.19	1217.58	978.52	837.25	744.84	680.30
40000	3615.05	1944.22	1391.52	1118.31	956.85	851.24	777.49
45000	4066.93	2187.25	1565.45	1258.09	1076.46	957.65	874.68
50000	4518.82	2430.28	1739.39	1397.88	1196.07	1064.05	971.86
55000	4970.70	2673.30	1913.33	1537.67	1315.67	1170.46	1069.05
56000	5061.07	2721.91	1948.12	1565.63	1339.60	1191.74	1088.49
57000	5151.45	2770.51	1982.91	1593.59	1363.52	1213.02	1107.93
58000	5241.83	2819.12	2017.70	1621.54	1387.44	1234.30	1127.36
59000	5332.20	2867.73	2052.48	1649.50	1411.36	1255.58	1146.80
60000	5422.58	2916.33	2087.27	1677.46	1435.28	1276.86	1166.24
61000	5512.96	2964.94	2122.06	1705.42	1459.20	1298.14	1185.67
62000	5603.33	3013.54	2156.85	1733.37	1483.12	1319.42	1205.11
63000	5693.71	3062.15	2191.64	1761.33	1507.05	1340.70	1224.55
64000	5784.08	3110.75	2226.42	1789.29	1530.97	1361.98	1243.99
65000	5874.46	3159.36	2261.21	1817.25	1554.89	1383.27	1263.42
70000	6326.34	3402.39	2435.15	1957.03	1674.50	1489.67	1360.61
75000	6778.22	3645.41	2609.09	2096.82	1794.10	1596.08	1457.80
80000	7230.11	3888.44	2783.03	2236.61	1913.71	1702.48	1554.98
85000	7681.99	4131.47	2956.97	2376.40	2033.32	1808.89	1652.17
90000	8133.87	4374.50	3130.91	2516.19	2152.92	1915.29	1749.36
95000	8585.75	4617.52	3304.85	2655.98	2272.53	2021.70	1846.54
100000	9037.63	4860.55	3478.79	2795.76	2392.14	2128.10	1943.73
105000	9489.51	5103.58	3652.73	2935.55	2511.74	2234.51	2040.91
110000	9941.40	5346.61	3826.67	3075.34	2631.35	2340.91	2138.10
120000	10845.16	5832.66	4174.55	3354.92	2870.56	2553.72	2332.47
130000	11748.92	6318.72	4522.42	3634.49	3109.78	2766.53	2526.85
140000	12652.69	6804.77	4870.30	3914.07	3348.99	2979.34	2721.22
150000	13556.45	7290.83	5218.18	4193.65	3588.20	3192.15	2915.59
160000	14460.21	7776.88	5566.06	4473.22	3827.42	3404.96	3109.97
175000	15815.86	8505.96	6087.88	4892.59	4186.24	3724.18	3401.52
200000	18075.26	9721.10	6957.58	5591.53	4784.27	4256.20	3887.46
250000	22594.08	12151.38	8696.97	6989.41	5980.34	5320.25	4859.32
500000	45188.16	24302.76	17393.94	13978.82	11960.68	10640.51	9718.64
1000000	90376.32	48605.51	34787.88	27957.64	23921.36	21281.02	19437.28

MONTHLY PAYMENTS 15.25%

AMOUNT	8 YEARS	9 YEARS	10 YEARS	11 YEARS	12 YEARS	13 YEARS	14 YEARS
100	1.81	1.71	1.63	1.57	1.52	1.48	1.44
200	3.62	3.41	3.26	3.13	3.03	2.95	2.89
500	9.05	8.54	8.14	7.83	7.59	7.38	7.22
1000	18.09	17.07	16.29	15.67	15.17	14.77	14.44
2000	36.18	34.15	32.57	31.33	30.34	29.54	28.88
3000	54.27	51.22	48.86	47.00	45.51	44.30	43.32
4000	72.36	68.29	65.15	62.67	60.68	59.07	57.76
5000	90.45	85.37	81.43	78.33	75.85	73.84	72.19
6000	108.54	102.44	97.72	94.00	91.02	88.61	86.63
7000	126.63	119.52	114.01	109.67	106.19	103.37	101.07
8000	144.72	136.59	130.30	125.33	121.36	118.14	115.51
9000	162.81	153.66	146.58	141.00	136.53	132.91	129.95
10000	180.90	170.74	162.87	156.67	151.70	147.68	144.39
11000	198.99	187.81	179.16	172.33	166.87	162.45	158.83
12000	217.08	204.88	195.44	188.00	182.04	177.21	173.27
13000	235.17	221.96	211.73	203.67	197.21	191.98	187.70
14000	253.27	239.03	228.02	219.33	212.38	206.75	202.14
15000	271.36	256.10	244.30	235.00	227.55	221.52	216.58
20000	361.81	341.47	325.74	313.33	303.40	295.36	288.78
25000	452.26	426.84	407.17	391.66	379.25	369.19	360.97
30000	542.71	512.21	488.61	470.00	455.10	443.03	433.16
35000	633.16	597.58	570.04	548.33	530.95	516.87	505.36
40000	723.61	682.94	651.48	626.66	606.80	590.71	577.55
45000	814.07	768.31	732.91	705.00	682.65	664.55	649.74
50000	904.52	853.68	814.35	783.33	758.50	738.39	721.94
55000	994.97	939.05	895.78	861.66	834.35	812.23	794.13
56000	1013.06	956.12	912.07	877.33	849.52	827.00	808.57
57000	1031.15	973.20	928.36	893.00	864.69	841.76	823.01
58000	1049.24	990.27	944.64	908.66	879.86	856.53	837.45
59000	1067.33	1007.34	960.93	924.33	895.03	871.30	851.89
60000	1085.42	1024.42	977.22	940.00	910.20	886.07	866.33
61000	1103.51	1041.49	993.50	955.66	925.37	900.83	880.76
62000	1121.60	1058.56	1009.79	971.33	940.54	915.60	895.20
63000	1139.69	1075.64	1026.08	987.00	955.71	930.37	909.64
64000	1157.78	1092.71	1042.36	1002.66	970.88	945.14	924.08
65000	1175.87	1109.78	1058.65	1018.33	986.05	959.91	938.52
70000	1266.33	1195.15	1140.09	1096.66	1061.90	1033.74	1010.71
75000	1356.78	1280.52	1221.52	1174.99	1137.75	1107.58	1082.91
80000	1447.23	1365.89	1302.95	1253.32	1213.60	1181.42	1155.10
85000	1537.68	1451.26	1384.39	1331.66	1289.45	1255.26	1227.29
90000	1628.13	1536.63	1465.82	1409.99	1365.30	1329.10	1299.49
95000	1718.59	1621.99	1547.26	1488.33	1441.15	1402.94	1371.68
100000	1809.04	1707.36	1628.69	1566.66	1517.00	1476.78	1443.88
105000	1899.49	1792.73	1710.13	1644.99	1592.85	1550.62	1516.07
110000	1989.94	1878.10	1791.56	1723.32	1668.70	1624.46	1588.26
120000	2170.84	2048.83	1954.43	1879.99	1820.40	1772.13	1732.65
130000	2351.75	2219.57	2117.30	2036.66	1972.10	1919.81	1877.04
140000	2532.65	2390.31	2280.17	2193.32	2123.80	2067.49	2021.43
150000	2713.56	2561.04	2443.04	2349.99	2275.51	2215.17	2165.81
160000	2894.46	2731.78	2605.91	2506.65	2427.21	2362.85	2310.20
175000	3165.81	2987.88	2850.21	2741.65	2654.76	2584.36	2526.78
200000	3618.07	3414.72	3257.39	3133.32	3034.01	2953.56	2887.75
250000	4522.59	4268.40	4071.73	3916.65	3792.51	3691.95	3609.69
500000	9045.18	8536.81	8143.47	7833.29	7585.02	7383.89	7219.38
1000000	18090.37	17073.61	16286.93	15666.59	15170.03	14767.78	14438.76

15.25% MONTHLY PAYMENTS

AMOUNT	15 YEARS	16 YEARS	17 YEARS	18 YEARS	19 YEARS	20 YEARS	21 YEARS
100	1.42	1.39	1.38	1.36	1.35	1.34	1.33
200	2.83	2.79	2.75	2.72	2.69	2.67	2.65
500	7.08	6.97	6.88	6.80	6.73	6.68	6.63
1000	14.17	13.94	13.75	13.60	13.46	13.35	13.26
2000	28.33	27.88	27.51	27.19	26.93	26.71	26.52
3000	42.50	41.83	41.26	40.79	40.39	40.06	39.78
4000	56.67	55.77	55.02	54.39	53.86	53.41	53.03
5000	70.84	69.71	68.77	67.99	67.32	66.76	66.29
6000	85.00	83.65	82.53	81.58	80.79	80.12	79.55
7000	99.17	97.60	96.28	95.18	94.25	93.47	92.81
8000	113.34	111.54	110.04	108.78	107.72	106.82	106.07
9000	127.51	125.48	123.79	122.37	121.18	120.18	119.33
10000	141.67	139.42	137.55	135.97	134.65	133.53	132.58
11000	155.84	153.37	151.30	149.57	148.11	146.88	145.84
12000	170.01	167.31	165.05	163.17	161.58	160.24	159.10
13000	184.18	181.25	178.81	176.76	175.04	173.59	172.36
14000	198.34	195.19	192.56	190.36	188.51	186.94	185.62
15000	212.51	209.14	206.32	203.96	201.97	200.29	198.88
20000	283.35	278.85	275.09	271.94	269.29	267.06	265.17
25000	354.19	348.56	343.86	339.93	336.62	333.82	331.46
30000	425.02	418.27	412.64	407.92	403.94	400.59	397.75
35000	495.86	487.98	481.41	475.90	471.27	467.35	464.04
40000	566.70	557.70	550.18	543.89	538.59	534.12	530.34
45000	637.54	627.41	618.96	611.87	605.91	600.88	596.63
50000	708.37	697.12	687.73	679.86	673.24	667.65	662.92
55000	779.21	766.83	756.50	747.84	740.56	734.41	729.21
56000	793.38	780.77	770.26	761.44	754.03	747.77	742.47
57000	807.55	794.72	784.01	775.04	767.49	761.12	755.73
58000	821.71	808.66	797.77	788.64	780.96	774.47	768.99
59000	835.88	822.60	811.52	802.23	794.42	787.83	782.25
60000	850.05	836.54	825.27	815.83	807.88	801.18	795.50
61000	864.22	850.49	839.03	829.43	821.35	814.53	808.76
62000	878.38	864.43	852.78	843.02	834.81	827.89	822.02
63000	892.55	878.37	866.54	856.62	848.28	841.24	835.28
64000	906.72	892.31	880.29	870.22	861.74	854.59	848.54
65000	920.89	906.26	894.05	883.82	875.21	867.94	861.80
70000	991.72	975.97	962.82	951.80	942.53	934.71	928.09
75000	1062.56	1045.68	1031.59	1019.79	1009.86	1001.47	994.38
80000	1133.40	1115.39	1100.37	1087.77	1077.18	1068.24	1060.67
85000	1204.24	1185.10	1169.14	1155.76	1144.50	1135.00	1126.97
90000	1275.07	1254.82	1237.91	1223.75	1211.83	1201.77	1193.26
95000	1345.91	1324.53	1306.68	1291.73	1279.15	1268.53	1259.55
100000	1416.75	1394.24	1375.46	1359.72	1346.47	1335.30	1325.84
105000	1487.59	1463.95	1444.23	1427.70	1413.80	1402.06	1392.13
110000	1558.42	1533.66	1513.00	1495.69	1481.12	1468.83	1458.43
120000	1700.10	1673.09	1650.55	1631.66	1615.77	1602.36	1591.01
130000	1841.77	1812.51	1788.10	1767.63	1750.42	1735.89	1723.59
140000	1983.45	1951.93	1925.64	1903.60	1885.06	1869.42	1856.18
150000	2125.12	2091.36	2063.19	2039.58	2019.71	2002.95	1988.76
160000	2266.80	2230.78	2200.73	2175.55	2154.36	2136.48	2121.35
175000	2479.31	2439.92	2407.05	2379.50	2356.33	2336.77	2320.22
200000	2833.50	2788.48	2750.92	2719.43	2692.95	2670.60	2651.68
250000	3541.87	3485.60	3438.64	3399.29	3366.19	3338.25	3314.60
500000	7083.75	6971.20	6877.29	6798.58	6732.37	6676.49	6629.21
1000000	14167.50	13942.39	13754.58	13597.17	13464.75	13352.99	13258.41

MONTHLY PAYMENTS 15.25%

AMOUNT	22 YEARS	23 YEARS	24 YEARS	25 YEARS	30 YEARS	35 YEARS	40 YEARS
100	1.32	1.31	1.31	1.30	1.28	1.28	1.27
200	2.64	2.62	2.61	2.60	2.57	2.55	2.55
500	6.59	6.56	6.53	6.50	6.42	6.39	6.37
1000	13.18	13.11	13.05	13.00	12.84	12.77	12.74
2000	26.36	26.22	26.10	26.01	25.69	25.54	25.48
3000	39.53	39.33	39.16	39.01	38.53	38.32	38.21
4000	52.71	52.44	52.21	52.01	51.38	51.09	50.95
5000	65.89	65.55	65.26	65.01	64.22	63.86	63.69
6000	79.07	78.66	78.31	78.02	77.07	76.63	76.43
7000	92.25	91.77	91.36	91.02	89.91	89.40	89.17
8000	105.43	104.88	104.42	104.02	102.76	102.17	101.90
9000	118.60	117.99	117.47	117.02	115.60	114.95	114.64
10000	131.78	131.10	130.52	130.03	128.45	127.72	127.38
11000	144.96	144.21	143.57	143.03	141.29	140.49	140.12
12000	158.14	157.32	156.62	156.03	154.14	153.26	152.86
13000	171.32	170.43	169.68	169.03	166.98	166.03	165.59
14000	184.49	183.54	182.73	182.04	179.82	178.81	178.33
15000	197.67	196.65	195.78	195.04	192.67	191.58	191.07
20000	263.56	262.20	261.04	260.05	256.89	255.44	254.76
25000	329.46	327.75	326.30	325.06	321.11	319.30	318.45
30000	395.35	393.30	391.56	390.08	385.34	383.16	382.14
35000	461.24	458.85	456.82	455.09	449.56	447.01	445.83
40000	527.13	524.40	522.08	520.10	513.78	510.87	509.52
45000	593.02	589.95	587.34	585.12	578.01	574.73	573.21
50000	658.91	655.50	652.60	650.13	642.23	638.59	636.90
55000	724.80	721.05	717.86	715.14	706.45	702.45	700.59
56000	737.98	734.16	730.91	728.14	719.30	715.22	713.33
57000	751.16	747.27	743.97	741.15	732.14	727.99	726.07
58000	764.34	760.38	757.02	754.15	744.99	740.77	738.81
59000	777.51	773.49	770.07	767.15	757.83	753.54	751.54
60000	790.69	786.60	783.12	780.15	770.68	766.31	764.28
61000	803.87	799.71	796.17	793.16	783.52	779.08	777.02
62000	817.05	812.82	809.23	806.16	796.36	791.85	789.76
63000	830.23	825.93	822.28	819.16	809.21	804.63	802.50
64000	843.41	839.04	835.33	832.17	822.05	817.40	815.23
65000	856.58	852.15	848.38	845.17	834.90	830.17	827.97
70000	922.47	917.70	913.64	910.18	899.12	894.03	891.66
75000	988.37	983.25	978.90	975.19	963.34	957.89	955.35
80000	1054.26	1048.80	1044.16	1040.21	1027.57	1021.75	1019.04
85000	1120.15	1114.35	1109.42	1105.22	1091.79	1085.61	1082.73
90000	1186.04	1179.90	1174.68	1170.23	1156.01	1149.47	1146.42
95000	1251.93	1245.45	1239.94	1235.25	1220.24	1213.32	1210.11
100000	1317.82	1311.00	1305.20	1300.26	1284.46	1277.18	1273.80
105000	1383.71	1376.55	1370.46	1365.27	1348.68	1341.04	1337.49
110000	1449.60	1442.10	1435.72	1430.28	1412.90	1404.90	1401.18
120000	1581.38	1573.21	1566.24	1560.31	1541.35	1532.62	1528.56
130000	1713.17	1704.31	1696.76	1690.34	1669.80	1660.34	1655.94
140000	1844.95	1835.41	1827.28	1820.36	1798.24	1788.06	1783.32
150000	1976.73	1966.51	1957.80	1950.39	1926.69	1915.78	1910.70
160000	2108.51	2097.61	2088.32	2080.41	2055.13	2043.49	2038.08
175000	2306.19	2294.26	2284.11	2275.45	2247.80	2235.07	2229.15
200000	2635.64	2622.01	2610.41	2600.52	2568.92	2554.37	2547.60
250000	3294.55	3277.51	3263.01	3250.65	3211.15	3192.96	3184.51
500000	6589.10	6555.02	6526.02	6501.29	6422.29	6385.92	6369.01
1000000	13178.20	13110.04	13052.03	13002.58	12844.59	12771.84	12738.02

15.50%   MONTHLY PAYMENTS

AMOUNT	1 YEAR	2 YEARS	3 YEARS	4 YEARS	5 YEARS	6 YEARS	7 YEARS
100	9.05	4.87	3.49	2.81	2.41	2.14	1.96
200	18.10	9.74	6.98	5.62	4.81	4.28	3.92
500	45.25	24.36	17.46	14.04	12.03	10.71	9.79
1000	90.49	48.72	34.91	28.08	24.05	21.42	19.58
2000	180.99	97.45	69.82	56.17	48.11	42.83	39.16
3000	271.48	146.17	104.73	84.25	72.16	64.25	58.74
4000	361.98	194.90	139.64	112.34	96.21	85.67	78.31
5000	452.47	243.62	174.55	140.42	120.27	107.09	97.89
6000	542.97	292.35	209.46	168.51	144.32	128.50	117.47
7000	633.46	341.07	244.37	196.59	168.37	149.92	137.05
8000	723.96	389.80	279.29	224.68	192.43	171.34	156.63
9000	814.45	438.52	314.20	252.76	216.48	192.76	176.21
10000	904.94	487.25	349.11	280.85	240.53	214.17	195.78
11000	995.44	535.97	384.02	308.93	264.59	235.59	215.36
12000	1085.93	584.69	418.93	337.02	288.64	257.01	234.94
13000	1176.43	633.42	453.84	365.10	312.69	278.43	254.52
14000	1266.92	682.14	488.75	393.19	336.74	299.84	274.10
15000	1357.42	730.87	523.66	421.27	360.80	321.26	293.68
20000	1809.89	974.49	698.21	561.70	481.06	428.35	391.57
25000	2262.36	1218.11	872.77	702.12	601.33	535.44	489.46
30000	2714.83	1461.74	1047.32	842.55	721.60	642.52	587.35
35000	3167.30	1705.36	1221.87	982.97	841.86	749.61	685.24
40000	3619.78	1948.98	1396.43	1123.39	962.13	856.70	783.13
45000	4072.25	2192.60	1570.98	1263.82	1082.39	963.79	881.03
50000	4524.72	2436.23	1745.53	1404.24	1202.66	1070.87	978.92
55000	4977.19	2679.85	1920.09	1544.67	1322.93	1177.96	1076.81
56000	5067.69	2728.57	1955.00	1572.75	1346.98	1199.38	1096.39
57000	5158.18	2777.30	1989.91	1600.84	1371.03	1220.80	1115.97
58000	5248.68	2826.02	2024.82	1628.92	1395.09	1242.21	1135.54
59000	5339.17	2874.75	2059.73	1657.01	1419.14	1263.63	1155.12
60000	5429.66	2923.47	2094.64	1685.09	1443.19	1285.05	1174.70
61000	5520.16	2972.20	2129.55	1713.18	1467.24	1306.47	1194.28
62000	5610.65	3020.92	2164.46	1741.26	1491.30	1327.88	1213.86
63000	5701.15	3069.65	2199.37	1769.35	1515.35	1349.30	1233.44
64000	5791.64	3118.37	2234.28	1797.43	1539.40	1370.72	1253.01
65000	5882.14	3167.10	2269.19	1825.52	1563.46	1392.14	1272.59
70000	6334.61	3410.72	2443.75	1965.94	1683.72	1499.22	1370.48
75000	6787.08	3654.34	2618.30	2106.36	1803.99	1606.31	1468.38
80000	7239.55	3897.96	2792.85	2246.79	1924.26	1713.40	1566.27
85000	7692.03	4141.59	2967.41	2387.21	2044.52	1820.49	1664.16
90000	8144.50	4385.21	3141.96	2527.64	2164.79	1927.57	1762.05
95000	8596.97	4628.83	3316.51	2668.06	2285.05	2034.66	1859.94
100000	9049.44	4872.45	3491.07	2808.49	2405.32	2141.75	1957.83
105000	9501.91	5116.08	3665.62	2948.91	2525.59	2248.84	2055.73
110000	9954.39	5359.70	3840.17	3089.33	2645.85	2355.92	2153.62
120000	10859.33	5846.95	4189.28	3370.18	2886.38	2570.10	2349.40
130000	11764.27	6334.19	4538.39	3651.03	3126.91	2784.27	2545.19
140000	12669.22	6821.44	4887.50	3931.88	3367.45	2998.45	2740.97
150000	13574.16	7308.68	5236.60	4212.73	3607.98	3212.62	2936.75
160000	14479.11	7795.93	5585.71	4493.58	3848.51	3426.80	3132.54
175000	15836.52	8526.79	6109.37	4914.85	4209.31	3748.06	3426.21
200000	18098.88	9744.91	6982.14	5616.97	4810.64	4283.50	3915.67
250000	22623.60	12181.14	8727.67	7021.21	6013.30	5354.37	4894.59
500000	45247.21	24362.27	17455.34	14042.43	12026.60	10708.74	9789.17
1000000	90494.42	48724.54	34910.68	28084.86	24053.19	21417.49	19578.35

MONTHLY PAYMENTS 15.50%

AMOUNT	8 YEARS	9 YEARS	10 YEARS	11 YEARS	12 YEARS	13 YEARS	14 YEARS
100	1.82	1.72	1.64	1.58	1.53	1.49	1.46
200	3.65	3.44	3.29	3.16	3.07	2.99	2.92
500	9.12	8.61	8.22	7.91	7.67	7.47	7.30
1000	18.24	17.22	16.44	15.82	15.33	14.93	14.61
2000	36.47	34.45	32.88	31.65	30.66	29.87	29.22
3000	54.71	51.67	49.32	47.47	46.00	44.80	43.82
4000	72.94	68.89	65.76	63.30	61.33	59.73	58.43
5000	91.18	86.12	82.21	79.12	76.66	74.67	73.04
6000	109.42	103.34	98.65	94.95	91.99	89.60	87.65
7000	127.65	120.56	115.09	110.77	107.32	104.53	102.26
8000	145.89	137.79	131.53	126.60	122.66	119.47	116.86
9000	164.12	155.01	147.97	142.42	137.99	134.40	131.47
10000	182.36	172.24	164.41	158.25	153.32	149.33	146.08
11000	200.60	189.46	180.85	174.07	168.65	164.27	160.69
12000	218.83	206.68	197.29	189.90	183.98	179.20	175.29
13000	237.07	223.91	213.73	205.72	199.32	194.13	189.90
14000	255.30	241.13	230.17	221.55	214.65	209.07	204.51
15000	273.54	258.35	246.62	237.37	229.98	224.00	219.12
20000	364.72	344.47	328.82	316.49	306.64	298.67	292.16
25000	455.90	430.59	411.03	395.62	383.30	373.34	365.20
30000	547.08	516.71	493.23	474.74	459.96	448.00	438.24
35000	638.26	602.82	575.44	553.87	536.62	522.67	511.28
40000	729.44	688.94	657.64	632.99	613.28	597.34	584.32
45000	820.62	775.06	739.85	712.11	689.94	672.01	657.36
50000	911.80	861.18	822.05	791.24	766.60	746.67	730.39
55000	1002.98	947.29	904.26	870.36	843.26	821.34	803.43
56000	1021.21	964.52	920.70	886.19	858.59	836.27	818.04
57000	1039.45	981.74	937.14	902.01	873.93	851.21	832.65
58000	1057.68	998.96	953.58	917.84	889.26	866.14	847.26
59000	1075.92	1016.19	970.02	933.66	904.59	881.07	861.87
60000	1094.16	1033.41	986.46	949.48	919.92	896.01	876.47
61000	1112.39	1050.64	1002.90	965.31	935.25	910.94	891.08
62000	1130.63	1067.86	1019.35	981.13	950.59	925.87	905.69
63000	1148.86	1085.08	1035.79	996.96	965.92	940.81	920.30
64000	1167.10	1102.31	1052.23	1012.78	981.25	955.74	934.91
65000	1185.33	1119.53	1068.67	1028.61	996.58	970.67	949.51
70000	1276.51	1205.65	1150.87	1107.73	1073.24	1045.34	1022.55
75000	1367.69	1291.76	1233.08	1186.86	1149.90	1120.01	1095.59
80000	1458.87	1377.88	1315.28	1265.98	1226.56	1194.68	1168.63
85000	1550.05	1464.00	1397.49	1345.10	1303.22	1269.34	1241.67
90000	1641.23	1550.12	1479.69	1424.23	1379.88	1344.01	1314.71
95000	1732.41	1636.23	1561.90	1503.35	1456.54	1418.68	1387.75
100000	1823.59	1722.35	1644.11	1582.47	1533.20	1493.35	1460.79
105000	1914.77	1808.47	1726.31	1661.60	1609.86	1568.01	1533.83
110000	2005.95	1894.59	1808.52	1740.72	1686.52	1642.68	1606.87
120000	2188.31	2066.82	1972.93	1898.97	1839.85	1792.01	1752.95
130000	2370.67	2239.06	2137.34	2057.22	1993.17	1941.35	1899.03
140000	2553.03	2411.29	2301.75	2215.46	2146.49	2090.68	2045.11
150000	2735.39	2583.53	2466.16	2373.71	2299.81	2240.02	2191.18
160000	2917.75	2755.76	2630.57	2531.96	2453.13	2389.35	2337.26
175000	3191.29	3014.12	2877.18	2769.33	2683.11	2613.35	2556.38
200000	3647.18	3444.71	3288.21	3164.95	3066.41	2986.69	2921.58
250000	4558.98	4305.88	4110.26	3956.19	3833.01	3733.36	3651.97
500000	9117.96	8611.76	8220.53	7912.37	7666.02	7466.73	7303.95
1000000	18235.92	17223.53	16441.05	15824.74	15332.04	14933.46	14607.90

15.50%   MONTHLY PAYMENTS

AMOUNT	15 YEARS	16 YEARS	17 YEARS	18 YEARS	19 YEARS	20 YEARS	21 YEARS
100	1.43	1.41	1.39	1.38	1.36	1.35	1.34
200	2.87	2.82	2.79	2.76	2.73	2.71	2.69
500	7.17	7.06	6.97	6.89	6.82	6.77	6.72
1000	14.34	14.12	13.93	13.78	13.65	13.54	13.45
2000	28.68	28.24	27.87	27.56	27.30	27.08	26.89
3000	43.02	42.35	41.80	41.33	40.94	40.62	40.34
4000	57.36	56.47	55.73	55.11	54.59	54.16	53.79
5000	71.70	70.59	69.66	68.89	68.24	67.69	67.23
6000	86.04	84.71	83.60	82.67	81.89	81.23	80.68
7000	100.38	98.83	97.53	96.45	95.54	94.77	94.12
8000	114.72	112.94	111.46	110.23	109.19	108.31	107.57
9000	129.06	127.06	125.40	124.00	122.83	121.85	121.02
10000	143.40	141.18	139.33	137.78	136.48	135.39	134.46
11000	157.74	155.30	153.26	151.56	150.13	148.93	147.91
12000	172.08	169.41	167.20	165.34	163.78	162.47	161.36
13000	186.42	183.53	181.13	179.12	177.43	176.00	174.80
14000	200.76	197.65	195.06	192.89	191.08	189.54	188.25
15000	215.10	211.77	208.99	206.67	204.72	203.08	201.70
20000	286.80	282.36	278.66	275.56	272.97	270.78	268.93
25000	358.50	352.95	348.32	344.45	341.21	338.47	336.16
30000	430.20	423.54	417.99	413.35	409.45	406.16	403.39
35000	501.90	494.13	487.65	482.24	477.69	473.86	470.62
40000	573.60	564.71	557.32	551.13	545.93	541.55	537.85
45000	645.30	635.30	626.98	620.02	614.17	609.25	605.09
50000	717.00	705.89	696.65	688.91	682.41	676.94	672.32
55000	788.69	776.48	766.31	757.80	750.65	744.63	739.55
56000	803.03	790.60	780.24	771.58	764.30	758.17	753.00
57000	817.37	804.72	794.18	785.36	777.95	771.71	766.44
58000	831.71	818.84	808.11	799.14	791.60	785.25	779.89
59000	846.05	832.95	822.04	812.91	805.25	798.79	793.34
60000	860.39	847.07	835.98	826.69	818.90	812.33	806.78
61000	874.73	861.19	849.91	840.47	832.54	825.87	820.23
62000	889.07	875.31	863.84	854.25	846.19	839.41	833.67
63000	903.41	889.43	877.77	868.03	859.84	852.94	847.12
64000	917.75	903.54	891.71	881.80	873.49	866.48	860.57
65000	932.09	917.66	905.64	895.58	887.14	880.02	874.01
70000	1003.79	988.25	975.30	964.47	955.38	947.72	941.25
75000	1075.49	1058.84	1044.97	1033.36	1023.62	1015.41	1008.48
80000	1147.19	1129.43	1114.63	1102.26	1091.86	1083.10	1075.71
85000	1218.89	1200.02	1184.30	1171.15	1160.10	1150.80	1142.94
90000	1290.59	1270.61	1253.96	1240.04	1228.34	1218.49	1210.17
95000	1362.29	1341.20	1323.63	1308.93	1296.58	1286.19	1277.40
100000	1433.99	1411.79	1393.29	1377.82	1364.83	1353.88	1344.64
105000	1505.69	1482.38	1462.96	1446.71	1433.07	1421.57	1411.87
110000	1577.39	1552.97	1532.62	1515.60	1501.31	1489.27	1479.10
120000	1720.79	1694.14	1671.95	1653.38	1637.79	1624.66	1613.56
130000	1864.19	1835.32	1811.28	1791.17	1774.27	1760.04	1748.03
140000	2007.59	1976.50	1950.61	1928.95	1910.76	1895.43	1882.49
150000	2150.99	2117.68	2089.94	2066.73	2047.24	2030.82	2016.95
160000	2294.38	2258.86	2229.27	2204.51	2183.72	2166.21	2151.42
175000	2509.48	2470.63	2438.26	2411.18	2388.45	2369.29	2353.11
200000	2867.98	2823.57	2786.58	2755.64	2729.65	2707.76	2689.27
250000	3584.98	3529.47	3483.23	3444.55	3412.07	3384.70	3361.59
500000	7169.95	7058.93	6966.46	6889.10	6824.13	6769.40	6723.18
1000000	14339.90	14117.87	13932.92	13778.19	13648.26	13538.81	13446.36

MONTHLY PAYMENTS   15.50%

AMOUNT	22 YEARS	23 YEARS	24 YEARS	25 YEARS	30 YEARS	35 YEARS	40 YEARS
100	1.34	1.33	1.32	1.32	1.30	1.30	1.29
200	2.67	2.66	2.65	2.64	2.61	2.60	2.59
500	6.68	6.65	6.62	6.60	6.52	6.49	6.47
1000	13.37	13.30	13.25	13.20	13.05	12.98	12.94
2000	26.74	26.60	26.49	26.39	26.09	25.95	25.89
3000	40.10	39.91	39.74	39.59	39.14	38.93	38.83
4000	53.47	53.21	52.98	52.79	52.18	51.90	51.78
5000	66.84	66.51	66.23	65.99	65.23	64.88	64.72
6000	80.21	79.81	79.47	79.18	78.27	77.86	77.66
7000	93.58	93.11	92.72	92.38	91.32	90.83	90.61
8000	106.94	106.41	105.96	105.58	104.36	103.81	103.55
9000	120.31	119.72	119.21	118.78	117.41	116.78	116.50
10000	133.68	133.02	132.45	131.97	130.45	129.76	129.44
11000	147.05	146.32	145.70	145.17	143.50	142.73	142.38
12000	160.42	159.62	158.94	158.37	156.54	155.71	155.33
13000	173.79	172.92	172.19	171.57	169.59	168.69	168.27
14000	187.15	186.22	185.44	184.76	182.63	181.66	181.22
15000	200.52	199.53	198.68	197.96	195.68	194.64	194.16
20000	267.36	266.04	264.91	263.95	260.90	259.52	258.88
25000	334.20	332.54	331.13	329.94	326.13	324.40	323.60
30000	401.04	399.05	397.36	395.92	391.36	389.28	388.32
35000	467.88	465.56	463.59	461.91	456.58	454.15	453.04
40000	534.72	532.07	529.82	527.90	521.81	519.03	517.76
45000	601.57	598.58	596.04	593.89	587.03	583.91	582.48
50000	668.41	665.09	662.27	659.87	652.26	648.79	647.20
55000	735.25	731.60	728.50	725.86	717.48	713.67	711.92
56000	748.61	744.90	741.74	739.06	730.53	726.65	724.86
57000	761.98	758.20	754.99	752.25	743.57	739.62	737.81
58000	775.35	771.50	768.23	765.45	756.62	752.60	750.75
59000	788.72	784.80	781.48	778.65	769.66	765.57	763.70
60000	802.09	798.11	794.72	791.85	782.71	778.55	776.64
61000	815.46	811.41	807.97	805.04	795.76	791.53	789.58
62000	828.82	824.71	821.21	818.24	808.80	804.50	802.53
63000	842.19	838.01	834.46	831.44	821.85	817.48	815.47
64000	855.56	851.31	847.71	844.64	834.89	830.45	828.42
65000	868.93	864.61	860.95	857.83	847.94	843.43	841.36
70000	935.77	931.12	927.18	923.82	913.16	908.31	906.08
75000	1002.61	997.63	993.40	989.81	978.39	973.19	970.80
80000	1069.45	1064.14	1059.63	1055.80	1043.61	1038.07	1035.52
85000	1136.29	1130.65	1125.86	1121.78	1108.84	1102.95	1100.24
90000	1203.13	1197.16	1192.09	1187.77	1174.07	1167.83	1164.96
95000	1269.97	1263.67	1258.31	1253.76	1239.29	1232.71	1229.68
100000	1336.81	1330.18	1324.54	1319.75	1304.52	1297.58	1294.40
105000	1403.65	1396.68	1390.77	1385.73	1369.74	1362.46	1359.12
110000	1470.49	1463.19	1456.99	1451.72	1434.97	1427.34	1423.84
120000	1604.17	1596.21	1589.45	1583.69	1565.42	1557.10	1553.28
130000	1737.86	1729.23	1721.90	1715.67	1695.87	1686.86	1682.72
140000	1871.54	1862.25	1854.36	1847.64	1826.32	1816.62	1812.16
150000	2005.22	1995.26	1986.81	1979.62	1956.78	1946.38	1941.60
160000	2138.90	2128.28	2119.26	2111.59	2087.23	2076.14	2071.04
175000	2339.42	2327.81	2317.94	2309.55	2282.90	2270.77	2265.20
200000	2673.62	2660.35	2649.08	2639.49	2609.03	2595.17	2588.80
250000	3342.03	3325.44	3311.35	3299.36	3261.29	3243.96	3236.00
500000	6684.06	6650.88	6622.70	6598.73	6522.58	6487.92	6472.00
1000000	13368.12	13301.76	13245.39	13197.45	13045.17	12975.85	12944.00

15.75%   MONTHLY PAYMENTS

AMOUNT	1 YEAR	2 YEARS	3 YEARS	4 YEARS	5 YEARS	6 YEARS	7 YEARS
100	9.06	4.88	3.50	2.82	2.42	2.16	1.97
200	18.12	9.77	7.01	5.64	4.84	4.31	3.94
500	45.31	24.42	17.52	14.11	12.09	10.78	9.86
1000	90.61	48.84	35.03	28.21	24.19	21.55	19.72
2000	181.23	97.69	70.07	56.42	48.37	43.11	39.44
3000	271.84	146.53	105.10	84.64	72.56	64.66	59.16
4000	362.45	195.37	140.13	112.85	96.74	86.22	78.88
5000	453.06	244.22	175.17	141.06	120.93	107.77	98.60
6000	543.68	293.06	210.20	169.27	145.11	129.33	118.32
7000	634.29	341.91	245.24	197.49	169.30	150.88	138.04
8000	724.90	390.75	280.27	225.70	193.48	172.44	157.76
9000	815.51	439.59	315.30	253.91	217.67	193.99	177.48
10000	906.13	488.44	350.34	282.12	241.85	215.54	197.20
11000	996.74	537.28	385.37	310.34	266.04	237.10	216.92
12000	1087.35	586.12	420.40	338.55	290.23	258.65	236.64
13000	1177.96	634.97	455.44	366.76	314.41	280.21	256.36
14000	1268.58	683.81	490.47	394.97	338.60	301.76	276.08
15000	1359.19	732.66	525.51	423.19	362.78	323.32	295.80
20000	1812.25	976.87	700.67	564.25	483.71	431.09	394.40
25000	2265.31	1221.09	875.84	705.31	604.64	538.86	493.00
30000	2718.38	1465.31	1051.01	846.37	725.56	646.63	591.60
35000	3171.44	1709.53	1226.18	987.43	846.49	754.41	690.20
40000	3624.50	1953.75	1401.35	1128.50	967.42	862.18	788.80
45000	4077.57	2197.97	1576.52	1269.56	1088.34	969.95	887.40
50000	4530.63	2442.19	1751.69	1410.62	1209.27	1077.72	986.00
55000	4983.69	2686.41	1926.86	1551.68	1330.20	1185.49	1084.60
56000	5074.31	2735.25	1961.89	1579.89	1354.38	1207.05	1104.32
57000	5164.92	2784.09	1996.92	1608.11	1378.57	1228.60	1124.04
58000	5255.53	2832.94	2031.96	1636.32	1402.75	1250.16	1143.76
59000	5346.14	2881.78	2066.99	1664.53	1426.94	1271.71	1163.48
60000	5436.76	2930.62	2102.02	1692.74	1451.13	1293.27	1183.20
61000	5527.37	2979.47	2137.06	1720.96	1475.31	1314.82	1202.92
62000	5617.98	3028.31	2172.09	1749.17	1499.50	1336.37	1222.64
63000	5708.59	3077.16	2207.13	1777.38	1523.68	1357.93	1242.36
64000	5799.21	3126.00	2242.16	1805.59	1547.87	1379.48	1262.08
65000	5889.82	3174.84	2277.19	1833.81	1572.05	1401.04	1281.80
70000	6342.88	3419.06	2452.36	1974.87	1692.98	1508.81	1380.40
75000	6795.94	3663.28	2627.53	2115.93	1813.91	1616.58	1479.00
80000	7249.01	3907.50	2802.70	2256.99	1934.83	1724.35	1577.60
85000	7702.07	4151.72	2977.87	2398.05	2055.76	1832.13	1676.19
90000	8155.13	4395.94	3153.04	2539.12	2176.69	1939.90	1774.79
95000	8608.20	4640.16	3328.20	2680.18	2297.62	2047.67	1873.39
100000	9061.26	4884.37	3503.37	2821.24	2418.54	2155.44	1971.99
105000	9514.32	5128.59	3678.54	2962.30	2539.47	2263.22	2070.59
110000	9967.39	5372.81	3853.71	3103.36	2660.40	2370.99	2169.19
120000	10873.51	5861.25	4204.05	3385.49	2902.25	2586.53	2366.39
130000	11779.64	6349.69	4554.39	3667.61	3144.11	2802.08	2563.59
140000	12685.76	6838.12	4904.72	3949.74	3385.96	3017.62	2760.79
150000	13591.89	7326.56	5255.06	4231.86	3627.81	3233.16	2957.99
160000	14498.02	7815.00	5605.40	4513.98	3869.67	3448.71	3155.19
175000	15857.20	8547.65	6130.90	4937.17	4232.45	3772.03	3450.99
200000	18122.52	9768.75	7006.75	5642.48	4837.08	4310.89	3943.99
250000	22653.15	12210.94	8758.43	7053.10	6046.36	5388.61	4929.99
500000	45306.30	24421.87	17516.87	14106.20	12092.71	10777.22	9859.97
1000000	90612.59	48843.74	35033.73	28212.41	24185.42	21554.43	19719.94

MONTHLY PAYMENTS 15.75%

AMOUNT	8 YEARS	9 YEARS	10 YEARS	11 YEARS	12 YEARS	13 YEARS	14 YEARS
100	1.84	1.74	1.66	1.60	1.55	1.51	1.48
200	3.68	3.47	3.32	3.20	3.10	3.02	2.96
500	9.19	8.69	8.30	7.99	7.75	7.55	7.39
1000	18.38	17.37	16.60	15.98	15.49	15.10	14.78
2000	36.76	34.75	33.19	31.97	30.99	30.20	29.56
3000	55.15	52.12	49.79	47.95	46.48	45.30	44.33
4000	73.53	69.50	66.38	63.93	61.98	60.40	59.11
5000	91.91	86.87	82.98	79.92	77.47	75.50	73.89
6000	110.29	104.24	99.58	95.90	92.97	90.60	88.67
7000	128.67	121.62	116.17	111.89	108.46	105.70	103.44
8000	147.06	138.99	132.77	127.87	123.96	120.80	118.22
9000	165.44	156.37	149.36	143.85	139.45	135.90	133.00
10000	183.82	173.74	165.96	159.84	154.95	151.00	147.78
11000	202.20	191.11	182.55	175.82	170.44	166.10	162.56
12000	220.58	208.49	199.15	191.80	185.94	181.20	177.33
13000	238.97	225.86	215.75	207.79	201.43	196.30	192.11
14000	257.35	243.24	232.34	223.77	216.93	211.40	206.89
15000	275.73	260.61	248.94	239.75	232.42	226.50	221.67
20000	367.64	347.48	331.92	319.67	309.90	302.00	295.56
25000	459.55	434.35	414.90	399.59	387.37	377.50	369.45
30000	551.46	521.22	497.88	479.51	464.84	453.00	443.33
35000	643.37	608.09	580.85	559.43	542.32	528.50	517.22
40000	735.28	694.96	663.83	639.34	619.79	604.00	591.11
45000	827.19	781.83	746.81	719.26	697.27	679.49	665.00
50000	919.10	868.70	829.79	799.18	774.74	754.99	738.89
55000	1011.01	955.57	912.77	879.10	852.21	830.49	812.78
56000	1029.40	972.95	929.37	895.08	867.71	845.59	827.56
57000	1047.78	990.32	945.96	911.07	883.20	860.69	842.33
58000	1066.16	1007.70	962.56	927.05	898.70	875.79	857.11
59000	1084.54	1025.07	979.16	943.03	914.19	890.89	871.89
60000	1102.92	1042.44	995.75	959.02	929.69	905.99	886.67
61000	1121.31	1059.82	1012.35	975.00	945.18	921.09	901.45
62000	1139.69	1077.19	1028.94	990.98	960.68	936.19	916.22
63000	1158.07	1094.57	1045.54	1006.97	976.17	951.29	931.00
64000	1176.45	1111.94	1062.13	1022.95	991.67	966.39	945.78
65000	1194.83	1129.31	1078.73	1038.93	1007.16	981.49	960.56
70000	1286.74	1216.19	1161.71	1118.85	1084.63	1056.99	1034.45
75000	1378.65	1303.06	1244.69	1198.77	1162.11	1132.49	1108.34
80000	1470.57	1389.93	1327.67	1278.69	1239.58	1207.99	1182.22
85000	1562.48	1476.80	1410.65	1358.61	1317.06	1283.49	1256.11
90000	1654.39	1563.67	1493.63	1438.52	1394.53	1358.99	1330.00
95000	1746.30	1650.54	1576.61	1518.44	1472.00	1434.49	1403.89
100000	1838.21	1737.41	1659.58	1598.36	1549.48	1509.99	1477.78
105000	1930.12	1824.28	1742.56	1678.28	1626.95	1585.49	1551.67
110000	2022.03	1911.15	1825.54	1758.20	1704.43	1660.99	1625.56
120000	2205.85	2084.89	1991.50	1918.03	1859.37	1811.99	1773.34
130000	2389.67	2258.63	2157.46	2077.87	2014.32	1962.98	1921.11
140000	2573.49	2432.37	2323.42	2237.71	2169.27	2113.98	2068.89
150000	2757.31	2606.11	2489.38	2397.54	2324.22	2264.98	2216.67
160000	2941.13	2779.85	2655.34	2557.38	2479.17	2415.98	2364.45
175000	3216.86	3040.46	2904.27	2797.13	2711.59	2642.48	2586.12
200000	3676.41	3474.81	3319.17	3196.72	3098.96	3019.98	2955.56
250000	4595.52	4343.52	4148.96	3995.90	3873.70	3774.97	3694.45
500000	9191.03	8687.04	8297.92	7991.80	7747.39	7549.94	7388.90
1000000	18382.06	17374.07	16595.85	15983.61	15494.78	15099.88	14777.80

15.75%　　　MONTHLY PAYMENTS

AMOUNT	15 YEARS	16 YEARS	17 YEARS	18 YEARS	19 YEARS	20 YEARS	21 YEARS
100	1.45	1.43	1.41	1.40	1.38	1.37	1.36
200	2.90	2.86	2.82	2.79	2.77	2.75	2.73
500	7.26	7.15	7.06	6.98	6.92	6.86	6.82
1000	14.51	14.29	14.11	13.96	13.83	13.73	13.64
2000	29.03	28.59	28.22	27.92	27.67	27.45	27.27
3000	43.54	42.88	42.34	41.88	41.50	41.18	40.91
4000	58.05	57.18	56.45	55.84	55.33	54.90	54.54
5000	72.57	71.47	70.56	69.80	69.16	68.63	68.18
6000	87.08	85.76	84.67	83.76	83.00	82.35	81.81
7000	101.59	100.06	98.78	97.72	96.83	96.08	95.45
8000	116.10	114.35	112.90	111.68	110.66	109.80	109.08
9000	130.62	128.65	127.01	125.64	124.49	123.53	122.72
10000	145.13	142.94	141.12	139.60	138.33	137.25	136.35
11000	159.64	157.24	155.23	153.56	152.16	150.98	149.99
12000	174.16	171.53	169.34	167.52	165.99	164.70	163.62
13000	188.67	185.82	183.46	181.48	179.82	178.43	177.26
14000	203.18	200.12	197.57	195.44	193.66	192.15	190.89
15000	217.70	214.41	211.68	209.40	207.49	205.88	204.53
20000	290.26	285.88	282.24	279.20	276.65	274.51	272.70
25000	362.83	357.35	352.80	349.00	345.81	343.13	340.88
30000	435.39	428.82	423.36	418.80	414.98	411.76	409.05
35000	507.96	500.29	493.92	488.60	484.14	480.39	477.23
40000	580.52	571.76	564.48	558.40	553.30	549.01	545.40
45000	653.09	643.23	635.04	628.20	622.46	617.64	613.58
50000	725.65	714.71	705.60	698.00	691.63	686.27	681.75
55000	798.22	786.18	776.16	767.80	760.79	754.89	749.93
56000	812.73	800.47	790.27	781.76	774.62	768.62	763.56
57000	827.25	814.76	804.39	795.72	788.45	782.34	777.20
58000	841.76	829.06	818.50	809.68	802.29	796.07	790.83
59000	856.27	843.35	832.61	823.64	816.12	809.79	804.47
60000	870.78	857.65	846.72	837.60	829.95	823.52	818.10
61000	885.30	871.94	860.83	851.56	843.78	837.25	831.74
62000	899.81	886.23	874.95	865.52	857.62	850.97	845.37
63000	914.32	900.53	889.06	879.48	871.45	864.70	859.01
64000	928.84	914.82	903.17	893.44	885.28	878.42	872.64
65000	943.35	929.12	917.28	907.40	899.11	892.15	886.28
70000	1015.92	1000.59	987.84	977.20	968.28	960.77	954.45
75000	1088.48	1072.06	1058.40	1047.00	1037.44	1029.40	1022.63
80000	1161.05	1143.53	1128.96	1116.80	1106.60	1098.03	1090.80
85000	1233.61	1215.00	1199.52	1186.60	1175.76	1166.65	1158.98
90000	1306.18	1286.47	1270.08	1256.40	1244.93	1235.28	1227.15
95000	1378.74	1357.94	1340.64	1326.20	1314.09	1303.91	1295.33
100000	1451.31	1429.41	1411.20	1396.00	1383.25	1372.53	1363.50
105000	1523.87	1500.88	1481.76	1465.80	1452.41	1441.16	1431.68
110000	1596.44	1572.35	1552.32	1535.60	1521.58	1509.79	1499.85
120000	1741.57	1715.29	1693.44	1675.20	1659.90	1647.04	1636.20
130000	1886.70	1858.23	1834.56	1814.80	1798.23	1784.29	1772.55
140000	2031.83	2001.18	1975.68	1954.40	1936.55	1921.55	1908.90
150000	2176.96	2144.12	2116.80	2094.00	2074.83	2058.80	2045.25
160000	2322.09	2287.06	2257.93	2233.59	2213.20	2196.05	2181.60
175000	2539.79	2501.47	2469.61	2442.99	2420.69	2401.93	2386.13
200000	2902.62	2858.82	2822.41	2791.99	2766.50	2745.07	2727.00
250000	3628.27	3573.53	3528.01	3489.99	3458.13	3431.33	3408.75
500000	7256.54	7147.05	7056.02	6979.98	6916.25	6862.67	6817.50
1000000	14513.08	14294.11	14112.03	13959.97	13832.50	13725.34	13635.00

MONTHLY PAYMENTS 15.75%

AMOUNT	22 YEARS	23 YEARS	24 YEARS	25 YEARS	30 YEARS	35 YEARS	40 YEARS
100	1.36	1.35	1.34	1.34	1.32	1.32	1.32
200	2.71	2.70	2.69	2.68	2.65	2.64	2.63
500	6.78	6.75	6.72	6.70	6.62	6.59	6.58
1000	13.56	13.49	13.44	13.39	13.25	13.18	13.15
2000	27.12	26.99	26.88	26.79	26.49	26.36	26.30
3000	40.68	40.48	40.32	40.18	39.74	39.54	39.45
4000	54.23	53.98	53.76	53.57	52.98	52.72	52.60
5000	67.79	67.47	67.20	66.96	66.23	65.90	65.75
6000	81.35	80.96	80.64	80.36	79.48	79.08	78.90
7000	94.91	94.46	94.08	93.75	92.72	92.26	92.05
8000	108.47	107.95	107.51	107.14	105.97	105.44	105.20
9000	122.03	121.45	120.95	120.54	119.22	118.62	118.35
10000	135.59	134.94	134.39	133.93	132.46	131.80	131.50
11000	149.15	148.44	147.83	147.32	145.71	144.98	144.65
12000	162.70	161.93	161.27	160.71	158.95	158.16	157.80
13000	176.26	175.42	174.71	174.11	172.20	171.34	170.95
14000	189.82	188.92	188.15	187.50	185.45	184.52	184.10
15000	203.38	202.41	201.59	200.89	198.69	197.70	197.25
20000	271.17	269.88	268.79	267.86	264.92	263.60	263.00
25000	338.97	337.35	335.98	334.82	331.15	329.50	328.75
30000	406.76	404.82	403.18	401.79	397.39	395.40	394.50
35000	474.55	472.29	470.38	468.75	463.62	461.30	460.26
40000	542.35	539.76	537.57	535.72	529.85	527.21	526.01
45000	610.14	607.23	604.77	602.68	596.08	593.11	591.76
50000	677.93	674.71	671.97	669.64	662.31	659.01	657.51
55000	745.73	742.18	739.16	736.61	728.54	724.91	723.26
56000	759.29	755.67	752.60	750.00	741.79	738.09	736.41
57000	772.85	769.16	766.04	763.40	755.03	751.27	749.56
58000	786.40	782.66	779.48	776.79	768.28	764.45	762.71
59000	799.96	796.15	792.92	790.18	781.52	777.63	775.86
60000	813.52	809.65	806.36	803.57	794.77	790.81	789.01
61000	827.08	823.14	819.80	816.97	808.02	803.99	802.16
62000	840.64	836.63	833.24	830.36	821.26	817.17	815.31
63000	854.20	850.13	846.68	843.75	834.51	830.35	828.46
64000	867.76	863.62	860.12	857.15	847.75	843.53	841.61
65000	881.31	877.12	873.56	870.54	861.00	856.71	854.76
70000	949.11	944.59	940.76	937.50	927.23	922.61	920.51
75000	1016.90	1012.06	1007.95	1004.47	993.46	988.51	986.26
80000	1084.70	1079.53	1075.15	1071.43	1059.69	1054.41	1052.01
85000	1152.49	1147.00	1142.35	1138.40	1125.92	1120.31	1117.76
90000	1220.28	1214.47	1209.54	1205.36	1192.16	1186.21	1183.51
95000	1288.08	1281.94	1276.74	1272.33	1258.39	1252.11	1249.27
100000	1355.87	1349.41	1343.94	1339.29	1324.62	1318.01	1315.02
105000	1423.66	1416.88	1411.13	1406.25	1390.85	1383.91	1380.77
110000	1491.46	1484.35	1478.33	1473.22	1457.08	1449.82	1446.52
120000	1627.04	1619.29	1612.72	1607.15	1589.54	1581.62	1578.02
130000	1762.63	1754.23	1747.12	1741.08	1722.00	1713.42	1709.52
140000	1898.22	1889.17	1881.51	1875.01	1854.46	1845.22	1841.02
150000	2033.80	2024.12	2015.90	2008.93	1986.93	1977.02	1972.52
160000	2169.39	2159.06	2150.30	2142.86	2119.39	2108.82	2104.03
175000	2372.77	2361.47	2351.89	2343.76	2318.08	2306.52	2301.28
200000	2711.74	2698.82	2687.87	2678.58	2649.23	2636.03	2630.03
250000	3389.67	3373.53	3359.84	3348.22	3311.54	3295.03	3287.54
500000	6779.34	6747.05	6719.68	6696.45	6623.09	6590.07	6575.08
1000000	13558.69	13494.10	13439.36	13392.90	13246.17	13180.14	13150.16

16.00%   MONTHLY PAYMENTS

AMOUNT	1 YEAR	2 YEARS	3 YEARS	4 YEARS	5 YEARS	6 YEARS	7 YEARS
100	9.07	4.90	3.52	2.83	2.43	2.17	1.99
200	18.15	9.79	7.03	5.67	4.86	4.34	3.97
500	45.37	24.48	17.58	14.17	12.16	10.85	9.93
1000	90.73	48.96	35.16	28.34	24.32	21.69	19.86
2000	181.46	97.93	70.31	56.68	48.64	43.38	39.72
3000	272.19	146.89	105.47	85.02	72.95	65.08	59.59
4000	362.92	195.85	140.63	113.36	97.27	86.77	79.45
5000	453.65	244.82	175.79	141.70	121.59	108.46	99.31
6000	544.39	293.78	210.94	170.04	145.91	130.15	119.17
7000	635.12	342.74	246.10	198.38	170.23	151.84	139.03
8000	725.85	391.70	281.26	226.72	194.54	173.53	158.90
9000	816.58	440.67	316.41	255.06	218.86	195.23	178.76
10000	907.31	489.63	351.57	283.40	243.18	216.92	198.62
11000	998.04	538.59	386.73	311.74	267.50	238.61	218.48
12000	1088.77	587.56	421.88	340.08	291.82	260.30	238.34
13000	1179.50	636.52	457.04	368.42	316.13	281.99	258.21
14000	1270.23	685.48	492.20	396.76	340.45	303.69	278.07
15000	1360.96	734.45	527.36	425.10	364.77	325.38	297.93
20000	1814.62	979.26	703.14	566.81	486.36	433.84	397.24
25000	2268.27	1224.08	878.93	708.51	607.95	542.30	496.55
30000	2721.93	1468.89	1054.71	850.21	729.54	650.76	595.86
35000	3175.58	1713.71	1230.50	991.91	851.13	759.21	695.17
40000	3629.23	1958.52	1406.28	1133.61	972.72	867.67	794.48
45000	4082.89	2203.34	1582.07	1275.31	1094.31	976.13	893.79
50000	4536.54	2448.16	1757.85	1417.01	1215.90	1084.59	993.10
55000	4990.20	2692.97	1933.64	1558.72	1337.49	1193.05	1092.41
56000	5080.93	2741.93	1968.79	1587.06	1361.81	1214.74	1112.28
57000	5171.66	2790.90	2003.95	1615.40	1386.13	1236.43	1132.14
58000	5262.39	2839.86	2039.11	1643.74	1410.45	1258.13	1152.00
59000	5353.12	2888.82	2074.26	1672.08	1434.77	1279.82	1171.86
60000	5443.85	2937.79	2109.42	1700.42	1459.08	1301.51	1191.72
61000	5534.58	2986.75	2144.58	1728.76	1483.40	1323.20	1211.59
62000	5625.31	3035.71	2179.74	1757.10	1507.72	1344.89	1231.45
63000	5716.04	3084.68	2214.89	1785.44	1532.04	1366.59	1251.31
64000	5806.77	3133.64	2250.05	1813.78	1556.36	1388.28	1271.17
65000	5897.51	3182.60	2285.21	1842.12	1580.67	1409.97	1291.03
70000	6351.16	3427.42	2460.99	1983.82	1702.26	1518.43	1390.34
75000	6804.81	3672.23	2636.78	2125.52	1823.85	1626.89	1489.65
80000	7258.47	3917.05	2812.56	2267.22	1945.44	1735.35	1588.97
85000	7712.12	4161.86	2988.35	2408.92	2067.03	1843.81	1688.28
90000	8165.78	4406.68	3164.13	2550.63	2188.63	1952.27	1787.59
95000	8619.43	4651.50	3339.92	2692.33	2310.22	2060.72	1886.90
100000	9073.09	4896.31	3515.70	2834.03	2431.81	2169.18	1986.21
105000	9526.74	5141.13	3691.49	2975.73	2553.40	2277.64	2085.52
110000	9980.39	5385.94	3867.27	3117.43	2674.99	2386.10	2184.83
120000	10887.70	5875.57	4218.84	3400.83	2918.17	2603.02	2383.45
130000	11795.01	6365.20	4570.41	3684.24	3161.35	2819.94	2582.07
140000	12702.32	6854.84	4921.98	3967.64	3404.53	3036.86	2780.69
150000	13609.63	7344.47	5273.55	4251.04	3647.71	3253.78	2979.31
160000	14516.94	7834.10	5625.13	4534.44	3890.89	3470.69	3177.93
175000	15877.90	8568.54	6152.48	4959.55	4255.66	3796.07	3475.86
200000	18146.17	9792.62	7031.41	5668.06	4863.61	4338.37	3972.41
250000	22682.71	12240.78	8789.26	7085.07	6079.51	5422.96	4965.52
500000	45365.43	24481.56	17578.52	14170.14	12159.03	10845.92	9931.03
1000000	90730.86	48963.11	35157.03	28340.28	24318.06	21691.84	19862.06

MONTHLY PAYMENTS 16.00%

AMOUNT	8 YEARS	9 YEARS	10 YEARS	11 YEARS	12 YEARS	13 YEARS	14 YEARS
100	1.85	1.75	1.68	1.61	1.57	1.53	1.49
200	3.71	3.51	3.35	3.23	3.13	3.05	2.99
500	9.26	8.76	8.38	8.07	7.83	7.63	7.47
1000	18.53	17.53	16.75	16.14	15.66	15.27	14.95
2000	37.06	35.05	33.50	32.29	31.32	30.53	29.90
3000	55.59	52.58	50.25	48.43	46.97	45.80	44.85
4000	74.12	70.10	67.01	64.57	62.63	61.07	59.79
5000	92.64	87.63	83.76	80.72	78.29	76.34	74.74
6000	111.17	105.15	100.51	96.86	93.95	91.60	89.69
7000	129.70	122.68	117.26	113.00	109.61	106.87	104.64
8000	148.23	140.20	134.01	129.15	125.27	122.14	119.59
9000	166.76	157.73	150.76	145.29	140.92	137.40	134.54
10000	185.29	175.25	167.51	161.43	156.58	152.67	149.48
11000	203.82	192.78	184.26	177.57	172.24	167.94	164.43
12000	222.35	210.30	201.02	193.72	187.90	183.20	179.38
13000	240.87	227.83	217.77	209.86	203.56	198.47	194.33
14000	259.40	245.35	234.52	226.00	219.22	213.74	209.28
15000	277.93	262.88	251.27	242.15	234.87	229.01	224.23
20000	370.58	350.51	335.03	322.86	313.17	305.34	298.97
25000	463.22	438.13	418.78	403.58	391.46	381.68	373.71
30000	555.86	525.76	502.54	484.30	469.75	458.01	448.45
35000	648.51	613.38	586.30	565.01	548.04	534.35	523.20
40000	741.15	701.01	670.05	645.73	626.33	610.68	597.94
45000	833.80	788.64	753.81	726.44	704.62	687.02	672.68
50000	926.44	876.26	837.57	807.16	782.91	763.35	747.42
55000	1019.08	963.89	921.32	887.87	861.20	839.69	822.16
56000	1037.61	981.41	938.07	904.02	876.86	854.95	837.11
57000	1056.14	998.94	954.82	920.16	892.52	870.22	852.06
58000	1074.67	1016.46	971.58	936.30	908.18	885.49	867.01
59000	1093.20	1033.99	988.33	952.45	923.84	900.76	881.96
60000	1111.73	1051.52	1005.08	968.59	939.50	916.02	896.91
61000	1130.26	1069.04	1021.83	984.73	955.15	931.29	911.86
62000	1148.78	1086.57	1038.58	1000.88	970.81	946.56	926.80
63000	1167.31	1104.09	1055.33	1017.02	986.47	961.82	941.75
64000	1185.84	1121.62	1072.08	1033.16	1002.13	977.09	956.70
65000	1204.37	1139.14	1088.84	1049.31	1017.79	992.36	971.65
70000	1297.02	1226.77	1172.59	1130.02	1096.08	1068.69	1046.39
75000	1389.66	1314.39	1256.35	1210.74	1174.37	1145.03	1121.13
80000	1482.30	1402.02	1340.10	1291.45	1252.66	1221.36	1195.88
85000	1574.95	1489.65	1423.86	1372.17	1330.95	1297.70	1270.62
90000	1667.59	1577.27	1507.62	1452.89	1409.24	1374.03	1345.36
95000	1760.23	1664.90	1591.37	1533.60	1487.53	1450.37	1420.10
100000	1852.88	1752.53	1675.13	1614.32	1565.83	1526.70	1494.85
105000	1945.52	1840.15	1758.89	1695.03	1644.12	1603.04	1569.59
110000	2038.17	1927.78	1842.64	1775.75	1722.41	1679.37	1644.33
120000	2223.45	2103.03	2010.16	1937.18	1878.99	1832.05	1793.81
130000	2408.74	2278.28	2177.67	2098.61	2035.57	1984.72	1943.30
140000	2594.03	2453.54	2345.18	2260.04	2192.16	2137.39	2092.78
150000	2779.32	2628.79	2512.70	2421.48	2348.74	2290.06	2242.27
160000	2964.61	2804.04	2680.21	2582.91	2505.32	2442.73	2391.75
175000	3242.54	3066.92	2931.48	2825.06	2740.19	2671.73	2615.98
200000	3705.76	3505.05	3350.26	3228.63	3131.65	3053.41	2989.69
250000	4632.20	4381.31	4187.83	4035.79	3914.56	3816.76	3737.11
500000	9264.39	8762.63	8375.66	8071.59	7829.13	7633.52	7474.23
1000000	18528.79	17525.25	16751.31	16143.17	15658.25	15267.04	14948.45

16.00%   MONTHLY PAYMENTS

AMOUNT	15 YEARS	16 YEARS	17 YEARS	18 YEARS	19 YEARS	20 YEARS	21 YEARS
100	1.47	1.45	1.43	1.41	1.40	1.39	1.38
200	2.94	2.89	2.86	2.83	2.80	2.78	2.76
500	7.34	7.24	7.15	7.07	7.01	6.96	6.91
1000	14.69	14.47	14.29	14.14	14.02	13.91	13.82
2000	29.37	28.94	28.58	28.28	28.03	27.83	27.65
3000	44.06	43.41	42.88	42.43	42.05	41.74	41.47
4000	58.75	57.88	57.17	56.57	56.07	55.65	55.30
5000	73.44	72.36	71.46	70.71	70.09	69.56	69.12
6000	88.12	86.83	85.75	84.85	84.10	83.48	82.95
7000	102.81	101.30	100.04	99.00	98.12	97.39	96.77
8000	117.50	115.77	114.34	113.14	112.14	111.30	110.59
9000	132.18	130.24	128.63	127.28	126.16	125.21	124.42
10000	146.87	144.71	142.92	141.42	140.17	139.13	138.24
11000	161.56	159.18	157.21	155.57	154.19	153.04	152.07
12000	176.24	173.65	171.50	169.71	168.21	166.95	165.89
13000	190.93	188.12	185.79	183.85	182.23	180.86	179.72
14000	205.62	202.60	200.09	197.99	196.24	194.78	193.54
15000	220.31	217.07	214.38	212.14	210.26	208.69	207.36
20000	293.74	289.42	285.84	282.85	280.35	278.25	276.49
25000	367.18	361.78	357.30	353.56	350.44	347.81	345.61
30000	440.61	434.13	428.76	424.27	420.52	417.38	414.73
35000	514.05	506.49	500.22	494.99	490.61	486.94	483.85
40000	587.48	578.84	571.68	565.70	560.70	556.50	552.97
45000	660.92	651.20	643.13	636.41	630.79	626.07	622.09
50000	734.35	723.56	714.59	707.12	700.87	695.63	691.22
55000	807.79	795.91	786.05	777.84	770.96	765.19	760.34
56000	822.47	810.38	800.35	791.98	784.98	779.10	774.16
57000	837.16	824.85	814.64	806.12	799.00	793.02	787.99
58000	851.85	839.32	828.93	820.26	813.01	806.93	801.81
59000	866.53	853.80	843.22	834.41	827.03	820.84	815.63
60000	881.22	868.27	857.51	848.55	841.05	834.75	829.46
61000	895.91	882.74	871.80	862.69	855.07	848.67	843.28
62000	910.59	897.21	886.10	876.83	869.08	862.58	857.11
63000	925.28	911.68	900.39	890.98	883.10	876.49	870.93
64000	939.97	926.15	914.68	905.12	897.12	890.40	884.76
65000	954.66	940.62	928.97	919.26	911.14	904.32	898.58
70000	1028.09	1012.98	1000.43	989.97	981.22	973.88	967.70
75000	1101.53	1085.33	1071.89	1060.69	1051.31	1043.44	1036.82
80000	1174.96	1157.69	1143.35	1131.40	1121.40	1113.00	1105.94
85000	1248.40	1230.04	1214.81	1202.11	1191.48	1182.57	1175.07
90000	1321.83	1302.40	1286.27	1272.82	1261.57	1252.13	1244.19
95000	1395.27	1374.75	1357.73	1343.53	1331.66	1321.69	1313.31
100000	1468.70	1447.11	1429.19	1414.25	1401.75	1391.26	1382.43
105000	1542.14	1519.47	1500.65	1484.96	1471.83	1460.82	1451.55
110000	1615.57	1591.82	1572.11	1555.67	1541.92	1530.38	1520.67
120000	1762.44	1736.53	1715.03	1697.10	1682.10	1669.51	1658.92
130000	1909.31	1881.24	1857.94	1838.52	1822.27	1808.63	1797.16
140000	2056.18	2025.95	2000.86	1979.95	1962.44	1947.76	1935.40
150000	2203.05	2170.67	2143.78	2121.37	2102.62	2086.88	2073.65
160000	2349.92	2315.38	2286.70	2262.80	2242.79	2226.01	2211.89
175000	2570.23	2532.44	2501.08	2474.93	2453.06	2434.70	2419.25
200000	2937.40	2894.22	2858.38	2828.49	2803.49	2782.51	2764.86
250000	3671.75	3617.78	3572.97	3535.62	3504.37	3478.14	3456.08
500000	7343.50	7235.55	7145.94	7071.24	7008.73	6956.28	6912.15
1000000	14687.01	14471.10	14291.88	14142.47	14017.46	13912.56	13824.30

MONTHLY PAYMENTS 16.00%

AMOUNT	22 YEARS	23 YEARS	24 YEARS	25 YEARS	30 YEARS	35 YEARS	40 YEARS
100	1.37	1.37	1.36	1.36	1.34	1.34	1.34
200	2.75	2.74	2.73	2.72	2.69	2.68	2.67
500	6.87	6.84	6.82	6.79	6.72	6.69	6.68
1000	13.75	13.69	13.63	13.59	13.45	13.38	13.36
2000	27.50	27.37	27.27	27.18	26.90	26.77	26.71
3000	41.25	41.06	40.90	40.77	40.34	40.15	40.07
4000	55.00	54.75	54.54	54.36	53.79	53.54	53.43
5000	68.75	68.44	68.17	67.94	67.24	66.92	66.78
6000	82.50	82.12	81.80	81.53	80.69	80.31	80.14
7000	96.25	95.81	95.44	95.12	94.13	93.69	93.50
8000	110.00	109.50	109.07	108.71	107.58	107.08	106.85
9000	123.75	123.18	122.71	122.30	121.03	120.46	120.21
10000	137.50	136.87	136.34	135.89	134.48	133.85	133.56
11000	151.25	150.56	149.97	149.48	147.92	147.23	146.92
12000	165.00	164.24	163.61	163.07	161.37	160.62	160.28
13000	178.75	177.93	177.24	176.66	174.82	174.00	173.63
14000	192.50	191.62	190.87	190.24	188.27	187.39	186.99
15000	206.25	205.31	204.51	203.83	201.71	200.77	200.35
20000	275.00	273.74	272.68	271.78	268.95	267.69	267.13
25000	343.75	342.18	340.85	339.72	336.19	334.62	333.91
30000	412.50	410.61	409.02	407.67	403.43	401.54	400.69
35000	481.25	479.05	477.19	475.61	470.66	468.46	467.48
40000	550.00	547.48	545.36	543.56	537.90	535.39	534.26
45000	618.75	615.92	613.53	611.50	605.14	602.31	601.04
50000	687.50	684.35	681.70	679.44	672.38	669.23	667.82
55000	756.24	752.79	749.86	747.39	739.62	736.16	734.61
56000	769.99	766.48	763.50	760.98	753.06	749.54	747.96
57000	783.74	780.16	777.13	774.57	766.51	762.93	761.32
58000	797.49	793.85	790.77	788.16	779.96	776.31	774.68
59000	811.24	807.54	804.40	801.74	793.41	789.70	788.03
60000	824.99	821.22	818.03	815.33	806.85	803.08	801.39
61000	838.74	834.91	831.67	828.92	820.30	816.47	814.75
62000	852.49	848.60	845.30	842.51	833.75	829.85	828.10
63000	866.24	862.28	858.94	856.10	847.20	843.24	841.46
64000	879.99	875.97	872.57	869.69	860.64	856.62	854.82
65000	893.74	889.66	886.20	883.28	874.09	870.01	868.17
70000	962.49	958.09	954.37	951.22	941.33	936.93	934.95
75000	1031.24	1026.53	1022.54	1019.17	1008.57	1003.85	1001.74
80000	1099.99	1094.96	1090.71	1087.11	1075.81	1070.78	1068.52
85000	1168.74	1163.40	1158.88	1155.06	1143.04	1137.70	1135.30
90000	1237.49	1231.84	1227.05	1223.00	1210.28	1204.62	1202.08
95000	1306.24	1300.27	1295.22	1290.94	1277.52	1271.55	1268.87
100000	1374.99	1368.71	1363.39	1358.89	1344.76	1338.47	1335.65
105000	1443.74	1437.14	1431.56	1426.83	1411.99	1405.39	1402.43
110000	1512.49	1505.58	1499.73	1494.78	1479.23	1472.32	1469.21
120000	1649.99	1642.45	1636.07	1630.67	1613.71	1606.16	1602.78
130000	1787.49	1779.32	1772.41	1766.56	1748.18	1740.01	1736.34
140000	1924.99	1916.19	1908.75	1902.44	1882.66	1873.86	1869.91
150000	2062.49	2053.06	2045.09	2038.33	2017.14	2007.70	2003.47
160000	2199.98	2189.93	2181.42	2174.22	2151.61	2141.55	2137.04
175000	2406.23	2395.24	2385.93	2378.06	2353.32	2342.32	2337.38
200000	2749.98	2737.41	2726.78	2717.78	2689.51	2676.94	2671.30
250000	3437.48	3421.76	3408.48	3397.22	3361.89	3346.17	3339.12
500000	6874.95	6843.53	6816.95	6794.44	6723.78	6692.35	6678.24
1000000	13749.90	13687.06	13633.91	13588.89	13447.57	13384.69	13356.48

16.25% MONTHLY PAYMENTS

AMOUNT	1 YEAR	2 YEARS	3 YEARS	4 YEARS	5 YEARS	6 YEARS	7 YEARS
100	9.08	4.91	3.53	2.85	2.45	2.18	2.00
200	18.17	9.82	7.06	5.69	4.89	4.37	4.00
500	45.42	24.54	17.64	14.23	12.23	10.91	10.00
1000	90.85	49.08	35.28	28.47	24.45	21.83	20.00
2000	181.70	98.17	70.56	56.94	48.90	43.66	40.01
3000	272.55	147.25	105.84	85.41	73.35	65.49	60.01
4000	363.40	196.33	141.12	113.87	97.80	87.32	80.02
5000	454.25	245.41	176.40	142.34	122.26	109.15	100.02
6000	545.10	294.50	211.68	170.81	146.71	130.98	120.03
7000	635.94	343.58	246.96	199.28	171.16	152.81	140.03
8000	726.79	392.66	282.24	227.75	195.61	174.64	160.04
9000	817.64	441.74	317.53	256.22	220.06	196.47	180.04
10000	908.49	490.83	352.81	284.68	244.51	218.30	200.05
11000	999.34	539.91	388.09	313.15	268.96	240.13	220.05
12000	1090.19	588.99	423.37	341.62	293.41	261.96	240.06
13000	1181.04	638.07	458.65	370.09	317.86	283.79	260.06
14000	1271.89	687.16	493.93	398.56	342.32	305.62	280.07
15000	1362.74	736.24	529.21	427.03	366.77	327.45	300.07
20000	1816.98	981.65	705.61	569.37	489.02	436.59	400.09
25000	2271.23	1227.07	882.01	711.71	611.28	545.74	500.12
30000	2725.48	1472.48	1058.42	854.05	733.53	654.89	600.14
35000	3179.72	1717.89	1234.82	996.40	855.79	764.04	700.16
40000	3633.97	1963.31	1411.22	1138.74	978.04	873.19	800.19
45000	4088.21	2208.72	1587.63	1281.08	1100.30	982.34	900.21
50000	4542.46	2454.13	1764.03	1423.42	1222.55	1091.49	1000.24
55000	4996.71	2699.55	1940.43	1565.77	1344.81	1200.63	1100.26
56000	5087.56	2748.63	1975.71	1594.24	1369.26	1222.46	1120.26
57000	5178.40	2797.71	2010.99	1622.70	1393.71	1244.29	1140.27
58000	5269.25	2846.79	2046.27	1651.17	1418.16	1266.12	1160.27
59000	5360.10	2895.88	2081.55	1679.64	1442.61	1287.95	1180.28
60000	5450.95	2944.96	2116.83	1708.11	1467.07	1309.78	1200.28
61000	5541.80	2994.04	2152.12	1736.58	1491.52	1331.61	1220.29
62000	5632.65	3043.12	2187.40	1765.05	1515.97	1353.44	1240.29
63000	5723.50	3092.21	2222.68	1793.51	1540.42	1375.27	1260.30
64000	5814.35	3141.29	2257.96	1821.98	1564.87	1397.10	1280.30
65000	5905.20	3190.37	2293.24	1850.45	1589.32	1418.93	1300.31
70000	6359.44	3435.79	2469.64	1992.79	1711.58	1528.08	1400.33
75000	6813.69	3681.20	2646.04	2135.14	1833.83	1637.23	1500.35
80000	7267.94	3926.61	2822.45	2277.48	1956.09	1746.38	1600.38
85000	7722.18	4172.02	2998.85	2419.82	2078.34	1855.53	1700.40
90000	8176.43	4417.44	3175.25	2562.16	2200.60	1964.67	1800.42
95000	8630.67	4662.85	3351.66	2704.51	2322.85	2073.82	1900.45
100000	9084.92	4908.26	3528.06	2846.85	2445.11	2182.97	2000.47
105000	9539.17	5153.68	3704.46	2989.19	2567.36	2292.12	2100.49
110000	9993.41	5399.09	3880.86	3131.53	2689.62	2401.27	2200.52
120000	10901.90	5889.92	4233.67	3416.22	2934.13	2619.57	2400.57
130000	11810.40	6380.74	4586.48	3700.90	3178.64	2837.86	2600.61
140000	12718.89	6871.57	4939.28	3985.59	3423.15	3056.16	2800.66
150000	13627.38	7362.40	5292.09	4270.27	3667.66	3274.46	3000.71
160000	14535.87	7853.22	5644.89	4554.96	3912.17	3492.75	3200.75
175000	15898.61	8589.46	6174.10	4981.98	4278.94	3820.20	3500.82
200000	18169.84	9816.53	7056.12	5693.70	4890.22	4365.94	4000.94
250000	22712.30	12270.66	8820.15	7117.12	6112.77	5457.43	5001.18
500000	45424.60	24541.32	17640.29	14234.24	12225.54	10914.86	10002.36
1000000	90849.21	49082.65	35280.58	28468.48	24451.09	21829.72	20004.71

MONTHLY PAYMENTS 16.25%

AMOUNT	8 YEARS	9 YEARS	10 YEARS	11 YEARS	12 YEARS	13 YEARS	14 YEARS
100	1.87	1.77	1.69	1.63	1.58	1.54	1.51
200	3.74	3.54	3.38	3.26	3.16	3.09	3.02
500	9.34	8.84	8.45	8.15	7.91	7.72	7.56
1000	18.68	17.68	16.91	16.30	15.82	15.43	15.12
2000	37.35	35.35	33.81	32.61	31.64	30.87	30.24
3000	56.03	53.03	50.72	48.91	47.47	46.30	45.36
4000	74.70	70.71	67.63	65.21	63.29	61.74	60.48
5000	93.38	88.39	84.54	81.52	79.11	77.17	75.60
6000	112.06	106.06	101.44	97.82	94.93	92.61	90.72
7000	130.73	123.74	118.35	114.12	110.76	108.04	105.84
8000	149.41	141.42	135.26	130.43	126.58	123.48	120.96
9000	168.08	159.09	152.17	146.73	142.40	138.91	136.08
10000	186.76	176.77	169.07	163.03	158.22	154.35	151.20
11000	205.44	194.45	185.98	179.34	174.05	169.78	166.32
12000	224.11	212.12	202.89	195.64	189.87	185.22	181.44
13000	242.79	229.80	219.80	211.94	205.69	200.65	196.56
14000	261.47	247.48	236.70	228.25	221.51	216.09	211.68
15000	280.14	265.16	253.61	244.55	237.34	231.52	226.80
20000	373.52	353.54	338.15	326.07	316.45	308.70	302.40
25000	466.90	441.93	422.69	407.59	395.56	385.87	378.00
30000	560.28	530.31	507.22	489.10	474.67	463.05	453.60
35000	653.66	618.70	591.76	570.62	553.79	540.22	529.19
40000	747.04	707.08	676.30	652.14	632.90	617.40	604.79
45000	840.42	795.47	760.83	733.65	712.01	694.57	680.39
50000	933.80	883.85	845.37	815.17	791.12	771.75	755.99
55000	1027.18	972.24	929.91	896.69	870.23	848.92	831.59
56000	1045.86	989.92	946.82	912.99	886.06	864.36	846.71
57000	1064.54	1007.59	963.72	929.30	901.88	879.79	861.83
58000	1083.21	1025.27	980.63	945.60	917.70	895.23	876.95
59000	1101.89	1042.95	997.54	961.90	933.52	910.66	892.07
60000	1120.57	1060.62	1014.45	978.21	949.35	926.10	907.19
61000	1139.24	1078.30	1031.35	994.51	965.17	941.53	922.31
62000	1157.92	1095.98	1048.26	1010.81	980.99	956.97	937.43
63000	1176.59	1113.65	1065.17	1027.12	996.81	972.40	952.55
64000	1195.27	1131.33	1082.08	1043.42	1012.64	987.84	967.67
65000	1213.95	1149.01	1098.98	1059.72	1028.46	1003.27	982.79
70000	1307.33	1237.39	1183.52	1141.24	1107.57	1080.45	1058.39
75000	1400.71	1325.78	1268.06	1222.76	1186.68	1157.62	1133.99
80000	1494.09	1414.16	1352.60	1304.27	1265.80	1234.80	1209.59
85000	1587.47	1502.55	1437.13	1385.79	1344.91	1311.97	1285.19
90000	1680.85	1590.93	1521.67	1467.31	1424.02	1389.15	1360.79
95000	1774.23	1679.32	1606.21	1548.83	1503.13	1466.32	1436.39
100000	1867.61	1767.71	1690.74	1630.34	1582.24	1543.49	1511.99
105000	1960.99	1856.09	1775.28	1711.86	1661.36	1620.67	1587.58
110000	2054.37	1944.48	1859.82	1793.38	1740.47	1697.84	1663.18
120000	2241.13	2121.25	2028.89	1956.41	1898.69	1852.19	1814.38
130000	2427.89	2298.02	2197.97	2119.45	2056.92	2006.54	1965.58
140000	2614.65	2474.79	2367.04	2282.48	2215.14	2160.89	2116.78
150000	2801.41	2651.56	2536.12	2445.51	2373.37	2315.24	2267.98
160000	2988.17	2828.33	2705.19	2608.55	2531.59	2469.59	2419.18
175000	3268.32	3093.48	2958.80	2853.10	2768.93	2701.12	2645.97
200000	3735.22	3535.41	3381.49	3260.69	3164.49	3086.99	3023.97
250000	4669.02	4419.26	4226.86	4075.86	3955.61	3858.74	3779.96
500000	9338.04	8838.53	8453.72	8151.72	7911.22	7717.47	7559.93
1000000	18676.09	17677.06	16907.44	16303.43	15822.44	15434.94	15119.85

16.25%　　　　MONTHLY PAYMENTS

AMOUNT	15 YEARS	16 YEARS	17 YEARS	18 YEARS	19 YEARS	20 YEARS	21 YEARS
100	1.49	1.46	1.45	1.43	1.42	1.41	1.40
200	2.97	2.93	2.89	2.87	2.84	2.82	2.80
500	7.43	7.32	7.24	7.16	7.10	7.05	7.01
1000	14.86	14.65	14.47	14.33	14.20	14.10	14.01
2000	29.72	29.30	28.94	28.65	28.41	28.20	28.03
3000	44.59	43.95	43.42	42.98	42.61	42.30	42.04
4000	59.45	58.60	57.89	57.30	56.81	56.40	56.06
5000	74.31	73.24	72.36	71.63	71.02	70.50	70.07
6000	89.17	87.89	86.83	85.95	85.22	84.60	84.09
7000	104.03	102.54	101.31	100.28	99.42	98.70	98.10
8000	118.89	117.19	115.78	114.61	113.62	112.80	112.11
9000	133.76	131.84	130.25	128.93	127.83	126.90	126.13
10000	148.62	146.49	144.72	143.26	142.03	141.00	140.14
11000	163.48	161.14	159.20	157.58	156.23	155.11	154.16
12000	178.34	175.79	173.67	171.91	170.44	169.21	168.17
13000	193.20	190.43	188.14	186.23	184.64	183.31	182.19
14000	208.06	205.08	202.61	200.56	198.84	197.41	196.20
15000	222.93	219.73	217.09	214.89	213.05	211.51	210.21
20000	297.23	292.98	289.45	286.51	284.06	282.01	280.29
25000	371.54	366.22	361.81	358.14	355.08	352.51	350.36
30000	445.85	439.47	434.17	429.77	426.09	423.01	420.43
35000	520.16	512.71	506.54	501.40	497.11	493.52	490.50
40000	594.47	585.95	578.90	573.03	568.12	564.02	560.57
45000	668.78	659.20	651.26	644.66	639.14	634.52	630.64
50000	743.08	732.44	723.62	716.28	710.16	705.02	700.71
55000	817.39	805.69	795.99	787.91	781.17	775.53	770.78
56000	832.25	820.33	810.46	802.24	795.37	789.63	784.80
57000	847.12	834.98	824.93	816.56	809.58	803.73	798.81
58000	861.98	849.63	839.40	830.89	823.78	817.83	812.83
59000	876.84	864.28	853.88	845.22	837.98	831.93	826.84
60000	891.70	878.93	868.35	859.54	852.19	846.03	840.86
61000	906.56	893.58	882.82	873.87	866.39	860.13	854.87
62000	921.42	908.23	897.29	888.19	880.59	874.23	868.88
63000	936.29	922.88	911.77	902.52	894.80	888.33	882.90
64000	951.15	937.53	926.24	916.84	909.00	902.43	896.91
65000	966.01	952.17	940.71	931.17	923.20	916.53	910.93
70000	1040.32	1025.42	1013.07	1002.80	994.22	987.03	981.00
75000	1114.63	1098.66	1085.43	1074.43	1065.23	1057.53	1051.07
80000	1188.93	1171.91	1157.80	1146.06	1136.25	1128.04	1121.14
85000	1263.24	1245.15	1230.16	1217.68	1207.26	1198.54	1191.21
90000	1337.55	1318.40	1302.52	1289.31	1278.28	1269.04	1261.28
95000	1411.86	1391.64	1374.88	1360.94	1349.30	1339.54	1331.35
100000	1486.17	1464.88	1447.25	1432.57	1420.31	1410.05	1401.43
105000	1560.48	1538.13	1519.61	1504.20	1491.33	1480.55	1471.50
110000	1634.78	1611.37	1591.97	1575.83	1562.34	1551.05	1541.57
120000	1783.40	1757.86	1736.70	1719.08	1704.37	1692.05	1681.71
130000	1932.02	1904.35	1881.42	1862.34	1846.41	1833.06	1821.85
140000	2080.64	2050.84	2026.14	2005.60	1988.44	1974.06	1962.00
150000	2229.25	2197.33	2170.87	2148.85	2130.47	2115.07	2102.14
160000	2377.87	2343.81	2315.59	2292.11	2272.50	2256.07	2242.28
175000	2600.79	2563.55	2532.68	2507.00	2485.55	2467.58	2452.50
200000	2972.34	2929.77	2894.49	2865.14	2840.62	2820.09	2802.85
250000	3715.42	3662.21	3618.12	3581.42	3550.78	3525.11	3503.56
500000	7430.84	7324.42	7236.23	7162.84	7101.56	7050.23	7007.13
1000000	14861.68	14648.84	14472.46	14325.69	14203.12	14100.46	14014.26

MONTHLY PAYMENTS 16.25%

AMOUNT	22 YEARS	23 YEARS	24 YEARS	25 YEARS	30 YEARS	35 YEARS	40 YEARS
100	1.39	1.39	1.38	1.38	1.36	1.36	1.36
200	2.79	2.78	2.77	2.76	2.73	2.72	2.71
500	6.97	6.94	6.91	6.89	6.82	6.79	6.78
1000	13.94	13.88	13.83	13.79	13.65	13.59	13.56
2000	27.88	27.76	27.66	27.57	27.30	27.18	27.13
3000	41.83	41.64	41.49	41.36	40.95	40.77	40.69
4000	55.77	55.52	55.32	55.14	54.60	54.36	54.25
5000	69.71	69.40	69.15	68.93	68.25	67.95	67.81
6000	83.65	83.28	82.97	82.71	81.90	81.54	81.38
7000	97.59	97.16	96.80	96.50	95.55	95.13	94.94
8000	111.53	111.04	110.63	110.28	109.19	108.72	108.50
9000	125.48	124.93	124.46	124.07	122.84	122.31	122.07
10000	139.42	138.81	138.29	137.85	136.49	135.89	135.63
11000	153.36	152.69	152.12	151.64	150.14	149.48	149.19
12000	167.30	166.57	165.95	165.42	163.79	163.07	162.76
13000	181.24	180.45	179.78	179.21	177.44	176.66	176.32
14000	195.18	194.33	193.61	193.00	191.09	190.25	189.88
15000	209.13	208.21	207.44	206.78	204.74	203.84	203.44
20000	278.83	277.61	276.58	275.71	272.99	271.79	271.26
25000	348.54	347.02	345.73	344.64	341.23	339.74	339.07
30000	418.25	416.42	414.87	413.56	409.48	407.68	406.89
35000	487.96	485.82	484.02	482.49	477.73	475.63	474.70
40000	557.67	555.22	553.16	551.42	545.97	543.58	542.52
45000	627.38	624.63	622.31	620.34	614.22	611.53	610.33
50000	697.09	694.03	691.45	689.27	682.47	679.47	678.15
55000	766.80	763.43	760.60	758.20	750.71	747.42	745.96
56000	780.74	777.31	774.42	771.98	764.36	761.01	759.53
57000	794.68	791.19	788.25	785.77	778.01	774.60	773.09
58000	808.62	805.08	802.08	799.55	791.66	788.19	786.65
59000	822.56	818.96	815.91	813.34	805.31	801.78	800.22
60000	836.50	832.84	829.74	827.12	818.96	815.37	813.78
61000	850.45	846.72	843.57	840.91	832.61	828.96	827.34
62000	864.39	860.60	857.40	854.70	846.26	842.55	840.90
63000	878.33	874.48	871.23	868.48	859.91	856.14	854.47
64000	892.27	888.36	885.06	882.27	873.56	869.73	868.03
65000	906.21	902.24	898.89	896.05	887.21	883.32	881.59
70000	975.92	971.64	968.03	964.98	955.45	951.26	949.41
75000	1045.63	1041.05	1037.18	1033.91	1023.70	1019.21	1017.22
80000	1115.34	1110.45	1106.32	1102.83	1091.95	1087.16	1085.04
85000	1185.05	1179.85	1175.47	1171.76	1160.19	1155.11	1152.85
90000	1254.76	1249.25	1244.61	1240.69	1228.44	1223.05	1220.67
95000	1324.46	1318.66	1313.76	1309.61	1296.69	1291.00	1288.48
100000	1394.17	1388.06	1382.90	1378.54	1364.93	1358.95	1356.30
105000	1463.88	1457.46	1452.05	1447.47	1433.18	1426.90	1424.11
110000	1533.59	1526.87	1521.19	1516.40	1501.43	1494.84	1491.93
120000	1673.01	1665.67	1659.48	1654.25	1637.92	1630.74	1627.56
130000	1812.43	1804.48	1797.77	1792.10	1774.42	1766.63	1763.19
140000	1951.84	1943.29	1936.06	1929.96	1910.91	1902.53	1898.82
150000	2091.26	2082.09	2074.35	2067.81	2047.40	2038.42	2034.45
160000	2230.68	2220.90	2212.64	2205.67	2183.90	2174.32	2170.07
175000	2439.80	2429.11	2420.08	2412.45	2388.64	2378.16	2373.52
200000	2788.35	2776.12	2765.80	2757.08	2729.87	2717.90	2712.59
250000	3485.43	3470.15	3457.25	3446.35	3412.34	3397.37	3390.74
500000	6970.87	6940.30	6914.51	6892.71	6824.67	6794.75	6781.48
1000000	13941.73	13880.61	13829.01	13785.41	13649.35	13589.50	13562.97

16.50%   MONTHLY PAYMENTS

AMOUNT	1 YEAR	2 YEARS	3 YEARS	4 YEARS	5 YEARS	6 YEARS	7 YEARS
100	9.10	4.92	3.54	2.86	2.46	2.20	2.01
200	18.19	9.84	7.08	5.72	4.92	4.39	4.03
500	45.48	24.60	17.70	14.30	12.29	10.98	10.07
1000	90.97	49.20	35.40	28.60	24.58	21.97	20.15
2000	181.94	98.40	70.81	57.19	49.17	43.94	40.30
3000	272.90	147.61	106.21	85.79	73.75	65.90	60.44
4000	363.87	196.81	141.62	114.39	98.34	87.87	80.59
5000	454.84	246.01	177.02	142.99	122.92	109.84	100.74
6000	545.81	295.21	212.43	171.58	147.51	131.81	120.89
7000	636.77	344.42	247.83	200.18	172.09	153.78	141.04
8000	727.74	393.62	283.24	228.78	196.68	175.74	161.18
9000	818.71	442.82	318.64	257.37	221.26	197.71	181.33
10000	909.68	492.02	354.04	285.97	245.85	219.68	201.48
11000	1000.64	541.23	389.45	314.57	270.43	241.65	221.63
12000	1091.61	590.43	424.85	343.16	295.01	263.62	241.77
13000	1182.58	639.63	460.26	371.76	319.60	285.58	261.92
14000	1273.55	688.83	495.66	400.36	344.18	307.55	282.07
15000	1364.51	738.04	531.07	428.96	368.77	329.52	302.22
20000	1819.35	984.05	708.09	571.94	491.69	439.36	402.96
25000	2274.19	1230.06	885.11	714.93	614.61	549.20	503.70
30000	2729.03	1476.07	1062.13	857.91	737.54	659.04	604.44
35000	3183.87	1722.08	1239.15	1000.90	860.46	768.88	705.18
40000	3638.71	1968.09	1416.18	1143.88	983.38	878.72	805.92
45000	4093.54	2214.11	1593.20	1286.87	1106.30	988.56	906.66
50000	4548.38	2460.12	1770.22	1429.85	1229.23	1098.40	1007.39
55000	5003.22	2706.13	1947.24	1572.84	1352.15	1208.24	1108.13
56000	5094.19	2755.33	1982.65	1601.43	1376.73	1230.21	1128.28
57000	5185.16	2804.53	2018.05	1630.03	1401.32	1252.18	1148.43
58000	5276.12	2853.74	2053.45	1658.63	1425.90	1274.15	1168.58
59000	5367.09	2902.94	2088.86	1687.22	1450.49	1296.12	1188.73
60000	5458.06	2952.14	2124.26	1715.82	1475.07	1318.08	1208.87
61000	5549.02	3001.34	2159.67	1744.42	1499.66	1340.05	1229.02
62000	5639.99	3050.55	2195.07	1773.01	1524.24	1362.02	1249.17
63000	5730.96	3099.75	2230.48	1801.61	1548.82	1383.99	1269.32
64000	5821.93	3148.95	2265.88	1830.21	1573.41	1405.96	1289.46
65000	5912.90	3198.15	2301.28	1858.81	1597.99	1427.92	1309.61
70000	6367.73	3444.16	2478.31	2001.79	1720.92	1537.76	1410.35
75000	6822.57	3690.18	2655.33	2144.78	1843.84	1647.60	1511.09
80000	7277.41	3936.19	2832.35	2287.76	1966.76	1757.44	1611.83
85000	7732.25	4182.20	3009.37	2430.75	2089.68	1867.28	1712.57
90000	8187.09	4428.21	3186.39	2573.73	2212.61	1977.13	1813.31
95000	8641.93	4674.22	3363.42	2716.72	2335.53	2086.97	1914.05
100000	9096.76	4920.24	3540.44	2859.70	2458.45	2196.81	2014.79
105000	9551.60	5166.25	3717.46	3002.69	2581.37	2306.65	2115.53
110000	10006.44	5412.26	3894.48	3145.67	2704.30	2416.49	2216.27
120000	10916.12	5904.28	4248.53	3431.64	2950.14	2636.17	2417.75
130000	11825.79	6396.31	4602.57	3717.61	3195.99	2855.85	2619.23
140000	12735.47	6888.33	4956.61	4003.58	3441.83	3075.53	2820.70
150000	13645.15	7380.35	5310.66	4289.55	3687.68	3295.21	3022.18
160000	14554.82	7872.38	5664.70	4575.52	3933.52	3514.89	3223.66
175000	15919.34	8610.41	6195.77	5004.48	4302.29	3844.41	3525.88
200000	18193.53	9840.47	7080.88	5719.40	4916.90	4393.61	4029.58
250000	22741.91	12300.59	8851.10	7149.25	6146.13	5492.01	5036.97
500000	45483.82	24601.18	17702.19	14298.50	12292.26	10984.03	10073.94
1000000	90967.64	49202.35	35404.38	28597.01	24584.52	21968.06	20147.89

MONTHLY PAYMENTS 16.50%

AMOUNT	8 YEARS	9 YEARS	10 YEARS	11 YEARS	12 YEARS	13 YEARS	14 YEARS
100	1.88	1.78	1.71	1.65	1.60	1.56	1.53
200	3.76	3.57	3.41	3.29	3.20	3.12	3.06
500	9.41	8.91	8.53	8.23	7.99	7.80	7.65
1000	18.82	17.83	17.06	16.46	15.99	15.60	15.29
2000	37.65	35.66	34.13	32.93	31.97	31.21	30.58
3000	56.47	53.49	51.19	49.39	47.96	46.81	45.88
4000	75.30	71.32	68.26	65.86	63.95	62.41	61.17
5000	94.12	89.15	85.32	82.32	79.94	78.02	76.46
6000	112.94	106.98	102.39	98.79	95.92	93.62	91.75
7000	131.77	124.81	119.45	115.25	111.91	109.22	107.04
8000	150.59	142.64	136.51	131.72	127.90	124.83	122.34
9000	169.42	160.47	153.58	148.18	143.89	140.43	137.63
10000	188.24	178.29	170.64	164.64	159.87	156.04	152.92
11000	207.06	196.12	187.71	181.11	175.86	171.64	168.21
12000	225.89	213.95	204.77	197.57	191.85	187.24	183.50
13000	244.71	231.78	221.83	214.04	207.84	202.85	198.80
14000	263.54	249.61	238.90	230.50	223.82	218.45	214.09
15000	282.36	267.44	255.96	246.97	239.81	234.05	229.38
20000	376.48	356.59	341.28	329.29	319.75	312.07	305.84
25000	470.60	445.74	426.61	411.61	399.68	390.09	382.30
30000	564.72	534.88	511.93	493.93	479.62	468.11	458.76
35000	658.84	624.03	597.25	576.25	559.56	546.12	535.22
40000	752.96	713.18	682.57	658.58	639.49	624.14	611.68
45000	847.08	802.33	767.89	740.90	719.43	702.16	688.14
50000	941.20	891.47	853.21	823.22	799.37	780.18	764.60
55000	1035.32	980.62	938.53	905.54	879.30	858.20	841.06
56000	1054.14	998.45	955.60	922.01	895.29	873.80	856.35
57000	1072.97	1016.28	972.66	938.47	911.28	889.40	871.64
58000	1091.79	1034.11	989.73	954.93	927.27	905.01	886.93
59000	1110.61	1051.94	1006.79	971.40	943.25	920.61	902.23
60000	1129.44	1069.77	1023.85	987.86	959.24	936.21	917.52
61000	1148.26	1087.60	1040.92	1004.33	975.23	951.82	932.81
62000	1167.09	1105.43	1057.98	1020.79	991.21	967.42	948.10
63000	1185.91	1123.26	1075.05	1037.26	1007.20	983.02	963.39
64000	1204.73	1141.09	1092.11	1053.72	1023.19	998.63	978.69
65000	1223.56	1158.92	1109.17	1070.18	1039.18	1014.23	993.98
70000	1317.68	1248.06	1194.50	1152.51	1119.11	1092.25	1070.44
75000	1411.80	1337.21	1279.82	1234.83	1199.05	1170.27	1146.90
80000	1505.92	1426.36	1365.14	1317.15	1278.99	1248.29	1223.36
85000	1600.04	1515.51	1450.46	1399.47	1358.92	1326.30	1299.82
90000	1694.16	1604.65	1535.78	1481.79	1438.86	1404.32	1376.28
95000	1788.28	1693.80	1621.10	1564.12	1518.80	1482.34	1452.74
100000	1882.40	1782.95	1706.42	1646.44	1598.73	1560.36	1529.20
105000	1976.52	1872.10	1791.74	1728.76	1678.67	1638.37	1605.66
110000	2070.64	1961.24	1877.07	1811.08	1758.61	1716.39	1682.12
120000	2258.88	2139.54	2047.71	1975.73	1918.48	1872.43	1835.04
130000	2447.12	2317.83	2218.35	2140.37	2078.35	2028.46	1987.96
140000	2635.36	2496.13	2388.99	2305.01	2238.23	2184.50	2140.88
150000	2823.60	2674.42	2559.63	2469.66	2398.10	2340.54	2293.80
160000	3011.84	2852.72	2730.28	2634.30	2557.97	2496.57	2446.72
175000	3294.19	3120.16	2986.24	2881.27	2797.78	2730.62	2676.10
200000	3764.79	3565.90	3412.85	3292.88	3197.47	3120.71	3058.40
250000	4705.99	4457.37	4266.06	4116.10	3996.83	3900.89	3822.99
500000	9411.99	8914.74	8532.11	8232.19	7993.67	7801.78	7645.99
1000000	18823.97	17829.48	17064.23	16464.38	15987.34	15603.57	15291.98

16.50% MONTHLY PAYMENTS

AMOUNT	15 YEARS	16 YEARS	17 YEARS	18 YEARS	19 YEARS	20 YEARS	21 YEARS
100	1.50	1.48	1.47	1.45	1.44	1.43	1.42
200	3.01	2.97	2.93	2.90	2.88	2.86	2.84
500	7.52	7.41	7.33	7.25	7.19	7.14	7.10
1000	15.04	14.83	14.65	14.51	14.39	14.29	14.20
2000	30.07	29.65	29.31	29.02	28.78	28.58	28.41
3000	45.11	44.48	43.96	43.53	43.17	42.87	42.61
4000	60.15	59.31	58.62	58.04	57.56	57.16	56.82
5000	75.19	74.14	73.27	72.55	71.95	71.45	71.02
6000	90.22	88.96	87.92	87.06	86.34	85.73	85.23
7000	105.26	103.79	102.58	101.57	100.73	100.02	99.43
8000	120.30	118.62	117.23	116.08	115.12	114.31	113.64
9000	135.33	133.45	131.88	130.59	129.51	128.60	127.84
10000	150.37	148.27	146.54	145.10	143.89	142.89	142.05
11000	165.41	163.10	161.19	159.61	158.28	157.18	156.25
12000	180.45	177.93	175.85	174.12	172.67	171.47	170.46
13000	195.48	192.75	190.50	188.62	187.06	185.76	184.66
14000	210.52	207.58	205.15	203.13	201.45	200.05	198.87
15000	225.56	222.41	219.81	217.64	215.84	214.34	213.07
20000	300.74	296.55	293.08	290.19	287.79	285.78	284.10
25000	375.93	370.68	366.34	362.74	359.74	357.23	355.12
30000	451.11	444.82	439.61	435.29	431.68	428.67	426.15
35000	526.30	518.96	512.88	507.84	503.63	500.12	497.17
40000	601.48	593.09	586.15	580.38	575.58	571.56	568.19
45000	676.67	667.23	659.42	652.93	647.53	643.01	639.22
50000	751.85	741.36	732.69	725.48	719.47	714.45	710.24
55000	827.04	815.50	805.96	798.03	791.42	785.90	781.27
56000	842.08	830.33	820.61	812.54	805.81	800.18	795.47
57000	857.11	845.16	835.26	827.05	820.20	814.47	809.68
58000	872.15	859.98	849.92	841.56	834.59	828.76	823.88
59000	887.19	874.81	864.57	856.07	848.98	843.05	838.09
60000	902.23	889.64	879.23	870.58	863.37	857.34	852.29
61000	917.26	904.47	893.88	885.09	877.76	871.63	866.50
62000	932.30	919.29	908.53	899.60	892.15	885.92	880.70
63000	947.34	934.12	923.19	914.11	906.54	900.21	894.90
64000	962.37	948.95	937.84	928.61	920.92	914.50	909.11
65000	977.41	963.77	952.49	943.12	935.31	928.79	923.31
70000	1052.60	1037.91	1025.76	1015.67	1007.26	1000.23	994.34
75000	1127.78	1112.05	1099.03	1088.22	1079.21	1071.68	1065.36
80000	1202.97	1186.18	1172.30	1160.77	1151.16	1143.12	1136.39
85000	1278.15	1260.32	1245.57	1233.32	1223.10	1214.57	1207.41
90000	1353.34	1334.46	1318.84	1305.86	1295.05	1286.01	1278.44
95000	1428.52	1408.59	1392.11	1378.41	1367.00	1357.46	1349.46
100000	1503.71	1482.73	1465.38	1450.96	1438.94	1428.90	1420.48
105000	1578.89	1556.87	1538.64	1523.51	1510.89	1500.35	1491.51
110000	1654.08	1631.00	1611.91	1596.06	1582.84	1571.79	1562.53
120000	1804.45	1779.28	1758.45	1741.15	1726.73	1714.68	1704.58
130000	1954.82	1927.55	1904.99	1886.25	1870.63	1857.57	1846.63
140000	2105.19	2075.82	2051.53	2031.34	2014.52	2000.46	1988.68
150000	2255.56	2224.09	2198.06	2176.44	2158.42	2143.35	2130.73
160000	2405.93	2372.37	2344.60	2321.54	2302.31	2286.24	2272.77
175000	2631.49	2594.78	2564.41	2539.18	2518.15	2500.58	2485.85
200000	3007.42	2965.46	2930.75	2901.92	2877.89	2857.80	2840.97
250000	3759.27	3706.82	3663.44	3627.40	3597.36	3572.25	3551.21
500000	7518.54	7413.65	7326.88	7254.80	7194.72	7144.50	7102.42
1000000	15037.09	14827.30	14653.76	14509.61	14389.45	14289.01	14204.84

MONTHLY PAYMENTS   16.50%

AMOUNT	22 YEARS	23 YEARS	24 YEARS	25 YEARS	30 YEARS	35 YEARS	40 YEARS
100	1.41	1.41	1.40	1.40	1.39	1.38	1.38
200	2.83	2.81	2.80	2.80	2.77	2.76	2.75
500	7.07	7.04	7.01	6.99	6.93	6.90	6.88
1000	14.13	14.07	14.02	13.98	13.85	13.79	13.77
2000	28.27	28.15	28.05	27.96	27.70	27.59	27.54
3000	42.40	42.22	42.07	41.95	41.55	41.38	41.31
4000	56.54	56.30	56.10	55.93	55.41	55.18	55.08
5000	70.67	70.37	70.12	69.91	69.26	68.97	68.85
6000	84.81	84.45	84.15	83.89	83.11	82.77	82.62
7000	98.94	98.52	98.17	97.88	96.96	96.56	96.39
8000	113.07	112.60	112.20	111.86	110.81	110.36	110.16
9000	127.21	126.67	126.22	125.84	124.66	124.15	123.93
10000	141.34	140.75	140.25	139.82	138.51	137.95	137.70
11000	155.48	154.82	154.27	153.81	152.37	151.74	151.47
12000	169.61	168.90	168.30	167.79	166.22	165.53	165.24
13000	183.74	182.97	182.32	181.77	180.07	179.33	179.00
14000	197.88	197.05	196.35	195.75	193.92	193.12	192.77
15000	212.01	211.12	210.37	209.74	207.77	206.92	206.54
20000	282.68	281.49	280.49	279.65	277.03	275.89	275.39
25000	353.35	351.87	350.62	349.56	346.29	344.86	344.24
30000	424.03	422.24	420.74	419.47	415.54	413.84	413.09
35000	494.70	492.62	490.86	489.39	484.80	482.81	481.94
40000	565.37	562.99	560.99	559.30	554.06	551.78	550.78
45000	636.04	633.36	631.11	629.21	623.32	620.75	619.63
50000	706.71	703.74	701.23	699.12	692.57	689.73	688.48
55000	777.38	774.11	771.36	769.03	761.83	758.70	757.33
56000	791.51	788.18	785.38	783.02	775.68	772.49	771.10
57000	805.65	802.26	799.41	797.00	789.53	786.29	784.87
58000	819.78	816.33	813.43	810.98	803.39	800.08	798.64
59000	833.92	830.41	827.46	824.96	817.24	813.88	812.41
60000	848.05	844.48	841.48	838.95	831.09	827.67	826.18
61000	862.18	858.56	855.50	852.93	844.94	841.47	839.95
62000	876.32	872.63	869.53	866.91	858.79	855.26	853.71
63000	890.45	886.71	883.55	880.89	872.64	869.06	867.48
64000	904.59	900.78	897.58	894.88	886.49	882.85	881.25
65000	918.72	914.86	911.60	908.86	900.35	896.65	895.02
70000	989.39	985.23	981.73	978.77	969.60	965.62	963.87
75000	1060.06	1055.60	1051.85	1048.68	1038.86	1034.59	1032.72
80000	1130.73	1125.98	1121.97	1118.60	1108.12	1103.56	1101.57
85000	1201.40	1196.35	1192.10	1188.51	1177.38	1172.54	1170.42
90000	1272.08	1266.73	1262.22	1258.42	1246.63	1241.51	1239.26
95000	1342.75	1337.10	1332.34	1328.33	1315.89	1310.48	1308.11
100000	1413.42	1407.47	1402.47	1398.24	1385.15	1379.45	1376.96
105000	1484.09	1477.85	1472.59	1468.16	1454.41	1448.43	1445.81
110000	1554.76	1548.22	1542.71	1538.07	1523.66	1517.40	1514.66
120000	1696.10	1688.97	1682.96	1677.89	1662.18	1655.34	1652.35
130000	1837.44	1829.71	1823.21	1817.72	1800.69	1793.29	1790.05
140000	1978.78	1970.46	1963.45	1957.54	1939.21	1931.24	1927.74
150000	2120.13	2111.21	2103.70	2097.37	2077.72	2069.18	2065.44
160000	2261.47	2251.96	2243.95	2237.19	2216.24	2207.13	2203.13
175000	2473.48	2463.08	2454.32	2446.93	2424.01	2414.04	2409.68
200000	2826.83	2814.95	2804.93	2796.49	2770.30	2758.91	2753.92
250000	3533.54	3518.68	3506.17	3495.61	3462.87	3448.63	3442.40
500000	7067.08	7037.36	7012.33	6991.22	6925.74	6897.27	6884.80
1000000	14134.17	14074.73	14024.66	13982.45	13851.48	13794.54	13769.59

16.75% MONTHLY PAYMENTS

AMOUNT	1 YEAR	2 YEARS	3 YEARS	4 YEARS	5 YEARS	6 YEARS	7 YEARS
100	9.11	4.93	3.55	2.87	2.47	2.21	2.03
200	18.22	9.86	7.11	5.75	4.94	4.42	4.06
500	45.54	24.66	17.76	14.36	12.36	11.05	10.15
1000	91.09	49.32	35.53	28.73	24.72	22.11	20.29
2000	182.17	98.64	71.06	57.45	49.44	44.21	40.58
3000	273.26	147.97	106.59	86.18	74.16	66.32	60.87
4000	364.34	197.29	142.11	114.90	98.87	88.43	81.17
5000	455.43	246.61	177.64	143.63	123.59	110.53	101.46
6000	546.52	295.93	213.17	172.36	148.31	132.64	121.75
7000	637.60	345.26	248.70	201.08	173.03	154.75	142.04
8000	728.69	394.58	284.23	229.81	197.75	176.85	162.33
9000	819.78	443.90	319.76	258.53	222.47	198.96	182.62
10000	910.86	493.22	355.28	287.26	247.18	221.07	202.92
11000	1001.95	542.54	390.81	315.98	271.90	243.18	223.21
12000	1093.03	591.87	426.34	344.71	296.62	265.28	243.50
13000	1184.12	641.19	461.87	373.44	321.34	287.39	263.79
14000	1275.21	690.51	497.40	402.16	346.06	309.50	284.08
15000	1366.29	739.83	532.93	430.89	370.78	331.60	304.37
20000	1821.72	986.44	710.57	574.52	494.37	442.14	405.83
25000	2277.15	1233.06	888.21	718.15	617.96	552.67	507.29
30000	2732.58	1479.67	1065.85	861.78	741.55	663.21	608.75
35000	3188.02	1726.28	1243.50	1005.41	865.14	773.74	710.21
40000	3643.45	1972.89	1421.14	1149.03	988.73	884.27	811.66
45000	4098.88	2219.50	1598.78	1292.66	1112.33	994.81	913.12
50000	4554.31	2466.11	1776.42	1436.29	1235.92	1105.34	1014.58
55000	5009.74	2712.72	1954.06	1579.92	1359.51	1215.88	1116.04
56000	5100.82	2762.04	1989.59	1608.65	1384.23	1237.98	1136.33
57000	5191.91	2811.37	2025.12	1637.37	1408.95	1260.09	1156.62
58000	5283.00	2860.69	2060.65	1666.10	1433.66	1282.20	1176.91
59000	5374.08	2910.01	2096.18	1694.83	1458.38	1304.30	1197.20
60000	5465.17	2959.33	2131.71	1723.55	1483.10	1326.41	1217.50
61000	5556.26	3008.66	2167.23	1752.28	1507.82	1348.52	1237.79
62000	5647.34	3057.98	2202.76	1781.00	1532.54	1370.63	1258.08
63000	5738.43	3107.30	2238.29	1809.73	1557.26	1392.73	1278.37
64000	5829.51	3156.62	2273.82	1838.46	1581.97	1414.84	1298.66
65000	5920.60	3205.94	2309.35	1867.18	1606.69	1436.95	1318.95
70000	6376.03	3452.56	2486.99	2010.81	1730.29	1547.48	1420.41
75000	6831.46	3699.17	2664.63	2154.44	1853.88	1658.01	1521.87
80000	7286.89	3945.78	2842.27	2298.07	1977.47	1768.55	1623.33
85000	7742.32	4192.39	3019.92	2441.70	2101.06	1879.08	1724.78
90000	8197.75	4439.00	3197.56	2585.33	2224.65	1989.62	1826.24
95000	8653.18	4685.61	3375.20	2728.96	2348.24	2100.15	1927.70
100000	9108.61	4932.22	3552.84	2872.59	2471.84	2210.69	2029.16
105000	9564.05	5178.83	3730.49	3016.22	2595.43	2321.22	2130.62
110000	10019.48	5425.44	3908.13	3159.84	2719.02	2431.76	2232.07
120000	10930.34	5918.67	4263.41	3447.10	2966.20	2652.82	2434.99
130000	11841.20	6411.89	4618.70	3734.36	3213.39	2873.89	2637.91
140000	12752.06	6905.11	4973.98	4021.62	3460.57	3094.96	2840.82
150000	13662.92	7398.33	5329.26	4308.88	3707.75	3316.03	3043.74
160000	14573.78	7891.56	5684.55	4596.14	3954.94	3537.10	3246.65
175000	15940.08	8631.39	6217.48	5027.04	4325.71	3868.70	3551.03
200000	18217.23	9864.44	7105.69	5745.17	4943.67	4421.37	4058.32
250000	22771.54	12330.56	8882.11	7181.47	6179.59	5526.72	5072.90
500000	45543.08	24661.11	17764.22	14362.93	12359.18	11053.43	10145.79
1000000	91086.15	49322.22	35528.43	28725.86	24718.35	22106.86	20291.59

MONTHLY PAYMENTS 16.75%

AMOUNT	8 YEARS	9 YEARS	10 YEARS	11 YEARS	12 YEARS	13 YEARS	14 YEARS
100	1.90	1.80	1.72	1.66	1.62	1.58	1.55
200	3.79	3.60	3.44	3.33	3.23	3.15	3.09
500	9.49	8.99	8.61	8.31	8.08	7.89	7.73
1000	18.97	17.98	17.22	16.63	16.15	15.77	15.46
2000	37.94	35.97	34.44	33.25	32.31	31.55	30.93
3000	56.92	53.95	51.67	49.88	48.46	47.32	46.39
4000	75.89	71.93	68.89	66.50	64.61	63.09	61.86
5000	94.86	89.91	86.11	83.13	80.76	78.86	77.32
6000	113.83	107.90	103.33	99.76	96.92	94.64	92.79
7000	132.81	125.88	120.55	116.38	113.07	110.41	108.25
8000	151.78	143.86	137.77	133.01	129.22	126.18	123.72
9000	170.75	161.84	155.00	149.63	145.38	141.96	139.18
10000	189.72	179.83	172.22	166.26	161.53	157.73	154.65
11000	208.70	197.81	189.44	182.89	177.68	173.50	170.11
12000	227.67	215.79	206.66	199.51	193.84	189.27	185.58
13000	246.64	233.77	223.88	216.14	209.99	205.05	201.04
14000	265.61	251.76	241.10	232.76	226.14	220.82	216.51
15000	284.59	269.74	258.33	249.39	242.29	236.59	231.97
20000	379.45	359.65	344.43	332.52	323.06	315.46	309.30
25000	474.31	449.56	430.54	415.65	403.82	394.32	386.62
30000	569.17	539.48	516.65	498.78	484.59	473.19	463.94
35000	664.03	629.39	602.76	581.91	565.35	552.05	541.27
40000	758.90	719.30	688.87	665.04	646.12	630.92	618.59
45000	853.76	809.21	774.98	748.17	726.88	709.78	695.92
50000	948.62	899.13	861.08	831.30	807.65	788.65	773.24
55000	1043.48	989.04	947.19	914.43	888.41	867.51	850.57
56000	1062.46	1007.02	964.41	931.06	904.56	883.28	866.03
57000	1081.43	1025.00	981.64	947.68	920.72	899.06	881.50
58000	1100.40	1042.99	998.86	964.31	936.87	914.83	896.96
59000	1119.37	1060.97	1016.08	980.93	953.02	930.60	912.42
60000	1138.35	1078.95	1033.30	997.56	969.18	946.37	927.89
61000	1157.32	1096.93	1050.52	1014.19	985.33	962.15	943.35
62000	1176.29	1114.92	1067.74	1030.81	1001.48	977.92	958.82
63000	1195.26	1132.90	1084.97	1047.44	1017.63	993.69	974.28
64000	1214.24	1150.88	1102.19	1064.06	1033.79	1009.47	989.75
65000	1233.21	1168.86	1119.41	1080.69	1049.94	1025.24	1005.21
70000	1328.07	1258.78	1205.52	1163.82	1130.71	1104.10	1082.54
75000	1422.93	1348.69	1291.63	1246.95	1211.47	1182.97	1159.86
80000	1517.79	1438.60	1377.73	1330.08	1292.23	1261.83	1237.19
85000	1612.66	1528.51	1463.84	1413.21	1373.00	1340.70	1314.51
90000	1707.52	1618.43	1549.95	1496.34	1453.76	1419.56	1391.83
95000	1802.38	1708.34	1636.06	1579.47	1534.53	1498.43	1469.16
100000	1897.24	1798.25	1722.17	1662.60	1615.29	1577.29	1546.48
105000	1992.10	1888.17	1808.28	1745.73	1696.06	1656.16	1623.81
110000	2086.97	1978.08	1894.38	1828.86	1776.82	1735.02	1701.13
120000	2276.69	2157.90	2066.60	1995.12	1938.35	1892.75	1855.78
130000	2466.42	2337.73	2238.82	2161.38	2099.88	2050.48	2010.43
140000	2656.14	2517.55	2411.03	2327.64	2261.41	2208.21	2165.08
150000	2845.86	2697.38	2583.25	2493.90	2422.94	2365.94	2319.72
160000	3035.59	2877.20	2755.47	2660.16	2584.47	2523.67	2474.37
175000	3320.17	3146.94	3013.79	2909.55	2826.76	2760.26	2706.34
200000	3794.49	3596.51	3444.33	3325.20	3230.59	3154.58	3092.96
250000	4743.11	4495.63	4305.42	4156.50	4038.23	3943.23	3866.21
500000	9486.21	8991.26	8610.84	8313.01	8076.47	7886.45	7732.41
1000000	18972.43	17982.53	17221.67	16626.01	16152.94	15772.91	15464.82

16.75%　　　MONTHLY PAYMENTS

AMOUNT	15 YEARS	16 YEARS	17 YEARS	18 YEARS	19 YEARS	20 YEARS	21 YEARS
100	1.52	1.50	1.48	1.47	1.46	1.45	1.44
200	3.04	3.00	2.97	2.94	2.92	2.90	2.88
500	7.61	7.50	7.42	7.35	7.29	7.24	7.20
1000	15.21	15.01	14.84	14.69	14.58	14.48	14.40
2000	30.43	30.01	29.67	29.39	29.15	28.96	28.79
3000	45.64	45.02	44.51	44.08	43.73	43.43	43.19
4000	60.85	60.03	59.34	58.78	58.31	57.91	57.58
5000	76.07	75.03	74.18	73.47	72.88	72.39	71.98
6000	91.28	90.04	89.01	88.17	87.46	86.87	86.38
7000	106.49	105.05	103.85	102.86	102.04	101.35	100.77
8000	121.71	120.05	118.69	117.55	116.61	115.83	115.17
9000	136.92	135.06	133.52	132.25	131.19	130.30	129.56
10000	152.13	150.06	148.36	146.94	145.76	144.78	143.96
11000	167.35	165.07	163.19	161.64	160.34	159.26	158.36
12000	182.56	180.08	178.03	176.33	174.92	173.74	172.75
13000	197.77	195.08	192.86	191.02	189.49	188.22	187.15
14000	212.98	210.09	207.70	205.72	204.07	202.69	201.54
15000	228.20	225.10	222.54	220.41	218.65	217.17	215.94
20000	304.26	300.13	296.72	293.88	291.53	289.56	287.92
25000	380.33	375.16	370.89	367.36	364.41	361.95	359.90
30000	456.40	450.19	445.07	440.83	437.29	434.35	431.88
35000	532.46	525.23	519.25	514.30	510.18	506.74	503.86
40000	608.53	600.26	593.43	587.77	583.06	579.13	575.84
45000	684.59	675.29	667.61	661.24	655.94	651.52	647.82
50000	760.66	750.32	741.79	734.71	728.82	723.91	719.80
55000	836.73	825.36	815.97	808.18	801.70	796.30	791.78
56000	851.94	840.36	830.80	822.88	816.28	810.78	806.18
57000	867.15	855.37	845.64	837.57	830.86	825.26	820.57
58000	882.37	870.38	860.47	852.26	845.43	839.74	834.97
59000	897.58	885.38	875.31	866.96	860.01	854.21	849.37
60000	912.79	900.39	890.15	881.65	874.59	868.69	863.76
61000	928.01	915.39	904.98	896.35	889.16	883.17	878.16
62000	943.22	930.40	919.82	911.04	903.74	897.65	892.55
63000	958.43	945.41	934.65	925.73	918.32	912.13	906.95
64000	973.65	960.41	949.49	940.43	932.89	926.60	921.35
65000	988.86	975.42	964.32	955.12	947.47	941.08	935.74
70000	1064.92	1050.45	1038.50	1028.59	1020.35	1013.47	1007.72
75000	1140.99	1125.49	1112.68	1102.07	1093.23	1085.86	1079.70
80000	1217.06	1200.52	1186.86	1175.54	1166.12	1158.26	1151.68
85000	1293.12	1275.55	1261.04	1249.01	1239.00	1230.65	1223.66
90000	1369.19	1350.58	1335.22	1322.48	1311.88	1303.04	1295.64
95000	1445.26	1425.61	1409.40	1395.95	1384.76	1375.43	1367.62
100000	1521.32	1500.65	1483.58	1469.42	1457.64	1447.82	1439.60
105000	1597.39	1575.68	1557.75	1542.89	1530.53	1520.21	1511.58
110000	1673.45	1650.71	1631.93	1616.36	1603.41	1592.60	1583.56
120000	1825.59	1800.78	1780.29	1763.30	1749.17	1737.38	1727.52
130000	1977.72	1950.84	1928.65	1910.25	1894.94	1882.17	1871.48
140000	2129.85	2100.91	2077.01	2057.19	2040.70	2026.95	2015.44
150000	2281.98	2250.97	2225.36	2204.13	2186.47	2171.73	2159.40
160000	2434.11	2401.04	2373.72	2351.07	2332.23	2316.51	2303.37
175000	2662.31	2626.13	2596.26	2571.49	2550.88	2533.68	2519.31
200000	3042.64	3001.29	2967.15	2938.84	2915.29	2895.64	2879.21
250000	3803.30	3751.62	3708.94	3673.55	3644.11	3619.55	3599.01
500000	7606.61	7503.23	7417.88	7347.10	7288.22	7239.10	7198.02
1000000	15213.21	15006.47	14835.75	14694.21	14576.44	14478.20	14396.03

MONTHLY PAYMENTS   16.75%

AMOUNT	22 YEARS	23 YEARS	24 YEARS	25 YEARS	30 YEARS	35 YEARS	40 YEARS
100	1.43	1.43	1.42	1.42	1.41	1.40	1.40
200	2.87	2.85	2.84	2.84	2.81	2.80	2.80
500	7.16	7.13	7.11	7.09	7.03	7.00	6.99
1000	14.33	14.27	14.22	14.18	14.05	14.00	13.98
2000	28.65	28.54	28.44	28.36	28.11	28.00	27.95
3000	42.98	42.81	42.66	42.54	42.16	42.00	41.93
4000	57.31	57.08	56.88	56.72	56.22	56.00	55.91
5000	71.64	71.35	71.10	70.90	70.27	70.00	69.88
6000	85.96	85.62	85.33	85.08	84.32	84.00	83.86
7000	100.29	99.89	99.55	99.26	98.38	98.00	97.83
8000	114.62	114.16	113.77	113.44	112.43	112.00	111.81
9000	128.94	128.42	127.99	127.62	126.49	126.00	125.79
10000	143.27	142.69	142.21	141.80	140.54	140.00	139.76
11000	157.60	156.96	156.43	155.98	154.59	154.00	153.74
12000	171.93	171.23	170.65	170.16	168.65	168.00	167.72
13000	186.25	185.50	184.87	184.34	182.70	182.00	181.69
14000	200.58	199.77	199.09	198.52	196.76	196.00	195.67
15000	214.91	214.04	213.31	212.70	210.81	210.00	209.65
20000	286.54	285.39	284.42	283.60	281.08	280.00	279.53
25000	358.18	356.74	355.52	354.50	351.35	349.99	349.41
30000	429.82	428.08	426.63	425.40	421.62	419.99	419.29
35000	501.45	499.43	497.73	496.30	491.89	489.99	489.17
40000	573.09	570.78	568.83	567.20	562.16	559.99	559.05
45000	644.72	642.12	639.94	638.10	632.43	629.99	628.94
50000	716.36	713.47	711.04	709.00	702.70	699.99	698.82
55000	788.00	784.82	782.15	779.90	772.97	769.99	768.70
56000	802.32	799.09	796.37	794.08	787.02	783.99	782.68
57000	816.65	813.36	810.59	808.26	801.08	797.99	796.65
58000	830.98	827.63	824.81	822.44	815.13	811.99	810.63
59000	845.30	841.89	839.03	836.62	829.18	825.99	824.60
60000	859.63	856.16	853.25	850.80	843.24	839.99	838.58
61000	873.96	870.43	867.47	864.98	857.29	853.99	852.56
62000	888.29	884.70	881.69	879.16	871.35	867.99	866.53
63000	902.61	898.97	895.91	893.34	885.40	881.99	880.51
64000	916.94	913.24	910.13	907.52	899.45	895.99	894.49
65000	931.27	927.51	924.35	921.70	913.51	909.99	908.46
70000	1002.90	998.86	995.46	992.60	983.78	979.99	978.34
75000	1074.54	1070.21	1066.56	1063.50	1054.05	1049.98	1048.23
80000	1146.17	1141.55	1137.67	1134.40	1124.32	1119.98	1118.11
85000	1217.81	1212.90	1208.77	1205.30	1194.59	1189.98	1187.99
90000	1289.45	1284.25	1279.88	1276.20	1264.86	1259.98	1257.87
95000	1361.08	1355.59	1350.98	1347.10	1335.13	1329.98	1327.75
100000	1432.72	1426.94	1422.08	1418.00	1405.40	1399.98	1397.64
105000	1504.35	1498.29	1493.19	1488.90	1475.67	1469.98	1467.52
110000	1575.99	1569.63	1564.29	1559.80	1545.94	1539.98	1537.40
120000	1719.26	1712.33	1706.50	1701.60	1686.47	1679.98	1677.16
130000	1862.53	1855.02	1848.71	1843.40	1827.01	1819.97	1816.93
140000	2005.81	1997.72	1990.92	1985.20	1967.55	1959.97	1956.69
150000	2149.08	2140.41	2133.13	2127.00	2108.09	2099.97	2096.45
160000	2292.35	2283.10	2275.33	2268.80	2248.63	2239.97	2236.22
175000	2507.26	2497.15	2488.65	2481.49	2459.44	2449.96	2445.86
200000	2865.44	2853.88	2844.17	2835.99	2810.79	2799.96	2795.27
250000	3581.80	3567.35	3555.21	3544.99	3513.49	3499.95	3494.09
500000	7163.59	7134.70	7110.42	7089.99	7026.98	6999.90	6988.18
1000000	14327.19	14269.40	14220.84	14179.97	14053.96	13999.80	13976.35

17.00% MONTHLY PAYMENTS

AMOUNT	1 YEAR	2 YEARS	3 YEARS	4 YEARS	5 YEARS	6 YEARS	7 YEARS
100	9.12	4.94	3.57	2.89	2.49	2.22	2.04
200	18.24	9.89	7.13	5.77	4.97	4.45	4.09
500	45.60	24.72	17.83	14.43	12.43	11.12	10.22
1000	91.20	49.44	35.65	28.86	24.85	22.25	20.44
2000	182.41	98.88	71.31	57.71	49.71	44.49	40.87
3000	273.61	148.33	106.96	86.57	74.56	66.74	61.31
4000	364.82	197.77	142.61	115.42	99.41	88.98	81.74
5000	456.02	247.21	178.26	144.28	124.26	111.23	102.18
6000	547.23	296.65	213.92	173.13	149.12	133.48	122.61
7000	638.43	346.10	249.57	201.99	173.97	155.72	143.05
8000	729.64	395.54	285.22	230.84	198.82	177.97	163.49
9000	820.84	444.98	320.87	259.70	223.67	200.22	183.92
10000	912.05	494.42	356.53	288.55	248.53	222.46	204.36
11000	1003.25	543.86	392.18	317.41	273.38	244.71	224.79
12000	1094.46	593.31	427.83	346.26	298.23	266.95	245.23
13000	1185.66	642.75	463.49	375.12	323.08	289.20	265.67
14000	1276.87	692.19	499.14	403.97	347.94	311.45	286.10
15000	1368.07	741.63	534.79	432.83	372.79	333.69	306.54
20000	1824.10	988.85	713.05	577.10	497.05	444.92	408.72
25000	2280.12	1236.06	891.32	721.38	621.31	556.15	510.90
30000	2736.14	1483.27	1069.58	865.65	745.58	667.38	613.07
35000	3192.17	1730.48	1247.85	1009.93	869.84	778.61	715.25
40000	3648.19	1977.69	1426.11	1154.20	994.10	889.85	817.43
45000	4104.21	2224.90	1604.37	1298.48	1118.37	1001.08	919.61
50000	4560.24	2472.11	1782.64	1442.75	1242.63	1112.31	1021.79
55000	5016.26	2719.32	1960.90	1587.03	1366.89	1223.54	1123.97
56000	5107.47	2768.77	1996.55	1615.88	1391.74	1245.78	1144.41
57000	5198.67	2818.21	2032.21	1644.74	1416.60	1268.03	1164.84
58000	5289.88	2867.65	2067.86	1673.59	1441.45	1290.28	1185.28
59000	5381.08	2917.09	2103.51	1702.45	1466.30	1312.52	1205.71
60000	5472.29	2966.54	2139.16	1731.30	1491.15	1334.77	1226.15
61000	5563.49	3015.98	2174.82	1760.16	1516.01	1357.01	1246.58
62000	5654.69	3065.42	2210.47	1789.01	1540.86	1379.26	1267.02
63000	5745.90	3114.86	2246.12	1817.87	1565.71	1401.51	1287.46
64000	5837.10	3164.30	2281.77	1846.72	1590.56	1423.75	1307.89
65000	5928.31	3213.75	2317.43	1875.58	1615.42	1446.00	1328.33
70000	6384.33	3460.96	2495.69	2019.85	1739.68	1557.23	1430.51
75000	6840.36	3708.17	2673.95	2164.13	1863.94	1668.46	1532.69
80000	7296.38	3955.38	2852.22	2308.40	1988.21	1779.69	1634.86
85000	7752.40	4202.59	3030.48	2452.68	2112.47	1890.92	1737.04
90000	8208.43	4449.80	3208.75	2596.95	2236.73	2002.15	1839.22
95000	8664.45	4697.02	3387.01	2741.23	2360.99	2113.38	1941.40
100000	9120.48	4944.23	3565.27	2885.50	2485.26	2224.61	2043.58
105000	9576.50	5191.44	3743.54	3029.78	2609.52	2335.84	2145.76
110000	10032.52	5438.65	3921.80	3174.05	2733.78	2447.07	2247.94
120000	10944.57	5933.07	4278.33	3462.61	2982.31	2669.54	2452.30
130000	11856.62	6427.49	4634.85	3751.16	3230.83	2892.00	2656.65
140000	12768.67	6921.92	4991.38	4039.71	3479.36	3114.46	2861.01
150000	13680.71	7416.34	5347.91	4328.26	3727.89	3336.92	3065.37
160000	14592.76	7910.76	5704.44	4616.81	3976.41	3559.38	3269.73
175000	15960.83	8652.40	6239.23	5049.63	4349.20	3893.07	3576.27
200000	18240.95	9888.45	7130.55	5771.01	4970.52	4449.23	4087.16
250000	22801.19	12360.57	8913.18	7213.76	6213.14	5561.53	5108.95
500000	45602.38	24721.13	17826.36	14427.52	12426.29	11123.07	10217.90
1000000	91204.75	49442.26	35652.73	28855.04	24852.58	22246.13	20435.80

MONTHLY PAYMENTS 17.00%

AMOUNT	8 YEARS	9 YEARS	10 YEARS	11 YEARS	12 YEARS	13 YEARS	14 YEARS
100	1.91	1.81	1.74	1.68	1.63	1.59	1.56
200	3.82	3.63	3.48	3.36	3.26	3.19	3.13
500	9.56	9.07	8.69	8.39	8.16	7.97	7.82
1000	19.12	18.14	17.38	16.79	16.32	15.94	15.64
2000	38.24	36.27	34.76	33.58	32.64	31.89	31.28
3000	57.36	54.41	52.14	50.36	48.96	47.83	46.92
4000	76.49	72.54	69.52	67.15	65.28	63.77	62.55
5000	95.61	90.68	86.90	83.94	81.60	79.71	78.19
6000	114.73	108.82	104.28	100.73	97.92	95.66	93.83
7000	133.85	126.95	121.66	117.52	114.23	111.60	109.47
8000	152.97	145.09	139.04	134.31	130.55	127.54	125.11
9000	172.09	163.23	156.42	151.09	146.87	143.49	140.75
10000	191.21	181.36	173.80	167.88	163.19	159.43	156.38
11000	210.34	199.50	191.18	184.67	179.51	175.37	172.02
12000	229.46	217.63	208.56	201.46	195.83	191.32	187.66
13000	248.58	235.77	225.94	218.25	212.15	207.26	203.30
14000	267.70	253.91	243.32	235.04	228.47	223.20	218.94
15000	286.82	272.04	260.70	251.82	244.79	239.14	234.58
20000	382.43	362.72	347.60	335.77	326.38	318.86	312.77
25000	478.04	453.40	434.49	419.71	407.98	398.57	390.96
30000	573.64	544.09	521.39	503.65	489.58	478.29	469.15
35000	669.25	634.77	608.29	587.59	571.17	558.00	547.34
40000	764.86	725.45	695.19	671.53	652.77	637.72	625.54
45000	860.47	816.13	782.09	755.47	734.37	717.43	703.73
50000	956.07	906.81	868.99	839.42	815.96	797.15	781.92
55000	1051.68	997.49	955.89	923.36	897.56	876.86	860.11
56000	1070.80	1015.63	973.27	940.15	913.88	892.81	875.75
57000	1089.92	1033.76	990.65	956.93	930.20	908.75	891.39
58000	1109.04	1051.90	1008.03	973.72	946.52	924.69	907.03
59000	1128.17	1070.04	1025.41	990.51	962.83	940.63	922.66
60000	1147.29	1088.17	1042.79	1007.30	979.15	956.58	938.30
61000	1166.41	1106.31	1060.17	1024.09	995.47	972.52	953.94
62000	1185.53	1124.44	1077.55	1040.88	1011.79	988.46	969.58
63000	1204.65	1142.58	1094.93	1057.66	1028.11	1004.41	985.22
64000	1223.77	1160.72	1112.30	1074.45	1044.43	1020.35	1000.86
65000	1242.89	1178.85	1129.68	1091.24	1060.75	1036.29	1016.49
70000	1338.50	1269.53	1216.58	1175.18	1142.35	1116.01	1094.69
75000	1434.11	1360.21	1303.48	1259.12	1223.94	1195.72	1172.88
80000	1529.72	1450.90	1390.38	1343.07	1305.54	1275.44	1251.07
85000	1625.32	1541.58	1477.28	1427.01	1387.13	1355.15	1329.26
90000	1720.93	1632.26	1564.18	1510.95	1468.73	1434.87	1407.45
95000	1816.54	1722.94	1651.08	1594.89	1550.33	1514.58	1485.65
100000	1912.15	1813.62	1737.98	1678.83	1631.92	1594.30	1563.84
105000	2007.75	1904.30	1824.88	1762.77	1713.52	1674.01	1642.03
110000	2103.36	1994.98	1911.77	1846.72	1795.12	1753.72	1720.22
120000	2294.57	2176.34	2085.57	2014.60	1958.31	1913.15	1876.61
130000	2485.79	2357.70	2259.37	2182.48	2121.50	2072.58	2032.99
140000	2677.00	2539.07	2433.17	2350.36	2284.69	2232.01	2189.37
150000	2868.22	2720.43	2606.96	2518.25	2447.88	2391.44	2345.76
160000	3059.43	2901.79	2780.76	2686.13	2611.08	2550.87	2502.14
175000	3346.25	3173.83	3041.46	2937.96	2855.87	2790.02	2736.72
200000	3824.29	3627.24	3475.95	3357.66	3263.85	3188.59	3127.68
250000	4780.36	4534.05	4344.94	4197.08	4079.81	3985.74	3909.60
500000	9560.73	9068.09	8689.88	8394.16	8159.61	7971.48	7819.19
1000000	19121.45	18136.19	17379.77	16788.32	16319.23	15942.95	15638.38

17.00%   MONTHLY PAYMENTS

AMOUNT	15 YEARS	16 YEARS	17 YEARS	18 YEARS	19 YEARS	20 YEARS	21 YEARS
100	1.54	1.52	1.50	1.49	1.48	1.47	1.46
200	3.08	3.04	3.00	2.98	2.95	2.93	2.92
500	7.70	7.59	7.51	7.44	7.38	7.33	7.29
1000	15.39	15.19	15.02	14.88	14.76	14.67	14.59
2000	30.78	30.37	30.04	29.76	29.53	29.34	29.18
3000	46.17	45.56	45.06	44.64	44.29	44.00	43.76
4000	61.56	60.75	60.07	59.52	59.06	58.67	58.35
5000	76.95	75.93	75.09	74.40	73.82	73.34	72.94
6000	92.34	91.12	90.11	89.28	88.58	88.01	87.53
7000	107.73	106.30	105.13	104.16	103.35	102.68	102.11
8000	123.12	121.49	120.15	119.04	118.11	117.34	116.70
9000	138.51	136.68	135.17	133.92	132.88	132.01	131.29
10000	153.90	151.86	150.18	148.79	147.64	146.68	145.88
11000	169.29	167.05	165.20	163.67	162.40	161.35	160.47
12000	184.68	182.24	180.22	178.55	177.17	176.02	175.05
13000	200.07	197.42	195.24	193.43	191.93	190.68	189.64
14000	215.46	212.61	210.26	208.31	206.70	205.35	204.23
15000	230.85	227.80	225.28	223.19	221.46	220.02	218.82
20000	307.80	303.73	300.37	297.59	295.28	293.36	291.76
25000	384.75	379.66	375.46	371.99	369.10	366.70	364.70
30000	461.70	455.59	450.55	446.38	442.92	440.04	437.63
35000	538.65	531.52	525.65	520.78	516.74	513.38	510.57
40000	615.60	607.45	600.74	595.18	590.56	586.72	583.51
45000	692.55	683.39	675.83	669.58	664.38	660.06	656.45
50000	769.50	759.32	750.92	743.97	738.20	733.40	729.39
55000	846.45	835.25	826.01	818.37	812.02	806.74	802.33
56000	861.84	850.44	841.03	833.25	826.79	821.41	816.92
57000	877.23	865.62	856.05	848.13	841.55	836.08	831.51
58000	892.62	880.81	871.07	863.01	856.32	850.74	846.09
59000	908.01	895.99	886.09	877.89	871.08	865.41	860.68
60000	923.40	911.18	901.11	892.77	885.85	880.08	875.27
61000	938.79	926.37	916.12	907.65	900.61	894.75	889.86
62000	954.18	941.55	931.14	922.53	915.37	909.42	904.44
63000	969.57	956.74	946.16	937.41	930.14	924.08	919.03
64000	984.96	971.93	961.18	952.29	944.90	938.75	933.62
65000	1000.35	987.11	976.20	967.17	959.67	953.42	948.21
70000	1077.30	1063.04	1051.29	1041.56	1033.49	1026.76	1021.15
75000	1154.25	1138.98	1126.38	1115.96	1107.31	1100.10	1094.09
80000	1231.20	1214.91	1201.47	1190.36	1181.13	1173.44	1167.03
85000	1308.15	1290.84	1276.57	1264.76	1254.95	1246.78	1239.96
90000	1385.10	1366.77	1351.66	1339.15	1328.77	1320.12	1312.90
95000	1462.05	1442.70	1426.75	1413.55	1402.59	1393.46	1385.84
100000	1539.00	1518.63	1501.84	1487.95	1476.41	1466.80	1458.78
105000	1615.95	1594.57	1576.94	1562.34	1550.23	1540.14	1531.72
110000	1692.90	1670.50	1652.03	1636.74	1624.05	1613.48	1604.66
120000	1846.81	1822.36	1802.21	1785.54	1771.69	1760.16	1750.54
130000	2000.71	1974.22	1952.40	1934.33	1919.33	1906.84	1896.42
140000	2154.61	2126.09	2102.58	2083.13	2066.97	2053.52	2042.29
150000	2308.51	2277.95	2252.77	2231.92	2214.61	2200.20	2188.17
160000	2462.41	2429.81	2402.95	2380.72	2362.25	2346.88	2334.05
175000	2693.26	2657.61	2628.23	2603.91	2583.71	2566.90	2552.87
200000	3078.01	3037.27	3003.69	2975.89	2952.82	2933.60	2917.56
250000	3847.51	3796.59	3754.61	3719.87	3691.02	3667.00	3646.95
500000	7695.02	7593.17	7509.22	7439.74	7382.04	7334.00	7293.91
1000000	15390.04	15186.34	15018.43	14879.47	14764.09	14668.01	14587.82

MONTHLY PAYMENTS   17.00%

AMOUNT	22 YEARS	23 YEARS	24 YEARS	25 YEARS	30 YEARS	35 YEARS	40 YEARS
100	1.45	1.45	1.44	1.44	1.43	1.42	1.42
200	2.90	2.89	2.88	2.88	2.85	2.84	2.84
500	7.26	7.23	7.21	7.19	7.13	7.10	7.09
1000	14.52	14.46	14.42	14.38	14.26	14.21	14.18
2000	29.04	28.93	28.84	28.76	28.51	28.41	28.37
3000	43.56	43.39	43.25	43.13	42.77	42.62	42.55
4000	58.08	57.86	57.67	57.51	57.03	56.82	56.73
5000	72.60	72.32	72.09	71.89	71.28	71.03	70.92
6000	87.12	86.79	86.51	86.27	85.54	85.23	85.10
7000	101.65	101.25	100.92	100.65	99.80	99.44	99.28
8000	116.17	115.72	115.34	115.02	114.05	113.64	113.47
9000	130.69	130.18	129.76	129.40	128.31	127.85	127.65
10000	145.21	144.65	144.18	143.78	142.57	142.05	141.83
11000	159.73	159.11	158.59	158.16	156.82	156.26	156.02
12000	174.25	173.58	173.01	172.54	171.08	170.46	170.20
13000	188.77	188.04	187.43	186.91	185.34	184.67	184.38
14000	203.29	202.50	201.85	201.29	199.59	198.87	198.57
15000	217.81	216.97	216.26	215.67	213.85	213.08	212.75
20000	290.42	289.29	288.35	287.56	285.14	284.11	283.66
25000	363.02	361.62	360.44	359.45	356.42	355.13	354.58
30000	435.62	433.94	432.53	431.34	427.70	426.16	425.50
35000	508.23	506.26	504.61	503.23	498.99	497.18	496.41
40000	580.83	578.58	576.70	575.12	570.27	568.21	567.33
45000	653.43	650.91	648.79	647.01	641.55	639.24	638.25
50000	726.04	723.23	720.88	718.90	712.84	710.26	709.16
55000	798.64	795.55	792.96	790.79	784.12	781.29	780.08
56000	813.16	810.02	807.38	805.17	798.38	795.49	794.26
57000	827.68	824.48	821.80	819.54	812.63	809.70	808.44
58000	842.20	838.95	836.22	833.92	826.89	823.91	822.63
59000	856.73	853.41	850.63	848.30	841.15	838.11	836.81
60000	871.25	867.88	865.05	862.68	855.41	852.32	850.99
61000	885.77	882.34	879.47	877.06	869.66	866.52	865.18
62000	900.29	896.81	893.89	891.43	883.92	880.73	879.36
63000	914.81	911.27	908.30	905.81	898.18	894.93	893.54
64000	929.33	925.73	922.72	920.19	912.43	909.14	907.73
65000	943.85	940.20	937.14	934.57	926.69	923.34	921.91
70000	1016.45	1012.52	1009.23	1006.46	997.97	994.37	992.83
75000	1089.06	1084.85	1081.31	1078.35	1069.26	1065.39	1063.74
80000	1161.66	1157.17	1153.40	1150.24	1140.54	1136.42	1134.66
85000	1234.27	1229.49	1225.49	1222.13	1211.82	1207.45	1205.58
90000	1306.87	1301.81	1297.58	1294.02	1283.11	1278.47	1276.49
95000	1379.47	1374.14	1369.66	1365.91	1354.39	1349.50	1347.41
100000	1452.08	1446.46	1441.75	1437.80	1425.68	1420.53	1418.32
105000	1524.68	1518.78	1513.84	1509.69	1496.96	1491.55	1489.24
110000	1597.28	1591.11	1585.93	1581.58	1568.24	1562.58	1560.16
120000	1742.49	1735.75	1730.10	1725.36	1710.81	1704.63	1701.99
130000	1887.70	1880.40	1874.28	1869.14	1853.38	1846.68	1843.82
140000	2032.91	2025.05	2018.45	2012.92	1995.95	1988.74	1985.65
150000	2178.11	2169.69	2162.63	2156.69	2138.51	2130.79	2127.49
160000	2323.32	2314.34	2306.80	2300.47	2281.08	2272.84	2269.32
175000	2541.13	2531.31	2523.06	2516.14	2494.93	2485.92	2482.07
200000	2904.15	2892.92	2883.50	2875.59	2851.35	2841.05	2836.65
250000	3630.19	3616.15	3604.38	3594.49	3564.19	3551.32	3545.81
500000	7260.38	7232.30	7208.76	7188.98	7128.38	7102.63	7091.62
1000000	14520.77	14464.61	14417.51	14377.97	14256.75	14205.26	14183.24

17.25% MONTHLY PAYMENTS

AMOUNT	1 YEAR	2 YEARS	3 YEARS	4 YEARS	5 YEARS	6 YEARS	7 YEARS
100	9.13	4.96	3.58	2.90	2.50	2.24	2.06
200	18.26	9.91	7.16	5.80	5.00	4.48	4.12
500	45.66	24.78	17.89	14.49	12.49	11.19	10.29
1000	91.32	49.56	35.78	28.98	24.99	22.39	20.58
2000	182.65	99.12	71.55	57.97	49.97	44.77	41.16
3000	273.97	148.69	107.33	86.95	74.96	67.16	61.74
4000	365.29	198.25	143.11	115.94	99.95	89.54	82.32
5000	456.62	247.81	178.89	144.92	124.94	111.93	102.90
6000	547.94	297.37	214.66	173.91	149.92	134.32	123.48
7000	639.26	346.94	250.44	202.89	174.91	156.70	144.06
8000	730.59	396.50	286.22	231.88	199.90	179.09	164.64
9000	821.91	446.06	322.00	260.86	224.88	201.47	185.22
10000	913.23	495.62	357.77	289.85	249.87	223.86	205.81
11000	1004.56	545.19	393.55	318.83	274.86	246.24	226.39
12000	1095.88	594.75	429.33	347.81	299.85	268.63	246.97
13000	1187.20	644.31	465.10	376.80	324.83	291.02	267.55
14000	1278.53	693.87	500.88	405.78	349.82	313.40	288.13
15000	1369.85	743.44	536.66	434.77	374.81	335.79	308.71
20000	1826.47	991.25	715.55	579.69	499.74	447.72	411.61
25000	2283.09	1239.06	894.43	724.61	624.68	559.65	514.51
30000	2739.70	1486.87	1073.32	869.54	749.62	671.58	617.42
35000	3196.32	1734.69	1252.20	1014.46	874.55	783.51	720.32
40000	3652.94	1982.50	1431.09	1159.38	999.49	895.43	823.22
45000	4109.55	2230.31	1609.98	1304.30	1124.42	1007.36	926.12
50000	4566.17	2478.12	1788.86	1449.23	1249.36	1119.29	1029.03
55000	5022.79	2725.94	1967.75	1594.15	1374.30	1231.22	1131.93
56000	5114.11	2775.50	2003.53	1623.13	1399.28	1253.61	1152.51
57000	5205.44	2825.06	2039.30	1652.12	1424.27	1275.99	1173.09
58000	5296.76	2874.62	2075.08	1681.10	1449.26	1298.38	1193.67
59000	5388.08	2924.19	2110.86	1710.09	1474.24	1320.77	1214.25
60000	5479.41	2973.75	2146.64	1739.07	1499.23	1343.15	1234.83
61000	5570.73	3023.31	2182.41	1768.06	1524.22	1365.54	1255.41
62000	5662.05	3072.87	2218.19	1797.04	1549.21	1387.92	1275.99
63000	5753.38	3122.44	2253.97	1826.03	1574.19	1410.31	1296.57
64000	5844.70	3172.00	2289.75	1855.01	1599.18	1432.69	1317.15
65000	5936.02	3221.56	2325.52	1884.00	1624.17	1455.08	1337.74
70000	6392.64	3469.37	2504.41	2028.92	1749.10	1567.01	1440.64
75000	6849.26	3717.19	2683.30	2173.84	1874.04	1678.94	1543.54
80000	7305.87	3965.00	2862.18	2318.76	1998.98	1790.87	1646.44
85000	7762.49	4212.81	3041.07	2463.69	2123.91	1902.80	1749.35
90000	8219.11	4460.62	3219.95	2608.61	2248.85	2014.73	1852.25
95000	8675.73	4708.43	3398.84	2753.53	2373.78	2126.66	1955.15
100000	9132.34	4956.25	3577.73	2898.45	2498.72	2238.59	2058.05
105000	9588.96	5204.06	3756.61	3043.38	2623.66	2350.52	2160.96
110000	10045.58	5451.87	3935.50	3188.30	2748.59	2462.44	2263.86
120000	10958.81	5947.50	4293.27	3478.15	2998.46	2686.30	2469.66
130000	11872.05	6443.12	4651.05	3767.99	3248.34	2910.16	2675.47
140000	12785.28	6938.75	5008.82	4057.84	3498.21	3134.02	2881.28
150000	13698.52	7434.37	5366.59	4347.68	3748.08	3357.88	3087.08
160000	14611.75	7930.00	5724.36	4637.53	3997.95	3581.74	3292.89
175000	15981.60	8673.43	6261.02	5072.30	4372.76	3917.53	3601.59
200000	18264.69	9912.49	7155.45	5796.91	4997.44	4477.17	4116.11
250000	22830.86	12390.62	8944.32	7246.14	6246.80	5596.46	5145.14
500000	45661.72	24781.24	17888.64	14492.27	12493.60	11192.93	10290.27
1000000	91323.44	49562.47	35777.27	28984.55	24987.20	22385.86	20580.54

MONTHLY PAYMENTS   17.25%

AMOUNT	8 YEARS	9 YEARS	10 YEARS	11 YEARS	12 YEARS	13 YEARS	14 YEARS
100	1.93	1.83	1.75	1.70	1.65	1.61	1.58
200	3.85	3.66	3.51	3.39	3.30	3.22	3.16
500	9.64	9.15	8.77	8.48	8.24	8.06	7.91
1000	19.27	18.29	17.54	16.95	16.49	16.11	15.81
2000	38.54	36.58	35.08	33.90	32.97	32.23	31.63
3000	57.81	54.87	52.62	50.85	49.46	48.34	47.44
4000	77.08	73.16	70.15	67.81	65.94	64.45	63.25
5000	96.36	91.45	87.69	84.76	82.43	80.57	79.06
6000	115.63	109.74	105.23	101.71	98.92	96.68	94.88
7000	134.90	128.03	122.77	118.66	115.40	112.80	110.69
8000	154.17	146.32	140.31	135.61	131.89	128.91	126.50
9000	173.44	164.61	157.85	152.56	148.38	145.02	142.31
10000	192.71	182.90	175.39	169.51	164.86	161.14	158.13
11000	211.98	201.20	192.92	186.46	181.35	177.25	173.94
12000	231.25	219.49	210.46	203.42	197.83	193.36	189.75
13000	250.52	237.78	228.00	220.37	214.32	209.48	205.56
14000	269.79	256.07	245.54	237.32	230.81	225.59	221.38
15000	289.07	274.36	263.08	254.27	247.29	241.71	237.19
20000	385.42	365.81	350.77	339.03	329.72	322.27	316.25
25000	481.78	457.26	438.46	423.78	412.16	402.84	395.32
30000	578.13	548.71	526.16	508.54	494.59	483.41	474.38
35000	674.49	640.17	613.85	593.30	577.02	563.98	553.44
40000	770.84	731.62	701.54	678.05	659.45	644.55	632.51
45000	867.20	823.07	789.23	762.81	741.88	725.12	711.57
50000	963.55	914.52	876.93	847.56	824.31	805.68	790.63
55000	1059.91	1005.98	964.62	932.32	906.74	886.25	869.70
56000	1079.18	1024.27	982.16	949.27	923.23	902.37	885.51
57000	1098.45	1042.56	999.69	966.22	939.71	918.48	901.32
58000	1117.72	1060.85	1017.23	983.18	956.20	934.59	917.13
59000	1136.99	1079.14	1034.77	1000.13	972.69	950.71	932.95
60000	1156.26	1097.43	1052.31	1017.08	989.17	966.82	948.76
61000	1175.53	1115.72	1069.85	1034.03	1005.66	982.94	964.57
62000	1194.81	1134.01	1087.39	1050.98	1022.15	999.05	980.38
63000	1214.08	1152.30	1104.93	1067.93	1038.63	1015.16	996.20
64000	1233.35	1170.59	1122.46	1084.88	1055.12	1031.28	1012.01
65000	1252.62	1188.88	1140.00	1101.83	1071.60	1047.39	1027.82
70000	1348.97	1280.33	1227.70	1186.59	1154.03	1127.96	1106.88
75000	1445.33	1371.78	1315.39	1271.35	1236.47	1208.53	1185.95
80000	1541.68	1463.24	1403.08	1356.10	1318.90	1289.10	1265.01
85000	1638.04	1554.69	1490.77	1440.86	1401.33	1369.66	1344.07
90000	1734.39	1646.14	1578.47	1525.62	1483.76	1450.23	1423.14
95000	1830.75	1737.59	1666.16	1610.37	1566.19	1530.80	1502.20
100000	1927.10	1829.05	1753.85	1695.13	1648.62	1611.37	1581.26
105000	2023.46	1920.50	1841.54	1779.89	1731.05	1691.94	1660.33
110000	2119.82	2011.95	1929.24	1864.64	1813.48	1772.51	1739.39
120000	2312.53	2194.85	2104.62	2034.16	1978.35	1933.64	1897.52
130000	2505.24	2377.76	2280.01	2203.67	2143.21	2094.78	2055.64
140000	2697.95	2560.66	2455.39	2373.18	2308.07	2255.92	2213.77
150000	2890.66	2743.57	2630.78	2542.69	2472.93	2417.05	2371.90
160000	3083.37	2926.47	2806.16	2712.21	2637.79	2578.19	2530.02
175000	3372.43	3200.83	3069.24	2966.48	2885.09	2819.90	2767.21
200000	3854.21	3658.09	3507.70	3390.26	3297.24	3222.74	3162.53
250000	4817.76	4572.61	4384.63	4237.82	4121.55	4028.42	3953.16
500000	9635.52	9145.23	8769.25	8475.65	8243.11	8056.85	7906.32
1000000	19271.05	18290.46	17538.50	16951.30	16486.21	16113.69	15812.64

17.25%   MONTHLY PAYMENTS

AMOUNT	15 YEARS	16 YEARS	17 YEARS	18 YEARS	19 YEARS	20 YEARS	21 YEARS
100	1.56	1.54	1.52	1.51	1.50	1.49	1.48
200	3.11	3.07	3.04	3.01	2.99	2.97	2.96
500	7.78	7.68	7.60	7.53	7.48	7.43	7.39
1000	15.57	15.37	15.20	15.07	14.95	14.86	14.78
2000	31.14	30.73	30.40	30.13	29.90	29.72	29.56
3000	46.70	46.10	45.61	45.20	44.86	44.58	44.34
4000	62.27	61.47	60.81	60.26	59.81	59.43	59.12
5000	77.84	76.83	76.01	75.33	74.76	74.29	73.90
6000	93.41	92.20	91.21	90.39	89.71	89.15	88.68
7000	108.97	107.57	106.41	105.46	104.67	104.01	103.46
8000	124.54	122.94	121.61	120.52	119.62	118.87	118.24
9000	140.11	138.30	136.82	135.59	134.57	133.73	133.02
10000	155.68	153.67	152.02	150.65	149.52	148.58	147.80
11000	171.24	169.04	167.22	165.72	164.48	163.44	162.58
12000	186.81	184.40	182.42	180.78	179.43	178.30	177.36
13000	202.38	199.77	197.62	195.85	194.38	193.16	192.14
14000	217.95	215.14	212.83	210.92	209.33	208.02	206.92
15000	233.51	230.50	228.03	225.98	224.29	222.88	221.70
20000	311.35	307.34	304.04	301.31	299.05	297.17	295.60
25000	389.19	384.17	380.04	376.63	373.81	371.46	369.50
30000	467.03	461.01	456.05	451.96	448.57	445.75	443.41
35000	544.86	537.84	532.06	527.29	523.33	520.04	517.31
40000	622.70	614.68	608.07	602.62	598.09	594.34	591.21
45000	700.54	691.51	684.08	677.94	672.86	668.63	665.11
50000	778.38	768.34	760.09	753.27	747.62	742.92	739.01
55000	856.22	845.18	836.10	828.60	822.38	817.21	812.91
56000	871.78	860.55	851.30	843.66	837.33	832.07	827.69
57000	887.35	875.91	866.50	858.73	852.28	846.93	842.47
58000	902.92	891.28	881.70	873.79	867.24	861.79	857.25
59000	918.49	906.65	896.91	888.86	882.19	876.65	872.03
60000	934.05	922.01	912.11	903.92	897.14	891.51	886.81
61000	949.62	937.38	927.31	918.99	912.09	906.36	901.59
62000	965.19	952.75	942.51	934.05	927.05	921.22	916.37
63000	980.76	968.11	957.71	949.12	942.00	936.08	931.15
64000	996.32	983.48	972.91	964.19	956.95	950.94	945.93
65000	1011.89	998.85	988.12	979.25	971.90	965.80	960.71
70000	1089.73	1075.68	1064.13	1054.58	1046.66	1040.09	1034.61
75000	1167.57	1152.52	1140.13	1129.90	1121.43	1114.38	1108.51
80000	1245.41	1229.35	1216.14	1205.23	1196.19	1188.67	1182.41
85000	1323.24	1306.19	1292.15	1280.56	1270.95	1262.97	1256.32
90000	1401.08	1383.02	1368.16	1355.89	1345.71	1337.26	1330.22
95000	1478.92	1459.86	1444.17	1431.21	1420.47	1411.55	1404.12
100000	1556.76	1536.69	1520.18	1506.54	1495.24	1485.84	1478.02
105000	1634.59	1613.52	1596.19	1581.87	1570.00	1560.13	1551.92
110000	1712.43	1690.36	1672.20	1657.19	1644.76	1634.43	1625.82
120000	1868.11	1844.03	1824.21	1807.85	1794.28	1783.01	1773.62
130000	2023.78	1997.70	1976.23	1958.50	1943.81	1931.59	1921.42
140000	2179.46	2151.37	2128.25	2109.16	2093.33	2080.18	2069.23
150000	2335.14	2305.03	2280.27	2259.81	2242.85	2228.76	2217.03
160000	2490.81	2458.70	2432.29	2410.46	2392.38	2377.35	2364.83
175000	2724.32	2689.21	2660.31	2636.44	2616.66	2600.22	2586.53
200000	3113.51	3073.38	3040.36	3013.08	2990.47	2971.68	2956.04
250000	3891.89	3841.72	3800.45	3766.35	3738.09	3714.60	3695.05
500000	7783.79	7683.45	7600.89	7532.70	7476.18	7429.21	7390.09
1000000	15567.57	15366.90	15201.79	15065.39	14952.36	14858.42	14780.18

MONTHLY PAYMENTS 17.25%

AMOUNT	22 YEARS	23 YEARS	24 YEARS	25 YEARS	30 YEARS	35 YEARS	40 YEARS
100	1.47	1.47	1.46	1.46	1.45	1.44	1.44
200	2.94	2.93	2.92	2.92	2.89	2.88	2.88
500	7.36	7.33	7.31	7.29	7.23	7.21	7.20
1000	14.71	14.66	14.61	14.58	14.46	14.41	14.39
2000	29.43	29.32	29.23	29.15	28.92	28.82	28.78
3000	44.14	43.98	43.84	43.73	43.38	43.23	43.17
4000	58.86	58.64	58.46	58.31	57.84	57.64	57.56
5000	73.57	73.30	73.07	72.88	72.30	72.05	71.95
6000	88.29	87.96	87.69	87.46	86.76	86.47	86.34
7000	103.00	102.62	102.30	102.03	101.22	100.88	100.73
8000	117.72	117.28	116.92	116.61	115.68	115.29	115.12
9000	132.43	131.94	131.53	131.19	130.14	129.70	129.51
10000	147.15	146.60	146.15	145.76	144.60	144.11	143.90
11000	161.86	161.26	160.76	160.34	159.06	158.52	158.29
12000	176.58	175.92	175.38	174.92	173.52	172.93	172.68
13000	191.29	190.58	189.99	189.49	187.98	187.34	187.07
14000	206.01	205.24	204.61	204.07	202.44	201.75	201.46
15000	220.72	219.90	219.22	218.65	216.90	216.16	215.85
20000	294.30	293.21	292.29	291.53	289.20	288.22	287.80
25000	367.87	366.51	365.37	364.41	361.50	360.27	359.76
30000	441.45	439.81	438.44	437.29	433.80	432.33	431.71
35000	515.02	513.11	511.51	510.17	506.10	504.38	503.66
40000	588.60	586.41	584.59	583.06	578.39	576.44	575.61
45000	662.17	659.71	657.66	655.94	650.69	648.49	647.56
50000	735.74	733.02	730.73	728.82	722.99	720.55	719.51
55000	809.32	806.32	803.81	801.70	795.29	792.60	791.46
56000	824.03	820.98	818.42	816.28	809.75	807.01	805.85
57000	838.75	835.64	833.04	830.86	824.21	821.42	820.24
58000	853.46	850.30	847.65	845.43	838.67	835.83	834.63
59000	868.18	864.96	862.27	860.01	853.13	850.24	849.02
60000	882.89	879.62	876.88	874.58	867.59	864.66	863.41
61000	897.61	894.28	891.49	889.16	882.05	879.07	877.80
62000	912.32	908.94	906.11	903.74	896.51	893.48	892.19
63000	927.04	923.60	920.72	918.31	910.97	907.89	906.58
64000	941.75	938.26	935.34	932.89	925.43	922.30	920.97
65000	956.47	952.92	949.95	947.47	939.89	936.71	935.37
70000	1030.04	1026.22	1023.03	1020.35	1012.19	1008.76	1007.32
75000	1103.62	1099.52	1096.10	1093.23	1084.49	1080.82	1079.27
80000	1177.19	1172.83	1169.17	1166.11	1156.79	1152.87	1151.22
85000	1250.77	1246.13	1242.25	1239.00	1229.09	1224.93	1223.17
90000	1324.34	1319.43	1315.32	1311.88	1301.39	1296.98	1295.12
95000	1397.91	1392.73	1388.39	1384.76	1373.69	1369.04	1367.07
100000	1471.49	1466.03	1461.47	1457.64	1445.99	1441.09	1439.02
105000	1545.06	1539.33	1534.54	1530.52	1518.29	1513.15	1510.97
110000	1618.64	1612.64	1607.61	1603.41	1590.58	1585.20	1582.93
120000	1765.79	1759.24	1753.76	1749.17	1735.18	1729.31	1726.83
130000	1912.94	1905.84	1899.91	1894.93	1879.78	1873.42	1870.73
140000	2060.09	2052.45	2046.05	2040.70	2024.38	2017.53	2014.63
150000	2207.23	2199.05	2192.20	2186.46	2168.98	2161.64	2158.53
160000	2354.38	2345.65	2338.35	2332.23	2313.58	2305.75	2302.44
175000	2575.11	2565.56	2557.57	2550.87	2530.48	2521.91	2518.29
200000	2942.98	2932.07	2922.93	2915.28	2891.97	2882.18	2878.05
250000	3678.72	3665.08	3653.67	3644.10	3614.96	3602.73	3597.56
500000	7357.45	7330.17	7307.33	7288.21	7229.93	7205.46	7195.12
1000000	14714.89	14660.33	14614.67	14576.41	14459.86	14410.92	14390.23

17.50%

MONTHLY PAYMENTS

AMOUNT	1 YEAR	2 YEARS	3 YEARS	4 YEARS	5 YEARS	6 YEARS	7 YEARS
100	9.14	4.97	3.59	2.91	2.51	2.25	2.07
200	18.29	9.94	7.18	5.82	5.02	4.51	4.15
500	45.72	24.84	17.95	14.56	12.56	11.26	10.36
1000	91.44	49.68	35.90	29.11	25.12	22.53	20.73
2000	182.88	99.37	71.80	58.23	50.24	45.05	41.45
3000	274.33	149.05	107.71	87.34	75.37	67.58	62.18
4000	365.77	198.73	143.61	116.46	100.49	90.10	82.90
5000	457.21	248.41	179.51	145.57	125.61	112.63	103.63
6000	548.65	298.10	215.41	174.69	150.73	135.16	124.35
7000	640.10	347.78	251.31	203.80	175.86	157.68	145.08
8000	731.54	397.46	287.22	232.91	200.98	180.21	165.81
9000	822.98	447.15	323.12	262.03	226.10	202.73	186.53
10000	914.42	496.83	359.02	291.14	251.22	225.26	207.26
11000	1005.86	546.51	394.92	320.26	276.34	247.79	227.98
12000	1097.31	596.19	430.82	349.37	301.47	270.31	248.71
13000	1188.75	645.88	466.73	378.49	326.59	292.84	269.44
14000	1280.19	695.56	502.63	407.60	351.71	315.36	290.16
15000	1371.63	745.24	538.53	436.72	376.83	337.89	310.89
20000	1828.84	993.66	718.04	582.29	502.44	450.52	414.52
25000	2286.06	1242.07	897.55	727.86	628.06	563.15	518.14
30000	2743.27	1490.49	1077.06	873.43	753.67	675.78	621.77
35000	3200.48	1738.90	1256.57	1019.00	879.28	788.41	725.40
40000	3657.69	1987.31	1436.08	1164.57	1004.89	901.04	829.03
45000	4114.90	2235.73	1615.59	1310.15	1130.50	1013.67	932.66
50000	4572.11	2484.14	1795.10	1455.72	1256.11	1126.30	1036.29
55000	5029.32	2732.56	1974.61	1601.29	1381.72	1238.93	1139.92
56000	5120.76	2782.24	2010.52	1630.40	1406.84	1261.46	1160.64
57000	5212.21	2831.92	2046.42	1659.52	1431.97	1283.98	1181.37
58000	5303.65	2881.61	2082.32	1688.63	1457.09	1306.51	1202.10
59000	5395.09	2931.29	2118.22	1717.75	1482.21	1329.04	1222.82
60000	5486.53	2980.97	2154.12	1746.86	1507.33	1351.56	1243.55
61000	5577.97	3030.65	2190.03	1775.98	1532.46	1374.09	1264.27
62000	5669.42	3080.34	2225.93	1805.09	1557.58	1396.61	1285.00
63000	5760.86	3130.02	2261.83	1834.21	1582.70	1419.14	1305.73
64000	5852.30	3179.70	2297.73	1863.32	1607.82	1441.67	1326.45
65000	5943.74	3229.39	2333.63	1892.43	1632.94	1464.19	1347.18
70000	6400.95	3477.80	2513.14	2038.01	1758.55	1576.82	1450.81
75000	6858.17	3726.21	2692.65	2183.58	1884.17	1689.45	1554.43
80000	7315.38	3974.63	2872.17	2329.15	2009.78	1802.08	1658.06
85000	7772.59	4223.04	3051.68	2474.72	2135.39	1914.71	1761.69
90000	8229.80	4471.46	3231.19	2620.29	2261.00	2027.34	1865.32
95000	8687.01	4719.87	3410.70	2765.87	2386.61	2139.97	1968.95
100000	9144.22	4968.28	3590.21	2911.44	2512.22	2252.60	2072.58
105000	9601.43	5216.70	3769.72	3057.01	2637.83	2365.23	2176.21
110000	10058.64	5465.11	3949.23	3202.58	2763.44	2477.87	2279.84
120000	10973.06	5961.94	4308.25	3493.72	3014.67	2703.13	2487.10
130000	11887.49	6458.77	4667.27	3784.87	3265.89	2928.39	2694.35
140000	12801.91	6955.60	5026.29	4076.01	3517.11	3153.65	2901.61
150000	13716.33	7452.43	5385.31	4367.16	3768.33	3378.91	3108.87
160000	14630.75	7949.26	5744.33	4658.30	4019.55	3604.17	3316.13
175000	16002.39	8694.50	6282.86	5095.02	4396.39	3942.06	3627.01
200000	18288.44	9936.57	7180.41	5822.87	5024.44	4505.21	4145.16
250000	22860.55	12420.71	8975.52	7278.59	6280.55	5631.51	5181.45
500000	45721.10	24841.42	17951.03	14557.19	12561.11	11263.02	10362.90
1000000	91442.20	49682.85	35902.07	29114.37	25122.21	22526.05	20725.79

MONTHLY PAYMENTS 17.50%

AMOUNT	8 YEARS	9 YEARS	10 YEARS	11 YEARS	12 YEARS	13 YEARS	14 YEARS
100	1.94	1.84	1.77	1.71	1.67	1.63	1.60
200	3.88	3.69	3.54	3.42	3.33	3.26	3.20
500	9.71	9.22	8.85	8.56	8.33	8.14	7.99
1000	19.42	18.45	17.70	17.11	16.65	16.29	15.99
2000	38.84	36.89	35.40	34.23	33.31	32.57	31.98
3000	58.26	55.34	53.09	51.34	49.96	48.86	47.96
4000	77.68	73.78	70.79	68.46	66.62	65.14	63.95
5000	97.11	92.23	88.49	85.57	83.27	81.43	79.94
6000	116.53	110.67	106.19	102.69	99.92	97.71	95.93
7000	135.95	129.12	123.89	119.80	116.58	114.00	111.91
8000	155.37	147.56	141.58	136.92	133.23	130.28	127.90
9000	174.79	166.01	159.28	154.03	149.88	146.57	143.89
10000	194.21	184.45	176.98	171.15	166.54	162.85	159.88
11000	213.63	202.90	194.68	188.26	183.19	179.14	175.86
12000	233.05	221.34	212.37	205.38	199.85	195.42	191.85
13000	252.48	239.79	230.07	222.49	216.50	211.71	207.84
14000	271.90	258.23	247.77	239.61	233.15	227.99	223.83
15000	291.32	276.68	265.47	256.72	249.81	244.28	239.81
20000	388.42	368.91	353.96	342.30	333.08	325.70	319.75
25000	485.53	461.13	442.45	427.87	416.35	407.13	399.69
30000	582.64	553.36	530.94	513.45	499.62	488.55	479.63
35000	679.74	645.59	619.43	599.02	582.89	569.98	559.57
40000	776.85	737.81	707.92	684.60	666.15	651.40	639.50
45000	873.95	830.04	796.40	770.17	749.42	732.83	719.44
50000	971.06	922.27	884.89	855.75	832.69	814.26	799.38
55000	1068.17	1014.49	973.38	941.32	915.96	895.68	879.32
56000	1087.59	1032.94	991.08	958.44	932.62	911.97	895.30
57000	1107.01	1051.38	1008.78	975.55	949.27	928.25	911.29
58000	1126.43	1069.83	1026.48	992.67	965.92	944.54	927.28
59000	1145.85	1088.27	1044.17	1009.78	982.58	960.82	943.27
60000	1165.27	1106.72	1061.87	1026.90	999.23	977.11	959.26
61000	1184.69	1125.17	1079.57	1044.01	1015.89	993.39	975.24
62000	1204.12	1143.61	1097.27	1061.13	1032.54	1009.68	991.23
63000	1223.54	1162.06	1114.97	1078.24	1049.19	1025.96	1007.22
64000	1242.96	1180.50	1132.66	1095.36	1065.85	1042.25	1023.21
65000	1262.38	1198.95	1150.36	1112.47	1082.50	1058.53	1039.19
70000	1359.48	1291.17	1238.85	1198.05	1165.77	1139.96	1119.13
75000	1456.59	1383.40	1327.34	1283.62	1249.04	1221.38	1199.07
80000	1553.70	1475.63	1415.83	1369.19	1332.31	1302.81	1279.01
85000	1650.80	1567.85	1504.32	1454.77	1415.58	1384.24	1358.94
90000	1747.91	1660.08	1592.81	1540.34	1498.85	1465.66	1438.88
95000	1845.01	1752.31	1681.30	1625.92	1582.12	1547.09	1518.82
100000	1942.12	1844.53	1769.79	1711.49	1665.39	1628.51	1598.76
105000	2039.23	1936.76	1858.28	1797.07	1748.66	1709.94	1678.70
110000	2136.33	2028.99	1946.77	1882.64	1831.93	1791.36	1758.63
120000	2330.55	2213.44	2123.75	2053.79	1998.46	1954.21	1918.51
130000	2524.76	2397.89	2300.72	2224.94	2165.00	2117.07	2078.39
140000	2718.97	2582.35	2477.70	2396.09	2331.54	2279.92	2238.26
150000	2913.18	2766.80	2654.68	2567.24	2498.08	2442.77	2398.14
160000	3107.39	2951.25	2831.66	2738.39	2664.62	2605.62	2558.01
175000	3398.71	3227.93	3097.13	2995.11	2914.43	2849.90	2797.83
200000	3884.24	3689.07	3539.58	3422.99	3330.77	3257.02	3197.52
250000	4855.30	4611.33	4424.47	4278.73	4163.47	4071.28	3996.90
500000	9710.61	9222.67	8848.94	8557.47	8326.94	8142.56	7993.79
1000000	19421.21	18445.33	17697.88	17114.94	16653.87	16285.12	15987.59

17.50%　　　MONTHLY PAYMENTS

AMOUNT	15 YEARS	16 YEARS	17 YEARS	18 YEARS	19 YEARS	20 YEARS	21 YEARS
100	1.57	1.55	1.54	1.53	1.51	1.50	1.50
200	3.15	3.11	3.08	3.05	3.03	3.01	2.99
500	7.87	7.77	7.69	7.63	7.57	7.52	7.49
1000	15.75	15.55	15.39	15.25	15.14	15.05	14.97
2000	31.49	31.10	30.77	30.50	30.28	30.10	29.95
3000	47.24	46.64	46.16	45.76	45.42	45.15	44.92
4000	62.98	62.19	61.54	61.01	60.56	60.20	59.89
5000	78.73	77.74	76.93	76.26	75.71	75.25	74.87
6000	94.47	93.29	92.31	91.51	90.85	90.30	89.84
7000	110.22	108.84	107.70	106.76	105.99	105.35	104.81
8000	125.97	124.39	123.09	122.02	121.13	120.40	119.78
9000	141.71	139.93	138.47	137.27	136.27	135.44	134.76
10000	157.46	155.48	153.86	152.52	151.41	150.49	149.73
11000	173.20	171.03	169.24	167.77	166.55	165.54	164.70
12000	188.95	186.58	184.63	183.02	181.69	180.59	179.68
13000	204.70	202.13	200.02	198.28	196.84	195.64	194.65
14000	220.44	217.67	215.40	213.53	211.98	210.69	209.62
15000	236.19	233.22	230.79	228.78	227.12	225.74	224.60
20000	314.92	310.96	307.72	305.04	302.82	300.99	299.46
25000	393.64	388.70	384.64	381.30	378.53	376.24	374.33
30000	472.37	466.44	461.57	457.56	454.24	451.48	449.19
35000	551.10	544.18	538.50	533.82	529.94	526.73	524.06
40000	629.83	621.93	615.43	610.08	605.65	601.98	598.92
45000	708.56	699.67	692.36	686.34	681.36	677.22	673.79
50000	787.29	777.41	769.29	762.60	757.06	752.47	748.66
55000	866.02	855.15	846.22	838.86	832.77	827.72	823.52
56000	881.76	870.70	861.60	854.11	847.91	842.77	838.49
57000	897.51	886.24	876.99	869.36	863.05	857.82	853.47
58000	913.26	901.79	892.38	884.61	878.19	872.87	868.44
59000	929.00	917.34	907.76	899.87	893.33	887.92	883.41
60000	944.75	932.89	923.15	915.12	908.47	902.97	898.39
61000	960.49	948.44	938.53	930.37	923.62	918.01	913.36
62000	976.24	963.98	953.92	945.62	938.76	933.06	928.33
63000	991.98	979.53	969.31	960.87	953.90	948.11	943.31
64000	1007.73	995.08	984.69	976.12	969.04	963.16	958.28
65000	1023.48	1010.63	1000.08	991.38	984.18	978.21	973.25
70000	1102.20	1088.37	1077.01	1067.64	1059.89	1053.46	1048.12
75000	1180.93	1166.11	1153.93	1143.90	1135.59	1128.71	1122.98
80000	1259.66	1243.85	1230.86	1220.16	1211.30	1203.95	1197.85
85000	1338.39	1321.59	1307.79	1296.42	1287.01	1279.20	1272.71
90000	1417.12	1399.33	1384.72	1372.68	1362.71	1354.45	1347.58
95000	1495.85	1477.07	1461.65	1448.94	1438.42	1429.69	1422.44
100000	1574.58	1554.81	1538.58	1525.19	1514.12	1504.94	1497.31
105000	1653.31	1632.55	1615.51	1601.45	1589.83	1580.19	1572.18
110000	1732.04	1710.29	1692.44	1677.71	1665.54	1655.44	1647.04
120000	1889.49	1865.78	1846.30	1830.23	1816.95	1805.93	1796.77
130000	2046.95	2021.26	2000.15	1982.75	1968.36	1956.42	1946.50
140000	2204.41	2176.74	2154.01	2135.27	2119.77	2106.92	2096.23
150000	2361.87	2332.22	2307.87	2287.79	2271.19	2257.41	2245.97
160000	2519.33	2487.70	2461.73	2440.31	2422.60	2407.91	2395.70
175000	2755.52	2720.92	2692.51	2669.09	2649.72	2633.65	2620.29
200000	3149.16	3109.63	3077.16	3050.39	3028.25	3009.88	2994.62
250000	3936.45	3887.03	3846.45	3812.99	3785.31	3762.35	3743.28
500000	7872.89	7774.06	7692.90	7625.97	7570.62	7524.71	7486.55
1000000	15745.78	15548.13	15385.79	15251.95	15141.24	15049.42	14973.10

MONTHLY PAYMENTS 17.50%

AMOUNT	22 YEARS	23 YEARS	24 YEARS	25 YEARS	30 YEARS	35 YEARS	40 YEARS
100	1.49	1.49	1.48	1.48	1.47	1.46	1.46
200	2.98	2.97	2.96	2.96	2.93	2.92	2.92
500	7.45	7.43	7.41	7.39	7.33	7.31	7.30
1000	14.91	14.86	14.81	14.78	14.66	14.62	14.60
2000	29.82	29.71	29.62	29.55	29.33	29.23	29.19
3000	44.73	44.57	44.44	44.33	43.99	43.85	43.79
4000	59.64	59.43	59.25	59.10	58.65	58.47	58.39
5000	74.55	74.28	74.06	73.88	73.32	73.08	72.99
6000	89.46	89.14	88.87	88.65	87.98	87.70	87.58
7000	104.37	104.00	103.69	103.43	102.64	102.32	102.18
8000	119.28	118.85	118.50	118.20	117.31	116.93	116.78
9000	134.19	133.71	133.31	132.98	131.97	131.55	131.38
10000	149.10	148.57	148.12	147.75	146.63	146.17	145.97
11000	164.01	163.42	162.94	162.53	161.30	160.78	160.57
12000	178.91	178.28	177.75	177.30	175.96	175.40	175.17
13000	193.82	193.14	192.56	192.08	190.62	190.02	189.77
14000	208.73	207.99	207.37	206.85	205.29	204.63	204.36
15000	223.64	222.85	222.18	221.63	219.95	219.25	218.96
20000	298.19	297.13	296.25	295.51	293.27	292.34	291.95
25000	372.74	371.41	370.31	369.38	366.58	365.42	364.93
30000	447.29	445.70	444.37	443.26	439.90	438.50	437.92
35000	521.83	519.98	518.43	517.14	513.21	511.59	510.91
40000	596.38	594.26	592.49	591.01	586.53	584.67	583.89
45000	670.93	668.54	666.55	664.89	659.85	657.75	656.88
50000	745.48	742.83	740.61	738.76	733.16	730.84	729.87
55000	820.03	817.11	814.68	812.64	806.48	803.92	802.85
56000	834.93	831.97	829.49	827.42	821.14	818.54	817.45
57000	849.84	846.82	844.30	842.19	835.81	833.15	832.05
58000	864.75	861.68	859.11	856.97	850.47	847.77	846.65
59000	879.66	876.54	873.93	871.74	865.13	862.39	861.24
60000	894.57	891.39	888.74	886.52	879.80	877.01	875.84
61000	909.48	906.25	903.55	901.29	894.46	891.62	890.44
62000	924.39	921.11	918.36	916.07	909.12	906.24	905.03
63000	939.30	935.96	933.17	930.84	923.78	920.86	919.63
64000	954.21	950.82	947.99	945.62	938.45	935.47	934.23
65000	969.12	965.68	962.80	960.39	953.11	950.09	948.83
70000	1043.67	1039.96	1036.86	1034.27	1026.43	1023.17	1021.81
75000	1118.22	1114.24	1110.92	1108.15	1099.74	1096.26	1094.80
80000	1192.76	1188.52	1184.98	1182.02	1173.06	1169.34	1167.79
85000	1267.31	1262.81	1259.04	1255.90	1246.38	1242.42	1240.77
90000	1341.86	1337.09	1333.11	1329.78	1319.69	1315.51	1313.76
95000	1416.41	1411.37	1407.17	1403.65	1393.01	1388.59	1386.75
100000	1490.95	1485.65	1481.23	1477.53	1466.33	1461.68	1459.73
105000	1565.50	1559.94	1555.29	1551.41	1539.64	1534.76	1532.72
110000	1640.05	1634.22	1629.35	1625.28	1612.96	1607.84	1605.71
120000	1789.15	1782.79	1777.48	1773.04	1759.59	1754.01	1751.68
130000	1938.24	1931.35	1925.60	1920.79	1906.22	1900.18	1897.65
140000	2087.34	2079.92	2073.72	2068.54	2052.86	2046.35	2043.63
150000	2236.43	2228.48	2221.84	2216.29	2199.49	2192.51	2189.60
160000	2385.53	2377.05	2369.97	2364.05	2346.12	2338.68	2335.57
175000	2609.17	2599.90	2592.15	2585.68	2566.07	2557.93	2554.53
200000	2981.91	2971.31	2962.46	2955.06	2932.65	2923.35	2919.47
250000	3727.39	3714.14	3703.07	3693.82	3665.81	3654.19	3649.33
500000	7454.77	7428.27	7406.15	7387.65	7331.63	7308.38	7298.67
1000000	14909.55	14856.55	14812.29	14775.30	14663.25	14616.75	14597.33

17.75% MONTHLY PAYMENTS

AMOUNT	1 YEAR	2 YEARS	3 YEARS	4 YEARS	5 YEARS	6 YEARS	7 YEARS
100	9.16	4.98	3.60	2.92	2.53	2.27	2.09
200	18.31	9.96	7.21	5.85	5.05	4.53	4.17
500	45.78	24.90	18.01	14.62	12.63	11.33	10.44
1000	91.56	49.80	36.03	29.24	25.26	22.67	20.87
2000	183.12	99.61	72.05	58.49	50.52	45.33	41.74
3000	274.68	149.41	108.08	87.73	75.77	68.00	62.61
4000	366.24	199.21	144.11	116.98	101.03	90.67	83.49
5000	457.81	249.02	180.14	146.22	126.29	113.33	104.36
6000	549.37	298.82	216.16	175.47	151.55	136.00	125.23
7000	640.93	348.62	252.19	204.71	176.80	158.67	146.10
8000	732.49	398.43	288.22	233.96	202.06	181.33	166.97
9000	824.05	448.23	324.24	263.20	227.32	204.00	187.84
10000	915.61	498.03	360.27	292.45	252.58	226.67	208.72
11000	1007.17	547.84	396.30	321.69	277.83	249.33	229.59
12000	1098.73	597.64	432.33	350.93	303.09	272.00	250.46
13000	1190.29	647.44	468.35	380.18	328.35	294.67	271.33
14000	1281.85	697.25	504.38	409.42	353.61	317.33	292.20
15000	1373.42	747.05	540.41	438.67	378.86	340.00	313.07
20000	1831.22	996.07	720.54	584.89	505.15	453.33	417.43
25000	2289.03	1245.08	900.68	731.11	631.44	566.67	521.79
30000	2746.83	1494.10	1080.81	877.34	757.73	680.00	626.15
35000	3204.64	1743.12	1260.95	1023.56	884.02	793.33	730.50
40000	3662.44	1992.14	1441.08	1169.78	1010.30	906.67	834.86
45000	4120.25	2241.15	1621.22	1316.00	1136.59	1020.00	939.22
50000	4578.05	2490.17	1801.36	1462.23	1262.88	1133.33	1043.58
55000	5035.86	2739.19	1981.49	1608.45	1389.17	1246.67	1147.94
56000	5127.42	2788.99	2017.52	1637.69	1414.43	1269.33	1168.81
57000	5218.98	2838.79	2053.55	1666.94	1439.68	1292.00	1189.68
58000	5310.54	2888.60	2089.57	1696.18	1464.94	1314.67	1210.55
59000	5402.10	2938.40	2125.60	1725.43	1490.20	1337.33	1231.42
60000	5493.66	2988.20	2161.63	1754.67	1515.46	1360.00	1252.29
61000	5585.22	3038.01	2197.65	1783.92	1540.72	1382.67	1273.17
62000	5676.79	3087.81	2233.68	1813.16	1565.97	1405.33	1294.04
63000	5768.35	3137.61	2269.71	1842.41	1591.23	1428.00	1314.91
64000	5859.91	3187.42	2305.73	1871.65	1616.49	1450.67	1335.78
65000	5951.47	3237.22	2341.76	1900.89	1641.75	1473.33	1356.65
70000	6409.27	3486.24	2521.90	2047.12	1768.03	1586.67	1461.01
75000	6867.08	3735.25	2702.03	2193.34	1894.32	1700.00	1565.37
80000	7324.88	3984.27	2882.17	2339.56	2020.61	1813.34	1669.72
85000	7782.69	4233.29	3062.30	2485.78	2146.90	1926.67	1774.08
90000	8240.50	4482.31	3242.44	2632.01	2273.19	2040.00	1878.44
95000	8698.30	4731.32	3422.58	2778.23	2399.47	2153.34	1982.80
100000	9156.11	4980.34	3602.71	2924.45	2525.76	2266.67	2087.16
105000	9613.91	5229.36	3782.85	3070.68	2652.05	2380.00	2191.51
110000	10071.72	5478.37	3962.98	3216.90	2778.34	2493.34	2295.87
120000	10987.33	5976.41	4323.25	3509.34	3030.91	2720.00	2504.59
130000	11902.94	6474.44	4683.52	3801.79	3283.49	2946.67	2713.30
140000	12818.55	6972.47	5043.79	4094.23	3536.07	3173.34	2922.02
150000	13734.16	7470.51	5404.07	4386.68	3788.64	3400.00	3130.73
160000	14649.77	7968.54	5764.34	4679.12	4041.22	3626.67	3339.45
175000	16023.18	8715.59	6304.74	5117.79	4420.08	3966.67	3652.52
200000	18312.21	9960.68	7205.42	5848.91	5051.52	4533.34	4174.31
250000	22890.26	12450.85	9006.78	7311.13	6314.41	5666.67	5217.89
500000	45780.53	24901.70	18013.55	14622.26	12628.81	11333.35	10435.78
1000000	91561.06	49803.39	36027.11	29244.53	25257.62	22666.69	20871.56

MONTHLY PAYMENTS   17.75%

AMOUNT	8 YEARS	9 YEARS	10 YEARS	11 YEARS	12 YEARS	13 YEARS	14 YEARS
100	1.96	1.86	1.79	1.73	1.68	1.65	1.62
200	3.91	3.72	3.57	3.46	3.36	3.29	3.23
500	9.79	9.30	8.93	8.64	8.41	8.23	8.08
1000	19.57	18.60	17.86	17.28	16.82	16.46	16.16
2000	39.14	37.20	35.72	34.56	33.64	32.91	32.33
3000	58.72	55.80	53.57	51.84	50.47	49.37	48.49
4000	78.29	74.40	71.43	69.12	67.29	65.83	64.65
5000	97.86	93.00	89.29	86.40	84.11	82.29	80.82
6000	117.43	111.60	107.15	103.68	100.93	98.74	96.98
7000	137.00	130.21	125.01	120.95	117.76	115.20	113.14
8000	156.58	148.81	142.86	138.23	134.58	131.66	129.31
9000	176.15	167.41	160.72	155.51	151.40	148.12	145.47
10000	195.72	186.01	178.58	172.79	168.22	164.57	161.63
11000	215.29	204.61	196.44	190.07	185.04	181.03	177.80
12000	234.86	223.21	214.29	207.35	201.87	197.49	193.96
13000	254.44	241.81	232.15	224.63	218.69	213.94	210.12
14000	274.01	260.41	250.01	241.91	235.51	230.40	226.28
15000	293.58	279.01	267.87	259.19	252.33	246.86	242.45
20000	391.44	372.02	357.16	345.58	336.44	329.14	323.26
25000	489.30	465.02	446.45	431.98	420.56	411.43	404.08
30000	587.16	558.02	535.74	518.38	504.67	493.72	484.90
35000	685.02	651.03	625.03	604.77	588.78	576.00	565.71
40000	782.88	744.03	714.32	691.17	672.89	658.29	646.53
45000	880.74	837.04	803.60	777.57	757.00	740.58	727.34
50000	978.60	930.04	892.89	863.96	841.11	822.86	808.16
55000	1076.46	1023.04	982.18	950.36	925.22	905.15	888.98
56000	1096.03	1041.65	1000.04	967.64	942.04	921.60	905.14
57000	1115.60	1060.25	1017.90	984.92	958.87	938.06	921.30
58000	1135.17	1078.85	1035.76	1002.20	975.69	954.52	937.47
59000	1154.74	1097.45	1053.62	1019.47	992.51	970.98	953.63
60000	1174.32	1116.05	1071.47	1036.75	1009.33	987.43	969.79
61000	1193.89	1134.65	1089.33	1054.03	1026.15	1003.89	985.96
62000	1213.46	1153.25	1107.19	1071.31	1042.98	1020.35	1002.12
63000	1233.03	1171.85	1125.05	1088.59	1059.80	1036.81	1018.28
64000	1252.60	1190.45	1142.90	1105.87	1076.62	1053.26	1034.45
65000	1272.18	1209.05	1160.76	1123.15	1093.44	1069.72	1050.61
70000	1370.04	1302.06	1250.05	1209.55	1177.55	1152.01	1131.42
75000	1467.89	1395.06	1339.34	1295.94	1261.67	1234.29	1212.24
80000	1565.75	1488.06	1428.63	1382.34	1345.78	1316.58	1293.06
85000	1663.61	1581.07	1517.92	1468.73	1429.89	1398.86	1373.87
90000	1761.47	1674.07	1607.21	1555.13	1514.00	1481.15	1454.69
95000	1859.33	1767.08	1696.50	1641.53	1598.11	1563.44	1535.51
100000	1957.19	1860.08	1785.79	1727.92	1682.22	1645.72	1616.32
105000	2055.05	1953.09	1875.08	1814.32	1766.33	1728.01	1697.14
110000	2152.91	2046.09	1964.37	1900.72	1850.44	1810.30	1777.95
120000	2348.63	2232.10	2142.95	2073.51	2018.66	1974.87	1939.59
130000	2544.35	2418.11	2321.52	2246.30	2186.89	2139.44	2101.22
140000	2740.07	2604.11	2500.10	2419.09	2355.11	2304.01	2262.85
150000	2935.79	2790.12	2678.68	2591.88	2523.33	2468.58	2424.48
160000	3131.51	2976.13	2857.26	2764.68	2691.55	2633.16	2586.11
175000	3425.09	3255.14	3125.13	3023.87	2943.89	2880.02	2828.56
200000	3914.39	3720.16	3571.58	3455.85	3364.44	3291.45	3232.64
250000	4892.98	4650.20	4464.47	4319.81	4205.55	4114.31	4040.80
500000	9785.97	9300.41	8928.94	8639.62	8411.10	8228.62	8081.61
1000000	19571.93	18600.81	17857.88	17279.23	16822.20	16457.23	16163.21

17.75%　　　MONTHLY PAYMENTS

AMOUNT	15 YEARS	16 YEARS	17 YEARS	18 YEARS	19 YEARS	20 YEARS	21 YEARS
100	1.59	1.57	1.56	1.54	1.53	1.52	1.52
200	3.18	3.15	3.11	3.09	3.07	3.05	3.03
500	7.96	7.87	7.79	7.72	7.67	7.62	7.58
1000	15.92	15.73	15.57	15.44	15.33	15.24	15.17
2000	31.85	31.46	31.14	30.88	30.66	30.48	30.33
3000	47.77	47.19	46.71	46.32	45.99	45.72	45.50
4000	63.70	62.92	62.28	61.76	61.32	60.96	60.67
5000	79.62	78.65	77.85	77.20	76.65	76.20	75.83
6000	95.55	94.38	93.42	92.63	91.98	91.45	91.00
7000	111.47	110.11	108.99	108.07	107.32	106.69	106.17
8000	127.40	125.84	124.56	123.51	122.65	121.93	121.33
9000	143.32	141.57	140.13	138.95	137.98	137.17	136.50
10000	159.25	157.30	155.70	154.39	153.31	152.41	151.67
11000	175.17	173.03	171.27	169.83	168.64	167.65	166.83
12000	191.10	188.76	186.85	185.27	183.97	182.89	182.00
13000	207.02	204.49	202.42	200.71	199.30	198.13	197.17
14000	222.95	220.22	217.99	216.15	214.63	213.37	212.33
15000	238.87	235.95	233.56	231.59	229.96	228.61	227.50
20000	318.49	314.60	311.41	308.78	306.61	304.82	303.33
25000	398.12	393.25	389.26	385.98	383.27	381.02	379.16
30000	477.74	471.90	467.11	463.17	459.92	457.23	455.00
35000	557.36	550.55	544.97	540.37	536.58	533.43	530.83
40000	636.99	629.20	622.82	617.57	613.23	609.64	606.66
45000	716.61	707.85	700.67	694.76	689.88	685.84	682.50
50000	796.23	786.50	778.52	771.96	766.54	762.05	758.33
55000	875.86	865.15	856.37	849.15	843.19	838.25	834.16
56000	891.78	880.88	871.95	864.59	858.52	853.50	849.33
57000	907.71	896.61	887.52	880.03	873.85	868.74	864.49
58000	923.63	912.34	903.09	895.47	889.18	883.98	879.66
59000	939.56	928.07	918.66	910.91	904.51	899.22	894.83
60000	955.48	943.80	934.23	926.35	919.84	914.46	909.99
61000	971.40	959.53	949.80	941.79	935.17	929.70	925.16
62000	987.33	975.26	965.37	957.23	950.50	944.94	940.33
63000	1003.25	990.99	980.94	972.67	965.84	960.18	955.49
64000	1019.18	1006.72	996.51	988.10	981.17	975.42	970.66
65000	1035.10	1022.45	1012.08	1003.54	996.50	990.66	985.83
70000	1114.73	1101.10	1089.93	1080.74	1073.15	1066.87	1061.66
75000	1194.35	1179.75	1167.78	1157.93	1149.80	1143.07	1137.49
80000	1273.97	1258.40	1245.64	1235.13	1226.46	1219.28	1213.32
85000	1353.60	1337.05	1323.49	1312.33	1303.11	1295.48	1289.16
90000	1433.22	1415.70	1401.34	1389.52	1379.76	1371.69	1364.99
95000	1512.84	1494.35	1479.19	1466.72	1456.42	1447.89	1440.82
100000	1592.47	1573.00	1557.04	1543.91	1533.07	1524.10	1516.66
105000	1672.09	1651.65	1634.90	1621.11	1609.73	1600.30	1592.49
110000	1751.71	1730.30	1712.75	1698.30	1686.38	1676.51	1668.32
120000	1910.96	1887.60	1868.45	1852.70	1839.69	1828.92	1819.99
130000	2070.21	2044.90	2024.16	2007.09	1992.99	1981.33	1971.65
140000	2229.45	2202.20	2179.86	2161.48	2146.30	2133.74	2123.32
150000	2388.70	2359.50	2335.57	2315.87	2299.61	2286.15	2274.98
160000	2547.95	2516.80	2491.27	2470.26	2452.92	2438.56	2426.65
175000	2786.82	2752.75	2724.83	2701.85	2682.88	2667.17	2654.15
200000	3184.93	3146.00	3114.09	3087.83	3066.14	3048.20	3033.31
250000	3981.17	3932.50	3892.61	3859.78	3832.68	3810.25	3791.64
500000	7962.33	7865.01	7785.22	7719.56	7665.36	7620.50	7583.28
1000000	15924.67	15730.02	15570.45	15439.13	15330.72	15240.99	15166.56

MONTHLY PAYMENTS 17.75%

AMOUNT	22 YEARS	23 YEARS	24 YEARS	25 YEARS	30 YEARS	35 YEARS	40 YEARS
100	1.51	1.51	1.50	1.50	1.49	1.48	1.48
200	3.02	3.01	3.00	2.99	2.97	2.96	2.96
500	7.55	7.53	7.51	7.49	7.43	7.41	7.40
1000	15.10	15.05	15.01	14.97	14.87	14.82	14.80
2000	30.21	30.11	30.02	29.95	29.73	29.65	29.61
3000	45.31	45.16	45.03	44.92	44.60	44.47	44.41
4000	60.42	60.21	60.04	59.90	59.47	59.29	59.22
5000	75.52	75.27	75.05	74.87	74.33	74.11	74.02
6000	90.63	90.32	90.06	89.85	89.20	88.94	88.83
7000	105.73	105.37	105.07	104.82	104.07	103.76	103.63
8000	120.84	120.43	120.08	119.80	118.94	118.58	118.44
9000	135.94	135.48	135.09	134.77	133.80	133.40	133.24
10000	151.05	150.53	150.10	149.75	148.67	148.23	148.05
11000	166.15	165.59	165.11	164.72	163.54	163.05	162.85
12000	181.26	180.64	180.12	179.70	178.40	177.87	177.65
13000	196.36	195.69	195.13	194.67	193.27	192.70	192.46
14000	211.47	210.75	210.15	209.64	208.14	207.52	207.26
15000	226.57	225.80	225.16	224.62	223.00	222.34	222.07
20000	302.09	301.06	300.21	299.49	297.34	296.46	296.09
25000	377.62	376.33	375.26	374.36	371.67	370.57	370.11
30000	453.14	451.60	450.31	449.24	446.01	444.68	444.14
35000	528.67	526.86	525.36	524.11	520.34	518.80	518.16
40000	604.19	602.13	600.41	598.98	594.68	592.91	592.18
45000	679.71	677.40	675.47	673.86	669.01	667.02	666.20
50000	755.24	752.66	750.52	748.73	743.35	741.14	740.23
55000	830.76	827.93	825.57	823.60	817.68	815.25	814.25
56000	845.86	842.98	840.58	838.58	832.55	830.07	829.05
57000	860.97	858.04	855.59	853.55	847.41	844.90	843.86
58000	876.07	873.09	870.60	868.53	862.28	859.72	858.66
59000	891.18	888.14	885.61	883.50	877.15	874.54	873.47
60000	906.28	903.19	900.62	898.48	892.02	889.37	888.27
61000	921.39	918.25	915.63	913.45	906.88	904.19	903.08
62000	936.49	933.30	930.64	928.43	921.75	919.01	917.88
63000	951.60	948.35	945.65	943.40	936.62	933.83	932.69
64000	966.70	963.41	960.66	958.37	951.48	948.66	947.49
65000	981.81	978.46	975.67	973.35	966.35	963.48	962.29
70000	1057.33	1053.73	1050.73	1048.22	1040.68	1037.59	1036.32
75000	1132.85	1128.99	1125.78	1123.09	1115.02	1111.71	1110.34
80000	1208.38	1204.26	1200.83	1197.97	1189.35	1185.82	1184.36
85000	1283.90	1279.53	1275.88	1272.84	1263.69	1259.93	1258.39
90000	1359.42	1354.79	1350.93	1347.71	1338.02	1334.05	1332.41
95000	1434.95	1430.06	1425.98	1422.59	1412.36	1408.16	1406.43
100000	1510.47	1505.32	1501.04	1497.46	1486.69	1482.28	1480.45
105000	1586.00	1580.59	1576.09	1572.33	1561.03	1556.39	1554.48
110000	1661.52	1655.86	1651.14	1647.21	1635.36	1630.50	1628.50
120000	1812.57	1806.39	1801.24	1796.95	1784.03	1778.73	1776.54
130000	1963.61	1956.92	1951.35	1946.70	1932.70	1926.96	1924.59
140000	2114.66	2107.45	2101.45	2096.44	2081.37	2075.19	2072.63
150000	2265.71	2257.99	2251.55	2246.19	2230.04	2223.41	2220.68
160000	2416.75	2408.52	2401.66	2395.94	2378.71	2371.64	2368.73
175000	2643.33	2634.32	2626.81	2620.55	2601.71	2593.98	2590.79
200000	3020.94	3010.65	3002.07	2994.92	2973.38	2964.55	2960.91
250000	3776.18	3763.31	3752.59	3743.65	3716.73	3705.69	3701.13
500000	7552.36	7526.62	7505.18	7487.30	7433.46	7411.38	7402.27
1000000	15104.72	15053.25	15010.37	14974.60	14866.92	14822.76	14804.53

18.00% MONTHLY PAYMENTS

AMOUNT	1 YEAR	2 YEARS	3 YEARS	4 YEARS	5 YEARS	6 YEARS	7 YEARS
100	9.17	4.99	3.62	2.94	2.54	2.28	2.10
200	18.34	9.98	7.23	5.87	5.08	4.56	4.20
500	45.84	24.96	18.08	14.69	12.70	11.40	10.51
1000	91.68	49.92	36.15	29.37	25.39	22.81	21.02
2000	183.36	99.85	72.30	58.75	50.79	45.62	42.04
3000	275.04	149.77	108.46	88.12	76.18	68.42	63.05
4000	366.72	199.70	144.61	117.50	101.57	91.23	84.07
5000	458.40	249.62	180.76	146.87	126.97	114.04	105.09
6000	550.08	299.54	216.91	176.25	152.36	136.85	126.11
7000	641.76	349.47	253.07	205.62	177.75	159.65	147.12
8000	733.44	399.39	289.22	235.00	203.15	182.46	168.14
9000	825.12	449.32	325.37	264.37	228.54	205.27	189.16
10000	916.80	499.24	361.52	293.75	253.93	228.08	210.18
11000	1008.48	549.17	397.68	323.12	279.33	250.89	231.20
12000	1100.16	599.09	433.83	352.50	304.72	273.69	252.21
13000	1191.84	649.01	469.98	381.87	330.11	296.50	273.23
14000	1283.52	698.94	506.13	411.25	355.51	319.31	294.25
15000	1375.20	748.86	542.29	440.62	380.90	342.12	315.27
20000	1833.60	998.48	723.05	587.50	507.87	456.16	420.36
25000	2292.00	1248.10	903.81	734.37	634.84	570.19	525.45
30000	2750.40	1497.72	1084.57	881.25	761.80	684.23	630.54
35000	3208.80	1747.34	1265.33	1028.12	888.77	798.27	735.62
40000	3667.20	1996.96	1446.10	1175.00	1015.74	912.31	840.71
45000	4125.60	2246.58	1626.86	1321.87	1142.70	1026.35	945.80
50000	4584.00	2496.21	1807.62	1468.75	1269.67	1140.39	1050.89
55000	5042.40	2745.83	1988.38	1615.62	1396.64	1254.43	1155.98
56000	5134.08	2795.75	2024.53	1645.00	1422.03	1277.24	1177.00
57000	5225.76	2845.67	2060.69	1674.37	1447.43	1300.04	1198.02
58000	5317.44	2895.60	2096.84	1703.75	1472.82	1322.85	1219.03
59000	5409.12	2945.52	2132.99	1733.12	1498.21	1345.66	1240.05
60000	5500.80	2995.45	2169.14	1762.50	1523.61	1368.47	1261.07
61000	5592.48	3045.37	2205.30	1791.87	1549.00	1391.28	1282.09
62000	5684.16	3095.29	2241.45	1821.25	1574.39	1414.08	1303.11
63000	5775.84	3145.22	2277.60	1850.62	1599.79	1436.89	1324.12
64000	5867.52	3195.14	2313.75	1880.00	1625.18	1459.70	1345.14
65000	5959.20	3245.07	2349.91	1909.37	1650.57	1482.51	1366.16
70000	6417.60	3494.69	2530.67	2056.25	1777.54	1596.55	1471.35
75000	6876.00	3744.31	2711.43	2203.12	1904.51	1710.58	1576.34
80000	7334.40	3993.93	2892.19	2350.00	2031.47	1824.62	1681.43
85000	7792.80	4243.55	3072.95	2496.87	2158.44	1938.66	1786.52
90000	8251.20	4493.17	3253.72	2643.75	2285.41	2052.70	1891.61
95000	8709.60	4742.79	3434.48	2790.62	2412.38	2166.74	1996.69
100000	9168.00	4992.41	3615.24	2937.50	2539.34	2280.78	2101.78
105000	9626.40	5242.03	3796.00	3084.37	2666.31	2394.82	2206.87
110000	10084.80	5491.65	3976.76	3231.25	2793.28	2508.86	2311.95
120000	11001.60	5990.89	4338.29	3525.00	3047.21	2736.93	2522.14
130000	11918.40	6490.13	4699.81	3818.75	3301.15	2965.01	2732.32
140000	12835.20	6989.37	5061.34	4112.50	3555.08	3193.09	2942.50
150000	13752.00	7488.62	5422.86	4406.25	3809.01	3421.17	3152.68
160000	14668.80	7987.86	5784.38	4700.00	4062.95	3649.25	3362.85
175000	16044.00	8736.72	6326.67	5140.62	4443.85	3991.36	3678.12
200000	18336.00	9984.82	7230.48	5875.00	5078.69	4561.56	4203.57
250000	22920.00	12481.03	9038.10	7343.75	6348.36	5701.95	5254.46
500000	45840.00	24962.05	18076.20	14687.50	12696.71	11403.90	10508.92
1000000	91679.99	49924.10	36152.40	29375.00	25393.43	22807.79	21017.84

MONTHLY PAYMENTS 18.00%

AMOUNT	8 YEARS	9 YEARS	10 YEARS	11 YEARS	12 YEARS	13 YEARS	14 YEARS
100	1.97	1.88	1.80	1.74	1.70	1.66	1.63
200	3.94	3.75	3.60	3.49	3.40	3.33	3.27
500	9.86	9.38	9.01	8.72	8.50	8.32	8.17
1000	19.72	18.76	18.02	17.44	16.99	16.63	16.34
2000	39.45	37.51	36.04	34.89	33.98	33.26	32.68
3000	59.17	56.27	54.06	52.33	50.97	49.89	49.02
4000	78.89	75.03	72.07	69.78	67.96	66.52	65.36
5000	98.62	93.78	90.09	87.22	84.96	83.15	81.70
6000	118.34	112.54	108.11	104.67	101.95	99.78	98.04
7000	138.06	131.30	126.13	122.11	118.94	116.41	114.38
8000	157.79	150.06	144.15	139.55	135.93	133.04	130.72
9000	177.51	168.81	162.17	157.00	152.92	149.67	147.06
10000	197.23	187.57	180.19	174.44	169.91	166.30	163.40
11000	216.96	206.33	198.20	191.89	186.90	182.93	179.73
12000	236.68	225.08	216.22	209.33	203.89	199.56	196.07
13000	256.40	243.84	234.24	226.77	220.89	216.19	212.41
14000	276.12	262.60	252.26	244.22	237.88	232.82	228.75
15000	295.85	281.35	270.28	261.66	254.87	249.45	245.09
20000	394.46	375.14	360.37	348.88	339.82	332.60	326.79
25000	493.08	468.92	450.46	436.10	424.78	415.75	408.49
30000	591.70	562.71	540.56	523.33	509.74	498.90	490.19
35000	690.31	656.49	630.65	610.55	594.69	582.05	571.88
40000	788.93	750.28	720.74	697.77	679.65	665.20	653.58
45000	887.54	844.06	810.83	784.99	764.60	748.35	735.28
50000	986.16	937.84	900.93	872.21	849.56	831.50	816.98
55000	1084.78	1031.63	991.02	959.43	934.52	914.65	898.67
56000	1104.50	1050.39	1009.04	976.87	951.51	931.28	915.01
57000	1124.22	1069.14	1027.06	994.32	968.50	947.91	931.35
58000	1143.95	1087.90	1045.07	1011.76	985.49	964.54	947.69
59000	1163.67	1106.66	1063.09	1029.21	1002.48	981.17	964.03
60000	1183.39	1125.41	1081.11	1046.65	1019.47	997.80	980.37
61000	1203.12	1144.17	1099.13	1064.09	1036.46	1014.43	996.71
62000	1222.84	1162.93	1117.15	1081.54	1053.45	1031.06	1013.05
63000	1242.56	1181.68	1135.17	1098.98	1070.45	1047.69	1029.39
64000	1262.29	1200.44	1153.19	1116.43	1087.44	1064.32	1045.73
65000	1282.01	1219.20	1171.20	1133.87	1104.43	1080.95	1062.07
70000	1380.62	1312.98	1261.30	1221.09	1189.38	1164.10	1143.77
75000	1479.24	1406.77	1351.39	1308.31	1274.34	1247.25	1225.46
80000	1577.86	1500.55	1441.48	1395.53	1359.30	1330.40	1307.16
85000	1676.47	1594.34	1531.57	1482.76	1444.25	1413.55	1388.86
90000	1775.09	1688.12	1621.67	1569.98	1529.21	1496.70	1470.56
95000	1873.71	1781.90	1711.76	1657.20	1614.16	1579.85	1552.25
100000	1972.32	1875.69	1801.85	1744.42	1699.12	1663.00	1633.95
105000	2070.94	1969.47	1891.94	1831.64	1784.08	1746.15	1715.65
110000	2169.55	2063.26	1982.04	1918.86	1869.03	1829.30	1797.35
120000	2366.79	2250.83	2162.22	2093.30	2038.94	1995.60	1960.74
130000	2564.02	2438.40	2342.41	2267.74	2208.86	2161.90	2124.14
140000	2761.25	2625.96	2522.59	2442.19	2378.77	2328.20	2287.53
150000	2958.48	2813.53	2702.78	2616.63	2548.68	2494.50	2450.93
160000	3155.71	3001.10	2882.96	2791.07	2718.59	2660.80	2614.32
175000	3451.56	3282.46	3153.24	3052.73	2973.46	2910.25	2859.41
200000	3944.64	3751.38	3603.70	3488.84	3398.24	3326.00	3267.90
250000	4930.80	4689.22	4504.63	4361.04	4247.80	4157.50	4084.88
500000	9861.61	9378.44	9009.26	8722.09	8495.60	8315.00	8169.75
1000000	19723.21	18756.89	18018.52	17444.18	16991.20	16630.01	16339.50

18.00%   MONTHLY PAYMENTS

AMOUNT	15 YEARS	16 YEARS	17 YEARS	18 YEARS	19 YEARS	20 YEARS	21 YEARS
100	1.61	1.59	1.58	1.56	1.55	1.54	1.54
200	3.22	3.18	3.15	3.13	3.10	3.09	3.07
500	8.05	7.96	7.88	7.81	7.76	7.72	7.68
1000	16.10	15.91	15.76	15.63	15.52	15.43	15.36
2000	32.21	31.83	31.51	31.25	31.04	30.87	30.72
3000	48.31	47.74	47.27	46.88	46.56	46.30	46.08
4000	64.42	63.65	63.02	62.51	62.08	61.73	61.44
5000	80.52	79.56	78.78	78.13	77.60	77.17	76.80
6000	96.63	95.48	94.53	93.76	93.12	92.60	92.16
7000	112.73	111.39	110.29	109.39	108.65	108.03	107.52
8000	128.83	127.30	126.05	125.02	124.17	123.46	122.88
9000	144.94	143.21	141.80	140.64	139.69	138.90	138.24
10000	161.04	159.13	157.56	156.27	155.21	154.33	153.61
11000	177.15	175.04	173.31	171.90	170.73	169.76	168.97
12000	193.25	190.95	189.07	187.52	186.25	185.20	184.33
13000	209.35	206.86	204.82	203.15	201.77	200.63	199.69
14000	225.46	222.78	220.58	218.78	217.29	216.06	215.05
15000	241.56	238.69	236.34	234.40	232.81	231.50	230.41
20000	322.08	318.25	315.11	312.54	310.42	308.66	307.21
25000	402.61	397.81	393.89	390.67	388.02	385.83	384.01
30000	483.13	477.38	472.67	468.81	465.62	462.99	460.82
35000	563.65	556.94	551.45	546.94	543.23	540.16	537.62
40000	644.17	636.50	630.23	625.08	620.83	617.32	614.42
45000	724.69	716.07	709.01	703.21	698.44	694.49	691.22
50000	805.21	795.63	787.79	781.35	776.04	771.66	768.03
55000	885.73	875.19	866.57	859.48	853.64	848.82	844.83
56000	901.84	891.10	882.32	875.11	869.16	864.25	860.19
57000	917.94	907.02	898.08	890.73	884.68	879.69	875.55
58000	934.04	922.93	913.83	906.36	900.21	895.12	890.91
59000	950.15	938.84	929.59	921.99	915.73	910.55	906.27
60000	966.25	954.75	945.34	937.61	931.25	925.99	921.63
61000	982.36	970.67	961.10	953.24	946.77	941.42	936.99
62000	998.46	986.58	976.86	968.87	962.29	956.85	952.35
63000	1014.57	1002.49	992.61	984.50	977.81	972.29	967.71
64000	1030.67	1018.40	1008.37	1000.12	993.33	987.72	983.08
65000	1046.77	1034.32	1024.12	1015.75	1008.85	1003.15	998.44
70000	1127.29	1113.88	1102.90	1093.88	1086.45	1080.32	1075.24
75000	1207.82	1193.44	1181.68	1172.02	1164.06	1157.48	1152.04
80000	1288.34	1273.00	1260.46	1250.15	1241.66	1234.65	1228.84
85000	1368.86	1352.57	1339.24	1328.29	1319.27	1311.81	1305.65
90000	1449.38	1432.13	1418.02	1406.42	1396.87	1388.98	1382.45
95000	1529.90	1511.69	1496.79	1484.56	1474.47	1466.15	1459.25
100000	1610.42	1591.26	1575.57	1562.69	1552.08	1543.31	1536.05
105000	1690.94	1670.82	1654.35	1640.83	1629.68	1620.48	1612.86
110000	1771.46	1750.38	1733.13	1718.96	1707.29	1697.64	1689.66
120000	1932.51	1909.51	1890.69	1875.23	1862.49	1851.97	1843.27
130000	2093.55	2068.63	2048.24	2031.50	2017.70	2006.30	1996.87
140000	2254.59	2227.76	2205.80	2187.77	2172.91	2160.64	2150.48
150000	2415.63	2386.88	2363.36	2344.04	2328.12	2314.97	2304.08
160000	2576.67	2546.01	2520.92	2500.31	2483.33	2469.30	2457.69
175000	2818.24	2784.70	2757.25	2734.71	2716.14	2700.80	2688.10
200000	3220.84	3182.51	3151.15	3125.38	3104.16	3086.62	3072.11
250000	4026.05	3978.14	3938.93	3906.73	3880.20	3858.28	3840.14
500000	8052.11	7956.28	7877.86	7813.46	7760.39	7716.56	7680.27
1000000	16104.21	15912.56	15755.73	15626.91	15520.78	15433.12	15360.55

MONTHLY PAYMENTS 18.00%

AMOUNT	22 YEARS	23 YEARS	24 YEARS	25 YEARS	30 YEARS	35 YEARS	40 YEARS
100	1.53	1.53	1.52	1.52	1.51	1.50	1.50
200	3.06	3.05	3.04	3.03	3.01	3.01	3.00
500	7.65	7.63	7.60	7.59	7.54	7.51	7.51
1000	15.30	15.25	15.21	15.17	15.07	15.03	15.01
2000	30.60	30.50	30.42	30.35	30.14	30.06	30.02
3000	45.90	45.75	45.63	45.52	45.21	45.09	45.04
4000	61.20	61.00	60.84	60.70	60.28	60.12	60.05
5000	76.50	76.25	76.04	75.87	75.35	75.14	75.06
6000	91.80	91.50	91.25	91.05	90.43	90.17	90.07
7000	107.10	106.75	106.46	106.22	105.50	105.20	105.08
8000	122.40	122.00	121.67	121.39	120.57	120.23	120.09
9000	137.70	137.25	136.88	136.57	135.64	135.26	135.11
10000	153.00	152.50	152.09	151.74	150.71	150.29	150.12
11000	168.30	167.75	167.30	166.92	165.78	165.32	165.13
12000	183.60	183.00	182.51	182.09	180.85	180.35	180.14
13000	198.90	198.26	197.72	197.27	195.92	195.38	195.15
14000	214.21	213.51	212.92	212.44	210.99	210.40	210.17
15000	229.51	228.76	228.13	227.61	226.06	225.43	225.18
20000	306.01	305.01	304.18	303.49	301.42	300.58	300.24
25000	382.51	381.26	380.22	379.36	376.77	375.72	375.30
30000	459.01	457.51	456.27	455.23	452.13	450.87	450.35
35000	535.51	533.76	532.31	531.10	527.48	526.01	525.41
40000	612.02	610.02	608.35	606.97	602.83	601.16	600.47
45000	688.52	686.27	684.40	682.84	678.19	676.30	675.53
50000	765.02	762.52	760.44	758.71	753.54	751.45	750.59
55000	841.52	838.77	836.49	834.59	828.90	826.59	825.65
56000	856.82	854.02	851.70	849.76	843.97	841.62	840.66
57000	872.12	869.27	866.91	864.94	859.04	856.65	855.67
58000	887.42	884.52	882.11	880.11	874.11	871.68	870.69
59000	902.72	899.77	897.32	895.28	889.18	886.71	885.70
60000	918.02	915.02	912.53	910.46	904.25	901.74	900.71
61000	933.32	930.28	927.74	925.63	919.32	916.76	915.72
62000	948.62	945.53	942.95	940.81	934.39	931.79	930.73
63000	963.92	960.78	958.16	955.98	949.46	946.82	945.74
64000	979.22	976.03	973.37	971.16	964.53	961.85	960.76
65000	994.52	991.28	988.58	986.33	979.61	976.88	975.77
70000	1071.03	1067.53	1064.62	1062.20	1054.96	1052.02	1050.83
75000	1147.53	1143.78	1140.67	1138.07	1130.31	1127.17	1125.89
80000	1224.03	1220.03	1216.71	1213.94	1205.67	1202.31	1200.95
85000	1300.53	1296.28	1292.75	1289.82	1281.02	1277.46	1276.00
90000	1377.03	1372.54	1368.80	1365.69	1356.38	1352.60	1351.06
95000	1453.54	1448.79	1444.84	1441.56	1431.73	1427.75	1426.12
100000	1530.04	1525.04	1520.89	1517.43	1507.09	1502.89	1501.18
105000	1606.54	1601.29	1596.93	1593.30	1582.44	1578.04	1576.24
110000	1683.04	1677.55	1672.98	1669.17	1657.79	1653.18	1651.30
120000	1836.05	1830.05	1825.06	1820.92	1808.50	1803.47	1801.42
130000	1989.05	1982.55	1977.15	1972.66	1959.21	1953.76	1951.54
140000	2142.05	2135.06	2129.24	2124.40	2109.92	2104.05	2101.66
150000	2295.06	2287.56	2281.33	2276.14	2260.63	2254.34	2251.77
160000	2448.06	2440.07	2433.42	2427.89	2411.34	2404.63	2401.89
175000	2677.57	2668.82	2661.55	2655.50	2637.40	2630.06	2627.07
200000	3060.08	3050.08	3041.77	3034.86	3014.17	3005.78	3002.36
250000	3825.09	3812.60	3802.22	3793.57	3767.71	3757.23	3752.96
500000	7650.19	7625.21	7604.44	7587.15	7535.43	7514.46	7505.91
1000000	15300.38	15250.41	15208.87	15174.30	15070.85	15028.92	15011.82

18.25%　　　MONTHLY PAYMENTS

AMOUNT	1 YEARS	2 YEARS	3 YEARS	4 YEARS	5 YEARS	6 YEARS	7 YEARS
100	9.18	5.00	3.63	2.95	2.55	2.29	2.12
200	18.36	10.01	7.26	5.90	5.11	4.59	4.23
500	45.90	25.02	18.14	14.75	12.76	11.47	10.58
1000	91.80	50.04	36.28	29.51	25.53	22.95	21.16
2000	183.60	100.09	72.56	59.01	51.06	45.90	42.33
3000	275.40	150.13	108.83	88.52	76.59	68.85	63.49
4000	367.20	200.18	145.11	118.02	102.12	91.80	84.66
5000	459.00	250.22	181.39	147.53	127.65	114.75	105.82
6000	550.79	300.27	217.67	177.03	153.18	137.70	126.99
7000	642.59	350.31	253.95	206.54	178.71	160.65	148.15
8000	734.39	400.36	290.22	236.05	204.24	183.59	169.32
9000	826.19	450.40	326.50	265.55	229.77	206.54	190.48
10000	917.99	500.45	362.78	295.06	255.30	229.49	211.65
11000	1009.79	550.49	399.06	324.56	280.83	252.44	232.81
12000	1101.59	600.54	435.34	354.07	306.36	275.39	253.98
13000	1193.39	650.58	471.61	383.58	331.89	298.34	275.14
14000	1285.19	700.63	507.89	413.08	357.41	321.29	296.30
15000	1376.99	750.67	544.17	442.59	382.94	344.24	317.47
20000	1835.98	1000.90	725.56	590.12	510.59	458.99	423.29
25000	2294.98	1251.12	906.95	737.64	638.24	573.73	529.12
30000	2753.97	1501.35	1088.34	885.17	765.89	688.48	634.94
35000	3212.97	1751.57	1269.73	1032.70	893.54	803.23	740.76
40000	3671.96	2001.80	1451.12	1180.23	1021.18	917.97	846.59
45000	4130.96	2252.02	1632.51	1327.76	1148.83	1032.72	952.41
50000	4589.95	2502.25	1813.90	1475.29	1276.48	1147.47	1058.23
55000	5048.95	2752.47	1995.29	1622.82	1404.13	1262.21	1164.05
56000	5140.74	2802.52	2031.56	1652.32	1429.66	1285.16	1185.22
57000	5232.54	2852.56	2067.84	1681.83	1455.19	1308.11	1206.38
58000	5324.34	2902.61	2104.12	1711.34	1480.72	1331.06	1227.55
59000	5416.14	2952.65	2140.40	1740.84	1506.25	1354.01	1248.71
60000	5507.94	3002.70	2176.68	1770.35	1531.78	1376.96	1269.88
61000	5599.74	3052.74	2212.95	1799.85	1557.31	1399.91	1291.04
62000	5691.54	3102.79	2249.23	1829.36	1582.84	1422.86	1312.21
63000	5783.34	3152.83	2285.51	1858.87	1608.37	1445.81	1333.37
64000	5875.14	3202.88	2321.79	1888.37	1633.90	1468.76	1354.54
65000	5966.94	3252.92	2358.07	1917.88	1659.43	1491.71	1375.70
70000	6425.93	3503.15	2539.46	2065.41	1787.07	1606.45	1481.52
75000	6884.93	3753.37	2720.84	2212.93	1914.72	1721.20	1587.35
80000	7343.92	4003.60	2902.23	2360.46	2042.37	1835.95	1693.17
85000	7802.92	4253.82	3083.62	2507.99	2170.02	1950.69	1798.99
90000	8261.91	4504.05	3265.01	2655.52	2297.67	2065.44	1904.82
95000	8720.91	4754.27	3446.40	2803.05	2425.31	2180.19	2010.64
100000	9179.90	5004.50	3627.79	2950.58	2552.96	2294.93	2116.46
105000	9638.90	5254.72	3809.18	3098.11	2680.61	2409.68	2222.29
110000	10097.89	5504.95	3990.57	3245.64	2808.26	2524.43	2328.11
120000	11015.88	6005.40	4353.35	3540.70	3063.55	2753.92	2539.76
130000	11933.87	6505.85	4716.13	3835.75	3318.85	2983.42	2751.40
140000	12851.86	7006.30	5078.91	4130.81	3574.15	3212.91	2963.05
150000	13769.85	7506.75	5441.69	4425.87	3829.44	3442.40	3174.69
160000	14687.84	8007.20	5804.47	4720.93	4084.74	3671.90	3386.34
175000	16064.83	8757.87	6348.64	5163.51	4467.68	4016.14	3703.81
200000	18359.80	10009.00	7255.59	5901.16	5105.92	4589.87	4232.93
250000	22949.75	12511.25	9069.48	7376.45	6382.41	5737.34	5291.16
500000	45899.51	25022.49	18138.97	14752.90	12764.81	11474.67	10582.31
1000000	91799.01	50044.98	36277.93	29505.80	25529.62	22949.35	21164.63

MONTHLY PAYMENTS 18.25%

AMOUNT	8 YEARS	9 YEARS	10 YEARS	11 YEARS	12 YEARS	13 YEARS	14 YEARS
100	1.99	1.89	1.82	1.76	1.72	1.68	1.65
200	3.98	3.78	3.64	3.52	3.43	3.36	3.30
500	9.94	9.46	9.09	8.80	8.58	8.40	8.26
1000	19.88	18.91	18.18	17.61	17.16	16.80	16.52
2000	39.75	37.83	36.36	35.22	34.32	33.61	33.03
3000	59.63	56.74	54.54	52.83	51.48	50.41	49.55
4000	79.50	75.65	72.72	70.44	68.64	67.21	66.07
5000	99.38	94.57	90.90	88.05	85.80	84.02	82.58
6000	119.25	113.48	109.08	105.66	102.97	100.82	99.10
7000	139.13	132.39	127.26	123.27	120.13	117.62	115.62
8000	159.00	151.31	145.44	140.88	137.29	134.43	132.13
9000	178.88	170.22	163.62	158.49	154.45	151.23	148.65
10000	198.75	189.14	181.80	176.10	171.61	168.03	165.16
11000	218.63	208.05	199.98	193.71	188.77	184.84	181.68
12000	238.50	226.96	218.16	211.32	205.93	201.64	198.20
13000	258.38	245.88	236.34	228.93	223.09	218.44	214.71
14000	278.25	264.79	254.52	246.54	240.25	235.25	231.23
15000	298.13	283.70	272.70	264.15	257.41	252.05	247.75
20000	397.50	378.27	363.60	352.20	343.22	336.07	330.33
25000	496.88	472.84	454.49	440.24	429.02	420.09	412.91
30000	596.25	567.41	545.39	528.29	514.83	504.10	495.49
35000	695.63	661.97	636.29	616.34	600.63	588.12	578.08
40000	795.00	756.54	727.19	704.39	686.43	672.14	660.66
45000	894.38	851.11	818.09	792.44	772.24	756.16	743.24
50000	993.75	945.68	908.99	880.49	858.04	840.17	825.82
55000	1093.13	1040.25	999.89	968.54	943.85	924.19	908.40
56000	1113.00	1059.16	1018.07	986.15	961.01	940.99	924.92
57000	1132.88	1078.07	1036.25	1003.76	978.17	957.80	941.44
58000	1152.75	1096.99	1054.43	1021.37	995.33	974.60	957.95
59000	1172.63	1115.90	1072.61	1038.98	1012.49	991.40	974.47
60000	1192.50	1134.81	1090.79	1056.59	1029.65	1008.21	990.99
61000	1212.38	1153.73	1108.97	1074.20	1046.81	1025.01	1007.50
62000	1232.25	1172.64	1127.15	1091.81	1063.97	1041.81	1024.02
63000	1252.13	1191.55	1145.33	1109.42	1081.13	1058.62	1040.54
64000	1272.00	1210.47	1163.51	1127.03	1098.29	1075.42	1057.05
65000	1291.88	1229.38	1181.69	1144.63	1115.45	1092.22	1073.57
70000	1391.25	1323.95	1272.58	1232.68	1201.26	1176.24	1156.15
75000	1490.63	1418.52	1363.48	1320.73	1287.06	1260.26	1238.73
80000	1590.00	1513.08	1454.38	1408.78	1372.87	1344.28	1321.32
85000	1689.38	1607.65	1545.28	1496.83	1458.67	1428.29	1403.90
90000	1788.75	1702.22	1636.18	1584.88	1544.48	1512.31	1486.48
95000	1888.13	1796.79	1727.08	1672.93	1630.28	1596.33	1569.06
100000	1987.51	1891.36	1817.98	1760.98	1716.08	1680.34	1651.65
105000	2086.88	1985.92	1908.88	1849.03	1801.89	1764.36	1734.23
110000	2186.26	2080.49	1999.78	1937.07	1887.69	1848.38	1816.81
120000	2385.01	2269.63	2181.57	2113.17	2059.30	2016.41	1981.97
130000	2583.76	2458.76	2363.37	2289.27	2230.91	2184.45	2147.14
140000	2782.51	2647.90	2545.17	2465.37	2402.52	2352.48	2312.30
150000	2981.26	2837.03	2726.97	2641.47	2574.13	2520.52	2477.47
160000	3180.01	3026.17	2908.76	2817.56	2745.74	2688.55	2642.63
175000	3478.13	3309.87	3181.46	3081.71	3003.15	2940.60	2890.38
200000	3975.01	3782.71	3635.96	3521.95	3432.17	3360.69	3303.29
250000	4968.76	4728.39	4544.94	4402.44	4290.21	4200.86	4129.11
500000	9937.53	9456.78	9089.89	8804.88	8580.42	8401.72	8258.23
1000000	19875.05	18913.56	18179.78	17609.77	17160.84	16803.45	16516.45

18.25%   MONTHLY PAYMENTS

AMOUNT	15 YEARS	16 YEARS	17 YEARS	18 YEARS	19 YEARS	20 YEARS	21 YEARS
100	1.63	1.61	1.59	1.58	1.57	1.56	1.56
200	3.26	3.22	3.19	3.16	3.14	3.13	3.11
500	8.14	8.05	7.97	7.91	7.86	7.81	7.78
1000	16.28	16.10	15.94	15.82	15.71	15.63	15.56
2000	32.57	32.19	31.88	31.63	31.42	31.25	31.11
3000	48.85	48.29	47.82	47.45	47.13	46.88	46.67
4000	65.14	64.38	63.77	63.26	62.85	62.50	62.22
5000	81.42	80.48	79.71	79.08	78.56	78.13	77.78
6000	97.71	96.57	95.65	94.89	94.27	93.75	93.33
7000	113.99	112.67	111.59	110.71	109.98	109.38	108.89
8000	130.28	128.77	127.53	126.52	125.69	125.01	124.44
9000	146.56	144.86	143.47	142.34	141.40	140.63	140.00
10000	162.84	160.96	159.42	158.15	157.11	156.26	155.55
11000	179.13	177.05	175.36	173.97	172.83	171.88	171.11
12000	195.41	193.15	191.30	189.78	188.54	187.51	186.66
13000	211.70	209.24	207.24	205.60	204.25	203.14	202.22
14000	227.98	225.34	223.18	221.41	219.96	218.76	217.77
15000	244.27	241.44	239.12	237.23	235.67	234.39	233.33
20000	325.69	321.91	318.83	316.31	314.23	312.52	311.10
25000	407.11	402.39	398.54	395.38	392.79	390.64	388.88
30000	488.53	482.87	478.25	474.46	471.34	468.77	466.65
35000	569.95	563.35	557.96	553.54	549.90	546.90	544.43
40000	651.38	643.83	637.67	632.61	628.46	625.03	622.20
45000	732.80	724.31	717.37	711.69	707.01	703.16	699.98
50000	814.22	804.79	797.08	790.76	785.57	781.29	777.75
55000	895.64	885.27	876.79	869.84	864.13	859.42	855.53
56000	911.93	901.36	892.73	885.66	879.84	875.04	871.08
57000	928.21	917.46	908.67	901.47	895.55	890.67	886.64
58000	944.50	933.55	924.61	917.29	911.26	906.30	902.19
59000	960.78	949.65	940.56	933.10	926.97	921.92	917.75
60000	977.06	965.74	956.50	948.92	942.68	937.55	933.30
61000	993.35	981.84	972.44	964.73	958.40	953.17	948.86
62000	1009.63	997.94	988.38	980.55	974.11	968.80	964.41
63000	1025.92	1014.03	1004.32	996.36	989.82	984.42	979.97
64000	1042.20	1030.13	1020.26	1012.18	1005.53	1000.05	995.52
65000	1058.49	1046.22	1036.21	1027.99	1021.24	1015.68	1011.08
70000	1139.91	1126.70	1115.91	1107.07	1099.80	1093.80	1088.85
75000	1221.33	1207.18	1195.62	1186.15	1178.36	1171.93	1166.63
80000	1302.75	1287.66	1275.33	1265.22	1256.91	1250.06	1244.40
85000	1384.17	1368.14	1355.04	1344.30	1335.47	1328.19	1322.18
90000	1465.60	1448.62	1434.75	1423.38	1414.03	1406.32	1399.95
95000	1547.02	1529.09	1514.45	1502.45	1492.58	1484.45	1477.73
100000	1628.44	1609.57	1594.16	1581.53	1571.14	1562.58	1555.50
105000	1709.86	1690.05	1673.87	1660.61	1649.70	1640.71	1633.28
110000	1791.28	1770.53	1753.58	1739.68	1728.26	1718.84	1711.05
120000	1954.13	1931.49	1913.00	1897.84	1885.37	1875.09	1866.61
130000	2116.97	2092.44	2072.41	2055.99	2042.48	2031.35	2022.16
140000	2279.82	2253.40	2231.83	2214.14	2199.60	2187.61	2177.71
150000	2442.66	2414.36	2391.24	2372.29	2356.71	2343.87	2333.26
160000	2605.50	2575.32	2550.66	2530.45	2513.83	2500.12	2488.81
175000	2849.77	2816.75	2789.78	2767.68	2749.50	2734.51	2722.13
200000	3256.88	3219.15	3188.33	3163.06	3142.28	3125.16	3111.01
250000	4071.10	4023.93	3985.41	3953.82	3927.85	3906.44	3888.76
500000	8142.20	8047.86	7970.81	7907.65	7855.71	7812.89	7777.52
1000000	16284.40	16095.73	15941.63	15815.29	15711.41	15625.78	15555.04

MONTHLY PAYMENTS 18.25%

AMOUNT	22 YEARS	23 YEARS	24 YEARS	25 YEARS	30 YEARS	35 YEARS	40 YEARS
100	1.55	1.54	1.54	1.54	1.53	1.52	1.52
200	3.10	3.09	3.08	3.07	3.06	3.05	3.04
500	7.75	7.72	7.70	7.69	7.64	7.62	7.61
1000	15.50	15.45	15.41	15.37	15.28	15.24	15.22
2000	30.99	30.90	30.82	30.75	30.55	30.47	30.44
3000	46.49	46.34	46.22	46.12	45.83	45.71	45.66
4000	61.99	61.79	61.63	61.50	61.10	60.94	60.88
5000	77.48	77.24	77.04	76.87	76.38	76.18	76.10
6000	92.98	92.69	92.45	92.25	91.65	91.41	91.32
7000	108.48	108.14	107.85	107.62	106.93	106.65	106.53
8000	123.97	123.58	123.26	123.00	122.20	121.88	121.75
9000	139.47	139.03	138.67	138.37	137.48	137.12	136.97
10000	154.97	154.48	154.08	153.74	152.75	152.35	152.19
11000	170.46	169.93	169.49	169.12	168.03	167.59	167.41
12000	185.96	185.38	184.89	184.49	183.30	182.82	182.63
13000	201.45	200.82	200.30	199.87	198.58	198.06	197.85
14000	216.95	216.27	215.71	215.24	213.85	213.29	213.07
15000	232.45	231.72	231.12	230.62	229.13	228.53	228.29
20000	309.93	308.96	308.16	307.49	305.50	304.70	304.38
25000	387.41	386.20	385.19	384.36	381.88	380.88	380.48
30000	464.90	463.44	462.23	461.23	458.25	457.06	456.58
35000	542.38	540.68	539.27	538.10	534.63	533.23	532.67
40000	619.86	617.92	616.31	614.98	611.00	609.41	608.77
45000	697.34	695.16	693.35	691.85	687.38	685.59	684.86
50000	774.83	772.40	770.39	768.72	763.75	761.76	760.96
55000	852.31	849.64	847.43	845.59	840.13	837.94	837.06
56000	867.80	865.09	862.84	860.97	855.40	853.17	852.27
57000	883.30	880.54	878.24	876.34	870.68	868.41	867.49
58000	898.80	895.99	893.65	891.71	885.95	883.64	882.71
59000	914.29	911.43	909.06	907.09	901.23	898.88	897.93
60000	929.79	926.88	924.47	922.46	916.50	914.11	913.15
61000	945.29	942.33	939.88	937.84	931.78	929.35	928.37
62000	960.78	957.78	955.28	953.21	947.05	944.58	943.59
63000	976.28	973.23	970.69	968.59	962.33	959.82	958.81
64000	991.78	988.67	986.10	983.96	977.60	975.05	974.03
65000	1007.27	1004.12	1001.51	999.34	992.88	990.29	989.25
70000	1084.76	1081.36	1078.55	1076.21	1069.25	1066.47	1065.34
75000	1162.24	1158.60	1155.58	1153.08	1145.63	1142.64	1141.44
80000	1239.72	1235.84	1232.62	1229.95	1222.00	1218.82	1217.54
85000	1317.20	1313.08	1309.66	1306.82	1298.38	1294.99	1293.63
90000	1394.69	1390.32	1386.70	1383.69	1374.75	1371.17	1369.73
95000	1472.17	1467.56	1463.74	1460.57	1451.13	1447.35	1445.82
100000	1549.65	1544.80	1540.78	1537.44	1527.50	1523.52	1521.92
105000	1627.13	1622.04	1617.82	1614.31	1603.88	1599.70	1598.02
110000	1704.62	1699.28	1694.86	1691.18	1680.25	1675.88	1674.11
120000	1859.58	1853.76	1848.93	1844.93	1833.00	1828.23	1826.30
130000	2014.55	2008.24	2003.01	1998.67	1985.75	1980.58	1978.50
140000	2169.51	2162.72	2157.09	2152.41	2138.50	2132.93	2130.69
150000	2324.48	2317.20	2311.17	2306.16	2291.25	2285.28	2282.88
160000	2479.44	2471.68	2465.25	2459.90	2444.01	2437.64	2435.07
175000	2711.89	2703.40	2696.36	2690.52	2673.13	2666.17	2663.36
200000	3099.30	3089.60	3081.56	3074.88	3055.01	3047.05	3043.84
250000	3874.13	3862.01	3851.95	3843.60	3818.76	3808.81	3804.80
500000	7748.26	7724.01	7703.90	7687.19	7637.52	7617.61	7609.60
1000000	15496.52	15448.02	15407.79	15374.39	15275.03	15235.23	15219.20

18.50% MONTHLY PAYMENTS

AMOUNT	1 YEAR	2 YEARS	3 YEARS	4 YEARS	5 YEARS	6 YEARS	7 YEARS
100	9.19	5.02	3.64	2.96	2.57	2.31	2.13
200	18.38	10.03	7.28	5.93	5.13	4.62	4.26
500	45.96	25.08	18.20	14.82	12.83	11.55	10.66
1000	91.92	50.17	36.40	29.64	25.67	23.09	21.31
2000	183.84	100.33	72.81	59.27	51.33	46.18	42.62
3000	275.75	150.50	109.21	88.91	77.00	69.27	63.94
4000	367.67	200.66	145.61	118.55	102.66	92.37	85.25
5000	459.59	250.83	182.02	148.18	128.33	115.46	106.56
6000	551.50	301.00	218.42	177.82	154.00	138.55	127.87
7000	643.43	351.16	254.83	207.46	179.66	161.64	149.18
8000	735.34	401.33	291.23	237.10	205.33	184.73	170.50
9000	827.26	451.49	327.63	266.73	231.00	207.82	191.81
10000	919.18	501.66	364.04	296.37	256.66	230.91	213.12
11000	1011.10	551.83	400.44	326.01	282.33	254.00	234.43
12000	1103.02	601.99	436.84	355.64	307.99	277.10	255.74
13000	1194.94	652.16	473.25	385.28	333.66	300.19	277.05
14000	1286.85	702.32	509.65	414.92	359.33	323.28	298.37
15000	1378.77	752.49	546.06	444.55	384.99	346.37	319.68
20000	1838.36	1003.32	728.07	592.74	513.32	461.83	426.24
25000	2297.95	1254.15	910.09	740.92	641.66	577.28	532.80
30000	2757.54	1504.98	1092.11	889.11	769.99	692.74	639.36
35000	3217.13	1755.81	1274.13	1037.29	898.32	808.20	745.92
40000	3676.72	2006.64	1456.15	1185.48	1026.65	923.65	852.48
45000	4136.32	2257.47	1638.17	1333.66	1154.98	1039.11	959.04
50000	4595.91	2508.30	1820.19	1481.85	1283.31	1154.57	1065.60
55000	5055.50	2759.13	2002.20	1630.03	1411.64	1270.02	1172.16
56000	5147.41	2809.30	2038.61	1659.67	1437.31	1293.12	1193.47
57000	5239.33	2859.46	2075.01	1689.30	1462.97	1316.21	1214.78
58000	5331.25	2909.63	2111.42	1718.94	1488.64	1339.30	1236.09
59000	5423.17	2959.80	2147.82	1748.58	1514.31	1362.39	1257.40
60000	5515.09	3009.96	2184.22	1778.21	1539.97	1385.48	1278.72
61000	5607.01	3060.13	2220.63	1807.85	1565.64	1408.57	1300.03
62000	5698.92	3110.29	2257.03	1837.49	1591.30	1431.66	1321.34
63000	5790.84	3160.46	2293.43	1867.13	1616.97	1454.76	1342.65
64000	5882.76	3210.63	2329.84	1896.76	1642.64	1477.85	1363.96
65000	5974.68	3260.79	2366.24	1926.40	1668.30	1500.94	1385.27
70000	6434.27	3511.62	2548.26	2074.58	1796.63	1616.39	1491.83
75000	6893.86	3762.45	2730.28	2222.77	1924.97	1731.85	1598.39
80000	7353.45	4013.28	2912.30	2370.95	2053.30	1847.31	1704.95
85000	7813.04	4264.11	3094.32	2519.14	2181.63	1962.77	1811.51
90000	8272.63	4514.94	3276.33	2667.32	2309.96	2078.22	1918.07
95000	8732.22	4765.77	3458.35	2815.51	2438.29	2193.68	2024.63
100000	9191.81	5016.60	3640.37	2963.69	2566.62	2309.14	2131.19
105000	9651.40	5267.43	3822.39	3111.88	2694.95	2424.59	2237.75
110000	10110.99	5518.26	4004.41	3260.06	2823.28	2540.05	2344.31
120000	11030.17	6019.92	4368.45	3556.43	3079.95	2770.96	2557.43
130000	11949.36	6521.58	4732.48	3852.80	3336.61	3001.88	2770.55
140000	12868.54	7023.24	5096.52	4149.17	3593.27	3232.79	2983.67
150000	13787.72	7524.90	5460.56	4445.54	3849.93	3463.70	3196.79
160000	14706.90	8026.56	5824.59	4741.91	4106.59	3694.62	3409.91
175000	16085.67	8779.05	6370.65	5186.46	4491.59	4040.99	3729.59
200000	18383.62	10033.21	7280.74	5927.38	5133.24	4618.27	4262.38
250000	22979.53	12541.51	9100.93	7409.23	6416.55	5772.84	5327.98
500000	45959.06	25083.01	18201.86	14818.46	12833.10	11545.68	10655.96
1000000	91918.12	50166.03	36403.71	29636.92	25666.21	23091.35	21311.92

MONTHLY PAYMENTS   18.50%

AMOUNT	8 YEARS	9 YEARS	10 YEARS	11 YEARS	12 YEARS	13 YEARS	14 YEARS
100	2.00	1.91	1.83	1.78	1.73	1.70	1.67
200	4.01	3.81	3.67	3.56	3.47	3.40	3.34
500	10.01	9.54	9.17	8.89	8.67	8.49	8.35
1000	20.03	19.07	18.34	17.78	17.33	16.98	16.69
2000	40.05	38.14	36.68	35.55	34.66	33.96	33.39
3000	60.08	57.21	55.02	53.33	51.99	50.93	50.08
4000	80.11	76.28	73.37	71.10	69.32	67.91	66.78
5000	100.14	95.35	91.71	88.88	86.66	84.89	83.47
6000	120.16	114.42	110.05	106.66	103.99	101.87	100.16
7000	140.19	133.50	128.39	124.43	121.32	118.84	116.86
8000	160.22	152.57	146.73	142.21	138.65	135.82	133.55
9000	180.25	171.64	165.07	159.98	155.98	152.80	150.25
10000	200.27	190.71	183.42	177.76	173.31	169.78	166.94
11000	220.30	209.78	201.76	195.54	190.64	186.75	183.63
12000	240.33	228.85	220.10	213.31	207.97	203.73	200.33
13000	260.36	247.92	238.44	231.09	225.30	220.71	217.02
14000	280.38	266.99	256.78	248.86	242.64	237.69	233.72
15000	300.41	286.06	275.12	266.64	259.97	254.66	250.41
20000	400.55	381.42	366.83	355.52	346.62	339.55	333.88
25000	500.69	476.77	458.54	444.40	433.28	424.44	417.35
30000	600.82	572.12	550.25	533.28	519.93	509.33	500.82
35000	700.96	667.48	641.96	622.16	606.59	594.21	584.29
40000	801.10	762.83	733.67	711.04	693.25	679.10	667.76
45000	901.23	858.19	825.37	799.92	779.90	763.99	751.23
50000	1001.37	953.54	917.08	888.80	866.56	848.88	834.70
55000	1101.51	1048.89	1008.79	977.68	953.21	933.76	918.17
56000	1121.54	1067.97	1027.13	995.46	970.54	950.74	934.87
57000	1141.56	1087.04	1045.47	1013.23	987.88	967.72	951.56
58000	1161.59	1106.11	1063.82	1031.01	1005.21	984.70	968.25
59000	1181.62	1125.18	1082.16	1048.78	1022.54	1001.67	984.95
60000	1201.65	1144.25	1100.50	1066.56	1039.87	1018.65	1001.64
61000	1221.67	1163.32	1118.84	1084.34	1057.20	1035.63	1018.34
62000	1241.70	1182.39	1137.18	1102.11	1074.53	1052.61	1035.03
63000	1261.73	1201.46	1155.52	1119.89	1091.86	1069.58	1051.73
64000	1281.76	1220.53	1173.87	1137.66	1109.19	1086.56	1068.42
65000	1301.78	1239.60	1192.21	1155.44	1126.52	1103.54	1085.11
70000	1401.92	1334.96	1283.92	1244.32	1213.18	1188.43	1168.58
75000	1502.06	1430.31	1375.62	1333.20	1299.84	1273.31	1252.05
80000	1602.20	1525.67	1467.33	1422.08	1386.49	1358.20	1335.52
85000	1702.33	1621.02	1559.04	1510.96	1473.15	1443.09	1418.99
90000	1802.47	1716.37	1650.75	1599.84	1559.80	1527.98	1502.46
95000	1902.61	1811.73	1742.46	1688.72	1646.46	1612.87	1585.93
100000	2002.74	1907.08	1834.17	1777.60	1733.11	1697.75	1669.41
105000	2102.88	2002.44	1925.87	1866.48	1819.77	1782.64	1752.88
110000	2203.02	2097.79	2017.58	1955.36	1906.43	1867.53	1836.35
120000	2403.29	2288.50	2201.00	2133.12	2079.74	2037.30	2003.29
130000	2603.57	2479.21	2384.42	2310.88	2253.05	2207.08	2170.23
140000	2803.84	2669.91	2567.83	2488.64	2426.36	2376.85	2337.17
150000	3004.12	2860.62	2751.25	2666.40	2599.67	2546.63	2504.11
160000	3204.39	3051.33	2934.66	2844.16	2772.98	2716.41	2671.05
175000	3504.80	3337.39	3209.79	3110.80	3032.95	2971.07	2921.46
200000	4005.49	3814.16	3668.33	3555.20	3466.23	3395.51	3338.81
250000	5006.86	4767.70	4585.41	4444.00	4332.79	4244.38	4173.51
500000	10013.72	9535.41	9170.83	8888.00	8665.57	8488.77	8347.03
1000000	20027.44	19070.82	18341.65	17775.99	17331.14	16977.53	16694.05

18.50% MONTHLY PAYMENTS

AMOUNT	15 YEARS	16 YEARS	17 YEARS	18 YEARS	19 YEARS	20 YEARS	21 YEARS
100	1.65	1.63	1.61	1.60	1.59	1.58	1.58
200	3.29	3.26	3.23	3.20	3.18	3.16	3.15
500	8.23	8.14	8.06	8.00	7.95	7.91	7.88
1000	16.47	16.28	16.13	16.00	15.90	15.82	15.75
2000	32.93	32.56	32.26	32.01	31.81	31.64	31.50
3000	49.40	48.84	48.38	48.01	47.71	47.46	47.25
4000	65.86	65.12	64.51	64.02	63.61	63.28	63.00
5000	82.33	81.40	80.64	80.02	79.51	79.09	78.75
6000	98.79	97.68	96.77	96.03	95.42	94.91	94.50
7000	115.26	113.96	112.90	112.03	111.32	110.73	110.25
8000	131.72	130.24	129.02	128.03	127.22	126.55	126.00
9000	148.19	146.52	145.15	144.04	143.12	142.37	141.75
10000	164.65	162.80	161.28	160.04	159.03	158.19	157.50
11000	181.12	179.07	177.41	176.05	174.93	174.01	173.25
12000	197.58	195.35	193.54	192.05	190.83	189.83	189.00
13000	214.05	211.63	209.67	208.06	206.73	205.65	204.75
14000	230.51	227.91	225.79	224.06	222.64	221.47	220.50
15000	246.98	244.19	241.92	240.06	238.54	237.28	236.25
20000	329.30	325.59	322.56	320.08	318.05	316.38	315.00
25000	411.63	406.99	403.20	400.11	397.56	395.47	393.75
30000	493.96	488.39	483.84	480.13	477.08	474.57	472.50
35000	576.28	569.78	564.48	560.15	556.59	553.66	551.25
40000	658.61	651.18	645.12	640.17	636.10	632.76	630.00
45000	740.94	732.58	725.77	720.19	715.62	711.85	708.75
50000	823.26	813.98	806.41	800.21	795.13	790.95	787.50
55000	905.59	895.37	887.05	880.23	874.64	870.04	866.25
56000	922.05	911.65	903.17	896.24	890.55	885.86	882.00
57000	938.52	927.93	919.30	912.24	906.45	901.68	897.75
58000	954.98	944.21	935.43	928.25	922.35	917.50	913.50
59000	971.45	960.49	951.56	944.25	938.25	933.32	929.25
60000	987.91	976.77	967.69	960.25	954.16	949.14	945.00
61000	1004.38	993.05	983.82	976.26	970.06	964.96	960.75
62000	1020.84	1009.33	999.94	992.26	985.96	980.78	976.50
63000	1037.31	1025.61	1016.07	1008.27	1001.86	996.59	992.25
64000	1053.77	1041.89	1032.20	1024.27	1017.77	1012.41	1008.00
65000	1070.24	1058.17	1048.33	1040.28	1033.67	1028.23	1023.75
70000	1152.57	1139.57	1128.97	1120.30	1113.18	1107.33	1102.50
75000	1234.89	1220.96	1209.61	1200.32	1192.69	1186.42	1181.25
80000	1317.22	1302.36	1290.25	1280.34	1272.21	1265.52	1260.00
85000	1399.54	1383.76	1370.89	1360.36	1351.72	1344.61	1338.75
90000	1481.87	1465.16	1451.53	1440.38	1431.23	1423.71	1417.50
95000	1564.20	1546.55	1532.17	1520.40	1510.75	1502.80	1496.25
100000	1646.52	1627.95	1612.81	1600.42	1590.26	1581.90	1575.00
105000	1728.85	1709.35	1693.45	1680.45	1669.77	1660.99	1653.75
110000	1811.18	1790.75	1774.09	1760.47	1749.29	1740.09	1732.50
120000	1975.83	1953.54	1935.37	1920.51	1908.31	1898.28	1890.00
130000	2140.48	2116.34	2096.66	2080.55	2067.34	2056.47	2047.50
140000	2305.13	2279.13	2257.94	2240.59	2226.36	2214.66	2205.00
150000	2469.79	2441.93	2419.22	2400.64	2385.39	2372.84	2362.50
160000	2634.44	2604.72	2580.50	2560.68	2544.41	2531.03	2520.01
175000	2881.42	2848.92	2822.42	2800.74	2782.95	2768.32	2756.26
200000	3293.05	3255.90	3225.62	3200.85	3180.52	3163.79	3150.01
250000	4116.31	4069.88	4032.03	4001.06	3975.65	3954.74	3937.51
500000	8232.62	8139.76	8064.06	8002.12	7951.30	7909.48	7875.02
1000000	16465.23	16279.52	16128.12	16004.25	15902.59	15818.97	15750.03

MONTHLY PAYMENTS 18.50%

AMOUNT	22 YEARS	23 YEARS	24 YEARS	25 YEARS	30 YEARS	35 YEARS	40 YEARS
100	1.57	1.56	1.56	1.56	1.55	1.54	1.54
200	3.14	3.13	3.12	3.11	3.10	3.09	3.09
500	7.85	7.82	7.80	7.79	7.74	7.72	7.71
1000	15.69	15.65	15.61	15.57	15.48	15.44	15.43
2000	31.39	31.29	31.21	31.15	30.96	30.88	30.85
3000	47.08	46.94	46.82	46.72	46.44	46.33	46.28
4000	62.77	62.58	62.43	62.30	61.92	61.77	61.71
5000	78.47	78.23	78.04	77.87	77.40	77.21	77.13
6000	94.16	93.88	93.64	93.45	92.88	92.65	92.56
7000	109.85	109.52	109.25	109.02	108.36	108.09	107.99
8000	125.54	125.17	124.86	124.60	123.84	123.53	123.41
9000	141.24	140.81	140.46	140.17	139.32	138.98	138.84
10000	156.93	156.46	156.07	155.75	154.79	154.42	154.27
11000	172.62	172.11	171.68	171.32	170.27	169.86	169.69
12000	188.32	187.75	187.29	186.90	185.75	185.30	185.12
13000	204.01	203.40	202.89	202.47	201.23	200.74	200.55
14000	219.70	219.04	218.50	218.05	216.71	216.18	215.97
15000	235.40	234.69	234.11	233.62	232.19	231.63	231.40
20000	313.86	312.92	312.14	311.50	309.59	308.83	308.53
25000	392.33	391.15	390.18	389.37	386.99	386.04	385.67
30000	470.79	469.38	468.21	467.25	464.38	463.25	462.80
35000	549.26	547.61	546.25	545.12	541.78	540.46	539.93
40000	627.72	625.84	624.28	622.99	619.18	617.67	617.07
45000	706.19	704.07	702.32	700.87	696.58	694.88	694.20
50000	784.66	782.30	780.36	778.74	773.97	772.08	771.33
55000	863.12	860.53	858.39	856.62	851.37	849.29	848.47
56000	878.81	876.18	874.00	872.19	866.85	864.73	863.89
57000	894.51	891.83	889.61	887.77	882.33	880.18	879.32
58000	910.20	907.47	905.21	903.34	897.81	895.62	894.75
59000	925.89	923.12	920.82	918.92	913.29	911.06	910.17
60000	941.59	938.76	936.43	934.49	928.77	926.50	925.60
61000	957.28	954.41	952.03	950.07	944.25	941.94	941.03
62000	972.97	970.06	967.64	965.64	959.73	957.38	956.45
63000	988.67	985.70	983.25	981.22	975.21	972.83	971.88
64000	1004.36	1001.35	998.86	996.79	990.68	988.27	987.31
65000	1020.05	1016.99	1014.46	1012.36	1006.16	1003.71	1002.73
70000	1098.52	1095.22	1092.50	1090.24	1083.56	1080.92	1079.87
75000	1176.98	1173.45	1170.53	1168.11	1160.96	1158.13	1157.00
80000	1255.45	1251.68	1248.57	1245.99	1238.36	1235.33	1234.13
85000	1333.91	1329.92	1326.60	1323.86	1315.75	1312.54	1311.26
90000	1412.38	1408.15	1404.64	1401.74	1393.15	1389.75	1388.40
95000	1490.85	1486.38	1482.68	1479.61	1470.55	1466.96	1465.53
100000	1569.31	1564.61	1560.71	1557.48	1547.94	1544.17	1542.66
105000	1647.78	1642.84	1638.75	1635.36	1625.34	1621.38	1619.80
110000	1726.24	1721.07	1716.78	1713.23	1702.74	1698.58	1696.93
120000	1883.17	1877.53	1872.85	1868.98	1857.53	1853.00	1851.20
130000	2040.11	2033.99	2028.92	2024.73	2012.33	2007.42	2005.46
140000	2197.04	2190.45	2185.00	2180.48	2167.12	2161.83	2159.73
150000	2353.97	2346.91	2341.07	2336.23	2321.92	2316.25	2314.00
160000	2510.90	2503.37	2497.14	2491.97	2476.71	2470.67	2468.26
175000	2746.30	2738.06	2731.24	2725.60	2708.90	2702.29	2699.66
200000	3138.62	3129.21	3121.42	3114.97	3095.89	3088.34	3085.33
250000	3923.28	3911.52	3901.78	3893.71	3869.86	3860.42	3856.66
500000	7846.56	7823.03	7803.56	7787.42	7739.72	7720.84	7713.32
1000000	15693.12	15646.06	15607.11	15574.84	15479.45	15441.68	15426.64

18.75%   MONTHLY PAYMENTS

AMOUNT	1 YEAR	2 YEARS	3 YEARS	4 YEARS	5 YEARS	6 YEARS	7 YEARS
100	9.20	5.03	3.65	2.98	2.58	2.32	2.15
200	18.41	10.06	7.31	5.95	5.16	4.65	4.29
500	46.02	25.14	18.26	14.88	12.90	11.62	10.73
1000	92.04	50.29	36.53	29.77	25.80	23.23	21.46
2000	184.07	100.57	73.06	59.54	51.61	46.47	42.92
3000	276.11	150.86	109.59	89.31	77.41	69.70	64.38
4000	368.15	201.15	146.12	119.07	103.21	92.94	85.84
5000	460.19	251.44	182.65	148.84	129.02	116.17	107.30
6000	552.22	301.72	219.18	178.61	154.82	139.40	128.76
7000	644.26	352.01	255.71	208.38	180.62	162.64	150.22
8000	736.30	402.30	292.24	238.15	206.43	185.87	171.68
9000	828.34	452.59	328.77	267.92	232.23	209.10	193.14
10000	920.37	502.87	365.30	297.68	258.03	232.34	214.60
11000	1012.41	553.16	401.83	327.45	283.84	255.57	236.06
12000	1104.45	603.45	438.36	357.22	309.64	278.81	257.52
13000	1196.48	653.73	474.89	386.99	335.44	302.04	278.98
14000	1288.52	704.02	511.42	416.76	361.24	325.27	300.44
15000	1380.56	754.31	547.95	446.53	387.05	348.51	321.90
20000	1840.75	1005.74	730.59	595.37	516.06	464.68	429.19
25000	2300.93	1257.18	913.24	744.21	645.08	580.85	536.49
30000	2761.12	1508.62	1095.89	893.05	774.10	697.01	643.79
35000	3221.31	1760.05	1278.54	1041.89	903.11	813.18	751.09
40000	3681.49	2011.49	1461.19	1190.73	1032.13	929.35	858.39
45000	4141.68	2262.93	1643.84	1339.58	1161.14	1045.52	965.69
50000	4601.87	2514.36	1826.49	1488.42	1290.16	1161.69	1072.99
55000	5062.05	2765.80	2009.14	1637.26	1419.18	1277.86	1180.28
56000	5154.09	2816.09	2045.67	1667.03	1444.98	1301.09	1201.74
57000	5246.13	2866.37	2082.20	1696.80	1470.78	1324.33	1223.20
58000	5338.16	2916.66	2118.73	1726.56	1496.58	1347.56	1244.66
59000	5430.20	2966.95	2155.25	1756.33	1522.39	1370.80	1266.12
60000	5522.24	3017.23	2191.78	1786.10	1548.19	1394.03	1287.58
61000	5614.28	3067.52	2228.31	1815.87	1573.99	1417.26	1309.04
62000	5706.31	3117.81	2264.84	1845.64	1599.80	1440.50	1330.50
63000	5798.35	3168.10	2301.37	1875.41	1625.60	1463.73	1351.96
64000	5890.39	3218.38	2337.90	1905.17	1651.40	1486.96	1373.42
65000	5982.42	3268.67	2374.43	1934.94	1677.21	1510.20	1394.88
70000	6442.61	3520.11	2557.08	2083.78	1806.22	1626.37	1502.18
75000	6902.80	3771.54	2739.73	2232.63	1935.24	1742.54	1609.48
80000	7362.98	4022.98	2922.38	2381.47	2064.25	1858.71	1716.78
85000	7823.17	4274.42	3105.03	2530.31	2193.27	1974.87	1824.08
90000	8283.36	4525.85	3287.68	2679.15	2322.29	2091.04	1931.37
95000	8743.54	4777.29	3470.33	2827.99	2451.30	2207.21	2038.67
100000	9203.73	5028.72	3652.97	2976.84	2580.32	2323.38	2145.97
105000	9663.92	5280.16	3835.62	3125.68	2709.33	2439.55	2253.27
110000	10124.10	5531.60	4018.27	3274.52	2838.35	2555.72	2360.57
120000	11044.48	6034.47	4383.57	3572.20	3096.38	2788.06	2575.17
130000	11964.85	6537.34	4748.87	3869.89	3354.41	3020.40	2789.76
140000	12885.22	7040.21	5114.16	4167.57	3612.45	3252.73	3004.36
150000	13805.60	7543.09	5479.46	4465.25	3870.48	3485.07	3218.96
160000	14725.97	8045.96	5844.76	4762.94	4128.51	3717.41	3433.55
175000	16106.53	8800.27	6392.71	5209.46	4515.56	4065.92	3755.45
200000	18407.46	10057.45	7305.95	5953.67	5160.64	4646.76	4291.94
250000	23009.33	12571.81	9132.44	7442.09	6450.80	5808.45	5364.93
500000	46018.65	25143.62	18264.87	14884.18	12901.59	11616.91	10729.86
1000000	92037.31	50287.24	36529.74	29768.36	25803.19	23233.81	21459.72

MONTHLY PAYMENTS 18.75%

AMOUNT	8 YEARS	9 YEARS	10 YEARS	11 YEARS	12 YEARS	13 YEARS	14 YEARS
100	2.02	1.92	1.85	1.79	1.75	1.72	1.69
200	4.04	3.85	3.70	3.59	3.50	3.43	3.37
500	10.09	9.61	9.25	8.97	8.75	8.58	8.44
1000	20.18	19.23	18.50	17.94	17.50	17.15	16.87
2000	40.36	38.46	37.01	35.89	35.00	34.30	33.74
3000	60.54	57.69	55.51	53.83	52.51	51.46	50.62
4000	80.72	76.91	74.02	71.77	70.01	68.61	67.49
5000	100.90	96.14	92.52	89.71	87.51	85.76	84.36
6000	121.08	115.37	111.02	107.66	105.01	102.91	101.23
7000	141.26	134.60	129.53	125.60	122.51	120.07	118.11
8000	161.44	153.83	148.03	143.54	140.02	137.22	134.98
9000	181.62	173.06	166.54	161.49	157.52	154.37	151.85
10000	201.80	192.29	185.04	179.43	175.02	171.52	168.72
11000	221.98	211.52	203.55	197.37	192.52	188.67	185.60
12000	242.16	230.74	222.05	215.31	210.02	205.83	202.47
13000	262.34	249.97	240.55	233.26	227.53	222.98	219.34
14000	282.53	269.20	259.06	251.20	245.03	240.13	236.21
15000	302.71	288.43	277.56	269.14	262.53	257.28	253.08
20000	403.61	384.57	370.08	358.86	350.04	343.05	337.45
25000	504.51	480.72	462.60	448.57	437.55	428.81	421.81
30000	605.41	576.86	555.12	538.29	525.06	514.57	506.17
35000	706.31	673.00	647.64	628.00	612.57	600.33	590.53
40000	807.22	769.15	740.17	717.71	700.08	686.09	674.89
45000	908.12	865.29	832.69	807.43	787.59	771.85	759.25
50000	1009.02	961.43	925.21	897.14	875.10	857.61	843.61
55000	1109.92	1057.58	1017.73	986.86	962.61	943.37	927.98
56000	1130.10	1076.80	1036.23	1004.80	980.12	960.53	944.85
57000	1150.28	1096.03	1054.74	1022.74	997.62	977.68	961.72
58000	1170.46	1115.26	1073.24	1040.69	1015.12	994.83	978.59
59000	1190.64	1134.49	1091.74	1058.63	1032.62	1011.98	995.46
60000	1210.82	1153.72	1110.25	1076.57	1050.12	1029.14	1012.34
61000	1231.00	1172.95	1128.75	1094.51	1067.63	1046.29	1029.21
62000	1251.18	1192.18	1147.26	1112.46	1085.13	1063.44	1046.08
63000	1271.36	1211.41	1165.76	1130.40	1102.63	1080.59	1062.95
64000	1291.54	1230.63	1184.27	1148.34	1120.13	1097.74	1079.83
65000	1311.72	1249.86	1202.77	1166.29	1137.64	1114.90	1096.70
70000	1412.63	1346.01	1295.29	1256.00	1225.15	1200.66	1181.06
75000	1513.53	1442.15	1387.81	1345.71	1312.66	1286.42	1265.42
80000	1614.43	1538.29	1480.33	1435.43	1400.17	1372.18	1349.78
85000	1715.33	1634.44	1572.85	1525.14	1487.68	1457.94	1434.14
90000	1816.23	1730.58	1665.37	1614.86	1575.19	1543.70	1518.51
95000	1917.14	1826.72	1757.89	1704.57	1662.70	1629.46	1602.87
100000	2018.04	1922.87	1850.41	1794.28	1750.21	1715.23	1687.23
105000	2118.94	2019.01	1942.93	1884.00	1837.72	1800.99	1771.59
110000	2219.84	2115.15	2035.46	1973.71	1925.23	1886.75	1855.95
120000	2421.65	2307.44	2220.50	2153.14	2100.25	2058.27	2024.67
130000	2623.45	2499.73	2405.54	2332.57	2275.27	2229.79	2193.40
140000	2825.25	2692.01	2590.58	2512.00	2450.29	2401.32	2362.12
150000	3027.06	2884.30	2775.62	2691.43	2625.31	2572.84	2530.84
160000	3228.86	3076.59	2960.66	2870.86	2800.33	2744.36	2699.57
175000	3531.57	3365.02	3238.22	3140.00	3062.86	3001.65	2952.65
200000	4036.08	3845.73	3700.83	3588.57	3500.42	3430.45	3374.46
250000	5045.09	4807.16	4626.04	4485.71	4375.52	4288.07	4218.07
500000	10090.19	9614.33	9252.07	8971.42	8751.04	8576.13	8436.14
1000000	20180.38	19228.66	18504.14	17942.85	17502.08	17152.26	16872.28

18.75% MONTHLY PAYMENTS

AMOUNT	15 YEARS	16 YEARS	17 YEARS	18 YEARS	19 YEARS	20 YEARS	21 YEARS
100	1.66	1.65	1.63	1.62	1.61	1.60	1.59
200	3.33	3.29	3.26	3.24	3.22	3.20	3.19
500	8.32	8.23	8.16	8.10	8.05	8.01	7.97
1000	16.65	16.46	16.32	16.19	16.09	16.01	15.95
2000	33.29	32.93	32.63	32.39	32.19	32.03	31.89
3000	49.94	49.39	48.95	48.58	48.28	48.04	47.84
4000	66.59	65.86	65.26	64.78	64.38	64.05	63.78
5000	83.23	82.32	81.58	80.97	80.47	80.06	79.73
6000	99.88	98.78	97.89	97.16	96.57	96.08	95.67
7000	116.53	115.25	114.21	113.36	112.66	112.09	111.62
8000	133.17	131.71	130.52	129.55	128.75	128.10	127.56
9000	149.82	148.18	146.84	145.74	144.85	144.11	143.51
10000	166.47	164.64	163.15	161.94	160.94	160.13	159.45
11000	183.11	181.10	179.47	178.13	177.04	176.14	175.40
12000	199.76	197.57	195.78	194.33	193.13	192.15	191.35
13000	216.41	214.03	212.10	210.52	209.23	208.16	207.29
14000	233.05	230.49	228.41	226.71	225.32	224.18	223.24
15000	249.70	246.96	244.73	242.91	241.41	240.19	239.18
20000	332.93	329.28	326.30	323.88	321.89	320.25	318.91
25000	416.17	411.60	407.88	404.84	402.36	400.32	398.64
30000	499.40	493.92	489.46	485.81	482.83	480.38	478.36
35000	582.63	576.24	571.03	566.78	563.30	560.44	558.09
40000	665.87	658.56	652.61	647.75	643.77	640.51	637.82
45000	749.10	740.88	734.18	728.72	724.24	720.57	717.55
50000	832.33	823.20	815.76	809.69	804.72	800.63	797.27
55000	915.57	905.52	897.34	890.66	885.19	880.70	877.00
56000	932.21	921.98	913.65	906.85	901.28	896.71	892.95
57000	948.86	938.44	929.97	923.04	917.38	912.72	908.89
58000	965.51	954.91	946.28	939.24	933.47	928.73	924.84
59000	982.15	971.37	962.60	955.43	949.56	944.75	940.78
60000	998.80	987.84	978.91	971.63	965.66	960.76	956.73
61000	1015.45	1004.30	995.23	987.82	981.75	976.77	972.68
62000	1032.09	1020.76	1011.54	1004.01	997.85	992.78	988.62
63000	1048.74	1037.23	1027.86	1020.21	1013.94	1008.80	1004.57
64000	1065.39	1053.69	1044.17	1036.40	1030.04	1024.81	1020.51
65000	1082.03	1070.16	1060.49	1052.60	1046.13	1040.82	1036.46
70000	1165.27	1152.47	1142.06	1133.56	1126.60	1120.89	1116.18
75000	1248.50	1234.79	1223.64	1214.53	1207.07	1200.95	1195.91
80000	1331.74	1317.11	1305.22	1295.50	1287.54	1281.01	1275.64
85000	1414.97	1399.43	1386.79	1376.47	1368.02	1361.08	1355.37
90000	1498.20	1481.75	1468.37	1457.44	1448.49	1441.14	1435.09
95000	1581.44	1564.07	1549.95	1538.41	1528.96	1521.20	1514.82
100000	1664.67	1646.39	1631.52	1619.38	1609.43	1601.27	1594.55
105000	1747.90	1728.71	1713.10	1700.35	1689.90	1681.33	1674.28
110000	1831.14	1811.03	1794.67	1781.31	1770.37	1761.39	1754.00
120000	1997.60	1975.67	1957.83	1943.25	1931.32	1921.52	1913.46
130000	2164.07	2140.31	2120.98	2105.19	2092.26	2081.65	2072.91
140000	2330.54	2304.95	2284.13	2267.13	2253.20	2241.77	2232.37
150000	2497.00	2469.59	2447.28	2429.07	2414.15	2401.90	2391.82
160000	2663.47	2634.23	2610.43	2591.00	2575.09	2562.03	2551.28
175000	2913.17	2881.19	2855.16	2833.91	2816.50	2802.22	2790.46
200000	3329.34	3292.79	3263.04	3238.75	3218.86	3202.53	3189.10
250000	4161.67	4115.98	4078.80	4048.44	4023.58	4003.17	3986.37
500000	8323.34	8231.96	8157.61	8096.89	8047.16	8006.33	7972.75
1000000	16646.69	16463.93	16315.21	16193.77	16094.31	16012.66	15945.50

MONTHLY PAYMENTS 18.75%

AMOUNT	22 YEARS	23 YEARS	24 YEARS	25 YEARS	30 YEARS	35 YEARS	40 YEARS
100	1.59	1.58	1.58	1.58	1.57	1.56	1.56
200	3.18	3.17	3.16	3.16	3.14	3.13	3.13
500	7.95	7.92	7.90	7.89	7.84	7.82	7.82
1000	15.89	15.84	15.81	15.78	15.68	15.65	15.63
2000	31.78	31.69	31.61	31.55	31.37	31.30	31.27
3000	47.67	47.53	47.42	47.33	47.05	46.94	46.90
4000	63.56	63.38	63.23	63.10	62.74	62.59	62.54
5000	79.45	79.22	79.03	78.88	78.42	78.24	78.17
6000	95.34	95.07	94.84	94.65	94.10	93.89	93.80
7000	111.23	110.91	110.65	110.43	109.79	109.54	109.44
8000	127.12	126.76	126.45	126.21	125.47	125.19	125.07
9000	143.01	142.60	142.26	141.98	141.16	140.83	140.71
10000	158.90	158.45	158.07	157.76	156.84	156.48	156.34
11000	174.79	174.29	173.87	173.53	172.52	172.13	171.98
12000	190.68	190.13	189.68	189.31	188.21	187.78	187.61
13000	206.57	205.98	205.49	205.08	203.89	203.43	203.24
14000	222.46	221.82	221.30	220.86	219.58	219.08	218.88
15000	238.35	237.67	237.10	236.63	235.26	234.72	234.51
20000	317.80	316.89	316.14	315.51	313.68	312.97	312.68
25000	397.25	396.11	395.17	394.39	392.10	391.21	390.85
30000	476.70	475.34	474.20	473.27	470.52	469.45	469.02
35000	556.16	554.56	553.24	552.15	548.94	547.69	547.20
40000	635.61	633.78	632.27	631.03	627.36	625.93	625.37
45000	715.06	713.00	711.31	709.90	705.78	704.17	703.54
50000	794.51	792.23	790.34	788.78	784.20	782.41	781.71
55000	873.96	871.45	869.37	867.66	862.62	860.65	859.88
56000	889.85	887.29	885.18	883.44	878.31	876.30	875.51
57000	905.74	903.14	900.99	899.21	893.99	891.95	891.15
58000	921.63	918.98	916.80	914.99	909.68	907.60	906.78
59000	937.52	934.83	932.60	930.76	925.36	923.25	922.42
60000	953.41	950.67	948.41	946.54	941.04	938.90	938.05
61000	969.30	966.52	964.22	962.31	956.73	954.54	953.68
62000	985.19	982.36	980.02	978.09	972.41	970.19	969.32
63000	1001.08	998.20	995.83	993.87	988.10	985.84	984.95
64000	1016.97	1014.05	1011.64	1009.64	1003.78	1001.49	1000.59
65000	1032.86	1029.89	1027.44	1025.42	1019.47	1017.14	1016.22
70000	1112.31	1109.12	1106.48	1104.30	1097.89	1095.38	1094.39
75000	1191.76	1188.34	1185.51	1183.17	1176.31	1173.62	1172.56
80000	1271.21	1267.56	1264.55	1262.05	1254.73	1251.86	1250.73
85000	1350.66	1346.78	1343.58	1340.93	1333.15	1330.10	1328.90
90000	1430.11	1426.01	1422.61	1419.81	1411.57	1408.34	1407.07
95000	1509.57	1505.23	1501.65	1498.69	1489.99	1486.58	1485.25
100000	1589.02	1584.45	1580.68	1577.57	1568.41	1564.83	1563.42
105000	1668.47	1663.67	1659.72	1656.44	1646.83	1643.07	1641.59
110000	1747.92	1742.90	1738.75	1735.32	1725.25	1721.31	1719.76
120000	1906.82	1901.34	1896.82	1893.08	1882.09	1877.79	1876.10
130000	2065.72	2059.79	2054.89	2050.83	2038.93	2034.27	2032.44
140000	2224.62	2218.23	2212.95	2208.59	2195.77	2190.76	2188.78
150000	2383.52	2376.68	2371.02	2366.35	2352.61	2347.24	2345.12
160000	2542.43	2535.12	2529.09	2524.10	2509.45	2503.72	2501.47
175000	2780.78	2772.79	2766.19	2760.74	2744.71	2738.44	2735.98
200000	3178.03	3168.90	3161.36	3155.13	3136.82	3129.65	3126.83
250000	3972.54	3961.13	3951.70	3943.91	3921.02	3912.06	3908.54
500000	7945.08	7922.26	7903.41	7887.83	7842.04	7824.13	7817.08
1000000	15890.16	15844.52	15806.82	15775.65	15684.08	15648.25	15634.16

19.00% MONTHLY PAYMENTS

AMOUNT	1 YEAR	2 YEARS	3 YEARS	4 YEARS	5 YEARS	6 YEARS	7 YEARS
100	9.22	5.04	3.67	2.99	2.59	2.34	2.16
200	18.43	10.08	7.33	5.98	5.19	4.68	4.32
500	46.08	25.20	18.33	14.95	12.97	11.69	10.80
1000	92.16	50.41	36.66	29.90	25.94	23.38	21.61
2000	184.31	100.82	73.31	59.80	51.88	46.75	43.22
3000	276.47	151.23	109.97	89.70	77.82	70.13	64.82
4000	368.63	201.63	146.62	119.60	103.76	93.51	86.43
5000	460.78	252.04	183.28	149.50	129.70	116.88	108.04
6000	552.94	302.45	219.94	179.40	155.64	140.26	129.65
7000	645.10	352.86	256.59	209.30	181.58	163.64	151.26
8000	737.25	403.27	293.25	239.20	207.52	187.01	172.86
9000	829.41	453.68	329.90	269.10	233.46	210.39	194.47
10000	921.57	504.09	366.56	299.00	259.41	233.77	216.08
11000	1013.72	554.49	403.22	328.90	285.35	257.14	237.69
12000	1105.88	604.90	439.87	358.80	311.29	280.52	259.30
13000	1198.04	655.31	476.53	388.70	337.23	303.90	280.90
14000	1290.19	705.72	513.18	418.60	363.17	327.27	302.51
15000	1382.35	756.13	549.84	448.50	389.11	350.65	324.12
20000	1843.13	1008.17	733.12	598.00	518.81	467.53	432.16
25000	2303.91	1260.22	916.40	747.50	648.51	584.42	540.20
30000	2764.70	1512.26	1099.68	897.00	778.22	701.30	648.24
35000	3225.48	1764.30	1282.96	1046.50	907.92	818.19	756.28
40000	3686.26	2016.34	1466.24	1196.00	1037.62	935.07	864.32
45000	4147.05	2268.39	1649.52	1345.51	1167.32	1051.95	972.36
50000	4607.83	2520.43	1832.80	1495.01	1297.03	1168.84	1080.40
55000	5068.61	2772.47	2016.08	1644.51	1426.73	1285.72	1188.44
56000	5160.77	2822.88	2052.74	1674.41	1452.67	1309.10	1210.05
57000	5252.92	2873.29	2089.39	1704.31	1478.61	1332.47	1231.66
58000	5345.08	2923.70	2126.05	1734.21	1504.55	1355.85	1253.27
59000	5437.24	2974.11	2162.71	1764.11	1530.49	1379.23	1274.87
60000	5529.39	3024.52	2199.36	1794.01	1556.43	1402.60	1296.48
61000	5621.55	3074.93	2236.02	1823.91	1582.37	1425.98	1318.09
62000	5713.71	3125.33	2272.67	1853.81	1608.31	1449.36	1339.70
63000	5805.86	3175.74	2309.33	1883.71	1634.25	1472.73	1361.31
64000	5898.02	3226.15	2345.99	1913.61	1660.20	1496.11	1382.91
65000	5990.18	3276.56	2382.64	1943.51	1686.14	1519.49	1404.52
70000	6450.96	3528.60	2565.92	2093.01	1815.84	1636.37	1512.56
75000	6911.74	3780.65	2749.20	2242.51	1945.54	1753.25	1620.60
80000	7372.53	4032.69	2932.48	2392.01	2075.24	1870.14	1728.64
85000	7833.31	4284.73	3115.76	2541.51	2204.95	1987.02	1836.68
90000	8294.09	4536.78	3299.04	2691.01	2334.65	2103.91	1944.72
95000	8754.87	4788.82	3482.32	2840.51	2464.35	2220.79	2052.76
100000	9215.66	5040.86	3665.60	2990.01	2594.06	2337.67	2160.80
105000	9676.44	5292.90	3848.88	3139.51	2723.76	2454.56	2268.84
110000	10137.22	5544.95	4032.16	3289.01	2853.46	2571.44	2376.88
120000	11058.79	6049.03	4398.72	3588.01	3112.87	2805.21	2592.96
130000	11980.36	6553.12	4765.28	3887.02	3372.27	3038.97	2809.04
140000	12901.92	7057.21	5131.84	4186.02	3631.68	3272.74	3025.12
150000	13823.49	7561.29	5498.40	4485.02	3891.08	3506.51	3241.20
160000	14745.05	8065.38	5864.96	4784.02	4150.49	3740.28	3457.28
175000	16127.40	8821.51	6414.80	5232.52	4539.60	4090.93	3781.40
200000	18431.32	10081.72	7331.20	5980.03	5188.11	4675.34	4321.60
250000	23039.14	12602.15	9164.01	7475.03	6485.14	5844.18	5402.00
500000	46078.29	25204.31	18328.01	14950.06	12970.28	11688.36	10804.01
1000000	92156.58	50408.62	36656.02	29900.12	25940.55	23376.72	21608.02

MONTHLY PAYMENTS   19.00%

AMOUNT	8 YEARS	9 YEARS	10 YEARS	11 YEARS	12 YEARS	13 YEARS	14 YEARS
100	2.03	1.94	1.87	1.81	1.77	1.73	1.71
200	4.07	3.88	3.73	3.62	3.53	3.47	3.41
500	10.17	9.69	9.33	9.06	8.84	8.66	8.53
1000	20.33	19.39	18.67	18.11	17.67	17.33	17.05
2000	40.67	38.77	37.33	36.22	35.35	34.66	34.10
3000	61.00	58.16	56.00	54.33	53.02	51.98	51.15
4000	81.34	77.55	74.67	72.44	70.69	69.31	68.20
5000	101.67	96.94	93.34	90.55	88.37	86.64	85.26
6000	122.00	116.32	112.00	108.66	106.04	103.97	102.31
7000	142.34	135.71	130.67	126.77	123.72	121.29	119.36
8000	162.67	155.10	149.34	144.88	141.39	138.62	136.41
9000	183.00	174.48	168.01	162.99	159.06	155.95	153.46
10000	203.34	193.87	186.67	181.10	176.74	173.28	170.51
11000	223.67	213.26	205.34	199.21	194.41	190.60	187.56
12000	244.01	232.64	224.01	217.32	212.08	207.93	204.61
13000	264.34	252.03	242.67	235.43	229.76	225.26	221.66
14000	284.67	271.42	261.34	253.54	247.43	242.59	238.72
15000	305.01	290.81	280.01	271.65	265.10	259.91	255.77
20000	406.68	387.74	373.34	362.21	353.47	346.55	341.02
25000	508.35	484.68	466.68	452.76	441.84	433.19	426.28
30000	610.02	581.61	560.02	543.31	530.21	519.83	511.53
35000	711.69	678.55	653.35	633.86	618.58	606.47	596.79
40000	813.35	775.48	746.69	724.41	706.95	693.10	682.05
45000	915.02	872.42	840.03	814.96	795.31	779.74	767.30
50000	1016.69	969.35	933.36	905.52	883.68	866.38	852.56
55000	1118.36	1066.29	1026.70	996.07	972.05	953.02	937.81
56000	1138.70	1085.68	1045.37	1014.18	989.72	970.35	954.86
57000	1159.03	1105.06	1064.03	1032.29	1007.40	987.67	971.92
58000	1179.36	1124.45	1082.70	1050.40	1025.07	1005.00	988.97
59000	1199.70	1143.84	1101.37	1068.51	1042.75	1022.33	1006.02
60000	1220.03	1163.22	1120.03	1086.62	1060.42	1039.66	1023.07
61000	1240.37	1182.61	1138.70	1104.73	1078.09	1056.99	1040.12
62000	1260.70	1202.00	1157.37	1122.84	1095.77	1074.31	1057.17
63000	1281.03	1221.39	1176.04	1140.95	1113.44	1091.64	1074.22
64000	1301.37	1240.77	1194.70	1159.06	1131.11	1108.97	1091.27
65000	1321.70	1260.16	1213.37	1177.17	1148.79	1126.30	1108.32
70000	1423.37	1357.10	1306.71	1267.72	1237.16	1212.93	1193.58
75000	1525.04	1454.03	1400.04	1358.27	1325.52	1299.57	1278.84
80000	1626.71	1550.97	1493.38	1448.83	1413.89	1386.21	1364.09
85000	1728.38	1647.90	1586.72	1539.38	1502.26	1472.85	1449.35
90000	1830.05	1744.84	1680.05	1629.93	1590.63	1559.49	1534.60
95000	1931.72	1841.77	1773.39	1720.48	1679.00	1646.12	1619.86
100000	2033.39	1938.71	1866.72	1811.03	1767.36	1732.76	1705.11
105000	2135.06	2035.64	1960.06	1901.58	1855.73	1819.40	1790.37
110000	2236.73	2132.58	2053.40	1992.14	1944.10	1906.04	1875.63
120000	2440.06	2326.45	2240.07	2173.24	2120.84	2079.31	2046.14
130000	2643.40	2520.32	2426.74	2354.34	2297.57	2252.59	2216.65
140000	2846.74	2714.19	2613.41	2535.45	2474.31	2425.87	2387.16
150000	3050.08	2908.06	2800.09	2716.55	2651.05	2599.14	2557.67
160000	3253.42	3101.93	2986.76	2897.65	2827.78	2772.42	2728.18
175000	3558.43	3392.74	3266.77	3169.31	3092.89	3032.33	2983.95
200000	4066.77	3877.42	3733.45	3622.07	3534.73	3465.52	3410.23
250000	5083.47	4846.77	4666.81	4527.58	4418.41	4331.91	4262.79
500000	10166.93	9693.54	9333.62	9055.16	8836.82	8663.81	8525.57
1000000	20333.86	19387.08	18667.24	18110.33	17673.65	17327.62	17051.15

19.00%　　　MONTHLY PAYMENTS

AMOUNT	15 YEARS	16 YEARS	17 YEARS	18 YEARS	19 YEARS	20 YEARS	21 YEARS
100	1.68	1.66	1.65	1.64	1.63	1.62	1.61
200	3.37	3.33	3.30	3.28	3.26	3.24	3.23
500	8.41	8.32	8.25	8.19	8.14	8.10	8.07
1000	16.83	16.65	16.50	16.38	16.29	16.21	16.14
2000	33.66	33.30	33.01	32.77	32.57	32.41	32.28
3000	50.49	49.95	49.51	49.15	48.86	48.62	48.42
4000	67.32	66.60	66.01	65.54	65.15	64.83	64.57
5000	84.14	83.24	82.51	81.92	81.43	81.03	80.71
6000	100.97	99.89	99.02	98.30	97.72	97.24	96.85
7000	117.80	116.54	115.52	114.69	114.01	113.45	112.99
8000	134.63	133.19	132.02	131.07	130.29	129.65	129.13
9000	151.46	149.84	148.53	147.45	146.58	145.86	145.27
10000	168.29	166.49	165.03	163.84	162.87	162.07	161.41
11000	185.12	183.14	181.53	180.22	179.15	178.28	177.56
12000	201.95	199.79	198.03	196.61	195.44	194.48	193.70
13000	218.77	216.44	214.54	212.99	211.73	210.69	209.84
14000	235.60	233.08	231.04	229.37	228.01	226.90	225.98
15000	252.43	249.73	247.54	245.76	244.30	243.10	242.12
20000	336.58	332.98	330.06	327.68	325.73	324.14	322.83
25000	420.72	416.22	412.57	409.60	407.16	405.17	403.54
30000	504.86	499.47	495.09	491.52	488.60	486.21	484.24
35000	589.01	582.71	577.60	573.43	570.03	567.24	564.95
40000	673.15	665.96	660.12	655.35	651.46	648.27	645.66
45000	757.29	749.20	742.63	737.27	732.89	729.31	726.36
50000	841.44	832.45	825.14	819.19	814.33	810.34	807.07
55000	925.58	915.69	907.66	901.11	895.76	891.38	887.78
56000	942.41	932.34	924.16	917.50	912.05	907.58	903.92
57000	959.24	948.99	940.66	933.88	928.33	923.79	920.06
58000	976.07	965.64	957.17	950.26	944.62	940.00	936.20
59000	992.90	982.29	973.67	966.65	960.91	956.20	952.34
60000	1009.73	998.94	990.17	983.03	977.19	972.41	968.49
61000	1026.55	1015.58	1006.68	999.41	993.48	988.62	984.63
62000	1043.38	1032.23	1023.18	1015.80	1009.77	1004.82	1000.77
63000	1060.21	1048.88	1039.68	1032.18	1026.05	1021.03	1016.91
64000	1077.04	1065.53	1056.18	1048.57	1042.34	1037.24	1033.05
65000	1093.87	1082.18	1072.69	1064.95	1058.63	1053.45	1049.19
70000	1178.01	1165.42	1155.20	1146.87	1140.06	1134.48	1129.90
75000	1262.16	1248.67	1237.72	1228.79	1221.49	1215.51	1210.61
80000	1346.30	1331.91	1320.23	1310.71	1302.92	1296.55	1291.31
85000	1430.44	1415.16	1402.74	1392.63	1384.36	1377.58	1372.02
90000	1514.59	1498.40	1485.26	1474.55	1465.79	1458.62	1452.73
95000	1598.73	1581.65	1567.77	1556.47	1547.22	1539.65	1533.44
100000	1682.88	1664.89	1650.29	1638.38	1628.66	1620.68	1614.14
105000	1767.02	1748.14	1732.80	1720.30	1710.09	1701.72	1694.85
110000	1851.16	1831.38	1815.32	1802.22	1791.52	1782.75	1775.56
120000	2019.45	1997.87	1980.35	1966.06	1954.39	1944.82	1936.97
130000	2187.74	2164.36	2145.37	2129.90	2117.25	2106.89	2098.39
140000	2356.03	2330.85	2310.40	2293.74	2280.12	2268.96	2259.80
150000	2524.31	2497.34	2475.43	2457.58	2442.98	2431.03	2421.21
160000	2692.60	2663.83	2640.46	2621.41	2605.85	2593.10	2582.63
175000	2945.03	2913.56	2888.00	2867.17	2850.15	2836.20	2824.75
200000	3365.75	3329.79	3300.58	3276.77	3257.31	3241.37	3228.29
250000	4207.19	4162.23	4125.72	4095.96	4071.64	4051.71	4035.36
500000	8414.38	8324.46	8251.44	8191.92	8143.28	8103.42	8070.71
1000000	16828.76	16648.93	16502.88	16383.84	16286.55	16206.85	16141.43

MONTHLY PAYMENTS 19.00%

AMOUNT	22 YEARS	23 YEARS	24 YEARS	25 YEARS	30 YEARS	35 YEARS	40 YEARS
100	1.61	1.60	1.60	1.60	1.59	1.59	1.58
200	3.22	3.21	3.20	3.20	3.18	3.17	3.17
500	8.04	8.02	8.00	7.99	7.94	7.93	7.92
1000	16.09	16.04	16.01	15.98	15.89	15.85	15.84
2000	32.18	32.09	32.01	31.95	31.78	31.71	31.68
3000	48.26	48.13	48.02	47.93	47.67	47.56	47.53
4000	64.35	64.17	64.03	63.91	63.56	63.42	63.37
5000	80.44	80.22	80.03	79.88	79.44	79.27	79.21
6000	96.53	96.26	96.04	95.86	95.33	95.13	95.05
7000	112.61	112.30	112.05	111.84	111.22	110.98	110.89
8000	128.70	128.35	128.06	127.81	127.11	126.84	126.73
9000	144.79	144.39	144.06	143.79	143.00	142.69	142.58
10000	160.88	160.43	160.07	159.77	158.89	158.55	158.42
11000	176.96	176.48	176.08	175.74	174.78	174.40	174.26
12000	193.05	192.52	192.08	191.72	190.67	190.26	190.10
13000	209.14	208.56	208.09	207.70	206.56	206.11	205.94
14000	225.23	224.61	224.10	223.68	222.44	221.97	221.78
15000	241.31	240.65	240.10	239.65	238.33	237.82	237.63
20000	321.75	320.87	320.14	319.54	317.78	317.10	316.83
25000	402.19	401.08	400.17	399.42	397.22	396.37	396.04
30000	482.63	481.30	480.21	479.30	476.67	475.65	475.25
35000	563.07	561.52	560.24	559.19	556.11	554.92	554.46
40000	643.51	641.73	640.28	639.07	635.56	634.20	633.67
45000	723.94	721.95	720.31	718.96	715.00	713.47	712.88
50000	804.38	802.17	800.34	798.84	794.45	792.75	792.09
55000	884.82	882.39	880.38	878.72	873.89	872.02	871.30
56000	900.91	898.43	896.39	894.70	889.78	887.88	887.14
57000	917.00	914.47	912.39	910.68	905.67	903.73	902.98
58000	933.08	930.52	928.40	926.65	921.56	919.59	918.82
59000	949.17	946.56	944.41	942.63	937.45	935.44	934.66
60000	965.26	962.60	960.41	958.61	953.34	951.30	950.50
61000	981.35	978.65	976.42	974.58	969.22	967.15	966.35
62000	997.43	994.69	992.43	990.56	985.11	983.01	982.19
63000	1013.52	1010.73	1008.43	1006.54	1001.00	998.86	998.03
64000	1029.61	1026.78	1024.44	1022.52	1016.89	1014.72	1013.87
65000	1045.70	1042.82	1040.45	1038.49	1032.78	1030.57	1029.71
70000	1126.14	1123.04	1120.48	1118.38	1112.22	1109.85	1108.92
75000	1206.57	1203.25	1200.52	1198.26	1191.67	1189.12	1188.13
80000	1287.01	1283.47	1280.55	1278.14	1271.11	1268.40	1267.34
85000	1367.45	1363.69	1360.59	1358.03	1350.56	1347.67	1346.55
90000	1447.89	1443.90	1440.62	1437.91	1430.00	1426.95	1425.76
95000	1528.33	1524.12	1520.65	1517.80	1509.45	1506.22	1504.97
100000	1608.76	1604.34	1600.69	1597.68	1588.89	1585.49	1584.17
105000	1689.20	1684.55	1680.72	1677.56	1668.34	1664.77	1663.38
110000	1769.64	1764.77	1760.76	1757.45	1747.78	1744.04	1742.59
120000	1930.52	1925.20	1920.83	1917.22	1906.67	1902.59	1901.01
130000	2091.39	2085.64	2080.90	2076.98	2065.56	2061.14	2059.43
140000	2252.27	2246.07	2240.96	2236.75	2224.45	2219.69	2217.84
150000	2413.15	2406.51	2401.03	2396.52	2383.34	2378.24	2376.26
160000	2574.02	2566.94	2561.10	2556.29	2542.23	2536.79	2534.68
175000	2815.34	2807.59	2801.21	2795.94	2780.56	2774.62	2772.31
200000	3217.53	3208.67	3201.38	3195.36	3177.78	3170.99	3168.35
250000	4021.91	4010.84	4001.72	3994.20	3972.23	3963.74	3960.44
500000	8043.82	8021.69	8003.44	7988.40	7944.46	7927.47	7920.87
1000000	16087.64	16043.37	16006.89	15976.80	15888.92	15854.95	15841.75

19.50% MONTHLY PAYMENTS

AMOUNT	1 YEAR	2 YEARS	3 YEARS	4 YEARS	5 YEARS	6 YEARS	7 YEARS
100	9.24	5.07	3.69	3.02	2.62	2.37	2.19
200	18.48	10.13	7.38	6.03	5.24	4.73	4.38
500	46.20	25.33	18.45	15.08	13.11	11.83	10.95
1000	92.40	50.65	36.91	30.16	26.22	23.66	21.91
2000	184.79	101.30	73.82	60.33	52.43	47.33	43.81
3000	277.19	151.96	110.73	90.49	78.65	70.99	65.72
4000	369.58	202.61	147.64	120.66	104.87	94.66	87.62
5000	461.98	253.26	184.55	150.82	131.08	118.32	109.53
6000	554.37	303.91	221.46	180.99	157.30	141.98	131.44
7000	646.77	354.56	258.37	211.15	183.52	165.65	153.34
8000	739.16	405.22	295.27	241.32	209.73	189.31	175.25
9000	831.56	455.87	332.18	271.48	235.95	212.97	197.16
10000	923.95	506.52	369.09	301.65	262.16	236.64	219.06
11000	1016.35	557.17	406.00	331.81	288.38	260.30	240.97
12000	1108.74	607.82	442.91	361.98	314.60	283.97	262.87
13000	1201.14	658.47	479.82	392.14	340.81	307.63	284.78
14000	1293.54	709.13	516.73	422.30	367.03	331.29	306.69
15000	1385.93	759.78	553.64	452.47	393.25	354.96	328.59
20000	1847.91	1013.04	738.19	603.29	524.33	473.28	438.12
25000	2309.88	1266.30	922.73	754.12	655.41	591.60	547.65
30000	2771.86	1519.56	1107.28	904.94	786.49	709.92	657.18
35000	3233.84	1772.82	1291.83	1055.76	917.58	828.24	766.71
40000	3695.81	2026.08	1476.37	1206.58	1048.66	946.56	876.24
45000	4157.79	2279.33	1660.92	1357.41	1179.74	1064.87	985.78
50000	4619.77	2532.59	1845.47	1508.23	1310.82	1183.19	1095.31
55000	5081.75	2785.85	2030.01	1659.05	1441.90	1301.51	1204.84
56000	5174.14	2836.51	2066.92	1689.22	1468.12	1325.18	1226.74
57000	5266.54	2887.16	2103.83	1719.38	1494.34	1348.84	1248.65
58000	5358.93	2937.81	2140.74	1749.55	1520.55	1372.51	1270.55
59000	5451.33	2988.46	2177.65	1779.71	1546.77	1396.17	1292.46
60000	5543.72	3039.11	2214.56	1809.88	1572.99	1419.83	1314.37
61000	5636.12	3089.76	2251.47	1840.04	1599.20	1443.50	1336.27
62000	5728.51	3140.42	2288.38	1870.21	1625.42	1467.16	1358.18
63000	5820.91	3191.07	2325.29	1900.37	1651.64	1490.82	1380.09
64000	5913.30	3241.72	2362.20	1930.53	1677.85	1514.49	1401.99
65000	6005.70	3292.37	2399.11	1960.70	1704.07	1538.15	1423.90
70000	6467.68	3545.63	2583.65	2111.52	1835.15	1656.47	1533.43
75000	6929.65	3798.89	2768.20	2262.35	1966.23	1774.79	1642.96
80000	7391.63	4052.15	2952.74	2413.17	2097.32	1893.11	1752.49
85000	7853.61	4305.41	3137.29	2563.99	2228.40	2011.43	1862.02
90000	8315.58	4558.67	3321.84	2714.81	2359.48	2129.75	1971.55
95000	8777.56	4811.93	3506.38	2865.64	2490.56	2248.07	2081.08
100000	9239.54	5065.19	3690.93	3016.46	2621.64	2366.39	2190.61
105000	9701.51	5318.45	3875.48	3167.28	2752.73	2484.71	2300.14
110000	10163.49	5571.71	4060.02	3318.11	2883.81	2603.03	2409.67
120000	11087.44	6078.23	4429.12	3619.75	3145.97	2839.67	2628.73
130000	12011.40	6584.74	4798.21	3921.40	3408.14	3076.30	2847.80
140000	12935.35	7091.26	5167.30	4223.04	3670.30	3312.94	3066.86
150000	13859.31	7597.78	5536.40	4524.69	3932.47	3549.58	3285.92
160000	14783.26	8104.30	5905.49	4826.34	4194.63	3786.22	3504.98
175000	16169.19	8864.08	6459.13	5278.81	4587.88	4141.18	3833.57
200000	18479.07	10130.38	7381.86	6032.92	5243.29	4732.78	4381.22
250000	23098.84	12662.97	9227.33	7541.15	6554.11	5915.97	5476.53
500000	46197.69	25325.94	18454.66	15082.30	13108.22	11831.94	10953.06
1000000	92395.37	50651.88	36909.31	30164.60	26216.45	23663.88	21906.12

MONTHLY PAYMENTS   19.50%

AMOUNT	8 YEARS	9 YEARS	10 YEARS	11 YEARS	12 YEARS	13 YEARS	14 YEARS
100	2.06	1.97	1.90	1.84	1.80	1.77	1.74
200	4.13	3.94	3.80	3.69	3.60	3.54	3.48
500	10.32	9.85	9.50	9.22	9.01	8.84	8.71
1000	20.64	19.71	19.00	18.45	18.02	17.68	17.41
2000	41.28	39.41	37.99	36.89	36.04	35.36	34.82
3000	61.93	59.12	56.99	55.34	54.06	53.04	52.23
4000	82.57	78.82	75.98	73.79	72.07	70.72	69.64
5000	103.21	98.53	94.98	92.24	90.09	88.40	87.05
6000	123.85	118.23	113.97	110.68	108.11	106.08	104.46
7000	144.50	137.94	132.97	129.13	126.13	123.76	121.87
8000	165.14	157.65	151.96	147.58	144.15	141.44	139.29
9000	185.78	177.35	170.96	166.02	162.17	159.12	156.70
10000	206.42	197.06	189.95	184.47	180.19	176.80	174.11
11000	227.07	216.76	208.95	202.92	198.21	194.48	191.52
12000	247.71	236.47	227.94	221.37	216.22	212.16	208.93
13000	268.35	256.17	246.94	239.81	234.24	229.84	226.34
14000	288.99	275.88	265.93	258.26	252.26	247.52	243.75
15000	309.64	295.58	284.93	276.71	270.28	265.20	261.16
20000	412.85	394.11	379.90	368.94	360.37	353.60	348.21
25000	516.06	492.64	474.88	461.18	450.47	442.01	435.27
30000	619.27	591.17	569.86	553.41	540.56	530.41	522.32
35000	722.49	689.70	664.83	645.65	630.65	618.81	609.37
40000	825.70	788.23	759.81	737.89	720.75	707.21	696.43
45000	928.91	886.75	854.78	830.12	810.84	795.61	783.48
50000	1032.12	985.28	949.76	922.36	900.93	884.01	870.54
55000	1135.34	1083.81	1044.74	1014.59	991.03	972.41	957.59
56000	1155.98	1103.52	1063.73	1033.04	1009.04	990.09	975.00
57000	1176.62	1123.22	1082.73	1051.49	1027.06	1007.77	992.41
58000	1197.26	1142.93	1101.72	1069.93	1045.08	1025.45	1009.82
59000	1217.91	1162.63	1120.72	1088.38	1063.10	1043.13	1027.23
60000	1238.55	1182.34	1139.71	1106.83	1081.12	1060.81	1044.64
61000	1259.19	1202.05	1158.71	1125.27	1099.14	1078.49	1062.05
62000	1279.83	1221.75	1177.70	1143.72	1117.16	1096.17	1079.46
63000	1300.47	1241.46	1196.70	1162.17	1135.17	1113.85	1096.87
64000	1321.12	1261.16	1215.69	1180.62	1153.19	1131.53	1114.29
65000	1341.76	1280.87	1234.69	1199.06	1171.21	1149.21	1131.70
70000	1444.97	1379.40	1329.67	1291.30	1261.31	1237.61	1218.75
75000	1548.18	1477.92	1424.64	1383.53	1351.40	1326.02	1305.80
80000	1651.40	1576.45	1519.62	1475.77	1441.49	1414.42	1392.86
85000	1754.61	1674.98	1614.59	1568.01	1531.59	1502.82	1479.91
90000	1857.82	1773.51	1709.57	1660.24	1621.68	1591.22	1566.96
95000	1961.03	1872.04	1804.55	1752.48	1711.77	1679.62	1654.02
100000	2064.25	1970.57	1899.52	1844.71	1801.86	1768.02	1741.07
105000	2167.46	2069.09	1994.50	1936.95	1891.96	1856.42	1828.12
110000	2270.67	2167.62	2089.47	2029.18	1982.05	1944.82	1915.18
120000	2477.10	2364.68	2279.43	2213.66	2162.24	2121.63	2089.28
130000	2683.52	2561.74	2469.38	2398.13	2342.42	2298.43	2263.39
140000	2889.94	2758.79	2659.33	2582.60	2522.61	2475.23	2437.50
150000	3096.37	2955.85	2849.28	2767.07	2702.80	2652.03	2611.61
160000	3302.79	3152.91	3039.24	2951.54	2882.98	2828.83	2785.71
175000	3612.43	3448.49	3324.16	3228.25	3153.26	3094.04	3046.87
200000	4128.49	3941.13	3799.04	3689.43	3603.73	3536.04	3482.14
250000	5160.62	4926.41	4748.81	4611.78	4504.66	4420.05	4352.68
500000	10321.23	9852.83	9497.61	9223.56	9009.32	8840.11	8705.35
1000000	20642.46	19705.66	18995.22	18447.13	18018.65	17680.21	17410.71

19.50%　　　　MONTHLY PAYMENTS

AMOUNT	15 YEARS	16 YEARS	17 YEARS	18 YEARS	19 YEARS	20 YEARS	21 YEARS
100	1.72	1.70	1.69	1.68	1.67	1.66	1.65
200	3.44	3.40	3.38	3.35	3.33	3.32	3.31
500	8.60	8.51	8.44	8.38	8.34	8.30	8.27
1000	17.19	17.02	16.88	16.77	16.67	16.60	16.53
2000	34.39	34.04	33.76	33.53	33.35	33.19	33.07
3000	51.58	51.06	50.64	50.30	50.02	49.79	49.60
4000	68.78	68.08	67.52	67.06	66.69	66.39	66.14
5000	85.97	85.10	84.40	83.83	83.36	82.98	82.67
6000	103.17	102.12	101.28	100.59	100.04	99.58	99.21
7000	120.36	119.14	118.16	117.36	116.71	116.18	115.74
8000	137.56	136.17	135.04	134.12	133.38	132.77	132.28
9000	154.75	153.19	151.92	150.89	150.05	149.37	148.81
10000	171.95	170.21	168.80	167.66	166.73	165.97	165.35
11000	189.14	187.23	185.68	184.42	183.40	182.56	181.88
12000	206.34	204.25	202.56	201.19	200.07	199.16	198.42
13000	223.53	221.27	219.44	217.95	216.74	215.76	214.95
14000	240.73	238.29	236.32	234.72	233.42	232.35	231.48
15000	257.92	255.31	253.20	251.48	250.09	248.95	248.02
20000	343.89	340.41	337.60	335.31	333.45	331.93	330.69
25000	429.87	425.52	422.00	419.14	416.81	414.92	413.37
30000	515.84	510.62	506.40	502.97	500.18	497.90	496.04
35000	601.81	595.72	590.80	586.80	583.54	580.88	578.71
40000	687.79	680.83	675.20	670.62	666.90	663.87	661.38
45000	773.76	765.93	759.59	754.45	750.26	746.85	744.06
50000	859.74	851.03	843.99	838.28	833.63	829.83	826.73
55000	945.71	936.14	928.39	922.11	916.99	912.82	909.40
56000	962.90	953.16	945.27	938.87	933.66	929.41	925.94
57000	980.10	970.18	962.15	955.64	950.34	946.01	942.47
58000	997.29	987.20	979.03	972.40	967.01	962.61	959.01
59000	1014.49	1004.22	995.91	989.17	983.68	979.20	975.54
60000	1031.68	1021.24	1012.79	1005.93	1000.35	995.80	992.08
61000	1048.88	1038.26	1029.67	1022.70	1017.03	1012.40	1008.61
62000	1066.07	1055.28	1046.55	1039.47	1033.70	1028.99	1025.15
63000	1083.27	1072.30	1063.43	1056.23	1050.37	1045.59	1041.68
64000	1100.46	1089.32	1080.31	1073.00	1067.04	1062.19	1058.22
65000	1117.66	1106.34	1097.19	1089.76	1083.72	1078.78	1074.75
70000	1203.63	1191.45	1181.59	1173.59	1167.08	1161.77	1157.42
75000	1289.60	1276.55	1265.99	1257.42	1250.44	1244.75	1240.10
80000	1375.58	1361.65	1350.39	1341.25	1333.80	1327.73	1322.77
85000	1461.55	1446.76	1434.79	1425.07	1417.17	1410.71	1405.44
90000	1547.52	1531.86	1519.19	1508.90	1500.53	1493.70	1488.12
95000	1633.50	1616.96	1603.59	1592.73	1583.89	1576.68	1570.79
100000	1719.47	1702.07	1687.99	1676.56	1667.25	1659.66	1653.46
105000	1805.44	1787.17	1772.39	1760.39	1750.62	1742.65	1736.13
110000	1891.42	1872.27	1856.79	1844.21	1833.98	1825.63	1818.81
120000	2063.36	2042.48	2025.59	2011.87	2000.71	1991.60	1984.15
130000	2235.31	2212.69	2194.38	2179.53	2167.43	2157.56	2149.50
140000	2407.26	2382.89	2363.18	2347.18	2334.16	2323.53	2314.85
150000	2579.21	2553.10	2531.98	2514.84	2500.88	2489.50	2480.19
160000	2751.15	2723.31	2700.78	2682.49	2667.61	2655.46	2645.54
175000	3009.07	2978.62	2953.98	2933.98	2917.70	2904.41	2893.56
200000	3438.94	3404.13	3375.98	3353.12	3334.51	3319.33	3306.92
250000	4298.68	4255.17	4219.97	4191.40	4168.14	4149.16	4133.65
500000	8597.35	8510.34	8439.94	8382.79	8336.27	8298.32	8267.31
1000000	17194.70	17020.67	16879.88	16765.58	16672.55	16596.65	16534.61

MONTHLY PAYMENTS   19.50%

AMOUNT	22 YEARS	23 YEARS	24 YEARS	25 YEARS	30 YEARS	35 YEARS	40 YEARS
100	1.65	1.64	1.64	1.64	1.63	1.63	1.63
200	3.30	3.29	3.28	3.28	3.26	3.25	3.25
500	8.24	8.22	8.20	8.19	8.15	8.13	8.13
1000	16.48	16.44	16.41	16.38	16.30	16.27	16.26
2000	32.97	32.88	32.82	32.76	32.60	32.54	32.51
3000	49.45	49.33	49.22	49.14	48.90	48.81	48.77
4000	65.94	65.77	65.63	65.52	65.20	65.07	65.03
5000	82.42	82.21	82.04	81.90	81.50	81.34	81.29
6000	98.90	98.65	98.45	98.28	97.80	97.61	97.54
7000	115.39	115.10	114.86	114.66	114.09	113.88	113.80
8000	131.87	131.54	131.26	131.04	130.39	130.15	130.06
9000	148.35	147.98	147.67	147.42	146.69	146.42	146.31
10000	164.84	164.42	164.08	163.80	162.99	162.69	162.57
11000	181.32	180.86	180.49	180.18	179.29	178.96	178.83
12000	197.81	197.31	196.90	196.56	195.59	195.22	195.09
13000	214.29	213.75	213.31	212.94	211.89	211.49	211.34
14000	230.77	230.19	229.71	229.32	228.19	227.76	227.60
15000	247.26	246.63	246.12	245.70	244.49	244.03	243.86
20000	329.68	328.84	328.16	327.60	325.98	325.37	325.14
25000	412.10	411.06	410.20	409.50	407.48	406.72	406.43
30000	494.52	493.27	492.24	491.40	488.98	488.06	487.71
35000	576.93	575.48	574.28	573.30	570.47	569.40	569.00
40000	659.35	657.69	656.32	655.20	651.97	650.75	650.28
45000	741.77	739.90	738.36	737.10	733.46	732.09	731.57
50000	824.19	822.11	820.40	819.00	814.96	813.43	812.85
55000	906.61	904.32	902.44	900.90	896.46	894.78	894.14
56000	923.09	920.76	918.85	917.28	912.76	911.05	910.40
57000	939.58	937.21	935.26	933.66	929.05	927.31	926.65
58000	956.06	953.65	951.67	950.04	945.35	943.58	942.91
59000	972.55	970.09	968.08	966.42	961.65	959.85	959.17
60000	989.03	986.53	984.49	982.80	977.95	976.12	975.43
61000	1005.51	1002.98	1000.89	999.18	994.25	992.39	991.68
62000	1022.00	1019.42	1017.30	1015.56	1010.55	1008.66	1007.94
63000	1038.48	1035.86	1033.71	1031.94	1026.85	1024.93	1024.20
64000	1054.97	1052.30	1050.12	1048.32	1043.15	1041.19	1040.45
65000	1071.45	1068.74	1066.53	1064.70	1059.45	1057.46	1056.71
70000	1153.87	1150.96	1148.57	1146.60	1140.94	1138.81	1138.00
75000	1236.29	1233.17	1230.61	1228.50	1222.44	1220.15	1219.28
80000	1318.71	1315.38	1312.65	1310.40	1303.94	1301.49	1300.57
85000	1401.13	1397.59	1394.69	1392.31	1385.43	1382.84	1381.85
90000	1483.55	1479.80	1476.73	1474.21	1466.93	1464.18	1463.14
95000	1565.96	1562.01	1558.77	1556.11	1548.42	1545.52	1544.42
100000	1648.38	1644.22	1640.81	1638.01	1629.92	1626.87	1625.71
105000	1730.80	1726.43	1722.85	1719.91	1711.42	1708.21	1706.99
110000	1813.22	1808.64	1804.89	1801.81	1792.91	1789.55	1788.28
120000	1978.06	1973.07	1968.97	1965.61	1955.90	1952.24	1950.85
130000	2142.90	2137.49	2133.05	2129.41	2118.90	2114.93	2113.42
140000	2307.74	2301.91	2297.13	2293.21	2281.89	2277.61	2275.99
150000	2472.58	2466.33	2461.21	2457.01	2444.88	2440.30	2438.56
160000	2637.41	2630.76	2625.29	2620.81	2607.87	2602.99	2601.13
175000	2884.67	2877.39	2871.42	2866.51	2852.36	2847.02	2844.99
200000	3296.75	3288.44	3281.62	3276.01	3259.84	3253.73	3251.42
250000	4120.96	4110.56	4102.02	4095.02	4074.80	4067.17	4064.27
500000	8241.92	8221.11	8204.04	8190.03	8149.60	8134.33	8128.55
1000000	16483.84	16442.22	16408.09	16380.06	16299.20	16268.67	16257.09

20.00%   MONTHLY PAYMENTS

AMOUNT	1 YEAR	2 YEARS	3 YEARS	4 YEARS	5 YEARS	6 YEARS	7 YEARS
100	9.26	5.09	3.72	3.04	2.65	2.40	2.22
200	18.53	10.18	7.43	6.09	5.30	4.79	4.44
500	46.32	25.45	18.58	15.22	13.25	11.98	11.10
1000	92.63	50.90	37.16	30.43	26.49	23.95	22.21
2000	185.27	101.79	74.33	60.86	52.99	47.91	44.41
3000	277.90	152.69	111.49	91.29	79.48	71.86	66.62
4000	370.54	203.58	148.65	121.72	105.98	95.81	88.82
5000	463.17	254.48	185.82	152.15	132.47	119.76	111.03
6000	555.81	305.37	222.98	182.58	158.96	143.72	133.24
7000	648.44	356.27	260.15	213.01	185.46	167.67	155.44
8000	741.08	407.17	297.31	243.44	211.95	191.62	177.65
9000	833.71	458.06	334.47	273.87	238.44	215.58	199.86
10000	926.35	508.96	371.64	304.30	264.94	239.53	222.06
11000	1018.98	559.85	408.80	334.73	291.43	263.48	244.27
12000	1111.61	610.75	445.96	365.16	317.93	287.43	266.47
13000	1204.25	661.65	483.13	395.59	344.42	311.39	288.68
14000	1296.88	712.54	520.29	426.03	370.91	335.34	310.89
15000	1389.52	763.44	557.45	456.46	397.41	359.29	333.09
20000	1852.69	1017.92	743.27	608.61	529.88	479.06	444.12
25000	2315.86	1272.40	929.09	760.76	662.35	598.82	555.15
30000	2779.04	1526.87	1114.91	912.91	794.82	718.58	666.19
35000	3242.21	1781.35	1300.73	1065.06	927.29	838.35	777.22
40000	3705.38	2035.83	1486.54	1217.21	1059.76	958.11	888.25
45000	4168.55	2290.31	1672.36	1369.37	1192.22	1077.88	999.28
50000	4631.73	2544.79	1858.18	1521.52	1324.69	1197.64	1110.31
55000	5094.90	2799.27	2044.00	1673.67	1457.16	1317.41	1221.34
56000	5187.53	2850.16	2081.16	1704.10	1483.66	1341.36	1243.55
57000	5280.17	2901.06	2118.32	1734.53	1510.15	1365.31	1265.75
58000	5372.80	2951.96	2155.49	1764.96	1536.65	1389.26	1287.96
59000	5465.44	3002.85	2192.65	1795.39	1563.14	1413.22	1310.17
60000	5558.07	3053.75	2229.82	1825.82	1589.63	1437.17	1332.37
61000	5650.70	3104.64	2266.98	1856.25	1616.13	1461.12	1354.58
62000	5743.34	3155.54	2304.14	1886.68	1642.62	1485.08	1376.78
63000	5835.97	3206.44	2341.31	1917.11	1669.11	1509.03	1398.99
64000	5928.61	3257.33	2378.47	1947.54	1695.61	1532.98	1421.20
65000	6021.24	3308.23	2415.63	1977.97	1722.10	1556.93	1443.40
70000	6484.42	3562.71	2601.45	2130.13	1854.57	1676.70	1554.43
75000	6947.59	3817.19	2787.27	2282.28	1987.04	1796.46	1665.46
80000	7410.76	4071.66	2973.09	2434.43	2119.51	1916.23	1776.50
85000	7873.93	4326.14	3158.90	2586.58	2251.98	2035.99	1887.53
90000	8337.11	4580.62	3344.72	2738.73	2384.45	2155.75	1998.56
95000	8800.28	4835.10	3530.54	2890.88	2516.92	2275.52	2109.59
100000	9263.45	5089.58	3716.36	3043.04	2649.39	2395.28	2220.62
105000	9726.62	5344.06	3902.18	3195.19	2781.86	2515.05	2331.65
110000	10189.80	5598.54	4087.99	3347.34	2914.33	2634.81	2442.68
120000	11116.14	6107.50	4459.63	3651.64	3179.27	2874.34	2664.74
130000	12042.49	6616.45	4831.27	3955.95	3444.20	3113.87	2886.81
140000	12968.83	7125.41	5202.90	4260.25	3709.14	3353.40	3108.87
150000	13895.18	7634.37	5574.54	4564.55	3974.08	3592.92	3330.93
160000	14821.52	8143.33	5946.17	4868.86	4239.02	3832.45	3552.99
175000	16211.04	8906.77	6503.63	5325.31	4636.43	4191.74	3886.08
200000	18526.90	10179.16	7432.72	6086.07	5298.78	4790.57	4441.24
250000	23158.63	12723.95	9290.90	7607.59	6623.47	5988.21	5551.55
500000	46317.25	25447.90	18581.79	15215.18	13246.94	11976.41	11103.10
1000000	92634.51	50895.80	37163.58	30430.36	26493.88	23952.83	22206.20

MONTHLY PAYMENTS 20.00%

AMOUNT	8 YEARS	9 YEARS	10 YEARS	11 YEARS	12 YEARS	13 YEARS	14 YEARS
100	2.10	2.00	1.93	1.88	1.84	1.80	1.78
200	4.19	4.01	3.87	3.76	3.67	3.61	3.55
500	10.48	10.01	9.66	9.39	9.18	9.02	8.89
1000	20.95	20.03	19.33	18.79	18.37	18.04	17.77
2000	41.91	40.05	38.65	37.57	36.73	36.07	35.55
3000	62.86	60.08	57.98	56.36	55.10	54.11	53.32
4000	83.81	80.11	77.30	75.15	73.46	72.14	71.09
5000	104.77	100.13	96.63	93.93	91.83	90.18	88.86
6000	125.72	120.16	115.95	112.72	110.20	108.21	106.64
7000	146.67	140.19	135.28	131.50	128.56	126.25	124.41
8000	167.63	160.21	154.60	150.29	146.93	144.28	142.18
9000	188.58	180.24	173.93	169.08	165.29	162.32	159.95
10000	209.53	200.27	193.26	187.86	183.66	180.35	177.73
11000	230.49	220.29	212.58	206.65	202.03	198.39	195.50
12000	251.44	240.32	231.91	225.44	220.39	216.42	213.27
13000	272.39	260.34	251.23	244.22	238.76	234.46	231.04
14000	293.34	280.37	270.56	263.01	257.13	252.49	248.82
15000	314.30	300.40	289.88	281.80	275.49	270.53	266.59
20000	419.06	400.53	386.51	375.73	367.32	360.70	355.45
25000	523.83	500.66	483.14	469.66	459.15	450.88	444.32
30000	628.60	600.80	579.77	563.59	550.98	541.06	533.18
35000	733.36	700.93	676.39	657.52	642.81	631.23	622.04
40000	838.13	801.06	773.02	751.45	734.64	721.41	710.91
45000	942.89	901.19	869.65	845.39	826.47	811.58	799.77
50000	1047.66	1001.33	966.28	939.32	918.30	901.76	888.63
55000	1152.43	1101.46	1062.91	1033.25	1010.13	991.94	977.50
56000	1173.38	1121.48	1082.23	1052.04	1028.50	1009.97	995.27
57000	1194.33	1141.51	1101.56	1070.82	1046.87	1028.01	1013.04
58000	1215.29	1161.54	1120.88	1089.61	1065.23	1046.04	1030.81
59000	1236.24	1181.56	1140.21	1108.39	1083.60	1064.08	1048.59
60000	1257.19	1201.59	1159.53	1127.18	1101.97	1082.11	1066.36
61000	1278.15	1221.62	1178.86	1145.97	1120.33	1100.15	1084.13
62000	1299.10	1241.64	1198.19	1164.75	1138.70	1118.18	1101.90
63000	1320.05	1261.67	1217.51	1183.54	1157.06	1136.22	1119.68
64000	1341.00	1281.70	1236.84	1202.33	1175.43	1154.25	1137.45
65000	1361.96	1301.72	1256.16	1221.11	1193.80	1172.29	1155.22
70000	1466.72	1401.86	1352.79	1315.04	1285.63	1262.47	1244.09
75000	1571.49	1501.99	1449.42	1408.98	1377.46	1352.64	1332.95
80000	1676.26	1602.12	1546.05	1502.91	1469.29	1442.82	1421.81
85000	1781.02	1702.25	1642.67	1596.84	1561.12	1532.99	1510.68
90000	1885.79	1802.39	1739.30	1690.77	1652.95	1623.17	1599.54
95000	1990.55	1902.52	1835.93	1784.70	1744.78	1713.35	1688.40
100000	2095.32	2002.65	1932.56	1878.63	1836.61	1803.52	1777.27
105000	2200.09	2102.78	2029.18	1972.57	1928.44	1893.70	1866.13
110000	2304.85	2202.92	2125.81	2066.50	2020.27	1983.87	1954.99
120000	2514.38	2403.18	2319.07	2254.36	2203.93	2164.23	2132.72
130000	2723.92	2603.45	2512.32	2442.22	2387.59	2344.58	2310.44
140000	2933.45	2803.71	2705.58	2630.09	2571.25	2524.93	2488.17
150000	3142.98	3003.98	2898.84	2817.95	2754.91	2705.28	2665.90
160000	3352.51	3204.24	3092.09	3005.81	2938.57	2885.64	2843.62
175000	3666.81	3504.64	3381.97	3287.61	3214.06	3156.16	3110.21
200000	4190.64	4005.30	3865.11	3757.27	3673.22	3607.04	3554.53
250000	5238.30	5006.63	4831.39	4696.59	4591.52	4508.81	4443.16
500000	10476.60	10013.25	9662.78	9393.17	9183.04	9017.61	8886.33
1000000	20953.20	20026.50	19325.57	18786.34	18366.09	18035.22	17772.65

20.00%　　　MONTHLY PAYMENTS

AMOUNT	15 YEARS	16 YEARS	17 YEARS	18 YEARS	19 YEARS	20 YEARS	21 YEARS
100	1.76	1.74	1.73	1.71	1.71	1.70	1.69
200	3.51	3.48	3.45	3.43	3.41	3.40	3.39
500	8.78	8.70	8.63	8.57	8.53	8.49	8.46
1000	17.56	17.39	17.26	17.15	17.06	16.99	16.93
2000	35.13	34.79	34.52	34.30	34.12	33.98	33.86
3000	52.69	52.18	51.78	51.45	51.18	50.96	50.79
4000	70.25	69.58	69.04	68.60	68.24	67.95	67.72
5000	87.81	86.97	86.30	85.75	85.30	84.94	84.65
6000	105.38	104.37	103.55	102.90	102.36	101.93	101.58
7000	122.94	121.76	120.81	120.05	119.42	118.92	118.51
8000	140.50	139.16	138.07	137.19	136.48	135.91	135.44
9000	158.07	156.55	155.33	154.34	153.54	152.89	152.37
10000	175.63	173.95	172.59	171.49	170.60	169.88	169.29
11000	193.19	191.34	189.85	188.64	187.67	186.87	186.22
12000	210.76	208.74	207.11	205.79	204.73	203.86	203.15
13000	228.32	226.13	224.37	222.94	221.79	220.85	220.08
14000	245.88	243.53	241.63	240.09	238.85	237.84	237.01
15000	263.44	260.92	258.89	257.24	255.91	254.82	253.94
20000	351.26	347.89	345.18	342.99	341.21	339.76	338.59
25000	439.07	434.87	431.48	428.73	426.51	424.71	423.24
30000	526.89	521.84	517.77	514.48	511.81	509.65	507.88
35000	614.70	608.81	604.07	600.23	597.12	594.59	592.53
40000	702.52	695.79	690.36	685.97	682.42	679.53	677.18
45000	790.33	782.76	776.66	771.72	767.72	764.47	761.83
50000	878.15	869.73	862.95	857.47	853.02	849.41	846.47
55000	965.96	956.71	949.25	943.21	938.33	934.35	931.12
56000	983.53	974.10	966.51	960.36	955.39	951.34	948.05
57000	1001.09	991.50	983.76	977.51	972.45	968.33	964.98
58000	1018.65	1008.89	1001.02	994.66	989.51	985.32	981.91
59000	1036.21	1026.28	1018.28	1011.81	1006.57	1002.31	998.84
60000	1053.78	1043.68	1035.54	1028.96	1023.63 .	1019.29	1015.77
61000	1071.34	1061.07	1052.80	1046.11	1040.69	1036.28	1032.70
62000	1088.90	1078.47	1070.06	1063.26	1057.75	1053.27	1049.63
63000	1106.47	1095.86	1087.32	1080.41	1074.81	1070.26	1066.56
64000	1124.03	1113.26	1104.58	1097.56	1091.87	1087.25	1083.49
65000	1141.59	1130.65	1121.84	1114.71	1108.93	1104.24	1100.42
70000	1229.41	1217.63	1208.13	1200.46	1194.23	1189.18	1185.06
75000	1317.22	1304.60	1294.43	1286.20	1279.53	1274.12	1269.71
80000	1405.04	1391.57	1380.72	1371.95	1364.84	1359.06	1354.36
85000	1492.85	1478.55	1467.02	1457.70	1450.14	1444.00	1439.01
90000	1580.67	1565.52	1553.31	1543.44	1535.44	1528.94	1523.65
95000	1668.48	1652.49	1639.61	1629.19	1620.74	1613.88	1608.30
100000	1756.30	1739.47	1725.90	1714.94	1706.05	1698.82	1692.95
105000	1844.11	1826.44	1812.20	1800.68	1791.35	1783.77	1777.59
110000	1931.93	1913.41	1898.49	1886.43	1876.65	1868.71	1862.24
120000	2107.56	2087.36	2071.08	2057.92	2047.26	2038.59	2031.54
130000	2283.19	2261.31	2243.67	2229.42	2217.86	2208.47	2200.83
140000	2458.82	2435.25	2416.26	2400.91	2388.47	2378.35	2370.13
150000	2634.44	2609.20	2588.85	2572.40	2559.07	2548.24	2539.42
160000	2810.07	2783.15	2761.44	2743.90	2729.67	2718.12	2708.72
175000	3073.52	3044.07	3020.33	3001.14	2985.58	2972.94	2962.66
200000	3512.59	3478.93	3451.81	3429.87	3412.09	3397.65	3385.90
250000	4390.74	4348.67	4314.76	4287.34	4265.12	4247.06	4232.37
500000	8781.48	8697.33	8629.51	8574.68	8530.23	8494.12	8464.74
1000000	17562.97	17394.66	17259.03	17149.36	17060.46	16988.25	16929.48

MONTHLY PAYMENTS   20.00%

AMOUNT	22 YEARS	23 YEARS	24 YEARS	25 YEARS	30 YEARS	35 YEARS	40 YEARS
100	1.69	1.68	1.68	1.68	1.67	1.67	1.67
200	3.38	3.37	3.36	3.36	3.34	3.34	3.33
500	8.44	8.42	8.41	8.39	8.36	8.34	8.34
1000	16.88	16.84	16.81	16.78	16.71	16.68	16.67
2000	33.76	33.69	33.62	33.57	33.42	33.37	33.35
3000	50.64	50.53	50.43	50.35	50.13	50.05	50.02
4000	67.53	67.37	67.24	67.14	66.84	66.73	66.69
5000	84.41	84.21	84.05	83.92	83.55	83.41	83.36
6000	101.29	101.06	100.86	100.71	100.26	100.10	100.04
7000	118.17	117.90	117.67	117.49	116.97	116.78	116.71
8000	135.05	134.74	134.48	134.28	133.68	133.46	133.38
9000	151.93	151.58	151.30	151.06	150.39	150.15	150.05
10000	168.82	168.43	168.11	167.85	167.10	166.83	166.73
11000	185.70	185.27	184.92	184.63	183.81	183.51	183.40
12000	202.58	202.11	201.73	201.41	200.52	200.19	200.07
13000	219.46	218.95	218.54	218.20	217.23	216.88	216.74
14000	236.34	235.80	235.35	234.98	233.94	233.56	233.42
15000	253.22	252.64	252.16	251.77	250.65	250.24	250.09
20000	337.63	336.85	336.21	335.69	334.20	333.66	333.45
25000	422.04	421.06	420.26	419.61	417.75	417.07	416.82
30000	506.45	505.28	504.32	503.54	501.31	500.48	500.18
35000	590.86	589.49	588.37	587.46	584.86	583.90	583.54
40000	675.26	673.70	672.42	671.38	668.41	667.31	666.91
45000	759.67	757.91	756.48	755.30	751.96	750.73	750.27
50000	844.08	842.13	840.53	839.23	835.51	834.14	833.63
55000	928.49	926.34	924.58	923.15	919.06	917.55	917.00
56000	945.37	943.18	941.39	939.93	935.77	934.24	933.67
57000	962.25	960.02	958.20	956.72	952.48	950.92	950.34
58000	979.13	976.87	975.01	973.50	969.19	967.60	967.01
59000	996.01	993.71	991.83	990.29	985.90	984.28	983.69
60000	1012.89	1010.55	1008.64	1007.07	1002.61	1000.97	1000.36
61000	1029.78	1027.39	1025.45	1023.86	1019.32	1017.65	1017.03
62000	1046.66	1044.24	1042.26	1040.64	1036.03	1034.33	1033.70
63000	1063.54	1061.08	1059.07	1057.42	1052.74	1051.02	1050.38
64000	1080.42	1077.92	1075.88	1074.21	1069.45	1067.70	1067.05
65000	1097.30	1094.76	1092.69	1090.99	1086.16	1084.38	1083.72
70000	1181.71	1178.98	1176.74	1174.92	1169.71	1167.79	1167.08
75000	1266.12	1263.19	1260.79	1258.84	1253.26	1251.21	1250.45
80000	1350.53	1347.40	1344.85	1342.76	1336.81	1334.62	1333.81
85000	1434.93	1431.61	1428.90	1426.68	1420.37	1418.04	1417.17
90000	1519.34	1515.83	1512.95	1510.61	1503.92	1501.45	1500.54
95000	1603.75	1600.04	1597.01	1594.53	1587.47	1584.86	1583.90
100000	1688.16	1684.25	1681.06	1678.45	1671.02	1668.28	1667.26
105000	1772.57	1768.46	1765.11	1762.37	1754.57	1751.69	1750.63
110000	1856.97	1852.68	1849.17	1846.30	1838.12	1835.11	1833.99
120000	2025.79	2021.10	2017.27	2014.14	2005.22	2001.93	2000.72
130000	2194.61	2189.53	2185.38	2181.99	2172.32	2168.76	2167.44
140000	2363.42	2357.95	2353.48	2349.83	2339.43	2335.59	2334.17
150000	2532.24	2526.38	2521.59	2517.68	2506.53	2502.42	2500.90
160000	2701.05	2694.80	2689.70	2685.52	2673.63	2669.25	2667.62
175000	2954.28	2947.44	2941.85	2937.29	2924.28	2919.49	2917.71
200000	3376.32	3368.50	3362.12	3356.90	3342.04	3336.56	3334.53
250000	4220.40	4210.63	4202.65	4196.13	4177.55	4170.70	4168.16
500000	8440.79	8421.25	8405.30	8392.26	8355.09	8341.39	8336.32
1000000	16881.58	16842.51	16810.60	16784.52	16710.19	16682.78	16672.64

Annual Amortization Tables

When a mortgage loan is taken out, the annual amortization of that loan is often overlooked. The annual amortization tables in this section will help you to truly understand a mortgage loan. They show the amount of interest paid and the amount of principal paid in any particular year. They also indicate the total amount of interest paid since the beginning of the mortgage and the total amount of the payments. The current balance column indicates how much is still owed on the mortgage at the end of each year.

These tables are based on a mortgage loan amount of $10,000 with constant monthly payments and interest rate. It is assumed that the first payment is due one month from inception, and that all payments are made when due. The example that follows will help you understand how to use the tables.

Mr. Brown has been paying on a 20-year, 8% mortgage for seven years. The original amount of the loan was $40,000 How much does he still owe?

First find the 8%, 20-year table. Follow across the seventh year row to the current balance column and find $8,096.61. Since Mr. Brown borrowed $40,000 and the table is based on $10,000, multiply all numbers by four. The total still owed by Mr. Brown is $32,386.44. You can also see that $662.69 multiplied by four, or $2,650.76, was paid in interest this year, and $1,364.16 was paid on the principal. During the past seven years Mr. Brown has paid $28,104.40 of which $20,490.84 was interest.

5.00% Annual Amortization
$10,000 Loan Amount

20 Year Term
Payment $66.00

Yr.	Interest This Year	Principal This Year	Interest To Date	Payments To Date	Current Balance
1	$493.22	$298.73	$493.22	$791.95	$9,701.27
2	$477.93	$314.01	$971.15	$1,583.89	$9,387.25
3	$461.87	$330.08	$1,433.01	$2,375.84	$9,057.17
4	$444.98	$346.97	$1,877.99	$3,167.79	$8,710.21
5	$427.23	$364.72	$2,305.22	$3,959.73	$8,345.49
6	$408.57	$383.38	$2,713.79	$4,751.68	$7,962.11
7	$388.95	$402.99	$3,102.74	$5,543.63	$7,559.11
8	$368.34	$423.61	$3,471.08	$6,335.58	$7,135.50
9	$346.66	$445.28	$3,817.74	$7,127.52	$6,690.22
10	$323.88	$468.07	$4,141.62	$7,919.47	$6,222.15
11	$299.93	$492.01	$4,441.55	$8,711.42	$5,730.14
12	$274.76	$517.19	$4,716.32	$9,503.36	$5,212.95
13	$248.30	$543.65	$4,964.62	$10,295.31	$4,669.31
14	$220.49	$571.46	$5,185.10	$11,087.26	$4,097.85
15	$191.25	$600.70	$5,376.36	$11,879.20	$3,497.15
16	$160.52	$631.43	$5,536.87	$12,671.15	$2,865.72
17	$128.21	$663.73	$5,665.09	$13,463.10	$2,201.99
18	$94.25	$697.69	$5,759.34	$14,255.04	$1,504.30
19	$58.56	$733.39	$5,817.90	$15,046.99	$770.91
20	$21.04	$770.91	$5,838.94	$15,838.94	$0.00

5.00% Annual Amortization
$10,000 Loan Amount

25 Year Term
Payment $58.46

Yr.	Interest This Year	Principal This Year	Interest To Date	Payments To Date	Current Balance
1	$495.32	$206.19	$495.32	$701.51	$9,793.81
2	$484.77	$216.74	$980.09	$1,403.02	$9,577.07
3	$473.68	$227.83	$1,453.77	$2,104.52	$9,349.24
4	$462.02	$239.48	$1,915.79	$2,806.03	$9,109.76
5	$449.77	$251.74	$2,365.56	$3,507.54	$8,858.02
6	$436.89	$264.62	$2,802.45	$4,209.05	$8,593.40
7	$423.35	$278.15	$3,225.80	$4,910.56	$8,315.25
8	$409.12	$292.39	$3,634.93	$5,612.06	$8,022.86
9	$394.16	$307.34	$4,029.09	$6,313.57	$7,715.52
10	$378.44	$323.07	$4,407.53	$7,015.08	$7,392.45
11	$361.91	$339.60	$4,769.44	$7,716.59	$7,052.85
12	$344.54	$356.97	$5,113.97	$8,418.10	$6,695.88
13	$326.27	$375.24	$5,440.25	$9,119.60	$6,320.64
14	$307.07	$394.43	$5,747.32	$9,821.11	$5,926.21
15	$286.89	$414.61	$6,034.21	$10,522.62	$5,511.59
16	$265.68	$435.83	$6,299.90	$11,224.13	$5,075.77
17	$243.38	$458.12	$6,543.28	$11,925.64	$4,617.64
18	$219.95	$481.56	$6,763.23	$12,627.14	$4,136.08
19	$195.31	$506.20	$6,958.53	$13,328.65	$3,629.88
20	$169.41	$532.10	$7,127.94	$14,030.16	$3,097.78
21	$142.19	$559.32	$7,270.13	$14,731.67	$2,538.46
22	$113.57	$587.94	$7,383.70	$15,433.18	$1,950.53
23	$83.49	$618.02	$7,467.19	$16,134.69	$1,332.51
24	$51.87	$649.64	$7,519.07	$16,836.19	$682.87
25	$18.64	$682.87	$7,537.70	$17,537.70	$0.00

5.00% Annual Amortization
$10,000 Loan Amount

15 Year Term
Payment $79.08

Yr.	Interest This Year	Principal This Year	Interest To Date	Payments To Date	Current Balance
1	$489.57	$459.39	$489.57	$948.95	$9,540.61
2	$466.06	$482.89	$955.63	$1,897.90	$9,057.73
3	$441.36	$507.59	$1,396.99	$2,846.86	$8,550.13
4	$415.39	$533.56	$1,812.38	$3,795.81	$8,016.57
5	$388.09	$560.86	$2,200.47	$4,744.76	$7,455.71
6	$359.40	$589.56	$2,559.87	$5,693.71	$6,866.15
7	$329.23	$619.72	$2,889.10	$6,642.67	$6,246.43
8	$297.53	$651.42	$3,186.63	$7,591.62	$5,595.01
9	$264.20	$684.75	$3,450.83	$8,540.57	$4,910.26
10	$229.17	$719.79	$3,679.99	$9,489.52	$4,190.47
11	$192.34	$756.61	$3,872.34	$10,438.48	$3,433.86
12	$153.63	$795.32	$4,025.97	$11,387.43	$2,638.54
13	$112.94	$836.01	$4,138.91	$12,336.38	$1,802.53
14	$70.17	$878.78	$4,209.08	$13,285.33	$923.74
15	$25.21	$923.74	$4,234.29	$14,234.29	$0.00

5.00% Annual Amortization
$10,000 Loan Amount

30 Year Term
Payment $53.68

Yr.	Interest This Year	Principal This Year	Interest To Date	Payments To Date	Current Balance
1	$496.65	$147.54	$496.65	$644.19	$9,852.46
2	$489.10	$155.08	$985.75	$1,288.37	$9,697.38
3	$481.17	$163.02	$1,466.92	$1,932.56	$9,534.36
4	$472.83	$171.36	$1,939.74	$2,576.74	$9,363.00
5	$464.06	$180.13	$2,403.80	$3,220.93	$9,182.87
6	$454.84	$189.34	$2,858.65	$3,865.12	$8,993.53
7	$445.16	$199.03	$3,303.80	$4,509.30	$8,794.50
8	$434.97	$209.21	$3,738.78	$5,153.49	$8,585.29
9	$424.27	$219.92	$4,163.05	$5,797.67	$8,365.37
10	$413.02	$231.17	$4,576.07	$6,441.86	$8,134.21
11	$401.19	$242.99	$4,977.26	$7,086.05	$7,891.21
12	$388.76	$255.43	$5,366.02	$7,730.23	$7,635.79
13	$375.69	$268.49	$5,741.71	$8,374.42	$7,367.29
14	$361.96	$282.23	$6,103.66	$9,018.60	$7,085.06
15	$347.52	$296.67	$6,451.18	$9,662.79	$6,788.39
16	$332.34	$311.85	$6,783.52	$10,306.98	$6,476.54
17	$316.38	$327.80	$7,099.90	$10,951.16	$6,148.74
18	$299.61	$344.57	$7,399.51	$11,595.35	$5,804.16
19	$281.98	$362.20	$7,681.49	$12,239.53	$5,441.96
20	$263.45	$380.73	$7,944.95	$12,883.72	$5,061.23
21	$243.97	$400.21	$8,188.92	$13,527.90	$4,661.01
22	$223.49	$420.69	$8,412.41	$14,172.09	$4,240.32
23	$201.97	$442.21	$8,614.39	$14,816.28	$3,798.11
24	$179.35	$464.84	$8,793.74	$15,460.46	$3,333.27
25	$155.57	$488.62	$8,949.30	$16,104.65	$2,844.66
26	$130.57	$513.62	$9,079.87	$16,748.83	$2,331.04
27	$104.29	$539.90	$9,184.16	$17,393.02	$1,791.14
28	$76.67	$567.52	$9,260.83	$18,037.21	$1,223.63
29	$47.63	$596.55	$9,308.47	$18,681.39	$627.07
30	$17.11	$627.07	$9,325.58	$19,325.58	$0.00

5.50% Annual Amortization
$10,000 Loan Amount

20 Year Term
Payment $68.79

Yr.	Interest This Year	Principal This Year	Interest To Date	Payments To Date	Current Balance
1	$542.95	$282.52	$542.95	$825.46	$9,717.48
2	$527.01	$298.45	$1,069.96	$1,650.93	$9,419.03
3	$510.18	$315.29	$1,580.14	$2,476.39	$9,103.74
4	$492.39	$333.07	$2,072.53	$3,301.86	$8,770.67
5	$473.61	$351.86	$2,546.14	$4,127.32	$8,418.81
6	$453.76	$371.71	$2,999.89	$4,952.79	$8,047.11
7	$432.79	$392.67	$3,432.68	$5,778.25	$7,654.43
8	$410.64	$414.82	$3,843.33	$6,603.72	$7,239.61
9	$387.24	$438.22	$4,230.57	$7,429.18	$6,801.38
10	$362.52	$462.94	$4,593.09	$8,254.65	$6,338.44
11	$336.41	$489.06	$4,929.50	$9,080.11	$5,849.38
12	$308.82	$516.64	$5,238.32	$9,905.58	$5,332.74
13	$279.68	$545.79	$5,518.00	$10,731.04	$4,786.95
14	$248.89	$576.57	$5,766.89	$11,556.51	$4,210.38
15	$216.37	$609.10	$5,983.26	$12,381.97	$3,601.29
16	$182.01	$643.45	$6,165.27	$13,207.44	$2,957.83
17	$145.72	$679.75	$6,310.98	$14,032.90	$2,278.08
18	$107.37	$718.09	$6,418.35	$14,858.37	$1,559.99
19	$66.87	$758.60	$6,485.22	$15,683.83	$801.39
20	$24.07	$801.39	$6,509.30	$16,509.30	$0.00

5.50% Annual Amortization
$10,000 Loan Amount

25 Year Term
Payment $61.41

Yr.	Interest This Year	Principal This Year	Interest To Date	Payments To Date	Current Balance
1	$545.22	$191.69	$545.22	$736.90	$9,808.31
2	$534.40	$202.50	$1,079.62	$1,473.81	$9,605.81
3	$522.98	$213.92	$1,602.60	$2,210.71	$9,391.88
4	$510.91	$225.99	$2,113.51	$2,947.62	$9,165.89
5	$498.17	$238.74	$2,611.68	$3,684.52	$8,927.15
6	$484.70	$252.21	$3,096.38	$4,421.43	$8,674.95
7	$470.47	$266.43	$3,566.85	$5,158.33	$8,408.51
8	$455.44	$281.46	$4,022.29	$5,895.24	$8,127.05
9	$439.57	$297.34	$4,461.86	$6,632.14	$7,829.71
10	$422.79	$314.11	$4,884.65	$7,369.05	$7,515.60
11	$405.08	$331.83	$5,289.73	$8,105.95	$7,183.77
12	$386.36	$350.55	$5,676.09	$8,842.86	$6,833.23
13	$366.58	$370.32	$6,042.67	$9,579.76	$6,462.91
14	$345.70	$391.21	$6,388.37	$10,316.67	$6,071.70
15	$323.63	$413.28	$6,712.00	$11,053.57	$5,658.42
16	$300.32	$436.59	$7,012.31	$11,790.48	$5,221.83
17	$275.69	$461.22	$7,288.00	$12,527.38	$4,760.62
18	$249.67	$487.23	$7,537.68	$13,264.29	$4,273.39
19	$222.19	$514.72	$7,759.87	$14,001.19	$3,758.67
20	$193.16	$543.75	$7,953.02	$14,738.10	$3,214.92
21	$162.48	$574.42	$8,115.51	$15,475.00	$2,640.50
22	$130.08	$606.82	$8,245.59	$16,211.91	$2,033.68
23	$95.85	$641.05	$8,341.44	$16,948.81	$1,392.63
24	$59.69	$677.21	$8,401.13	$17,685.72	$715.41
25	$21.49	$715.41	$8,422.62	$18,422.62	$0.00

5.50% Annual Amortization
$10,000 Loan Amount

15 Year Term
Payment $81.71

Yr.	Interest This Year	Principal This Year	Interest To Date	Payments To Date	Current Balance
1	$538.98	$441.52	$538.98	$980.50	$9,558.48
2	$514.08	$466.43	$1,053.06	$1,961.00	$9,092.06
3	$487.77	$492.74	$1,540.82	$2,941.50	$8,599.32
4	$459.97	$520.53	$2,000.79	$3,922.00	$8,078.79
5	$430.61	$549.89	$2,431.40	$4,902.50	$7,528.90
6	$399.59	$580.91	$2,830.99	$5,883.00	$6,947.99
7	$366.82	$613.68	$3,197.81	$6,863.50	$6,334.31
8	$332.21	$648.29	$3,530.02	$7,844.00	$5,686.02
9	$295.64	$684.86	$3,825.66	$8,824.50	$5,001.16
10	$257.01	$723.49	$4,082.67	$9,805.00	$4,277.66
11	$216.20	$764.30	$4,298.86	$10,785.50	$3,513.36
12	$173.08	$807.42	$4,471.94	$11,766.00	$2,705.94
13	$127.54	$852.96	$4,599.48	$12,746.50	$1,852.98
14	$79.42	$901.08	$4,678.91	$13,727.00	$951.90
15	$28.60	$951.90	$4,707.50	$14,707.50	$0.00

5.50% Annual Amortization
$10,000 Loan Amount

30 Year Term
Payment $56.78

Yr.	Interest This Year	Principal This Year	Interest To Date	Payments To Date	Current Balance
1	$546.64	$134.71	$546.64	$681.35	$9,865.29
2	$539.04	$142.31	$1,085.68	$1,362.69	$9,722.98
3	$531.01	$150.33	$1,616.69	$2,044.04	$9,572.65
4	$522.53	$158.81	$2,139.22	$2,725.39	$9,413.83
5	$513.57	$167.77	$2,652.79	$3,406.73	$9,246.06
6	$504.11	$177.24	$3,156.90	$4,088.08	$9,068.82
7	$494.11	$187.23	$3,651.02	$4,769.43	$8,881.59
8	$483.55	$197.80	$4,134.57	$5,450.77	$8,683.79
9	$472.39	$208.95	$4,606.96	$6,132.12	$8,474.84
10	$460.61	$220.74	$5,067.57	$6,813.47	$8,254.10
11	$448.16	$233.19	$5,515.72	$7,494.81	$8,020.91
12	$435.00	$246.35	$5,950.72	$8,176.16	$7,774.56
13	$421.11	$260.24	$6,371.83	$8,857.51	$7,514.32
14	$406.43	$274.92	$6,778.26	$9,538.86	$7,239.40
15	$390.92	$290.43	$7,169.17	$10,220.20	$6,948.97
16	$374.54	$306.81	$7,543.71	$10,901.55	$6,642.16
17	$357.23	$324.12	$7,900.94	$11,582.90	$6,318.04
18	$338.95	$342.40	$8,239.89	$12,264.24	$5,975.64
19	$319.63	$361.71	$8,559.52	$12,945.59	$5,613.93
20	$299.23	$382.12	$8,858.75	$13,626.94	$5,231.81
21	$277.67	$403.67	$9,136.42	$14,308.28	$4,828.14
22	$254.90	$426.44	$9,391.33	$14,989.63	$4,401.70
23	$230.85	$450.50	$9,622.18	$15,670.98	$3,951.20
24	$205.44	$475.91	$9,827.61	$16,352.32	$3,475.29
25	$178.59	$502.75	$10,006.21	$17,033.67	$2,972.54
26	$150.23	$531.11	$10,156.44	$17,715.02	$2,441.42
27	$120.27	$561.07	$10,276.71	$18,396.36	$1,880.35
28	$88.63	$592.72	$10,365.34	$19,077.71	$1,287.63
29	$55.19	$626.16	$10,420.53	$19,759.06	$661.48
30	$19.87	$661.48	$10,440.40	$20,440.40	$0.00

6.00% Annual Amortization
$10,000 Loan Amount

20 Year Term
Payment $71.64

Yr.	Interest This Year	Principal This Year	Interest To Date	Payments To Date	Current Balance
1	$592.74	$266.98	$592.74	$859.72	$9,733.02
2	$576.27	$283.45	$1,169.01	$1,719.43	$9,449.57
3	$558.79	$300.93	$1,727.80	$2,579.15	$9,148.64
4	$540.23	$319.49	$2,268.02	$3,438.87	$8,829.15
5	$520.52	$339.20	$2,788.55	$4,298.59	$8,489.96
6	$499.60	$360.12	$3,288.15	$5,158.30	$8,129.84
7	$477.39	$382.33	$3,765.54	$6,018.02	$7,747.52
8	$453.81	$405.91	$4,219.35	$6,877.74	$7,341.61
9	$428.77	$430.94	$4,648.12	$7,737.46	$6,910.67
10	$402.19	$457.52	$5,050.31	$8,597.17	$6,453.14
11	$373.97	$485.74	$5,424.29	$9,456.89	$5,967.40
12	$344.02	$515.70	$5,768.31	$10,316.61	$5,451.70
13	$312.21	$547.51	$6,080.51	$11,176.32	$4,904.19
14	$278.44	$581.28	$6,358.95	$12,036.04	$4,322.91
15	$242.59	$617.13	$6,601.54	$12,895.76	$3,705.78
16	$204.52	$655.19	$6,806.06	$13,755.48	$3,050.59
17	$164.11	$695.60	$6,970.18	$14,615.19	$2,354.98
18	$121.27	$738.51	$7,091.38	$15,474.91	$1,616.47
19	$75.66	$784.06	$7,167.04	$16,334.63	$832.42
20	$27.30	$832.42	$7,194.35	$17,194.35	$0.00

6.00% Annual Amortization
$10,000 Loan Amount

25 Year Term
Payment $64.43

Yr.	Interest This Year	Principal This Year	Interest To Date	Payments To Date	Current Balance
1	$595.16	$178.00	$595.16	$773.16	$9,822.00
2	$584.18	$188.98	$1,179.34	$1,546.32	$9,633.01
3	$572.52	$200.64	$1,751.86	$2,319.49	$9,432.37
4	$560.15	$213.01	$2,312.01	$3,092.65	$9,219.36
5	$547.01	$226.15	$2,859.02	$3,865.81	$8,993.21
6	$533.06	$240.10	$3,392.08	$4,638.97	$8,753.11
7	$518.25	$254.91	$3,910.33	$5,412.13	$8,498.20
8	$502.53	$270.63	$4,412.86	$6,185.29	$8,227.57
9	$485.84	$287.32	$4,898.70	$6,958.46	$7,940.24
10	$468.12	$305.05	$5,366.81	$7,731.62	$7,635.20
11	$449.30	$323.86	$5,816.12	$8,504.78	$7,311.34
12	$429.33	$343.83	$6,245.44	$9,277.94	$6,967.50
13	$408.12	$365.04	$6,653.56	$10,051.10	$6,602.46
14	$385.61	$387.56	$7,039.17	$10,824.26	$6,214.91
15	$361.70	$411.46	$7,400.87	$11,597.43	$5,803.45
16	$336.32	$436.84	$7,737.19	$12,370.59	$5,366.61
17	$309.38	$463.78	$8,046.57	$13,143.75	$4,902.83
18	$280.78	$492.39	$8,327.35	$13,916.91	$4,410.44
19	$250.41	$522.76	$8,577.76	$14,690.07	$3,887.68
20	$218.16	$555.00	$8,795.92	$15,463.23	$3,332.69
21	$183.93	$589.23	$8,979.85	$16,236.40	$2,743.46
22	$147.59	$625.57	$9,127.44	$17,009.56	$2,117.88
23	$109.01	$664.16	$9,236.45	$17,782.72	$1,453.73
24	$68.04	$705.12	$9,304.49	$18,555.88	$748.61
25	$24.55	$748.61	$9,329.04	$19,329.04	$0.00

6.00% Annual Amortization
$10,000 Loan Amount

15 Year Term
Payment $84.39

Yr.	Interest This Year	Principal This Year	Interest To Date	Payments To Date	Current Balance
1	$588.46	$424.17	$588.46	$1,012.63	$9,575.83
2	$562.30	$450.33	$1,150.76	$2,025.26	$9,125.50
3	$534.52	$478.10	$1,685.29	$3,037.88	$8,647.40
4	$505.04	$507.59	$2,190.32	$4,050.51	$8,139.81
5	$473.73	$538.90	$2,664.05	$5,063.14	$7,600.91
6	$440.49	$572.14	$3,104.54	$6,075.77	$7,028.77
7	$405.20	$607.43	$3,509.74	$7,088.40	$6,421.35
8	$367.74	$644.89	$3,877.48	$8,101.03	$5,776.46
9	$327.96	$684.67	$4,205.44	$9,113.65	$5,091.79
10	$285.73	$726.89	$4,491.18	$10,126.28	$4,364.90
11	$240.90	$771.73	$4,732.08	$11,138.91	$3,593.17
12	$193.30	$819.33	$4,925.38	$12,151.54	$2,773.84
13	$142.77	$869.86	$5,068.15	$13,164.17	$1,903.98
14	$89.12	$923.51	$5,157.27	$14,176.79	$980.47
15	$32.16	$980.47	$5,189.42	$15,189.42	$0.00

6.00% Annual Amortization
$10,000 Loan Amount

30 Year Term
Payment $59.96

Yr.	Interest This Year	Principal This Year	Interest To Date	Payments To Date	Current Balance
1	$596.66	$122.80	$596.66	$719.46	$9,877.20
2	$589.09	$130.38	$1,185.74	$1,438.92	$9,746.82
3	$581.04	$138.42	$1,766.79	$2,158.38	$9,608.41
4	$572.51	$146.95	$2,339.30	$2,877.84	$9,461.45
5	$563.44	$156.02	$2,902.74	$3,597.30	$9,305.44
6	$553.82	$165.64	$3,456.56	$4,316.76	$9,139.80
7	$543.60	$175.86	$4,000.16	$5,036.22	$8,963.94
8	$532.76	$186.70	$4,532.92	$5,755.69	$8,777.24
9	$521.24	$198.22	$5,054.16	$6,475.15	$8,579.02
10	$509.02	$210.44	$5,563.18	$7,194.61	$8,368.57
11	$496.04	$223.42	$6,059.22	$7,914.07	$8,145.15
12	$482.26	$237.20	$6,541.47	$8,633.53	$7,907.94
13	$467.63	$251.83	$7,009.10	$9,352.99	$7,656.11
14	$452.09	$267.37	$7,461.19	$10,072.45	$7,388.74
15	$435.60	$283.86	$7,896.79	$10,791.91	$7,104.88
16	$418.10	$301.37	$8,314.89	$11,511.37	$6,803.52
17	$399.51	$319.95	$8,714.40	$12,230.83	$6,483.57
18	$379.77	$339.69	$9,094.17	$12,950.29	$6,143.88
19	$358.82	$360.64	$9,452.99	$13,669.75	$5,783.24
20	$336.58	$382.88	$9,789.57	$14,389.21	$5,400.36
21	$312.96	$406.50	$10,102.53	$15,108.67	$4,993.86
22	$287.89	$431.57	$10,390.43	$15,828.13	$4,562.29
23	$261.27	$458.19	$10,651.70	$16,547.59	$4,104.11
24	$233.01	$486.45	$10,884.71	$17,267.06	$3,617.66
25	$203.01	$516.45	$11,087.72	$17,986.52	$3,101.21
26	$171.16	$548.30	$11,258.88	$18,705.98	$2,552.91
27	$137.34	$582.12	$11,396.22	$19,425.44	$1,970.78
28	$101.43	$618.03	$11,497.66	$20,144.90	$1,352.76
29	$63.32	$656.14	$11,560.97	$20,864.36	$696.61
30	$22.85	$696.61	$11,583.82	$21,583.82	$0.00

6.50% Annual Amortization
$10,000 Loan Amount

20 Year Term
Payment $74.56

Yr.	Interest This Year	Principal This Year	Interest To Date	Payments To Date	Current Balance
1	$642.58	$252.11	$642.58	$894.69	$9,747.89
2	$625.69	$268.99	$1,268.27	$1,789.38	$9,478.89
3	$607.68	$287.01	$1,875.95	$2,684.06	$9,191.88
4	$588.46	$306.23	$2,464.40	$3,578.75	$8,885.65
5	$567.95	$326.74	$3,032.35	$4,473.44	$8,558.91
6	$546.06	$348.62	$3,578.42	$5,368.13	$8,210.29
7	$522.72	$371.97	$4,101.13	$6,262.81	$7,838.32
8	$497.81	$396.88	$4,598.94	$7,157.50	$7,441.44
9	$471.23	$423.46	$5,070.16	$8,052.19	$7,017.97
10	$442.87	$451.82	$5,513.03	$8,946.88	$6,566.15
11	$412.61	$482.08	$5,925.63	$9,841.57	$6,084.07
12	$380.32	$514.37	$6,305.95	$10,736.25	$5,569.70
13	$345.87	$548.82	$6,651.83	$11,630.94	$5,020.89
14	$309.12	$585.57	$6,960.94	$12,525.63	$4,435.31
15	$269.90	$624.79	$7,230.84	$13,420.32	$3,810.53
16	$228.06	$666.63	$7,458.90	$14,315.00	$3,143.89
17	$183.41	$711.28	$7,642.31	$15,209.69	$2,432.62
18	$135.78	$758.91	$7,778.09	$16,104.38	$1,673.71
19	$84.95	$809.74	$7,863.04	$16,999.07	$863.97
20	$30.72	$863.97	$7,893.76	$17,893.76	$0.00

6.50% Annual Amortization
$10,000 Loan Amount

25 Year Term
Payment $67.52

Yr.	Interest This Year	Principal This Year	Interest To Date	Payments To Date	Current Balance
1	$645.14	$165.11	$645.14	$810.25	$9,834.89
2	$634.08	$176.17	$1,279.22	$1,620.50	$9,658.72
3	$622.28	$187.97	$1,901.50	$2,430.75	$9,470.76
4	$609.69	$200.55	$2,511.20	$3,240.99	$9,270.20
5	$596.26	$213.99	$3,107.46	$4,051.24	$9,056.22
6	$581.93	$228.32	$3,689.39	$4,861.49	$8,827.90
7	$566.64	$243.61	$4,256.03	$5,671.74	$8,584.29
8	$550.33	$259.92	$4,806.36	$6,481.99	$8,324.37
9	$532.92	$277.33	$5,339.28	$7,292.24	$8,047.04
10	$514.35	$295.90	$5,853.62	$8,102.49	$7,751.14
11	$494.53	$315.72	$6,348.15	$8,912.73	$7,435.42
12	$473.38	$336.86	$6,821.53	$9,722.98	$7,098.55
13	$450.82	$359.43	$7,272.36	$10,533.23	$6,739.13
14	$426.75	$383.50	$7,699.11	$11,343.48	$6,355.63
15	$401.07	$409.18	$8,100.18	$12,153.73	$5,946.45
16	$373.66	$436.58	$8,473.84	$12,963.98	$5,509.86
17	$344.43	$465.82	$8,818.27	$13,774.23	$5,044.04
18	$313.23	$497.02	$9,131.50	$14,584.47	$4,547.02
19	$279.94	$530.31	$9,411.44	$15,394.72	$4,016.72
20	$244.43	$565.82	$9,655.87	$16,204.97	$3,450.89
21	$206.53	$603.72	$9,862.40	$17,015.22	$2,847.18
22	$166.10	$644.15	$10,028.50	$17,825.47	$2,203.03
23	$122.96	$687.29	$10,151.46	$18,635.72	$1,515.74
24	$76.93	$733.32	$10,228.39	$19,445.97	$782.43
25	$27.82	$782.43	$10,256.21	$20,256.21	$0.00

6.50% Annual Amortization
$10,000 Loan Amount

15 Year Term
Payment $87.11

Yr.	Interest This Year	Principal This Year	Interest To Date	Payments To Date	Current Balance
1	$638.01	$407.32	$638.01	$1,045.33	$9,592.68
2	$610.73	$434.60	$1,248.74	$2,090.66	$9,158.08
3	$581.62	$463.71	$1,830.36	$3,135.99	$8,694.37
4	$550.57	$494.76	$2,380.92	$4,181.32	$8,199.61
5	$517.43	$527.90	$2,898.36	$5,226.64	$7,671.71
6	$482.08	$563.25	$3,380.43	$6,271.97	$7,108.46
7	$444.36	$600.97	$3,824.79	$7,317.30	$6,507.49
8	$404.11	$641.22	$4,228.90	$8,362.63	$5,866.27
9	$361.16	$684.17	$4,590.06	$9,407.96	$5,182.10
10	$315.34	$729.99	$4,905.40	$10,453.29	$4,452.11
11	$266.46	$778.87	$5,171.86	$11,498.62	$3,673.24
12	$214.29	$831.04	$5,386.15	$12,543.95	$2,842.20
13	$158.64	$886.69	$5,544.79	$13,589.27	$1,955.51
14	$99.25	$946.08	$5,644.04	$14,634.60	$1,009.44
15	$35.89	$1,009.44	$5,679.93	$15,679.93	$0.00

6.50% Annual Amortization
$10,000 Loan Amount

30 Year Term
Payment $63.21

Yr.	Interest This Year	Principal This Year	Interest To Date	Payments To Date	Current Balance
1	$646.71	$111.77	$646.71	$758.48	$9,888.23
2	$639.22	$119.26	$1,285.93	$1,516.96	$9,768.97
3	$631.24	$127.25	$1,917.17	$2,275.44	$9,641.72
4	$622.71	$135.77	$2,539.88	$3,033.93	$9,505.96
5	$613.62	$144.86	$3,153.51	$3,792.41	$9,361.10
6	$603.92	$154.56	$3,757.43	$4,550.89	$9,206.54
7	$593.57	$164.91	$4,351.00	$5,309.37	$9,041.62
8	$582.52	$175.96	$4,933.52	$6,067.85	$8,865.67
9	$570.74	$187.74	$5,504.26	$6,826.33	$8,677.93
10	$558.17	$200.31	$6,062.43	$7,584.82	$8,477.61
11	$544.75	$213.73	$6,607.18	$8,343.30	$8,263.88
12	$530.44	$228.04	$7,137.62	$9,101.78	$8,035.84
13	$515.17	$243.32	$7,652.78	$9,860.26	$7,792.52
14	$498.87	$259.61	$8,151.65	$10,618.74	$7,532.91
15	$481.48	$277.00	$8,633.14	$11,377.22	$7,255.91
16	$462.93	$295.55	$9,096.07	$12,135.71	$6,960.37
17	$443.14	$315.34	$9,539.21	$12,894.19	$6,645.02
18	$422.02	$336.46	$9,961.23	$13,652.67	$6,308.56
19	$399.49	$359.00	$10,360.72	$14,411.15	$5,949.57
20	$375.44	$383.04	$10,736.16	$15,169.63	$5,566.53
21	$349.79	$408.69	$11,085.95	$15,928.11	$5,157.84
22	$322.42	$436.06	$11,408.37	$16,686.60	$4,721.78
23	$293.22	$465.26	$11,701.59	$17,445.08	$4,256.51
24	$262.06	$496.42	$11,963.65	$18,203.56	$3,760.09
25	$228.81	$529.67	$12,192.46	$18,962.04	$3,230.42
26	$193.34	$565.14	$12,385.79	$19,720.52	$2,665.27
27	$155.49	$602.99	$12,541.28	$20,479.00	$2,062.28
28	$115.11	$643.38	$12,656.39	$21,237.49	$1,418.90
29	$72.02	$686.46	$12,728.41	$21,995.97	$732.44
30	$26.04	$732.44	$12,754.45	$22,754.45	$0.00

7.00% Annual Amortization
$10,000 Loan Amount
20 Year Term
Payment $77.53

Yr.	Interest This Year	Principal This Year	Interest To Date	Payments To Date	Current Balance
1	$692.46	$237.90	$692.46	$930.36	$9,762.10
2	$675.27	$255.09	$1,367.73	$1,860.72	$9,507.01
3	$656.83	$273.53	$2,024.56	$2,791.08	$9,233.48
4	$637.05	$293.31	$2,661.61	$3,721.43	$8,940.17
5	$615.85	$314.51	$3,277.46	$4,651.79	$8,625.66
6	$593.11	$337.25	$3,870.57	$5,582.15	$8,288.42
7	$568.73	$361.63	$4,439.30	$6,512.51	$7,926.79
8	$542.59	$387.77	$4,981.89	$7,442.87	$7,539.02
9	$514.56	$415.80	$5,496.45	$8,373.23	$7,123.22
10	$484.50	$445.86	$5,980.95	$9,303.59	$6,677.37
11	$452.27	$478.09	$6,433.22	$10,233.95	$6,199.28
12	$417.71	$512.65	$6,850.93	$11,164.30	$5,686.63
13	$380.65	$549.71	$7,231.58	$12,094.66	$5,136.92
14	$340.91	$589.45	$7,572.49	$13,025.02	$4,547.47
15	$298.30	$632.06	$7,870.80	$13,955.38	$3,915.41
16	$252.61	$677.75	$8,123.40	$14,885.74	$3,237.66
17	$203.61	$726.74	$8,327.02	$15,816.10	$2,510.92
18	$151.08	$779.28	$8,478.09	$16,746.46	$1,731.64
19	$94.74	$835.62	$8,572.84	$17,676.82	$896.02
20	$34.34	$896.02	$8,607.17	$18,607.17	$0.00

7.00% Annual Amortization
$10,000 Loan Amount
25 Year Term
Payment $70.68

Yr.	Interest This Year	Principal This Year	Interest To Date	Payments To Date	Current Balance
1	$695.15	$152.98	$695.15	$848.14	$9,847.02
2	$684.09	$164.04	$1,379.25	$1,696.27	$9,682.98
3	$672.24	$175.90	$2,051.48	$2,544.41	$9,507.08
4	$659.52	$188.61	$2,711.00	$3,392.54	$9,318.46
5	$645.89	$202.25	$3,356.89	$4,240.68	$9,116.22
6	$631.26	$216.87	$3,988.16	$5,088.81	$8,899.35
7	$615.59	$232.55	$4,603.74	$5,936.95	$8,666.80
8	$598.78	$249.36	$5,202.52	$6,785.08	$8,417.44
9	$580.75	$267.38	$5,783.27	$7,633.22	$8,150.05
10	$561.42	$286.71	$6,344.69	$8,481.35	$7,863.34
11	$540.69	$307.44	$6,885.38	$9,329.49	$7,555.90
12	$518.47	$329.67	$7,403.85	$10,177.62	$7,226.23
13	$494.64	$353.50	$7,898.49	$11,025.76	$6,872.74
14	$469.08	$379.05	$8,367.58	$11,873.89	$6,493.68
15	$441.68	$406.45	$8,809.26	$12,722.03	$6,087.23
16	$412.30	$435.84	$9,221.56	$13,570.16	$5,651.40
17	$380.79	$467.34	$9,602.35	$14,418.30	$5,184.05
18	$347.01	$501.13	$9,949.36	$15,266.43	$4,682.93
19	$310.78	$537.35	$10,260.14	$16,114.57	$4,145.57
20	$271.94	$576.20	$10,532.08	$16,962.70	$3,569.38
21	$230.28	$617.85	$10,762.36	$17,810.84	$2,951.52
22	$185.62	$662.52	$10,947.98	$18,658.97	$2,289.01
23	$137.73	$710.41	$11,085.70	$19,507.11	$1,578.60
24	$86.37	$761.77	$11,172.07	$20,355.24	$816.83
25	$31.30	$816.83	$11,203.38	$21,203.38	$0.00

7.00% Annual Amortization
$10,000 Loan Amount

15 Year Term
Payment $89.88

Yr.	Interest This Year	Principal This Year	Interest To Date	Payments To Date	Current Balance
1	$687.61	$390.98	$687.61	$1,078.59	$9,609.02
2	$659.35	$419.24	$1,346.96	$2,157.19	$9,189.78
3	$629.04	$449.55	$1,976.01	$3,235.78	$8,740.23
4	$596.54	$482.05	$2,572.55	$4,314.38	$8,258.18
5	$561.70	$516.90	$3,134.25	$5,392.97	$7,741.28
6	$524.33	$554.26	$3,658.58	$6,471.56	$7,187.02
7	$484.26	$594.33	$4,142.84	$7,550.16	$6,592.69
8	$441.30	$637.29	$4,584.14	$8,628.75	$5,955.39
9	$395.23	$683.36	$4,979.37	$9,707.35	$5,272.03
10	$345.83	$732.77	$5,325.20	$10,785.94	$4,539.26
11	$292.86	$785.74	$5,618.06	$11,864.53	$3,753.52
12	$236.06	$842.54	$5,854.11	$12,943.13	$2,910.99
13	$175.15	$903.45	$6,029.26	$14,021.72	$2,007.54
14	$109.84	$968.76	$6,139.10	$15,100.31	$1,038.79
15	$39.81	$1,038.79	$6,178.91	$16,178.91	$0.00

7.00% Annual Amortization
$10,000 Loan Amount

30 Year Term
Payment $66.53

Yr.	Interest This Year	Principal This Year	Interest To Date	Payments To Date	Current Balance
1	$696.78	$101.58	$696.78	$798.36	$9,898.42
2	$689.44	$108.92	$1,386.22	$1,596.73	$9,789.49
3	$681.56	$116.80	$2,067.79	$2,395.09	$9,672.70
4	$673.12	$125.24	$2,740.91	$3,193.45	$9,547.45
5	$664.07	$134.30	$3,404.97	$3,991.81	$9,413.16
6	$654.36	$144.00	$4,059.33	$4,790.18	$9,269.16
7	$643.95	$154.41	$4,703.28	$5,588.54	$9,114.74
8	$632.79	$165.58	$5,336.07	$6,386.90	$8,949.17
9	$620.82	$177.55	$5,956.89	$7,185.27	$8,771.62
10	$607.98	$190.38	$6,564.87	$7,983.63	$8,581.24
11	$594.22	$204.14	$7,159.09	$8,781.99	$8,377.09
12	$579.46	$218.90	$7,738.55	$9,580.36	$8,158.19
13	$563.64	$234.73	$8,302.19	$10,378.72	$7,923.47
14	$546.67	$251.69	$8,848.86	$11,177.08	$7,671.78
15	$528.47	$269.89	$9,377.33	$11,975.44	$7,401.89
16	$508.96	$289.40	$9,886.30	$12,773.81	$7,112.49
17	$488.04	$310.32	$10,374.34	$13,572.17	$6,802.17
18	$465.61	$332.75	$10,839.95	$14,370.53	$6,469.42
19	$441.56	$356.81	$11,281.51	$15,168.90	$6,112.61
20	$415.76	$382.60	$11,697.27	$15,967.26	$5,730.01
21	$388.10	$410.26	$12,085.37	$16,765.62	$5,319.75
22	$358.45	$439.92	$12,443.82	$17,563.99	$4,879.83
23	$326.64	$471.72	$12,770.46	$18,362.35	$4,408.11
24	$292.54	$505.82	$13,063.01	$19,160.71	$3,902.29
25	$255.98	$542.38	$13,318.99	$19,959.07	$3,359.91
26	$216.77	$581.59	$13,535.75	$20,757.44	$2,778.32
27	$174.73	$623.64	$13,710.48	$21,555.80	$2,154.68
28	$129.64	$668.72	$13,840.12	$22,354.16	$1,485.96
29	$81.30	$717.06	$13,921.42	$23,152.53	$768.90
30	$29.46	$768.90	$13,950.89	$23,950.89	$0.00

7.50% Annual Amortization
$10,000 Loan Amount
20 Year Term
Payment $80.56

Yr.	Interest This Year	Principal This Year	Interest To Date	Payments To Date	Current Balance
1	$742.39	$224.32	$742.39	$966.71	$9,775.68
2	$724.98	$241.73	$1,467.37	$1,933.42	$9,533.95
3	$706.21	$260.50	$2,173.58	$2,900.14	$9,273.45
4	$685.99	$280.72	$2,859.57	$3,866.85	$8,992.73
5	$664.20	$302.52	$3,523.77	$4,833.56	$8,690.21
6	$640.71	$326.00	$4,164.48	$5,800.27	$8,364.21
7	$615.40	$351.31	$4,779.88	$6,766.98	$8,012.90
8	$588.13	$378.58	$5,368.01	$7,733.69	$7,634.32
9	$558.74	$407.97	$5,926.75	$8,700.41	$7,226.34
10	$527.07	$439.64	$6,453.82	$9,667.12	$6,786.70
11	$492.94	$473.78	$6,946.75	$10,633.83	$6,312.92
12	$456.16	$510.56	$7,402.91	$11,600.54	$5,802.37
13	$416.52	$550.19	$7,819.43	$12,567.25	$5,252.18
14	$373.81	$592.90	$8,193.24	$13,533.97	$4,659.27
15	$327.78	$638.93	$8,521.02	$14,500.68	$4,020.34
16	$278.18	$688.54	$8,799.19	$15,467.39	$3,331.80
17	$224.72	$741.99	$9,023.92	$16,434.10	$2,589.81
18	$167.12	$799.59	$9,191.04	$17,400.81	$1,790.22
19	$105.05	$861.67	$9,296.08	$18,367.52	$928.56
20	$38.15	$928.56	$9,334.24	$19,334.24	$0.00

7.50% Annual Amortization
$10,000 Loan Amount
25 Year Term
Payment $73.90

Yr.	Interest This Year	Principal This Year	Interest To Date	Payments To Date	Current Balance
1	$745.20	$141.59	$745.20	$886.79	$9,858.41
2	$734.21	$152.58	$1,479.40	$1,773.58	$9,705.83
3	$722.36	$164.43	$2,201.77	$2,660.37	$9,541.40
4	$709.60	$177.19	$2,911.36	$3,547.16	$9,364.20
5	$695.84	$190.95	$3,607.20	$4,433.95	$9,173.25
6	$681.02	$205.77	$4,288.22	$5,320.74	$8,967.48
7	$665.04	$221.75	$4,953.26	$6,207.53	$8,745.73
8	$647.83	$238.96	$5,601.09	$7,094.32	$8,506.77
9	$629.28	$257.51	$6,230.36	$7,981.10	$8,249.26
10	$609.28	$277.51	$6,839.65	$8,867.89	$7,971.75
11	$587.74	$299.05	$7,427.39	$9,754.68	$7,672.70
12	$564.52	$322.27	$7,991.91	$10,641.47	$7,350.44
13	$539.51	$347.28	$8,531.42	$11,528.26	$7,003.15
14	$512.55	$374.24	$9,043.96	$12,415.05	$6,628.91
15	$483.49	$403.30	$9,527.45	$13,301.84	$6,225.61
16	$452.18	$434.61	$9,979.64	$14,188.63	$5,791.01
17	$418.44	$468.35	$10,398.08	$15,075.42	$5,322.66
18	$382.08	$504.70	$10,780.16	$15,962.21	$4,817.95
19	$342.90	$543.89	$11,123.07	$16,849.00	$4,274.07
20	$300.68	$586.11	$11,423.75	$17,735.79	$3,687.96
21	$255.18	$631.61	$11,678.92	$18,622.58	$3,056.35
22	$206.14	$680.64	$11,885.07	$19,509.37	$2,375.70
23	$153.30	$733.48	$12,038.37	$20,396.16	$1,642.22
24	$96.36	$790.43	$12,134.74	$21,282.95	$851.79
25	$35.00	$851.79	$12,169.74	$22,169.74	$0.00

7.50% Annual Amortization
$10,000 Loan Amount

15 Year Term
Payment $92.70

Yr.	Interest This Year	Principal This Year	Interest To Date	Payments To Date	Current Balance
1	$737.28	$375.14	$737.28	$1,112.41	$9,624.86
2	$708.16	$404.26	$1,445.43	$2,224.83	$9,220.61
3	$676.77	$435.64	$2,122.21	$3,337.24	$8,784.96
4	$642.95	$469.46	$2,765.16	$4,449.66	$8,315.50
5	$606.51	$505.91	$3,371.67	$5,562.07	$7,809.59
6	$567.23	$545.18	$3,938.90	$6,674.49	$7,264.41
7	$524.91	$587.51	$4,463.81	$7,786.90	$6,676.90
8	$479.30	$633.12	$4,943.10	$8,899.32	$6,043.78
9	$430.15	$682.27	$5,373.25	$10,011.73	$5,361.52
10	$377.18	$735.23	$5,750.43	$11,124.15	$4,626.28
11	$320.10	$792.31	$6,070.54	$12,236.56	$3,833.97
12	$258.59	$853.82	$6,329.13	$13,348.98	$2,980.15
13	$192.31	$920.11	$6,521.44	$14,461.39	$2,060.05
14	$120.88	$991.54	$6,642.32	$15,573.81	$1,068.51
15	$43.90	$1,068.51	$6,686.22	$16,686.22	$0.00

7.50% Annual Amortization
$10,000 Loan Amount

30 Year Term
Payment $69.92

Yr.	Interest This Year	Principal This Year	Interest To Date	Payments To Date	Current Balance
1	$746.87	$92.18	$746.87	$839.06	$9,907.82
2	$739.72	$99.34	$1,486.59	$1,678.11	$9,808.48
3	$732.01	$107.05	$2,218.60	$2,517.17	$9,701.42
4	$723.69	$115.36	$2,942.29	$3,356.23	$9,586.06
5	$714.74	$124.32	$3,657.03	$4,195.29	$9,461.74
6	$705.09	$133.97	$4,362.12	$5,034.34	$9,327.77
7	$694.69	$144.37	$5,056.81	$5,873.40	$9,183.40
8	$683.48	$155.58	$5,740.29	$6,712.46	$9,027.83
9	$671.40	$167.66	$6,411.69	$7,551.52	$8,860.17
10	$658.39	$180.67	$7,070.07	$8,390.57	$8,679.50
11	$644.36	$194.70	$7,714.43	$9,229.63	$8,484.80
12	$629.25	$209.81	$8,343.68	$10,068.69	$8,274.99
13	$612.96	$226.10	$8,956.63	$10,907.75	$8,048.89
14	$595.40	$243.65	$9,552.04	$11,746.80	$7,805.24
15	$576.49	$262.57	$10,128.53	$12,585.86	$7,542.67
16	$556.10	$282.95	$10,684.63	$13,424.92	$7,259.71
17	$534.14	$304.92	$11,218.77	$14,263.98	$6,954.79
18	$510.47	$328.59	$11,729.24	$15,103.03	$6,626.20
19	$484.96	$354.10	$12,214.20	$15,942.09	$6,272.10
20	$457.47	$381.59	$12,671.66	$16,781.15	$5,890.51
21	$427.84	$411.21	$13,099.51	$17,620.21	$5,479.30
22	$395.92	$443.14	$13,495.43	$18,459.26	$5,036.16
23	$361.52	$477.54	$13,856.95	$19,298.32	$4,558.63
24	$324.45	$514.61	$14,181.39	$20,137.38	$4,044.01
25	$284.50	$554.56	$14,465.89	$20,976.44	$3,489.45
26	$241.44	$597.61	$14,707.33	$21,815.49	$2,891.84
27	$195.05	$644.01	$14,902.38	$22,654.55	$2,247.83
28	$145.05	$694.00	$15,047.43	$23,493.61	$1,553.82
29	$91.18	$747.88	$15,138.61	$24,332.66	$805.94
30	$33.12	$805.94	$15,171.72	$25,171.72	$0.00

8.00% Annual Amortization
$10,000 Loan Amount
20 Year Term
Payment $83.64

Yr.	Interest This Year	Principal This Year	Interest To Date	Payments To Date	Current Balance
1	$792.36	$211.37	$792.36	$1,003.73	$9,788.63
2	$774.82	$228.91	$1,567.18	$2,007.46	$9,559.72
3	$755.82	$247.91	$2,323.00	$3,011.18	$9,311.81
4	$735.24	$268.49	$3,058.24	$4,014.91	$9,043.33
5	$712.96	$290.77	$3,771.20	$5,018.64	$8,752.56
6	$688.82	$314.90	$4,460.02	$6,022.37	$8,437.65
7	$662.69	$341.04	$5,122.71	$7,026.10	$8,096.61
8	$634.38	$369.35	$5,757.09	$8,029.82	$7,727.27
9	$603.73	$400.00	$6,360.82	$9,033.55	$7,327.27
10	$570.53	$433.20	$6,931.34	$10,037.28	$6,894.06
11	$534.57	$469.16	$7,465.91	$11,041.01	$6,424.91
12	$495.63	$508.10	$7,961.54	$12,044.74	$5,916.81
13	$453.46	$550.27	$8,415.00	$13,048.47	$5,366.54
14	$407.79	$595.94	$8,822.79	$14,052.19	$4,770.60
15	$358.32	$645.40	$9,181.11	$15,055.92	$4,125.19
16	$304.76	$698.97	$9,485.87	$16,059.65	$3,426.22
17	$246.74	$756.99	$9,732.61	$17,063.38	$2,669.23
18	$183.91	$819.82	$9,916.52	$18,067.11	$1,849.41
19	$115.87	$887.86	$10,032.39	$19,070.83	$961.55
20	$42.17	$961.55	$10,074.56	$20,074.56	$0.00

8.00% Annual Amortization
$10,000 Loan Amount
25 Year Term
Payment $77.18

Yr.	Interest This Year	Principal This Year	Interest To Date	Payments To Date	Current Balance
1	$795.27	$130.91	$795.27	$926.18	$9,869.09
2	$784.40	$141.78	$1,579.67	$1,852.36	$9,727.31
3	$772.64	$153.54	$2,352.31	$2,778.54	$9,573.77
4	$759.89	$166.29	$3,112.20	$3,704.72	$9,407.48
5	$746.09	$180.09	$3,858.29	$4,630.90	$9,227.39
6	$731.14	$195.04	$4,589.43	$5,557.08	$9,032.36
7	$714.96	$211.22	$5,304.39	$6,483.26	$8,821.13
8	$697.42	$228.76	$6,001.81	$7,409.44	$8,592.38
9	$678.44	$247.74	$6,680.25	$8,335.62	$8,344.64
10	$657.87	$268.30	$7,338.13	$9,261.79	$8,076.33
11	$635.61	$290.57	$7,973.73	$10,187.97	$7,785.76
12	$611.49	$314.69	$8,585.22	$11,114.15	$7,471.07
13	$585.37	$340.81	$9,170.59	$12,040.33	$7,130.25
14	$557.08	$369.10	$9,727.67	$12,966.51	$6,761.16
15	$526.45	$399.73	$10,254.12	$13,892.69	$6,361.42
16	$493.27	$432.91	$10,747.38	$14,818.87	$5,928.51
17	$457.34	$468.84	$11,204.72	$15,745.05	$5,459.67
18	$418.42	$507.76	$11,623.15	$16,671.23	$4,951.92
19	$376.28	$549.90	$11,999.43	$17,597.41	$4,402.02
20	$330.64	$595.54	$12,330.07	$18,523.59	$3,806.48
21	$281.21	$644.97	$12,611.28	$19,449.77	$3,161.51
22	$227.68	$698.50	$12,838.95	$20,375.95	$2,463.00
23	$169.70	$756.48	$13,008.66	$21,302.13	$1,706.53
24	$106.91	$819.26	$13,115.57	$22,228.31	$887.26
25	$38.92	$887.26	$13,154.49	$23,154.49	$0.00

8.00% Annual Amortization
$10,000 Loan Amount

15 Year Term
Payment $95.57

Yr.	Interest This Year	Principal This Year	Interest To Date	Payments To Date	Current Balance
1	$787.00	$359.78	$787.00	$1,146.78	$9,640.22
2	$757.14	$389.65	$1,544.13	$2,293.57	$9,250.57
3	$724.80	$421.99	$2,268.93	$3,440.35	$8,828.58
4	$689.77	$457.01	$2,958.70	$4,587.13	$8,371.57
5	$651.84	$494.94	$3,610.54	$5,733.91	$7,876.63
6	$610.76	$536.02	$4,221.30	$6,880.70	$7,340.60
7	$566.27	$580.51	$4,787.57	$8,027.48	$6,760.09
8	$518.09	$628.70	$5,305.65	$9,174.26	$6,131.39
9	$465.91	$680.88	$5,771.56	$10,321.04	$5,450.52
10	$409.39	$737.39	$6,180.95	$11,467.83	$4,713.13
11	$348.19	$798.59	$6,529.14	$12,614.61	$3,914.53
12	$281.91	$864.88	$6,811.05	$13,761.39	$3,049.66
13	$210.12	$936.66	$7,021.17	$14,908.17	$2,113.00
14	$132.38	$1,014.40	$7,153.55	$16,054.96	$1,098.60
15	$48.19	$1,098.60	$7,201.74	$17,201.74	$0.00

8.00% Annual Amortization
$10,000 Loan Amount

30 Year Term
Payment $73.38

Yr.	Interest This Year	Principal This Year	Interest To Date	Payments To Date	Current Balance
1	$796.98	$83.54	$796.98	$880.52	$9,916.46
2	$790.05	$90.47	$1,587.03	$1,761.03	$9,825.99
3	$782.54	$97.98	$2,369.57	$2,641.55	$9,728.01
4	$774.41	$106.11	$3,143.97	$3,522.07	$9,621.90
5	$765.60	$114.92	$3,909.57	$4,402.59	$9,506.99
6	$756.06	$124.46	$4,665.63	$5,283.10	$9,382.53
7	$745.73	$134.79	$5,411.37	$6,163.62	$9,247.74
8	$734.54	$145.97	$6,145.91	$7,044.14	$9,101.77
9	$722.43	$158.09	$6,868.34	$7,924.66	$8,943.68
10	$709.31	$171.21	$7,577.65	$8,805.17	$8,772.47
11	$695.10	$185.42	$8,272.74	$9,685.69	$8,587.05
12	$679.71	$200.81	$8,952.45	$10,566.21	$8,386.24
13	$663.04	$217.48	$9,615.49	$11,446.73	$8,168.76
14	$644.99	$235.53	$10,260.48	$12,327.24	$7,933.23
15	$625.44	$255.08	$10,885.92	$13,207.76	$7,678.16
16	$604.27	$276.25	$11,490.19	$14,088.28	$7,401.91
17	$581.34	$299.18	$12,071.53	$14,968.80	$7,102.73
18	$556.51	$324.01	$12,628.04	$15,849.31	$6,778.72
19	$529.62	$350.90	$13,157.65	$16,729.83	$6,427.82
20	$500.49	$380.03	$13,658.15	$17,610.35	$6,047.80
21	$468.95	$411.57	$14,127.10	$18,490.87	$5,636.23
22	$434.79	$445.73	$14,561.89	$19,371.38	$5,190.50
23	$397.80	$482.72	$14,959.68	$20,251.90	$4,707.78
24	$357.73	$522.79	$15,317.41	$21,132.42	$4,184.99
25	$314.34	$566.18	$15,631.75	$22,012.94	$3,618.81
26	$267.35	$613.17	$15,899.09	$22,893.45	$3,005.64
27	$216.45	$664.06	$16,115.55	$23,773.97	$2,341.58
28	$161.34	$719.18	$16,276.88	$24,654.49	$1,622.39
29	$101.64	$778.87	$16,378.53	$25,535.01	$843.52
30	$37.00	$843.52	$16,415.52	$26,415.52	$0.00

| **8.50% Annual Amortization** | | | **20 Year Term** | |
| $10,000 Loan Amount | | | Payment $86.78 | |

Yr.	Interest This Year	Principal This Year	Interest To Date	Payments To Date	Current Balance
1	$842.36	$199.02	$842.36	$1,041.39	$9,800.98
2	$824.77	$216.61	$1,667.14	$2,082.78	$9,584.36
3	$805.63	$235.76	$2,472.76	$3,124.16	$9,348.60
4	$784.79	$256.60	$3,257.55	$4,165.55	$9,092.00
5	$762.11	$279.28	$4,019.66	$5,206.94	$8,812.72
6	$737.42	$303.97	$4,757.08	$6,248.33	$8,508.75
7	$710.55	$330.84	$5,467.63	$7,289.72	$8,177.91
8	$681.31	$360.08	$6,148.94	$8,331.10	$7,817.84
9	$649.48	$391.91	$6,798.42	$9,372.49	$7,425.93
10	$614.84	$426.55	$7,413.26	$10,413.88	$6,999.38
11	$577.14	$464.25	$7,990.40	$11,455.27	$6,535.13
12	$536.10	$505.29	$8,526.50	$12,496.65	$6,029.85
13	$491.44	$549.95	$9,017.94	$13,538.04	$5,479.90
14	$442.83	$598.56	$9,460.77	$14,579.43	$4,881.34
15	$389.92	$651.47	$9,850.69	$15,620.82	$4,229.87
16	$332.34	$709.05	$10,183.03	$16,662.21	$3,520.82
17	$269.66	$771.72	$10,452.69	$17,703.59	$2,749.10
18	$201.45	$839.94	$10,654.15	$18,744.98	$1,909.16
19	$127.21	$914.18	$10,781.35	$19,786.37	$994.98
20	$46.40	$994.98	$10,827.76	$20,827.76	$0.00

| **8.50% Annual Amortization** | | | **25 Year Term** | |
| $10,000 Loan Amount | | | Payment $80.52 | |

Yr.	Interest This Year	Principal This Year	Interest To Date	Payments To Date	Current Balance
1	$845.36	$120.91	$845.36	$966.27	$9,879.09
2	$834.67	$131.60	$1,680.04	$1,932.55	$9,747.49
3	$823.04	$143.23	$2,503.08	$2,898.82	$9,604.26
4	$810.38	$155.89	$3,313.46	$3,865.09	$9,448.37
5	$796.60	$169.67	$4,110.06	$4,831.36	$9,278.70
6	$781.61	$184.67	$4,891.67	$5,797.64	$9,094.03
7	$765.28	$200.99	$5,656.95	$6,763.91	$8,893.04
8	$747.52	$218.76	$6,404.47	$7,730.18	$8,674.29
9	$728.18	$238.09	$7,132.65	$8,696.45	$8,436.19
10	$707.14	$259.14	$7,839.78	$9,662.73	$8,177.06
11	$684.23	$282.04	$8,524.01	$10,629.00	$7,895.01
12	$659.30	$306.97	$9,183.31	$11,595.27	$7,588.04
13	$632.17	$334.11	$9,815.48	$12,561.54	$7,253.93
14	$602.63	$363.64	$10,418.11	$13,527.82	$6,890.30
15	$570.49	$395.78	$10,988.60	$14,494.09	$6,494.52
16	$535.51	$430.76	$11,524.11	$15,460.36	$6,063.75
17	$497.43	$468.84	$12,021.55	$16,426.63	$5,594.91
18	$455.99	$510.28	$12,477.54	$17,392.91	$5,084.63
19	$410.89	$555.38	$12,888.43	$18,359.18	$4,529.25
20	$361.80	$604.48	$13,250.22	$19,325.45	$3,924.77
21	$308.37	$657.91	$13,558.59	$20,291.72	$3,266.87
22	$250.21	$716.06	$13,808.80	$21,258.00	$2,550.81
23	$186.92	$779.35	$13,995.72	$22,224.27	$1,771.46
24	$118.03	$848.24	$14,113.76	$23,190.54	$923.22
25	$43.06	$923.22	$14,156.81	$24,156.81	$0.00

8.50% Annual Amortization
$10,000 Loan Amount
15 Year Term
Payment $98.47

Yr.	Interest This Year	Principal This Year	Interest To Date	Payments To Date	Current Balance
1	$836.77	$344.92	$836.77	$1,181.69	$9,655.08
2	$806.28	$375.41	$1,643.05	$2,363.37	$9,279.67
3	$773.10	$408.59	$2,416.15	$3,545.06	$8,871.08
4	$736.98	$444.71	$3,153.13	$4,726.75	$8,426.38
5	$697.67	$484.01	$3,850.80	$5,908.44	$7,942.36
6	$654.89	$526.80	$4,505.69	$7,090.12	$7,415.57
7	$608.33	$573.36	$5,114.02	$8,271.81	$6,842.21
8	$557.65	$624.04	$5,671.67	$9,453.50	$6,218.17
9	$502.49	$679.20	$6,174.16	$10,635.19	$5,538.97
10	$442.45	$739.23	$6,616.61	$11,816.87	$4,799.74
11	$377.11	$804.58	$6,993.72	$12,998.56	$3,995.16
12	$305.99	$875.69	$7,299.72	$14,180.25	$3,119.47
13	$228.59	$953.10	$7,528.31	$15,361.94	$2,166.37
14	$144.35	$1,037.34	$7,672.66	$16,543.62	$1,129.03
15	$52.66	$1,129.03	$7,725.31	$17,725.31	$0.00

8.50% Annual Amortization
$10,000 Loan Amount
30 Year Term
Payment $76.89

Yr.	Interest This Year	Principal This Year	Interest To Date	Payments To Date	Current Balance
1	$847.10	$75.60	$847.10	$922.70	$9,924.40
2	$840.42	$82.28	$1,687.52	$1,845.39	$9,842.13
3	$833.15	$89.55	$2,520.66	$2,768.09	$9,752.57
4	$825.23	$97.47	$3,345.89	$3,690.78	$9,655.11
5	$816.61	$106.08	$4,162.51	$4,613.48	$9,549.03
6	$807.24	$115.46	$4,969.75	$5,536.18	$9,433.57
7	$797.03	$125.66	$5,766.78	$6,458.87	$9,307.90
8	$785.93	$136.77	$6,552.70	$7,381.57	$9,171.13
9	$773.84	$148.86	$7,326.54	$8,304.27	$9,022.27
10	$760.68	$162.02	$8,087.22	$9,226.96	$8,860.25
11	$746.36	$176.34	$8,833.57	$10,149.66	$8,683.92
12	$730.77	$191.93	$9,564.34	$11,072.35	$8,491.99
13	$713.81	$208.89	$10,278.15	$11,995.05	$8,283.10
14	$695.34	$227.35	$10,973.49	$12,917.75	$8,055.74
15	$675.25	$247.45	$11,648.74	$13,840.44	$7,808.29
16	$653.37	$269.32	$12,302.11	$14,763.14	$7,538.97
17	$629.57	$293.13	$12,931.68	$15,685.84	$7,245.84
18	$603.66	$319.04	$13,535.33	$16,608.53	$6,926.80
19	$575.46	$347.24	$14,110.79	$17,531.23	$6,579.56
20	$544.76	$377.93	$14,655.55	$18,453.92	$6,201.63
21	$511.36	$411.34	$15,166.91	$19,376.62	$5,790.29
22	$475.00	$447.70	$15,641.91	$20,299.32	$5,342.60
23	$435.43	$487.27	$16,077.34	$21,222.01	$4,855.33
24	$392.36	$530.34	$16,469.70	$22,144.71	$4,324.99
25	$345.48	$577.22	$16,815.18	$23,067.40	$3,747.78
26	$294.46	$628.24	$17,109.64	$23,990.10	$3,119.54
27	$238.93	$683.77	$17,348.57	$24,912.80	$2,435.77
28	$178.49	$744.21	$17,527.06	$25,835.49	$1,691.57
29	$112.71	$809.99	$17,639.77	$26,758.19	$881.58
30	$41.11	$881.58	$17,680.89	$27,680.89	$0.00

| **9.00% Annual Amortization** | | | **20 Year Term** | |
| **$10,000 Loan Amount** | | | **Payment $89.97** | |
Yr.	Interest This Year	Principal This Year	Interest To Date	Payments To Date	Current Balance
1	$892.40	$187.27	$892.40	$1,079.67	$9,812.73
2	$874.83	$204.84	$1,767.23	$2,159.34	$9,607.89
3	$855.62	$224.05	$2,622.85	$3,239.01	$9,383.84
4	$834.60	$245.07	$3,457.45	$4,318.68	$9,138.77
5	$811.61	$268.06	$4,269.06	$5,398.36	$8,870.70
6	$786.46	$293.21	$5,055.53	$6,478.03	$8,577.50
7	$758.96	$320.71	$5,814.48	$7,557.70	$8,256.79
8	$728.87	$350.80	$6,543.36	$8,637.37	$7,905.99
9	$695.97	$383.70	$7,239.33	$9,717.04	$7,522.29
10	$659.97	$419.70	$7,899.30	$10,796.71	$7,102.59
11	$620.60	$459.07	$8,519.90	$11,876.38	$6,643.52
12	$577.54	$502.13	$9,097.44	$12,956.05	$6,141.39
13	$530.44	$549.24	$9,627.88	$14,035.72	$5,592.15
14	$478.91	$600.76	$10,106.79	$15,115.40	$4,991.40
15	$422.56	$657.11	$10,529.35	$16,195.07	$4,334.28
16	$360.92	$718.75	$10,890.27	$17,274.74	$3,615.53
17	$293.49	$786.18	$11,183.76	$18,354.41	$2,829.35
18	$219.74	$859.93	$11,403.50	$19,434.08	$1,969.42
19	$139.08	$940.59	$11,542.58	$20,513.75	$1,028.83
20	$50.84	$1,028.83	$11,593.42	$21,593.42	$0.00

| **9.00% Annual Amortization** | | | **25 Year Term** | |
| **$10,000 Loan Amount** | | | **Payment $83.92** | |
Yr.	Interest This Year	Principal This Year	Interest To Date	Payments To Date	Current Balance
1	$895.47	$111.56	$895.47	$1,007.04	$9,888.44
2	$885.01	$122.03	$1,780.48	$2,014.07	$9,766.41
3	$873.56	$133.48	$2,654.04	$3,021.11	$9,632.93
4	$861.04	$146.00	$3,515.08	$4,028.14	$9,486.94
5	$847.34	$159.69	$4,362.42	$5,035.18	$9,327.24
6	$832.36	$174.67	$5,194.79	$6,042.21	$9,152.57
7	$815.98	$191.06	$6,010.76	$7,049.25	$8,961.51
8	$798.06	$208.98	$6,808.82	$8,056.29	$8,752.53
9	$778.45	$228.58	$7,587.27	$9,063.32	$8,523.95
10	$757.01	$250.03	$8,344.28	$10,070.36	$8,273.92
11	$733.55	$273.48	$9,077.83	$11,077.39	$8,000.44
12	$707.90	$299.14	$9,785.73	$12,084.43	$7,701.31
13	$679.84	$327.20	$10,465.57	$13,091.46	$7,374.11
14	$649.15	$357.89	$11,114.72	$14,098.50	$7,016.22
15	$615.57	$391.46	$11,730.29	$15,105.53	$6,624.76
16	$578.85	$428.18	$12,309.14	$16,112.57	$6,196.57
17	$538.68	$468.35	$12,847.83	$17,119.61	$5,728.22
18	$494.75	$512.29	$13,342.58	$18,126.64	$5,215.94
19	$446.69	$560.34	$13,789.27	$19,133.68	$4,655.60
20	$394.13	$612.90	$14,183.40	$20,140.71	$4,042.69
21	$336.64	$670.40	$14,520.04	$21,147.75	$3,372.29
22	$273.75	$733.29	$14,793.79	$22,154.78	$2,639.00
23	$204.96	$802.08	$14,998.75	$23,161.82	$1,836.93
24	$129.72	$877.32	$15,128.47	$24,168.86	$959.61
25	$47.42	$959.61	$15,175.89	$25,175.89	$0.00

9.00% Annual Amortization
$10,000 Loan Amount

15 Year Term
Payment $101.43

Yr.	Interest This Year	Principal This Year	Interest To Date	Payments To Date	Current Balance
1	$886.59	$330.53	$886.59	$1,217.12	$9,669.47
2	$855.58	$361.54	$1,742.17	$2,434.24	$9,307.93
3	$821.66	$395.46	$2,563.83	$3,651.36	$8,912.47
4	$784.57	$432.55	$3,348.40	$4,868.48	$8,479.92
5	$743.99	$473.13	$4,092.39	$6,085.60	$8,006.79
6	$699.61	$517.51	$4,792.00	$7,302.72	$7,489.28
7	$651.06	$566.06	$5,443.06	$8,519.84	$6,923.23
8	$597.96	$619.16	$6,041.03	$9,736.96	$6,304.07
9	$539.88	$677.24	$6,580.91	$10,954.08	$5,626.83
10	$476.35	$740.77	$7,057.26	$12,171.20	$4,886.06
11	$406.86	$810.26	$7,464.13	$13,388.32	$4,075.81
12	$330.62	$886.26	$7,794.48	$14,605.44	$3,189.54
13	$247.72	$969.40	$8,042.70	$15,822.56	$2,220.14
14	$156.78	$1,060.34	$8,199.48	$17,039.68	$1,159.80
15	$57.31	$1,159.80	$8,256.80	$18,256.80	$0.00

9.00% Annual Amortization
$10,000 Loan Amount

30 Year Term
Payment $80.46

Yr.	Interest This Year	Principal This Year	Interest To Date	Payments To Date	Current Balance
1	$897.23	$68.32	$897.23	$965.55	$9,931.68
2	$890.82	$74.73	$1,788.05	$1,931.09	$9,856.95
3	$883.81	$81.74	$2,671.85	$2,896.64	$9,775.21
4	$876.14	$89.41	$3,548.00	$3,862.19	$9,685.81
5	$867.75	$97.79	$4,415.75	$4,827.74	$9,588.01
6	$858.58	$106.97	$5,274.33	$5,793.28	$9,481.05
7	$848.55	$117.00	$6,122.88	$6,758.83	$9,364.05
8	$837.57	$127.98	$6,960.45	$7,724.38	$9,236.07
9	$825.57	$139.98	$7,786.01	$8,689.92	$9,096.09
10	$812.43	$153.11	$8,598.45	$9,655.47	$8,942.97
11	$798.07	$167.48	$9,396.52	$10,621.02	$8,775.50
12	$782.36	$183.19	$10,178.88	$11,586.57	$8,592.31
13	$765.18	$200.37	$10,944.05	$12,552.11	$8,391.94
14	$746.38	$219.17	$11,690.43	$13,517.66	$8,172.77
15	$725.82	$239.73	$12,416.26	$14,483.21	$7,933.05
16	$703.33	$262.21	$13,119.59	$15,448.75	$7,670.83
17	$678.74	$286.81	$13,798.32	$16,414.30	$7,384.02
18	$651.83	$313.72	$14,450.16	$17,379.85	$7,070.31
19	$622.40	$343.15	$15,072.56	$18,345.40	$6,727.16
20	$590.21	$375.33	$15,662.77	$19,310.94	$6,351.83
21	$555.00	$410.54	$16,217.77	$20,276.49	$5,941.28
22	$516.49	$449.06	$16,734.27	$21,242.04	$5,492.23
23	$474.37	$491.18	$17,208.63	$22,207.58	$5,001.05
24	$428.29	$537.26	$17,636.92	$23,173.13	$4,463.79
25	$377.89	$587.65	$18,014.82	$24,138.68	$3,876.14
26	$322.77	$642.78	$18,337.58	$25,104.23	$3,233.36
27	$262.47	$703.08	$18,600.05	$26,069.77	$2,530.28
28	$196.52	$769.03	$18,796.57	$27,035.32	$1,761.25
29	$124.38	$841.17	$18,920.95	$28,000.87	$920.08
30	$45.47	$920.08	$18,966.41	$28,966.41	$0.00

9.50% Annual Amortization
$10,000 Loan Amount

20 Year Term
Payment $93.21

Yr.	Interest This Year	Principal This Year	Interest To Date	Payments To Date	Current Balance
1	$942.46	$176.09	$942.46	$1,118.56	$9,823.91
2	$924.99	$193.57	$1,867.45	$2,237.11	$9,630.34
3	$905.78	$212.78	$2,773.23	$3,355.67	$9,417.55
4	$884.66	$233.90	$3,657.88	$4,474.23	$9,183.65
5	$861.44	$257.11	$4,519.33	$5,592.79	$8,926.54
6	$835.93	$282.63	$5,355.25	$6,711.34	$8,643.91
7	$807.87	$310.68	$6,163.13	$7,829.90	$8,333.22
8	$777.04	$341.52	$6,940.17	$8,948.46	$7,991.71
9	$743.15	$375.41	$7,683.31	$10,067.02	$7,616.29
10	$705.89	$412.67	$8,389.20	$11,185.57	$7,203.62
11	$664.93	$453.63	$9,054.13	$12,304.13	$6,750.00
12	$619.91	$498.65	$9,674.04	$13,422.69	$6,251.35
13	$570.42	$548.14	$10,244.45	$14,541.25	$5,703.21
14	$516.02	$602.54	$10,760.47	$15,659.80	$5,100.67
15	$456.22	$662.34	$11,216.69	$16,778.36	$4,438.33
16	$390.48	$728.08	$11,607.17	$17,896.92	$3,710.25
17	$318.22	$800.34	$11,925.39	$19,015.48	$2,909.91
18	$238.79	$879.77	$12,164.18	$20,134.03	$2,030.15
19	$151.47	$967.08	$12,315.65	$21,252.59	$1,063.06
20	$55.49	$1,063.06	$12,371.15	$22,371.15	$0.00

9.50% Annual Amortization
$10,000 Loan Amount

25 Year Term
Payment $87.37

Yr.	Interest This Year	Principal This Year	Interest To Date	Payments To Date	Current Balance
1	$945.60	$102.84	$945.60	$1,048.44	$9,897.16
2	$935.39	$113.04	$1,880.99	$2,096.87	$9,784.12
3	$924.17	$124.26	$2,805.16	$3,145.31	$9,659.86
4	$911.84	$136.60	$3,717.00	$4,193.74	$9,523.26
5	$898.28	$150.15	$4,615.29	$5,242.18	$9,373.11
6	$883.38	$165.05	$5,498.67	$6,290.62	$9,208.05
7	$867.00	$181.44	$6,365.67	$7,339.05	$9,026.62
8	$848.99	$199.44	$7,214.66	$8,387.49	$8,827.17
9	$829.20	$219.24	$8,043.86	$9,435.92	$8,607.94
10	$807.44	$241.00	$8,851.30	$10,484.36	$8,366.94
11	$783.52	$264.91	$9,634.82	$11,532.80	$8,102.03
12	$757.23	$291.21	$10,392.05	$12,581.23	$7,810.82
13	$728.33	$320.11	$11,120.38	$13,629.67	$7,490.71
14	$696.56	$351.88	$11,816.94	$14,678.10	$7,138.83
15	$661.64	$386.80	$12,478.57	$15,726.54	$6,752.03
16	$623.25	$425.19	$13,101.82	$16,774.98	$6,326.84
17	$581.05	$467.39	$13,682.87	$17,823.41	$5,859.45
18	$534.66	$513.78	$14,217.53	$18,871.85	$5,345.68
19	$483.67	$564.77	$14,701.19	$19,920.28	$4,780.91
20	$427.62	$620.82	$15,128.81	$20,968.72	$4,160.09
21	$366.00	$682.43	$15,494.81	$22,017.16	$3,477.66
22	$298.27	$750.16	$15,793.09	$23,065.59	$2,727.49
23	$223.82	$824.62	$16,016.91	$24,114.03	$1,902.88
24	$141.98	$906.46	$16,158.88	$25,162.46	$996.42
25	$52.02	$996.42	$16,210.90	$26,210.90	$0.00

9.50% Annual Amortization
$10,000 Loan Amount

15 Year Term
Payment $104.42

Yr.	Interest This Year	Principal This Year	Interest To Date	Payments To Date	Current Balance
1	$936.45	$316.62	$936.45	$1,253.07	$9,683.38
2	$905.03	$348.04	$1,841.47	$2,506.14	$9,335.34
3	$870.48	$382.59	$2,711.96	$3,759.21	$8,952.75
4	$832.51	$420.56	$3,544.47	$5,012.28	$8,532.19
5	$790.77	$462.30	$4,335.24	$6,265.35	$8,069.89
6	$744.89	$508.18	$5,080.13	$7,518.42	$7,561.72
7	$694.46	$558.61	$5,774.59	$8,771.49	$7,003.10
8	$639.01	$614.06	$6,413.60	$10,024.56	$6,389.05
9	$578.07	$675.00	$6,991.68	$11,277.63	$5,714.05
10	$511.08	$741.99	$7,502.75	$12,530.70	$4,972.06
11	$437.44	$815.63	$7,940.19	$13,783.77	$4,156.43
12	$356.49	$896.58	$8,296.68	$15,036.84	$3,259.85
13	$267.51	$985.56	$8,564.19	$16,289.91	$2,274.28
14	$169.69	$1,083.38	$8,733.88	$17,542.97	$1,190.90
15	$62.17	$1,190.90	$8,796.04	$18,796.04	$0.00

9.50% Annual Amortization
$10,000 Loan Amount

30 Year Term
Payment $84.09

Yr.	Interest This Year	Principal This Year	Interest To Date	Payments To Date	Current Balance
1	$947.36	$61.66	$947.36	$1,009.03	$9,938.34
2	$941.24	$67.78	$1,888.60	$2,018.05	$9,870.55
3	$934.51	$74.51	$2,823.12	$3,027.08	$9,796.04
4	$927.12	$81.91	$3,750.23	$4,036.10	$9,714.13
5	$918.99	$90.04	$4,669.22	$5,045.13	$9,624.10
6	$910.05	$98.97	$5,579.28	$6,054.15	$9,525.13
7	$900.23	$108.79	$6,479.51	$7,063.18	$9,416.33
8	$889.43	$119.59	$7,368.94	$8,072.20	$9,296.74
9	$877.56	$131.46	$8,246.50	$9,081.23	$9,165.28
10	$864.52	$144.51	$9,111.02	$10,090.25	$9,020.77
11	$850.17	$158.85	$9,961.20	$11,099.28	$8,861.92
12	$834.41	$174.62	$10,795.61	$12,108.30	$8,687.31
13	$817.08	$191.95	$11,612.68	$13,117.33	$8,495.36
14	$798.03	$211.00	$12,410.71	$14,126.35	$8,284.36
15	$777.09	$231.94	$13,187.80	$15,135.38	$8,052.43
16	$754.07	$254.96	$13,941.87	$16,144.40	$7,797.47
17	$728.77	$280.26	$14,670.64	$17,153.43	$7,517.21
18	$700.95	$308.08	$15,371.59	$18,162.45	$7,209.13
19	$670.37	$338.65	$16,041.96	$19,171.48	$6,870.48
20	$636.76	$372.26	$16,678.72	$20,180.50	$6,498.22
21	$599.82	$409.21	$17,278.54	$21,189.53	$6,089.02
22	$559.21	$449.82	$17,837.75	$22,198.55	$5,639.20
23	$514.56	$494.46	$18,352.31	$23,207.58	$5,144.73
24	$465.49	$543.54	$18,817.80	$24,216.60	$4,601.20
25	$411.54	$597.48	$19,229.34	$25,225.63	$4,003.71
26	$352.24	$656.78	$19,581.58	$26,234.65	$3,346.93
27	$287.06	$721.97	$19,868.64	$27,243.68	$2,624.97
28	$215.41	$793.62	$20,084.05	$28,252.70	$1,831.35
29	$136.64	$872.38	$20,220.69	$29,261.73	$958.97
30	$50.06	$958.97	$20,270.75	$30,270.75	$0.00

10.00% Annual Amortization
$10,000 Loan Amount

20 Year Term
Payment $96.50

Yr.	Interest This Year	Principal This Year	Interest To Date	Payments To Date	Current Balance
1	$992.55	$165.47	$992.55	$1,158.03	$9,834.53
2	$975.22	$182.80	$1,967.78	$2,316.05	$9,651.73
3	$956.08	$201.94	$2,923.86	$3,474.08	$9,449.78
4	$934.94	$223.09	$3,858.80	$4,632.10	$9,226.69
5	$911.58	$246.45	$4,770.37	$5,790.13	$8,980.24
6	$885.77	$272.26	$5,656.14	$6,948.16	$8,707.99
7	$857.26	$300.76	$6,513.41	$8,106.18	$8,407.22
8	$825.77	$332.26	$7,339.17	$9,264.21	$8,074.97
9	$790.98	$367.05	$8,130.15	$10,422.23	$7,707.92
10	$752.54	$405.48	$8,882.69	$11,580.26	$7,302.43
11	$710.08	$447.94	$9,592.77	$12,738.29	$6,854.49
12	$663.18	$494.85	$10,255.95	$13,896.31	$6,359.64
13	$611.36	$546.67	$10,867.31	$15,054.34	$5,812.97
14	$554.12	$603.91	$11,421.42	$16,212.36	$5,209.06
15	$490.88	$667.15	$11,912.30	$17,370.39	$4,541.91
16	$421.02	$737.01	$12,333.32	$18,528.42	$3,804.90
17	$343.84	$814.18	$12,677.16	$19,686.44	$2,990.72
18	$258.59	$899.44	$12,935.75	$20,844.47	$2,091.28
19	$164.41	$993.62	$13,100.16	$22,002.49	$1,097.66
20	$60.36	$1,097.66	$13,160.52	$23,160.52	$0.00

10.00% Annual Amortization
$10,000 Loan Amount

25 Year Term
Payment $90.87

Yr.	Interest This Year	Principal This Year	Interest To Date	Payments To Date	Current Balance
1	$995.74	$94.70	$995.74	$1,090.44	$9,905.30
2	$985.82	$104.62	$1,981.56	$2,180.88	$9,800.68
3	$974.87	$115.58	$2,956.42	$3,271.32	$9,685.10
4	$962.76	$127.68	$3,919.19	$4,361.76	$9,557.42
5	$949.39	$141.05	$4,868.58	$5,452.20	$9,416.38
6	$934.62	$155.82	$5,803.21	$6,542.65	$9,260.56
7	$918.31	$172.13	$6,721.51	$7,633.09	$9,088.43
8	$900.28	$190.16	$7,621.80	$8,723.53	$8,898.27
9	$880.37	$210.07	$8,502.17	$9,813.97	$8,688.20
10	$858.38	$232.07	$9,360.55	$10,904.41	$8,456.14
11	$834.07	$256.37	$10,194.62	$11,994.85	$8,199.77
12	$807.23	$283.21	$11,001.85	$13,085.29	$7,916.56
13	$777.57	$312.87	$11,779.42	$14,175.73	$7,603.69
14	$744.81	$345.63	$12,524.24	$15,266.17	$7,258.06
15	$708.62	$381.82	$13,232.86	$16,356.61	$6,876.24
16	$668.64	$421.80	$13,901.50	$17,447.05	$6,454.44
17	$624.47	$465.97	$14,525.97	$18,537.50	$5,988.47
18	$575.68	$514.76	$15,101.65	$19,627.94	$5,473.71
19	$521.78	$568.67	$15,623.42	$20,718.38	$4,905.05
20	$462.23	$628.21	$16,085.65	$21,808.82	$4,276.83
21	$396.45	$693.99	$16,482.10	$22,899.26	$3,582.84
22	$323.78	$766.66	$16,805.88	$23,989.70	$2,816.18
23	$243.50	$846.94	$17,049.37	$25,080.14	$1,969.23
24	$154.81	$935.63	$17,204.18	$26,170.58	$1,033.60
25	$56.84	$1,033.60	$17,261.02	$27,261.02	$0.00

10.00% Annual Amortization
$10,000 Loan Amount

15 Year Term
Payment $107.46

Yr.	Interest This Year	Principal This Year	Interest To Date	Payments To Date	Current Balance
1	$986.35	$303.17	$986.35	$1,289.53	$9,696.83
2	$954.61	$334.92	$1,940.96	$2,579.05	$9,361.91
3	$919.54	$369.99	$2,860.50	$3,868.58	$8,991.92
4	$880.80	$408.73	$3,741.30	$5,158.10	$8,583.19
5	$838.00	$451.53	$4,579.29	$6,447.63	$8,131.66
6	$790.72	$498.81	$5,370.01	$7,737.16	$7,632.85
7	$738.48	$551.04	$6,108.49	$9,026.68	$7,081.81
8	$680.78	$608.74	$6,789.27	$10,316.21	$6,473.06
9	$617.04	$672.49	$7,406.31	$11,605.74	$5,800.58
10	$546.62	$742.91	$7,952.93	$12,895.26	$5,057.67
11	$468.83	$820.70	$8,421.76	$14,184.79	$4,236.97
12	$382.89	$906.64	$8,804.65	$15,474.31	$3,330.33
13	$287.95	$1,001.57	$9,092.60	$16,763.84	$2,328.76
14	$183.08	$1,106.45	$9,275.68	$18,053.37	$1,222.31
15	$67.22	$1,222.31	$9,342.89	$19,342.89	$0.00

10.00% Annual Amortization
$10,000 Loan Amount

30 Year Term
Payment $87.76

Yr.	Interest This Year	Principal This Year	Interest To Date	Payments To Date	Current Balance
1	$997.50	$55.59	$997.50	$1,053.09	$9,944.41
2	$991.68	$61.41	$1,989.18	$2,106.17	$9,883.00
3	$985.25	$67.84	$2,974.42	$3,159.26	$9,815.16
4	$978.14	$74.94	$3,952.57	$4,212.34	$9,740.22
5	$970.30	$82.79	$4,922.86	$5,265.43	$9,657.43
6	$961.63	$91.46	$5,884.49	$6,318.52	$9,565.97
7	$952.05	$101.04	$6,836.54	$7,371.60	$9,464.94
8	$941.47	$111.62	$7,778.01	$8,424.69	$9,353.32
9	$929.78	$123.30	$8,707.79	$9,477.77	$9,230.02
10	$916.87	$136.22	$9,624.66	$10,530.86	$9,093.80
11	$902.61	$150.48	$10,527.27	$11,583.94	$8,943.32
12	$886.85	$166.24	$11,414.12	$12,637.03	$8,777.09
13	$869.44	$183.64	$12,283.56	$13,690.12	$8,593.44
14	$850.21	$202.87	$13,133.77	$14,743.20	$8,390.57
15	$828.97	$224.12	$13,962.74	$15,796.29	$8,166.46
16	$805.50	$247.58	$14,768.25	$16,849.37	$7,918.87
17	$779.58	$273.51	$15,547.82	$17,902.46	$7,645.36
18	$750.94	$302.15	$16,298.76	$18,955.55	$7,343.21
19	$719.30	$333.79	$17,018.06	$20,008.63	$7,009.43
20	$684.35	$368.74	$17,702.40	$21,061.72	$6,640.69
21	$645.73	$407.35	$18,348.14	$22,114.80	$6,233.33
22	$603.08	$450.01	$18,951.22	$23,167.89	$5,783.33
23	$555.96	$497.13	$19,507.17	$24,220.98	$5,286.20
24	$503.90	$549.18	$20,011.08	$25,274.06	$4,737.01
25	$446.39	$606.69	$20,457.47	$26,327.15	$4,130.32
26	$382.87	$670.22	$20,840.34	$27,380.23	$3,460.10
27	$312.69	$740.40	$21,153.02	$28,433.32	$2,719.70
28	$235.16	$817.93	$21,388.18	$29,486.40	$1,901.77
29	$149.51	$903.58	$21,537.69	$30,539.49	$998.19
30	$54.89	$998.19	$21,592.58	$31,592.58	$0.00

10.50% Annual Amortization
$10,000 Loan Amount

20 Year Term
Payment $99.84

Yr.	Interest This Year	Principal This Year	Interest To Date	Payments To Date	Current Balance
1	$1,042.66	$155.39	$1,042.66	$1,198.06	$9,844.61
2	$1,025.54	$172.52	$2,068.20	$2,396.11	$9,672.09
3	$1,006.53	$191.53	$3,074.73	$3,594.17	$9,480.56
4	$985.42	$212.64	$4,060.15	$4,792.22	$9,267.92
5	$961.99	$236.07	$5,022.13	$5,990.28	$9,031.85
6	$935.97	$262.09	$5,958.10	$7,188.34	$8,769.77
7	$907.09	$290.97	$6,865.19	$8,386.39	$8,478.80
8	$875.02	$323.03	$7,740.21	$9,584.45	$8,155.76
9	$839.42	$358.63	$8,579.63	$10,782.50	$7,797.13
10	$799.90	$398.16	$9,379.53	$11,980.56	$7,398.97
11	$756.02	$442.04	$10,135.55	$13,178.61	$6,956.93
12	$707.31	$490.75	$10,842.85	$14,376.67	$6,466.18
13	$653.22	$544.83	$11,496.08	$15,574.73	$5,921.35
14	$593.18	$604.87	$12,089.26	$16,772.78	$5,316.48
15	$526.52	$671.53	$12,615.78	$17,970.84	$4,644.95
16	$452.52	$745.54	$13,068.30	$19,168.89	$3,899.41
17	$370.36	$827.70	$13,438.66	$20,366.95	$3,071.71
18	$279.14	$918.91	$13,717.80	$21,565.01	$2,152.79
19	$177.87	$1,020.18	$13,895.67	$22,763.06	$1,132.61
20	$65.45	$1,132.61	$13,961.12	$23,961.12	$0.00

10.50% Annual Amortization
$10,000 Loan Amount

25 Year Term
Payment $94.42

Yr.	Interest This Year	Principal This Year	Interest To Date	Payments To Date	Current Balance
1	$1,045.89	$87.13	$1,045.89	$1,133.02	$9,912.87
2	$1,036.28	$96.73	$2,082.17	$2,266.04	$9,816.13
3	$1,025.62	$107.39	$3,107.79	$3,399.05	$9,708.74
4	$1,013.79	$119.23	$4,121.58	$4,532.07	$9,589.51
5	$1,000.65	$132.37	$5,122.23	$5,665.09	$9,457.14
6	$986.06	$146.96	$6,108.29	$6,798.11	$9,310.18
7	$969.87	$163.15	$7,078.16	$7,931.13	$9,147.03
8	$951.89	$181.13	$8,030.04	$9,064.14	$8,965.90
9	$931.92	$201.09	$8,961.96	$10,197.16	$8,764.80
10	$909.76	$223.26	$9,871.73	$11,330.18	$8,541.55
11	$885.16	$247.86	$10,756.89	$12,463.20	$8,293.69
12	$857.84	$275.17	$11,614.73	$13,596.22	$8,018.51
13	$827.52	$305.50	$12,442.25	$14,729.23	$7,713.02
14	$793.85	$339.17	$13,236.10	$15,862.25	$7,373.85
15	$756.48	$376.54	$13,992.58	$16,995.27	$6,997.31
16	$714.98	$418.04	$14,707.56	$18,128.29	$6,579.27
17	$668.91	$464.11	$15,376.47	$19,261.31	$6,115.16
18	$617.76	$515.25	$15,994.23	$20,394.32	$5,599.91
19	$560.98	$572.04	$16,555.21	$21,527.34	$5,027.87
20	$497.94	$635.08	$17,053.15	$22,660.36	$4,392.79
21	$427.95	$705.07	$17,481.10	$23,793.38	$3,687.72
22	$350.25	$782.77	$17,831.35	$24,926.40	$2,904.96
23	$263.99	$869.03	$18,095.34	$26,059.42	$2,035.93
24	$168.22	$964.80	$18,263.56	$27,192.43	$1,071.12
25	$61.89	$1,071.12	$18,325.45	$28,325.45	$0.00

10.50% Annual Amortization
$10,000 Loan Amount

15 Year Term
Payment $110.54

Yr.	Interest This Year	Principal This Year	Interest To Date	Payments To Date	Current Balance
1	$1,036.30	$290.18	$1,036.30	$1,326.48	$9,709.82
2	$1,004.32	$322.16	$2,040.62	$2,652.96	$9,387.66
3	$968.82	$357.66	$3,009.44	$3,979.44	$9,030.00
4	$929.40	$397.08	$3,938.84	$5,305.91	$8,632.92
5	$885.64	$440.84	$4,824.48	$6,632.39	$8,192.08
6	$837.06	$489.42	$5,661.54	$7,958.87	$7,702.67
7	$783.12	$543.35	$6,444.66	$9,285.35	$7,159.31
8	$723.25	$603.23	$7,167.91	$10,611.83	$6,556.08
9	$656.77	$669.71	$7,824.67	$11,938.31	$5,886.37
10	$582.96	$743.52	$8,407.64	$13,264.79	$5,142.85
11	$501.02	$825.45	$8,908.66	$14,591.27	$4,317.39
12	$410.06	$916.42	$9,318.72	$15,917.74	$3,400.97
13	$309.06	$1,017.42	$9,627.78	$17,244.22	$2,383.56
14	$196.94	$1,129.54	$9,824.72	$18,570.70	$1,254.02
15	$72.46	$1,254.02	$9,897.18	$19,897.18	$0.00

10.50% Annual Amortization
$10,000 Loan Amount

30 Year Term
Payment $91.47

Yr.	Interest This Year	Principal This Year	Interest To Date	Payments To Date	Current Balance
1	$1,047.64	$50.05	$1,047.64	$1,097.69	$9,949.95
2	$1,042.12	$55.57	$2,089.76	$2,195.37	$9,894.38
3	$1,036.00	$61.69	$3,125.76	$3,293.06	$9,832.69
4	$1,029.20	$68.49	$4,154.95	$4,390.75	$9,764.21
5	$1,021.65	$76.04	$5,176.61	$5,488.44	$9,688.17
6	$1,013.27	$84.42	$6,189.88	$6,586.12	$9,603.75
7	$1,003.97	$93.72	$7,193.85	$7,683.81	$9,510.04
8	$993.64	$104.05	$8,187.49	$8,781.50	$9,405.99
9	$982.17	$115.51	$9,169.66	$9,879.18	$9,290.48
10	$969.45	$128.24	$10,139.11	$10,976.87	$9,162.24
11	$955.31	$142.37	$11,094.42	$12,074.56	$9,019.86
12	$939.62	$158.06	$12,034.04	$13,172.25	$8,861.80
13	$922.20	$175.48	$12,956.25	$14,269.93	$8,686.31
14	$902.86	$194.82	$13,859.11	$15,367.62	$8,491.49
15	$881.39	$216.29	$14,740.50	$16,465.31	$8,275.20
16	$857.56	$240.13	$15,598.06	$17,562.99	$8,035.07
17	$831.09	$266.59	$16,429.16	$18,660.68	$7,768.47
18	$801.71	$295.97	$17,230.87	$19,758.37	$7,472.50
19	$769.10	$328.59	$17,999.97	$20,856.06	$7,143.91
20	$732.89	$364.80	$18,732.85	$21,953.74	$6,779.11
21	$692.68	$405.00	$19,425.54	$23,051.43	$6,374.11
22	$648.05	$449.64	$20,073.59	$24,149.12	$5,924.47
23	$598.50	$499.19	$20,672.09	$25,246.80	$5,425.28
24	$543.49	$554.20	$21,215.58	$26,344.49	$4,871.08
25	$482.41	$615.27	$21,697.99	$27,442.18	$4,255.81
26	$414.61	$683.08	$22,112.59	$28,539.87	$3,572.73
27	$339.33	$758.36	$22,451.92	$29,637.55	$2,814.37
28	$255.76	$841.93	$22,707.68	$30,735.24	$1,972.44
29	$162.97	$934.72	$22,870.65	$31,832.93	$1,037.72
30	$59.96	$1,037.72	$22,930.61	$32,930.61	$0.00

11.00% Annual Amortization
$10,000 Loan Amount

20 Year Term
Payment $103.22

Yr.	Interest This Year	Principal This Year	Interest To Date	Payments To Date	Current Balance
1	$1,092.79	$145.83	$1,092.79	$1,238.63	$9,854.17
2	$1,075.92	$162.71	$2,168.71	$2,477.25	$9,691.46
3	$1,057.09	$181.54	$3,225.80	$3,715.88	$9,509.92
4	$1,036.08	$202.54	$4,261.88	$4,954.50	$9,307.38
5	$1,012.64	$225.98	$5,274.52	$6,193.13	$9,081.39
6	$986.49	$252.13	$6,261.02	$7,431.76	$8,829.26
7	$957.32	$281.31	$7,218.33	$8,670.38	$8,547.95
8	$924.76	$313.86	$8,143.10	$9,909.01	$8,234.09
9	$888.44	$350.18	$9,031.54	$11,147.63	$7,883.91
10	$847.92	$390.71	$9,879.46	$12,386.26	$7,493.20
11	$802.71	$435.92	$10,682.17	$13,624.89	$7,057.28
12	$752.27	$486.36	$11,434.43	$14,863.51	$6,570.92
13	$695.98	$542.64	$12,130.42	$16,102.14	$6,028.28
14	$633.19	$605.44	$12,763.61	$17,340.76	$5,422.84
15	$563.13	$675.50	$13,326.74	$18,579.39	$4,747.35
16	$484.96	$753.66	$13,811.70	$19,818.02	$3,993.68
17	$397.75	$840.88	$14,209.45	$21,056.64	$3,152.81
18	$300.44	$938.18	$14,509.89	$22,295.27	$2,214.62
19	$191.88	$1,046.75	$14,701.77	$23,533.90	$1,167.88
20	$70.75	$1,167.88	$14,772.52	$24,772.52	$0.00

11.00% Annual Amortization
$10,000 Loan Amount

25 Year Term
Payment $98.01

Yr.	Interest This Year	Principal This Year	Interest To Date	Payments To Date	Current Balance
1	$1,096.04	$80.09	$1,096.04	$1,176.14	$9,919.91
2	$1,086.77	$89.36	$2,182.82	$2,352.27	$9,830.54
3	$1,076.43	$99.70	$3,259.25	$3,528.41	$9,730.84
4	$1,064.89	$111.24	$4,324.14	$4,704.54	$9,619.60
5	$1,052.02	$124.11	$5,376.16	$5,880.68	$9,495.49
6	$1,037.66	$138.48	$6,413.82	$7,056.81	$9,357.01
7	$1,021.64	$154.50	$7,435.46	$8,232.95	$9,202.51
8	$1,003.76	$172.38	$8,439.22	$9,409.09	$9,030.13
9	$983.81	$192.33	$9,423.03	$10,585.22	$8,837.81
10	$961.55	$214.58	$10,384.58	$11,761.36	$8,623.22
11	$936.72	$239.41	$11,321.30	$12,937.49	$8,383.81
12	$909.02	$267.12	$12,230.32	$14,113.63	$8,116.69
13	$878.11	$298.03	$13,108.43	$15,289.76	$7,818.67
14	$843.62	$332.52	$13,952.05	$16,465.90	$7,486.15
15	$805.14	$370.99	$14,757.19	$17,642.04	$7,115.16
16	$762.21	$413.92	$15,519.40	$18,818.17	$6,701.23
17	$714.31	$461.82	$16,233.72	$19,994.31	$6,239.41
18	$660.87	$515.27	$16,894.59	$21,170.44	$5,724.14
19	$601.24	$574.89	$17,495.83	$22,346.58	$5,149.25
20	$534.72	$641.42	$18,030.55	$23,522.71	$4,507.84
21	$460.52	$715.64	$18,491.05	$24,698.85	$3,792.20
22	$377.68	$798.45	$18,868.73	$25,874.99	$2,993.74
23	$285.29	$890.85	$19,154.01	$27,051.12	$2,102.89
24	$182.20	$993.94	$19,336.21	$28,227.26	$1,108.96
25	$67.18	$1,108.96	$19,403.39	$29,403.39	$0.00

11.00% Annual Amortization
$10,000 Loan Amount

15 Year Term
Payment $113.66

Yr.	Interest This Year	Principal This Year	Interest To Date	Payments To Date	Current Balance
1	$1,086.28	$277.64	$1,086.28	$1,363.92	$9,722.36
2	$1,054.15	$309.77	$2,140.43	$2,727.83	$9,412.60
3	$1,018.31	$345.61	$3,158.74	$4,091.75	$9,066.99
4	$978.31	$385.60	$4,137.05	$5,455.67	$8,681.38
5	$933.69	$430.23	$5,070.74	$6,819.58	$8,251.16
6	$883.91	$480.01	$5,954.64	$8,183.50	$7,771.15
7	$828.36	$535.56	$6,783.00	$9,547.41	$7,235.59
8	$766.38	$597.53	$7,549.39	$10,911.33	$6,638.06
9	$697.24	$666.68	$8,246.63	$12,275.25	$5,971.38
10	$620.09	$743.82	$8,866.72	$13,639.16	$5,227.55
11	$534.02	$829.90	$9,400.73	$15,003.08	$4,397.66
12	$437.98	$925.93	$9,838.72	$16,367.00	$3,471.72
13	$330.83	$1,033.08	$10,169.55	$17,730.91	$2,438.64
14	$211.29	$1,152.63	$10,380.84	$19,094.83	$1,286.01
15	$77.91	$1,286.01	$10,458.74	$20,458.74	$0.00

11.00% Annual Amortization
$10,000 Loan Amount

30 Year Term
Payment $95.23

Yr.	Interest This Year	Principal This Year	Interest To Date	Payments To Date	Current Balance
1	$1,097.78	$45.01	$1,097.78	$1,142.79	$9,954.99
2	$1,092.57	$50.22	$2,190.34	$2,285.58	$9,904.77
3	$1,086.76	$56.03	$3,277.10	$3,428.36	$9,848.73
4	$1,080.27	$62.52	$4,357.37	$4,571.15	$9,786.22
5	$1,073.04	$69.75	$5,430.40	$5,713.94	$9,716.46
6	$1,064.97	$77.82	$6,495.37	$6,856.73	$9,638.64
7	$1,055.96	$86.83	$7,551.33	$7,999.52	$9,551.81
8	$1,045.91	$96.88	$8,597.24	$9,142.30	$9,454.94
9	$1,034.70	$108.09	$9,631.94	$10,285.09	$9,346.85
10	$1,022.19	$120.59	$10,654.14	$11,427.88	$9,226.26
11	$1,008.24	$134.55	$11,662.38	$12,570.67	$9,091.71
12	$992.67	$150.12	$12,655.04	$13,713.46	$8,941.59
13	$975.30	$167.49	$13,630.34	$14,856.24	$8,774.10
14	$955.92	$186.87	$14,586.26	$15,999.03	$8,587.22
15	$934.29	$208.50	$15,520.55	$17,141.82	$8,378.73
16	$910.16	$232.62	$16,430.71	$18,284.61	$8,146.10
17	$883.24	$259.54	$17,313.95	$19,427.40	$7,886.56
18	$853.21	$289.58	$18,167.17	$20,570.19	$7,596.98
19	$819.70	$323.09	$18,986.87	$21,712.97	$7,273.89
20	$782.31	$360.47	$19,769.18	$22,855.76	$6,913.42
21	$740.60	$402.19	$20,509.78	$23,998.55	$6,511.23
22	$694.06	$448.73	$21,203.84	$25,141.34	$6,062.50
23	$642.13	$500.66	$21,845.97	$26,284.13	$5,561.85
24	$584.20	$558.59	$22,430.17	$27,426.91	$5,003.25
25	$519.56	$623.23	$22,949.73	$28,569.70	$4,380.02
26	$447.44	$695.35	$23,397.16	$29,712.49	$3,684.67
27	$366.97	$775.81	$23,764.14	$30,855.28	$2,908.86
28	$277.20	$865.59	$24,041.33	$31,998.07	$2,043.27
29	$177.03	$965.76	$24,218.37	$33,140.85	$1,077.51
30	$65.28	$1,077.51	$24,283.64	$34,283.64	$0.00

11.50% Annual Amortization
$10,000 Loan Amount

20 Year Term
Payment $106.64

Yr.	Interest This Year	Principal This Year	Interest To Date	Payments To Date	Current Balance
1	$1,142.94	$136.78	$1,142.94	$1,279.72	$9,863.22
2	$1,126.35	$153.36	$2,269.29	$2,559.43	$9,709.86
3	$1,107.76	$171.96	$3,377.05	$3,839.15	$9,537.91
4	$1,086.91	$192.81	$4,463.96	$5,118.86	$9,345.10
5	$1,063.53	$216.19	$5,527.48	$6,398.58	$9,128.91
6	$1,037.31	$242.40	$6,564.80	$7,678.29	$8,886.50
7	$1,007.92	$271.80	$7,572.71	$8,958.01	$8,614.71
8	$974.96	$304.76	$8,547.67	$10,237.72	$8,309.95
9	$938.01	$341.71	$9,485.68	$11,517.44	$7,968.24
10	$896.57	$383.15	$10,382.25	$12,797.16	$7,585.09
11	$850.11	$429.61	$11,232.36	$14,076.87	$7,155.49
12	$798.02	$481.70	$12,030.38	$15,356.59	$6,673.79
13	$739.61	$540.11	$12,769.98	$16,636.30	$6,133.68
14	$674.11	$605.60	$13,444.09	$17,916.02	$5,528.08
15	$600.68	$679.04	$14,044.77	$19,195.73	$4,849.04
16	$518.34	$761.38	$14,563.11	$20,475.45	$4,087.66
17	$426.01	$853.70	$14,989.12	$21,755.16	$3,233.96
18	$322.49	$957.22	$15,311.61	$23,034.88	$2,276.73
19	$206.42	$1,073.29	$15,518.04	$24,314.60	$1,203.44
20	$76.27	$1,203.44	$15,594.31	$25,594.31	$0.00

11.50% Annual Amortization
$10,000 Loan Amount

25 Year Term
Payment $101.65

Yr.	Interest This Year	Principal This Year	Interest To Date	Payments To Date	Current Balance
1	$1,146.20	$73.56	$1,146.20	$1,219.76	$9,926.44
2	$1,137.28	$82.48	$2,283.49	$2,439.53	$9,843.96
3	$1,127.28	$92.48	$3,410.77	$3,659.29	$9,751.48
4	$1,116.07	$103.70	$4,526.84	$4,879.05	$9,647.78
5	$1,103.49	$116.27	$5,630.33	$6,098.81	$9,531.51
6	$1,089.39	$130.37	$6,719.72	$7,318.58	$9,401.15
7	$1,073.59	$146.18	$7,793.31	$8,538.34	$9,254.97
8	$1,055.86	$163.90	$8,849.17	$9,758.10	$9,091.07
9	$1,035.99	$183.78	$9,885.16	$10,977.86	$8,907.29
10	$1,013.70	$206.06	$10,898.86	$12,197.63	$8,701.23
11	$988.72	$231.05	$11,887.57	$13,417.39	$8,470.18
12	$960.70	$259.06	$12,848.27	$14,637.15	$8,211.12
13	$929.28	$290.48	$13,777.56	$15,856.92	$7,920.64
14	$894.06	$325.70	$14,671.62	$17,076.68	$7,594.94
15	$854.57	$365.20	$15,526.18	$18,296.44	$7,229.74
16	$810.28	$409.48	$16,336.47	$19,516.20	$6,820.26
17	$760.63	$459.13	$17,097.10	$20,735.97	$6,361.13
18	$704.96	$514.81	$17,802.05	$21,955.73	$5,846.32
19	$642.53	$577.23	$18,444.59	$23,175.49	$5,269.09
20	$572.54	$647.23	$19,017.12	$24,395.26	$4,621.87
21	$494.05	$725.71	$19,511.18	$25,615.02	$3,896.16
22	$406.06	$813.71	$19,917.23	$26,834.78	$3,082.45
23	$307.39	$912.38	$20,224.62	$28,054.54	$2,170.07
24	$196.75	$1,023.01	$20,421.37	$29,274.31	$1,147.06
25	$72.70	$1,147.06	$20,494.07	$30,494.07	$0.00

11.50% Annual Amortization
$10,000 Loan Amount

15 Year Term
Payment $116.82

Yr.	Interest This Year	Principal This Year	Interest To Date	Payments To Date	Current Balance
1	$1,136.29	$265.53	$1,136.29	$1,401.83	$9,734.47
2	$1,104.09	$297.73	$2,240.39	$2,803.66	$9,436.73
3	$1,067.99	$333.84	$3,308.38	$4,205.48	$9,102.90
4	$1,027.51	$374.32	$4,335.89	$5,607.31	$8,728.58
5	$982.12	$419.71	$5,318.01	$7,009.14	$8,308.87
6	$931.23	$470.60	$6,249.24	$8,410.97	$7,838.27
7	$874.16	$527.66	$7,123.41	$9,812.79	$7,310.61
8	$810.18	$591.65	$7,933.58	$11,214.62	$6,718.96
9	$738.44	$663.39	$8,672.02	$12,616.45	$6,055.57
10	$657.99	$743.83	$9,330.02	$14,018.28	$5,311.74
11	$567.80	$834.03	$9,897.81	$15,420.11	$4,477.71
12	$466.66	$935.16	$10,364.48	$16,821.93	$3,542.54
13	$353.27	$1,048.56	$10,717.74	$18,223.76	$2,493.98
14	$226.12	$1,175.71	$10,943.86	$19,625.59	$1,318.27
15	$83.55	$1,318.27	$11,027.42	$21,027.42	$0.00

11.50% Annual Amortization
$10,000 Loan Amount

30 Year Term
Payment $99.03

Yr.	Interest This Year	Principal This Year	Interest To Date	Payments To Date	Current Balance
1	$1,147.91	$40.44	$1,147.91	$1,188.35	$9,959.56
2	$1,143.01	$45.34	$2,290.92	$2,376.70	$9,914.22
3	$1,137.51	$50.84	$3,428.43	$3,565.05	$9,863.38
4	$1,131.35	$57.00	$4,559.78	$4,753.40	$9,806.38
5	$1,124.43	$63.92	$5,684.21	$5,941.75	$9,742.47
6	$1,116.68	$71.67	$6,800.90	$7,130.10	$9,670.80
7	$1,107.99	$80.36	$7,908.89	$8,318.45	$9,590.44
8	$1,098.25	$90.10	$9,007.14	$9,506.80	$9,500.35
9	$1,087.32	$101.02	$10,094.47	$10,695.15	$9,399.32
10	$1,075.07	$113.28	$11,169.54	$11,883.50	$9,286.05
11	$1,061.34	$127.01	$12,230.88	$13,071.85	$9,159.04
12	$1,045.94	$142.41	$13,276.82	$14,260.20	$9,016.62
13	$1,028.67	$159.68	$14,305.49	$15,448.55	$8,856.94
14	$1,009.31	$179.04	$15,314.80	$16,636.90	$8,677.90
15	$987.60	$200.75	$16,302.39	$17,825.25	$8,477.14
16	$963.25	$225.10	$17,265.64	$19,013.60	$8,252.05
17	$935.96	$252.39	$18,201.60	$20,201.95	$7,999.65
18	$905.35	$283.00	$19,106.95	$21,390.29	$7,716.66
19	$871.04	$317.31	$19,977.99	$22,578.64	$7,399.34
20	$832.56	$355.79	$20,810.55	$23,766.99	$7,043.55
21	$789.42	$398.93	$21,599.96	$24,955.34	$6,644.62
22	$741.04	$447.31	$22,341.00	$26,143.69	$6,197.31
23	$686.80	$501.55	$23,027.81	$27,332.04	$5,695.76
24	$625.98	$562.37	$23,653.79	$28,520.39	$5,133.40
25	$557.79	$630.56	$24,211.58	$29,708.74	$4,502.84
26	$481.33	$707.02	$24,692.91	$30,897.09	$3,795.82
27	$395.60	$792.75	$25,088.51	$32,085.44	$3,003.07
28	$299.47	$888.88	$25,387.98	$33,273.79	$2,114.19
29	$191.68	$996.67	$25,579.66	$34,462.14	$1,117.52
30	$70.83	$1,117.52	$25,650.49	$35,650.49	$0.00

12.00% Annual Amortization
$10,000 Loan Amount

20 Year Term
Payment $110.11

Yr.	Interest This Year	Principal This Year	Interest To Date	Payments To Date	Current Balance
1	$1,193.10	$128.20	$1,193.10	$1,321.30	$9,871.80
2	$1,176.84	$144.46	$2,369.94	$2,642.61	$9,727.34
3	$1,158.52	$162.78	$3,528.46	$3,963.91	$9,564.55
4	$1,137.88	$183.43	$4,666.34	$5,285.21	$9,381.12
5	$1,114.61	$206.69	$5,780.95	$6,606.52	$9,174.43
6	$1,088.40	$232.91	$6,869.35	$7,927.82	$8,941.53
7	$1,058.86	$262.44	$7,928.21	$9,249.12	$8,679.08
8	$1,025.58	$295.73	$8,953.78	$10,570.43	$8,383.36
9	$988.07	$333.23	$9,941.85	$11,891.73	$8,050.12
10	$945.81	$375.50	$10,887.66	$13,213.03	$7,674.63
11	$898.19	$423.12	$11,785.85	$14,534.34	$7,251.51
12	$844.52	$476.78	$12,630.37	$15,855.64	$6,774.73
13	$784.06	$537.25	$13,414.43	$17,176.94	$6,237.48
14	$715.92	$605.38	$14,130.35	$18,498.25	$5,632.10
15	$639.14	$682.16	$14,769.49	$19,819.55	$4,949.94
16	$552.63	$768.68	$15,322.11	$21,140.85	$4,181.26
17	$455.14	$866.16	$15,777.25	$22,462.16	$3,315.10
18	$345.29	$976.02	$16,122.54	$23,783.46	$2,339.08
19	$221.50	$1,099.80	$16,344.04	$25,104.76	$1,239.28
20	$82.02	$1,239.28	$16,426.07	$26,426.07	$0.00

12.00% Annual Amortization
$10,000 Loan Amount

25 Year Term
Payment $105.32

Yr.	Interest This Year	Principal This Year	Interest To Date	Payments To Date	Current Balance
1	$1,196.37	$67.50	$1,196.37	$1,263.87	$9,932.50
2	$1,187.81	$76.06	$2,384.17	$2,527.74	$9,856.44
3	$1,178.16	$85.71	$3,562.33	$3,791.61	$9,770.73
4	$1,167.29	$96.58	$4,729.62	$5,055.48	$9,674.15
5	$1,155.04	$108.83	$5,884.67	$6,319.34	$9,565.32
6	$1,141.24	$122.63	$7,025.90	$7,583.21	$9,442.69
7	$1,125.69	$138.18	$8,151.59	$8,847.08	$9,304.51
8	$1,108.16	$155.71	$9,259.75	$10,110.95	$9,148.80
9	$1,088.41	$175.45	$10,348.17	$11,374.82	$8,973.35
10	$1,066.16	$197.71	$11,414.33	$12,638.69	$8,775.64
11	$1,041.09	$222.78	$12,455.42	$13,902.56	$8,552.86
12	$1,012.83	$251.04	$13,468.25	$15,166.43	$8,301.82
13	$981.00	$282.87	$14,449.25	$16,430.30	$8,018.95
14	$945.12	$318.75	$15,394.37	$17,694.17	$7,700.20
15	$904.70	$359.17	$16,299.06	$18,958.03	$7,341.03
16	$859.14	$404.73	$17,158.20	$20,221.90	$6,936.30
17	$807.81	$456.06	$17,966.02	$21,485.77	$6,480.25
18	$749.97	$513.89	$18,715.99	$22,749.64	$5,966.35
19	$684.80	$579.07	$19,400.79	$24,013.51	$5,387.28
20	$611.36	$652.51	$20,012.15	$25,277.38	$4,734.77
21	$528.60	$735.26	$20,540.76	$26,541.25	$3,999.51
22	$435.35	$828.51	$20,976.11	$27,805.12	$3,171.00
23	$330.28	$933.59	$21,306.39	$29,068.99	$2,237.40
24	$211.88	$1,051.99	$21,518.27	$30,332.86	$1,185.41
25	$78.46	$1,185.41	$21,596.72	$31,596.72	$0.00

12.00% Annual Amortization
$10,000 Loan Amount

15 Year Term
Payment $120.02

Yr.	Interest This Year	Principal This Year	Interest To Date	Payments To Date	Current Balance
1	$1,186.34	$253.86	$1,186.34	$1,440.20	$9,746.14
2	$1,154.14	$286.06	$2,340.48	$2,880.40	$9,460.08
3	$1,117.86	$322.34	$3,458.34	$4,320.61	$9,137.74
4	$1,076.98	$363.22	$4,535.33	$5,760.81	$8,774.52
5	$1,030.92	$409.28	$5,566.24	$7,201.01	$8,365.23
6	$979.01	$461.19	$6,545.25	$8,641.21	$7,904.04
7	$920.52	$519.68	$7,465.77	$10,081.41	$7,384.36
8	$854.61	$585.59	$8,320.38	$11,521.61	$6,798.77
9	$780.34	$659.86	$9,100.72	$12,961.82	$6,138.91
10	$696.66	$743.55	$9,797.38	$14,402.02	$5,395.36
11	$602.35	$837.85	$10,399.73	$15,842.22	$4,557.51
12	$496.09	$944.11	$10,895.83	$17,282.42	$3,613.41
13	$376.36	$1,063.84	$11,272.19	$18,722.62	$2,549.56
14	$241.44	$1,198.77	$11,513.62	$20,162.82	$1,350.80
15	$89.40	$1,350.80	$11,603.03	$21,603.03	$0.00

12.00% Annual Amortization
$10,000 Loan Amount

30 Year Term
Payment $102.86

Yr.	Interest This Year	Principal This Year	Interest To Date	Payments To Date	Current Balance
1	$1,198.05	$36.29	$1,198.05	$1,234.34	$9,963.71
2	$1,193.44	$40.89	$2,391.49	$2,468.67	$9,922.82
3	$1,188.26	$46.08	$3,579.75	$3,703.01	$9,876.75
4	$1,182.42	$51.92	$4,762.17	$4,937.34	$9,824.83
5	$1,175.83	$58.50	$5,938.00	$6,171.68	$9,766.32
6	$1,168.41	$65.92	$7,106.41	$7,406.01	$9,700.40
7	$1,160.05	$74.29	$8,266.46	$8,640.35	$9,626.11
8	$1,150.63	$83.71	$9,417.09	$9,874.68	$9,542.41
9	$1,140.01	$94.32	$10,557.10	$11,109.02	$9,448.08
10	$1,128.05	$106.28	$11,685.15	$12,343.35	$9,341.80
11	$1,114.57	$119.76	$12,799.72	$13,577.69	$9,222.04
12	$1,099.38	$134.95	$13,899.10	$14,812.02	$9,087.08
13	$1,082.27	$152.07	$14,981.37	$16,046.36	$8,935.01
14	$1,062.98	$171.35	$16,044.35	$17,280.69	$8,763.66
15	$1,041.25	$193.09	$17,085.60	$18,515.03	$8,570.57
16	$1,016.76	$217.58	$18,102.36	$19,749.36	$8,353.00
17	$989.17	$245.17	$19,091.52	$20,983.70	$8,107.83
18	$958.07	$276.26	$20,049.60	$22,218.03	$7,831.56
19	$923.04	$311.30	$20,972.63	$23,452.37	$7,520.26
20	$883.55	$350.78	$21,856.19	$24,686.70	$7,169.48
21	$839.07	$395.27	$22,695.25	$25,921.04	$6,774.22
22	$788.94	$445.40	$23,484.19	$27,155.37	$6,328.82
23	$732.45	$501.89	$24,216.64	$28,389.71	$5,826.93
24	$668.80	$565.54	$24,885.44	$29,624.04	$5,261.39
25	$597.07	$637.26	$25,482.51	$30,858.38	$4,624.13
26	$516.25	$718.08	$25,998.76	$32,092.71	$3,906.05
27	$425.18	$809.15	$26,423.94	$33,327.05	$3,096.90
28	$322.56	$911.77	$26,746.50	$34,561.38	$2,185.12
29	$206.92	$1,027.41	$26,953.43	$35,795.72	$1,157.71
30	$76.62	$1,157.71	$27,030.05	$37,030.05	$0.00

12.50% Annual Amortization
$10,000 Loan Amount

20 Year Term
Payment $113.61

Yr.	Interest This Year	Principal This Year	Interest To Date	Payments To Date	Current Balance
1	$1,243.27	$120.09	$1,243.27	$1,363.37	$9,879.91
2	$1,227.37	$136.00	$2,470.65	$2,726.74	$9,743.91
3	$1,209.36	$154.01	$3,680.01	$4,090.11	$9,589.90
4	$1,188.97	$174.40	$4,868.98	$5,453.47	$9,415.50
5	$1,165.88	$197.49	$6,034.86	$6,816.84	$9,218.01
6	$1,139.73	$223.64	$7,174.58	$8,180.21	$8,994.37
7	$1,110.11	$253.26	$8,284.70	$9,543.58	$8,741.12
8	$1,076.58	$286.79	$9,361.27	$10,906.95	$8,454.32
9	$1,038.60	$324.77	$10,399.88	$12,270.32	$8,129.56
10	$995.60	$367.77	$11,395.47	$13,633.69	$7,761.79
11	$946.90	$416.47	$12,342.37	$14,997.06	$7,345.32
12	$891.75	$471.62	$13,234.12	$16,360.42	$6,873.70
13	$829.30	$534.07	$14,063.42	$17,723.79	$6,339.63
14	$758.58	$604.79	$14,822.01	$19,087.16	$5,734.85
15	$678.50	$684.87	$15,500.51	$20,450.53	$5,049.98
16	$587.81	$775.56	$16,088.32	$21,813.90	$4,274.42
17	$485.12	$878.25	$16,573.43	$23,177.27	$3,396.17
18	$368.82	$994.55	$16,942.25	$24,540.64	$2,401.62
19	$237.13	$1,126.24	$17,179.38	$25,904.00	$1,275.37
20	$87.99	$1,275.37	$17,267.37	$27,267.37	$0.00

12.50% Annual Amortization
$10,000 Loan Amount

25 Year Term
Payment $109.04

Yr.	Interest This Year	Principal This Year	Interest To Date	Payments To Date	Current Balance
1	$1,246.53	$61.89	$1,246.53	$1,308.42	$9,938.11
2	$1,238.34	$70.09	$2,484.87	$2,616.85	$9,868.02
3	$1,229.06	$79.37	$3,713.93	$3,925.27	$9,788.65
4	$1,218.55	$89.88	$4,932.48	$5,233.70	$9,698.78
5	$1,206.65	$101.78	$6,139.13	$6,542.12	$9,597.00
6	$1,193.17	$115.25	$7,332.30	$7,850.55	$9,481.75
7	$1,177.91	$130.52	$8,510.20	$9,158.97	$9,351.23
8	$1,160.63	$147.80	$9,670.83	$10,467.40	$9,203.43
9	$1,141.06	$167.37	$10,811.89	$11,775.82	$9,036.06
10	$1,118.89	$189.53	$11,930.78	$13,084.25	$8,846.53
11	$1,093.80	$214.63	$13,024.57	$14,392.67	$8,631.90
12	$1,065.38	$243.05	$14,089.95	$15,701.10	$8,388.85
13	$1,033.19	$275.23	$15,123.14	$17,009.52	$8,113.62
14	$996.75	$311.68	$16,119.89	$18,317.95	$7,801.94
15	$955.47	$352.95	$17,075.36	$19,626.37	$7,448.99
16	$908.74	$399.69	$17,984.10	$20,934.80	$7,049.30
17	$855.81	$452.61	$18,839.91	$22,243.22	$6,596.69
18	$795.88	$512.54	$19,635.79	$23,551.65	$6,084.15
19	$728.01	$580.41	$20,363.81	$24,860.07	$5,503.73
20	$651.16	$657.27	$21,014.96	$26,168.50	$4,846.46
21	$564.12	$744.30	$21,579.08	$27,476.92	$4,102.16
22	$465.57	$842.86	$22,044.65	$28,785.35	$3,259.30
23	$353.96	$954.47	$22,398.61	$30,093.77	$2,304.83
24	$227.57	$1,080.85	$22,626.18	$31,402.20	$1,223.98
25	$84.45	$1,223.98	$22,710.62	$32,710.62	$0.00

12.50% Annual Amortization
$10,000 Loan Amount

15 Year Term
Payment $123.25

Yr.	Interest This Year	Principal This Year	Interest To Date	Payments To Date	Current Balance
1	$1,236.41	$242.61	$1,236.41	$1,479.03	$9,757.39
2	$1,204.29	$274.74	$2,440.70	$2,958.05	$9,482.65
3	$1,167.91	$311.12	$3,608.60	$4,437.08	$9,171.53
4	$1,126.71	$352.32	$4,735.31	$5,916.11	$8,819.21
5	$1,080.06	$398.97	$5,815.37	$7,395.13	$8,420.24
6	$1,027.23	$451.80	$6,842.60	$8,874.16	$7,968.44
7	$967.40	$511.63	$7,810.00	$10,353.19	$7,456.81
8	$899.65	$579.37	$8,709.65	$11,832.21	$6,877.44
9	$822.93	$656.09	$9,532.59	$13,311.24	$6,221.35
10	$736.06	$742.97	$10,268.64	$14,790.26	$5,478.38
11	$637.68	$841.35	$10,906.32	$16,269.29	$4,637.03
12	$526.27	$952.76	$11,432.59	$17,748.32	$3,684.27
13	$400.11	$1,078.92	$11,832.70	$19,227.34	$2,605.35
14	$257.24	$1,221.78	$12,089.94	$20,706.37	$1,383.57
15	$95.46	$1,383.57	$12,185.40	$22,185.40	$0.00

12.50% Annual Amortization
$10,000 Loan Amount

30 Year Term
Payment $106.73

Yr.	Interest This Year	Principal This Year	Interest To Date	Payments To Date	Current Balance
1	$1,248.18	$32.53	$1,248.18	$1,280.71	$9,967.47
2	$1,243.87	$36.84	$2,492.05	$2,561.42	$9,930.63
3	$1,238.99	$41.72	$3,731.04	$3,842.13	$9,888.91
4	$1,233.47	$47.24	$4,964.51	$5,122.84	$9,841.67
5	$1,227.21	$53.50	$6,191.72	$6,403.55	$9,788.18
6	$1,220.13	$60.58	$7,411.85	$7,684.26	$9,727.60
7	$1,212.11	$68.60	$8,623.96	$8,964.97	$9,658.99
8	$1,203.02	$77.69	$9,826.98	$10,245.67	$9,581.31
9	$1,192.74	$87.97	$11,019.72	$11,526.38	$9,493.33
10	$1,181.09	$99.62	$12,200.81	$12,807.09	$9,393.71
11	$1,167.90	$112.81	$13,368.70	$14,087.80	$9,280.90
12	$1,152.96	$127.75	$14,521.66	$15,368.51	$9,153.15
13	$1,136.04	$144.67	$15,657.70	$16,649.22	$9,008.48
14	$1,116.88	$163.82	$16,774.58	$17,929.93	$8,844.65
15	$1,095.19	$185.52	$17,869.78	$19,210.64	$8,659.14
16	$1,070.63	$210.08	$18,940.40	$20,491.35	$8,449.05
17	$1,042.81	$237.90	$19,983.21	$21,772.06	$8,211.15
18	$1,011.31	$269.40	$20,994.52	$23,052.77	$7,941.75
19	$975.63	$305.08	$21,970.15	$24,333.48	$7,636.67
20	$935.24	$345.47	$22,905.39	$25,614.19	$7,291.20
21	$889.49	$391.22	$23,794.87	$26,894.90	$6,899.98
22	$837.69	$443.02	$24,632.56	$28,175.60	$6,456.96
23	$779.02	$501.69	$25,411.58	$29,456.31	$5,955.27
24	$712.59	$568.12	$26,124.17	$30,737.02	$5,387.15
25	$637.36	$643.35	$26,761.54	$32,017.73	$4,743.80
26	$552.17	$728.54	$27,313.71	$33,298.44	$4,015.27
27	$455.70	$825.01	$27,769.41	$34,579.15	$3,190.26
28	$346.46	$934.25	$28,115.87	$35,859.86	$2,256.01
29	$222.75	$1,057.96	$28,338.62	$37,140.57	$1,198.05
30	$82.66	$1,198.05	$28,421.28	$38,421.28	$0.00

13.00% Annual Amortization
$10,000 Loan Amount

20 Year Term
Payment $117.16

Yr.	Interest This Year	Principal This Year	Interest To Date	Payments To Date	Current Balance
1	$1,293.46	$112.43	$1,293.46	$1,405.89	$9,887.57
2	$1,277.94	$127.95	$2,571.39	$2,811.78	$9,759.61
3	$1,260.28	$145.61	$3,831.67	$4,217.67	$9,614.00
4	$1,240.18	$165.71	$5,071.85	$5,623.56	$9,448.28
5	$1,217.30	$188.59	$6,289.15	$7,029.45	$9,259.70
6	$1,191.27	$214.62	$7,480.42	$8,435.35	$9,045.08
7	$1,161.65	$244.24	$8,642.07	$9,841.24	$8,800.83
8	$1,127.93	$277.96	$9,770.00	$11,247.13	$8,522.87
9	$1,089.57	$316.33	$10,859.57	$12,653.02	$8,206.55
10	$1,045.90	$359.99	$11,905.47	$14,058.91	$7,846.56
11	$996.21	$409.68	$12,901.68	$15,464.80	$7,436.88
12	$939.66	$466.23	$13,841.34	$16,870.69	$6,970.65
13	$875.31	$530.58	$14,716.65	$18,276.58	$6,440.07
14	$802.07	$603.82	$15,518.73	$19,682.47	$5,836.25
15	$718.72	$687.17	$16,237.45	$21,088.36	$5,149.09
16	$623.87	$782.02	$16,861.32	$22,494.25	$4,367.07
17	$515.93	$889.96	$17,377.25	$23,900.14	$3,477.11
18	$393.09	$1,012.80	$17,770.34	$25,306.04	$2,464.31
19	$253.29	$1,152.60	$18,023.63	$26,711.93	$1,311.70
20	$94.19	$1,311.70	$18,117.82	$28,117.82	$0.00

13.00% Annual Amortization
$10,000 Loan Amount

25 Year Term
Payment $112.78

Yr.	Interest This Year	Principal This Year	Interest To Date	Payments To Date	Current Balance
1	$1,296.70	$56.70	$1,296.70	$1,353.40	$9,943.30
2	$1,288.87	$64.53	$2,585.57	$2,706.80	$9,878.77
3	$1,279.97	$73.44	$3,865.54	$4,060.21	$9,805.33
4	$1,269.83	$83.57	$5,135.37	$5,413.61	$9,721.76
5	$1,258.29	$95.11	$6,393.66	$6,767.01	$9,626.65
6	$1,245.17	$108.24	$7,638.83	$8,120.41	$9,518.42
7	$1,230.23	$123.18	$8,869.06	$9,473.82	$9,395.24
8	$1,213.22	$140.18	$10,082.28	$10,827.22	$9,255.06
9	$1,193.87	$159.53	$11,276.10	$12,180.62	$9,095.54
10	$1,171.85	$181.55	$12,448.01	$13,534.02	$8,913.99
11	$1,146.80	$206.61	$13,594.81	$14,887.43	$8,707.38
12	$1,118.28	$235.13	$14,713.08	$16,240.83	$8,472.26
13	$1,085.82	$267.58	$15,798.91	$17,594.23	$8,204.67
14	$1,048.89	$304.52	$16,847.79	$18,947.63	$7,900.16
15	$1,006.85	$346.55	$17,854.65	$20,301.04	$7,553.61
16	$959.02	$394.38	$18,813.67	$21,654.44	$7,159.23
17	$904.58	$448.82	$19,718.25	$23,007.84	$6,710.41
18	$842.63	$510.77	$20,560.88	$24,361.24	$6,199.63
19	$772.13	$581.28	$21,333.00	$25,714.64	$5,618.36
20	$691.89	$661.51	$22,024.90	$27,068.05	$4,956.85
21	$600.58	$752.82	$22,625.48	$28,421.45	$4,204.03
22	$496.67	$856.73	$23,122.15	$29,774.85	$3,347.29
23	$378.41	$974.99	$23,500.56	$31,128.25	$2,372.30
24	$243.83	$1,109.57	$23,744.39	$32,481.66	$1,262.73
25	$90.67	$1,262.73	$23,835.06	$33,835.06	$0.00

13.00% Annual Amortization
$10,000 Loan Amount

15 Year Term
Payment $126.52

Yr.	Interest This Year	Principal This Year	Interest To Date	Payments To Date	Current Balance
1	$1,286.51	$231.78	$1,286.51	$1,518.29	$9,768.22
2	$1,254.52	$263.77	$2,541.03	$3,036.58	$9,504.45
3	$1,218.11	$300.18	$3,759.14	$4,554.87	$9,204.27
4	$1,176.68	$341.62	$4,935.82	$6,073.16	$8,862.65
5	$1,129.52	$388.77	$6,065.34	$7,591.45	$8,473.89
6	$1,075.86	$442.43	$7,141.20	$9,109.74	$8,031.45
7	$1,014.79	$503.50	$8,155.99	$10,628.03	$7,527.95
8	$945.29	$573.00	$9,101.28	$12,146.32	$6,954.95
9	$866.20	$652.09	$9,967.47	$13,664.62	$6,302.86
10	$776.19	$742.10	$10,743.66	$15,182.91	$5,560.75
11	$673.75	$844.54	$11,417.41	$16,701.20	$4,716.21
12	$557.18	$961.11	$11,974.59	$18,219.49	$3,755.10
13	$424.51	$1,093.78	$12,399.10	$19,737.78	$2,661.32
14	$273.54	$1,244.75	$12,672.64	$21,256.07	$1,416.57
15	$101.72	$1,416.57	$12,774.36	$22,774.36	$0.00

13.00% Annual Amortization
$10,000 Loan Amount

30 Year Term
Payment $110.62

Yr.	Interest This Year	Principal This Year	Interest To Date	Payments To Date	Current Balance
1	$1,298.30	$29.13	$1,298.30	$1,327.44	$9,970.87
2	$1,294.28	$33.16	$2,592.59	$2,654.88	$9,937.71
3	$1,289.71	$37.73	$3,882.29	$3,982.32	$9,899.98
4	$1,284.50	$42.94	$5,166.79	$5,309.76	$9,857.03
5	$1,278.57	$48.87	$6,445.36	$6,637.20	$9,808.17
6	$1,271.83	$55.61	$7,717.19	$7,964.64	$9,752.55
7	$1,264.15	$63.29	$8,981.34	$9,292.08	$9,689.26
8	$1,255.41	$72.03	$10,236.75	$10,619.52	$9,617.23
9	$1,245.47	$81.97	$11,482.22	$11,946.95	$9,535.26
10	$1,234.16	$93.28	$12,716.37	$13,274.39	$9,441.98
11	$1,221.28	$106.16	$13,937.65	$14,601.83	$9,335.82
12	$1,206.63	$120.81	$15,144.28	$15,929.27	$9,215.01
13	$1,189.95	$137.49	$16,334.23	$17,256.71	$9,077.52
14	$1,170.97	$156.47	$17,505.20	$18,584.15	$8,921.05
15	$1,149.37	$178.06	$18,654.58	$19,911.59	$8,742.99
16	$1,124.80	$202.64	$19,779.37	$21,239.03	$8,540.34
17	$1,096.82	$230.61	$20,876.20	$22,566.47	$8,309.73
18	$1,064.99	$262.45	$21,941.19	$23,893.91	$8,047.28
19	$1,028.77	$298.67	$22,969.96	$25,221.35	$7,748.61
20	$987.54	$339.90	$23,957.50	$26,548.79	$7,408.71
21	$940.62	$386.82	$24,898.12	$27,876.23	$7,021.89
22	$887.23	$440.21	$25,785.35	$29,203.67	$6,581.68
23	$826.47	$500.97	$26,611.81	$30,531.11	$6,080.70
24	$757.31	$570.12	$27,369.13	$31,858.55	$5,510.58
25	$678.62	$648.82	$28,047.74	$33,185.99	$4,861.76
26	$589.06	$738.38	$28,636.80	$34,513.43	$4,123.38
27	$487.14	$840.30	$29,123.94	$35,840.86	$3,283.08
28	$371.15	$956.29	$29,495.10	$37,168.30	$2,326.79
29	$239.15	$1,088.29	$29,734.25	$38,495.74	$1,238.51
30	$88.93	$1,238.51	$29,823.18	$39,823.18	$0.00

13.50% Annual Amortization
$10,000 Loan Amount

20 Year Term
Payment $120.74

Yr.	Interest This Year	Principal This Year	Interest To Date	Payments To Date	Current Balance
1	$1,343.65	$105.20	$1,343.65	$1,448.85	$9,894.80
2	$1,328.53	$120.32	$2,672.18	$2,897.70	$9,774.48
3	$1,311.25	$137.60	$3,983.43	$4,346.55	$9,636.88
4	$1,291.48	$157.37	$5,274.91	$5,795.40	$9,479.51
5	$1,268.87	$179.98	$6,543.77	$7,244.25	$9,299.53
6	$1,243.01	$205.84	$7,786.78	$8,693.10	$9,093.68
7	$1,213.43	$235.42	$9,000.22	$10,141.95	$8,858.27
8	$1,179.61	$269.24	$10,179.83	$11,590.80	$8,589.03
9	$1,140.93	$307.92	$11,320.76	$13,039.65	$8,281.11
10	$1,096.69	$352.16	$12,417.44	$14,488.50	$7,928.95
11	$1,046.09	$402.76	$13,463.53	$15,937.35	$7,526.19
12	$988.22	$460.62	$14,451.76	$17,386.20	$7,065.56
13	$922.04	$526.80	$15,373.80	$18,835.05	$6,538.76
14	$846.36	$602.49	$16,220.16	$20,283.89	$5,936.26
15	$759.79	$689.06	$16,979.95	$21,732.74	$5,247.21
16	$660.79	$788.06	$17,640.75	$23,181.59	$4,459.15
17	$547.57	$901.28	$18,188.32	$24,630.44	$3,557.87
18	$418.08	$1,030.77	$18,606.40	$26,079.29	$2,527.10
19	$269.98	$1,178.87	$18,876.38	$27,528.14	$1,348.24
20	$100.61	$1,348.24	$18,976.99	$28,976.99	$0.00

13.50% Annual Amortization
$10,000 Loan Amount

25 Year Term
Payment $116.56

Yr.	Interest This Year	Principal This Year	Interest To Date	Payments To Date	Current Balance
1	$1,346.87	$51.91	$1,346.87	$1,398.77	$9,948.09
2	$1,339.41	$59.37	$2,686.27	$2,797.55	$9,888.73
3	$1,330.88	$67.89	$4,017.15	$4,196.32	$9,820.83
4	$1,321.12	$77.65	$5,338.28	$5,595.10	$9,743.18
5	$1,309.97	$88.81	$6,648.25	$6,993.87	$9,654.38
6	$1,297.21	$101.57	$7,945.45	$8,392.64	$9,552.81
7	$1,282.62	$116.16	$9,228.07	$9,791.42	$9,436.65
8	$1,265.93	$132.85	$10,494.00	$11,190.19	$9,303.81
9	$1,246.84	$151.93	$11,740.84	$12,588.96	$9,151.87
10	$1,225.01	$173.76	$12,965.85	$13,987.74	$8,978.11
11	$1,200.05	$198.73	$14,165.90	$15,386.51	$8,779.38
12	$1,171.49	$227.28	$15,337.39	$16,785.29	$8,552.11
13	$1,138.84	$259.93	$16,476.23	$18,184.06	$8,292.17
14	$1,101.49	$297.28	$17,577.73	$19,582.83	$7,994.89
15	$1,058.78	$339.99	$18,636.51	$20,981.61	$7,654.90
16	$1,009.94	$388.84	$19,646.45	$22,380.38	$7,266.06
17	$954.07	$444.70	$20,600.52	$23,779.16	$6,821.36
18	$890.17	$508.60	$21,490.69	$25,177.93	$6,312.76
19	$817.10	$581.67	$22,307.80	$26,576.70	$5,731.09
20	$733.53	$665.24	$23,041.33	$27,975.48	$5,065.85
21	$637.96	$760.82	$23,679.28	$29,374.25	$4,305.03
22	$528.64	$870.13	$24,207.93	$30,773.02	$3,434.91
23	$403.63	$995.14	$24,611.56	$32,171.80	$2,439.76
24	$260.65	$1,138.12	$24,872.21	$33,570.57	$1,301.64
25	$97.13	$1,301.64	$24,969.35	$34,969.35	$0.00

13.50% Annual Amortization
$10,000 Loan Amount

15 Year Term
Payment $129.83

Yr.	Interest This Year	Principal This Year	Interest To Date	Payments To Date	Current Balance
1	$1,336.64	$221.35	$1,336.64	$1,557.98	$9,778.65
2	$1,304.83	$253.15	$2,641.47	$3,115.96	$9,525.51
3	$1,268.46	$289.52	$3,909.93	$4,673.95	$9,235.99
4	$1,226.87	$331.12	$5,136.80	$6,231.93	$8,904.87
5	$1,179.29	$378.69	$6,316.09	$7,789.91	$8,526.18
6	$1,124.89	$433.10	$7,440.98	$9,347.89	$8,093.09
7	$1,062.66	$495.32	$8,503.64	$10,905.88	$7,597.77
8	$991.50	$566.49	$9,495.14	$12,463.86	$7,031.28
9	$910.11	$647.88	$10,405.25	$14,021.84	$6,383.41
10	$817.02	$740.96	$11,222.27	$15,579.82	$5,642.45
11	$710.57	$847.42	$11,932.84	$17,137.80	$4,795.03
12	$588.82	$969.17	$12,521.65	$18,695.79	$3,825.87
13	$449.57	$1,108.41	$12,971.22	$20,253.77	$2,717.45
14	$290.32	$1,267.66	$13,261.54	$21,811.75	$1,449.79
15	$108.19	$1,449.79	$13,369.73	$23,369.73	$0.00

13.50% Annual Amortization
$10,000 Loan Amount

30 Year Term
Payment $114.54

Yr.	Interest This Year	Principal This Year	Interest To Date	Payments To Date	Current Balance
1	$1,348.43	$26.07	$1,348.43	$1,374.49	$9,973.93
2	$1,344.68	$29.81	$2,693.11	$2,748.99	$9,944.12
3	$1,340.40	$34.10	$4,033.50	$4,123.48	$9,910.02
4	$1,335.50	$39.00	$5,369.00	$5,497.98	$9,871.02
5	$1,329.90	$44.60	$6,698.90	$6,872.47	$9,826.42
6	$1,323.49	$51.01	$8,022.39	$8,246.97	$9,775.42
7	$1,316.16	$58.34	$9,338.55	$9,621.46	$9,717.08
8	$1,307.78	$66.72	$10,646.32	$10,995.96	$9,650.37
9	$1,298.19	$76.30	$11,944.52	$12,370.45	$9,574.06
10	$1,287.23	$87.26	$13,231.75	$13,744.95	$9,486.80
11	$1,274.69	$99.80	$14,506.44	$15,119.44	$9,387.00
12	$1,260.35	$114.14	$15,766.79	$16,493.94	$9,272.86
13	$1,243.95	$130.54	$17,010.75	$17,868.43	$9,142.32
14	$1,225.20	$149.30	$18,235.94	$19,242.92	$8,993.02
15	$1,203.75	$170.75	$19,439.69	$20,617.42	$8,822.27
16	$1,179.22	$195.28	$20,618.91	$21,991.91	$8,627.00
17	$1,151.16	$223.33	$21,770.07	$23,366.41	$8,403.66
18	$1,119.07	$255.42	$22,889.14	$24,740.90	$8,148.24
19	$1,082.38	$292.12	$23,971.52	$26,115.40	$7,856.12
20	$1,040.41	$334.09	$25,011.92	$27,489.89	$7,522.03
21	$992.41	$382.09	$26,004.33	$28,864.39	$7,139.94
22	$937.51	$436.99	$26,941.84	$30,238.88	$6,702.96
23	$874.73	$499.77	$27,816.56	$31,613.38	$6,203.19
24	$802.92	$571.57	$28,619.49	$32,987.87	$5,631.62
25	$720.80	$653.69	$29,340.29	$34,362.37	$4,977.92
26	$626.88	$747.61	$29,967.17	$35,736.86	$4,230.31
27	$519.47	$855.03	$30,486.64	$37,111.35	$3,375.28
28	$396.62	$977.87	$30,883.26	$38,485.85	$2,397.41
29	$256.13	$1,118.37	$31,139.39	$39,860.34	$1,279.05
30	$95.45	$1,279.05	$31,234.84	$41,234.84	$0.00

14.00% Annual Amortization
$10,000 Loan Amount

20 Year Term
Payment $124.35

Yr.	Interest This Year	Principal This Year	Interest To Date	Payments To Date	Current Balance
1	$1,393.85	$98.38	$1,393.85	$1,492.22	$9,901.62
2	$1,379.15	$113.07	$2,773.00	$2,984.45	$9,788.55
3	$1,362.27	$129.96	$4,135.27	$4,476.67	$9,658.59
4	$1,342.86	$149.37	$5,478.13	$5,968.90	$9,509.23
5	$1,320.55	$171.67	$6,798.68	$7,461.12	$9,337.55
6	$1,294.92	$197.31	$8,093.59	$8,953.35	$9,140.24
7	$1,265.45	$226.78	$9,359.04	$10,445.57	$8,913.47
8	$1,231.58	$260.64	$10,590.62	$11,937.80	$8,652.82
9	$1,192.66	$299.57	$11,783.28	$13,430.02	$8,353.26
10	$1,147.92	$344.31	$12,931.20	$14,922.25	$8,008.95
11	$1,096.50	$395.73	$14,027.70	$16,414.47	$7,613.22
12	$1,037.40	$454.83	$15,065.10	$17,906.70	$7,158.40
13	$969.48	$522.75	$16,034.57	$19,398.92	$6,635.65
14	$891.41	$600.82	$16,925.98	$20,891.15	$6,034.83
15	$801.68	$690.55	$17,727.66	$22,383.37	$5,344.28
16	$698.55	$793.67	$18,426.21	$23,875.60	$4,550.61
17	$580.02	$912.20	$19,006.23	$25,367.82	$3,638.41
18	$443.79	$1,048.43	$19,450.02	$26,860.05	$2,589.97
19	$287.22	$1,205.01	$19,737.24	$28,352.27	$1,384.97
20	$107.26	$1,384.97	$19,844.50	$29,844.50	$0.00

14.00% Annual Amortization
$10,000 Loan Amount

25 Year Term
Payment $120.38

Yr.	Interest This Year	Principal This Year	Interest To Date	Payments To Date	Current Balance
1	$1,397.03	$47.48	$1,397.03	$1,444.51	$9,952.52
2	$1,389.94	$54.57	$2,786.97	$2,889.03	$9,897.94
3	$1,381.79	$62.73	$4,168.76	$4,333.54	$9,835.22
4	$1,372.42	$72.09	$5,541.18	$5,778.05	$9,763.12
5	$1,361.65	$82.86	$6,902.83	$7,222.57	$9,680.26
6	$1,349.92	$95.23	$8,252.11	$8,667.08	$9,585.03
7	$1,335.06	$109.46	$9,587.17	$10,111.59	$9,475.58
8	$1,318.71	$125.80	$10,905.88	$11,556.11	$9,349.77
9	$1,299.92	$144.59	$12,205.80	$13,000.62	$9,205.18
10	$1,278.33	$166.18	$13,484.13	$14,445.13	$9,039.00
11	$1,253.51	$191.00	$14,737.64	$15,889.65	$8,848.00
12	$1,224.99	$219.53	$15,962.63	$17,334.16	$8,628.47
13	$1,192.20	$252.31	$17,154.84	$18,778.67	$8,376.16
14	$1,154.52	$289.99	$18,309.36	$20,223.19	$8,086.17
15	$1,111.21	$333.30	$19,420.57	$21,667.70	$7,752.87
16	$1,061.44	$383.07	$20,482.01	$23,112.21	$7,369.80
17	$1,004.23	$440.28	$21,486.24	$24,556.73	$6,929.52
18	$938.48	$506.04	$22,424.72	$26,001.24	$6,423.48
19	$862.91	$581.61	$23,287.62	$27,445.75	$5,841.87
20	$776.05	$668.47	$24,063.67	$28,890.27	$5,173.41
21	$676.22	$768.30	$24,739.89	$30,334.78	$4,405.11
22	$561.48	$883.04	$25,301.36	$31,779.29	$3,522.07
23	$429.60	$1,014.91	$25,730.97	$33,223.80	$2,507.16
24	$278.03	$1,166.48	$26,009.00	$34,668.32	$1,340.68
25	$103.83	$1,340.68	$26,112.83	$36,112.83	$0.00

14.00% Annual Amortization
$10,000 Loan Amount

15 Year Term
Payment $133.17

Yr.	Interest This Year	Principal This Year	Interest To Date	Payments To Date	Current Balance
1	$1,386.78	$211.31	$1,386.78	$1,598.09	$9,788.69
2	$1,355.22	$242.87	$2,742.01	$3,196.18	$9,545.83
3	$1,318.95	$279.14	$4,060.96	$4,794.27	$9,266.69
4	$1,277.27	$320.82	$5,338.23	$6,392.36	$8,945.87
5	$1,229.36	$368.73	$6,567.58	$7,990.45	$8,577.14
6	$1,174.29	$423.80	$7,741.87	$9,588.54	$8,153.34
7	$1,111.00	$487.09	$8,852.87	$11,186.63	$7,666.24
8	$1,038.25	$559.84	$9,891.12	$12,784.72	$7,106.41
9	$954.65	$643.44	$10,845.77	$14,382.81	$6,462.96
10	$858.55	$739.54	$11,704.32	$15,980.90	$5,723.43
11	$748.11	$849.98	$12,452.43	$17,578.99	$4,873.45
12	$621.17	$976.92	$13,073.61	$19,177.08	$3,896.53
13	$475.28	$1,122.81	$13,548.88	$20,775.17	$2,773.72
14	$307.59	$1,290.50	$13,856.48	$22,373.26	$1,483.22
15	$114.87	$1,483.22	$13,971.34	$23,971.34	$0.00

14.00% Annual Amortization
$10,000 Loan Amount

30 Year Term
Payment $118.49

Yr.	Interest This Year	Principal This Year	Interest To Date	Payments To Date	Current Balance
1	$1,398.54	$23.30	$1,398.54	$1,421.85	$9,976.70
2	$1,395.06	$26.78	$2,793.60	$2,843.69	$9,949.91
3	$1,391.06	$30.78	$4,184.67	$4,265.54	$9,919.13
4	$1,386.46	$35.38	$5,571.13	$5,687.38	$9,883.75
5	$1,381.18	$40.67	$6,952.31	$7,109.23	$9,843.08
6	$1,375.11	$46.74	$8,327.42	$8,531.08	$9,796.34
7	$1,368.13	$53.72	$9,695.55	$9,952.92	$9,742.62
8	$1,360.11	$61.74	$11,055.65	$11,374.77	$9,680.88
9	$1,350.88	$70.96	$12,406.54	$12,796.61	$9,609.92
10	$1,340.29	$81.56	$13,746.82	$14,218.46	$9,528.36
11	$1,328.11	$93.74	$15,074.93	$15,640.31	$9,434.62
12	$1,314.11	$107.74	$16,389.04	$17,062.15	$9,326.89
13	$1,298.02	$123.83	$17,687.06	$18,484.00	$9,203.06
14	$1,279.53	$142.32	$18,966.58	$19,905.85	$9,060.74
15	$1,258.27	$163.58	$20,224.85	$21,327.69	$8,897.16
16	$1,233.84	$188.00	$21,458.69	$22,749.54	$8,709.16
17	$1,205.77	$216.08	$22,664.46	$24,171.38	$8,493.08
18	$1,173.50	$248.35	$23,837.95	$25,593.23	$8,244.72
19	$1,136.41	$285.44	$24,974.36	$27,015.08	$7,959.28
20	$1,093.78	$328.07	$26,068.14	$28,436.92	$7,631.22
21	$1,044.78	$377.06	$27,112.92	$29,858.77	$7,254.15
22	$988.47	$433.37	$28,101.39	$31,280.61	$6,820.78
23	$923.75	$498.10	$29,025.14	$32,702.46	$6,322.68
24	$849.36	$572.48	$29,874.51	$34,124.31	$5,750.20
25	$763.87	$657.98	$30,638.38	$35,546.15	$5,092.23
26	$665.61	$756.24	$31,303.98	$36,968.00	$4,335.98
27	$552.67	$869.18	$31,856.65	$38,389.84	$3,466.80
28	$422.86	$998.98	$32,279.51	$39,811.69	$2,467.82
29	$273.67	$1,148.17	$32,553.18	$41,233.54	$1,319.65
30	$102.20	$1,319.65	$32,655.38	$42,655.38	$0.00

14.50% Annual Amortization
$10,000 Loan Amount

20 Year Term
Payment $128.00

Yr.	Interest This Year	Principal This Year	Interest To Date	Payments To Date	Current Balance
1	$1,444.05	$91.95	$1,444.05	$1,536.00	$9,908.05
2	$1,429.79	$106.20	$2,873.84	$3,071.99	$9,801.85
3	$1,413.33	$122.67	$4,287.17	$4,607.99	$9,679.18
4	$1,394.31	$141.69	$5,681.48	$6,143.99	$9,537.49
5	$1,372.34	$163.65	$7,053.82	$7,679.99	$9,373.83
6	$1,346.97	$189.03	$8,400.79	$9,215.98	$9,184.81
7	$1,317.66	$218.33	$9,718.45	$10,751.98	$8,966.47
8	$1,283.82	$252.18	$11,002.27	$12,287.98	$8,714.29
9	$1,244.72	$291.28	$12,246.99	$13,823.98	$8,423.01
10	$1,199.56	$336.44	$13,446.55	$15,359.97	$8,086.57
11	$1,147.40	$388.60	$14,593.95	$16,895.97	$7,697.98
12	$1,087.15	$448.84	$15,681.10	$18,431.97	$7,249.13
13	$1,017.57	$518.43	$16,698.67	$19,967.97	$6,730.70
14	$937.19	$598.81	$17,635.86	$21,503.96	$6,131.89
15	$844.36	$691.64	$18,480.21	$23,039.96	$5,440.25
16	$737.13	$798.87	$19,217.34	$24,575.96	$4,641.38
17	$613.27	$922.72	$19,830.61	$26,111.95	$3,718.66
18	$470.22	$1,065.78	$20,300.83	$27,647.95	$2,652.88
19	$304.98	$1,231.01	$20,605.81	$29,183.95	$1,421.86
20	$114.13	$1,421.86	$20,719.95	$30,719.95	$0.00

14.50% Annual Amortization
$10,000 Loan Amount

25 Year Term
Payment $124.22

Yr.	Interest This Year	Principal This Year	Interest To Date	Payments To Date	Current Balance
1	$1,447.19	$43.41	$1,447.19	$1,490.60	$9,956.59
2	$1,440.46	$50.13	$2,887.65	$2,981.19	$9,906.46
3	$1,432.69	$57.91	$4,320.34	$4,471.79	$9,848.55
4	$1,423.71	$66.88	$5,744.05	$5,962.38	$9,781.67
5	$1,413.34	$77.25	$7,157.39	$7,452.98	$9,704.41
6	$1,401.36	$89.23	$8,558.76	$8,943.57	$9,615.18
7	$1,387.53	$103.07	$9,946.29	$10,434.17	$9,512.12
8	$1,371.55	$119.04	$11,317.84	$11,924.76	$9,393.07
9	$1,353.10	$137.50	$12,670.93	$13,415.36	$9,255.57
10	$1,331.78	$158.82	$14,002.71	$14,905.95	$9,096.76
11	$1,307.16	$183.44	$15,309.87	$16,396.55	$8,913.32
12	$1,278.72	$211.88	$16,588.58	$17,887.15	$8,701.44
13	$1,245.84	$244.73	$17,834.45	$19,377.74	$8,456.71
14	$1,207.93	$282.67	$19,042.38	$20,868.34	$8,174.04
15	$1,164.10	$326.49	$20,206.48	$22,358.93	$7,847.55
16	$1,113.48	$377.11	$21,319.96	$23,849.53	$7,470.43
17	$1,055.02	$435.58	$22,374.98	$25,340.12	$7,034.86
18	$987.49	$503.11	$23,362.47	$26,830.72	$6,531.75
19	$909.49	$581.11	$24,271.96	$28,321.31	$5,950.64
20	$819.40	$671.20	$25,091.36	$29,811.91	$5,279.45
21	$715.34	$775.26	$25,806.69	$31,302.51	$4,504.19
22	$595.15	$895.45	$26,401.84	$32,793.10	$3,608.74
23	$456.32	$1,034.28	$26,858.16	$34,283.70	$2,574.46
24	$295.97	$1,194.63	$27,154.13	$35,774.29	$1,379.84
25	$110.76	$1,379.84	$27,264.89	$37,264.89	$0.00

14.50% Annual Amortization
$10,000 Loan Amount

15 Year Term
Payment $136.55

Yr.	Interest This Year	Principal This Year	Interest To Date	Payments To Date	Current Balance
1	$1,436.95	$201.65	$1,436.95	$1,638.60	$9,798.35
2	$1,405.68	$232.92	$2,842.63	$3,277.20	$9,565.43
3	$1,369.57	$269.03	$4,212.20	$4,915.80	$9,296.40
4	$1,327.86	$310.74	$5,540.07	$6,554.40	$8,985.66
5	$1,279.69	$358.91	$6,819.76	$8,193.01	$8,626.75
6	$1,224.05	$414.56	$8,043.80	$9,831.61	$8,212.20
7	$1,159.77	$478.83	$9,203.58	$11,470.21	$7,733.37
8	$1,085.54	$553.06	$10,289.12	$13,108.81	$7,180.31
9	$999.79	$638.81	$11,288.91	$14,747.41	$6,541.50
10	$900.76	$737.84	$12,189.67	$16,386.01	$5,803.66
11	$786.37	$852.24	$12,976.03	$18,024.61	$4,951.42
12	$654.24	$984.36	$13,630.27	$19,663.21	$3,967.06
13	$501.63	$1,136.97	$14,131.90	$21,301.81	$2,830.09
14	$325.36	$1,313.24	$14,457.26	$22,940.41	$1,516.84
15	$121.76	$1,516.84	$14,579.02	$24,579.02	$0.00

14.50% Annual Amortization
$10,000 Loan Amount

30 Year Term
Payment $122.46

Yr.	Interest This Year	Principal This Year	Interest To Date	Payments To Date	Current Balance
1	$1,448.65	$20.81	$1,448.65	$1,469.47	$9,979.19
2	$1,445.43	$24.04	$2,894.08	$2,938.93	$9,955.14
3	$1,441.70	$27.77	$4,335.78	$4,408.40	$9,927.38
4	$1,437.39	$32.07	$5,773.17	$5,877.87	$9,895.30
5	$1,432.42	$37.05	$7,205.59	$7,347.34	$9,858.26
6	$1,426.68	$42.79	$8,632.27	$8,816.80	$9,815.47
7	$1,420.04	$49.42	$10,052.31	$10,286.27	$9,766.04
8	$1,412.38	$57.09	$11,464.69	$11,755.74	$9,708.96
9	$1,403.53	$65.94	$12,868.22	$13,225.20	$9,643.02
10	$1,393.31	$76.16	$14,261.53	$14,694.67	$9,566.86
11	$1,381.50	$87.97	$15,643.03	$16,164.14	$9,478.89
12	$1,367.86	$101.60	$17,010.89	$17,633.61	$9,377.29
13	$1,352.11	$117.36	$18,363.00	$19,103.07	$9,259.93
14	$1,333.92	$135.55	$19,696.92	$20,572.54	$9,124.38
15	$1,312.90	$156.57	$21,009.82	$22,042.01	$8,967.82
16	$1,288.63	$180.84	$22,298.45	$23,511.47	$8,786.98
17	$1,260.59	$208.88	$23,559.04	$24,980.94	$8,578.10
18	$1,228.21	$241.26	$24,787.25	$26,450.41	$8,336.84
19	$1,190.80	$278.66	$25,978.05	$27,919.88	$8,058.18
20	$1,147.60	$321.87	$27,125.65	$29,389.34	$7,736.31
21	$1,097.70	$371.77	$28,223.35	$30,858.81	$7,364.55
22	$1,040.06	$429.40	$29,263.42	$32,328.28	$6,935.14
23	$973.49	$495.98	$30,236.91	$33,797.74	$6,439.17
24	$896.60	$572.87	$31,133.51	$35,267.21	$5,866.30
25	$807.78	$661.68	$31,941.29	$36,736.68	$5,204.61
26	$705.20	$764.27	$32,646.49	$38,206.14	$4,440.34
27	$586.71	$882.76	$33,233.20	$39,675.61	$3,557.59
28	$449.85	$1,019.62	$33,683.05	$41,145.08	$2,537.97
29	$291.77	$1,177.69	$33,974.82	$42,614.55	$1,360.28
30	$109.19	$1,360.28	$34,084.01	$44,084.01	$0.00

15.00% Annual Amortization
$10,000 Loan Amount
20 Year Term
Payment $131.68

Yr.	Interest This Year	Principal This Year	Interest To Date	Payments To Date	Current Balance
1	$1,494.25	$85.89	$1,494.25	$1,580.15	$9,914.11
2	$1,480.45	$99.70	$2,974.70	$3,160.29	$9,814.40
3	$1,464.42	$115.73	$4,439.12	$4,740.44	$9,698.68
4	$1,445.81	$134.33	$5,884.93	$6,320.59	$9,564.34
5	$1,424.22	$155.93	$7,309.15	$7,900.74	$9,408.41
6	$1,399.15	$180.99	$8,708.31	$9,480.88	$9,227.42
7	$1,370.06	$210.09	$10,078.36	$11,061.03	$9,017.33
8	$1,336.29	$243.86	$11,414.65	$12,641.18	$8,773.47
9	$1,297.08	$283.06	$12,711.73	$14,221.33	$8,490.40
10	$1,251.58	$328.57	$13,963.31	$15,801.47	$8,161.84
11	$1,198.76	$381.39	$15,162.07	$17,381.62	$7,780.45
12	$1,137.45	$442.70	$16,299.52	$18,961.77	$7,337.75
13	$1,066.29	$513.86	$17,365.81	$20,541.92	$6,823.89
14	$983.68	$596.47	$18,349.49	$22,122.06	$6,227.42
15	$887.80	$692.35	$19,237.28	$23,702.21	$5,535.07
16	$776.50	$803.65	$20,013.78	$25,282.36	$4,731.42
17	$647.31	$932.84	$20,661.09	$26,862.51	$3,798.58
18	$497.35	$1,082.80	$21,158.43	$28,442.65	$2,715.78
19	$323.28	$1,256.87	$21,481.71	$30,022.80	$1,458.91
20	$121.24	$1,458.91	$21,602.95	$31,602.95	$0.00

15.00% Annual Amortization
$10,000 Loan Amount
25 Year Term
Payment $128.08

Yr.	Interest This Year	Principal This Year	Interest To Date	Payments To Date	Current Balance
1	$1,497.35	$39.65	$1,497.35	$1,537.00	$9,960.35
2	$1,490.97	$46.02	$2,988.32	$3,073.99	$9,914.33
3	$1,483.58	$53.42	$4,471.90	$4,610.99	$9,860.91
4	$1,474.99	$62.01	$5,946.88	$6,147.99	$9,798.90
5	$1,465.02	$71.98	$7,411.90	$7,684.98	$9,726.92
6	$1,453.45	$83.55	$8,865.35	$9,221.98	$9,643.37
7	$1,440.02	$96.98	$10,305.37	$10,758.98	$9,546.39
8	$1,424.43	$112.57	$11,729.80	$12,295.97	$9,433.82
9	$1,406.33	$130.66	$13,136.13	$13,832.97	$9,303.16
10	$1,385.33	$151.67	$14,521.46	$15,369.97	$9,151.49
11	$1,360.95	$176.05	$15,882.40	$16,906.96	$8,975.44
12	$1,332.64	$204.35	$17,215.05	$18,443.96	$8,771.09
13	$1,299.79	$237.20	$18,514.84	$19,980.96	$8,533.88
14	$1,261.66	$275.33	$19,776.50	$21,517.95	$8,258.55
15	$1,217.40	$319.60	$20,993.90	$23,054.95	$7,938.95
16	$1,166.02	$370.97	$22,159.93	$24,591.95	$7,567.98
17	$1,106.39	$430.61	$23,266.32	$26,128.94	$7,137.37
18	$1,037.17	$499.83	$24,303.49	$27,665.94	$6,637.54
19	$956.82	$580.18	$25,260.30	$29,202.94	$6,057.36
20	$863.55	$673.45	$26,123.85	$30,739.93	$5,383.92
21	$755.29	$781.71	$26,879.15	$32,276.93	$4,602.21
22	$629.63	$907.37	$27,508.77	$33,813.93	$3,694.85
23	$483.77	$1,053.23	$27,992.54	$35,350.92	$2,641.62
24	$314.45	$1,222.54	$28,306.99	$36,887.92	$1,419.07
25	$117.92	$1,419.07	$28,424.92	$38,424.92	$0.00

15.00% Annual Amortization
$10,000 Loan Amount

15 Year Term
Payment $139.96

Yr.	Interest This Year	Principal This Year	Interest To Date	Payments To Date	Current Balance
1	$1,487.13	$192.37	$1,487.13	$1,679.50	$9,807.63
2	$1,456.21	$223.30	$2,943.34	$3,359.01	$9,584.33
3	$1,420.31	$259.20	$4,363.64	$5,038.51	$9,325.13
4	$1,378.64	$300.86	$5,742.29	$6,718.02	$9,024.27
5	$1,330.28	$349.23	$7,072.56	$8,397.52	$8,675.04
6	$1,274.14	$405.37	$8,346.70	$10,077.03	$8,269.67
7	$1,208.97	$470.53	$9,555.67	$11,756.53	$7,799.14
8	$1,133.33	$546.17	$10,689.00	$13,436.04	$7,252.97
9	$1,045.53	$633.97	$11,734.53	$15,115.54	$6,618.99
10	$943.62	$735.89	$12,678.15	$16,795.05	$5,883.11
11	$825.32	$854.18	$13,503.47	$18,474.55	$5,028.92
12	$688.01	$991.50	$14,191.48	$20,154.05	$4,037.43
13	$528.62	$1,150.89	$14,720.10	$21,833.56	$2,886.54
14	$343.61	$1,335.90	$15,063.71	$23,513.06	$1,550.65
15	$128.86	$1,550.65	$15,192.57	$25,192.57	$0.00

15.00% Annual Amortization
$10,000 Loan Amount

30 Year Term
Payment $126.44

Yr.	Interest This Year	Principal This Year	Interest To Date	Payments To Date	Current Balance
1	$1,498.76	$18.58	$1,498.76	$1,517.33	$9,981.42
2	$1,495.77	$21.56	$2,994.53	$3,034.67	$9,959.86
3	$1,492.31	$25.03	$4,486.83	$4,552.00	$9,934.84
4	$1,488.28	$29.05	$5,975.12	$6,069.33	$9,905.78
5	$1,483.61	$33.72	$7,458.73	$7,586.66	$9,872.06
6	$1,478.19	$39.14	$8,936.92	$9,104.00	$9,832.92
7	$1,471.90	$45.43	$10,408.82	$10,621.33	$9,787.49
8	$1,464.59	$52.74	$11,873.41	$12,138.66	$9,734.75
9	$1,456.12	$61.22	$13,329.53	$13,656.00	$9,673.53
10	$1,446.28	$71.06	$14,775.80	$15,173.33	$9,602.48
11	$1,434.85	$82.48	$16,210.66	$16,690.66	$9,520.00
12	$1,421.59	$95.74	$17,632.25	$18,207.99	$9,424.26
13	$1,406.20	$111.13	$19,038.46	$19,725.33	$9,313.13
14	$1,388.34	$128.99	$20,426.80	$21,242.66	$9,184.14
15	$1,367.60	$149.73	$21,794.40	$22,759.99	$9,034.41
16	$1,343.53	$173.80	$23,137.93	$24,277.33	$8,860.61
17	$1,315.59	$201.74	$24,453.53	$25,794.66	$8,658.87
18	$1,283.16	$234.17	$25,736.69	$27,311.99	$8,424.70
19	$1,245.52	$271.81	$26,982.21	$28,829.32	$8,152.89
20	$1,201.83	$315.51	$28,184.04	$30,346.66	$7,837.38
21	$1,151.11	$366.23	$29,335.15	$31,863.99	$7,471.16
22	$1,092.23	$425.10	$30,427.38	$33,381.32	$7,046.06
23	$1,023.90	$493.43	$31,451.28	$34,898.65	$6,552.63
24	$944.58	$572.76	$32,395.86	$36,415.99	$5,979.87
25	$852.50	$664.83	$33,248.36	$37,933.32	$5,315.04
26	$745.63	$771.70	$33,993.99	$39,450.65	$4,543.33
27	$621.57	$895.76	$34,615.56	$40,967.99	$3,647.58
28	$477.58	$1,039.76	$35,093.14	$42,485.32	$2,607.82
29	$310.43	$1,206.90	$35,403.57	$44,002.65	$1,400.92
30	$116.42	$1,400.92	$35,519.98	$45,519.98	$0.00

15.50% Annual Amortization
$10,000 Loan Amount
20 Year Term
Payment $135.39

Yr.	Interest This Year	Principal This Year	Interest To Date	Payments To Date	Current Balance
1	$1,544.46	$80.20	$1,544.46	$1,624.66	$9,919.80
2	$1,531.11	$93.55	$3,075.57	$3,249.31	$9,826.26
3	$1,515.53	$109.12	$4,591.10	$4,873.97	$9,717.13
4	$1,497.36	$127.29	$6,088.47	$6,498.63	$9,589.84
5	$1,476.17	$148.49	$7,564.64	$8,123.28	$9,441.35
6	$1,451.45	$173.21	$9,016.08	$9,747.94	$9,268.14
7	$1,422.61	$202.05	$10,438.69	$11,372.60	$9,066.09
8	$1,388.97	$235.69	$11,827.65	$12,997.25	$8,830.40
9	$1,349.72	$274.93	$13,177.38	$14,621.91	$8,555.47
10	$1,303.95	$320.71	$14,481.32	$16,246.57	$8,234.76
11	$1,250.55	$374.11	$15,731.87	$17,871.23	$7,860.65
12	$1,188.26	$436.40	$16,920.13	$19,495.88	$7,424.25
13	$1,115.60	$509.06	$18,035.73	$21,120.54	$6,915.19
14	$1,030.84	$593.81	$19,066.57	$22,745.20	$6,321.38
15	$931.97	$692.68	$19,998.55	$24,369.85	$5,628.69
16	$816.64	$808.02	$20,815.19	$25,994.51	$4,820.68
17	$682.11	$942.55	$21,497.29	$27,619.17	$3,878.13
18	$525.17	$1,099.49	$22,022.47	$29,243.82	$2,778.64
19	$342.11	$1,282.55	$22,364.57	$30,868.48	$1,496.09
20	$128.56	$1,496.09	$22,493.14	$32,493.14	$0.00

15.50% Annual Amortization
$10,000 Loan Amount
25 Year Term
Payment $131.97

Yr.	Interest This Year	Principal This Year	Interest To Date	Payments To Date	Current Balance
1	$1,547.50	$36.19	$1,547.50	$1,583.69	$9,963.81
2	$1,541.47	$42.22	$3,088.97	$3,167.39	$9,921.59
3	$1,534.44	$49.25	$4,623.42	$4,751.08	$9,872.34
4	$1,526.24	$57.45	$6,149.66	$6,334.78	$9,814.89
5	$1,516.68	$67.02	$7,666.34	$7,918.47	$9,747.87
6	$1,505.52	$78.17	$9,171.86	$9,502.17	$9,669.70
7	$1,492.50	$91.19	$10,664.37	$11,085.86	$9,578.51
8	$1,477.32	$106.37	$12,141.69	$12,669.55	$9,472.13
9	$1,459.61	$124.08	$13,601.30	$14,253.25	$9,348.05
10	$1,438.95	$144.74	$15,040.25	$15,836.94	$9,203.31
11	$1,414.85	$168.84	$16,455.10	$17,420.64	$9,034.46
12	$1,386.74	$196.96	$17,841.84	$19,004.33	$8,837.51
13	$1,353.95	$229.75	$19,195.78	$20,588.03	$8,607.76
14	$1,315.69	$268.00	$20,511.48	$22,171.72	$8,339.76
15	$1,271.07	$312.62	$21,782.55	$23,755.41	$8,027.13
16	$1,219.02	$364.68	$23,001.57	$25,339.11	$7,662.46
17	$1,158.30	$425.39	$24,159.87	$26,922.80	$7,237.06
18	$1,087.47	$496.22	$25,247.34	$28,506.50	$6,740.84
19	$1,004.85	$578.84	$26,252.19	$30,090.19	$6,162.00
20	$908.47	$675.22	$27,160.66	$31,673.89	$5,486.78
21	$796.05	$787.64	$27,956.71	$33,257.58	$4,699.13
22	$664.91	$918.79	$28,621.62	$34,841.27	$3,780.35
23	$511.93	$1,071.76	$29,133.55	$36,424.97	$2,708.58
24	$333.48	$1,250.21	$29,467.03	$38,008.66	$1,458.37
25	$125.32	$1,458.37	$29,592.36	$39,592.36	$0.00

15.50% Annual Amortization
$10,000 Loan Amount

15 Year Term
Payment $143.40

Yr.	Interest This Year	Principal This Year	Interest To Date	Payments To Date	Current Balance
1	$1,537.33	$183.46	$1,537.33	$1,720.79	$9,816.54
2	$1,506.78	$214.01	$3,044.11	$3,441.58	$9,602.54
3	$1,471.15	$249.64	$4,515.26	$5,162.37	$9,352.90
4	$1,429.59	$291.20	$5,944.85	$6,883.15	$9,061.70
5	$1,381.10	$339.69	$7,325.95	$8,603.94	$8,722.01
6	$1,324.54	$396.24	$8,650.50	$10,324.73	$8,325.77
7	$1,258.57	$462.22	$9,909.07	$12,045.52	$7,863.55
8	$1,181.61	$539.18	$11,090.68	$13,766.31	$7,324.37
9	$1,091.84	$628.95	$12,182.51	$15,487.10	$6,695.42
10	$987.12	$733.67	$13,169.63	$17,207.88	$5,961.75
11	$864.96	$855.83	$14,034.59	$18,928.67	$5,105.92
12	$722.47	$998.32	$14,757.06	$20,649.46	$4,107.60
13	$556.25	$1,164.54	$15,313.30	$22,370.25	$2,943.06
14	$362.35	$1,358.44	$15,675.66	$24,091.04	$1,584.62
15	$136.17	$1,584.62	$15,811.83	$25,811.83	$0.00

15.50% Annual Amortization
$10,000 Loan Amount

30 Year Term
Payment $130.45

Yr.	Interest This Year	Principal This Year	Interest To Date	Payments To Date	Current Balance
1	$1,548.86	$16.56	$1,548.86	$1,565.42	$9,983.44
2	$1,546.10	$19.32	$3,094.95	$3,130.84	$9,964.11
3	$1,542.88	$22.54	$4,637.83	$4,696.26	$9,941.57
4	$1,539.13	$26.29	$6,176.96	$6,261.68	$9,915.28
5	$1,534.75	$30.67	$7,711.71	$7,827.10	$9,884.61
6	$1,529.64	$35.78	$9,241.36	$9,392.52	$9,848.84
7	$1,523.69	$41.73	$10,765.04	$10,957.94	$9,807.10
8	$1,516.74	$48.68	$12,281.78	$12,523.36	$9,758.42
9	$1,508.63	$56.79	$13,790.42	$14,088.78	$9,701.63
10	$1,499.18	$66.24	$15,289.59	$15,654.20	$9,635.39
11	$1,488.15	$77.27	$16,777.74	$17,219.62	$9,558.12
12	$1,475.28	$90.14	$18,253.03	$18,785.04	$9,467.98
13	$1,460.28	$105.15	$19,713.30	$20,350.46	$9,362.84
14	$1,442.77	$122.65	$21,156.07	$21,915.88	$9,240.18
15	$1,422.35	$143.07	$22,578.42	$23,481.30	$9,097.11
16	$1,398.53	$166.90	$23,976.94	$25,046.72	$8,930.22
17	$1,370.74	$194.68	$25,347.68	$26,612.15	$8,735.53
18	$1,338.32	$227.10	$26,686.00	$28,177.57	$8,508.44
19	$1,300.51	$264.91	$27,986.51	$29,742.99	$8,243.53
20	$1,256.40	$309.02	$29,242.92	$31,308.41	$7,934.51
21	$1,204.95	$360.47	$30,447.87	$32,873.83	$7,574.04
22	$1,144.93	$420.49	$31,592.80	$34,439.25	$7,153.56
23	$1,074.92	$490.50	$32,667.73	$36,004.67	$6,663.06
24	$993.26	$572.16	$33,660.98	$37,570.09	$6,090.90
25	$897.99	$667.43	$34,558.97	$39,135.51	$5,423.47
26	$786.86	$778.56	$35,345.84	$40,700.93	$4,644.91
27	$657.24	$908.18	$36,003.08	$42,266.35	$3,736.73
28	$506.02	$1,059.40	$36,509.10	$43,831.77	$2,677.33
29	$329.63	$1,235.79	$36,838.73	$45,397.19	$1,441.54
30	$123.88	$1,441.54	$36,962.61	$46,962.61	$0.00

16.00% Annual Amortization
$10,000 Loan Amount

20 Year Term
Payment $139.13

Yr.	Interest This Year	Principal This Year	Interest To Date	Payments To Date	Current Balance
1	$1,594.67	$74.84	$1,594.67	$1,669.51	$9,925.16
2	$1,581.78	$87.73	$3,176.45	$3,339.01	$9,837.43
3	$1,566.66	$102.84	$4,743.11	$5,008.52	$9,734.59
4	$1,548.95	$120.56	$6,292.06	$6,678.03	$9,614.03
5	$1,528.18	$141.33	$7,820.23	$8,347.54	$9,472.70
6	$1,503.83	$165.68	$9,324.06	$10,017.04	$9,307.02
7	$1,475.29	$194.22	$10,799.35	$11,686.55	$9,112.80
8	$1,441.83	$227.68	$12,241.19	$13,356.06	$8,885.13
9	$1,402.61	$266.90	$13,643.80	$15,025.56	$8,618.23
10	$1,356.63	$312.88	$15,000.43	$16,695.07	$8,305.36
11	$1,302.73	$366.78	$16,303.16	$18,364.58	$7,938.58
12	$1,239.55	$429.96	$17,542.70	$20,034.09	$7,508.62
13	$1,165.48	$504.03	$18,708.18	$21,703.59	$7,004.59
14	$1,078.65	$590.86	$19,786.83	$23,373.10	$6,413.73
15	$976.86	$692.65	$20,763.69	$25,042.61	$5,721.08
16	$857.54	$811.97	$21,621.23	$26,712.11	$4,909.11
17	$717.66	$951.85	$22,338.88	$28,381.62	$3,957.26
18	$553.68	$1,115.83	$22,892.57	$30,051.13	$2,841.44
19	$361.46	$1,308.05	$23,254.02	$31,720.64	$1,533.39
20	$136.12	$1,533.39	$23,390.14	$33,390.14	$0.00

16.00% Annual Amortization
$10,000 Loan Amount

25 Year Term
Payment $135.89

Yr.	Interest This Year	Principal This Year	Interest To Date	Payments To Date	Current Balance
1	$1,597.65	$33.02	$1,597.65	$1,630.67	$9,966.98
2	$1,591.96	$38.71	$3,189.61	$3,261.33	$9,928.27
3	$1,585.29	$45.37	$4,774.90	$4,892.00	$9,882.90
4	$1,577.48	$53.19	$6,352.38	$6,522.67	$9,829.71
5	$1,568.31	$62.35	$7,920.69	$8,153.33	$9,767.35
6	$1,557.57	$73.10	$9,478.26	$9,784.00	$9,694.26
7	$1,544.98	$85.69	$11,023.23	$11,414.67	$9,608.57
8	$1,530.22	$100.45	$12,553.45	$13,045.33	$9,508.12
9	$1,512.91	$117.76	$14,066.36	$14,676.00	$9,390.36
10	$1,492.63	$138.04	$15,558.99	$16,306.67	$9,252.32
11	$1,468.84	$161.82	$17,027.83	$17,937.33	$9,090.50
12	$1,440.97	$189.70	$18,468.80	$19,568.00	$8,900.80
13	$1,408.29	$222.38	$19,877.09	$21,198.67	$8,678.42
14	$1,369.98	$260.69	$21,247.06	$22,829.33	$8,417.73
15	$1,325.07	$305.60	$22,572.13	$24,460.00	$8,112.13
16	$1,272.42	$358.24	$23,844.56	$26,090.67	$7,753.89
17	$1,210.71	$419.96	$25,055.27	$27,721.33	$7,333.93
18	$1,138.36	$492.30	$26,193.63	$29,352.00	$6,841.63
19	$1,053.55	$577.11	$27,247.18	$30,982.67	$6,264.52
20	$954.13	$676.53	$28,201.32	$32,613.33	$5,587.98
21	$837.59	$793.08	$29,038.92	$34,244.00	$4,794.90
22	$700.96	$929.70	$29,739.86	$35,874.67	$3,865.20
23	$540.80	$1,089.87	$30,280.67	$37,505.33	$2,775.33
24	$353.05	$1,277.62	$30,633.71	$39,136.00	$1,497.71
25	$132.95	$1,497.71	$30,766.67	$40,766.67	$0.00

16.00% Annual Amortization
$10,000 Loan Amount

15 Year Term
Payment $146.87

Yr.	Interest This Year	Principal This Year	Interest To Date	Payments To Date	Current Balance
1	$1,587.54	$174.90	$1,587.54	$1,762.44	$9,825.10
2	$1,557.41	$205.03	$3,144.95	$3,524.88	$9,620.07
3	$1,522.09	$240.35	$4,667.05	$5,287.32	$9,379.72
4	$1,480.69	$281.75	$6,147.73	$7,049.76	$9,097.97
5	$1,432.15	$330.29	$7,579.88	$8,812.20	$8,767.68
6	$1,375.25	$387.19	$8,955.13	$10,574.65	$8,380.48
7	$1,308.55	$453.89	$10,263.68	$12,337.09	$7,926.59
8	$1,230.35	$532.09	$11,494.03	$14,099.53	$7,394.50
9	$1,138.69	$623.75	$12,632.72	$15,861.97	$6,770.75
10	$1,031.24	$731.20	$13,663.96	$17,624.41	$6,039.55
11	$905.27	$857.17	$14,569.23	$19,386.85	$5,182.38
12	$757.61	$1,004.83	$15,326.84	$21,149.29	$4,177.54
13	$584.50	$1,177.94	$15,911.34	$22,911.73	$2,999.61
14	$381.58	$1,380.86	$16,292.92	$24,674.17	$1,618.74
15	$143.70	$1,618.74	$16,436.61	$26,436.61	$0.00

16.00% Annual Amortization
$10,000 Loan Amount

30 Year Term
Payment $134.48

Yr.	Interest This Year	Principal This Year	Interest To Date	Payments To Date	Current Balance
1	$1,598.95	$14.76	$1,598.95	$1,613.71	$9,985.24
2	$1,596.41	$17.30	$3,195.35	$3,227.42	$9,967.94
3	$1,593.43	$20.28	$4,788.78	$4,841.13	$9,947.65
4	$1,589.93	$23.78	$6,378.71	$6,454.83	$9,923.88
5	$1,585.83	$27.87	$7,964.55	$8,068.54	$9,896.00
6	$1,581.03	$32.68	$9,545.58	$9,682.25	$9,863.33
7	$1,575.40	$38.30	$11,120.98	$11,295.96	$9,825.02
8	$1,568.81	$44.90	$12,689.79	$12,909.67	$9,780.12
9	$1,561.07	$52.64	$14,250.86	$14,523.38	$9,727.48
10	$1,552.00	$61.71	$15,802.86	$16,137.08	$9,665.78
11	$1,541.37	$72.34	$17,344.23	$17,750.79	$9,593.44
12	$1,528.91	$84.80	$18,873.14	$19,364.50	$9,508.64
13	$1,514.30	$99.41	$20,387.45	$20,978.21	$9,409.24
14	$1,497.18	$116.53	$21,884.62	$22,591.92	$9,292.71
15	$1,477.10	$136.61	$23,361.73	$24,205.63	$9,156.10
16	$1,453.57	$160.14	$24,815.29	$25,819.33	$8,995.96
17	$1,425.98	$187.73	$26,241.28	$27,433.04	$8,808.23
18	$1,393.64	$220.07	$27,634.92	$29,046.75	$8,588.17
19	$1,355.73	$257.98	$28,990.65	$30,660.46	$8,330.19
20	$1,311.29	$302.42	$30,301.94	$32,274.17	$8,027.77
21	$1,259.19	$354.52	$31,561.13	$33,887.88	$7,673.25
22	$1,198.12	$415.59	$32,759.25	$35,501.58	$7,257.66
23	$1,126.52	$487.18	$33,885.77	$37,115.29	$6,770.48
24	$1,042.60	$571.11	$34,928.37	$38,729.00	$6,199.37
25	$944.21	$669.50	$35,872.58	$40,342.71	$5,529.87
26	$828.88	$784.83	$36,701.46	$41,956.42	$4,745.04
27	$693.67	$920.04	$37,395.13	$43,570.13	$3,825.00
28	$535.18	$1,078.53	$37,930.30	$45,183.84	$2,746.47
29	$349.38	$1,264.33	$38,279.68	$46,797.54	$1,482.14
30	$131.57	$1,482.14	$38,411.25	$48,411.25	$0.00

16.50% Annual Amortization
$10,000 Loan Amount

20 Year Term
Payment $142.89

Yr.	Interest This Year	Principal This Year	Interest To Date	Payments To Date	Current Balance
1	$1,644.88	$69.80	$1,644.88	$1,714.68	$9,930.20
2	$1,632.45	$82.23	$3,277.32	$3,429.36	$9,847.96
3	$1,617.80	$96.88	$4,895.13	$5,144.04	$9,751.09
4	$1,600.55	$114.13	$6,495.68	$6,858.72	$9,636.96
5	$1,580.23	$134.45	$8,075.91	$8,573.40	$9,502.51
6	$1,556.29	$158.39	$9,632.20	$10,288.08	$9,344.12
7	$1,528.09	$186.59	$11,160.29	$12,002.77	$9,157.52
8	$1,494.86	$219.82	$12,655.15	$13,717.45	$8,937.70
9	$1,455.72	$258.96	$14,110.87	$15,432.13	$8,678.74
10	$1,409.60	$305.08	$15,520.47	$17,146.81	$8,373.66
11	$1,355.28	$359.40	$16,875.75	$18,861.49	$8,014.26
12	$1,291.28	$423.40	$18,167.03	$20,576.17	$7,590.86
13	$1,215.89	$498.80	$19,382.91	$22,290.85	$7,092.06
14	$1,127.07	$587.61	$20,509.98	$24,005.53	$6,504.45
15	$1,022.43	$692.25	$21,532.41	$25,720.21	$5,812.20
16	$899.16	$815.52	$22,431.57	$27,434.89	$4,996.68
17	$753.95	$960.74	$23,185.52	$29,149.57	$4,035.94
18	$582.87	$1,131.81	$23,768.38	$30,864.25	$2,904.13
19	$381.33	$1,333.35	$24,149.71	$32,578.93	$1,570.78
20	$143.90	$1,570.78	$24,293.62	$34,293.62	$0.00

16.50% Annual Amortization
$10,000 Loan Amount

25 Year Term
Payment $139.82

Yr.	Interest This Year	Principal This Year	Interest To Date	Payments To Date	Current Balance
1	$1,647.79	$30.10	$1,647.79	$1,677.89	$9,969.90
2	$1,642.43	$35.46	$3,290.22	$3,355.79	$9,934.43
3	$1,636.12	$41.78	$4,926.34	$5,033.68	$9,892.66
4	$1,628.68	$49.22	$6,555.01	$6,711.57	$9,843.44
5	$1,619.91	$57.98	$8,174.93	$8,389.47	$9,785.46
6	$1,609.59	$68.31	$9,784.51	$10,067.36	$9,717.15
7	$1,597.42	$80.47	$11,381.94	$11,745.26	$9,636.68
8	$1,583.10	$94.80	$12,965.03	$13,423.15	$9,541.88
9	$1,566.22	$111.68	$14,531.25	$15,101.04	$9,430.21
10	$1,546.33	$131.56	$16,077.58	$16,778.94	$9,298.64
11	$1,522.90	$154.99	$17,600.48	$18,456.83	$9,143.65
12	$1,495.30	$182.59	$19,095.78	$20,134.72	$8,961.06
13	$1,462.79	$215.11	$20,558.57	$21,812.62	$8,745.95
14	$1,424.48	$253.41	$21,983.05	$23,490.51	$8,492.54
15	$1,379.36	$298.53	$23,362.41	$25,168.40	$8,194.01
16	$1,326.20	$351.69	$24,688.61	$26,846.30	$7,842.32
17	$1,263.58	$414.32	$25,952.19	$28,524.19	$7,428.00
18	$1,189.80	$488.09	$27,141.99	$30,202.08	$6,939.91
19	$1,102.89	$575.01	$28,244.88	$31,879.98	$6,364.90
20	$1,000.50	$677.40	$29,245.37	$33,557.87	$5,687.50
21	$879.87	$798.02	$30,125.24	$35,235.77	$4,889.48
22	$737.77	$940.12	$30,863.01	$36,913.66	$3,949.35
23	$570.36	$1,107.53	$31,433.38	$38,591.55	$2,841.82
24	$373.15	$1,304.75	$31,806.53	$40,269.45	$1,537.08
25	$140.81	$1,537.08	$31,947.34	$41,947.34	$0.00

16.50% Annual Amortization
$10,000 Loan Amount

15 Year Term
Payment $150.37

Yr.	Interest This Year	Principal This Year	Interest To Date	Payments To Date	Current Balance
1	$1,637.77	$166.68	$1,637.77	$1,804.45	$9,833.32
2	$1,608.09	$196.36	$3,245.85	$3,608.90	$9,636.95
3	$1,573.12	$231.33	$4,818.97	$5,413.35	$9,405.62
4	$1,531.93	$272.52	$6,350.90	$7,217.80	$9,133.10
5	$1,483.40	$321.05	$7,834.30	$9,022.25	$8,812.05
6	$1,426.23	$378.22	$9,260.53	$10,826.70	$8,433.83
7	$1,358.88	$445.57	$10,619.42	$12,631.15	$7,988.26
8	$1,279.54	$524.91	$11,898.96	$14,435.60	$7,463.36
9	$1,186.07	$618.38	$13,085.03	$16,240.05	$6,844.98
10	$1,075.96	$728.49	$14,160.99	$18,044.50	$6,116.49
11	$946.24	$858.21	$15,107.23	$19,848.95	$5,258.27
12	$793.42	$1,011.03	$15,900.64	$21,653.40	$4,247.24
13	$613.38	$1,191.07	$16,514.03	$23,457.85	$3,056.17
14	$401.29	$1,403.16	$16,915.32	$25,262.30	$1,653.01
15	$151.44	$1,653.01	$17,066.75	$27,066.75	$0.00

16.50% Annual Amortization
$10,000 Loan Amount

30 Year Term
Payment $138.51

Yr.	Interest This Year	Principal This Year	Interest To Date	Payments To Date	Current Balance
1	$1,649.04	$13.14	$1,649.04	$1,662.18	$9,986.86
2	$1,646.70	$15.48	$3,295.73	$3,324.36	$9,971.38
3	$1,643.94	$18.24	$4,939.67	$4,986.53	$9,953.14
4	$1,640.69	$21.49	$6,580.36	$6,648.71	$9,931.65
5	$1,636.86	$25.31	$8,217.22	$8,310.89	$9,906.34
6	$1,632.36	$29.82	$9,849.58	$9,973.07	$9,876.51
7	$1,627.05	$35.13	$11,476.63	$11,635.24	$9,841.38
8	$1,620.79	$41.39	$13,097.42	$13,297.42	$9,800.00
9	$1,613.42	$48.76	$14,710.84	$14,959.60	$9,751.24
10	$1,604.74	$57.44	$16,315.58	$16,621.78	$9,693.80
11	$1,594.51	$67.67	$17,910.09	$18,283.95	$9,626.14
12	$1,582.46	$79.72	$19,492.55	$19,946.13	$9,546.42
13	$1,568.27	$93.91	$21,060.82	$21,608.31	$9,452.51
14	$1,551.55	$110.63	$22,612.37	$23,270.49	$9,341.88
15	$1,531.85	$130.33	$24,144.21	$24,932.67	$9,211.55
16	$1,508.64	$153.54	$25,652.85	$26,594.84	$9,058.01
17	$1,481.30	$180.88	$27,134.14	$28,257.02	$8,877.12
18	$1,449.09	$213.09	$28,583.23	$29,919.20	$8,664.03
19	$1,411.14	$251.04	$29,994.37	$31,581.38	$8,413.00
20	$1,366.44	$295.74	$31,360.82	$33,243.55	$8,117.26
21	$1,313.78	$348.40	$32,674.59	$34,905.73	$7,768.86
22	$1,251.74	$410.44	$33,926.34	$36,567.91	$7,358.43
23	$1,178.66	$483.52	$35,104.99	$38,230.09	$6,874.90
24	$1,092.56	$569.62	$36,197.55	$39,892.26	$6,305.28
25	$991.12	$671.05	$37,188.67	$41,554.44	$5,634.23
26	$871.63	$790.55	$38,060.30	$43,216.62	$4,843.68
27	$730.86	$931.32	$38,791.16	$44,878.80	$3,912.36
28	$565.02	$1,097.16	$39,356.18	$46,540.98	$2,815.21
29	$369.65	$1,292.52	$39,725.84	$48,203.15	$1,522.68
30	$139.50	$1,522.68	$39,865.33	$49,865.33	$0.00

17.00% Annual Amortization
$10,000 Loan Amount

20 Year Term
Payment $146.68

Yr.	Interest This Year	Principal This Year	Interest To Date	Payments To Date	Current Balance
1	$1,695.08	$65.08	$1,695.08	$1,760.16	$9,934.92
2	$1,683.12	$77.04	$3,378.20	$3,520.32	$9,857.88
3	$1,668.95	$91.21	$5,047.15	$5,280.48	$9,766.67
4	$1,652.18	$107.98	$6,699.33	$7,040.64	$9,658.68
5	$1,632.32	$127.84	$8,331.64	$8,800.80	$9,530.84
6	$1,608.81	$151.35	$9,940.45	$10,560.96	$9,379.49
7	$1,580.98	$179.18	$11,521.43	$12,321.12	$9,200.31
8	$1,548.03	$212.13	$13,069.46	$14,081.29	$8,988.17
9	$1,509.02	$251.14	$14,578.48	$15,841.45	$8,737.03
10	$1,462.83	$297.33	$16,041.31	$17,601.61	$8,439.70
11	$1,408.16	$352.00	$17,449.47	$19,361.77	$8,087.70
12	$1,343.43	$416.73	$18,792.90	$21,121.93	$7,670.97
13	$1,266.79	$493.37	$20,059.69	$22,882.09	$7,177.60
14	$1,176.07	$584.09	$21,235.76	$24,642.25	$6,593.51
15	$1,068.66	$691.50	$22,304.42	$26,402.41	$5,902.01
16	$941.50	$818.66	$23,245.91	$28,162.57	$5,083.34
17	$790.95	$969.21	$24,036.86	$29,922.73	$4,114.13
18	$612.72	$1,147.44	$24,649.59	$31,682.89	$2,966.69
19	$401.72	$1,358.44	$25,051.30	$33,443.05	$1,608.25
20	$151.91	$1,608.25	$25,203.21	$35,203.21	$0.00

17.00% Annual Amortization
$10,000 Loan Amount

25 Year Term
Payment $143.78

Yr.	Interest This Year	Principal This Year	Interest To Date	Payments To Date	Current Balance
1	$1,697.93	$27.43	$1,697.93	$1,725.36	$9,972.57
2	$1,692.88	$32.47	$3,390.81	$3,450.71	$9,940.10
3	$1,686.91	$38.44	$5,077.73	$5,176.07	$9,901.66
4	$1,679.84	$45.51	$6,757.57	$6,901.42	$9,856.15
5	$1,671.47	$53.88	$8,429.04	$8,626.78	$9,802.26
6	$1,661.57	$63.79	$10,090.61	$10,352.14	$9,738.47
7	$1,649.84	$75.52	$11,740.44	$12,077.49	$9,662.95
8	$1,635.95	$89.41	$13,376.39	$13,802.85	$9,573.55
9	$1,619.51	$105.85	$14,995.90	$15,528.20	$9,467.70
10	$1,600.04	$125.31	$16,595.94	$17,253.56	$9,342.38
11	$1,577.00	$148.36	$18,172.94	$18,978.91	$9,194.02
12	$1,549.72	$175.64	$19,722.65	$20,704.27	$9,018.38
13	$1,517.42	$207.94	$21,240.07	$22,429.63	$8,810.44
14	$1,479.18	$246.18	$22,719.25	$24,154.98	$8,564.27
15	$1,433.91	$291.45	$24,153.16	$25,880.34	$8,272.82
16	$1,380.31	$345.04	$25,533.47	$27,605.69	$7,927.78
17	$1,316.86	$408.49	$26,850.34	$29,331.05	$7,519.28
18	$1,241.75	$483.61	$28,092.08	$31,056.41	$7,035.67
19	$1,152.81	$572.54	$29,244.89	$32,781.76	$6,463.13
20	$1,047.53	$677.83	$30,292.42	$34,507.12	$5,785.30
21	$922.88	$802.48	$31,215.30	$36,232.47	$4,982.83
22	$775.31	$950.04	$31,990.61	$37,957.83	$4,032.78
23	$600.61	$1,124.75	$32,591.22	$39,683.19	$2,908.03
24	$393.77	$1,331.58	$32,984.99	$41,408.54	$1,576.45
25	$148.91	$1,576.45	$33,133.90	$43,133.90	$0.00

17.00% Annual Amortization **15 Year Term**
$10,000 Loan Amount **Payment $153.90**

Yr.	Interest This Year	Principal This Year	Interest To Date	Payments To Date	Current Balance
1	$1,688.00	$158.80	$1,688.00	$1,846.81	$9,841.20
2	$1,658.80	$188.00	$3,346.81	$3,693.61	$9,653.19
3	$1,624.23	$222.58	$4,971.03	$5,540.42	$9,430.62
4	$1,583.30	$263.51	$6,554.33	$7,387.22	$9,167.11
5	$1,534.84	$311.96	$8,089.18	$9,234.03	$8,855.15
6	$1,477.48	$369.33	$9,566.65	$11,080.83	$8,485.82
7	$1,409.56	$437.25	$10,976.21	$12,927.64	$8,048.57
8	$1,329.15	$517.65	$12,305.36	$14,774.44	$7,530.92
9	$1,233.96	$612.84	$13,539.32	$16,621.25	$6,918.08
10	$1,121.26	$725.54	$14,660.59	$18,468.05	$6,192.53
11	$987.84	$858.96	$15,648.43	$20,314.86	$5,333.57
12	$829.89	$1,016.92	$16,478.31	$22,161.66	$4,316.65
13	$642.88	$1,203.92	$17,121.20	$24,008.47	$3,112.73
14	$421.49	$1,425.31	$17,542.69	$25,855.27	$1,687.42
15	$159.39	$1,687.42	$17,702.08	$27,702.08	$0.00

17.00% Annual Amortization **30 Year Term**
$10,000 Loan Amount **Payment $142.57**

Yr.	Interest This Year	Principal This Year	Interest To Date	Payments To Date	Current Balance
1	$1,699.12	$11.69	$1,699.12	$1,710.81	$9,988.31
2	$1,696.97	$13.84	$3,396.08	$3,421.62	$9,974.46
3	$1,694.42	$16.39	$5,090.50	$5,132.43	$9,958.07
4	$1,691.41	$19.40	$6,781.91	$6,843.24	$9,938.67
5	$1,687.84	$22.97	$8,469.75	$8,554.05	$9,915.70
6	$1,683.61	$27.20	$10,153.36	$10,264.86	$9,888.50
7	$1,678.61	$32.20	$11,831.97	$11,975.67	$9,856.30
8	$1,672.69	$38.12	$13,504.67	$13,686.48	$9,818.18
9	$1,665.68	$45.13	$15,170.35	$15,397.29	$9,773.05
10	$1,657.38	$53.43	$16,827.73	$17,108.10	$9,719.63
11	$1,647.56	$63.25	$18,475.29	$18,818.91	$9,656.37
12	$1,635.93	$74.88	$20,111.22	$20,529.72	$9,581.49
13	$1,622.16	$88.65	$21,733.37	$22,240.54	$9,492.84
14	$1,605.85	$104.96	$23,339.23	$23,951.35	$9,387.88
15	$1,586.55	$124.26	$24,925.78	$25,662.16	$9,263.62
16	$1,563.70	$147.11	$26,489.48	$27,372.97	$9,116.51
17	$1,536.65	$174.16	$28,026.13	$29,083.78	$8,942.35
18	$1,504.62	$206.19	$29,530.76	$30,794.59	$8,736.17
19	$1,466.71	$244.10	$30,997.46	$32,505.40	$8,492.07
20	$1,421.82	$288.99	$32,419.28	$34,216.21	$8,203.08
21	$1,368.68	$342.13	$33,787.96	$35,927.02	$7,860.94
22	$1,305.76	$405.05	$35,093.72	$37,637.83	$7,455.89
23	$1,231.28	$479.53	$36,325.00	$39,348.64	$6,976.36
24	$1,143.09	$567.72	$37,468.09	$41,059.45	$6,408.64
25	$1,038.70	$672.11	$38,506.79	$42,770.26	$5,736.53
26	$915.10	$795.71	$39,421.89	$44,481.07	$4,940.82
27	$768.78	$942.04	$40,190.66	$46,191.88	$3,998.78
28	$595.54	$1,115.27	$40,786.21	$47,902.69	$2,883.52
29	$390.45	$1,320.36	$41,176.66	$49,613.50	$1,563.16
30	$147.65	$1,563.16	$41,324.31	$51,324.31	$0.00